SOUND
PICTURES

SOUND PICTURES

THE LIFE OF BEATLES PRODUCER

GEORGE MARTIN

THE LATER YEARS, 1966-2016

KENNETH WOMACK

CHICAGO
REVIEW
PRESS

An A Cappella Book

Published by Chicago Review Press Incorporated
814 North Franklin Street
Chicago, Illinois 60610
ISBN 978-0-912777-74-0

Library of Congress Cataloging-in-Publication Data

Names: Womack, Kenneth, author.
Title: Sound pictures: the life of Beatles producer George Martin: the later
   years, 1966-2016 / by Kenneth Womack.
Description: First edition. | Chicago, Illinois: Chicago Review Press, [2018]
   | Includes bibliographical references.
Identifiers: LCCN 2018009547 (print) | LCCN 2018011496 (ebook) | ISBN
   9780912777757 (adobe pdf) | ISBN 9780912777764 (kindle) | ISBN
   9780912777771 (epub) | ISBN 9780912777740 (cloth)
Subjects: LCSH: Martin, George, 1926-2016. | Sound recording executives and
   producers—England—Biography. | Beatles. | LCGFT: Biographies.
Classification: LCC ML429.M34 (ebook) | LCC ML429.M34 W67 2018 (print)
   | DDC 781.66/149092 [B] —dc23
LC record available at https://lccn.loc.gov/2018009547

Typesetting: Nord Compo

Printed in the United States of America
5 4 3 2 1

For Becca and PMo:
All You Need Is Love!

We should always remember that sensitiveness and emotion constitute the real content of a work of art.

—Maurice Ravel

CONTENTS

GET BACK TO WHERE YOU ONCE BELONGED

OR GEORGE MARTIN, it came in the form of a most unexpected telephone call. And from no less than Paul McCartney.

It was a late spring day in 1969, and England's most esteemed record producer was sitting in his office on London's Park Street, toiling away at AIR (Associated Independent Recording), the company he founded four years earlier after experiencing one rebuff too many at the hands of the vaunted EMI Group.

And what a rebuff it had been. After leading EMI's Parlophone Records label with a steady hand for more than a decade, the normally staid George simply couldn't take it anymore. Within the space of a scant eighteen months—from the autumn of 1962 through the spring of 1964—he had transformed Parlophone from a modest comedy imprint into EMI's most valuable, blue-chip musical property. His production had earned EMI a king's ransom many times over—tens of millions of pounds, quite literally—and what did he have to show for it? In 1963, his salary amounted to a paltry £3,000 during a year in which the records he produced held the number-one position on the British charts for a phenomenal thirty-seven weeks.[1]

But by the spring of 1969, the high tide of Beatlemania was just a memory. As the days and weeks passed since he had last seen the bandmates, the man whom the Beatles lovingly referred to as "Big George" had begun to assume that he would never work with the group again. Indeed, it was the longest he'd gone without seeing them since their February 1968 sojourn to Rishikesh in the company of the Maharishi Mahesh Yogi. Only this time, it was different. This time it had seemed eminently more *final*.

On the one hand, George was relieved by the respite, having grown tired of the emotional roller coaster. The heartbreak had simply become too much to bear. Yet on the other hand, he was terribly sad to see them go out with a whimper after such masterworks as *Rubber Soul, Revolver,* and *Sgt. Pepper's Lonely Hearts Club Band.* Surely, their last gasp wouldn't be in the form of the failed *Get Back* LP, with all of the attendant infighting and the would-be album's crude and haphazard production efforts?

"What a shame to end like this," George thought to himself at the time. But then, to his great surprise, Paul had phoned him out of the blue. So unexpected, yet at the same time, so very welcome to George's ears. Paul wasted little time in getting down to business: "We're going to make another record," he announced. "Would you like to produce it?" For his part, George's reply was immediate and firm. "Only if you let me produce it the way we used to," he answered. "We do want to do that," said Paul. "John included?" asked George, overbrimming with caution. "Yes," Paul replied. And then, as an afterthought: *"Honestly."*[2]

For all of his understandable hesitation in that call, George was undeniably intrigued. Only a short time later, he was back in the familiar environs of Studio 2, assisting Paul in nailing down a lead vocal in the service of a new and as of yet untitled Beatles album. But as Paul's fellow band members assembled in the studio in the coming days for one more stab at greatness, George worried, justifiably, whether or not they could recapture the magic of days gone by.

Was it even possible, at this late date, to take the Beatles' sad song and make it better?

1

YOU SAY
IT'S YOUR BIRTHDAY!

ON JANUARY 3, 1966, George Martin celebrated his fortieth birthday with his fiancée Judy Lockhart Smith by his side. With marriage in the offing, George's future shone brightly. On the professional front, he had just completed production work on *Rubber Soul*, the Beatles' latest studio album and their sixth straight UK chart-topper. The long-player had proven to be pioneering in every sense of the word. As George later observed, "I think *Rubber Soul* was the first of the albums that presented a new Beatles to the world. Up to this point, we had been making albums that were rather like a collection of their singles and now we really were beginning to think about albums as a bit of art in their own right. We were thinking about the album as an entity of its own, and *Rubber Soul* was the first one to emerge in this way." Like Paul McCartney, George perceived the album as a result of a growing collaboration between himself and the Beatles, as opposed to the more authoritative position that he had assumed with earlier projects. Previously, George "had a lot of control—we used to record the stuff, and leave him to mix it, pick a single, everything," Paul later remarked. "After a while though, we got so into recording we'd stay behind while he mixed it, watching what he was doing." But for his part, John Lennon had already begun to see the bandmates' working relationship with George evolving even further still. "We were getting better technically and musically, that's all. We finally took over the studio," John observed. "With *Rubber Soul*, we were more precise about making the album—that's all. We took over the cover and everything."[1]

Forced to produce the long-player between the Beatles' stints on the road, George had delivered *Rubber Soul* in breakneck fashion. Recorded between October 12 and November 15, 1965, the album was mastered for release and in the shops by December 3, along with the band's latest single, "Day Tripper" backed with "We Can Work It Out." In the space of slightly more than fifty days, George and the Beatles had brought sixteen new tracks to fruition and into the hands of Beatles fans across the globe. Such was the pace in those heady days of midperiod Beatlemania. As it happened, there was no rest for the bandmates, who performed eighteen concerts that same month on their UK winter tour. Not surprisingly, by the time the new year rolled around, the Beatles were drained. But the same could hardly be said for their producer, who had just concluded another banner year in which his acts had reigned atop the charts, and who also ended his long-standing employment with the EMI Group to establish a consortium of producers known as Associated Independent Recording—or AIR for short. But rather than giving in to exhaustion, George had been buoyed by the exhilarating experience of going into business for himself. As George later observed, "My workload was enormous so that I was spending more time in the studio than I was anywhere else. And I found myself completely and utterly wrapped up in my work."[2]

By Thursday, January 6, 1966, George was back in the studio with the Beatles. Only this time, George and the bandmates weren't in the studio to tackle new material for their waiting world of hungry consumers. And the studio, for that matter, wasn't the friendly environs of good old Number 2 at Abbey Road that they knew so well. Instead, George and the Beatles had gathered a few miles further south at Cine-Tele Sound Studios (CTS). Located in Kensington Gardens Square in London's tony Bayswater district, CTS opened for business in 1956, having been constructed in a converted banquet hall that formerly served Whiteley's Gentleman's Dining Club. With its ornate, crown-molded ceilings reaching a height of twenty-six feet, the banquet hall was rather large, measuring forty feet across and eighty-five feet deep. During its heyday, the hall had also functioned as a runway for parading the latest European fashions. But by the time that George and the Beatles alighted there in January 1966, the cavernous space enjoyed renown as the go-to place for cinema and television soundtrack recording. George himself had recorded there many times as the bandleader behind the George Martin Orchestra. In the mid-1960s, George lauded CTS as "the best film-recording studio in London." Indeed, as a converted recording studio space, it didn't disappoint. CTS could accommodate some sixty-five musicians and—most importantly for George's purposes—the room produced a natural reverberation of 0.8 seconds.[3]

When George and the bandmates assembled at CTS on that frigid Thursday morning, they had come expressly for the reverb. With only a matter of hours to spare, they had been tasked with touching up—if not rerecording entirely—the ragged audio from the group's August 15, 1965, performance at New York City's Shea Stadium, where they had delivered a record-setting concert for more than fifty-five thousand screaming fans. With its natural reverb, CTS seemed like the perfect venue for carrying out the necessary touch-up work for the audio portion of their thirty-four-minute gig. According to chief maintenance engineer Peter Harris, the building had one major drawback: "Underneath the studio were the storage cellars of the furniture company next door (Frederick Lawrence & Co.), so at crucial times you'd hear these steel-wheeled trolleys being trundled around downstairs. One had to rush round and beg the gentleman who controlled the loading bay to get these guys to lay off for a little while."[4]

As it happened, George and the Beatles' mission at CTS was time sensitive. BBC One was slated to broadcast a documentary devoted to the Shea Stadium concert on March 1, and the existing audio simply wasn't up to par. This issue was of paramount concern to the bandmates, given that manager Brian Epstein's NEMS Enterprises, along with the Beatles' Subafilms and American television personality Ed Sullivan, were acting as coproducers for the project. George and the Beatles had pointedly refused to release their 1964 and 1965 Hollywood Bowl performances given the atrocious state of the original recordings. But with NEMS's own money on the line, things were very different this time around. George and the Beatles needed to clean up the Shea recordings—and fast.

The Shea Stadium concert had originally been filmed under the direction of M. Clay Adams and cinematographer Andrew Laszlo, who deployed fourteen cameras to capture footage of the group and the unbridled euphoria of their multitudinous fans. The Shea audio had been recorded by Fred Bosch, a Cinerama engineer who had to resort to recording the vocals directly from the stadium's column speakers arrayed around the playing field. According to Bill Hanley, the engineer who mixed the Beatles' 1966 Shea concert, "The delay, combining those field speakers and the screaming house speakers, would have been atrocious; it would have been a horror show." During the 1965 concert, Bosch and Bob Fine, who served as the original sound mixer, were stationed below the elevated stage platform. As Fine's son Tom later observed, the mixers had been built "for P.A. and broadcast use. They weren't designed for a guy screaming rock and roll into a microphone. The overloading could have started at the input transformer."[5]

With the Beatles' raucous sound blaring through the stadium speakers blending with fifty-five thousand boisterous fans into an unholy cacophony, Bosch and Fine never really had a chance. As Tom Fine later observed, "Everything was really primitive then. You can't look at this from a modern perspective. These guys had small space and limited time. They just set up whatever worked. This was the beginning of stadium rock P.A.—it had never been done before." The Beatles performed a dozen songs during the thirty-four-minute show. Most of the band's lead vocals were heavily distorted given the brutal conditions inside the stadium. In truth, there was very little Fine could do to capture a passable recording. As Abbey Road engineer Sam Okell remarked, Fine was standing "in the middle of a baseball field, with headphones on and he can't hear anything. It's absolutely crazy they got anything."[6]

On the Wednesday afternoon before the CTS session, Martin and Adams assembled at Abbey Road to cobble together a game plan for salvaging the Shea recordings. Adams had flown in from New York City earlier in the week in order to work with George at CTS to bring the audio up to snuff—or, failing that, to a much less embarrassing sound than existed in the original recording. Working from Fine's mix, which Fine had prepared back on December 2, Martin and Adams had their work cut out for them. John Lennon and Paul McCartney's vocal recordings were particularly dreadful on "Twist and Shout" and "She's a Woman," while Ringo Starr's lead vocal was inexplicably dropped from "Act Naturally." A number of the songs suffered from recording hiccups and instrumental drops, especially "I'm Down," which featured Lennon playing a lively Vox Continental organ. In a January 10, 1966, letter to his son Michael, Adams described Martin as being "a fine person—very thoughtful, cooperative, and very 'giving' of himself. He has been recording the Beatles as their A&R (artists and repertoire) man ever since the beginning." Observing the CTS recording sessions the next day, Adams remarked that the bandmates "really look up to George Martin. Whenever they are recording, they do exactly what he tells them and they take his criticisms to the letter." Adams later joined Martin at AIR's Park Street offices, where he met Ron Richards, John Burgess, and Peter Sullivan, Martin's business partners in his post-EMI career.[7] For dubbing purposes, Adams had brought a rough cut of the documentary to serve as a guide for overdubbing the Beatles' new vocals and instrumentation onto Fine's December 2 mix. In Adams's recollections,

Martin quickly diagnosed the problem with the original recordings as being weak on the "low end"—namely, McCartney's bass and Starr's drums. Living in Central London, McCartney arrived at CTS first. In short order, roadie Mal Evans set up an amplifier and McCartney began recording new bass lines to accompany Fine's mix. Adams recalled that McCartney was "playing bass notes so loud they felt like they were loosening the fillings in your teeth."[8]

An hour later, the other three Beatles arrived. Only they couldn't get started, as their guitars hadn't been delivered to the studio. Eventually, Evans and Alf Bicknell, the Beatles' driver, managed to retrieve the bandmates' guitars, and by early afternoon they were finally ready to go. Adams had described their mission as needing to "fortify" Fine's mix, and the bandmates took to aping Adams at nearly every turn. "How are we doing, Clay, did we fortify that one okay?" McCartney asked. As the session proceeded, Martin led the Beatles through complete remakes of "Ticket to Ride," "I Feel Fine," and "Help!" With the bandmates unable to simply "fortify" "Twist and Shout" into shape, Martin helpfully provided Adams with unreleased audio for the song from the band's August 30, 1965, concert at the Hollywood Bowl, their last appearance in that august West Coast venue. Unable to salvage "Act Naturally," Martin provided Adams with the original master recording from the *Help!* long-player, which the Beatles' producer had "sweetened" with crowd noise. While Martin and the bandmates had to contend with less-than-stellar audio recordings, Adams was impressed with their ability to match their studio performances with the images on the documentary. As Adams's son Michael later recalled, "My dad said he was amazed by the Beatles' ability to sync precisely to picture, particularly when they were patching their vocals. They could match completely what they did onstage." By January 25, Adams had returned to New York City, where he prepared a mono mix of Martin's CTS recording. Broadcast on the BBC on March 1, *The Beatles at Shea Stadium* documentary wouldn't debut in the United States until January 10, 1967, when it was finally broadcast on ABC television.[9]

For George, recording in a pinch had long been the norm—whether he was working with the Beatles or carrying out his new freelance professional lifestyle with his partners at AIR. As it happened, life at AIR had started out rather slowly as far as hit making went. The Beatles were AIR's mainstay, "fireproof" act as far as their producer was concerned, and by this juncture their track record in the United Kingdom had resulted in six straight number-one long-players and eight chart-topping singles—nine if you count "Please Please Me," which landed the top spot on *New Musical Express* (*NME*) and *Melody Maker*, respectively, but came in second on *Record Retailer*, the official UK charts for much of the 1960s. But even with the Beatles' staggering sales returns, George needed to supplement AIR's balance sheet with a few hitmakers of their own if they were going to prosper, since the percentage he received for new acts was considerably higher. George was ever mindful of AIR's motto—"Built by producers, for producers"—and he knew that if his partnership was going to succeed in the long run, it would do so on the backs of a new stable of artists.[10]

As it happened, the new year had not been entirely kind to George. For the past several months, he had been devoting long hours between Beatles sessions to *Twang!!*, a new musical from the redoubtable Lionel Bart, the West End composer behind *Oliver!* Bart's latest work promised a burlesque musical revue of the Robin Hood legend. Given his work with the British comedy masters of the day, Martin seemed like a perfect complement for Bart's zany vision. Martin had subsequently been inked to prepare the soundtrack album for release with United Artists, the American record and film conglomerate who had signed him to a multirecord deal back in September 1964. He was no stranger to the theatrical world, having recorded live performances of *Beyond the Fringe* and *Flanders and Swan* during his Parlophone days. But *Twang!!* was less dependent upon Martin's expertise as producer and musical director. Working with Bart wasn't that different from collaborating with the Beatles, who had no formal training and couldn't compose in notation. As Martin later wrote, "There have been many great musicians who couldn't write a pop tune to save their lives. Equally, the pop world in particular has seen many who have known nothing of music but could write great tunes. Lionel Bart, for example, can't play an instrument." Instead, "he just whistles his tunes as he thinks of them." Musicals like *Twang!!* tended to take on lives of their own, and Bart's show was no different.[11]

Things had seemed promising on October 9, 1965, when George and the bandmates celebrated John's twenty-fifth birthday with the cast at Lionel's home to commemorate the musical's opening. But a preview performance in Manchester's Palace Theatre offered a glimpse of the horrid events to come. Indeed, the preview performance had gone so badly that the director, Joan Littlewood, promptly jumped ship. By the time that *Twang!!* opened in the West End's Shaftesbury Theatre in December 1965, disaster was clearly imminent. Collapsing under the weight of a poorly written script and—worse yet—a weak rendering of Robin Hood's typically charismatic personage, *Twang!!* closed in January 1966 after just forty-three performances. For his part, Bart lost his entire fortune in the fiasco. In an incredible irony, by the time that Martin's United Artists original cast soundtrack was released that same

January, the musical had already been mothballed. When the show closed, London critics were already condemning *Twang!!* as "the worst musical for years." Bart's theatrical disaster would not soon be forgotten. In 2015—sixteen years after the one-time musical impresario's death—the *Telegraph* ranked *Twang!!* as seventh on its roster of the ten worst musicals of all time.[12]

January also saw the release of Cilla Black's new single "Alfie" backed with "Night Time Is Here." Like "Anyone Who Had a Heart," which notched a number-one hit for Black and Martin in 1964, "Alfie" had been penned by the legendary American songwriting team of Burt Bacharach and Hal David, who had been inspired to write the song by the upcoming British film of the same name. Since 1957, Bacharach and David had landed thirty-three top-forty hits in the United States and United Kingdom alone, many of them with Dionne Warwick, the American chanteuse who was the principal interpreter of their music. Given the film's London setting, the film's producers recommended that Bacharach and David seek out a British singer for "Alfie." Black seemed like a natural choice, since Bacharach had personally selected Black to sing the Bacharach-David confection "Anyone Who Had a Heart."

For her part, Black initially jumped at the chance to interpret another Bacharach-David composition: "When Burt Bacharach first wrote to me from New York to tell me that he and Hal David, inspired by the film *Alfie*, had written another song especially for me, I was very excited and immediately ditched my plans to record an Italian ballad. When the demo disc arrived, however, I didn't like the song at all—and I hated the idea of singing about a guy called Alfie. That name, I thought, was really naff." Set for a UK release in March 1966, the movie starred Michael Caine in an unseemly role about the life and times of a narcissistic womanizer. Hoping that she could extricate herself from recording the song, Black announced that she'd only record "Alfie" if Bacharach prepared the arrangement. To her surprise—and Martin's great pleasure—the songwriter called her bluff, even agreeing to join Black and Martin in London, as he had done previously with "Anyone Who Had a Heart." When pushed even further, Bacharach offered to play the piano accompaniment himself if Black would agree to sing "Alfie." "By this time," Black later wrote, "coward that I was, I couldn't back out."[13]

Unbeknownst to Black, Bacharach had previously offered "Alfie" to Sandie Shaw, the reigning female vocalist of the Swinging Sixties who had previously struck pop gold with Bacharach and David's "(There's) Always Something There to Remind Me." Shaw was a shrewd choice, regularly making the round of British television programming on such hit shows as *Top of the Pops, Thank Your Lucky Stars*, and *Ready Steady Go!* After Shaw and her manager, Eve Taylor—who also represented Adam Faith, another AIR client—turned down the song, Bacharach offered it to Black. Martin and Epstein were eager to try their hand at another Bacharach-David composition, and Martin produced the session at Abbey Road during the autumn of 1965. Having commandeered the massive Studio 1 at Abbey Road, Martin arranged for a forty-eight-piece orchestra to join Black and Bacharach for the session, which Epstein filmed for promotional purposes.

With Bacharach conducting the orchestra and Martin in the control room, Black was joined on the recording by the Breakaways, her regular troupe of female backup singers who, like Black herself, hailed from Liverpool. The session turned out to be a protracted affair in which Black performed take after take of the song, never seeming to meet Bacharach's expectations. After eighteen takes, it was Martin who finally interrupted the proceedings. As Black recalled, Bacharach likely "would have continued way beyond this number if George Martin hadn't become exasperated and said, kindly but firmly, and in front of everyone, 'Burt, what exactly are you looking for here?'" Always the perfectionist, Bacharach answered, "That little bit of magic." Without missing a beat, Martin looked at Bacharach and replied, "I think we got that on take four." Released nearly four months in advance of the movie's UK premiere, "Alfie" was deployed by the movie's producers to build up buzz. To Martin's delight, Black's version of "Alfie" did just that, registering a UK top-ten hit over the coming months, although it barely succeeded in cracking the US *Billboard*'s Hot 100, where it languished at a paltry number ninety-five. But for Black, "Alfie" turned out to be a godsend, becoming one of her signature songs and, years later, prompting the title of the singer's autobiography, *What's It All About?*[14]

While Martin was pleased with Black's continuing popularity, he was on the lookout for more non-Beatles successes to add to his curriculum vitae. Acutely aware of the necessity of signing new talent, Martin flew to New York City in February. Over the next fortnight, he auditioned a few acts as potential clients for AIR but spent most of the trip attempting to ferret out new songs for his existing roster, falling back on his pre-Beatles mode of going to places like London's Tin Pan Alley or, in the latest case, New York City's Brill Building to check out the wares of professional songwriters. His visit managed to capture the attention of *Cash Box*, the weekly industry trade magazine that, as with the vaunted *Billboard*, tracked the sales activities of the hitmakers of the day. Described as the "musical director of the Beatles," Martin was reported by *Cash Box* to be on a mission "to seek-out and bring back material to be cut by the artists who are being recorded by AIR." Martin told *Cash Box* that there is a "dearth of great songs" and that he was on the lookout for material for new recordings from the likes of Matt Monro and Cilla Black. But Munro and Black were existing artists in his stable, of course. And what Martin really needed was new talent outside of AIR's existing roster. In March, Martin and his partners began making key moves in this direction with the hiring of Tony King, who had previously handled promotion for Decca Records before working exclusively for Andrew Loog Oldham and the Rolling Stones. Promoting AIR and its interest in signing new talent was a priority, and King's profile fit the bill. But as *Billboard* reported in early March, King inked a deal with AIR with the express promise from Martin and his partners that King would be able to produce his own acts in the near future.[15]

As it happened, some of AIR's first recordings were performed by a quintet of mods out of North West London—Kentish Town, to be exact—called the Action, whom George had signed when he was still in EMI's employ. Purveyors of an underground culture founded on a penchant for style and fashion, the mods often clashed with the rockers, their rival subculture, in a series of riotous conflicts in the mid-1960s. With the experimental mores of Swinging London already coming to the fore, the Action seemed like the perfect act for George and AIR to catch pop music's newest wave. In many ways, the Action typified the more edgy "London sound" associated with such contemporary bands as the Who, the Small Faces, the Kinks, and the Rolling Stones. While the Beatles lorded over the mainstream UK charts and BBC airwaves during this era, the mods and the rockers duked it out on pirate radio stations like Radio Caroline and Swinging Radio England. George was convinced that the Action were the next big thing, and he had signed them as Parlophone artists—and one of AIR's inaugural clients—shortly after leaving the EMI Group in 1965. Originally known as the Boys, the Action worked a crisp, driving beat with a hard-edged sound that George deployed to great effect on their searing debut single, "Land of a Thousand Dances" backed with "In My Lonely Room." Originally written and recorded by Chris Kenner, "Land of a Thousand Dances" proved to be a veritable flop in spite of receiving strong critical notices. For his part, George was floored, having learned to trust his hitmaking instincts after several years of working to transform Epstein's stable of artists into chart-toppers. While the Action's version of "Land of a Thousand Dances" failed to make even the slightest dent in the UK charts after its October 1965 release, the song would strike gold in the United States in 1966 with Wilson Pickett's rhythm-and-blues hit record. Not to be discouraged for long, George had entered the new year with big plans to navigate the Action to the top of the UK charts. In February 1966, he prepared the Action's next single, "I'll Keep Holding On" backed with "Hey Sha-Lo-Ney," for a Parlophone release. But like its predecessor, the Action's latest single failed to chart, as did their July 1966 follow-up, "Baby, You've Got It" backed with "Since I Lost My Baby." A remake of Maurice and the Radiants' 1954 rhythm-and-blues classic with Chess Records, "Baby, You've Got It" seemed like the perfect vehicle for the Action given its dance-music overtones and hard-driving tempo.[16]

While the Action's failure to crack the UK charts had left George more than a little flummoxed, he enjoyed decidedly more success, albeit short-lived, with David and Jonathan, who had been AIR's first official signing. A pop duo out of Bristol, David and Jonathan were composed of Roger Greenaway and Roger Cook. Drawing their names from the biblical story of the friendship between Hebrew King David and Prince Jonathan in the first book of Samuel, the duo had first come to George's attention as the songwriters behind the Fortunes' top-ten UK and US hit "You've Got Your Troubles," as well as "This Golden Ring." As it turned out, the pop duo owed the genesis of their name to George's fiancée and longtime assistant, Judy. "We couldn't call them the Two Rogers," George later wrote, "and we didn't like Cook and Greenaway, so Judy hit on the idea of the biblical characters David and Jonathan, really as an example of two people who were very close friends." David and Jonathan made their AIR debut with "Michelle" backed with "How Bitter the Taste of Love" on EMI's Columbia label. Produced and orchestrated by Martin, the duo's cover version of "Michelle," the standout Lennon-McCartney composition on the Beatles' *Rubber Soul* album, landed a top-fifteen showing on the UK charts. Greenaway later recalled that "George Martin asked us to do 'Michelle' as the Beatles weren't releasing it as a single. He did the whole orchestral arrangement and worked out our harmonies. Roger Cook has a range of three octaves, he can sing high or low, and I had a high voice. I was perfect for harmonies above him and he was perfect for harmonies below me." Given his expertise in vocal arrangement, George was able to devise the harmonies that really made David and Jonathan's vocals stand out. David and Jonathan continued their wave of success with "Lovers of the World Unite" backed with "Oh My Word," which topped out at number seven, demonstrating in the process that George's ear for spotting new talent was as sharp as ever.[17]

Yet with a paucity of new artists on AIR's roster, George continued his tour of the existing acts in his stable. As 1966 continued to roll forward, he reached several years back to Rolf Harris, the Australian entertainer with whom he'd scored a major hit with "Sun Arise." Harris was thrilled to be working with Martin, especially on the peculiar novelty tracks that had recently begun to characterize the musician's output. As Harris later recalled, "George Martin was into weird things long before the Beatles. He did those comedy tracks for Charlie Drake, and I was given to George because nobody else could figure out what to do with me." With Martin in the control booth, Harris had recorded "Jake the Peg" back in 1965. He enjoyed a hit with the novelty song back in his homeland, and his career was back on track. The song's irreverent lyrics about a three-legged man managed to catch fire with his audience, who enjoyed his stage antics. During his live performances of the song, Harris often donned a peg leg in order to enhance the comedic effect. Working with George, he recorded the long-player *The Man with a Microphone* on the strength of the momentum that he had established with "Jake the Peg" back in Australia. In a clear attempt to hearken back to Harris's earlier success, Martin produced the entertainer's performance of "That's What They Call the Didgeridoo," a reference to the Australian indigenous instrument that Martin had simulated on "Sun Arise" by virtue of recording two cellos, a double bass, a piano, and Harris's guttural sounds. A collection of comic skits and wacky compositions, *The Man with a Microphone* failed to chart in the United Kingdom and Australia alike, leaving George at a loss about how to recapture the success that they had enjoyed years earlier with "Sun Arise."[18]

During this period, George also parceled out time to repackage his 1965 United Artists release, *George Martin Scores Instrumental Versions of the Hits*, for distribution on EMI's Columbia TWO label. Compiled in the same manner in which he assembled his collection of *Help!*-themed instrumentals for Columbia TWO in mid-1965, the album was titled *. . . And I Love Her* and credited to George Martin and His Orchestra. With a comely model peering out seductively from its cover art, the album featured George's easy-listening arrangements of such songs as the Beatles' *A Hard Day's Night*–era "If I Fell" and "I'm Happy Just to Dance with You," the Rolling Stones' "Time Is on My Side," Petula Clark's "Downtown," and the Righteous Brothers' "You've Lost That Lovin' Feeling," among others. Although his long-players never set the world on fire—much less generated enough sales to make a serious dent in the record charts—George's easy-listening arrangements served a vital purpose by making inroads into adult demographics beyond the teenaged set. In a similar vein, George produced his old friend Ron Goodwin's latest long-player. One of Martin's first clients from his earliest days with Parlophone, Goodwin had enjoyed considerable success as a composer and conductor of movie soundtracks, including such films as *633 Squadron, Of*

Human Bondage, and, most recently, *Those Magnificent Men in Their Flaying Machines*. Titled *Adventure*, Goodwin's new album offered selections from his film scores, which he had conducted with the Ron Goodwin Orchestra and with Martin up in the booth. For his part, Goodwin was an unabashed admirer of Martin's, later describing him as a "first-class record producer and a very good musician. He was very well-informed technically about what you can and can't do in a recording studio, and he had a wonderful, natural talent for handling people. I've never seen him get upset on a session and I've never seen him upset anybody else. If anything went wrong, George knew how to handle it in such a way that the other person doesn't realize what's happening." And to Goodwin's mind, this latter aspect made him "the ideal producer."[19]

In March, Martin completed postproduction work on Black's new long-player, titled *Cilla Sings a Rainbow*. By the time that *Cilla Sings a Rainbow* was released on the Parlophone label on April 18, George would be hard at work on a project that would shift the trajectory of his career yet again. But in the interim, Black's latest long-player marked yet another strong showing for her collaboration with Martin, with the album topping out at number four on the UK charts, besting *Cilla*, which had captured the number-five position. The album was chock-full of cover versions, including some of the original compositions that Martin had secured for the chanteuse during his recent trip to New York City. *Cilla Sings a Rainbow* included yet another Bacharach-David number in "Make It Easy on Yourself," as well as a cover version of Lennon-McCartney's "Yesterday." Although it was not even a year old at this point, "Yesterday" was already well on its way to becoming the most covered song in pop-music history. For Black, the album's great highlight was the jaunty "Love's Just a Broken Heart (L'Amour Est Ce Qu'il Est)," which had been arranged by Martin, of course, and composed by Mort Shuman, Kenny Lynch, and Michele Vendome. For Black, it was especially poignant when the "Love's Just a Broken Heart" backed with "Yesterday" single notched the number-two spot on the UK charts. As she later wrote, "It was in many ways a surprise to lots of people that I was still having hits. I was supposed to be a flash in the pan, after all. This was the number I would sing when I topped the bill on *Sunday Night at the London Palladium*." The album's colorful cover art was shot by Robert Whitaker, a London photographer known for his pop-art designs and surrealistic vision.[20]

As he was putting the finishing touches on *Cilla Sings a Rainbow*, George found himself on the fringes of a lawsuit involving the Who and their estranged producer, American expatriate Shel Talmy. For his part, Martin had long admired Talmy, who had thrown caution to the wind and immigrated to the United Kingdom in 1962, slowly building up a stable of hit acts like the Kinks and the Who as an independent record producer. Martin admired the twenty-eight-year-old Talmy's pluck, and his own pursuit of the Action as potential hitmakers likely owed its genesis to the younger man's raucous-sounding records, especially his breakthrough work with the Kinks' lacerating "You Really Got Me." Like the other independents of his day, Talmy took considerable risk when he assumed out-of-pocket costs, including studio rental fees, studio musicians, and personnel expenses, but he stood to make big bucks if his records ascended the charts and generated strong sales receipts. Martin came to Talmy's defense after the young producer and the Who parted ways after a contractual disagreement. Talmy had signed the Who after watching them rehearse, and he recorded their breakout tune "I Can't Explain" in November 1964 at London's Pye Studios. But things came to a head after the December 1965 release of the Who's debut LP, *My Generation*, which scored a top-five showing in the United Kingdom and was likely denied the number-one spot because of the *Rubber Soul* juggernaut. The band's relationship with Talmy soured after they accused him of being in cahoots with Decca Records, the American distributor of their debut album, which was titled *The Who Sings My Generation* in the US marketplace. The Who blamed Talmy and Decca for the LP's lackluster showing in North America, and they decided to break their contract with their producer.[21]

The Who's lawsuit with Talmy came about after they released the song "Instant Party" as the B-side of "Substitute" on March 7, 1966. Knowing that the Who had simply rerecorded "Circles," an earlier Talmy production, and renamed it, Talmy leaped into action, seeking an emergency injunction. As the Who's Pete Townshend later recalled, "We did two versions of 'Circles,' which were both identical because they were both copies of my demo. Shel put in a High Court injunction, saying there was copyright in the recording. In other words, if you're a record producer and you produce a song with a group, and you make a creative contribution, then you own that sound. He took it to the high-court judge and he said things like 'And then on bar 36 I suggested to the lead guitarist that he play a diminuendo, forget the adagio, and play 36 bars modulating to the key of E flat,' which was all total bullshit—he used to fall asleep at the desk." In his sworn affidavit on Talmy's behalf, Martin attested to his long-standing and now vaunted place in the British record industry, which by this point spanned nearly sixteen years. With his bona fides established, Martin affirmed that the recordings of "Circles" and "Instant Party" were "substantially the same," albeit with "one or two minor and insignificant differences." For Martin, being called upon to provide expert testimony was a far cry from his more desperate, pre-Beatles times in 1960, when he had been accused by *Melody Maker* of "piracy" for recording a near-perfect copy of American phenom Brian Hyland's "Itsy Bitsy Teenie Weenie Yellow Polka Dot Bikini" with eighteen-year-old Brit Paul Hanford. As for Talmy and the Who, Martin's affidavit clearly made a difference, with the warring parties working out an agreement within the month in Talmy's favor in which the Who would provide the producer with a percentage of their future royalties.[22]

But by that juncture, George's mind had clearly drifted to more pressing matters. He had found himself in limbo with the Beatles across the early months of 1966, which was undoubtedly an issue of great concern for the producer, who was now an independent in his own right. The bandmates were at a crossroads of sorts after completing work on *Rubber Soul* in November and perhaps even more significantly, wrapping up their final UK concert tour with a pair of shows at the Capitol Cinema in Cardiff. They had privately decided that their touring days were coming to an end. For his part, Epstein doubted their resolve. But the evidence of their shifting intentions was hidden in plain sight.

During the 1963 and 1964 holiday seasons, Epstein had staged a series of sold-out Beatles Christmas concerts. But in December 1965, the bandmates simply weren't having it. The UK winter tour was their concession to Epstein's abiding desire to keep them in the public eye—but it would be one of their last. Like other rock 'n' roll impresarios, Epstein was concerned that the Beatles' fame could be fleeting—that they might end up being yet another "flash in the pan." After all, Beatlemania had been built, brick by brick, on the foundation of standout performances on Val Parnell's *Sunday Night at the London Palladium* in October 1963 and *The Ed Sullivan Show* in February 1964. But George understood the Beatles' frustrations, which went well beyond life on the road. He had long harbored concerns about their safety, as he had personally observed the tumult in such faraway locales as Colorado's Red Rocks Amphitheatre and California's Hollywood Bowl. At their last show in Cardiff, a fan had rushed the stage as John introduced "Day Tripper," reminding the bandmates yet again how vulnerable they were to the selfsame fans who had elevated them to global stardom. For Martin, the writing was clearly on the wall as far as the Beatles were concerned. "By 1966, the Beatles were in a car that was going downhill very fast," he later recalled. "This is not to say that their career was going downhill; but they were a media juggernaut that was increasingly out of their manager Brian Epstein's control—and everyone else's, for that matter. It wasn't so much that somebody was pressing the accelerator too hard; it was that nobody had their foot on the brake." And when it came to the Beatles, Martin increasingly recognized that he, too, was complicit in the band's headlong rush into the unknown, that he, too, had effectively taken his hand off the brake.[23]

2

"WHY CAN'T WE CUT A RECORD LIKE THAT?"

B Y THE EARLY MONTHS of 1966, it was far more than just concert tours—and the Beatles' prison-like progress from one faceless city to another—that plagued the bandmates. By this point, their collaboration with George had transformed their musical output from primitive beat numbers into more mature recordings that addressed weightier subject matter, including loneliness, infidelity, and the rage for individuality in such songs as "Yesterday," "Norwegian Wood (This Bird Has Flown)," and "Nowhere Man," respectively. By expanding their notions of the recording studio—and how technology could propel their visions into ever more vivid representations of sound and language—George had opened up a world of uncharted territory for the Beatles. With 1965's *Help!* and *Rubber Soul* long-players, the Beatles had grown their demographic considerably beyond teeny boppers and young adults. By the dawn of 1966, their fan base was bursting at the seams and now included legions of new fans who had seen themselves reflected in the band's evolving sound. But for all the adulation that they enjoyed, the Beatles themselves still felt isolated by their creative vision, which they increasingly found nearly impossible to re-create in front of thousands of screaming fans who wanted nothing more than to hear the likes of "She Loves You" and "I Want to Hold Your Hand" blaring from inadequate PA systems in far-flung concert halls across Great Britain and the United States. As Ringo later recalled, "The realization was really kicking in that nobody was listening. And that was okay at the beginning, but even worse than that was we were playing so bad. I just felt we're playing really bad. Why I joined the Beatles was because they were the best band in Liverpool. I always wanted to play with good players—that's what it was all about. First and foremost, we were musicians."[1]

By this point, the Beatles simply wanted their music to be *heard*, to be understood for what they had accomplished in just a few short years. As John had remarked to *NME*'s Keith Altham, "There are only about a hundred people in the world who really understand what our music is all about." In an August 24 press conference in Los Angeles at Capitol Records' famous tower, McCartney deployed humor in an effort to deflect a reporter's question about the significance of the band's music and its attendant meanings:

> Reporter: "I'd like to direct this question to Messrs. Lennon and McCartney. In a recent article, *Time* magazine put down pop music. And they referred to 'Day Tripper' as being about a prostitute . . . and 'Norwegian Wood' as being about a lesbian. . . . I just wanted to know what your intent was when you wrote it, and what your feeling is about the *Time* magazine criticism of the music that is being written today."
> McCartney: "We were just trying to write songs about prostitutes and lesbians, that's all."

And while they were clearly irritated by the culture's seeming inability to grasp the meaning behind their work, they were far more rankled by their increasingly slipshod stage work. By the mid-1960s, the Beatles' shoddy live performances had become a matter of concern for Paul, who worried that their musicianship was suffering under the harsh sonic conditions inherent in contemporary concert technology. "We were getting worse and worse as a band while all those people were screaming," he remembered. "It was lovely that they liked us, but we couldn't hear to play. So the only place we could develop was in the studio." But the Beatles also wanted their recordings to be made with the greatest possible fidelity, an aspect of their sound that they felt had been hampered by Abbey Road's outdated technology. George understood this perspective implicitly. Along with the bandmates, he had been clamoring for EMI to install newfangled equipment at Abbey Road, although their individual and collective voices inevitably fell on deaf ears given the austere nature of EMI's studio mind-set. It is a great irony that George and the Beatles, having generated millions of record sales, were unable to throw their weight around and demand technological enhancements at EMI Studios.[2]

But in truth, the recalcitrance had more to do with the sterile, paternalistic culture that existed at Abbey Road at the time as opposed to the band's stature in the recording industry. As George later recalled, "What EMI did for them was to put in special lighting," which essentially amounted to "three fluorescent tubes—one white, one red, and one blue." As Norman Smith pointed out, the Beatles "were screaming for more sophisticated equipment, more flexible equipment, that could give better definition." For his part, Harrison put things in decidedly more blunt terms, realizing the irony in the stark conditions under which the biggest band in the world produced their legendary records: "It was all done very clinically, that's the joke," he later remarked. "We were in this big white room that was very dirty and hadn't been painted in years, and it had all these old sound baffles hanging down that were all dirty and broken. There was this huge big hanging light, there was no window, no daylight. It was a very clinical, not very nice atmosphere. When you think of the songs that were made in that studio, it's amazing because there was no atmosphere in there, we had to make the atmosphere." In many ways, EMI's top-down approach to the recording studio—in elevating management's position over the needs of the real makers of music—underscored many of the reasons that Martin had cited for leaving the record conglomerate the previous fall.[3]

Unbeknownst to George at that time, the bandmates had begun taking concrete steps to do something about their lingering dismay over EMI Studios' intractable ways. In retrospect, they can be understood as engaging in a pointed effort to transform themselves from a touring band into a studio act. With this notion in mind, the Beatles dispatched Brian Epstein to Memphis, Tennessee, in March in order to scout out recording studios with equipment superior to the existing technology at Abbey Road. The bandmates were especially interested in being able to capture the "Stax sound" associated with such American acts as Wilson Pickett, Otis Redding, and Booker T. and the MG's, among others. Stax Studio was particularly alluring to the Beatles because of the unique sound that the facility produced due to the cinema's sharply sloping floor. As Paul remarked at the time, "The equipment in most British recording studios is much better than it is in the States. But there's some extra bit they get to the sound over there that we haven't quite got. You put a record of ours [on after] an American record and you'll find the American record is always a fraction louder and it has a lucid something I can't explain." The intent behind Paul's words about "most British recording studios" offered a subtle hint about how the Beatles viewed Abbey Road. But there were plenty of recent examples that the Beatles could recount—most significantly, the Rolling Stones' international hit "(I Can't

Get No) Satisfaction," which they had recorded at Chicago's Chess Studios and Hollywood's RCA Studios.

Like McCartney, Harrison was interested in capturing the raw and punchy American sound on their records. As he remarked to *Beatles Book Monthly*, the band's official fan club magazine, "Some terrific records have been made. They get these great band sounds as well. Wilson Pickett, Otis Redding and lots of them record in Memphis. Even if we didn't use some local musicians on the actual sessions, there'd be this great atmosphere. They concentrate on rhythm & blues and rock in Memphis." In a conversation with Beatles publicity officer Tony Barrow, Harrison made special note of American recording engineers, whom he suspected were superior to their British counterparts: "The recording engineers there are specialists. It's not just a job to them. They love our kind of music. There'd be this great atmosphere." He later pointed out that recording overseas might even act as a creative catalyst for the group, a means for testing their mettle as musicians in unfamiliar environs. "It'll shake up everything," said Harrison. "You don't grow as a band unless you shake things up, you know."[4]

John took things a step further, even going so far as to suggest that they might try their hand with an American producer to go along with their desire to record on American soil. As he later remarked, "Obviously we'd discussed not using George, even when we'd used him, just for a change. America being the dream place, we were always suspicious that American studios were much better than ours, than EMI. It wasn't so true, of course, when we got over there. It was just that the early Sun Records were something special, and a few records that [Phil] Spector and some other people had made. It was usually the man, and not the studio. So we often talked about Spector, that we'd like to work with him."[5]

But with Memphis in the offing, the man of the moment for Lennon was none other than Steve Cropper, the legendary guitarist with Booker T. and the MG's, as well as a member of the Stax house band. At twenty-four years old, Cropper was the hippest American producer in the business, as well as the composer behind such classic tunes as Pickett's "In the Midnight Hour" and Eddie Floyd's "Knock on Wood," among others. As for Cropper himself, the rhythm-and-blues guitarist had no idea why the Beatles were interested in working with him beyond the opportunity to record at Stax. As Cropper later remarked, "In those days there was not much mention of George Martin, at least in Memphis. We also didn't listen to much Beatle or pop music. Only what was played on radio. I just assumed from what I was told by Epstein that they wanted me to produce them. We never got far enough to discuss engineers or other musicians' involvement. Brian Epstein was around for a couple of days. He only came to the studio to discuss things so I didn't hang with him or anything. We talked a few times by phone when he returned to England."[6]

Things may have been proceeding casually as far as Cropper was concerned, but Epstein was serious enough to book a starting date of April 9 for the Beatles to begin working at Stax. For his part, Epstein had already been considering security issues and accommodations during the Beatles' visit. Elvis Presley had even offered to house the group and their entourage at Graceland. While Epstein had demanded that the band's visit be held in absolute secrecy, word got out on March 31, when the *Memphis Press-Scimitar* reported that the group would be arriving in two weeks to record at Stax with studio owner Jim Stewart as producer, Cropper serving as arranger, and Atlantic Records' Tom Dowd supervising the sessions. Upset by this turn of events, Epstein suggested an abrupt change of course in a telephone call with Cropper, who later recalled that "he contacted me and asked if I would be willing to come to New York and record them at Atlantic's studio. He felt the Beatles would be safer there. I told him I would be willing if that was what the band wanted."[7]

So why did the Beatles give up on their dream of recording at Stax with a bona fide American producer? And more importantly, where did Martin figure in these decisions regarding the band's immediate future? In 1964, he and Brian had formulated a rudimentary plan of releasing new Beatles product in the form of a new single every three months, two albums per year, and a feature film. From 1963 through 1965, they had produced six albums together, along with a whole raft of hit singles. But 1966, alas, would be different. It already appeared as though there would be no new Beatles film that year—indeed, only a few months earlier, they had rejected producer Walter Shenson's pitch for a third United Artists movie titled *A Talent for Loving* that would have depicted the four Beatles as Old West characters. But at this point, as Brian and the bandmates considered veering away from their planned annual output, George had seemingly been left out of the equation and was possibly even entirely in the dark about the Beatles' thinking. At the same time, there was little doubt that he agreed with the bandmates' position vis-à-vis American studios, and he, too, wanted to emulate the sound that they created. As Martin later wrote, American records "were technically streets ahead of us, and they could make these records that didn't just shout—they roared. I didn't know how they did it. But I wanted to find out all right." Like the Fab Four, he had been fascinated by that quintessentially American sound. As he later recalled, "The Beatles used to play me some of these records when we first met: the new, mostly black American rock 'n' roll records. When I first came across them their favorite artists were Chuck Berry, Carl Perkins, Bo Diddley, Jerry Lee Lewis, Fats Domino, Little Richard, Smokey Robinson, Roy Orbison, Buddy Holly, and, of course, Elvis Presley. 'Have a listen to this!' they would say. 'Don't you think that's great?' I would not hear what they heard, but I heard something that was interesting and good."[8]

Like the Beatles, Martin couldn't help but be impressed by the maximum volume of the recordings produced in American studios. As Martin later observed, by early 1966 "I had been a record producer for so long that whenever I listened to anything new I was not listening only to the music; I was listening to the way the recording had been made, technically. What amazed me," he added, "was the sheer technical ferocity of the stuff. The US studios managed to pack so much volume on to a disc, much more than we could over here in the UK. I could pick up the newly imported piece of 45 RPM vinyl, look at it, and actually see the ear-splitting loudness of the record before I had even put it on. It was, as they say, in the groove." Although he may not have been fully a part of the ongoing conversation about where and under what conditions the bandmates would record their follow-up long-player to *Rubber Soul*, he certainly grasped the nature of their desire to make a sizzling, American-style record in places like Stax. "Why can't we cut a record like that?" he would say to the Beatles. "If we had tried to cut a record as loud as that, the needle, probably the whole playing-arm of your Dansette record player would have jumped straight off the vinyl and fallen on the floor." Such was the nature of the technology at EMI Studios at the time. But understandably, George's mind was in a very different place in those early months of 1966. He had been busying himself with getting AIR off the ground, signing new acts, and scouting out future London recording studio spaces for himself and his partners.[9]

In the end, the Beatles' American recording plans may have collapsed almost entirely for financial reasons. *Almost.* "They wanted a fantastic amount of money to use the facilities there," Paul later recalled, strongly suspecting that it came down to capitalizing on the Beatles' wealth and name. "They were obviously trying to take us for a ride," he added. Years later, Martin would take this issue a step further, pointing out that recording in the United States simply wasn't realistic in terms of the bottom line: "From EMI's point of view," he recalled, "it wouldn't have made sense because every record would have had to bear the 1.5 percent AFM [American Federation of Musicians] levy. It wasn't feasible. Anyway, I had to do what EMI told me." This last fact was particularly relevant in terms of George's ongoing work with the Beatles, which was strictly governed by the deal that he had struck back in 1965 when he parted ways with the record conglomerate. But perhaps even more interestingly, George attributed the Beatles' change of heart to the simple fact that he "didn't want to record in the States." Was he still as integral as he believed himself to be in the Beatles' artistic calculus? Or had he become expendable now that the Beatles, at least to John's way of thinking, had finally taken over the studio? As historian Mark Lewisohn has observed, it is difficult to imagine a scenario in which George wouldn't have ensured that he remained integral to the Beatles' activities at this juncture. Martin underscored this point himself in his April 1966 remarks to Barrow, pointedly demonstrating his continuous central role in their creative brain trust. "If we ever do go out of London for sessions," said George, "it would be experimental. It's true that different local musical environments could have a strong effect on the Beatles. We wouldn't know what to expect in the way of results but it would be a new experience for all of us." According to Lewisohn, if Martin had felt threatened, it wasn't from Cropper but Stewart, who was a bona fide producer with a longer and more distinguished record than the rhythm-and-blues guitarist. "George Martin wouldn't have liked another producer in the mix," said Lewisohn.[10]

As it happened, the Beatles had been experiencing another transformation during roughly the same period in which they had pondered their recording venture in Memphis. And it would have far-reaching implications for George's working relationship with the band. For Paul, in particular, the post–*Rubber Soul* era was turning out to be "a very free, formless time for me," he later recalled. When he was still living with Jane Asher's family on Wimpole Street—the place where George Martin had taken oboe lessons during the late 1940s—Paul had made vital connections across literary London and the avant-garde art world. As he spent more and more time with the smart set, he began to realize his own intellectual deficits, recognizing that "people are saying things and painting things and writing things and composing things that are great. I must know what people are doing." In addition to studying the work of experimental composers such as Karlheinz Stockhausen and Luciano Berio, Paul took to reading contemporary poetry and broadening his literary horizons. Robert Fraser, the London art dealer and gallery owner who went by the name of "Groovy Bob," emerged as one of Paul's mentors, introducing him to such purveyors of the canvas and screen as Andy Warhol, Claes Oldenburg, Jim Dine, and Michelangelo Antonioni. Paul was also the first Beatle to up his musical game. With George's encouragement, Paul took piano lessons at the Guildhall School of Music and Drama, the producer's alma mater. McCartney wasn't the only member of the Beatles' inner circle who had considered spreading his wings. For a time, Martin had even considered learning how to play the guitar so he could better understand the Beatles' composition and performance practices. But he gave up quickly, realizing that he would never have the necessary time to learn how to play, much less master the instrument.[11]

During this same period, Paul became friends with John Dunbar and his wife, Marianne Faithfull. With Dunbar and Peter Asher, McCartney would help found the Indica Bookshop and Gallery, which emerged as the unofficial headquarters for bohemian London. As Dunbar later recalled, "We talked a lot about the music, all of the time. We used to play stuff and record stuff. Old blues, Jimmy Reed, Muddy Waters, all the old blues blokes." And oh, how they recorded stuff. Paul had procured a couple of Brenell reel-to-reel tape recorders from Dick James's son. "I used to experiment with them when I had an afternoon off, which was quite often," Paul later recalled. "We'd be playing in the evening, we'd be doing a radio show or something, and there was often quite a bit of time when I was just in the house on my own so I had a lot of time for this. I wasn't in a routine. . . . So I would sit around all day, creating little tapes." Paul became entranced by the idea of running the tape backward, later graduating to creating imaginative tape loops by splicing bits of tape into pieces and randomly joining them together courtesy of a bottle of EMI glue that he had picked up at Abbey Road.

Paul was particularly influenced by Stockhausen's *Gesang der Jünglinge*, a mid-1950s work by the renowned composer of electronic sound and one of the first great *musique concrète* classics. By disabling the Brenell's erase heads and allowing a continuous loop of tape to course through the machine, Paul found that the machine would be constantly overdubbing itself and, in so doing, creating a saturation effect that he could slow down or speed up at his discretion. "I used to make loops mainly with guitar or voices, or bongos, and then I'd record them off on to this other Brenell so that I had a series of loops," Paul recalled. "It would start with a thing that sounded like bees buzzing for a few seconds, then that would slow down and then an echo would kick in and then some high violins would come in, but they were speeded-up guitar playing a little thing, then behind them there would be a very slow ponderous drone. Quite a nice montage sound collage. The guitar would sound like seagulls. They were great little things and I had great plans for them, they were going to be little symphonies, all made with tape loops done by varispeeding the tape."[12]

Paul was so enthralled with his Brenell experiments that he outfitted the other Beatles' homes with machines of their own. Like Paul, John soon began making experimental recordings with his Brenell recorder. Lennon's tape loops were often accented with sounds produced on a Mellotron, which Martin later described as Lennon's "favorite toy of the moment. The Mellotron was a Heath Robinson contraption if ever there was one; you could virtually see the bits of string and rubber holding it together. It was as if a Neanderthal piano had impregnated a primitive electronic keyboard, and they'd named the deformed, dwarfish offspring 'Mellotron.'" Lennon had purchased the Mellotron in 1965, possessing one of the rare versions with a polished mahogany cabinet and gold serigraphy. Pink Floyd, a new band out of London Polytechnic, also had their hands on one of the rare models, which they would shortly put to use on their debut album, with Norman Smith, Martin's old protégé, sitting in as their producer. An electro-mechanical keyboard, the Mellotron created sound through a tape-replay system composed of eighteen prerecorded instruments. As Geoff Emerick later pointed out, the Mellotron was not without controversy: in Great Britain, "the Musicians' Union tried to stop manufacture because of the way it reproduced the sounds of other instruments." As for George Harrison, the quiet Beatle had recently purchased Kinfauns, a bungalow in Esher only a few miles away from Kenwood, Lennon's place in Weybridge, where he planned to install a home recording studio.[13]

In the meantime, Harrison was experiencing a renaissance of his own. Like McCartney, he had begun to realize that the Beatles' live shows were contributing to a deterioration of the bandmates' musicianship. The throes and screams of Beatlemania, Harrison feared, had led to the erosion of their sound, not to mention a roadblock in the way of their further development as musicians. As Harrison remarked at the time, "We have different audiences all the time and we play the same numbers—so we don't get much chance to develop. . . . I suppose I should have improved much more. If we pack it in one day I'll probably learn to play the guitar properly. Or chop it up." But as it turned out, there were still plenty of new vistas of musical discovery available to him. In early 1965, he had become enthralled by the sitar, the Hindustani fretted instrument, which he had discovered on the set of *Help!* For his part, Martin had accrued previous experience recording the instrument back in 1959 for Peter Sellers and the Goons when they lampooned *My Fair Lady*'s "Wouldn't It Be Loverly" complete with sitar accompaniment, which Martin had arranged via London's Asian Music Circle. More recently, Martin had gamely recorded Harrison playing the exotic instrument on *Rubber Soul*'s

"Norwegian Wood (This Bird Has Flown)," but the quiet Beatle was only just getting started. At the time, Harrison admitted that he was so smitten with the instrument that "sometimes before I go to sleep, I think what it would be like to be inside Ravi's sitar."[14]

Harrison had found his own way into the vaunted Asian Music Circle after breaking a sitar string during one of the sessions for "Norwegian Wood." He met Ravi Shankar, the Bengali-born musician and composer, by way of Ayana Angadi and his wife, Patricia. Together, the couple led the Asian Music Circle, which met in their home in Finchley. Founded in 1953, the circle had invited a number of eminent Indian musicians to London, including Vilayat Khan, Ali Akbar Khan, Alla Rakha, Chatur Lal, and Shankar, who was in his midforties by the time he met Harrison and had already emerged as the most prominent Indian musician of his day—and most especially as an accomplished practitioner of the sitar. After working with Shankar, Harrison devoted himself to mastering the difficult instrument in much the same way that he approached his craft as a guitarist. It was an effort that would alter the musical direction of the Beatles, with far-reaching and unforeseen implications.

On Wednesday, April 6, 1966, Martin and the Beatles reconvened at Abbey Road for the first time in more than four months. That evening, they settled down to work in Studio 3, smaller and in sharp contrast with Number 2, their regular EMI Studios recording venue. But the room change wasn't the only shift in evidence that night. Changes were clearly afoot, as George and the Beatles' long-standing engineer Norman "Normal" Smith had vacated his seat in the control room, having ascended to become the next Parlophone A&R head, George's old job before he left the EMI Group to go into business for himself. But things had gotten off to a rocky start for Smith after having been chastised by EMI chairman Sir Joseph Lockwood for what Lockwood had seen as impolitic behavior when Smith sent a letter in which he attempted to lure away one of a rival record company's artists. For his part, Smith realized how close he'd come to being fired. And while he may not have known it at the time, Sir Joseph didn't forget so easily either. Throughout 1966 and into the early months of 1967, the EMI chairman had tried to entice independent producer Joe Meek to take over as Parlophone's A&R head. For record-business folk like Martin and Smith, Meek was a household name. Martin had known the younger man since the mid-1950s, when Martin, then Parlophone A&R head, recorded Meek's "Put a Ring on Her Finger" with singer Eddie Silver. The record failed to chart in the United Kingdom but managed a top-thirty showing stateside. Meek's career began to take off after he produced Humphrey Lyttelton's hit single "Bad Penny Blues" for Parlophone. As the 1950s wore on, Meek quickly became known as one of London's quirkiest, albeit most gifted, producers.

Meek worked with Martin even more closely in 1958, when he produced pop duo Joy and David's "Whoopee!," with Martin sitting in on the Abbey Road session as supervisor. The two producers clashed almost immediately when it became clear to Meek that, at the time at least, the men had very different ideas about staging an artist's career. During the session, Meek asked Martin about Joy and David's chances at recording a hit track, to which Martin replied, "Yes, about their eighth record." For the aggressive Meek, eager to grow his reputation in the marketplace after landing a hit with Lyttelton, Martin's seeming conservatism was patently unacceptable. A few short years later, Meek became known far and wide as a technical wunderkind after landing an international hit with the Tornados' "Telstar." Penned by Meek and named in honor of the Telstar satellite that began orbiting the Earth in July 1962, "Telstar" featured a clavioline, an electronic, space-age-sounding keyboard. The instrumental topped the UK and US charts in 1962, earning a coveted Ivor Novello Award for Meek in the process. Earlier that same year, Meek had even had a shot at producing the Beatles before they came into Martin's orbit. Epstein had pitched the band to Meek, who "was no more impressed with their audition tape than anyone else, seeing the Beatles as just another noisy group covering other people's songs." Epstein had pleaded with the young producer to take on the Beatles. In the end, Epstein went home to Liverpool empty-handed once again, and Meek would later claim that any potential deal had fallen apart because, improbably under the circumstances, Epstein had demanded too high a percentage.[15]

As George well knew from his long experience in the esteemed halls of EMI, the record conglomerate was rife with political intrigue and warring factions. In this light, it is easy to understand why Sir Joseph may have been determined to unseat Smith over what might have seemed like a fairly minor infraction in protocol. As 1966 progressed, the EMI chairman would make several overtures to Meek about assuming Martin's former role with Parlophone. But by this time, Meek was a far cry from the eager young producer who had transformed "Telstar" into an international juggernaut. Fraught with paranoia and hooked on barbiturates, the skilled producer was hunkered down in his three-story home studio at 304 Holloway Road in Islington, not too far, as the crow flies, from George's boyhood haunts. Nestled above a leather-goods shop, Meek's studio had already seen a number of hits produced within its walls. In addition to "Telstar," 304 Holloway Road had witnessed such Meek productions as John Leyton's UK chart-topper "Johnny Remember Me" and the Honeycombs' number-one hit "Have I the Right?," which also managed to crack the top five in the American market. But during the intervening years, the once-promising producer had slipped further behind the competition. Back in the summer of 1965, he had listened to Martin's exquisite work on "Yesterday" with some friends, and everything came brutally into focus, if only briefly. "That's beautiful," he said aloud. "I don't need telling that." And while it had been nearly two years since Meek had struck gold with the Honeycombs, Lockwood was betting that the wunderkind might yet right his ship before it was too late. And he was hoping that the addle-minded Meek would leave his home studio behind and stake his future with Parlophone at Abbey Road.[16]

However tenuous it may have been at the time, Smith's promotion made way for young Geoff Emerick to serve as the Beatles' balance engineer, with Phil McDonald acting as technical engineer. Emerick, who would turn twenty years old in 1966, had already been working at Abbey Road for nearly four years, having begun as a novice "button pusher" at the tender age of fifteen, fresh off of completing his studies at North London's Crouch End Secondary Modern School. Emerick's preternatural ability to hear minute particulars of sound had earned him the nickname "Golden Ears" around the studio corridors. In truth, there was no standing rule that would have prevented Smith from serving as a producer in his own right while staying on as the Beatles' engineer. But Martin wasn't having it. Years later, Emerick would speculate about his older colleague's motives:

> With the benefit of hindsight, I can equally understand George Martin's adamant refusal to allow Norman to receive the promotion and remain as the Beatles' engineer. There was no way George wanted another producer in the room with him when he was working with "the boys"—that would undermine his authority and place him, and everyone else, for that matter, in an extremely awkward position. George always wanted the limelight to shine on him alone. Having a peer in the control room was completely unacceptable from his point of view. Having a wet-behind-the-ears 19-year-old rookie engineer, on the other hand, was fine. Simply put, I presented no threat to him.

If Martin had been concerned that Emerick secretly coveted his job, he had nothing about which to be even remotely concerned. "Having control over the sounds was my goal all along," Emerick later remarked, "and I was much happier tinkering with the controls of the mixing board and coming up with new sonic innovations than I would have been going through string arrangements and organizing session bookings."[17]

For his part, Emerick directed most of his anxiety on that first night in the producer's chair to the Beatles themselves. He had tossed and turned the night before, worried that the bandmates might not be receptive to the idea of having him in such a vaunted role. Events would shortly demonstrate that his worries had been entirely unfounded. Emerick's value to the bandmates at this crucial juncture in their careers lay in his technical know-how. While Martin was a master of orchestration and had a natural gift for shaping the work of his artists, he lacked the vast storehouse of knowledge in terms of engineering and the nuts and bolts of record production that his younger colleague had in spades. To his credit, Emerick made it his business to possess a working understanding of the latest studio trickery and sonic innovations. By this point, he had worked with Meek on several occasions at Abbey Road. "I was enthralled with the low end on his records and with their unique coloration, which I later learned was due to his home-built compressors," Emerick later wrote. "Joe's tapes were distinguished by their offbeat echoes and reverbs, also the result of his self-designed equipment. The only tool we had that was roughly equivalent was EMI's acoustic echo chamber, which sounded quite good—so good, in fact, that it was rarely available for mastering, because it was almost always in use by a recording session." For Emerick, talented producers like Meek challenged him to learn as much as he possibly could so that when his own opportunity to shine arrived, he would be prepared to act.[18]

It seems plausible in retrospect that George didn't want to record in the United States—or at least, not at that juncture when he was trying to make a go of it with AIR—and that the Beatles knew it. Emerick would later claim to have known about the April 6 Abbey Road session with the Beatles for a solid fortnight, suggesting that Stax was old news by mid- to late March. But the band's presence in the United Kingdom that evening also came down to something entirely different, something essential to the Beatles' DNA as artists—namely, Lennon and McCartney's impulsiveness as composers. The duo's creative caprice had always been characterized by a fervent desire to bring their vision to fruition as soon as reasonably possible after first having discovered the germ of an artistic idea—whether as a result of a collaborative writing session or, as was becoming the norm, their individual efforts. Paul would later describe this rage for creation as something akin to working "on heat"—the notion that he and John would become so overwhelmed by their creative impulses that they had to get into the studio as soon as possible in order to purge the latest composition from their synapses and get on to the next thing.[19]

For John and Paul, the past few months had seen their compositions beginning to accumulate at a precipitous rate. Having achieved new artistic heights with *Rubber Soul*, they were clearly ready to take their latest wares into the studio and bring them off—so that they could write new and better songs, of course! For Paul, the composition for which he was "on heat" may very well have been a little number that had come to him during a recent visit to Bristol, where he was in town to see Jane Asher performing on stage with the local Old Vic Company. Written from a detached perspective about an aging spinster and a lonely parish priest, Paul's latest song was a clear departure for him, eschewing the warmth and familiarity of personal pronouns for the cold eye of a novelist. The spinster, at least at this juncture, was called Miss Daisy Hawkins, although he felt that the name seemed too contrived. As he later recalled,

I was sitting at the piano when I thought of it. Just like Jimmy Durante. The first few bars just came to me. And I got this name in my head— "Daisy Hawkins picks up the rice in the church where a wedding has been." I don't know why. I can hear a whole song in one chord. In fact, I think you can hear a whole song in one note, if you listen hard enough. I couldn't think of much more, so I put it away for a day. Then the name "Father McCartney" came to me—and "all the lonely people." But I thought people would think it was supposed to be my dad, sitting knitting his socks. Dad's a happy lad. So I went through the telephone book and I got the name McKenzie. I was in Bristol when I decided Daisy Hawkins wasn't a good name. I walked round looking at the shops and I saw the name Rigby. You got that? *Quick pan to Bristol.* I can just see this all as a Hollywood musical.

With a surname in hand, Paul christened his spinster as Eleanor after actress Eleanor Bron, whom the Beatles had starred with in *Help!* during the previous year. As it happened, the name Eleanor Rigby may have been in Paul's subconscious for much longer still. Scant yards away from the field behind St. Peter's Church in Woolton, where Lennon and McCartney first met on July 6, 1957, lies a gravestone for one Eleanor Rigby, who had died in October 1939 at age forty-four and been buried along with her name.[20]

As for John, writerly inspiration for his latest composition had been brewing since the previous year. But he wouldn't be writing "on heat" until barely a week before George and the Beatles reconvened at Abbey Road on April 6. John had been expressly interested in capturing the essence of his recent psychedelic wanderings on record. In April 1965, his world had been transformed by the events that transpired at a dinner party with George Harrison and Pattie Boyd's dentist, John Riley, at the home of Riley's fiancée, Cyndy Bury. To Lennon's surprise and initial dismay, Riley slipped LSD—lysergic acid diethylamide, also known as "acid"—into his guests' coffee. As Cynthia Lennon later recalled, "It was done without our knowledge so we didn't know how to handle it. We didn't know the effect it was going to have on us. It was like sitting in this room and it suddenly became like the Albert Hall. Pattie and George were opposite, John was beside me, and they started disappearing in the distance. I wondered what on earth was happening. We just had to get out. I didn't know what was happening to me. It was more frightening than anything I'd ever experienced. I thought I would be like this for the rest of my life. John Riley said that we shouldn't leave the house because he'd given us LSD but we thought 'So? What's that?' It was a totally irresponsible thing to have done." Against Riley's advice, the Beatles and their wives soon fled the premises. That evening, Lennon later became frightened during an elevator ride to the Ad Lib nightclub, having been convinced by the experience of his acid trip that the building had caught on fire.[21]

In August 1965, John gave LSD another try during a stopover during the Beatles' summer American tour. At a rented house in Benedict Canyon outside of Los Angeles, Lennon dropped acid with Harrison, Starr, the Byrds' David Crosby, and actor Peter Fonda. Lennon and Harrison were eager to have a more positive experience than at the April dinner party with Riley and their wives, but things didn't go so well for Harrison, who began to fear that he was dying. Having once died on the operating table, Fonda's measured reassurances for the Beatles' guitarist would later serve as a source of inspiration for Lennon, who by early 1966 had begun to experiment regularly with LSD in the privacy of his Kenwood home. Having increasingly embraced the personal in his lyrics, his growing penchant for LSD soon emerged as prime subject matter for his next composition. It was during the week before George and the Beatles' April 6 session that John would finally discover the found object that would bring his idea into much greater clarity and focus. With Paul in tow, John had visited the Indica Bookshop, where he happened upon *The Psychedelic Experience: A Manual Based on the Tibetan Book of the*

Dead, coauthored by a trio of academics—Timothy Leary, Richard Alpert, and Ralph Metzner.

Formerly a Harvard professor of clinical psychology, Leary had been an early advocate of LSD as a source of personal transcendence that could be deployed as a treatment for psychological disorders. With *The Psychedelic Experience*, Leary had advanced this notion further still to compare his acid trips to the euphoria purportedly experienced by Buddhists and Hindus during various religious rites such as meditation and fasting. In the book, Leary drew his inspiration from *The Tibetan Book of the Dead*. But it would be Leary's reading of the ancient work that caught Lennon's fancy. In *The Psychedelic Experience*, Leary refashions the precursory text, which had been envisioned as a means for preparing Buddhists to experience the various states of dying and eventual rebirth, into a guidebook for dropping acid. In its central tenet, *The Tibetan Book of the Dead* challenges its readers' sense of reality, urging them to release the ego in order to fully experience a sense of rebirth. Metzner, one of Leary's coauthors, described *The Psychedelic Experience* as "a paradigm for a spiritually-oriented psychedelic experience." To Leary's mind, *The Tibetan Book of the Dead*'s imperative to sublimate the ego seemed like a valuable means for preparing the acid dropper to experience the life-altering throes of an LSD trip, which for many users, Harrison included, took on death-like proportions, much like those Tibetan monks who were understandably petrified as they encountered the seeming "void" of nonexistence prior to entering the afterlife. For Leary, assisting his devotees in having fulfilling acid trips was a key objective, prompting him to deploy pacific, welcoming language in his writings. "Trust your divinity, trust your brain, trust your companions," he recommended in *The Psychedelic Experience*. "Whenever in doubt, turn off your mind, relax, float downstream."[22]

Borrowing the first line of his latest composition without benefit of elision from *The Psychedelic Experience*, Lennon was raring to go. A few days before the April 6 session, he premiered his new song for Martin and McCartney at Brian Epstein's Belgravia home during a planning session for their upcoming long-player. George and Paul would later register surprise at how simple the song's musical structure seemed to be. And its esoteric, philosophical nature was in stark contrast to "Run for Your Life," the Lennon composition that had set *Rubber Soul* into motion during the previous autumn. As Paul looked on, he gauged George's reaction as John shared this most unusual song for their consideration. To Paul's surprise, George nodded his head, and said, in measured tones, "Very interesting, John. Very interesting." For his part, Paul could have envisioned things unfolding very differently. As he later remarked,

This is one thing I always gave George Martin great credit for. He was a slightly older man and we were pretty far out, but he didn't flinch at all when John played it to him, he just said, "Hmmm, I see, yes. Hmm hmm." He could have said, "Bloody hell, it's terrible!" I think George was always intrigued to see what direction we'd gone in, probably in his mind thinking, "How can I make this into a record?" But by that point he was starting to trust that we must know vaguely what we were doing, but the material was really outside of his realm.

When it came time for Harrison to preview the song, he chalked its mono-chord structure up to the bandmates' growing interest in Indian culture and thought. It was a deft innovation, to be certain, and one that Martin would be sure to exploit back at Abbey Road: after spending so many years in the service of discovering and combining so many different sounds, why not simplify instead, reducing the multifariousness of their sound into a single chord? "Indian music doesn't modulate; it just stays," Harrison later observed. "You pick what key you're in, and it stays in that key. . . . The whole song was on one chord. But there is a chord that is superimposed on top that does change: if it was in C, it changes down to B flat. That was like an overdub, but the basic sound all hangs on the one drone."[23]

In this instance, the "drone" was the sound of Harrison's tamboura, hearkening back to the Indian influences that he had first introduced with *Rubber Soul*. When he arrived at Abbey Road for the sessions associated with their new long-player, Harrison lugged the instrument's massive case on his back, which carried the long-necked, double-steel-stringed instrument safely inside its cocoon. As Emerick later recalled, Harrison "staggered into the studio under its weight—it's a huge instrument, and the case was the size of a small coffin—and brought it out with a grand gesture, displaying it proudly as we gathered around." Clearly, "Norwegian Wood" hadn't marked the end of Harrison's Indian fascination. With Lennon's strange new composition in the offing, Harrison was only just getting started. And with Lennon and Harrison ready to make their return to Abbey Road—and in spite of damned near everything they had said over the past few months—McCartney carried out a few finishing touches of his own. Pulling off his own strategic coup d'état, he had finally moved out of the Ashers' home on Wimpole Street for good. Since the previous April, he had been overseeing renovations on a three-story Regency townhouse that he had purchased for £40,000 on St. John's Wood's Cavendish Avenue, just mere steps away from EMI Studios' front stoop at 3 Abbey Road. In the past few months, he had installed a music room on the top floor where he could compose new material and create demos courtesy of his well-used Brenell recorders. And perhaps most importantly, he would be closer than ever to Abbey Road—and certainly closer than the other bandmates. Now the pieces were all in place, the songs were coming fast and furious, and Martin and the band were cued up and ready to go. With the meeting to organize their new album in their rearview mirror, the Beatles were finally ready to record the follow-up long-player to the groundbreaking *Rubber Soul*.[24]

3

EVERY SOUND THERE IS

FROM THE MOMENT that George and the Beatles began work on their as-of-yet untitled new album, things were very different indeed. For George, the planning session back at Brian Epstein's Belgravia home had offered only a mere glimpse at the new ideas and potential sounds that would be coming his way. As Martin later recalled, "Their ideas were beginning to become much more potent in the studio. They started telling me what they wanted, and pressing me for more ideas and for more ways of translating those ideas into reality." The Beatles' producer could tell that the American records that the bandmates consumed so voraciously were exerting a clear influence upon their sound, as well as their own interest in pushing the boundaries of recording artistry. "You can hear that the boys were listening to lots of American records and saying, 'Can we get this effect?' and so on. So they would want us to do radical things." As he worked ever more diligently to assist them in capturing the sounds and visions in their minds, the Beatles' relationship began to shift perceptibly in terms of Martin's role in their creative lives. As Paul observed, "Originally, George Martin was the Supreme Producer in the Sky and we wouldn't even dare ask to go into the control room. But, as things loosened up, we got invited in and George gave us a bit of the control of the tools; he let us have a go." As Harrison later recalled, "George Martin had a strong role in our lives in the studio, but as we got more confidence he and the others in EMI became more relaxed with us. I suppose as time went on they believed more in our ability because it was obvious that we'd had success. They eased off on the schoolteacher approach." Besides, Harrison added, "George Martin had become more our friend as well; we socialized with him. We gained more control each time that we got a Number One, and then when we'd go back in the studio we'd claw our way up until we took over the store."[1]

As Martin and the bandmates sat down to work on that very first evening back in the studio, a recurring issue of John's began to make its presence known. The very same man who had cut his teeth learning how to belt out rock 'n' roll tunes with the best of them back in the dank, raucous clubs of Hamburg was growing less confident in his vocals in the sterile sonic spaces of the recording studio. As Martin later recalled, Lennon "had an inborn dislike of his own voice which I could never understand. He was always saying to me, 'Do something with my voice! You know, put something on it. Smother it with tomato ketchup or something. Make it different.'" According to Geoff Emerick, "That was typical John Lennon. Despite the fact that he was one of the greatest rock 'n' roll singers of all time, he hated the sound of his own voice and was constantly imploring us to make him sound different. 'Can you squeeze that up there?' he would say, or 'Can you make it sound nasally?'" To remedy his issues with his own voice, John would provide George and Geoff with metaphors for altering his voice in very specific ways. In an earlier instance, John had asked George to imbue his voice with "the feel of James Dean gunning his motorcycle down a highway." But this time, he wanted something designed especially for the mood of his latest composition—the one that was inspired by *The Tibetan Book of the Dead* by way of Leary's *The Psychedelic Experience*. "Make me sound like the Dalai Lama chanting from a mountaintop," said John. He even asked Martin if it were possible to suspend him from the ceiling by a rope so that his voice would swell in volume and intensity as his body swung above the microphone. But Martin understandably demurred at the very thought of hanging the Beatle by a rope under any circumstances. At the same time, Martin intuitively knew what the Beatle wanted—namely, to minimize the sound quality of his own voice and to maximize his lyrics. "He said he wanted to hear the words, but he didn't want to hear him," George sagely remarked.[2]

When things finally got underway, Martin and his production team, which was composed of Emerick and Phil McDonald, busied themselves with the basic track. As had been their practice since the *Help!* album, the Beatles' fifth long-player, the bandmates rehearsed each new song with George rolling the tape. This arrangement afforded them the creative space to perfect various aspects of the composition and to enjoy the occasional happy accidents that occur during the recording process that often take a routine track and transform it into something truly special. By this point, John's new song went under the working title of "Mark I." As they readied their first attempt at capturing the track, Phil prepared one of Paul's simple tape loops composed of slowed-down, distorted acoustic guitar and percussion and cued it up. "Here it comes," George announced through the playback, as Paul and Ringo began recording a steady rhythm track of bass and drums, respectively. And that's when John unleashed his guide vocal to try the song out for size: "Turn off your mind, relax, and float downstream," he sang, occasionally flagging as he paused to take in the sound effects produced by the tape loops. A second take resulted in a breakdown, but by take three they had captured a strong recording of Paul and Ringo's basic track—sans tape loops, this time. The stage was set for the tape loops and other assorted sound effects that bring the song home. Everyone seemed to be satisfied. *Almost* everyone, that is.[3]

To his ears, John sounded nowhere close to the Dalai Lama on a mountaintop. Nor did he sound like his other variation on the theme, which he described as "a thousand chanting monks." As Geoff later recalled, "George Martin looked over at me with a nod as he reassured John. 'Got it. I'm sure Geoff and I will come up with something.' Which meant, of course, that he was sure Geoff would come up with something." For his part, Geoff was caught in a panic. It was his first session as George and the Beatles' lead engineer, and he wanted to impress them. As he later recalled, "The whole time, I kept thinking about what the Dalai Lama might sound like if he were standing on Highgate Hill, a few miles away from the studio. I began doing a mental inventory of the equipment we had on hand. Clearly, none of the standard studio tricks available at the mixing console would do the job alone. We also had an echo chamber, and lots of amplifiers in the studio, but I couldn't see how they could help, either. But perhaps there was one amplifier that might work, even though nobody had ever put a vocal through it." That's when he got it: Geoff knew that the studio's Hammond organ was connected to a Leslie speaker system, which was composed of a large wooden box containing an amp and two sets of revolving speakers emitting bass and treble, respectively. Named after Donald J. Leslie, the innovator behind the Vibratone sound, the Leslie speaker had been designed in order to soften the church-like sound of the Hammond organ by adopting a system of rotating baffles that create a vibrato effect. To Geoff's mind, it seemed just possible that John's voice might be properly modulated to his specifications if the engineer were to project it using the Leslie speaker system.[4]

With a solution suddenly in hand, Geoff was ready to take it to George for the producer's approval. This was EMI Studios, after all—the austere place

where white-coated studio personnel and strict rules and equipment policy
ruled the day. Sometimes painfully shy, Geoff made his pitch:

> "I think I have an idea about what to do for John's voice," I announced
> to George in the control room as we finished editing the loop. Excit-
> edly, I explained my concept to him. Though his brows furrowed for
> a moment, he nodded his assent. Then he went out into the studio
> and told the four Beatles . . . to take a tea break while "Geoff sorts out
> something for the vocal."

While the Beatles took their break, Ken Townsend, EMI Studios' veteran
maintenance engineer who had worked at Abbey Road since 1954, rewired
the Leslie speaker system to accommodate Geoff's plan. Together, Geoff and
Phil tested the newfangled piece of equipment by placing two microphones
adjacent to the Leslie speakers. To Geoff's ears, "it certainly sounded different enough; I could only hope that it would satisfy Lennon." As McCartney
and Harrison joined Martin and the others in the control room, Lennon
took his place in front of the mic. Using the empty track four to allow for
John's new vocal, George instructed Geoff to activate the Leslie effect for the
second half of the song, which was recording alongside George Harrison's
droning tamboura. The result was plain to see through the glass window in
the control room. A smiling Lennon gave a thumbs-up. As Emerick recalled,
"Lennon's voice sounded like it never had before, eerily disconnected, distant
yet compelling. The effect seemed to perfectly complement the esoteric lyrics
he was chanting." Meanwhile, back in the control room, McCartney and Harrison good-naturedly slapped each other on the back. "It's the Dalai Lennon!"
McCartney exclaimed. Looking over at his mentor, Emerick watched as Martin
gave him a wry grin. "Nice one, Geoff," he said. For the new balance engineer
on his first day on the job, it was a bravura moment. "For someone not prone
to paying compliments," Geoff later wrote, "that was high praise indeed. For
the first time that day, the butterflies in my midsection stopped fluttering."[5]
    But as it turned out, the best was yet to come. As John joined the oth-
ers in the control room to listen to the playback, he could barely contain
his exuberance. "That is bloody marvelous," he remarked. "I say, dear boy,"
John said to Geoff in a mock upper-class accent, "tell us all precisely how
you accomplished that little miracle." Geoff tried his best to explain how
he had reimagined the Leslie speakers' purpose in order to facilitate John's
request to alter his vocal, but the effort hardly mattered. When it came to

technical considerations, Lennon was usually at sea. As Emerick observed, "In my experience, there are few musicians who are technically savvy—their focus is on the musical content and nothing else, which is as it should be— but Lennon was more technically challenged than most." Already bursting with new ideas for creating unusual, avant-garde sounds, John pummeled Geoff with even greater sonic challenges. "Couldn't we get the same effect by dangling me from a rope and swinging me around the microphone instead?" he asked, laughing uproariously at his own suggestion. "Yer daft, John, you are," said Paul, teasing him over his outlandish suggestion. Meanwhile, back in the control room, Geoff could see George Martin cheerfully shaking his head in bemusement "like a schoolteacher enjoying the naïveté of one of his young charges."[6]

Amazingly, with Geoff occupying the second chair, George had overseen an incredible sonic discovery—and during their very first night back in the studio, no less. Perhaps the Beatles didn't have to go to America after all in order to land the "specialist" recording engineer of Harrison's dreams. Emerick had been right there all along—almost since the very day the bandmates first arrived at Abbey Road themselves. And as events would shortly prove, the Beatles and their new production team were only just getting started. By the time that they finished up work that evening, George and the Beatles had captured three takes of "Mark I." If there had been a turning point for the creative artistry that they had been working toward for just four short years, this was it. Nearly thirty years later—while listening to the song with Martin sitting at the mixing desk—Harrison and McCartney couldn't hold back their sense of reverence for what had occurred that night so long ago. "Ah, now we're talking!" said Harrison, as the tamboura's ominous drone materialized out of the ether. "We're talking serious music now," McCartney added. And it was the dawn of an incredibly serious and artful music indeed. "Turn off your mind, relax and float downstream." George and the Beatles were preparing to float downstream on the shoulders of their own new musical direction. The same folks who had catalyzed the British Invasion sound were now on the verge of something new and different—and, for the most part, it certainly wasn't rhythm and blues, which had been done before and widely by practitioners across the pop-music landscape.[7]

But as it turned out, George and the bandmates weren't the only people inspired by their recent musical and artistic leaps. In addition to Geoff Emerick, who was determined to earn his place in the balance engineer's chair in spite of his tender years, Ken Townsend had often heard Lennon complaining about the awkwardness and tedium of having to double-track his vocals by singing along with himself, as he had done most recently with "Mark I." Martin would often ask the Beatles to double-track their vocals in order to imbue their performances with more warmth and power, as they did to great effect with such earlier songs as McCartney's "All My Loving" and Lennon's "This Boy." As Townsend later recalled, "They would relate what sounds they wanted and we then had to go away and come back with a solution." For the Beatles—Lennon especially—double-tracking was, according to Townsend, "quite a laborious process, and they soon got fed up with it. So after one particularly trying nighttime session doing just that, I was driving home and I suddenly had an idea."[8]

Once he had perfected it, Townsend's innovation would have far-reaching implications—not just for Martin and the Beatles but for the whole of the recording industry. Townsend's resulting process, which balance engineer Stuart Eltham would dub as artificial double-tracking or ADT for short, involved taking the recording signal from the tape machine's playback head and recording it onto a second tape machine outfitted with a variable oscillator, a device that works by creating a rhythmic pulse. This pulsating sweep allows the recording speed to be altered before being fed back into the first tape machine, where it is merged with the original recording signal. Mark Lewisohn offers a useful metaphor for understanding the manner in which ADT operates: "In photography, the placement of a negative directly over another does not alter the image. The two become one. But move one slightly and the image widens. ADT does this with tape. One voice laid perfectly on top of another produces one image. But move the second voice by just a few milliseconds, and two separate images emerge." Better still, the deployment of ADT meant that studio personnel like Martin could save a track for other purposes, which, in the four-track world of EMI Studios in 1966, was of considerable advantage. Townsend's ingenious design meant that ADT's users could control the level of oscillation, which afforded balance engineers like Emerick the ability to create different kinds of artificial sounds and phasing effects that were not previously in the realm of possibility.[9]

Martin and the Beatles were ecstatic over Townsend's invention. Even Harrison got into the act, proclaiming that Townsend should receive a medal for his invention. Years later, his words would ring true after the EMI engineer—and later studio head—earned an MBE, the same award that the queen had bestowed upon the Beatles back in 1965. As for Lennon, ADT proved to be a turning point for the singer. According to Phil McDonald, "After Ken invented ADT, John used to say, 'Well, I've sung it once, lads, just track it for me.'" While Lennon pointedly eschewed learning about recording technology, he couldn't resist asking Martin about the inner workings of Townsend's innovation. As George later recalled, "I knew he'd never understand it, so I said 'Now listen, it's very simple. We take the original image and, we split it through a double vibrocated sploshing flange with double negative feedback.'" Picking up on the producer's tongue-in-cheek explanation, John replied, "You're pulling my leg, aren't you?" Not missing a beat, George said, "Well, let's flange it and see. From that moment on, whenever he wanted ADT, he would ask for his voice to be flanged, or call out for 'Ken's flanger.'" The name stuck, and even decades later, musicians and studio personnel often refer to ADT as *flanging*.[10]

While ADT emerged slightly too late to register any effect on the production of "Mark I," for which Lennon double-tracked his vocal the old-fashioned, onerous way, Townsend's process would figure prominently in Martin and Emerick's mixing activities associated with the album. During the afternoon session on April 7, George and the group continued working on "Mark I," adding more intentional deployment of tape loops than the day before in order to imbue the song with a stronger sense of imagery. With Paul's collection of tape loops at the ready, Geoff guided the bandmates through the maelstrom of Paul's assorted sonic experiments with the intention of whittling them down to a handful of sounds. As Geoff later recalled, "We played them every conceivable way: proper speed, sped up, slowed down, backwards, forwards. Every now and then, one of the Beatles would shout, 'That's a good one,' as we played through the lot." Eventually, the Beatles and their production team had selected five tape loops for deployment in "Mark I." Musicologist Ian MacDonald has helpfully identified the tape loops as follows:

1. A recording of McCartney's laughter, sped up to resemble the sound of a seagull (0:07)
2. An orchestral chord of B flat major (0:19)
3. A Mellotron on its flute setting (0:22)
4. A Mellotron strings sound, alternating between B flat and C in 6/8 time (0:38)
5. A sitar playing a rising scalar phrase, recorded with heavy saturation and sped up (0:56)

With John's original vision for "Mark I" finally beginning to take shape, George and the bandmates were faced with another dilemma. As Geoff remembered, "The problem was that we had only one extra tape machine.

Fortunately, there were plenty of other machines in the Abbey Road complex, all interconnected via wiring in the walls, and all the other studios just happened to be empty that afternoon." To George's mind, the only solution was to conduct a "live mix," which necessitated rounding up nearly all of the studio personnel to get the job done. As Geoff recalled, "What followed next was a scene that could have come out of a science fiction movie—or a Monty Python sketch. Every tape machine in every studio was commandeered and every available EMI employee was given the task of holding a pencil or drinking glass to give the loops the proper tensioning. In many instances, this meant they had to be standing out in the hallway, looking quite sheepish. Most of those people didn't have a clue what we were doing; they probably thought we were daft. They certainly weren't pop people, and they weren't that young either. Add in the fact that all of the technical staff were required to wear white lab coats, and the whole thing became totally surreal."[11]

As EMI Studios personnel busied themselves with keeping the tape loops taut, George and Geoff worked in the control room, hunching over the recording console as the Beatles shouted out instructions over their shoulders—"Let's have that seagull sound now!" George and Geoff hurriedly raised and lowered the faders on the desk as the sound of the Beatles' directions filled up the control room. "With each fader carrying a different loop," Geoff recalled, "the mixing desk acted like a synthesizer, and we played it like a musical instrument, too, carefully overdubbing textures to the prerecorded backing track." With the track nearly complete, Harrison suggested the idea of beginning the song with the sound of his tamboura. As Geoff later wrote, "George Harrison had said that the tamboura drone would be the perfect complement to John's song, and he was right. Having seen how well Paul's loops had worked, George wanted to contribute one of his own, so I recorded him playing a single note on the huge instrument—again using a close-miking technique—and turned it into a loop. It ended up becoming the sound that opens the track."[12]

By this juncture, nearly all of the available tracks had been filled, with the tape loops being relegated to track two of "Mark I." For the time being, track three would remain available for further adornment, and for just a little while longer, the song would be known among the Beatles' brain trust by its working title. But for his part, Martin recognized that this unusual recording represented a clear departure for himself and the Beatles in more ways than one. Sure, it was innovative in terms of its experimental nature. But as Martin later observed, it "was a weird track, because once we'd made it we could never reproduce it." Given the way in which the tape loops had been selected and assembled, with most of the personnel at Abbey Road in on the action,

Martin had succeeded in creating a unique artifact. "The mix we did then was a random thing that could never be done again," he remarked. "Nobody else was doing records like that at that time—not as far as I knew." Even better still, "Mark I" represented a pivotal moment in the musical evolution that George and the bandmates shared together—and the experience had left the producer reveling in a state of liberation unlike anything else he had known during his many years in the record business. "As the Beatles began kicking over the traces of popular musical conventions," he later wrote, "it gave me the freedom to do more of what I enjoyed: experimenting, building sound pictures, creating a whole atmosphere for a song, all the things I'd always loved doing anyway. It was a very happy marriage. I didn't have to ask anyone's permission: that was the wonderful thing, that autonomy, that power. As long as the five of us agreed, everyone else could go hang!"[13]

If the Beatles' latest long-player had a Motown, rhythm-and-blues-tinged moment, it was clearly in evidence with "Got to Get You into My Life," which George and the bandmates began recording that same evening. A brand-new McCartney composition ostensibly about the first flush of romantic love—but really concerning Paul's incipient, unquenchable passion for marijuana—"Got to Get You into My Life" began as an acoustic number. And at first, the song had nothing in common with the rhythm-and-blues sound for which the Beatles had openly hungered only a few weeks earlier. Take one featured a one-note introductory piece played by Martin on the Hammond organ, with Starr providing a hi-hat accompaniment. By take five, McCartney had added lead vocals against his acoustic rhythm track, with Lennon and Harrison layering spirited backing vocals across the refrain. The next day, Friday, April 8, George and the Beatles resumed work on "Got to Get You into My Life"—only this time they were back in the familiar confines of Number 2, the Abbey Road studio from whence they had recorded the balance of their work since first meeting George back in June 1962. As they continued work on Paul's song, George and the bandmates decided to remake "Got to Get You into My Life." They recorded a basic rhythm track consisting of McCartney's bass and Starr's drums, along with two fuzz guitars, played by Harrison and Lennon, respectively, on track two. Track three included a second bass guitar, with track four featuring McCartney's guide vocal. And with that, they would abandon work on "Got to Get You into My Life," save for the addition of a slight bit of guitar ornamentation the following week, until May 18, when the song would be entirely remade yet again.

After taking a weekend break, George and the Beatles were back in the studio for an afternoon session on Monday, April 11. As roadie Neil Aspinall later observed, a pattern began to emerge during this period in terms of the Beatles' working relationship with Martin, as well as in regard to their studio practices. "At this time I was in the studio with them when they were making records," said Aspinall, "and the pattern changed over the years." Moreover, "it was getting so that sessions would start at about two or three in the afternoon and go on until they finished, whatever the time was. At the beginning of the session, if there was a new song, whoever had written it would play the chords to George Martin on either guitar or piano, or they'd all be around a piano, playing it, learning the chords. If they were halfway through a song, they'd go straight in and do harmonies, or double-tracking, or a guitar solo or whatever. Sometimes, because it was all on four-track, they would have to mix down on to one track to give a bit of space to do the rest of it." During the April 11 session, the balance of their work would be devoted to a new Harrison composition that went under the working title of "Granny Smith" in honor, presumably, of the apple variety, a recurring image that would figure later, and very prominently, in the band's evolving story. For the quiet Beatle, "Granny Smith" would mark his first full-throated, Indian-flavored track, having previously adorned "Norwegian Wood (This Bird Has Flown)" and "Mark I" with Eastern-oriented instrumentation. With Harrison having brought his sitar along for the day's proceedings, Martin recorded a basic track with the Beatles' guitarist singing and providing his own acoustic guitar accompaniment, while McCartney delivered harmony vocals to accentuate the verses. As the session progressed, the recording became imminently more complex. For track two, Paul provided a fuzz bass part, depressing the volume pedal in order to heighten the notes during each refrain. Track three found Martin and the Beatles deploying studio musicians for only the third time in their career—not counting Martin himself, of course. Having been recruited by way of London's Asian Music Circle, Anil Bhagwat joined the flute and string players on "You've Got to Hide Your Love Away" and "Yesterday," respectively, as the only non-Beatles to grace the band's recordings. As Bhagwat later recalled, "The session came out of the blue. A chap called [Ayana] Angadi called me and asked if I was free that evening to work with George. I didn't know who he meant—he didn't say it was Harrison. It was only when a Rolls-Royce came to pick me up that I realized I'd be playing on a Beatles session. When I arrived at Abbey Road, there were girls everywhere with Thermos flasks, cakes, sandwiches, waiting for the Beatles to come out."[14]

With Bhagwat poised above the tabla, a pair of small, bongo-like drums, Martin recorded track three, which featured Harrison's first pass at the song's distinctive sitar melody. As Bhagwat sat down in Studio 2, Harrison was ready to impart instructions to the session player. "Once the session began, George [Harrison] told me what he wanted, and I tuned the tabla with him," Bhagwat later recalled. "He suggested I play something in the Ravi Shankar style, 16-beats, though he agreed that I should improvise. Indian music is all improvisation." For track three, Martin recorded Harrison's sitar and Bhagwat's tabla, later overdubbing a tamboura part from Harrison onto the same track. For Martin and Emerick, recording instruments like the sitar and tamboura was fraught with sonic challenges given the instruments' frequency variations, which were known to wreak havoc for Western studio personnel—particularly during the mixing and mastering processes. If instruments such as the sitar and tamboura were not recorded properly and carefully, the sound fluctuations could cause the consumer's stylus to jump during those phonograph record days. Emerick found that the key to recording such instruments involved using nonstandard microphones and, in violation of EMI Studio policy, placing the mics mere inches away from the instrument. Determined to impress the Beatles and capture the best possible sound as their new balance engineer, Geoff didn't mind skirting the rules in unusual situations—and besides, in his own words, "the sitar was about as nonstandard as you could get."[15]

As work on "Granny Smith" progressed even further, Harrison overdubbed a second sitar part onto track four, along with another fuzz guitar piece. By this point, Harrison's layered fuzz guitar parts had provided the song with a searing downbeat in contrast with the tune's liberating lyrics about a utopian world of uninhibited singing and lovemaking—and not necessarily in that order. Harrison concluded his work on "Granny Smith" with the recording of a thirty-four-second motto, consisting of swarmandal (an Indian instrument in the same vein as a table harp that emits a zither-like sound) and sitar, to introduce the song. At this point, the sixth take of the recording was marked as "best," and a mono acetate was prepared for Harrison to take home for further consideration. Before the day's work was over, Martin recorded another guitar overdub by Harrison for the still unfinished "Got to Get You into My Life." As for Bhagwat, the "Granny Smith" session had proven to be a much-treasured experience. "I was very lucky, they put my name on the record sleeve. I'm really proud of that, they were the greatest ever and my name is on the sleeve. It was one of the most exciting times of my life."[16]

As with *Rubber Soul*'s "Think for Yourself," "Granny Smith" found Harrison continuing to exert his songwriterly presence, which was no easy feat among a group that included the likes of Lennon and McCartney. For the whole of the band's recording career so far, Harrison had languished as the "junior" member of their creative team, a pecking order that was reinforced not only by Lennon and McCartney but by Martin, too. The elder statesman for the Beatles' brain trust had no problem making distinctions among the bandmates and their talents, determined as he invariably was to get the most out of their collective talents. No, the producer definitely wasn't above playing favorites. The stakes of authorship were significant in a highly competitive group like the Beatles, and to Martin's mind, Harrison was lagging behind the world-famous songwriting duo. But the stakes were high for Martin, too—and especially as he was working to get AIR off the ground. Yet he could already sense a shift, however slight, in Harrison's songwriting fortunes—and particularly as the bandmates slaved away on their new long-player. Martin later wrote that Harrison had "been awfully poor up to then. Some of the stuff he'd written was very boring. The impression is sometimes given that we put him down. I don't think we ever did that, but possibly we didn't encourage him enough. He'd write, but we wouldn't say, 'What've you got then, George?' We'd say, 'Oh, you've got some more, have you?' I must say that looking back, it was a bit hard on him. It was always slightly condescending. But it was natural, because the others were so talented." Martin was equally quick to admit that he, too, fell well short of being on an equal playing field with the likes of Lennon and McCartney, later remarking that "there is no doubt in my mind that the main talent of that whole era came from Paul and John. George, Ringo, and myself were subsidiary talents. We were not five equal people artistically: two were very strong, and the other three were also-rans."[17]

It was a political calculus that would shift ever more precipitously over the coming years—at times, so profoundly that even Martin and Emerick would find themselves caught up in the high-stakes world of the Beatles' creative matrix.

4

A RUBE GOLDBERG
APPROACH TO RECORDING

W HEN IT CAME TIME to select the tune that would be the A-side for the Beatles' next single, Martin relegated the opportunity—quite naturally at this point, given the band's internal political calculus—to Lennon and McCartney. At this juncture, the Beatles were in the midst of riding a winning streak in their homeland, with eleven consecutive number-one singles—the latest being the double A-sided "Day Tripper" backed with "We Can Work It Out," which was released in December 1965 and had rung in 1966 atop the UK charts. The pressure was definitely on to maintain the Beatles' commercial dominion in their home country, and the group's principal songwriters took the competition very seriously indeed, with John and Paul regularly vying to see who could land the next A-side. As Geoff Emerick later remarked, "In those days, singles were probably even more important than albums. After all, the singles were the records that the radio DJs spun endlessly, thus fueling album sales. They were also far more affordable than albums—a major factor for the typical teenage Beatles fan of the era, who had limited cash to spend." George had a long-standing policy about Beatles singles, demanding that the songs be brand new and not mere reissues of album tracks. "It was laudable insofar as it gave the buying public tremendous value for their money, but it also added greatly to the pressure the group was under," Geoff later wrote. "Not only did they have to periodically write and record musically cohesive collections of their songs, but at the same time they also had to keep cranking out commercial hits."[1]

By the time the Beatles had recorded the first handful of songs for their new album, George received a memo from EMI about the deadline for the band's next single, which the record conglomerate intended for general release by the end of May. John and Paul wasted little time getting down to business. As Geoff later remarked, "Whoever wrote the stronger song—with George Martin as referee—would win the prize: the prestigious A-side. The losing song would either be relegated to the B-side or be included on an album, with another, lesser song purloined to occupy the nether regions of the single." This time, it was Paul who acted first. "Gather 'round, lads, and have a listen to our next single," he announced during a session in Studio 3 on Wednesday, April 13, the same day that George and the bandmates were creating additional overdubs for "Granny Smith." Paul's new composition, "Paperback Writer," had everything that George was looking for—a catchy pop hook, clever lyrics, and a great melody to boot. Geoff remembered John giving his partner a sidelong glance as Paul unveiled his latest confection, but as events would later show, John wasn't down for the count just yet.[2]

For "Paperback Writer," McCartney wanted a heavy, thumping bass sound, the very same pulsating tones that the Beatles associated with contemporary Motown hits of the day. In the studio, Paul had been playing the Rickenbacker 4001S bass that he debuted on *Rubber Soul*'s "Drive My Car." With a fluid fret board, the Rickenbacker afforded him greater versatility, not to mention superior tonal definition, in contrast with his signature Höfner violin bass, which he had since relegated to concert appearances given the instrument's light weight. But now he wanted to take the Rickenbacker a step further and simulate the beefier "American" bass sound that he heard on tracks by the likes of Donald "Duck" Dunn and James Jamerson in the United States and, more recently, the Who's John Entwistle, who had broken off a spirited bass solo in the vein of American rhythm and blues in "My Generation," which had notched a top-five UK hit only a few months earlier. Always buoyed by any glint of competition, Paul was determined to make his mark as a bassist, and "Paperback Writer" proved to be the perfect vehicle for showcasing his skills. The song also presented yet another opportunity for George and Geoff to expand the capabilities of EMI Studios, which had already seen two major technological innovations in the span of a few short weeks. As the selfsame producer who had greeted the Beatles' innovative plans to shift their sound in new and dramatic ways with the guarded reply of "very interesting," George was now working steadfastly to advance, if not enlarge, the capacity of the recording studio in order to meet their creative expectations, and Geoff had proven himself to be the perfect engineer to make these shifts possible.

While "Mark I" was still a work in progress and wouldn't come to fruition for a few more weeks yet—when it would finally lose its working title, to boot—"Paperback Writer" exploded into being in fewer than forty-eight hours. As George led the bandmates through a rehearsal of Paul's new song, which had a crackling electric guitar intro, Geoff turned to the issue of addressing the bass player's aspirations for a punchier, more "American" sound from his Rickenbacker. As Lennon and McCartney taught Harrison the opening chords to "Paperback Writer," "inspiration struck" Emerick, who was ready to meet McCartney's demands and then some:

It occurred to me that since microphones are in fact simply loudspeakers wired in reverse (in technical terms, both are transducers that convert sound waves to electrical signals, and vice versa), so why not try using a loudspeaker as a microphone? Logically, it seemed that whatever can push bass signal out can also take it in—and that a large loudspeaker should be able to respond to low frequencies better than a small microphone. The more I thought about it, the more it made sense. I broached my plan, gingerly, to Phil McDonald. His response was somewhat predictable: "You're daft; you've completely gone around the twist." Ignoring him, I took a walk down the hall and talked it over with Ken Townsend, our maintenance engineer. He thought my idea had some merit. "Sounds plausible," he said. "Let's wire a speaker up that way and try it." Over the next few hours, while the boys rehearsed with George Martin, Ken and I conducted a few experiments. To my delight, the idea of using a speaker as a microphone seemed to work pretty well. Even though it didn't deliver a lot of signal and was kind of muffled, I was able to achieve a good bass sound by placing it up against the grille of a bass amplifier, speaker to speaker, and then routing the signal through a complicated setup of compressors and filters—including one huge experimental unit that I secretly borrowed from the office of Mr. Cook, the manager of the maintenance department.

At this juncture, it is worth noting that George and Geoff were more than shirking EMI Studios' recording policies, which were "archaic" and overly regimented in their eyes. But Geoff persisted, buoyed by George's interest in addressing the Beatles' needs at all costs, as well as the Beatles' vaunted place in the EMI pecking order.[3]

But even still, Paul was surprised when Geoff placed a large, bulky loudspeaker directly in front of his bass amplifier rather than the usual studio microphone. As for George, he paid little mind, having become used to Geoff's self-described "Rube Goldberg approach to recording." As the rehearsal continued unabated, Geoff returned to the control room, where he carefully raised the faders that carried the bass signal. Much of the bass work that Paul performed on the song was played on the lower strings, and to Geoff's satisfaction the notes didn't become muddy or less coherent with the new setup. Rather, to Geoff's ears the tones from Paul's instrument had become rounded out, and the sound that the microphone emitted was "absolutely huge—so much so that I became somewhat concerned that it might actually make the needle jump out of the groove when it was finally cut to vinyl." It was a legitimate fear—and one that would haunt George's work with the Beatles for the next several years. But in the short run, Geoff's solution had done the trick. Paul was delighted by the result. His bass performance assumed its own place in the song's musical palette alongside the lead guitar part that he had fashioned on his Epiphone Casino. Indeed, in many ways, Paul's bass sound had assumed the proportions of a lead instrument capable of driving the melody, as opposed to settling behind it in the rhythm section along with Ringo's drum cadence.[4]

As it happened, during the rehearsal "Paperback Writer" had taken yet another turn. At this early date in George and the bandmates' sessions circa April 1966, sudden left turns were the norm rather than being an anomaly. In this instance, Paul suggested a new introduction for the song, which was originally prefaced with a burst of lead guitar. As Paul later recalled, "I had the idea to do the harmonies, and we arranged that in the studio." For George, this meant that he could indulge one of his favorite aspects of working with the Beatles, conducting them as they prepared the trademark harmonies that had adorned such earlier songs as "This Boy" and "If I Fell." Martin later referred to Lennon, McCartney, and Harrison's complex harmonies at the beginning of "Paperback Writer" as "contrapuntal statements from the backing voices—no one had really done that before." He would also cite their inspiration, moreover, as being the Beach Boys' latest single, "Sloop John B," which was just beginning to make a splash on the British airwaves at the time. As the lead single from the Beach Boys' new album *Pet Sounds*, "Sloop John B" showcased the American band's characteristic soaring, "stacked" harmonies, as well as a prominent bass track—both of which managed to catch McCartney's ear. After the Beach Boys' Brian Wilson first heard *Rubber Soul*, he vowed to produce "the greatest rock album ever. That's how blown out I was over the Beatles." With his ambitions aroused, Wilson said, "I just made up my mind to do something that expressed what was in my heart and soul. I didn't care about sales. I just cared about the artistic merit of it." In a few short weeks, John and Paul would have their first opportunity to hear the Beach Boys album in its entirety, and the Beatles' own long-player would take yet more unexpected turns.[5]

As the April 13 session continued, with the Beatles' general rehearsal for the song having concluded after more than six hours, George called the proceedings to order. The bandmates attempted a first take for "Paperback Writer," with McCartney and Harrison playing their Epiphone Casino hollow-bodied guitars, Starr on drums, and Lennon playing the tambourine. During the breaks, Ringo can be heard tapping his sticks together to keep the beat. After the first take, which broke down after slightly less than a minute, Harrison complained that the others were speeding up, with McCartney registering his agreement. Moments later, take two ensued, and the Beatles executed a flawless rhythm track. At this juncture, given the length of the session, George and the band opted to pack it in for the day, with plans for plenty of overdubs in the offing at the next session. In addition to the debut of an exciting new Beatles track, April 13 also marked George and the group's inaugural session with tape operator Richard Lush, who had previously been serving as an apprentice at EMI Studios. As Lush later recalled, "I was pretty nervous. I'd worked with Cliff and the Shadows, and they were very easy going but I knew that Beatles sessions were private. One was rarely allowed to open the door and peek in, and I heard that they took a while to accept new people. It certainly took a while before they knew me as Richard. Until then it was 'who is that boy sitting in the corner hearing all of our music?' But everything worked out in the end." But not before he experienced a run-in with Beatle Paul, who accosted him with a dose of Liverpudlian humor. After introducing himself—"Erm, my name is Richard. I'm a button-pusher here"—he found himself face-to-face with McCartney, who replied, "Oh, yeah? Wanna fight?" For a moment, Lush stood uncertainly in the middle of the control room before he figured out that he had become the latest victim of one of the bandmates' famous studio pranks.[6]

On the afternoon of Thursday, April 14, George and the bandmates were back in Studio 3. With a basic rhythm track in hand for "Paperback Writer," they spent the next several hours experimenting with various overdubs in order to enhance McCartney's latest composition. As if the potential for innovation had become limitless by this point, McCartney suggested that Martin try playing a jangle-box or tack piano to accompany the evolving rhythm track associated with "Paperback Writer." At EMI Studios, the jangle-box piano was a Steinway upright piano that had been modified to create a percussive sound. This was accomplished when studio personnel brushed the piano's hammers with cellulose and retuned some of its strings in order to create the distinctive jangling effect. As with "Mark I," Emerick diverted the signal through the Leslie speaker system in order to enhance the effect of the jangle piano, although it was ultimately deleted from the final mix, as was Martin's Vox Continental organ part for "Paperback Writer." With various bits of experimentation having finally concluded, they began assembling the various component parts of "Paperback Writer" into a seamless whole. Having relegated the previous day's rhythm track to track one, Martin overdubbed McCartney's lead vocal on track three, with Lennon and Harrison's cascading backing vocals on track four. Track two was reserved for performing the various supplemental effects that they had been preparing, including McCartney's bass part and the aforementioned keyboard experiments from Martin himself. While Martin's jangle-box piano and organ parts were discarded, Lennon and Harrison adorned "Paperback Writer" with one final playful bit of fun, singing "Frère Jacques" at McCartney's instigation between the phrases of his lead vocals. Martin later confessed that he hadn't noticed the French nursery rhyme when it was originally recorded. "You can't really hear the words," he later explained, "because they are so soft. I must confess, I didn't spot this little diversion on the number, but George [Harrison] reassured me that it was just one of those weird things that happened for the sake of it. There was no connection whatever between the famous Brother Jack and the knack of writing paperbacks."[7]

Although the Beatles' next single had been slated for a May 30 release date in the United Kingdom, George and his production team didn't waste any time carrying out the mixing process for "Paperback Writer," for which they prepared mono masters during a 7:30 PM session. Working in the Studio 3 control room, George, Geoff, and Phil made two passes at creating the mix, for which Phil had assembled copious notes throughout the recording process. According to Phil's notes, track one's a cappella interludes were intentionally faded out in order to obscure Ringo's drumstick taps during the breaks. The harmony backing vocals were also treated with tape echo prior to each chorus, which was then slowed down in order to enhance the effect. The mixing session for "Paperback Writer" was pioneering in its complexity, clearly acting as a harbinger for things to come in George and the Beatles' universe. But in terms of the highly structured professional world of Abbey Road, postrecording edits such as the ones performed on behalf of "Paperback Writer" were discouraged. As Emerick later observed, "In the archaic EMI way of thinking, edits were frowned upon. Management didn't want anyone taking a razor to master tapes, so multitrack editing—which would allow us to join the start of one take onto the end of another—was rarely allowed in those days. Even during mixing, editing was discouraged, although it would have allowed us to create a mix in sections—something that was commonly done in most other recording studios. Somehow EMI just didn't care what was going on in the outside world: we'd have to get the mix right from start to finish. If we messed up the middle, or even if the very end of the fadeout wasn't quite right, we would have to start all over again; we couldn't just edit in a replacement for the bad bit. As a result, you got that adrenaline going, and the mixes themselves became performances."[8]

As Martin later pointed out, "Paperback Writer" proved to be yet another watershed moment given that it was "the first time that we have echo on a Beatles track." For "Paperback Writer," the mixing phase was especially crucial in order to ensure that the echo effect was created to Martin and the Beatles' specifications. According to Emerick, the "fluttering echo at the end of each chorus added at the mix stage" was "accomplished by routing the vocals into a separate two-track machine and then connecting that machine's output to its input. At the end of each chorus, Phil had the job of slowly increasing the record level until it just reached the point of feedback. If he went one notch too far, the echo would get out of control, so there were many attempts at doing the mix. Every time he'd go past that point, or not far enough, we'd have to stop and remix the entire song again." But the process didn't end with George's mixing session that evening. The real test for the revolutionary new track occurred during the disc-cutting phase, when George and Geoff knew that the high bass content in "Paperback Writer" would come under company scrutiny. By this point, Ken Townsend had already been reprimanded by EMI's chief technical engineer, Bill Livy, for incorrectly matching impedances in order to facilitate the loudspeaker-as-microphone scenario. Record companies were apprehensive about bass-heavy productions, fearing that styli might jump out of the grooves from too much low-end sound. When it came to "Paperback Writer," Tony Clark was assigned the task of cutting the master lacquer for the recording. As Clark later recalled, "Paperback Writer" was "EMI's first high-level cut, and I used a wonderful new machine just invented by the backroom boys, ATOC—Automatic Transient Overload Control. It was a huge box with flashing lights and what looked like the eye of a Cyclops staring out at you. But it did the trick. I did two cuts, one with ATOC and one without, played them to George Martin and he approved of the high-level one."[9]

For George and the Beatles, contending with EMI's recalcitrance had become par for the course in recent years—and particularly as they began to engage in more innovations and experiments in the studio. "EMI had very firm rules," Paul later remarked, "which we always had to break. It wasn't a willful arrogance, it was just that we felt we knew better. . . . We were always forcing them into things they didn't want to do." "Paperback Writer" was simply the latest in a long line of production examples in which George and the Beatles challenged existing studio norms. "We were always pushing ahead," said Paul, "'louder, further, longer, more, different.' I always wanted things to be different because we knew that people, generally, always want to move on, and if we hadn't pushed them, the guys would have stuck by the rulebooks and still been wearing ties. Anyway, you'd then find 'Oh, it worked!' and they were secretly glad because they had been the engineer who'd put three times the allowed value of treble on a song. I think they were quietly proud of all those things."[10]

As it turned out, there was no rest for the weary when it came to George and the bandmates. As with "Paperback Writer," "Rain" promised to continue George and the group's ongoing efforts to expand the capabilities of the recording studio. As John's entry in the sweepstakes to land the A-side of the next singles release, "Rain" had already been slated for the B-side of "Paperback Writer" by the time that it saw its Abbey Road debut during the evening session of Thursday, April 14. Like "Mark I," "Rain" found its origins in Lennon's recent forays into *The Psychedelic Experience*, particularly Leary's philosophy of being: "Whether you experience heaven or hell," Leary instructed his reader, "remember that it is your mind which creates them. Avoid grasping the one or fleeing the other. Avoid imposing the ego game on the experience." For John, "Rain" afforded him with the opportunity to espouse his personal belief in the inherent value of pure human experience. With the tape rolling, Martin led the bandmates in a rehearsal of Lennon's latest composition. As they prepared a basic track, McCartney continued the heavy bass sound that Emerick had facilitated with "Paperback Writer." Nevertheless, as the band pushed forward, they couldn't settle on a groove. The song seemed lifeless to them, as if it were missing an essential element. And that's when Martin hit upon the idea of manipulating the recording's tape speed in order to imbue the song with an unusual sonic palette. To accomplish the effect, he instructed Emerick to record the band's performance on a sped-up tape machine. They managed to capture this sound across five takes, with Harrison and Lennon's guitars and Starr's drums on track one and McCartney's bass on track two. At this point, the song's basic rhythm track took on a languid, more lethargic mien. With this effect in place, Martin recorded Lennon's lead vocal on track three. But even still, the process was far from complete. During postproduction, Lennon's voice would be slowed down perceptibly, which would ultimately result in his lead vocal seeming slightly fast on the master recording. In this way, Martin's recording of "Rain" reveals a unique arrangement, with different elements of the finished track being drawn from performances that had been captured at varying tape speeds.[11]

But as with so many of the Beatles' latest compositions, there were more surprises in store. With "Rain," the surprises began with Lennon back home at Kenwood and ended with Martin in the Abbey Road control room. After George and the Beatles concluded the "Rain" session in the wee hours of April 15, Phil McDonald prepared a reel-to-reel tape copy of the unfinished song for John to take home. When he returned to Kenwood, the Beatle—being stoned at the time after the long, chauffeur-driven ride back home from the city—mistakenly thread the tape backward into his home machine. But as he listened to the playback in his narcotized state, he was confronted with the unexpected sound of hearing his voice blaring back at him in gibberish as the tape unspooled in reverse. In Lennon's version, which he recounted several times over the ensuing years, he adored the effect upon that very first experience. Yet according to Harrison, Lennon's account wasn't entirely accurate. When the Beatles left the studio that night, each of the bandmates were given a reference tape to take home with them. Only Phil hadn't properly rewound the tapes before handing them over to the departing Beatles. This fact had slipped Lennon's mind by the time he returned to Kenwood. "I got home from the studio and I was stoned out of my mind on marijuana," Lennon later recalled. At this point, Harrison's account jibes with Lennon's, as Lennon apparently experienced an epiphany about adopting such an effect during the next session, where Martin and the group were scheduled to continue working on "Rain." What happened next, at least in Lennon's version, was that "I ran in the next day and said, 'I know what to do with it, I know.... Listen to this!'"[12]

Yet according to Martin, neither Lennon's account, which was later echoed by Emerick, nor Harrison's was true. Rather, the idea of intentionally manipulating recordings by playing them backward had been in Martin's bag of production tricks for many years. Back in 1962, he had even collaborated with the BBC's Radiophonics Workshop laboratories in the creation of a moderately successful single titled "Time Beat" and credited to Ray Cathode, Martin's pseudonym for the project. In the producer's account of the "Rain" tape-manipulation episode, it was Martin himself who suggested that they experiment with backward recording. In a similar vein to the episode back in October 1965 in which he had waited for an opportune moment to deploy his windup piano effect on John's "In My Life," George took advantage of a session break to tinker with John's latest creation. "I was always playing around with tapes, and I thought it might be fun to do something extra with John's voice. So I lifted a bit of his main vocal off the four-track, put it onto another spool, turned it around and then slid it back and forth until it fitted. John was out at the time but when he came back he was amazed. Again, it was backwards forever after that." The tape segment in question featured John's lead vocal track in which he sang the song's opening line, along with the phrase "sun shines rain," which George had lifted from the second verse and the chorus. With the tape reel in hand, George overdubbed the thirty-second segment onto the tail end of the song.[13]

Martin's words about the Beatles' growing penchant for experimentation—"it was backwards forever after that"—would prove to be very prescient indeed. Harrison, for one, was ecstatic over the possibilities that backward recording entailed. With "Rain," "George Martin turned the master upside down and played it back. We were excited to hear what it sounded like, and it was magic—the backwards guitarist! The way the note sounded, because of the attack and the decay, was brilliant. We got very excited and started doing that on overdub. And then there was a bit of backwards singing as well, which came out sounding like Indian singing." As Geoff later reported, tape manipulation very quickly became the norm for John, Paul, George, and Ringo. When they finished a new song, one of the Beatles inevitably said, "'Okay, that sounds great, now let's play it backwards or speeded up or slowed down.' They tried everything backwards," Geoff remembered, "just to see what things sounded like." Disc cutter Tony Clark was hardly surprised by the bandmates' newfound adoration for backward recordings. "It's because of the enveloping of sound," he later recalled. "It draws you in. It's like someone putting their arms around you." During the next session, a protracted, eleven-hour affair that was held in Studio 2 on Saturday, April 16, Martin and the Beatles created further refinements to "Rain," including the addition of ADT to Lennon's vocal as recorded during take five. This resulted in an audible slowing down of his voice, as noted previously. According to Geoff, "An off-shoot of ADT was that we had a big audio oscillator to alter the frequency of the tape machines. We would drive it through a power amp and the power amp would drive the capstan wheel and enable you to speed up or slow down the machine at will. John—or George if it was his song—used to sit in the control room on mixes and actually play the oscillator." In addition to the tape manipulation of John's voice, the day's session witnessed the superimposition of tambourine and backing vocals. And with that, the "Paperback Writer" backed with "Rain" single was complete. But after "Rain," the die had truly been cast: from henceforward, George and Geoff observed the Beatles clamoring for more and greater sonic effects, affording the producer and his gifted engineer with one new challenge after another.[14]

George and the Beatles recorded yet another new track, "Doctor Robert," during a Sunday, April 17, session in Studio 2. The latest composition from Lennon, "Doctor Robert" told the loosely fictionalized story of a Robert Freymann, a New York City physician who prescribed hallucinogens for his celebrity clientele. During the long session, Martin and the bandmates captured a basic rhythm track for the song over seven takes, with Lennon on rhythm guitar, McCartney on bass, Starr on drums, and Harrison shaking the maracas. Once the basic track had been completed, Harrison overdubbed a lead guitar part on his Epiphone Casino, Lennon added a harmonium, and McCartney tickled the ivories. Paul's piano part was likely deleted during the next session, which was held on Tuesday, April 19, when John recorded his lead vocal, which described how Dr. Robert's mysterious concoctions from his "special cup" will help you become "a new and better man" with a heightened capacity "to understand." John's vocal would subsequently be treated with ADT, which was swiftly becoming the knee-jerk recording technique of choice as George and the Beatles continued work on their new long-player.[15]

By this point, the new Lennon compositions were coming fast and furious. On Wednesday, April 20, he debuted "And Your Bird Can Sing" for George and the Beatles' consideration. The sessions for the band's new LP had been marked by bouts of innovation and experimentation so far. But on this particular day, the group seemed uncharacteristically derivative, at one point breaking down into a rash of giggles and histrionics as they tried to find their groove with John's latest song. Working a twelve-hour session in Studio 2, Martin observed as the Beatles attempted two takes of "And Your Bird Can Sing." The basic rhythm track consisted of Lennon and Harrison's electric guitars and Starr on drums. Track two was composed of Lennon's lead vocals, McCartney's bass, and a tambourine, likely shaken by Ringo. At this point, "And Your Bird Can Sing" sounded uncannily like a recording by the Byrds, the Roger McGuinn–fronted American band with a distinctive, chiming twelve-string Rickenbacker ambience. As the session wore on, Martin and the bandmates compiled a third track, with Lennon singing a second lead vocal while McCartney and Harrison sang harmonies. "And Your Bird Can Sing" was subjected to numerous overdubs, including one particular attempt that featured John and Paul devolving into nearly uncontrollable laughter, along with a coda filled with whistling before the song finally came to an end. Although "And Your Bird Can Sing" would see five remixes that day, it would be completely remade at a later date in a far more original—and serious—form.

The rest of the April 20 session was devoted to a standout composition from Harrison titled "Taxman." Even still, the derivative nature of the Beatles' work on this particular Wednesday was continued with "Taxman," which sported a basic rhythm that had been inspired by the "Batman Theme," a surf music ditty that had been popularized by the American television show starring Adam West and Burt Ward and had ascended the UK charts that same spring. "Batman Theme" had proven to be remarkably influential among British music circles—the Who would release a cover version on their *Ready Steady Who* EP later that year. Fortunately, the interconnections between "Taxman" and the "Batman Theme" would end with the songs' rhythm tracks. As it happened, "Taxman" had been inspired by Harrison's disgust over the exorbitant British tax code—especially the "supertax" to which high earners such as the Beatles were subjected. During a February 1966 interview with Maureen Cleave, Harrison likened Prime Minister Harold Wilson to the Sheriff of Nottingham, who became infamous in the legend of Robin Hood for his insatiable appetite for taxing England's citizenry into oblivion. "There he goes," Harrison remarked to Cleave, "Taking all the money and then moaning about deficits here, deficits there—always moaning about deficits." As the song evolved, Lennon had thrown in a lyric or two to heighten the song's acerbic wit. Martin supervised four takes of "Taxman" as the Beatles attempted to capture the basic rhythm track, which consisted of Harrison and Lennon's guitars, McCartney's bass, and Starr's drums. After the fourth take had been concluded, Martin and the group devolved into a lengthy discussion about the song's structure.[16]

The next session began on Thursday afternoon, when George and the Beatles continued working on "Taxman," which they remade across eleven takes in a session that sprawled into the wee hours of the next morning. The first ten takes were devoted solely to perfecting the song's intricate rhythm track, which reprised the instrumentation from the previous session. Martin supervised several overdubs, including Harrison's two lead vocal tracks, with harmonies from Lennon and McCartney, as well as Starr's tambourine part. At this point, the song included two vocal features that would later be excised, including Lennon and McCartney's "anybody got a bit of money" falsetto harmony, as well as a coda in which the bandmates sang "Taxman!" by parroting the conclusion of the "Batman Theme." In one of the session's highlights, McCartney performed a spectacular lead guitar solo, complete with a raga-like cadence. As Harrison remarked, "I was pleased to have him play that bit on 'Taxman.' If you notice, he did a little Indian bit on it for me." Martin would later reprise McCartney's blistering guitar part by flying the tape into the fade-out. This session also witnessed McCartney lazily counting off the song, an element that Martin would later deploy as an ironic introduction to the still-untitled long-player.[17]

On Friday, April 22, Martin and the Beatles brought two key tracks to fruition, including "Taxman," for which Lennon and McCartney fashioned a new harmony referring to the politicians of the day—"Ha, ha, Mister Wilson, ha, ha, Mister Heath"—in keeping with Harrison's original vision for the composition. Starr also superimposed a cowbell part onto the song. Up next was Lennon's "Mark I," which was finally completed after a number of adornments, including organ, tambourine, and piano overdubs on track three. Although ADT was available at this point, Lennon opted to manually double-track his voice in order to improve his lead vocal during the song's early verses, which he found to be too "thin sounding." At one juncture, McCartney added a backward guitar solo, which Martin and Emerick appended to the track by turning the tape around during the recording. At some point over the next few weeks, John would finally drop "Mark I" as the song's title, adopting a non sequitur from Ringo instead. The new title found its origins in a February 1964 BBC interview at London Airport in which Ringo had been asked about the notorious incident at the British embassy in Washington, DC, in which a lock of hair had been snipped from his scalp. "What happened, exactly?" David Coleman, the interviewer, asked. "I don't know," Ringo replied. "I was just doing an interview. Like I am now! I was talking away and—there it goes! I looked round and there were about 400 people, smiling. You can't blame anyone. I mean—what can you say?" At that point, John asked, "Well, what can you say?" to which Ringo answered, "Tomorrow never knows." Although he laughed uproariously at the time, Lennon must have stowed the line away in his memory banks for safekeeping, only to resurrect it as the title of what would become—for a time, at least—Martin and the Beatles' most outlandish and groundbreaking recording.[18]

On Tuesday, April 26, the Beatles' impressive fervor to complete their new album continued unabated, as they returned from the long weekend to remake "And Your Bird Can Sing." For George, the week would begin with a pair of sessions in which they tidied up a pair of tracks they had begun earlier in the month, only to end with a moment of pure artistry for the Beatles' producer akin to creating the orchestration for "Yesterday" or the windup piano solo for "In My Life." But first, George and the bandmates had their sights set on completing "And Your Bird Can Sing." As the lengthy session began that afternoon, it was clear from the start that the Byrds-influenced composition from the week before had been scuttled in favor of a guitar-laden rock fusion. Lennon was no less playful—"Okay, boys, quite brisk, moderato, foxtrot!" he announced as the session commenced—but he was clearly ready to get down to business. As "And Your Bird Can Sing" progressed over the next eleven takes, the composition was elevated to the key of E and trans-formed into a banquet of electric guitars, highlighted by a dual guitar solo from McCartney and Harrison on their Epiphone Casinos. As McCartney later recalled, "We wrote [the duet] at the session and learned it on the spot—but it was thought out. George [Harrison] learned it, then I learned the harmony to it, then we sat and played it." After take ten had been selected as the best, Lennon overdubbed his lead vocal, with McCartney and Harrison provid-ing harmonies. The voices were later treated with ADT during the remixing phase. While take ten captured their fancy, they also liked the coda for take six, which featured a splendid bass run from McCartney. Emerick dutifully edited the bass flutter onto take ten in postproduction.[19]

The next evening, April 27, Martin and his production team carried out a mono mixing session for "Taxman," "And Your Bird Can Sing," and the track that would come to be known as "Tomorrow Never Knows." Only this time, they were joined by the bandmates themselves, who were beginning to take a greater interest in the presentation of their work. As Phil McDonald later recalled, "They found that they could get more control of the sound that they wanted by actually being there for a mix." While eleven mixes were completed that evening, none would make it onto the new long-player—underscoring the increasing oversight and general artistic concern that the bandmates dedicated to their art. As it happened, the Beatles wouldn't begin recording that day until 11:30 PM, when they began working on a new Len-non composition in Studio 3—a song devoted to the act of sleeping, one of John's favorite pastimes. Maureen Cleave, the journalist from the *London Evening Standard* who had recently conducted an exposé devoted to all four Beatles, called him "possibly the laziest man in Britain." The songwriter echoed these words in "I'm Only Sleeping," singing "Everybody seems to think I'm lazy / I don't mind; I think they're crazy." As was their practice, Martin and the bandmates spent the lion's share of the session, which ran until three in the morning, refining the basic rhythm track, which featured Lennon and Harrison strumming their acoustic guitars, McCartney on bass, and Starr on drums. With the tape running fast in the spirit of "Rain," the Beatles recorded eleven takes, the last of which was noted as being the best. The manipulation of tape speed afforded "I'm Only Sleeping" with a lethargic, dreamlike quality upon playback, an effect that paralleled the mood of the song to a tee.[20]

For the time being, George and the Beatles would put "I'm Only Sleeping" aside to concentrate on "Eleanor Rigby," the composition that had emerged after Paul's visit to Bristol earlier in the year. On Thursday, April 28, George would supervise a session that saw the bandmates—in this instance, John and Paul—in the Studio 2 control room, while he toiled down below conducting a double string quartet. For George, "Eleanor Rigby" represented an opportunity to display the skills that he had learned back at the Guildhall School of Music and Drama back in the late 1940s, as well as during more than a decade as a professional A&R man. In moments such as these, the Beatles afforded him with a wide berth to show off his expertise. In this case, George pulled off one of the finest moments across his incredible career as he executed his superb score for "Eleanor Rigby" that evening at EMI Studios. Years later, he would recall that

> my score for "Eleanor Rigby" was influenced by Bernard Hermann's for the film *Fahrenheit 451*. Bernard Hermann was the favored composer for Alfred Hitchcock. He's since been revered for his work. His scoring on *Fahrenheit 451* used strings a great deal and also electronics, and I did notice in particular that the strings that he wrote were the very opposite of syrupy. They were jagged, spiky, very menacing. *Psycho* was similar. That kind of short attack that you get on his strings was very useful on "Eleanor Rigby." It had to be very *marcato*; it had to be an absolutely tight rhythm, which strings aren't noted for.

The score that George composed for "Eleanor Rigby" proved to be the epitome of marcato, which denotes music being played with great emphasis. And his orchestration for McCartney's tale about a lonely, dejected spinster was menacing and emphatic indeed. But Martin would later admit that he had been mistaken about *Fahrenheit 451*'s influence. François Truffaut's brilliant adaptation of Ray Bradbury's dystopian novel wouldn't premiere until the fall of 1966. Hermann's score for Hitchcock's *Psycho* was the more likely influence, having been in the cultural main since 1960. Its penetrating, staccato movements bear more than a passing resemblance to Martin's vision for "Eleanor Rigby," a composition that, as with Hermann's finest work, was truly the "opposite of syrupy."[21]

Recorded in its entirety with an octet of studio musicians during the April 28 session, Martin's magnificent arrangement for "Eleanor Rigby" had been brewing over the past several weeks along with the song's memorable lyrics about the corrosive power of loneliness. McCartney and Lennon had refined the lyrics at a recent writing session, also attended by Lennon's boyhood friend Pete Shotton, at the Beatle's Weybridge estate. And there would be more refinements yet to come in that regard. When it came to scoring "Eleanor Rigby," Martin not only drew upon Hermann's musical influence but upon McCartney's own vision for the song, which had been inspired by Antonio Vivaldi. Jane Asher had recently introduced McCartney to the work of the Venetian composer by way of *The Four Seasons*, Vivaldi's famous series of violin concertos. McCartney had begun the composition while vamping on an E minor chord in the basement music room at the Asher residence, later recording a demo version of the song at a Montagu Square studio. In this fashion, Paul captured his vision for the song's musical direction. When it came time for Martin to translate McCartney's vision onto the page, the songwriter only offered a single request: "I want the strings to sound really biting." As McCartney later recalled, "I thought of the backing, but it was George Martin who finished it off. I just go bash, bash on the piano. He knows what I mean." Did he ever.[22]

George later recalled that the composition process for his score for "Eleanor Rigby" ensued after "Paul came round to my flat one day, and he played the piano and I played the piano." Deftly scored around a series of E minor and C chords, Martin's arrangement not only wore its Hermann antecedents on its sleeve but also worked in unison with McCartney's lyrics to establish one of the most vivid musical tapestries in the Beatles' canon. Working through Laurie Gold, EMI's session organizer, Martin arranged for several of London's top chamber musicians to join him at Abbey Road. The octet included violists John Underwood and Steve Shingles; cellists Derek Simpson and Norman Jones; and violinists Jürgen Hess, Tony Gilbert, John Sharpe, and Sid Sax. For their part, Gilbert and Sax were veteran Beatles studio musicians, having performed on Martin's groundbreaking score for "Yesterday." As classical players at the top of their profession, the studio musicians were only vaguely familiar with the Beatles. But they were well acquainted with Martin—if only by reputation. London's premier session men had the greatest respect for George. They knew that sessions would start on time, be professional, and be well organized. With Lennon and McCartney up in the Studio 2 control room, the April 28 session was no different. In historian Steve Turner's account of the octet's performance, which typified the manner in which professional studio musicians approached such sessions during that era, "the musicians sat near each other, as they would have done for a concert, read the music that was on their music stands (and which didn't seem exceptional to them), and played when asked to. They weren't prepared by listening to a demo tape beforehand, and although they were always welcome to go to the control room, none of them were sufficiently interested to stay on to hear a playback." Over the next three hours, the octet performed fourteen takes of the score under Martin's direction.[23]

For the most part, the session was routine for Martin and the studio musicians alike. The key issue of the afternoon, which emerged between the first and second takes of the musicians' performance, was whether or not they should play the musical accompaniment to "Eleanor Rigby" with vibrato. This was no minor consideration. The use of vibrato would call to mind the sound of Annunzio Mantovani, the Anglo-Italian purveyor of light orchestral entertainment and a forerunner of Muzak (or elevator music). Known for his overdone cascading strings, Mantovani's compositions sold handsomely throughout the 1950s, but by the following decade, his music had become increasingly associated with an ersatz, easy-listening sound. For the likes of Lennon and McCartney, who had been feted in Western media of all stripes, sounding even remotely like Mantovani would have been strictly verboten.

For his part, Martin had a soft spot for the Mantovanis and Percy Faiths of his day. As Geoff later recalled, Paul in particular was fearful that the score would be "too cloying, too 'Mancini,'" in reference to the popular American composer of that era. So when it came to the score for "Eleanor Rigby," John and Paul and the members of the octet were squarely on the same page, as the studio musicians opted to dispense with vibrato in favor of a more classically oriented sound. Their impulse made all of the difference, bringing Martin's arrangement into stark relief, imbuing his score with darkening shades of fear and uncertainty—the perfect palette for McCartney's tale about a reclusive spinster and the doom that awaits her at the song's despairing conclusion, the dispiriting place where "no one was saved." But in the end, it was Martin who had the last laugh. While McCartney held deep suspicions about vibrato as being emblematic of the BBC's light program, Martin decided to test the younger man's resolve, instructing the musicians at one point to play two quick versions of the score—one with vibrato and the other without. "Can you hear the difference?" George called up to Paul in the control room. "Er, not much," the Beatle sheepishly admitted.[24]

While the musicians clearly held great respect for Martin, Emerick had a very different experience altogether in his dealings with London's finest string players. As the balance engineer, Emerick was responsible for miking the instruments. He was particularly concerned with capturing the "biting" sound that McCartney envisioned for "Eleanor Rigby." As Geoff later recalled, "String quartets were traditionally recorded with just one or two microphones, placed high, several feet up in the air so that the sound of the bows scraping couldn't be heard. But with Paul's directive in mind, I decided to close-mic the instruments, which was a new concept. The musicians were horrified! One of them gave me a look of disdain, rolled his eyes to the ceiling, and said under his breath, 'You can't do that, you know.'" With his confidence shaken and beginning to second-guess himself, Geoff pushed forward, placing the mics only an inch or so away from each instrument in order to record the sound that Paul desired. "It was a fine line," Geoff reasoned. "I didn't want to make the musicians so uncomfortable that they couldn't give their best performance, but my job was to achieve what Paul wanted. That was the sound he liked, and so that was the miking we used, despite the string players' unhappiness. To some degree, I could understand why they were so upset: they were scared of playing a bum note, and being under a microscope like that meant that any discrepancy in their playing was going to be magnified."[25]

But things didn't end there. As the musicians worked through successive takes of Martin's score, Emerick had to contend with the players continually shifting their chairs backward in order to ease away from the microphones. He could literally hear their chairs scraping from his place up in the booth above Studio 2. Between each take, Geoff was forced to leave the control room in order to move the mics closer to the instruments. "It was comic, really," Geoff later recalled. George finally decided to end the charade, instructing the musicians over the talkback to stop moving their chairs. As it was, the players couldn't wait to leave the studio, not even bothering to stick around to listen to the playback. But it hardly mattered. Martin and Emerick—not to mention Lennon and McCartney—were thrilled by the result. As with so many instances across the sessions devoted to the Beatles' latest long-player, recording Martin's score for "Eleanor Rigby" had found the band's production team working together to create new, uncharted vistas of sound in popular music.[26]

Years later, Shingles would remember things differently about his session work that day. Perhaps revealing a considerable degree of sour grapes, the viola player would later recall that "I got about £5" for a one-time session fee when "Eleanor Rigby" went on to earn "billions of pounds. And like idiots we gave them all our ideas for free." Shingles's remarks are problematic for a number of reasons. First, the going rate for the standard Musicians' Union session fee during that era was nine pounds, suggesting that Shingles was clearly underpaid by EMI. Second, the idea that the musicians' ideation was behind Martin's innovative score is difficult to believe, given the level of care and control that Martin exerted over his Beatles productions. As Julian Lloyd Webber later remarked, "People like Bobby Vee used cellos and Adam Faith had those plucked strings but cellos hadn't been used really effectively on rock 'n' roll records until the Beatles. George Martin was a very good arranger who knew what he was doing and he loved the sound of the cello. They are used beautifully on 'Yesterday' and especially 'Eleanor Rigby.'"[27]

After the players took their leave, Martin and Emerick had some tidying up to carry out before the next session. The octet had been recorded across all four tracks, with two instruments relegated to each track. Having chosen take fourteen as the best of the lot, they mixed down the recording, with the reduction being duly numbered as take fifteen. In so doing, they left space for overdubbing the vocals onto "Eleanor Rigby." On Friday, April 29, Martin and the Beatles reconvened in Studio 3 to continue working on McCartney's composition. During yet another session that began in the late afternoon and ranged into the wee hours of the next morning, the Beatles made great strides in bringing "Eleanor Rigby" and "I'm Only Sleeping" to fruition. Up first was McCartney's vocal, which was overdubbed onto Martin's string arrangement, with Harrison and Lennon providing the song's memorable refrain, "Ah, look at all the lonely people." At this point, McCartney's lead vocal was treated with ADT, three mono remixes were carried out (with the third being selected as the best), and the recording for "Eleanor Rigby" seemed to be complete—if only for the time being.

At this juncture, the Beatles turned back to Lennon's "I'm Only Sleeping," which they remade entirely. With the tape running, they rehearsed a new version of the song with a basic track featuring drums, vibraphone, and acoustic guitar. Only one take was seen through to completion that evening. Composed of acoustic guitars and percussion, this version of "I'm Only Sleeping" featured a vocal duet from Lennon and McCartney. As with the session associated with the song two days earlier, the vocals were recorded with the tape machine running fast and played back a half step lower in terms of pitch.

The remake featured a strong resemblance to "Daydream," a recent hit by the Lovin' Spoonful, a band that Lennon and Harrison had seen in concert in mid-April. After comparing their efforts this evening with the version of "I'm Only Sleeping" that they recorded on April 27, George and the Beatles clearly preferred the earlier version, and the remake was subsequently abandoned.

And with that, George and the Beatles took a much-needed, nearly weeklong break from working on *Rubber Soul*'s follow-up, the still-unnamed long-player that had already witnessed the bandmates, with vital technical assistance from Geoff, exploring more sonic frontiers than all of their previous work combined. Their new single, "Paperback Writer" backed with "Rain," was mixed and ready for release, promising to pick up where "Day Tripper" backed with "We Can Work It Out" had left off the previous December. Even the most casual of listeners would be able to glean the artistic trajectory that the Beatles were now daring to travel. In a hair over three weeks, they had managed to eclipse their own expectations, which had already proven to be mighty ambitious indeed. For his part, McCartney wore his determination on his sleeve, remarking that this new batch of recordings had been "purposely composed to sound unusual. They are sounds that nobody else has done yet. I mean, nobody *ever*." Leave it to Harrison to strike more measured tones about their accomplishments at roughly the midpoint of their latest project. "Musically we're only just starting," he remarked. "We've realized for our-selves that as far as recording is concerned most of the things that recording men have said were impossible for 39 years are in fact very possible. In the past, we've thought that the recording people knew what they were talking about. We believed them when they said we couldn't do this, or we couldn't do that. Now we know we can, and it's opening up a wide new field for us." As with McCartney, Harrison was sanguine enough to realize that it was their music that was blowing open the doors of artistic change, but at the same time the bandmates understood intuitively that it was Martin and Emerick who were the ones who were prying open the locks and recasting them for a new musical age.[28]

With their work in the studio having been completed for the month of April, a period in which they had committed to tape a spate of groundbreak-ing recordings, there was still plenty of mystery in the air. How would they go about arranging such a motley assortment of recordings into a cohesive whole? Where *Rubber Soul* had a folk-rock flavor that dominated the fall 1965 sessions, this new LP had been all over the place as the Beatles tried on a wide range of musical styles and genres—from brash psychedelia and a string octet to Indian music and bass-heavy rock confections. All of which raised the question: What would they call this revolutionary long-player anyway? How do you begin to name something that intentionally broaches the unnamable?

And to think that it had all started with the idea of making an honest-to-goodness American rhythm-and-blues album in Memphis.

5

COLLECTIVE MADNESS

FOR THE BEATLES, May 1966 began with a milestone—although nobody could have possibly known it at the time. For the fourth year in a row, they appeared at the annual New Musical Express Poll Winners' Concert. When they took the stage on May 1, the Beatles topped a roster of all-stars that included the Rolling Stones, the Who, the Yardbirds, the Spencer Davis Group (featuring Stevie Winwood), the Small Faces, Roy Orbison, and Cliff Richard and the Shadows, the act that the Fab Four had supplanted as England's greatest hitmakers only a few years earlier. Cliff Richard was also the mainstay of producer Norrie Paramor, Martin's one-time rival at EMI, as well as one of the driving forces behind his interest in landing a beat group of his own.

But on May 1, the Beatles—especially Lennon—were beside themselves. Already prisoners of their fame, they were forced to arrive at the venue, Wembley's Empire Pool, by entering the premises via the service entrance. Wearing white aprons and chefs' toques, they made their way into the venue disguised as culinary staff. But the real trouble was brewing backstage. With the Stones knocking out numbers like "The Last Time," "Play with Fire," and "(I Can't Get No) Satisfaction," the bandmates gathered up their instruments and prepared to go onstage. And that's when *NME*'s publisher Maurice Kinn informed Lennon that the Beatles wouldn't be going on until after the awards ceremony. For John, these were fighting words. He expected his band to take the stage immediately after the Rolling Stones. The Beatles were England's reigning superstars—the world's, really—and there was no way they would be playing second fiddle to the Stones. "We're not waiting," Lennon barked.

"We're going on now." Kinn told Lennon that he was powerless to accede
to the Beatle's wishes, having made a prior agreement with Andrew Loog
Oldham, the Stones' manager. For a moment, Lennon threatened that the
Beatles wouldn't play at all, but Kinn called his bluff, warning him that he
would be forced to announce that the band had cancelled their appearance
in front of ten thousand rowdy fans. Brian Epstein would be responsible
for any ensuing damages to the Empire Pool, while also being vulnerable to
NME for breach of contract. Fine, Brian countered, but ABC-TV would not
be allowed to film the Beatles' set following the awards ceremony. Watching
the scene unfold before him, Loog Oldham, who had once worked at NEMS,
was surprised to observe Epstein giving in so easily to Kinn. Worse yet, he
seemed to have lost his grip on the bandmates, who had formerly accepted
their manager's professional judgment without fail.[1]

For his part, Lennon wasn't even remotely pacified by Epstein's attempt
at détente. "You can't do this to us," Lennon roared at Kinn. "We will never
appear on one of your shows ever again." His words would prove to be very
prophetic indeed. After the Stones finished their set, the Beatles, clad in dark
suits and black turtlenecks, clambered onstage to accept their awards from
American television star Clint Walker. Wearing dark sunglasses, Lennon
took home the trophy for Great Britain's top vocal personality. Meanwhile,
the band was honored as the world's top vocal group. When the awards
ceremony concluded, the Beatles turned in a blistering set, clearly having
left the backstage acrimony behind them. The oldest number in the set was
1964's "I Feel Fine," which they followed with "Nowhere Man," "Day Tripper," "If I Needed Someone," and "I'm Down"—powerful evidence of how
far they'd come since the days of "Please Please Me" and "She Loves You."
But it was hardly lost on the Beatles that, their latest strides in the studio
notwithstanding, the lion's share of their recent work could not be reproduced on the stage given its complexity, as well as contemporary limitations
related to the equipment and technology of the day. After they completed
their fifteen-minute set, the bandmates loped off of the stage, leaving ten
thousand screaming fans in their wake, as well as their life as a working rock
'n' roll band in their home country. Not only would the Beatles never play
another show for Kinn, but they would never perform again before a paying
audience in the United Kingdom.[2]

Martin took advantage of the break in the Beatles' recording schedule to
attend to neglected AIR business that had been stacking up while he attended
to the most valuable act in his stable—in truth, the most valuable act in *anyone's* stable. In early 1966, Martin had been grooming a new act, Liverpool's

the Scaffold, for their recording debut. The group, which was primarily pop musical in style, also dabbled in comedy and poetry—a bizarre admixture of genre bending that was well ahead of its time. The Scaffold, who drew their name from the UK title of the Louis Malle film *Lift to the Scaffold*, was led by Mike McGear—the stage name for one Peter Michael McCartney, the younger brother of one of the principal songwriters in one of Martin's other bands. "We were satirists," McGear later remarked. "Our main thing was to comment on life. A ladies' barber, a Post Office engineer, and an English teacher, jobs for life." But they were also satirists in need of spectators with whom they could share their peculiar brand of humor. "We realized that when comedy got to a wider audience, it would be good to include music," said McGear. "We couldn't do rock 'n' roll because we couldn't sing or play instruments." But in contrast with his deal with the Beatles, Martin enjoyed a larger percentage of any potential success that the Scaffold would accrue, given his existing agreement with the EMI Group, which dictated that EMI had the right of first refusal on any of AIR's productions. If EMI opted to release the recordings, AIR would receive a royalty of 7 percent of the product's retail price. When it came to AIR's production of existing EMI artists, George and his partners, including former Decca A&R man Peter Sullivan and fellow EMI refugee John Burgess, would receive a producer's royalty amounting to 2 percent of the retail price. When it came to the Beatles, EMI was even less generous, reasoning that the band had been discovered and established via the parent company's investment. By way of his exit agreement with EMI, Martin's AIR productions of Beatles records entitled him to just 1 percent of the wholesale price, which amounted to 0.5 percent retail in the UK marketplace.[3]

With the Scaffold, McGear was joined by Roger McGough, who had previously studied French and geography at the University of Hull, where he began to pursue a life in poetry. McGough settled in Merseyside in the early 1960s, where he found work as a French teacher. At that juncture, he began working with John Gorman, a local telecommunications engineer, to organize regional arts events—namely, the Edinburgh Festival Fringe. It was at Gorman's instigation that the Scaffold was founded. At the time, McGear had been working as an apprentice hairdresser. He had originally considered "Mike Blank" as his nom de plume in order to avoid any suggestion that he was trading on his famous brother's surname, but he adopted the root word *gear* instead so as to draw upon its Scouser connotations of being "fab" or "cool." At Martin's encouragement, they had signed with Parlophone, the producer's old label. As McGear—who would return to using his original surname in the 1970s—later remarked, "George Martin was the Scaffold's producer, not because of my brother and his chums, but because of his work with Peter Sellers and Spike Milligan. George had recorded *Songs for Swingin' Sellers*, and Paul and I had fallen about laughing to those nice little sketches." With Martin on their team, the Scaffold naturally gravitated toward lobbying for Epstein to be their manager, given the long string of successes that the two men had enjoyed together. "Now that we were involved with George Martin and EMI," McGear later recalled, "we went to Brian Epstein and said, 'You've got all the pop groups, but can you do a theatre comedy group?' He goes, 'My dear boy!'—cause he was a failed actor—'Of *course*. We'd *love* to have you aboard.' So we thought, with his enormous NEMS agency, we had nothing to lose."[4]

By the time that they had started working in the studio with Martin, the Scaffold had a number of "nice little sketches" ready for their new producer's consideration. Chief among them were "2 Days Monday," for which Martin was quite partial, and "3 Blind Jellyfish." As McGear had observed, the producer had a penchant for comedy recordings that dated well back to the 1950s, and they were eager to try their hands at going national. Martin's score for "2 Days Monday," which he had selected as the A-side of the band's first single, began with the Scaffold's singers rotating their vocal parts against a solo tuba. As the song proceeded, Martin's score augmented its orchestration with violin and flute arrangements. A novelty song about the mundane and arbitrary nature of human existence, "2 Days Monday" was similar in structure to the well-known Christmas carol "A Partridge in a Pear Tree" given the Scaffold's repeating refrains and the manner in which they double-back on themselves as the song progresses. As with its holiday antecedent, "2 Days Monday" associated different themes with each day of the week, with Monday, for instance, finding the singer glum and dejected after a carefree weekend. Each verse ends with the ironic pronouncement, "Is everybody happy? You bet your life we are!" Released in May 1966 to Martin and the band's great excitement, "2 Days Monday" backed with "3 Blind Jellyfish" failed to make a dent in the UK charts. But in contrast with his early days with the Beatles, Martin was hardly content to record the requisite sides and exhaust the Scaffold's contract. Believing that the Scaffold had the makings of a 1960s-era Goons, he was more than prepared to invest more time and energy into their cause. And now that he was his own boss, and not under EMI's ever-watchful eye, he was free to pursue any act that struck his fancy.

Meanwhile, the Beatles devoted a good portion of their break to a series of in-depth interviews with Brian Matthew, the voice of BBC Radio Two's

Saturday Club program. Knowing the bandmates' penchant for cutting up in front of each other and landing the most sardonic punch lines possible, Matthew opted to meet with them individually in order to create an environment that would be conducive for more candid, unguarded responses. Matthew's concept was in a similar vein to Maureen Cleave's revealing series of interviews with the bandmates that had been published back in March in the *London Evening Standard*. Recorded to celebrate *Saturday Club*'s four hundredth episode and scheduled for a June 4 broadcast, Matthew's interviews addressed the bandmates' new long-player and their recent low profile after so many months and years of being front and center in terms of media saturation. Proffering questions about whether or not the Beatles intended to retire and why they were spending so much time on their new album, Matthew seemed eager to get to the heart of the group's apparently shifting concerns. For his part, Harrison got right to the point, telling Matthew, "We spend more time on recording now, because we prefer recording." Lennon echoed the quiet Beatle's perspective, reporting, "We've done half an LP in the time we'd take to do a whole LP and a couple of singles. We can't do it all y'know. But we like recording." John made a special point of noting that the band members were showing a greater interest in the mixing process, which had previously been the exclusive purview of producers and engineers.[5]

During his own sit-down with Matthew, Ringo lauded the carefree existence that he now enjoyed—a life in which he was no longer overwhelmed by nonstop touring, photo sessions, and other sundry promotional efforts. "We used to work every night, practically. We were always tired—and hungry. Now we have plenty of time off." Matthew concluded his interviews with McCartney, who spoke at great length about his personal cultural renaissance, as well as the ways in which he was challenging himself to be less narrow-minded: "When I was in Liverpool I went once or twice to the Liverpool Playhouse, a repertory theatre there, and I wasn't very keen on it. I used to go to see if I liked going to these plays, you know? I just never went back again. But I went when I came down to London. I went to something that wasn't like the plays they did in repertory. So, you see some great actors acting in a great play and you think, 'Wow! That is good.' I was wrong to say that theatre is just rubbish."[6]

While McCartney was proud to extol the manner in which he was broadening his horizons, he was loath to discover that not everyone was open to cultural change, that in art as in life, we have a tendency to pigeonhole each other. Paul was shortly to experience a referendum, of sorts, on the sonic strides that George and the Beatles had been attempting in the studio of late.

After the BBC interview with Matthew had concluded, Lennon and McCartney traipsed off to Dolly's, a trendy mid-1960s nightclub in Central London. With roadie Neil Aspinall and Rolling Stones guitarists Keith Richards and Brian Jones in tow, they met up with Bob Dylan, who was in the city on a layover on the eve of his upcoming European tour. Later that evening, the group joined Dylan in his suite at the Mayfair Hotel. With an acetate of "Tomorrow Never Knows" at the ready, McCartney couldn't wait to gauge the American folk luminary's reaction to the Beatles' avant-garde creation. "Oh, I get it," Dylan said blankly after listening to the track, "you don't want to be cute anymore." Quite suddenly, McCartney felt that he had been put in his place, that to people like Dylan—artists the Beatles had revered, even engaged in a kind of hero worship—they were a mere pop act. Worse yet, they were still those four mop-tops in Dylan's eyes, the product of good looks, catchy tunes, and great marketing. For his part, Martin had experienced the illusion of Beatlemania firsthand in February 1964, on the very same weekend in which the band had made its unforgettable American splash on *The Ed Sullivan Show*. In an image that he would carry for the rest of his life, Martin recalled walking along Fifth Avenue and seeing middle-aged men caught up in the furor and wearing Beatle wigs.[7]

In Martin's mind, it was a "collective madness" that didn't have any relation to the group's music or the incredible creative trajectory that he had witnessed as it developed over their ensuing albums, with each one trumping the last in artistry and scope. Back in his suite at the Mayfair Hotel, Dylan had no sooner finished listening to the Beatles' most experimental recording to date—and questioning their motives for making it in the first place—than he began sharing tracks from his latest, as-of-yet unreleased album, *Blonde on Blonde*. Like the Beatles' latest project, it would be a smorgasbord of styles and genres. And it would even make thinly veiled references to *Rubber Soul* both in terms of its slightly out-of-focus cover photograph, as well as Dylan's "4th Time Around," which borrowed liberally from the melody of John's "Norwegian Wood (This Bird Has Flown)." Had Dylan somehow missed the strides that Martin and the Beatles had made in 1965—the seminal varispeed piano adornment for "In My Life" or the groundbreaking string arrangement for "Yesterday," which had topped the US singles charts? Or the "plastic soul" inherent in such ear-popping tracks as "Drive My Car" and "Day Tripper"? Or even the British folk writ large in songs like "Norwegian Wood" and "Girl"?

A few weeks later, John and Paul would be treated to yet another eye-opening release—this time, in the form of the Beach Boys' *Pet Sounds*. Introduced by the Who's Keith Moon to the Beach Boys' Bruce Johnston at the

Scotch of St. James, Lennon and McCartney later joined Johnston at a party in his suite at the Waldorf Astoria. As the festivities got underway, Johnston spun the Beach Boys' still-unreleased long-player on a portable mono phonograph. Producer Kim Fowley was also in attendance, and he vividly recalled observing John and Paul playing canasta as *Pet Sounds* filled the room. As he looked on, the two Beatles drifted over to a piano, fingering various chords and whispering to each other as the tracks unfolded. "They were there to see what the competition was," Fowley later remarked. But "they didn't steal lyrics, or notes, or chords. They stole emotional impact and pathos." As Steve Turner astutely observed, the Beatles' principal songwriters witnessing firsthand the latest wares from the likes of Dylan and the Beach Boys was "the pop equivalent of an arms race." Years later, McCartney didn't mince words about the occasion in Johnston's suite, remarking that *Pet Sounds* "blew me out of the water."[8]

When they rejoined Martin at Abbey Road on Thursday, May 5, the Beatles were well rested and ready to resume work on their own long-player. Not surprisingly, they were eager to one-up their rivals, which they began doing in fine style by recording backward guitar solos for "I'm Only Sleeping" in a six-hour session that would last into the wee hours of May 6. As Martin supervised the protracted, late-night session in Studio 3, Harrison was determined to afford Lennon's dreamy composition with an otherworldly guitar duet. As Emerick looked on, the Beatles' lead guitarist created the melodic solo, and then, over the next few hours, began to plot out the order of the notes in reverse order. Martin recorded Harrison playing the solo on his electric guitar and then later playing the same solo using a fuzz box. In the final recording, the second guitar was superimposed on top of the first, affording a surrealistic feel to the recording. In addition to Harrison's backward guitar solo, Martin and Emerick recorded Harrison and McCartney playing a backward guitar duet for the song's outro. The result was a revelation, with the Beatles achieving a unique, previously unrealized sound on their guitars—even more groundbreaking, if that were possible, than the ethereal guitar work on "Tomorrow Never Knows." The next day, Martin and Emerick carried out tape reductions in order to combine the guitar parts. George and his production team were keenly aware of the need to carry out tape reductions in order to free up more recording real estate, as well as of the attendant dangers associated with overdoing it—tape being an inherently "lossy" medium. "On analog tape," Martin later wrote, "every time you transfer one track to another, you multiply the signal-to-noise ratio. Dirt comes up, all the background hiss and audio clutter, and this noise multiplies by the square of each tape-to-tape transfer. Two copies create four times the amount of noise; a third generation increases the noise by nine times! So I had to be very disciplined in keeping the track usage together." After carrying out the tape reduction for "Tomorrow Never Knows," the available fourth track on "I'm Only Sleeping" was deployed with Lennon double-tracking his lead vocal and McCartney and Harrison providing harmonies. Aside from a dose of ADT during the mixing phase, "I'm Only Sleeping" was finally complete.[9]

During an evening session in Studio 2 on Monday, May 9, Martin and the Beatles tried their hand at a new McCartney composition titled "For No One." Originally titled "Why Did It Die?" the song had been written during the Beatle's March Swiss ski vacation with his longtime girlfriend Jane Asher. With the tape running, George conducted ten takes in order to create the basic rhythm track, with Paul refining a piano part on track one and Ringo playing the drums on track two. After take ten had been selected as the best, Martin and McCartney hit upon the idea of adorning the track with a clavichord to enhance the song's baroque ambience. With a five-pound rental fee debited to the band's standing EMI recording budget, Martin helpfully procured a clavichord from his AIR London studios on nearby Park Street. At variance with EMI records, Martin would remember things differently: "On 'For No One,' the track was laid down on my own clavichord. I brought it in from my home, because I thought it had a nice sound. It was a very strange instrument to record, and Paul played it." A European keyboard that creates sound when a series of tiny metal blades known as tangents strike the instrument's brass or iron strings, the clavichord seemed to be the perfect complement to McCartney's nostalgic, bittersweet effusion about a fading, increasingly emotionless romance. With the borrowed and/or rented keyboard ready and available in Studio 2, McCartney overdubbed the clavichord on the available third track, with Starr providing maracas and hi-hat cymbal.[10]

Martin and the Beatles would not continue work on their unnamed long-player until the following week on May 14. In the meantime, Martin and Emerick conducted an afternoon mixing session in the Studio 3 control room on Thursday, May 12. EMI had recently been contacted by Capitol Records, the record conglomerate's US subsidiary, with a request for three tracks slated for the Beatles' new album. As had long been the American company's practice, they planned to release a new album of original material for the US marketplace. To be titled *Yesterday . . . and Today*, the album had been devised by Capitol as a means for exploiting the chart-topping success of the American "Yesterday" backed with "Act Naturally" single. Since the early days of American Beatlemania, Capitol had been consistently skimming material from the bandmates' official British releases in order to create more product for the bustling US record marketplace. Most recently, Capitol had culled tracks from the UK *Help!* and *Rubber Soul* releases in order to begin stockpiling songs for a new American long-player. But Capitol execs still needed a few tracks to fill out the planned album. Martin and the Beatles had been aware of this practice since its inception, but EMI's prevailing contract with their American subsidiary prevented them from doing anything about it.

The bandmates had complained about the state of affairs vis-à-vis their American discography as recently as August 1965 during a press conference associated with their appearance at the Hollywood Bowl. The Beatles could barely hide their disgust, with Harrison remarking that "the thing is, Capitol issues all sorts of mad stuff, you know. It's nothing to do with us. We take 14 tracks to be put out, but they keep a couple and put them out later." In itself, this practice countermanded the group's evolving notions of the long-player as more than a mere collection of songs but rather as an artistic statement. Capitol's discrepant American releases were "a drag, because we make an album to be like an album, a complete thing," McCartney observed. "We plan it, and they wreck it," Lennon added. Forced to comply with Capitol's request, Martin selected three new tracks—"Doctor Robert," "I'm Only Sleeping," and "And Your Bird Can Sing"—for inclusion on the American *Yesterday . . . and Today* album. With Emerick in tow and Jerry Boys sitting in the second engineer's chair in place of McDonald, Martin conducted mono mixing sessions for the three recordings, which were dutifully shipped to the United States via courier. He pointedly supervised the session knowing that additional mixing would very likely be necessary in order to capture fully the Beatles' vision for the tracks, much less his own.[11]

There was also yet another prevailing issue at play, and one that George and the group had found to be incredibly insulting over the past few years. George had long harbored ill will over Capitol Records' treatment of the Beatles. As Beatlemania broke in the United Kingdom, EMI's American subsidiary refused to release them stateside, believing—falsely, of course— that they wouldn't appeal to the North American marketplace. Much of this stonewalling had been at the hands of Dave E. Dexter Jr., the company's international A&R representative. Martin had been so incensed at the time that he blanched when Capitol Records president Alan Livingston referred to the Beatles as Capitol recording artists during their triumphant visit to American shores in February 1964.

In subsequent years, Capitol's studio personnel—under Dexter's orders— had taken to subjecting Martin's original Beatles mixes to the American company's so-called Duophonic sound. Capitol execs had long maintained that Martin's mixes were unsuitable for the vagaries of AM radio airplay. To remedy this issue, they subjected Martin's mixes to heavy doses of echo and reverb without Martin and the Beatles' consent. More recently, a new practice had developed at Capitol in which Martin's mono mixes would be transformed into Duophonic mixes to simulate a stereo sound for the American marketplace. To this end, Capitol personnel would create a Duophonic mix by simply redirecting the signal from Martin's mono mixes and splitting the left and right channels. To produce this fake stereo sound, the high end would be filtered in one direction, and the low end would filter toward the other. In so doing, these Duophonic mixes would create the sonic illusion of separation—and, hence, of true stereo. As Beatles historian Robert Rodriguez has noted, "The crassness with which their music was being treated in the world's largest market annoyed the Beatles, Brian, and George Martin to no end, but at this point in time they were powerless to stop it." While Martin may not have approved of Capitol's repackaging of Beatles albums during this period, he understood the pressure that the American company was under to provide new product for an insatiable record-buying marketplace. As Martin remarked at the time, "We now spend more and more time in the studios than ever before. The Beatles have come to accept that recording is their way of life. They accept their voluntary imprisonment of being in the studio as long as 14 hours at a time." And while consumers may hunger for yet more product, "there are no secret unissued Beatles tracks in case of emergency. Everything that the Beatles have recorded has been released. It has to be this way. The demand is so strong; it is difficult even keeping up with it."[12]

After another long weekend, Martin and the Beatles reconvened on Monday, May 14, for a recording session devoted to their new British long-player. After working through April at breakneck speed, May had been comparatively less productive for the band, who were staring at a looming June deadline for completing the album before embarking upon a series of German and Far Eastern tours and concluding the summer with another concert swing across the United States. Working an eleven-hour session in Studio 2 from early afternoon until well after midnight, Martin and the bandmates returned to Harrison's "Granny Smith," which they had abandoned more than a month earlier on April 13, as well as "Taxman," "Tomorrow Never Knows," and "For No One." Much of the session had been devoted to preparing a master reel of the best mixes of the songs thus far. For "Taxman," Martin instructed Emerick to append McCartney's April 21 count-off, while also creating four mono mixes of the song—none of which would be ultimately used for the long-player. The highlight of the session was McCartney's lead vocal overdub on "For No One." The Beatle can be heard practicing the opening lyrics and prepping for the recording by requesting "silence for the studio, over and out." Paul's vocal was recorded on the available fourth track and carried out with the tape running slow in order to increase the pitch of his voice during playback.[13]

The next afternoon, Wednesday, May 18, Martin and the bandmates returned to Studio 2 for an extended twelve-hour session to complete "Got to Get You into My Life," which hadn't seen any effort since April 8, when the rhythm track had been perfected. During the May 18 session, "Got to Get You into My Life" took a hard left turn from British pop fare into the world of American Motown flair with a big brass sound. Perhaps today was the day when the Beatles would finally catch that Stax Studio sound that they had yearned for only a few months earlier. But even "Got to Get You into My Life" was not standard Motown flair, just as "Mark I" was by no means a prototypical number from any beat band with provincial North Country origins—or any band anywhere in the history of time, for that matter. Over the past few weeks, McCartney had decided that the song's missing element was a horn section—indeed, "Got to Get You into My Life" would be the first Beatles recording with brass accompaniment. A few days earlier, Paul had begun to make good on that vision by inviting Jamaican trumpet player Eddie "Tan Tan" Thornton to work the session. Paul had seen Eddie, who was a member of Georgie Fame and the Blue Flames, performing at the Scotch of St. James on the same night that John and Paul first heard the Beach Boys' *Pet Sounds* in its entirety. The brass section also included tenor sax player Peter Coe, another member of the Blue Flames who landed the gig at the last minute after baritone sax player Glenn Hughes fell ill. A trio of freelance studio musicians—trumpeters Ian Hamer and Les Condon and tenor sax player Alan Branscombe—rounded out the brass section.

When they arrived at the session that afternoon, the studio musicians for "Got to Get You into My Life" enjoyed a rare glimpse inside the largely unseen world of Martin and the Beatles. As Coe later recalled, "The Beatles wanted a definite jazz feel," and from what the sax player could tell, "Paul and George Martin were in charge." Condon remembered that the experience "was interesting and unusual. I've never done a session quite like it before. The tune was a rhythm and bluesish sort of thing. We were only on one number. Apparently, the Beatles felt it needed something extra." But if the musicians arrived that day expecting sheet music, they were in for quite a surprise. In contrast with his earlier practices for such arrangements as

"Yesterday," "You've Got to Hide Your Love Away," and, most recently, "Eleanor Rigby," Martin hadn't prepared a score in advance for the musicians who were set to play on "Got to Get You into My Life." As Condon recalled, "As for the song's arrangement, well, they didn't have a thing written down! We just listened to what they had done and got an idea of what they wanted. Then we went ahead from there and gradually built up an arrangement. We tried a few things, and Paul and George Martin decided between them what would be used." Coe added, "There was nothing written down but Paul sat at the piano and showed us what he wanted and we played with the rhythm track in our headphones. I remember that we tried it a few times to get the feel right and then John Lennon, who was in the control room, suddenly rushed out, stuck his thumb aloft and shouted 'Got it!'" As for the other Beatles, Harrison was only slightly involved in the session, according to Coe, and Starr sat in a corner playing checkers.[14]

With the studio musicians having jotted down their own arrangements based upon McCartney's directives from the piano bench, Martin prepared to run the quintet through their paces. First, he instructed Emerick to free up space by erasing two of the original tracks. Second, Emerick purposefully set up the microphones in a configuration that was at variance with standing EMI policy in order to capture the big brass sound that McCartney desired. As Emerick later recalled, "I close-miked the instruments—actually put the mics right down into the bells instead of the standard technique of placing them four feet away—and then applied severe limiting to the sound." By recommending that the mics be placed at least a yard away from the instruments, EMI's guidelines had been designed to control the amount of air pressure to which the microphones would be subjected to avoid damage to their interior diaphragms during the recording process. But Emerick didn't care—and neither did Martin, for that matter. As had been clear throughout the sessions for their latest long-player, the Beatles' production team was willing to go to any lengths to satisfy their clients. Well, *almost* any lengths, that is.[15]

Later that evening, during the mixing portion of the May 18 session, McCartney complained that the studio musicians' performance, given that there were only five of them, had fallen short of his vision. "I wish we could make the brass sound bigger," he remarked to Martin. "Well, there's no way we're bringing them back in for another session," the Beatles' producer replied, "we've got to get the album wrapped up and there's no more budget for outside players anyway." Amazingly, in spite of Martin and the bandmates' incredible contribution to EMI's bottom line since "Please Please Me" had topped the charts in early 1963—and the unbreakable string of hit singles and albums that continued into the present day—EMI held the Beatles to a strict budgetary allotment. And for his part, Martin was in no position to create any overruns, which might very well cut into AIR's percentage of the Fab Four's sales receipts. But as usual, Emerick was ready with a solution. As he later recalled, "I came up with the idea of dubbing the horn track onto a fresh piece of two-track tape, then playing it back alongside the multitrack, but just slightly out of sync, which had the effect of doubling the horns." Quite suddenly, McCartney's brass quintet had been amplified into a dectet.[16]

With the brass track having come to fruition, Martin and Emerick were faced with a four-track tape that was filled to the brim. By this juncture, McCartney was no longer happy with his original lead vocals, which were deleted during a tape-to-tape deduction. With two additional tracks now free, the existing recording was labeled as take nine and was composed of the original bass/drums rhythm track and the decuple brass section. At this point, Paul added a fresh vocal to "Got to Get You into My Life," turning in a high-octane performance that left his colleagues dazzled. As Geoff remembered, "I loved Paul's singing on that song, too—he really let loose. At one point, while Paul was recording the lead vocal, John actually burst out of the control room to shout his encouragement—evidence of the camaraderie and teamwork that was so pervasive" during that period. After the available fourth track was appended with harmony vocals and an electric guitar overdub, Martin and Emerick created more mono mixes of "Got to Get You into My Life" and finally called it a night. The five studio musicians had been treated to the unique experience of being able to observe Martin and the Beatles working at EMI Studios. But perhaps even more significantly for them in the short run, the musicians enjoyed a financial boon after news of their work on a Beatles session was leaked in the trade papers. "That led to a lot of extra work for me," Thornton recalled. "Through working with the Beatles, I played with Jimi Hendrix, Sandie Shaw, the Small Faces, and the Rolling Stones."[17]

As with the "Got to Get You into My Life" session the night before, Martin and the bandmates' session on the evening of Friday, May 19, would prove to be yet another defining moment in terms of their increasing activities with studio musicians and their interactions with creative external forces vis-à-vis the Beatles' sound recordings. John, Paul, George, and Ringo had already spent much of the day working in the cavernous Studio 1 with American director Michael Lindsay-Hogg, who was shooting promotional videos for their upcoming single release, "Paperback Writer" backed with "Rain." In 1965, Lindsay-Hogg had broken into the British pop scene as the director of several episodes of *Ready Steady Go!*, the popular ATV vehicle with the slogan

"The weekend starts here!" and on which entertainers of the day debuted their latest wares. After completing their work with Lindsay-Hogg, the Beatles took a dinner break and then joined Martin and Emerick in cozy Studio 3, where they met Alan Civil, a thirty-six-year-old horn player. McCartney felt that a French horn solo would make for a sublime adornment to "For No One," and the Beatles' producer readily agreed. "We wanted a very special sound" for the baroque-sounding composition, "and French horn was what he [McCartney] chose."[18]

As Paul later recalled, "Occasionally we'd have an idea for some new kind of instrumentation, particularly for solos. . . . On 'For No One,' I was interested in the French horn, because it was an instrument I'd always loved from when I was a kid. It's a beautiful sound, so I went to George Martin and said, 'How can we go about this?' And he said, 'Well, let me get the very finest.' That was one of the great things about George. He knew how to obtain the best musicians and would suggest getting them. On this occasion, he suggested Alan Civil, who, like all these great blokes, looks quite ordinary at the session—but plays like an angel." After a long and distinguished career, Civil would very shortly be named as the principal horn player for the BBC Symphony Orchestra. A much sought-after musician, he had recently been approached by the Berlin Symphony Orchestra. Had he accepted a role as principal in Berlin, he would have been the first non-German to be appointed to such a culturally esteemed position in a nation where classical musicians are deeply revered.[19]

For his part, Civil was delighted to work with Martin again. The idea of working with the Beatles was a bonus. At this juncture, fewer than twenty studio musicians had contributed to Beatles songs, and Civil was about to find himself, for the space of a single evening at least, in the heart of the bandmates' world. As Civil remembered, "George Martin rang me up and said, 'We want a French horn *obbligato* on a Beatles song. Can you do it?' I knew George from his very early days at EMI because I'd been doing a lot of freelance work then. So I turned up at Abbey Road and all the bobbysoxers were hanging around outside and trying to look through the windows." What happened next is a matter of some dispute. Civil recalled thinking that "the song was called 'For Number One' because I saw 'For No One' written down somewhere. Anyway, they played the existing tape to me, which was complete. . . . Paul said, 'We want something there. Can you play something that fits in?' It was rather difficult to actually understand exactly what they wanted so I made something up which was middle register, a Baroque-style solo. I played it several times, each take wiping out the previous attempt.

For me it was just another day's work, the third session that day in fact, but it was very interesting." But what, exactly, did Civil play that evening? And who actually scored it—*if anyone?*[20]

In Civil's memory, it was McCartney who asked him to improvise a solo—"to make something up," as it were, in a baroque style. In itself, this level of ambiguity in terms of authorship would have rendered the notion of another Lennon-McCartney original even more vague than it had already become in recent years. But Civil was certainly up to the job. His skills as a horn player were beyond reproach, having been playing since his teen years, when he performed with the Royal Artillery Band and Orchestra at Woolwich. In 1955, he first ascended as principal with the Royal Philharmonic Orchestra when he was barely twenty-six years old. During the year in which he first met the Beatles, he was appointed as a professor at the Royal College of Music, leaving little doubt that he had the skills and acumen to carry out fewer than twenty seconds of improv. McCartney's memories of the session vary dramatically from Civil's. The Beatle later recalled humming the melody to Martin, who dutifully adapted McCartney's vision into musical notation. As Paul remembered, "George asked me, 'Now, what do you want him to play?' I said, 'Something like this,' and sang the solo to him, and he wrote it down."[21]

A scenario in which Martin created a written score makes eminently more sense, especially given what happened next. Up to this point, Martin had scored all of the notation for Beatles studio musicians—save for "Got to Get You into My Life," for which Paul had banged out the notes on the piano in full view of the players—and there is no reason to believe that Civil's session for "For No One" would be any different. According to Emerick, by this point the issue with studio musicians had little to do with the idea of bringing in outside help to generate new sounds for pop arrangements—the Beatles were quite comfortable with shaping the direction of their recordings with the freelance classical musicians in Martin's stable. Rather, it was a matter of their own professional musical limitations. After all, they had limited knowledge of instruments outside of the guitars, bass, and drums with which they were extremely familiar, much less any knowledge of how to compose notation for professional symphonic players like Civil. As Geoff later wrote, "The Beatles were perfectionists, and they didn't always understand the limitations of musical instruments. In particular, Paul's attitude toward outside musicians was 'You're being paid to do a job, so just do it.'" But it was more than that, of course. The pop-music scene was shifting rather precipitously, especially given the Beatles' apotheosis in world music. It was, to borrow Emerick's words, the makings of a generational, even a cultural clash: "My sense was that the classical musicians had had it so easy for so long, but that things were now changing. There was also a generational clash, because most of those outside musicians were quite a bit older than the Beatles. They were pleased to be there, pleased to have the credit on their resumes, but they didn't know how to relate to the music or the musicians—and the Beatles didn't really know how to relate to them, either. George Martin served as the middleman, as the bridge between the two generations." This aspect of the Beatles' evolving artistry had become apparent, most recently, during the "Eleanor Rigby" session in which Paul was unable to ascertain the difference between string performances with and without vibrato. In short, the Beatles simply didn't possess the vocabulary or the experience to understand the classical musicians' approach to their sessions with Martin and the band.[22]

With Martin's score for "For No One," this overarching issue reared its head, first, when it came to tuning up, and second, when Civil finally got a glimpse of the producer's arrangement. When the horn player first heard the recording of "For No One," he "thought it had been recorded in rather bad musical style, in that it was 'in the cracks,' neither B-flat nor B-major," he commented. "This posed a certain difficulty in tuning my instrument." Worse yet, Civil felt that studio trickery, which Martin and Emerick often employed in order to alter a song's pitch, was a poor substitute for solving the tuning problem. "I think they had a method of raising or lowering the pitch in this case," he said, "but it made the horn part for me a very, very awkward key, purely because these fellows just tuned their instruments to themselves and not to an A on the piano." This was the crux of the matter, of course, because rock performers in that era lacked today's electronic tuners and typically tuned the strings of their guitars to themselves without benefit of working against a well-tuned piano.[23]

Which brings us to the horn part itself. As noted, Martin most likely transcribed McCartney's humming into a musical score for Civil's benefit. But the problems didn't end there. As McCartney remembered the events of the day, "Towards the end of the session, when we were getting the piece down for Alan to play, George explained to me the range of the instrument: 'Well, it goes from here to this top E,' and I said, 'What if we ask him to play an F?'" In Paul's recollection, "George saw the joke and joined in the conspiracy. We came to the session and Alan looked up from his bit of paper: 'Eh, George? I think there's a mistake here—you've got a high F written down.' Then George and I said, 'Yeah,' and smiled back at him, and he knew what we were up to and played it. These great players will do it. Even though it's officially off the end of their instrument, they can do it, and they're quite into it occasionally. It's a nice little solo." On yet another occasion, Paul remembered the events as being friendly, even whimsical: "On the session, Alan Civil said, 'George?' and looked at us both. He said, 'George, you've written a D [*sic*],' and George and I just looked at him and held our nerve and said, 'Yes?' And he gave us a crafty look and went, 'Okay.'" Was this an instance in which Martin had acted as a "middleman," not only translating McCartney's ideas into a musical score but working as a buffer between the pop star and the classically trained musician?[24]

As it happened, Emerick took away a very different experience from the Beatles' interaction with Civil that day—one that was bolstered by Martin's own remarks, as well as the ensuing events that would transpire over their future recording sessions with studio musicians. As Geoff later wrote, "Alan was under a lot of pressure doing that overdub, because it was so hard to hit the high note in the solo. In fact, most people would have never written that part for a French horn player because it was too high to play, but that was the note Paul wanted to hear, and so that was the note he was going to get. We felt that Alan, being the best horn player in London, could actually hit it, even though most horn players couldn't. Alan was reluctant to even try it; he was actually breaking out into a sweat, telling everyone it really shouldn't be done. But eventually he gave it a go and pulled it off." Martin concurred with Emerick's description of the events that day in Studio 3, later recalling that "Paul didn't realize how brilliantly Alan Civil was doing. We got the definitive performance, and Paul said, 'Well, okay, I think you can do it better than that, can't you, Alan?' Alan nearly exploded. Of course, he didn't do it better than that, and the way we'd already heard it was the way you hear it now."[25]

Acting as middleman in this instance enabled Martin to quell Civil's concerns and draw an exemplary performance from the horn player while also keeping McCartney's professional naïveté and natural persistence in check. Both parties were satisfied with the result, with McCartney remembering Civil's "nice little solo" with great regard. For his part, Civil was delighted with the end result. As Emerick later recalled, "Though Alan was a wreck by the time he left that session, he was well pleased with what he'd done, because it was the performance of his life. In fact, he became a star in his own right because of that, but the problem was that, from that day on, arrangers would expect other horn players to be able to do what he had done, and they were often disappointed if they gave parts to other players of lesser ability." While it may have been touch-and-go when it came to hitting the high note, Civil would look back on his experience with Martin and the Beatles with a special fondness: "My friends would ask, 'What have you done this week?' and I would say, 'Oh, I played with Otto Klemperer and Rudolf Kempe'—that didn't mean anything to them. But to say that you'd played with the Beatles was amazing. The day would almost go into their diaries as being the day they met someone who'd played with the Beatles. Even now, while only a few people come up to me and say 'I do like your Mozart horn concertos,' so many others say, 'See that big grey-haired old chap over there?—he played with the Beatles!'" Given his stature among London's classical music set, Civil received a top-drawer session fee of fifty pounds for his work on "For No One." Perhaps even more significantly, when the eventual long-player was released, Civil was credited on the album sleeve, making him the first studio musician to be identified as a contributor to a Beatles recording.[26]

On Friday, May 20, Martin supervised a session in the Studio 2 control room with Emerick and McDonald. Meanwhile, the Beatles were across town with Lindsay-Hogg at Chiswick House, where they were carrying out additional photography among the eighteenth-century estate's lush gardens and conservatory for the "Paperback Writer" and "Rain" promotional videos. During the control room session back at Abbey Road, Martin prepared stereo mixes of "Doctor Robert," "I'm Only Sleeping," and "And Your Bird Can Sing," the same three songs for which he had created mono mixes a week earlier for inclusion on the *Yesterday . . . and Today* long-player, Capitol Records' upcoming American release. The ninety-minute session was remarkably brief in comparison to the production team's recent activities, and each song only required two iterations to perfect. As usual, Martin dispatched the mixes by courier to Capitol's famous Los Angeles headquarters at Hollywood and Vine. As it turned out, the stereo mixes of "Doctor Robert," "I'm Only Sleeping," and "And Your Bird Can Sing" must have arrived too late for the purposes of EMI's American subsidiary. With a June 20 release date scarcely a month away, nervous Capitol technicians produced fake stereo versions of the songs using the mono masters that Martin had shipped to California the previous week. They were ersatz versions, to say the least—and hardly up to Martin's standards. But this would be a minor consideration, as events would have it, after *Yesterday . . . and Today* finally made its way into American record shops in late June.[27]

Over the next week, Martin and the Beatles enjoyed a much-needed break. The Beatles were a month away from embarking upon a world tour, and George was overwhelmed with AIR business. He and his partners were determined to grow their talent pool beyond the paucity of acts that they had brought to their fledgling company in 1965. Martin was responsible for bringing the Beatles into the fold, of course, along with Cilla Black, Gerry and the Pacemakers, Billy J. Kramer and the Dakotas, and the Fourmost. For his part, Burgess's stable included Adam Faith, Manfred Mann, and Peter and Gordon. While Ron Richards counted P. J. Proby and the Hollies among his acts, Peter Sullivan was producing the likes of Lulu, Tom Jones, and Engelbert Humperdinck. In many ways, AIR's artists made for an impressive roster of mid-1960s pop acts, but the record business was a fickle game, as Martin well knew, and he was always on the lookout for the next fireproof act that could keep the company humming along for years. In those post–British Invasion years, critics and industry stalwarts alike were invariably crowing about this or that pop act being nothing more than "a flash in the pan" or, worse yet, a "one-hit wonder." In some cases, the derision was the express result of the so-called generation gap in which elders mocked their youthful progeny's taste in style and culture. Even in the heady days of 1966, the Beatles were still being hounded by such claims, as if theirs was a very ephemeral art—as if they would be here today, gone tomorrow. The Beatles themselves had always been cognizant of this possible career-ending fate. But by this point, there was little doubt that their place in the popular culture of their day was here to stay—even if they never managed to land another hit record again. In her March 1966 exposés of the four Beatles in the *London Evening Standard*, Maureen Cleave made this distinction clear: "It was this time three years ago that the Beatles first grew famous," she wrote in her article devoted to Lennon. "Ever since then, observers have anxiously tried to gauge whether their fame was on the wax or on the wane; they foretold the fall of the old Beatles, they searched diligently for the new Beatles (which was as pointless as looking for the new Big Ben). At last they have given up; the Beatles' fame is beyond question. It has nothing to do with whether they are rude or polite, married or unmarried, 25 or 45; whether they appear on *Top of the Pops* or do not appear on *Top of the Pops*." Simply put, Cleave concluded, "they are famous in the way the Queen is famous."[28]

6

ABRACADABRA

DURING THE WEEK of May 23, Martin and the Beatles were no doubt pleased to learn that *Rubber Soul* had entered its twenty-fifth straight week in the UK top ten, suggesting that their commercial dominion would hardly be ebbing any time soon. George and the bandmates were scheduled to resume work on the band's newest album on Thursday, May 26, in Studio 3, but as it turned out, George would be nowhere near the vicinity of EMI Studios. Instead, he was resting back in his flat on Baker Street, having been felled by a severe bout of food poisoning. In his place in the control room was none other than Judy Lockhart Smith, George's fiancée. At thirty-seven years old, she was three years George's junior. As far as the music business went, she held a longer tenure in the industry than her producer boyfriend, having joined Parlophone as a secretary in 1948, two years before Martin took a job as Oscar Preuss's assistant A&R man. Born November 13, 1928, Judy was the daughter of Kenneth Lockhart Smith, the chairman of the UK's Film Producer's Guild, as well as a graduate of the Bedford School and St. James's Secretarial College.[1]

As his bachelor days were nearing their end, George had enjoyed the company of a roommate in the form of his octogenarian father, Harry. Having worked as a journeyman carpenter for as long as he could, Harry had begun taking odd jobs as a caretaker or a night watchman in recent years in order to make ends meet. Things had come to a head in George's relationship with his father when his marriage to his first wife, Sheena, had finally disintegrated as a result of his long-running affair with Judy. As George later recalled,

"When my first marriage broke up, I was scared about telling him [Harry] because I was ashamed. One evening, I confessed what had happened, that it was no good—it was over. He was a dear man, and he said, 'I'm so glad because I've known for a long time you haven't been happy. Thank God for that.'" For his part, George had been relieved by his father's understanding demeanor—especially after the untimely death of his mother, Bertha, during the early weeks of his marriage to Sheena. Having died in her sleep in February 1948, Bertha was just fifty-three years old. For George, his reunion with Harry had been a long time coming indeed.[2]

During their years sharing his "pokey little flat in Upper Berkeley Street," George and Harry "got to know each other pretty well, and we even made some furniture together. I still have a sideboard he made. I used to take him along to recording sessions, which he loved, so he met people like Matt Monro, and was thrilled about what I did. He was knocked out by the success of the Beatles." During those years, Harry also became reacquainted with his grandchildren, thirteen-year-old Alexis and nine-year-old Gregory. For George's children, the sight of their grandfather lumbering in their direction was a source of great delight. "He was a true classic cockney," Gregory later recalled. "Always sprucely dressed in the same three-piece tweed suit, a cap on his head perched at a jaunty angle, a smile on his face. 'Pop,' as I called him, would bend down, slipping a half crown into my palm as he greeted me. 'There ya go, boy!' he'd say."[3]

By the time that the Beatles had begun recording their latest long-player, Harry had been unable to work. Indeed, he had recently been fired from his recent stint as a night watchman after he had fallen asleep on the job. Living on his pension, Harry had moved in with his sister in nearby Wimbledon as his son's nuptials approached. Concerned about his father's welfare, George had begun giving Harry a small allowance of ten pounds a week, which his father grudgingly accepted. To George's further relief, Harry had developed a great fondness for Judy, "and they got on like a house on fire." In many ways, George had Judy to thank for his latter-day reunion with his father. By the mid-1960s, and at his fiancée's bidding, the trio had begun spending many happy evenings in each other's company. For George, it was nothing short of a blessing after experiencing the familial trauma associated with his mother's death and the pall that it had cast over his first marriage.[4]

For as long as Judy had known George—and certainly since they had begun their romantic relationship during the 1950s—she had been an unerring source of support for him. As George made his way at EMI, she stoked his ambitions as he took on greater responsibility. And she had been there, step by step, as he plotted his future with the Beatles, a risky enterprise, given the band's North Country origins and unproven track record. When things really took off, Judy had been by George's side, helping to promote the Beatles' career through her offices at Parlophone. In a November 19, 1963, letter, she wrote movingly about the group's increasingly national profile after their appearance on Val Parnell's *Sunday Night at the London Palladium*, ground zero for British Beatlemania: "It is so exciting about the success of the Beatles—it is quite the most amazing thing the amount of excitement they have caused here. We have always been their great fans in the office and couldn't be more thrilled and proud." Shortly thereafter, she was by George's side as the group performed their legend-making set during their *Ed Sullivan Show* appearance in February 1964. And in the fall of 1965, when George left the EMI Group and formed AIR with his partners, she was there yet again, handling the clerical duties and staffing the office for her fiancé's new, highly risky venture.[5]

But on the evening of May 23, 1966, Judy was on the scene at Abbey Road to keep tabs on George's most valuable commodity, even going so far as to take his regular seat in the Studio 2 control room. While the Beatles and their production team had known and loved Judy for a long time by this point, there was little doubt about why she was there. As Emerick later recalled, she was there "to keep an eye on things, and I suppose to make sure we all behaved ourselves! She sat in George's place at the console making sure that the Beatles got everything they wanted, while I took the helm." Martin's absence cast a strange spell over the proceedings, as if the bandmates had been waiting for the opportunity to cut loose. As Geoff wrote, his sick day "had a liberating effect on the four Beatles—they behaved like a bunch of schoolboys with a substitute teacher filling in. As a result, there was a lot of clowning around that evening—silliness that George Martin would not have tolerated." Eventually, it was John Lennon who called things to order after breaking into a protracted fit of the giggles: "Come on, it's getting late and we still haven't made us a record!" When they finally settled down, the Beatles were primed and ready to record "Yellow Submarine," a new Lennon-McCartney composition written expressly for Ringo to sing. With the exception of *A Hard Day's Night*, all of the Beatles' studio albums had included a lead vocal from the band's drummer, and this new long-player would be no different. As an added bonus, Paul had originally conceived the song with children as its intended audience. "There isn't a single big word," McCartney later observed. "Kids will understand it easier than adults."[6]

With Judy up in the control room beside Geoff and Phil McDonald, the bandmates captured a basic rhythm track in four takes. Two tracks were composed of Lennon's Gibson acoustic, Starr's drums, and McCartney's bass, with Harrison on tambourine. Ringo then overdubbed his vocal onto take four, with all four Beatles recording backing vocals on the remaining track. Emerick sweetened "Yellow Submarine" by recording the vocals with the tape running slow in order to give the bandmates' voices a brighter quality upon playback. With the carefree atmosphere in the studio that evening, the Beatles were brimming with ideas, especially Lennon, who reveled in the song's whimsical nature. "At a certain point," Geoff later recalled, "John decided that the third verse needed some spicing up, so he dashed into the studio and began answering each of Ringo's sung lines in a silly voice that I further altered to make it sound like he was talking over a ship's megaphone." Having recorded this section of the song—"And we live / A life of ease, / Every one of us / Has all we need"—Emerick closed the six-hour session by creating a tape reduction that combined the vocal and instrumental tracks into one.[7]

As it turned out, Martin and the Beatles wouldn't be bringing "Yellow Submarine" to fruition just yet. In fact, George had become so ill that a solid week would elapse before he was ready to return to work at Abbey Road. On Wednesday, June 1, he returned to the friendly confines of Studio 2 for a twelve-hour session that would begin with a bit of controversy, albeit short-lived, only to end with one of the zaniest Beatles sessions on record. During George's illness, Phil had accidently erased the initial portion of John's megaphone overdub, the one in which he echoed Ringo's voice singing "And we live / A life of ease." Having deleted John's first two lines, Phil was beside himself with fear. As Geoff later recalled, it was "one of the few times his usually accurate drop-in skills failed him. From his station in the machine room, he got on the intercom and let George and me know of his gaffe while the Beatles were out of earshot. I could hear the distress in his voice and could sympathize—almost every assistant had made a similar mistake at one time or another." Sure enough, once John realized that the lines had been erased, he "wasn't too happy about it," Geoff remembered, "but rather than pin the blame on Phil, George and I quickly concocted a story about needing the track for one of the overdubs. We all tended to close ranks and protect one another at times like that, and I know that Phil was very relieved that he didn't have to face John's wrath."[8]

For much of the day, George and Geoff had been raiding the EMI library's sound effects records for ideas about how to bring the Beatles' yellow submarine to life. Curated in a "rickety green cabinet" by George's longtime friend and former colleague Stuart Eltham, the tape library was brimming with quirky outtakes and unique bits of sound—many of them originating from Martin's heyday of making comedy records for Parlophone. "The collection began in about 1956," Eltham later recalled, "when Peter Sellers, Spike Milligan, Michael Bentine, and others used to make records at Abbey Road. We started to keep bits and pieces. If we did a location recording somewhere we'd keep what outtakes were possible. Then I and people like Ken Townsend used to make recordings in our spare time." For Martin, looking for sound effects was a great joy, and he had a knack for ferreting out unusual sonic morsels from among EMI's vast storehouse. After they finished searching for nautical sound effects, the producer and the engineer turned their attention to a glaring, two-bar gap in the song after Ringo sings, "And the band begins to play." As Geoff later recalled, "Someone—probably Paul—came up with the idea of using a brass band. There was, of course, no way that a band could be booked to come in on such short notice, and in any event, George Martin probably wouldn't have allocated budget to hire them, not for such a short section. So instead, he came up with an ingenious solution." To George's mind, the answer was somewhere in the EMI library. The producer sent McDonald to gather up a selection of marches for consideration. After listening to several brass bands, Martin and McCartney selected a march that was written in the same key as "Yellow Submarine," likely choosing a passage from a recording of Georges Krier and Charles Helmer's 1906 composition, "Le Rêve Passe." At this point, Martin became concerned about the issue of copyright. According to British law at the time, reproducing more than a few seconds of a commercial sound recording required permission from the rights holder—most likely the publisher—who might opt to negotiate a royalty. Hoping to avoid the hassle of ferreting out the owner of the copyright for the march, Martin happened upon an idea: As Emerick later recalled, Martin "told me to record the section on a clean piece of two-track tape and then chop it into pieces, toss the pieces into the air, and splice them back together. The end result should have been random, but, somehow, when I pieced it back together, it came back nearly the same way it had been in the first place! No one could believe their ears; we were all thoroughly amazed." With time running short, George asked Geoff to "swap over two of the pieces," which the engineer then dutifully fed into the multitrack master tape, which he faded out very quickly in order to minimize the unauthorized usage. "That's why the solo is so brief, and that's why it sounds almost musical, but not quite," Emerick later wrote. "At least it's unrecognizable enough that EMI was never sued by the original copyright holder of the song."[9]

By this point, the Beatles had reassembled in the studio and were ready to get back to work on "Yellow Submarine." But what they did next may have been the most inexplicable moment across their recording career, which is saying something given the events later that night in Studio 2. Apparently, at some point during Martin's absence, the bandmates had hit upon the idea of inserting a spoken-word introduction to "Yellow Submarine." Years later, no one could remember exactly why a spoken-word intro was necessary for the song, but that didn't stop the Beatles' brain trust from whiling away several hours trying to turn it into something meaningful. Ringo's monologue may have been intended to memorialize a recent and well-publicized charity walk by physician Barbara Moore, who had marched from Stepney to Utrecht, which made for an impressive trek from the southernmost tip of England to the northernmost tip of Scotland. Earlier, in July 1960, Dr. Moore had carried out a thirty-two-hundred-mile charity walk from Los Angeles to New York City. As Geoff later recalled, "John, who often had his head buried in a newspaper when he wasn't playing guitar or singing, had written a short medieval-sounding poem that somehow tied the walk to the song title, and he was determined to have Ringo recite it, accompanied by the sound of marching feet." To create the requisite sound effect, Emerick "pulled out the old radio trick of shaking coal in a cardboard box to simulate footsteps." Sitting behind the microphone, Ringo recited John's poem, which the Beatles' drummer attempted to deliver in emotionless deadpan: "And we will march to free the day to see them gathered there, / from Land O'Groats to John O'Green, from Stepney to Utrecht, / to see a Yellow Submarine / We love it!" For Emerick's money, "the final result was, in a word, boring." Apparently, Martin and the bandmates agreed. Ironically, George and the Beatles would spend far more time and energy bringing the thirty-one-second monologue into being than they would devote to the rest of the song. And in the end, they would choose to delete the intro piece altogether, wasting considerable time in the process.[10]

And that's when the hilarity ensued—fun and games the likes of which had scarcely been visited upon one of George's sessions in all his years at Abbey Road. After a dinner break, the Beatles returned to Studio 2 with a bevy of friends in tow, including a number of contemporary rock's reigning glitterati. The Abbey Road air was rife with the skunky odor of marijuana, and it was precisely in this state that Lennon came up with the idea of simulating the sound of a submerging submarine. Quick on the draw, Emerick grabbed a mic and recorded the sound of Lennon blowing bubbles into a glass of water. And that's when "Lennon wanted to take things to the next level and have me record him actually singing underwater," Emerick recalled. "First, he tried singing while gargling. When that failed (he nearly choked), he began lobbying for a tank to be brought in so that he could be submerged." That's when Geoff came up with the idea of recording John's voice using a submerged microphone. With Martin looking on patiently, in spite of the inherent absurdity of the entire scheme, Mal Evans succeeded in waterproofing the mic by enclosing it inside a condom and then dunking it in a milk bottle filled with water. "Well done, Malcolm!" John exclaimed. "After all, we don't want the microphone to be getting in the family way, do we?" Lennon quickly shifted his attentions after Emerick was unable to register a strong enough signal to conduct the experiment, with the engineer later realizing, to his horror, that the microphone had been live, which meant that the Beatle might possibly have been electrocuted. At this point, Martin intervened—perhaps because his budget for the album was nearing depletion or, more likely, fearing for Lennon's safety. Things really got rolling when the group began raiding the trap room, the closet beneath the staircase in Studio 2 that was brimming with an odd assortment of sound effects. "The cupboard had everything," Emerick later recalled, "chains, ships bells, hand bells from wartime, tap dancing mats, whistles, homers, wind machines, thunder-storm machines—everything." By this point, Studio 2 had begun to resemble something "straight out of a Marx Brothers movie."[11]

As George and the bandmates prepared to superimpose sound effects onto "Yellow Submarine," even studio personnel got in on the fun, with John Skinner and Terry Condon providing the whooshing sounds that adorn the song's engine room ambience. "There was a metal bath in the trap room," Skinner recalled, "the type people used to bathe in in front of the fire. We filled it with water, got some old chains and swirled them around. It worked really well. I'm sure no one listening to the song realized what was making the noise." The Rolling Stones' Mick Jagger and Brian Jones were there, along with Marianne Faithfull, Mick's new girlfriend, and Pattie Boyd. In addition to Martin, roadies Neil Aspinall and Mal Evans joined in on the merriment, gleefully singing "we all live in a yellow submarine" to their hearts' content. In one of his favorite memories, Geoff recalled that "there was one particular shout that John did. The door to the echo chamber behind Studio 2 was open so he went and sat there, singing all that 'full speed ahead, Mr. Captain' stuff at the top of his voice." As if things couldn't get any more bizarre, colossal Mal Evans took to marching around the studio with a bass drum strapped to his chest, as the raucous band gathered up behind him, conga style, singing the song's catchy chorus. For George, recording "Yellow Submarine" made for one of his most cherished memories from his days with the Beatles. As he later remarked, "We used to try different things. That was always fun, and it made life a little bit more interesting. The most notable case was 'Yellow Submarine,' of course, where you can hear the noise of bubbles being blown into tanks, chains rattling, and that kind of thing. We actually did that in the studio. John got one of those little hand mikes, which he put into his Vox amp and was able to talk through. So all of that 'Full steam ahead' you hear was done live while the main vocal was going on, and we all had a giggle."[12]

Not surprisingly, George and the Beatles were positively knackered the next day—so much so that the next session, on Thursday, June 2, wouldn't begin until seven o'clock that evening. But in true Beatles style at this point, it ranged until 3:30 AM. With the month now in full swing, Martin had a looming, late-June deadline for completing the album, and the Beatles had a lengthy tour for which to prepare. It was a banner day for Harrison, who presented a third composition for inclusion on the album. For a time, the song went under the decidedly honest working title of "I Don't Know." But whatever it was called, the song would give the Beatles' lead guitarist an unprecedented three new tunes on the record, demonstrating the many ways in which he had recently elevated his prowess as a working songwriter in a band that included the likes of Lennon and McCartney. Harrison understandably took heat from his friends for his lack of imagination in assigning titles to his composition. In addition to the well-named "Taxman," his other composition on the album went under "Granny Smith." In a moment of levity, Lennon suggested that he call the new one "Granny Smith Part Friggin' Two!" In an instant of well-timed deadpan, Emerick suggested calling it "Laxton's Superb," in reference to another variety of British apple. The session commenced with five takes of the song's basic rhythm track, which included Harrison's lead guitar, McCartney's piano, and Starr's drums on a single track. Take three was selected as the best, and Harrison subsequently performed his lead vocal on the second track, with Lennon and McCartney providing harmonies on the third. The remaining track was devoted to another piano overdub from McCartney, along with Lennon on tambourine and maracas. After a tape reduction, the Beatles added handclaps to accentuate the final verse. At this juncture, Emerick observed that a very particular practice was developing with Martin in terms of recording Harrison's songs. For Geoff, it seemed rather ironic that "George [Harrison] was being given a certain amount of time to do his tracks, whereas the others [i.e., John and Paul] could spend as long as they wanted." Yet at the same time, "one felt under pressure when doing one of George's songs." It was as if Martin were unduly concerned about giving his principal and most accomplished songwriters as much space as they required to develop their ideas, yet he also recognized that Harrison was all too cognizant of his place in the pecking order. Like all great coaches, Martin didn't want his third-string player to feel slighted at not playing at the top of his game, which was clearly on the upswing in early 1966.[13]

During the Friday, June 3, session, Martin and the Beatles cleared up a number of odds and ends as the long-player began to take its final shape. First up was Harrison's latest composition, which was still variously called both "I Don't Know" and "Laxton's Superb" at this point. McCartney overdubbed a bass guitar part, and then Martin and his production team carried out four remixes, choosing take one as the best of the lot. With Harrison's song complete, they turned to "Yellow Submarine," for which a mono mix was prepared. At this juncture, they discarded Ringo's "Land O'Groats" monologue for good.

While Martin and the band took a much-deserved weekend break, their work was very much in the news. On June 3, the first advertisement for the upcoming single, "Paperback Writer" backed with "Rain," appeared in *NME*. Of particular note was the ad's illustration, a photograph of the bandmates donning white lab coats and surrounded by dismembered doll parts and slabs of raw meat. The Beatles had posed for the photo back on March 25 at Robert Whitaker's Chelsea studio. Titled by the photographer *A Somnambulant Adventure*, Whitaker's vision was to create a work of surreal pop art, as well as a satirical, pictorial critique of the group's overwhelming international fame. The next day, Saturday, June 4, saw the broadcast of the bandmates' BBC interviews with Brian Matthew, as well as the opening of the Indica Gallery's first official art exhibition. The gallery, like Whitaker's photograph, would figure prominently in Martin and the group's future. The weekend concluded with the premiere of Lindsay-Hogg's "Paperback Writer" promotional video on none other than CBS television's *The Ed Sullivan Show*.

By Monday, June 6, the realities of their predicament must have settled in, as George and the Beatles felt the pressure of their upcoming LP and tour deadlines. Simply put, they had two weeks to finish the album. By that point, the Beatles themselves would be on a plane and jetting toward the first gig of their world tour, and Martin had plans of his own. But first, there was plenty of housekeeping to do. In a session in the Studio 3 control room, Martin supervised tape copying and remixes with Emerick and the bandmates in tow for an assortment of songs, including "Laxton's Superb," which had been aptly renamed "I Want to Tell You," as well as "And Your Bird Can Sing," "For No One," "I'm Only Sleeping," and "Tomorrow Never Knows," which formally supplanted "Mark I" as the song's title during the session. Remix eleven was selected as the best, which would have brought "Tomorrow Never Knows" to fruition were it not for Martin, who had second thoughts, telephoning Emerick on July 14—as the album went into the cutting room—and opting for remix eight instead. Around midnight, as June 6 transitioned into June 7, McCartney—like Martin, ever the perfectionist—descended into the studio to overdub his lead vocal for "Eleanor Rigby" with a well-timed counterpoint to Lennon and Harrison's existing refrain, "Ah, look at all the lonely people." Understandably lost in the shuffle that day was the significance of June 6 in the personal and professional histories of Martin and the bandmates. It had been precisely four years since the Beatles—John, Paul, George, and Pete at that juncture—first ambled into EMI Studios, unpolished and bedraggled, and changed their producer's life forever in myriad and unexpected ways.

As far as Martin and the Beatles were concerned, the studio was dark on June 7, with the band spending the day at Harrison's Esher home, Kinfauns, where they rehearsed for the upcoming tour. Slated to begin with a pair of shows on June 24 in Munich, the Beatles were a long way from being concert ready. Save for the May 1 Poll Winners appearance, they hadn't performed live since December. Their diminutive eleven-song set list told the story, by omission, about how far the group had come in just four years under Martin's tutelage. "Paperback Writer" was the only recent addition to the lineup, save for "Day Tripper" and Rubber Soul's "If I Needed Someone" and "Nowhere Man." Outside of a scaled-down version of "Yesterday," along with the high-octane, show-closing "I'm Down," the rest of the set was composed entirely of early Beatles, a band that they barely resembled as they rehearsed in Harrison's home studio. And none of the entries on their set list reflected the remarkable technological strides that Martin and the group had made since Rubber Soul. Songs like "Eleanor Rigby" and "Tomorrow Never Knows" were all but impossible to reproduce in a live setting in the summer of 1966. Meanwhile, songs like Rubber Soul's "Norwegian Wood (This Bird Has Flown)" and "In My Life," with sitar and windup piano adornments, were hardly worth the trouble. And why reproduce weak versions of such stellar recordings in the first place? They'd worked too hard to advance their musicianship and recording artistry. Why diminish their attainments with second- or even third-rate performances of their most sublime recordings? But rehearsing their meager set list was only part of the bargain. When they left for West Germany later that month, they would be traveling tens of thousands of miles between late June and the tail end of August, a period in which they were scheduled to play thirteen shows in West Germany, Japan, and the Philippines, respectively, followed by nineteen concerts in the United States and Canada.

On Wednesday, June 8, the bandmates were back in Studio 2 to try their hand at a new McCartney composition. At the time, it was known as "A Good Day's Sunshine"—the working title of the song that would shortly become "Good Day Sunshine"—and like Lennon's "I'm Only Sleeping," it owed a clear debt of influence to the Lovin' Spoonful's "Daydream," which had recently topped out at number two on the UK charts. Interestingly, it was also on June 8 that sitar virtuoso Ravi Shankar appeared on the British teen music program *A Whole Scene Going*. Incredibly, roughly seven months after Harrison had debuted the sitar for a Western popular audience on *Rubber Soul*, the sitar was going mainstream, demonstrating yet again how deftly Martin had assisted the Beatles in widening their demographic since the early days of Beatlemania. In its own way, "Good Day Sunshine," with its pleasing lilt and gently rolling melody, had all the makings of a mainstream pop tune—a far cry, indeed, from the early, beat-music days at the onset of the Beatles' recording career with Martin. In yet another twelve-hour session that would roam into the wee hours of Thursday, June 9, the bandmates made short work of "Good Day Sunshine." With the tape running, they recorded three takes, with take one being selected as the best of the lot. The basic rhythm track featured bass, piano, and drums, with McCartney adding a lead vocal on a second, along with Lennon and Harrison providing spirited harmony vocals. The song's placid feel is belied by its time signature, which shifts among common, 5/4, and 3/4 time.

On Thursday, June 9, George and the Beatles would, for the most part, put the finishing touches on "Good Day Sunshine." During the approximately six-hour session that day, Martin and his production team supervised a series of overdubs and edits in the course of bringing McCartney's latest song to fruition. In addition to supplementing the song with more handclaps and well-placed cymbal crashes, the highlight of the day was Martin's honky-tonk-style piano solo. Performed on Studio 2's Hamburg Steinway baby grand, George recorded the solo for the middle eight of "Good Day Sunshine" using his windup piano effect. Over the years, he had deployed varispeed recording on Beatles records to great effect, including such gems as the solo portions of "A Hard Day's Night" and "In My Life." Recorded at half speed and an octave lower, Martin's honky-tonk piano was allotted to the recording's available fourth track. Recording the solo at fifty-six cycles per second afforded Martin's piano part with a gentle, rolling quality on playback. During the mixing phase, Paul's vocal for "Good Day Sunshine" was treated with ADT, imbuing it with greater texture. George and his team carried out six remixes before the session concluded, with the sixth being selected as the best. But like other tracks on the album, "Good Day Sunshine" would be remixed yet again before the long-player was put to bed. George and the Beatles' penchant for perfectionism—even in the face of looming deadlines—was growing by the day.

The studio would be dark for George and the Beatles on Friday, June 10—most likely, so that John and Paul could polish up new material to round out the long-player—but the day was loaded with significance in their world, which was shifting by the moment. The big story in the UK part of Beatledom that day was the much-anticipated release of "Paperback Writer" backed with "Rain"—the first new 45 rpm record from the band since back on December 3, with the release of "Day Tripper" backed with "We Can Work It Out." It had been twenty-seven weeks since the band's last single, which meant that Martin and Epstein's best-laid plans back in 1963 for four singles and two albums per year were not merely in great jeopardy but in all likelihood kaput as far as the 1966 calendar year was concerned. Not surprisingly—and almost automatically for George and the Beatles at this point—"Paperback Writer" emerged as a worldwide hit, eventually topping the charts in both the UK and US marketplaces. But somehow "Paperback Writer" would prove to be slightly different in the coming days, not shooting to the top of the pops in quite the same manner—and with somewhat less velocity—than the Beatles' previous chart-toppers. In contrast with all of their previous singles releases up to this point, "Paperback Writer" was a slick narrative about pop authorship as opposed to heteronormative romance, those trials and tribulations of conventional love that had seen the Beatles break sales records across the globe. But with a live BBC television performance set for the following week, the single was in for a major shot in the arm. Still, its sales receipts would be the weakest for any Beatles single since "Love Me Do" backed with "P.S. I Love You," which was released way back in October 1962. If Martin and the Beatles were concerned that the clear shift in their subject matter from romantic love to impressionist, narrative-driven composition would risk decreasing or even losing their audience, they didn't show it.

Back in the United States, "Paperback Writer" was faring much better, underscoring the Americans' insatiable appetite for new Beatles material. But another issue had been brewing for the past several days, and, for the pop-music juggernaut that George and Brian had so carefully built, it was a troubling harbinger of things to come. Capitol's repackaging of old and new Beatles material for the purposes of releasing the *Yesterday . . . and Today* album to tide over American consumers had created the band's first—and worst, at least for the next several weeks—instance of negative publicity that they had experienced thus far. It could all be traced back to Whitaker's photograph of the white-coated Beatles posing among doll parts and raw meat. Having selected the photo as the album's cover art—in spite of the fact that, according to the participants, that had never been Whitaker or the bandmates' intention—Capitol put the Beatles' largely pristine brand and squeaky-clean image at incredible risk. Alan Livingston would later claim that it was McCartney's idea to use the photograph as the album's cover as a commentary on US involvement in the Vietnam War. Regardless of agency, the cover photograph for *Yesterday . . . and Today* had emerged as a full-scale PR disaster during the fortnight before its scheduled release date of June 20. Advance copies had been sent to DJs and music reviewers, and the negative reaction was immediate and intense. The EMI Group's chairman, Sir Joseph Lockwood, ordered an immediate recall. On June 10, Capitol invoked what its executives dubbed as Operation Retrieve, recalling some 750,000 copies of the LP from its distributors. With the company's record plants in Los Angeles, California; Scranton, Pennsylvania; Winchester, Virginia; and Jacksonville, Illinois, working at full throttle, new covers were printed that featured the comparatively benign image of the bandmates playfully posing around a steamer trunk.

In the end, the cost for replacing the album cover and conducting the recall was approximately $250,000, although it proved to be a shrewd investment. By the end of July, *Yesterday . . . and Today* had ascended to the pinnacle of the American charts and was certified as the Beatles' latest gold record in a whole sea of the things. While Lennon and McCartney seemed puzzled by the backlash over the album cover and derided their critics as being "soft," Martin didn't mince words. He had toiled too long and too hard with Epstein to build the Beatles' empire, and risking everything over something as trivial as an album cover, and for what amounted to a compilation in his eyes, bordered on the ridiculous. He would later cite the decision to release the photograph as his first disagreement with the bandmates: "I thought it was disgusting and in poor taste. It suggested that they were madmen." For his part, Harrison later admitted to regretting his participation in the photo session, deriding Whitaker's concept as "gross, and I also thought it was stupid. Sometimes we all did stupid things thinking it was cool and hip when it was naïve and dumb; and that was one of them." While many of the discarded covers for *Yesterday . . . and Today* were relegated to a landfill, thousands survived when personnel at Capitol's record plants resorted to pasting the new cover over what came to be known as the "butcher" photograph, creating in the process what became one of the most sought-after Beatles artifacts among collectors.[14]

While they may not have fully realized it at the time, the Beatles and their brain trust had dodged a bullet with the fiasco regarding *Yesterday . . . and Today*. When Martin reconvened the band on June 14 in Studio 2, they were in the homestretch as far as their next album was concerned. Titled "Here, There, and Everywhere," Paul's breathtaking new composition had been inspired by his repeated listenings to the Beach Boys' *Pet Sounds*—especially, their exquisite multivoiced harmonies. Much of the session was spent with Martin directing and perfecting Lennon's, McCartney's, and Harrison's own harmonies, one of the trademarks of their sound since their earliest days with the producer, who had a knack for vocal arrangement. As Martin later recalled, "The harmonies on that are very simple, just basic triads which the boys hummed behind and found very easy to do. There's nothing very clever, no counterpoint, just moving block harmonies. Very simple to do, but very effective." As usual, George's own inherent modesty betrayed his skill in drawing out the bandmates' finest performances, especially as vocalists. As Geoff has observed, "George's real expertise was and still is in vocal harmony work, there's no doubt about that. That is his forte, grooming and working out those great harmonies." During the June 14 session, "Here, There, and Everywhere" would witness just four takes, with vocals being added to take four.[15]

With time quickly running out, the studio was dark yet again on June 15, when the Beatles were out getting their inoculations in advance of their extended foreign travel, as well as rehearsing for their live appearance on the popular weekly BBC music program *Top of the Pops*. The next evening, the Beatles—adorned in dark suits—mimed performances of "Paperback Writer" and "Rain" in order to promote their latest single to a rabid national television audience in their homeland. The event marked their final appearance on the TV program that, in the United Kingdom at least, could make or break a pop release. Joined by such contemporaries as Herman's Hermits, Gene Pitney, the Yardbirds, Cilla Black, and the Hollies—with the former two being fellow AIR artists—the Beatles would not be broken. The program also featured a prerecorded video by the Beach Boys, the Beatles' most relevant artistic competitors for the moment, for "Sloop John B." While they would briefly be denied the top spot by Frank Sinatra's classic "Strangers in the Night," "Paperback Writer" would unseat Old Blue Eyes the very next week. The moment wasn't lost on Patrick Doncaster, the *Daily Mirror*'s entertainment reporter, who ascertained that neither track on the new Beatles song had "any romance about them. Gone, gone, gone are the days of luv, luv, luv." Asked about this shift in the Beatles' compositions, McCartney remarked that "it's not our best single by any means, but we're very satisfied with it. We are experimenting all the time with our songs. We cannot stay in the same rut. We have got to move forward." And then, in his most telling observation about the shape of things to come, McCartney added, "Our new LP is going to shock a lot of people."[16]

On Thursday, June 16, George and the Beatles had very nearly brought that new long-player to fruition. In a nearly nine-hour session, they remade "Here, There, and Everywhere" over nine takes. After perfecting the basic rhythm track, which included McCartney's bass, Starr's drums, and Lennon's electric guitar, they began adding overdubs and edits to take thirteen, which had been deemed as the best. Take thirteen also featured Harrison playing his electric guitar using a volume pedal in order to ornament the song with a series of delicate swells. Martin's arrangement for Lennon's, McCartney's, and Harrison's gorgeous harmonies was overdubbed, along with McCartney's bass part, which was afforded its own track, as had become their recent practice in order to give the low end of the song increased definition and prominence. All four tracks had been rounded out by Starr's finger-brushed cymbals, along with well-timed finger clicks and assorted percussion. At that point, Martin instructed Emerick to carry out a tape-to-tape copy in order to free up available space for McCartney's lead vocal, which was recorded with the tape running slow in order to sound faster—and hence, brighter—on playback.

During this decidedly late moment in the production of the album, the bandmates had begun making overtures to Klaus Voormann, an old friend from their Hamburg days, as well as an artist and bass player in his own right, about devising a hand-drawn cover, perhaps a collage. They may not have had anything resembling a title at this point, but their vision about doing something different, about "shocking" their massive fan base, remained undeterred. Their original idea, vague as it was at this point, had been to assemble a montage of black-and-white photographs by Robert Freeman, the photographer behind all of their album covers, save for *Please Please Me*. After rejecting Freeman's attempt at fashioning the long-player's cover art, they had turned to Voormann, who had immigrated to the United Kingdom, where he played bass for a time in a trio out of Liverpool—managed by Epstein, quite naturally—called Paddy, Klaus, and Gibson. Lennon approached Voormann about the cover art shortly after Voormann's group had disbanded, and the Beatles' old German friend was eager to take up the challenge. Determined to capture the spirit of their new LP in his cover, Voormann joined Martin and the Beatles at Abbey Road, where they played him several of the tracks, including "Tomorrow Never Knows." At the artist's request, the bandmates collected old photographs of themselves, which would become part of Voormann's collage, arranged around four line drawings—crafted in the style of the Victorian art nouveau movement's Aubrey Beardsley—of Lennon, McCartney, Harrison, and Starr.

The big unveil was held shortly thereafter at EMI Studios, with the Beatles, George Martin and his fiancée Judy Lockhart Smith, and Brian Epstein in evidence. As the assemblage eagerly awaited Voormann's creation, he propped his cover art on top of a file cabinet. At first, his artwork was met with a kind of stunned silence—this was, after all, a very different Beatles album cover in comparison with everything that had come before. Voormann later recalled that he mistook the initial silence as indicative of a coming shockwave of abject disapproval. But his fears were entirely mistaken. McCartney finally broke the silence, pointing at the cover art and saying, "Hey! That's me sitting on a toilet!" At that point, the others inched closer to Voormann's collage. And sure enough, there was Paul perched on a toilet in an old Hamburg photo. "Well, we can't have that," said Martin. "No, it's great," McCartney countered. But Martin's reproachful voice carried the day, and the image was subsequently removed. Up next was Epstein, still feeling the sting of recent Beatles cover photographs gone awry. "Klaus, this is exactly what we needed," he remarked. "I was worried that this whole thing might not work. But now I know that this cover, this LP, will work. Thank you." No doubt concerned after the recent *Yesterday . . . and Today* PR disaster, Epstein was clearly relieved, reportedly even weeping at the sight of Voormann's work. But it was more than that, of course. Beatlemania's architect would have been fine with George and the bandmates moving forward in the same musical vein that they had been mining during the early years. Their recent, protracted bout of avant-garde experimentation, while brash and impressive even to the cautious Epstein, was a lot to take. How, he had to be wondering at this late date, would their audience take it once the new long-player had been loosed upon the world?[17]

While Epstein might have been concerned about audience share, Martin didn't harbor even remotely the same level of disquiet. As he later remarked to *Melody Maker*, "By this time we were so established that we could afford to take risks. . . . If people didn't like it, hard luck. It was . . . an indulgence, if you like, and we thought it was worthwhile." In and of itself, Voormann's design made for a novel, arresting cover, unlike anything in the contemporary pop-music marketplace. By design, the album's name wouldn't appear on the cover—not that they had a title at this juncture anyway. Consumers would be confronted by Voormann's stark line-drawings of the Beatles, expressionless amid a sea of mind-boggling images adorned among the bandmates ever-ranging locks of hair, the most conspicuous aspect of their celebrity in the heady days of early Beatlemania.[18]

On Friday, June 17, Martin convened the band for yet another session of tidying up loose ends. Up first was "Got to Get You into My Life," for which Harrison provided a sizzling guitar solo on his Sonic Blue Fender Stratocaster. The additional guitar overdub meant that Martin and Emerick had to discard previous mixes of the song. After rendering five new mixes, they selected the last one as the best before turning back to "Here, There, and Everywhere." At this point, McCartney recorded a new lead vocal overdub to supplement his existing vocals, thus necessitating a fresh remix. But Martin and the Beatles, rarely satisfied with anything short of perfection, would revisit the song at a later date—not that there were many more left at this point.

On Monday, June 20, George conducted a mixing session in the control room of Studio 1 with Geoff and the Beatles present. After carrying out a final remixing session for "Got to Get You into My Life" in order to bolster the song's brass accompaniment, Martin was able to close the book on the track that had taken the longest to record at this point in 1966—it was a record that would easily be eclipsed much later in the year. Work had begun way back on April 7, the second day of recording sessions for the album, and concluded on what would amount to the penultimate session for the untitled long-player. June 20 also marked the stateside release date for *Yesterday . . . and Today*, complete with new cover art in place of Whitaker's now notorious "butcher" photograph. It was somewhere around this time that Martin realized that they only had thirteen tracks in the hopper for an album that, like their previous efforts up to this point (save *A Hard Day's Night*), clocked in at fourteen songs, their standard allotment for their UK releases. While the number of tracks may seem trivial, it was a key issue for the record-buying public during that period. As Emerick later pointed out: "The LPs of that era were a lot more concise than today's CDs, but if they were too short, there would be complaints—or worse yet, returns—from consumers. Not only was there a release date set, and a hungry public clamoring to hear the finished album, but the Beatles were booked to begin a European tour just days after the sessions ended, so there was no time to spare."[19]

With just over thirty hours before they had to be on a jet bound for Munich, the bandmates joined Martin on Tuesday, June 21, in Studio 2 to record one last track for the long-player. But first, Martin conducted a three-hour mixing session in the Studio 3 control room. Harrison's "Granny

Smith"—soon to be rechristened as "Love You To"—was treated to a stereo remix, as was "I Want to Tell You" and "Here, There, and Everywhere." The control room blitz continued at 2:30 PM in Studio 2, where Martin's production team concocted mono and stereo mixes for "For No One," "Taxman," and "Doctor Robert," the latter two of which required additional edits to come to fruition. At 7:00 PM, the scene shifted to the floor of Studio 2, where Martin and the group began taking their passes at recording a new Lennon composition titled, somewhat apropos under the circumstances, "Untitled." Later to be renamed as "She Said She Said," the song memorialized the Beatles' acid-infused party with David Crosby and Peter Fonda in Los Angeles's Benedict Canyon back in August 1965. In particular, "She Said She Said" made reference to Fonda's near-death experiences on the operating table. As Fonda recounted his otherworldly sensations, a drug-addled Lennon asked the actor, "Who put all that shit in your head?" Written into the composition's lyrics as "who put all those things in your head / Things that make me feel like I'm mad / And you're making me feel like I've never been born," the song's narrative provided a near-perfect bookend for the LSD-influenced "Tomorrow Never Knows," which had inaugurated the current LP's sessions on April 6.

By this point, everyone was feeling the pressure. Deadline fever had claimed not only George and his production team, but the Beatles themselves. Even the band's roadies Neil Aspinall and Mal Evans had to work double-time to bring the album in for its photo finish. Having recently transferred the group's gear for transport to West Germany, Aspinall and Evans were forced to haul the bandmates' instruments back to Abbey Road in order to record the fourteenth song. For the next several hours, Martin and the bandmates toiled over "She Said She Said," only for the first time, McCartney would not be among their number, having become the first Beatle to walk out on a session. At least for Paul's sake, he wouldn't have to go very far, with his newly renovated home on Cavendish Avenue just around the corner from Abbey Road. As Neil and Mal set up the gear in Studio 2 that evening, Paul wilted under the mounting pressure—and possibly even John's cavalier attitude about recording "She Said She Said" from scratch. As Geoff later recalled, "John had always been the basher in the group—his attitude was 'Let's just get it done'—so it was no big surprise that we got the entire song recorded and mixed in nine hours, as opposed to the more than three days we spent on 'Here, There, and Everywhere.' Still, he made the group run through the song dozens of times before he was satisfied with the final result." But McCartney wouldn't be around to see it. As Paul later remembered, "I'm not sure, but I think it was one of the only Beatle records I never played on. I think we'd had a barney or something, and I said, 'Oh, fuck you!' and they said, 'Well, we'll do it.' I think George [Harrison] played bass."[20]

With the tape running, Martin and the remaining Beatles rehearsed some twenty-five takes of "She Said She Said" before attempting a basic rhythm track. Captured in three takes, the rhythm track featured Starr's drums, Harrison sitting in on bass, and Lennon and Harrison's electric guitars. After selecting take three as the best, Lennon's lead vocal was overdubbed onto the recording, along with Lennon and Harrison's backing vocals. At this point, Martin instructed Emerick to create a tape-to-tape reduction onto which additional overdubs were adorned, including another electric guitar and Lennon's organ part. Not wasting any time, Martin immediately conducted three mono remixes, and the song—and the album proper—was effectively complete at 3:45 AM on June 22. As Geoff later recalled, "For all of that, it still sounds scrappy and rough to me, it's got the ragged feel of a track that was done in the middle of the night, under pressure." But Geoff, for one, was hardly bothered by the breakneck pace that George and the Beatles had been running across their years together—and most especially since the sessions for *Rubber Soul*. He accepted their penchant for sprinting to the finish line as part of the chemistry that made Martin and the Beatles' relationship purr. "Incredibly," Emerick later wrote, the album "had been completed in just over ten weeks (we had most weekends off), with many songs taking only a few hours to get down on tape. It was always a matter of capturing the moment, and when you were working with the Beatles it had to be right. Exhausting as it was, both mentally and physically, it was a good way to work—really, the only way to work."[21]

After "She Said She Said" was put to bed, Martin quickly followed suit, remarking to the others as he left the studio that morning, "All right, boys, I'm just going for a lie-down." But as it turned out, there would be no rest for the weary. By 7:00 PM on Wednesday, June 22, he would be back in the Studio 3 control room with Emerick and Jerry Boys by his side to carry out a nearly seven-hour mono and stereo remixing session for several tracks, including "Eleanor Rigby," "She Said She Said," "Good Day Sunshine," "Yellow Submarine," and "Tomorrow Never Knows," which joined the other eight tracks already in the hopper.[22]

By this point, the Beatles had already left for Munich to begin their latest concert tour. Only this time, Martin wouldn't be along for the ride, as he had occasionally been in the past. Two days later, with the latest still-untitled Beatles album behind them for the most part, George and Judy made the short trip from her place at Manchester Square to the Marylebone Registry Office, where they made their vows for the public record. Judy's sixty-three-year-old father, Kenneth Lockhart Smith, and his old friend Ron Goodwin served as the couple's witnesses. With his divorce from Sheena having been finalized the previous February, George and Judy had certainly waited long enough. Sixteen years after they first met at Abbey Road, with George wearing his Fleet Air Arm great coat and the glint of an unknown future in his eye, they were man and wife. With Judy smiling brightly by his side, George had never been more certain about anything in his life. After the Beatles had returned to the United Kingdom, Brian Epstein held a dinner party in the newlyweds' honor. "All four Beatles came, with wives and girlfriends," George later recalled, "but Brian had no one, so we were 11 to dinner. As we started dinner, everyone took out their napkins. Brian looked around the table and said, 'Now, everyone, when you finish the meal, I want you to pass all your napkin rings back to Judy and George because you'll see on them. . . .' He broke off, and looked at us with pleased anticipation. We looked at the little rings. Each had an 'M' engraved on it." For George, "it was a lovely thing to do. But he was like that: immensely generous, imaginative, and impulsive."[23]

And now, with George and the Beatles' dazzling creation having finally come to fruition, it was all but impossible at that moment to imagine that the Beatles could top their brave new long-player, with its air of mystery and experimentation, slated for release in mid-August. The whole enterprise had begun with the notion of borrowing the distinctly American rhythm-and-blues sound that they thought they could glean with the likes of Steve Cropper and Stax Studio. But instead, they had discovered something different—something of their own making. As McCartney later recalled, when Martin and the bandmates finally completed the album, "we realized that we had found a new British sound almost by accident." And with Emerick coming to the fore, they had seemingly pulled out every stop, generated a handful of studio innovations in the bargain, and even advanced their sound to yet another level, with Lennon and McCartney having bested themselves as composers—and even Harrison getting in on the act and coming up aces. What more could they possibly accomplish?

7

THE JESUS CHRIST TOUR

W HAT GEORGE AND THE BEATLES needed now—*and quickly*—was a title. The album was mixed for mono and stereo, Klaus Voormann's magisterial cover was set, and the long-player was all but ready for release. But when it came to naming their latest masterwork, the bandmates kept coming up empty. Even before the Beatles departed for their world tour, they had bandied about a variety of titles—some of which were inexplicable, while others were clearly acts of desperation. It was Paul, in particular, who fretted about the long-player's presentation and ultimate reception. In the June 11, 1966, issue of *Disc and Music Echo*, he figured, "We'll lose some fans with it, but we'll also gain some. The fans we'll probably lose will be the ones who like the things about us that we never liked anyway." At one point, he listened to the latest mix of the album as he traipsed around West Germany with the other Beatles. In his already heightened state of paranoia about the LP, Paul deluded himself into believing that the entire album was out of tune. The other bandmates succeeded in allaying his fears, which most likely resulted from the extensive use of ADT and varispeed, with which Martin and his team had treated the album. Paul finally regained his confidence after John, his roommate during the band's West German gigs, observed, "I think your songs are better than mine." For McCartney, it was high praise indeed coming from his songwriter partner, who rarely complimented anyone about anything.[1]

It was in Munich that the Beatles came into the home stretch for selecting a title. For the longest time, *Abracadabra* had been the leading contender, only to be dismissed after one of the Beatles' entourage claimed that it had already been used by another artist. And then there was *Beatles on Safari*, which held sway—possibly because of its connotations of the exotic sounds and styles that the new long-player offered. It was also a sly reference to the Beach Boys' *Surfin' Safari*, much like the suggestion of *Freewheelin' Beatles* was an homage to Bob Dylan. Other titles made the rounds, including *Bubble and Squeak*, *Pendulum*, and perhaps the most bizarre of them all, *Fat Man and Bobby*. The Beatles were in their mid-twenties after all, a significant remove from Martin, the elder statesman in their tightly knit crew. At one point, Ringo playfully suggested *After Geography* as a play on the Rolling Stones' recent LP, *Aftermath*. Things began to come into focus in Tokyo on July 2 after McCartney offered up *Magic Circle*, which quickly morphed, courtesy of Lennon, into *Four Sides of the Circle*, and, shortly thereafter, *Four Sides of the Eternal Triangle*. And with all the talk of geometric concepts being tossed around, McCartney happened upon *Revolver*.[2]

Short and sweet, the title connoted the idea of a revolving record, a pun that held considerable appeal for McCartney's bandmates. They realized almost immediately that the title might possibly be interpreted as referring to a handgun, but that was the beauty of it, given that the term *revolver* might suggest a host of different objects, ideas, and philosophies. As Lennon later remarked, "It's just a name for an LP, and there's no meaning to it. Why does everyone want a reason every time you move? It means *Revolver*. It's all the things that *Revolver* means because that's what it means to us, *Revolver* and all the things we could think of to go with it." With a winner on their hands, the Beatles sent a telegraph from the Tokyo Hilton over to Martin in the United Kingdom, and the matter was concluded. The album would be called *Revolver*, which Martin took a liking to almost instantly. The notion of *Revolver* suggested the idea of revolution, which is exactly what the LP portended: a musical revolution founded upon a myriad of swirling styles and sonic innovations. *Revolver* represented the revolutionary, even evolutionary nature of the art that George and the Beatles had been pursuing during their four years together at stately Abbey Road. *Revolver* it would be.[3]

While George and the bandmates were delighted with their choice, not everyone approved. John and Paul's art circle friends from the Indica Gallery were decidedly unimpressed, deploring *Revolver* as a "terrible" title. But as Barry Miles later observed, John Dunbar and his ilk hadn't really appreciated *Rubber Soul* as a title either. And the handgun motif would ultimately find its way into the Beatles' world, in spite of their well-known chagrin for firearms and violence. In their advertisements for the album later that summer, Capitol Records depicted Voormann's cover art under the word *Bang!*, which had been rendered in an elaborate pop-art font. In truth, *Revolver* required very little in the way of publicity. When it was released in the United Kingdom on August 4, the long-player was met with almost universal acclaim, with the glaring exception of the Kinks' Ray Davies, who panned *Revolver* in *Disc and Music Echo*. The Kinks' cold war with the Beatles dated back to 1964, when the two groups shared the bill in Blackpool. As the band members crossed paths backstage, Lennon drew Davies's ire when he remarked, "We've lost our set-list, lads. Can we borrow yours?" For Davies, the implication was clear: the Kinks were second-rate hacks. His review for *Disc and Music Echo* served as payback. He described "Eleanor Rigby" as having been composed "to please music teachers in primary schools," while belittling "Yellow Submarine" as "a load of rubbish." Davies concluded by demeaning *Revolver* as a step backward from the artistry of *Rubber Soul*.[4]

Davies's review proved to be a minority opinion, with the lion's share of reviewers lauding *Revolver* as a quantum leap ahead of *Rubber Soul*'s creative heights. *Melody Maker*'s review opined that *"Rubber Soul* showed that the Beatles were bursting the bounds of the three-guitar-drums instrumentation, a formula which was, for the purposes of accompaniment and projection of their songs, almost spent. *Revolver* is confirmation of this. They'll never be able to copy this. Neither will the Beatles be able to reproduce a tenth of this material on a live performance. But who cares? Let John, Paul, George and Ringo worry about that when the time comes. Meanwhile, it is a brilliant album which underlines once and for all that the Beatles have definitely broken the bounds of what we used to call pop." In one of the most thoughtful analyses of the album, *Gramophone*'s jazz critic Peter Clayton observed that *Revolver* "really is an astonishing collection, and listening to it you realize that the distance the four odd young men have travelled since 'Love Me Do' in 1962 is musically even greater than it is materially. It isn't easy to describe what's here, since much of it involves things that are either new to pop music or which are being properly applied for the first time, and which can't be helpfully compared with anything. In fact, the impression you get is not of any one sound or flavor, but simply of smoking hot newness with plenty of flaws and imperfections but *fresh*."[5]

Meanwhile, *NME*'s Allen Evans lauded *Revolver*'s innovative "electronic effects" and took special note of the ways in which the bandmates' "individual personalities are now showing through loud and clear." In *Record Mirror*, Richard Green and Peter Jones praised the album as being "full of musical ingenuity" but recognized that the Beatles' penchant for experimentation would leave some listeners bristling. "There are parts that will split the pop fraternity neatly down the middle," they wrote, echoing McCartney's earlier concern about the risks inherent in loosing the Beatles' new sound upon a world that had grown used to the innocent pop morsels that had been fed to them by the Four Mop-Tops. The American press was equally complimentary, although the version of *Revolver* that they reviewed in the pages of their newspapers and magazines was conspicuously lacking the three tracks—"Doctor Robert," "I'm Only Sleeping," and "And Your Bird Can Sing"—that had been consigned stateside to the *Yesterday . . . and Today* LP. On the West Coast, *KRLA Beat* commended *Revolver* as "a musical creation of exceptional excellence," while Richard Goldstein, writing for the *Village Voice* in New York City, described the new long-player as "a revolutionary record" that was every bit "as important to the expansion of pop as was *Rubber Soul.*" Goldstein concluded that "it seems now that we will view this album in retrospect as a key work in the development of rock 'n' roll into an artistic pursuit." Leave it to Tony Thorpe, a top London session musician who came of age as *Revolver* first cast its long shadow over the history of pop music, to get to the heart of the matter, the original song that set the long-player into motion: "Nothing like the lyrics of 'Tomorrow Never Knows' had been written before. The whole approach to that track was straight out of John Lennon's head and George Martin was able to pick up on it and do what he did. It's a piece of art, it's a Picasso."[6]

As with *Rubber Soul, Revolver* was a sizable commercial success, holding dominion over the UK album charts for seven weeks and, in the United States, topping *Billboard*'s album charts for six weeks. But as it happened, *Revolver*'s exemplary critical notices and gargantuan sales receipts would easily be the best aspects about that long, hot summer for the Beatles. As it turned out, George would have precious little time to bask in the joy of his recent nuptials with Judy. The record business—Beatles and non-Beatles alike—intervened almost immediately. First up was Martin's new long-term contract with United Artists, which was reported in the July 9, 1966, issue of *Cash Box*. Announced by United Artists president Mike Stewart, the long-term worldwide agreement accounted for all future albums and singles by Martin as recording artist and bandleader. In his press release, Stewart lauded Martin for having registered some two hundred million record sales internationally by his artists—namely, the Beatles—at this point in his career. "In keeping with United Artists' long-term policy of associating with the greatest creative talent in the entertainment world," said Stewart, "we are delighted to welcome George Martin to our fold. In view of the tremendous successes he has achieved in the past in conjunction with UA and with other organizations, and the great artistry he has consistently displayed, we feel that we have indeed signed one of the giant talents of the music business." Of course, United Artists had actually welcomed George to the fold nearly two years earlier, in September 1964. By then, Martin had already scored a minor US hit for United Artists with "Ringo's Theme (This Boy)," an instrumental from the soundtrack for *A Hard Day's Night*.[7]

By the time he signed his latest contract with United Artists, George had released several albums as bandleader of the George Martin Orchestra—also represented variously as George Martin and His Orchestra. In addition to *Off the Beatle Track* and the soundtrack music for *A Hard Day's Night* in 1964, he had released *George Martin Scores Instrumental Versions of the Hits* and a collection of *Help!*-themed instrumentals in 1965. With his new United Artists contract in hand, George began preparations that summer for his next collection of instrumental hits, which he recorded with the George Martin Orchestra over the next several months. George's orchestra was composed of a host of leading studio musicians, including mainstays Neville Marriner and Raymond Keenlyside on violin, John Underwood on viola, and Joy Hall on cello. Titled *George Martin Instrumentally Salutes The Beatle Girls*, the collection made for a strange assortment. While it included cutting-edge instrumental versions of recent tracks from *Rubber Soul* and *Revolver*, the album inexplicably included "Yellow Submarine," which hardly fit the long-player's theme. Stranger yet, George's cover version of "Eleanor Rigby" featured a vocal arrangement, belying the album's instrumental claims. The liner notes laud George for never failing "to bring forth a new dimension to a song. Sometimes, this is done by a deft and unusual blending of instruments. Occasionally, it is handled by bestowing a beguine beat or a classical treatment to a tune that had only been previously heard as a strictly pop entry." The cover art for *George Martin Instrumentally Salutes The Beatle Girls* depicted the producer, holding a martini (naturally) and wearing a sheepish look, surrounded by comely, miniskirted models clutching Beatles albums.

July 1966 also saw Martin register a new composition, titled "By George! It's *The David Frost* Theme," with Noel Gay Music, the London firm led by his longtime colleague, record producer Terry Kennedy. In September, Martin would release his first United Artists single under his new contract, which featured "By George! It's *The David Frost* Theme" backed with "Serenade to a Double Scotch" as recorded by George Martin and His Orchestra. Martin had composed "By George! It's *The David Frost* Theme" expressly for his old friend, popular British TV personality and journalist David Frost. Martin's association with Frost had begun rather furtively in March 1962, when the producer blew the whistle on his rival Norrie Paramor's shady business practices to the young journalist, who was a fledgling reporter for *This Week*, London AR-TV's current affairs program. Martin's revelations about Paramor would finally hit the airwaves in November 1962, when Frost ridiculed him before a national television audience for the BBC's satirical program *That Was the Week That Was*. In 1963, Martin produced an album devoted to *That Was the Week That Was*, including Millicent Martin's famous theme song, "That Was the Week That Was, It's Over, Let It Go." In 1966, as Frost prepared to premiere his new variety program, *The David Frost Show*, he commissioned Martin to compose the theme. And so "By George! It's *The David Frost* Theme" was born. George was especially fond of his latest composition, particularly the song's punning reference to its author in the title. As for the music, he "opted for something very brash and showbizzy, a kind of Nelson Riddle–type, swinging, hip kind of tune."[8]

While things were slow going at first with AIR, George had begun enjoying some success of late with the Master Singers, a highly unusual vocal act made up of four schoolmasters. Well aware of their quirky nature, George saw the Master Singers as a throwback to his early years at EMI. "In spite of having to devote a great part of my time to the established artists like Cilla and the Beatles," he later wrote, "I still managed to find room for some of my old 'nutty' ideas." Led by John Horrex, a teacher at Abingdon School in Oxfordshire, the Master Singers, who performed a cappella "in a very good cathedral-plainsong approach to singing," were rounded out by Horrex's colleagues George Pratt, Geoff Keating, and Barry Montague. The Master Singers specialized in novelty recordings, much like the quirky artists who pocked Martin's Parlophone roster during the 1950s. The group came to his attention after they were discovered by Winston Churchill, the grandson of the British prime minister, who subsequently played one of their novelty songs on his BBC radio program. Their big break with the BBC led to a contract with Parlophone. During his A&R head days, George had first deployed them for the purposes of choral accompaniment in conjunction with Peter Sellers. In one of his last collaborations with the legendary British funnyman, Martin had recorded Sellers's sidesplitting parody of "A Hard Day's Night," which the comedian performed on the December 1965 broadcast of *The Music of Lennon and McCartney* TV special. Released to coincide with Granada Television's broadcast, Sellers's "A Hard Day's Night" backed with "Help!" single featured the Master Singers providing backup on the B-side, which lampooned the Beatles hit with Sellers exercising his archly satiric wit as the schoolmasters provided solemn harmonies in their "best ecclesiastical manner."[9]

After the single enjoyed a top-twenty showing on the British charts, Martin continued working with the Master Singers in the new year. In 1966, he produced three singles by the vocal group. For George, working with the novelty ensemble was a welcome return to his days as A&R head at Parlophone. It hearkened back to a riskier time in his career, a period characterized by George stewarding one idiosyncratic artist after another through the record trade as he tried to improve the standing of EMI's third label. In April 1966, as the Beatles began the *Revolver* sessions, George released the Master Singers' single "Highway Code" backed with "Rumbletum." Arranged by Horrex and Keating, "Highway Code" featured the schoolmasters delivering a literal, chant-like performance of the British highway code in all of its banality. Later that spring, "Highway Code" notched a number-twenty-five showing on the charts, an impressive result for a novelty act in the mid-1960s, when one breakthrough rock act after another seemed to be holding sway over the charts. As Martin later observed, "To a certain degree of surprise in the business, it became a hit, and I naturally wanted to follow it up. I asked them what else they could dream up, and they had the idea of recording the telephone directory. I thought that was marvelous." Produced by Martin, the group's follow-up single, naturally titled "Telephone Directory," briefly landed the producer and the schoolmasters in hot water after the General Post Office claimed that prevailing copyright laws had been violated when the Master Singers recited the names and telephone numbers of actual customers. "Sadly, the heavy hand of bureaucracy intervened," Martin lamented. "The Post Office declared: 'We won't allow you to do it. Joe Bloggs of Lanchester Drive might not want his address in a song.' My view was that Mr. Bloggs would have loved it; but the Post Office would have none of it, and the idea came to nothing." Forced to scrap "Telephone Directory," George and the group recorded "Weather Forecast" backed with "Roadilore." Another Anglican chant sung with deadpan solemnity, "Weather Forecast" saw the Master Singers performing a mundane weather report, with occasional sound effects, courtesy of the EMI library, deployed to establish the sound of wind and torrential rain. By this point, the band's one-joke repertoire may have been wearing thin with British listeners. "Weather Forecast" scored a paltry number-forty-five showing on the charts. The Master Singers would go their separate ways soon thereafter, although their demise had nothing to do with flagging record sales but rather with the simple fact that the bandmates' shifting careers took them to different parts of the country.[10]

By this time, another one of George's perennial acts, the Fourmost, were also on the wane. Between 1963 and 1965, George had managed to navigate the middling band toward a string of top-forty hits. One of the charter members of Brian Epstein's stable of Merseyside acts, the Fourmost were understandably reeling from the March 1966 death of Mike Millward, the band's guitarist and vocalist, who lost his battle with leukemia at just twenty-three years old. Having tapped George Peckham, a fellow Scouser and well-known personality on the Mersey beat scene, as Millward's replacement, the Fourmost were primed and ready to make another pass at the British charts. When it came time to "routine" new material, George helpfully suggested a cover version of the Beatles' "Here, There, and Everywhere," which the Fab Four had no plans to release as a single. The Fourmost were no strangers to covering Lennon-McCartney compositions, having charted hits with several of the songwriters' throwaways, including "Hello Little Girl" and "I'm in Love." But when it came time to produce "Here, There, and Everywhere," Martin was unavailable. Instead, he passed the Fourmost along to his AIR colleague Ron Richards, who supervised the recording session. With orchestration by composer and Manfred Mann multi-instrumentalist Mike Vickers, the Fourmost seemed poised, as with David and Jonathan's well-timed cover version of "Michelle," to transform a Beatles album cut into a hit.

Released later that summer, "Here, There, and Everywhere" backed with "You've Changed," a composition that had been penned by Mike O'Hara, the band's founding member, failed to register so much as a blip on the British charts. The group that had once been hailed as "the clown princes of Merseybeat" were clearly flailing under Epstein and Martin's tutelage, which by this point was bordering on outright neglect. Bill Harry, the influential editor of the *Mersey Beat* newspaper, didn't mince words. "It went wrong for the Fourmost," he later observed. "The Fourmost could have been so much bigger." As it was, the bandmates regularly grumbled to Tony Barrow about playing second fiddle to the Beatles in Epstein's eyes. And as the summer of 1966 went from bad to worse for their manager, the band's case for neglect was understandable. Later that year, after their next single, "Auntie Maggie's Remedy" backed with "Turn the Lights Down," fell flat, the Fourmost couldn't wait any longer. When the band went on hiatus, O'Hara left Epstein's stable for good, vowing to try his hand on the lucrative cabaret circuit instead.[11]

Meanwhile, as the summer wore on and George and Judy continued to bask in their postconnubial bliss, news began to trickle in about Epstein and the Beatles' experiences on tour. And it soon became clear that trouble was brewing across the globe with the bandmates. After routine gigs in West Germany, the scene had shifted to Japan, where the group was scheduled to play five shows in Tokyo's celebrated Budokan, the octagon-shaped arena that had been reserved for traditional Japanese martial arts. The idea of a Western pop group playing in that hallowed space led to a succession of death threats. As Martin later recalled, "We all took the threat seriously, not least because there was so much religious and conservative opposition in Japan to the forthcoming concerts." Afraid that the world's most famous musicians might be injured—or, worse yet, perish—on their soil, the Japanese government overreacted in spectacular fashion, dispatching some thirty-five thousand police officers to protect the Beatles during their brief visit. The bandmates were held as virtual prisoners in the Tokyo Hilton, and the concerts themselves were sterile affairs in which some three thousand police had been distributed among the venue's ten thousand spectators in order to maintain control. With such an overwhelming police presence, the Japanese fans were reluctant to go berserk in the same fashion as their Western counterparts. Gone were the screams and tumult to which the band had become accustomed, and suddenly, without the comforting veil of teenage chaos and clamor, the Beatles could be heard, loudly and clearly, as an unhappy quartet of sloppy, out-of-tune musicians. As a surviving television broadcast of the first concert plainly demonstrates, their stage act by this juncture was simply awful.[12]

On July 3, the tour pressed on, with the Beatles bringing their show to the Philippines for the first time. After landing in Manila, the bandmates were inexplicably whisked away to a yacht that was owned by a local media mogul. After some two hours, Epstein demanded that the group be removed from the vessel and provided with hotel accommodations in the city. When they finally checked into the Manila Hotel, the Beatles were blissfully unaware of an invitation from President Ferdinand Marcos and First Lady Imelda Marcos requesting their appearance at Malacañang Palace at eleven o'clock the following morning. But "since the British embassy fiasco," the group's assistant Peter Brown recalled, "the policy was never to go to those things." The next morning, the Beatles' entourage ignored further demands from Filipino officials that they go to the palace, where the First Lady and some two hundred children were now anxiously awaiting their appearance. After playing an afternoon concert for some thirty-five thousand fans and an evening performance for another fifty thousand spectators at José Rizal Memorial Stadium, the band started to realize that they were in dire straits when news reports began detailing their snubbing of the royal family. Later that night, a genuinely contrite Brian Epstein attempted to ameliorate the situation by expressing his regrets to the First Family on the Channel 5 News, but a burst of suspicious static rendered his apology all but unintelligible. The next day, the Beatles were suddenly ordered to pay income tax on concert receipts that they still hadn't received from Filipino promoter Ramon Ramos.

Even worse, the Beatles' governmental security detail had been suspended given their allegedly rude treatment of the First Lady, and the group and their entourage were left to their own devices as they rushed to the Manila International Airport in order to make their KLM flight to New Delhi before making their way back to London. But their ordeal wasn't over yet. They were jostled by an angry mob as they made their way to immigration, and things became even more dicey on the tarmac, when Mal Evans and press officer Tony Barrow were removed from the plane shortly before takeoff. The Beatles had been declared "illegal immigrants" by the Filipino government, and Mal and Tony spent some forty minutes negotiating the band's way out of the country. Stultified by what they considered to be their near-death experience in the South Pacific, the group roundly blamed Epstein for the disastrous turn of events. As Martin later recalled, "The whole country was up in arms. Although the concerts had been immensely successful, it seemed every Filipino was out for their [the band's] blood." George had observed the bandmates' growing disdain for Epstein, as well as the ways in which they all too easily found him culpable for any mishap that came their way, both large and small: "I don't think the Beatles really appreciated him as they should have done," he later observed. "Once they had success, they tended to blame Brian for not getting what was due to them, rather than applaud him for the success. They developed a very negative attitude. When it came to light that he had mishandled certain things, they were very vocal in their criticism that he was a rotten manager. Forgetting that without him they would not have existed in the first place."[13]

When the Beatles finally arrived back in London on July 8, they were relieved to be back on home soil. And they knew one thing for sure: their touring had taken a significant toll in more ways than one—and perhaps most troubling, in terms of the quality of their musicianship. As Ringo later recalled, "We were absolutely fed up with touring, and why were we fed up with touring? Because we were turning into such bad musicians. The volume of the audience was always greater than the volume of the band. For me personally, there was no chance I could do a fill because it would just disappear. So I ended up just sort of hanging on to the other guys' bums and trying to lip-read to see where we were." What a terrible predicament for any drummer—the group's master timekeeper—having to follow his bandmates' bouncing rear ends in order to maintain the beat. And then there was the Beatles' manager. For his part, Epstein had returned to the United Kingdom as a shell of his former self—and he was terribly ill to boot. It was precisely in this state that he retired for several days' recuperation before gearing up for the American leg of the tour, which was set to begin in Chicago on August 12. Diagnosed with mononucleosis, Epstein convalesced at his home in Belgravia before relocating on July 30 to the seaside village of Portmeirion in North Wales to continue his recuperation. He was joined in his rented Italianate villa by George and Judy, who were happy to continue their honeymoon in the company of the Beatles' manager, with whom they had socialized since Beatlemania's salad days. Brian was one of the couple's closest friends, and they were always "a happy trio when we had been able to spend time with him. He was pretty much part of the family."[14]

When George and Judy arrived at Brian's villa, it was clear that their host was not only out of sorts—felled by mononucleosis and the aftershocks of the Far East tour—but verging on what appeared to be a deep depression. As for himself, George was still smarting from his illness during the latter stages of the *Revolver* sessions. Not surprisingly, the idea of a seaside vacation held great appeal for him. As George later wrote, "When I was well enough, my wife Judy and I joined him [Brian] for a much-needed weekend of rest, relaxation, and strategic discussion." The Welsh coast seemed to fit the bill perfectly. In George's memories, Portmeirion was a "curious seaside hideaway built like some giant film set by the architect Clough Williams Ellis." As the couple's "strategic discussion" with Brian began to unfold, they came to understand that the band's manager had found himself at a crossroads. "As he took stock," George later recalled, "Brian came to realize that he had taken a great deal for granted in running the lives of his four famous charges. So far, they hadn't complained about the grueling round of concerts and appearances he put them through." As they observed their host, George and Judy could sense that Brian felt that he was on the precipice of becoming secondary to the Beatles' concerns. Brian seemed to perceive his own value in terms of the band's ceaseless place in the public's imagination, an end that he inevitably secured as they traipsed among the world's concert halls and arenas.[15]

Yet at the same time, George couldn't help noting Brian's inability to remain focused on his artists, especially his acts beyond the Beatles. "There is no doubt," George later wrote, "that Brian was losing control of his empire by this stage. He had slight delusions of grandeur. He pictured himself as a latter-day Diaghilev, believing that he was the man who had masterminded the greatest group on earth, and therefore he had the magic touch. So it had proven in 1963, but after a while he was bringing me artists that weren't any good, and I was even having to turn them down sometimes. Brian's empire was crumbling at the edges because he was tending not to devote as much time as he should to people, who therefore felt neglected." To George's mind, Brian's life was rendered even more complex by his homosexuality, which forced him to live on society's fringes. By this time, George later recalled, Brian's "private life was also getting more and more complicated. The strains of being a closeted homosexual were telling on him, at a time when morality laws in England were very stringent and it was still a criminal offense to be a practicing gay. I think Brian had a tough time within himself. He would love to have had a happy relationship with someone, and I think he secretly envied Judy and me. At times, he seemed to be floating away." But before George and Judy could devote additional time and energy to ministering to their host's attendant difficulties, more pressing matters came to the fore. Indeed, it was there, by the seaside in Portmeirion, that they learned the awful news about a storm that was gathering in the United States—one that would make Tokyo and Manila seem like child's play.[16]

As it turned out, the fuse had been lit way back in March, when Tony Barrow had intentionally shared Maureen Cleave's in-depth Beatles interviews with Art Unger, the influential editor of *Datebook*, an American teen magazine, in order to build up buzz for the Beatles' upcoming tour. Barrow and the Beatles had wisely befriended Unger during their previous visit to the United States both because they liked the affable American and for his access to a massive teen readership that still lived at the heart of the band's primary demographic. Following Barrow's lead, Unger reprinted the Cleave interviews in a special "shout-out" issue of *Datebook*. Knowing the Beatles would soon be alighting on American shores, Unger was looking for an opportunity to stir up the magazine's substantial audience base. When he republished Cleave's interviews on July 29, as George and Judy were busy back in London preparing to join Brian in scenic Portmeirion, Art adorned the cover of *Datebook* with eye-popping quotations that he had culled—out of context, no less—from the Maureen Cleave interviews:

McCartney: "It's a lousy country where anyone black is a dirty nigger."
Lennon: "I don't know which will go first—rock 'n' roll or Christianity."

As he worked the print and broadcast media to create interest in *Datebook*'s latest issue, Unger shared the Beatles feature with a number of DJs, including Tommy Charles and Doug Layton, who hosted a morning show on WAQY in Birmingham, Alabama.[17]

On the morning of July 29—before the *Datebook* issue had even hit the newsstands—Charles and Layton began talking up the story. Like others in the media, they had harbored a growing concern that perhaps the Beatles' pop-cultural dominion had run its course, that in spite of all of the unchecked adulation they received, they were not "godlike creatures." While Charles and Layton admitted that the Beatles "are as good as or better than any group today," they suggested that "it's time somebody stood up to them and told them to shut up." With the *Datebook* issue in their hands, they now had the ammunition to do just that. While McCartney's hot-button remark about American racism received scant attention, Lennon's observation about the decline of Christianity quickly caught fire among WAQY's Bible Belt listeners, who took particular issue with what they perceived to be Lennon's arrogance in elevating the Beatles over an entire religion. After gauging the red-hot level of their audience's vitriol, Charles and Layton contrived the idea of banning the Fab Four from their airwaves while also suggesting that listeners round up their Beatles records for a WAQY-sponsored bonfire during the group's upcoming tour. In fact, the Beatles would be within a few hundred miles of Birmingham on August 19, when they were scheduled to play a pair of shows in Memphis at the Mid-South Coliseum. But things really gathered momentum when Al Benn, Birmingham's bureau manager for United Press International (UPI), caught Charles and Layton's morning show. Smelling a scoop, he published a story about the *Datebook* feature and, quite suddenly, the localized Beatles furor in Birmingham went global, given UPI's incredible international reach at the time. After Benn's story ran on July 31, Unger realized that Barrow's gambit, and his own complicity in it, had gone terribly awry. He telephoned Epstein, who was still vacationing with the Martins in Wales, telling him that "this is getting a little out of hand here. They're planning to burn Beatles' records." At first, the Beatles' manager seemed surprisingly unfazed under the circumstances. "If they burn Beatles records, they've got to buy them first," he replied.[18]

Epstein and his houseguests began to take things much more seriously after the Beatles' manager received a phone call from none other than Sid Bernstein, along with Nat Weiss, Epstein's New York business partner. Bernstein had been instrumental in the rise of American Beatlemania through the band's February 1964 Carnegie Hall performances and their historical August 1965 Shea Stadium appearance, which they were gearing up to repeat on August 15 as part of their upcoming tour. Bernstein and Weiss's point was resoundingly clear: his illness and recuperation be damned, Epstein should travel to America at once, rouse his PR machine into operation, and do some emergency damage control. The prevailing view was that, fearing a backlash, promoters might begin canceling Beatles concerts. Huddled up with George and Judy, Brian hatched a plan: He would follow his advisers' instructions and fly to New York City in advance of the Beatles' American tour to launch a coordinated media response. Meanwhile, he would dispatch Martin back to London, where the producer would tape a prerecorded apology from Lennon that could be broadcast on American radio outlets in order to begin quelling the storm. Brian suggested that they deploy Derek Taylor, the ghostwriter behind the manager's autobiography, *A Cellarful of Noise*, to script the apology.[19]

For his part, Martin was ready to leap into action. In contrast with his anger and disappointment in the Beatles over the *Yesterday ... and Today* furor, which had blown through the bandmates' world just seven weeks earlier, Martin was flabbergasted by what he perceived to be a puritanical and unwarranted response to Lennon's remarks. Years later, George would lament the ways in which John had been misunderstood vis-à-vis the *Datebook* controversy. "Knowing the religious fanaticism one can find in the States, that didn't help matters," George wrote. "Of course, like so much that was said and reported at that time, the whole thing was blown up out of all proportion. I can't remember John's exact words, but I know his intention. He was slightly bemused by the effect the Beatles were having on the world, and his statement was factual. It was to the effect that 'When you look at it, we are actually more popular than Jesus.' That was true. Far fewer people went to church than listened to Beatles records and went to Beatles concerts. But he didn't mean that the Beatles were more important than Christ, which was how most people interpreted the remark. On the contrary, he was deploring the situation, regretting that it was the case."[20]

But by the time that Brian alighted in New York City on August 4, this plan of attack had been scrapped, if only temporarily. With Martin and the taped apology gambit on hold, Epstein woke up the next morning to a headline about Lennon's remark plastered across the front page of the *New York Times*. The UPI story included remarks from Maureen Cleave, who, like Martin, argued for readers to take the context of the Beatle's words into fuller consideration. Lennon "was simply observing that so weak was the state of Christianity that the Beatles were, to many people, better known than Jesus," Cleave observed in the UPI report. "He was deploring rather than approving this. He said things had reached a ridiculous state of affairs when human beings could be worshiped in this extraordinary way." Later, speaking with Pittsburgh's KDKA, she pointed out that John's words had been "taken out of context and did not accurately reflect the article or the subject as it was discussed." Like Martin, Cleave argued that in the interview Lennon had intended to communicate that "the power of Christianity was on the decline in the modern world and that things had reached such a ridiculous state that human beings (such as the Beatles) could be worshipped more religiously by people than their own religion."[21]

In spite of Cleave's efforts, the story simply wouldn't ebb, even seeming to gain momentum as the Beatles' American concert dates loomed. The perceived arrogance of John's remarks was quickly becoming the prevailing talking point in media reports. When interpreted within the context of his actual utterance, it's not a difficult leap for readers to make: "Christianity will go," Lennon said to Cleave. "It will vanish and shrink. I needn't argue about that; I'm right, and I will be proved right. We're more popular than Jesus now; I don't know which will go first—rock 'n' roll or Christianity. Jesus was all right but his disciples were thick and ordinary. It's them twisting it that ruins it for me."

Perhaps worse yet, reporters had begun sensing a major news scoop on their hands, steadfastly fanning the flames of the brush fire that had plunged the bandmates and their reps into a state of PR chaos and a frenzy of ill-conceived communication. At this juncture—and in very different circumstances—the focus of Epstein's efforts should have been entirely on *Revolver*, of course, which was released that same day back in the United Kingdom. But at this point, there wasn't a hint of media strategy at work in the Beatles' world, save for Brian's hastily arranged visit to the United States and the idea about George recording a taped apology from John. Even George Harrison had gotten into the act, ill-advisedly informing *Disc and Music Echo* that, having just completed the Far East leg of their tour, "We'll take a couple of weeks to recuperate before we go and get beaten up by the Americans." It may have been at this point that Epstein shifted his still-latent PR strategy, deciding to scrap the taped apology and putting an embargo on further commentary to the media, whether it be from the bandmates, Cleave, or anyone else associated with the organization. He contacted his assistant, Wendy Hanson, directing her to "please advise Beatles to continue not to speak to the press under any circumstances. Also, it is not necessary for John to make the tape with Martin. Please advise Maureen Cleave." No, Brian would be handling things himself from this point forward; he would deploy the very same charm and forthright personality that had helped to transform the Beatles into household names. Perhaps then he would end the scandal once and for all.[22]

For his part, Geoff Emerick later called Epstein's directive to Hanson about the taped apology into question, suggesting that the decision to scrap the idea had nothing to do with Epstein's evolving media strategy. As Geoff later remembered, George was ready to meet John at Abbey Road and make the recording forthwith, "but the problem was that John was away on holiday and unavailable to come into the studio in person. He was apparently willing to phone it in, but for some reason Brian deemed that unacceptable—not remorseful enough, perhaps? As a result, our technical boffins spent a few hurried days designing a dummy head into which John's telephoned apology would be played: the idea was that the cavities of this little plaster head would somehow make his voice more realistic, as if he were actually in the studio talking on a high-quality microphone instead of over a low-fidelity phone line." According to Emerick, the absurd plan eventually collapsed because "Lennon had changed his mind" about even bothering to make the recording with Martin in the first place. The Beatles' engineer was flummoxed, not merely at John's apparent disinclination to record the apology but also at EMI itself. "It just goes to show the lengths to which EMI would go to accommodate the Beatles," Emerick observed. "If it had been any other artist, they would never have devoted the time and resources to such a foolish idea."[23]

Sensing that time was increasingly of the essence in terms of staving off any further uproar, Epstein held a press conference on the afternoon of Friday, August 5, at New York City's Americana Hotel. Like Martin and Cleave, Epstein cast the controversy as being based upon a quotation that had been taken out of the larger context of Lennon's *London Evening Standard* interview. "What he said, and meant, was that he was astonished that in the last 50 years the church in England, and therefore Christ, had suffered a decline in interest," Epstein proclaimed. "He did not mean to boast about the Beatles' fame. He meant to point out that the Beatles' effect appeared to him to be a more immediate one upon, certainly, the younger generation." And that's when the Beatles' manager took the much-needed step of showing remorse, remarking that "in the circumstances, John is deeply concerned, and regrets that people with certain religious beliefs should have been offended in any way whatsoever." Coming a week after the *Datebook* issue hit the newsstands and five days after the UPI story made national headlines, the apology, such as it was communicated, was too little, too late. Brian fared much better when he took questions from the media. "They feel absolutely terrible," he replied with great earnestness when asked about the bandmates' feelings about the American furor and having become targets of resentment. When pressed further, Brian confessed that he was concerned about the bandmates' safety during the upcoming American jaunt, just as George had been throughout the group's high-profile concert tours. After praising US authorities for providing first-rate protection over the years, Brian vowed that "I shall watch the security personally," but in the end, he admitted, "one just hopes for the best."[24]

On that same day back in the United Kingdom, the release of *Revolver* had been accompanied by the arrival of a new Beatles single, "Yellow Submarine" backed with "Eleanor Rigby." By the time that the Beatles landed stateside the very next week, the single would be released in America as well. As the group traipsed across the country for the next several weeks and the controversy slowly began to subside, "Yellow Submarine" and "Eleanor Rigby" swirled about the airwaves, selling well over a million units in August 1966 and earning the Beatles their twenty-first American gold record. It made for a remarkable moment of cultural dissonance, as Lennon was lambasted across the media for his remarks even as his band's latest song ascended the charts, with American radio audiences happily singing along with a children's tune about living a life of whimsy in the land of submarines. When US DJs flipped over the record and played "Eleanor Rigby," they were ceding airtime to a tune that excoriated contemporary religious institutions for being unable, and worse, unwilling at times, to look out for the welfare of vulnerable parishioners like Eleanor Rigby. The ironic juxtaposition of Lennon's remarks about religion's wane and the thematics inherent in "Eleanor Rigby" was very stark indeed, yet in all likelihood lost on the mass culture of the day. In the United Kingdom, the double A-sided "Yellow Submarine" backed with "Eleanor Rigby" single not only notched the band their twelfth straight chart-topper, but it also was the first single to feature Ringo as lead vocalist. However, at the same time the "Yellow Submarine" backed with "Eleanor Rigby" single marked the end of an era. Composed of a pair of tracks that had been lifted directly from *Revolver*, the single broke Martin's long-standing tradition—his personal ethic, really—about not duplicating Beatles singles on long-players, a plan that he and Epstein had devised in order to ensure that Beatles fans enjoyed greater value for their money. But with the "Yellow Submarine" backed with "Eleanor Rigby" single, George and Brian's grand design had been intentionally scuttled for the sake of pure expediency. Over the years, Beatles albums had been released concurrently with new singles, of course. But as Robert Rodriguez has noted, the Beatles were simply "out of gas at the time of *Revolver*'s release, only two months after their last single, 'Paperback Writer' b/w 'Rain,' and tradition had them issuing a new single alongside a new album." Unfortunately, John and Paul were both spent as far as new material was concerned.[25]

As the group prepared to travel to the United States, John had taken to calling their upcoming spate of American concerts the "Jesus Christ" tour. He had no idea how discerning his words would prove to be. On August 11, they flew to Chicago and were driven directly to the Astor Tower Hotel, where Epstein and Barrow had arranged for a press conference so that Lennon could face the music, and, as their manager fervently hoped, stem the derisive anti-Beatles tide. "He was terrified," John's wife Cynthia later recalled. "What he'd said had affected the whole group. Their popularity was under the microscope but he was the one who had opened his mouth and put his foot in it." After being briefed by Epstein and Barrow, Lennon wasted little time in getting to the matter at hand: "I wasn't saying whatever they're saying I was saying," he remarked. "I'm sorry I said it really. I never meant it to be a lousy anti-religious thing. I apologize if that will make you happy. I still don't know quite what I've done. I've tried to tell you what I did do, but if you want me to apologize, if that will make you happy, then okay, I'm sorry."[26]

Over the next several days—as the Beatles traveled from one city to another—the controversy began to wane perceptibly. But the die had already been cast, as demonstrated by flagging ticket sales. During their August 15 return engagement at Shea Stadium, the fallout from the recent controversy could be observed in the stands, which were pocked with empty seats. "Some tickets for the Shea Stadium performance even had to be given away," Martin wrote. "This was incredible to Brian, as it was to me. It was the only time we could remember when the band had played to anything less than a full house. Brian's main fear on that last tour, like my own, was for the physical well-being of the Beatles." Lennon had publicly apologized numerous times by the time the band reached Memphis a week later, and the staged record burnings had all but stopped in the interim. They arrived at the Mid-South Coliseum in Memphis to the stomach-churning sight of a clutch of hooded Ku Klux Klansmen parading outside. That same day, a Christian revival meeting was held in the city as a demonstration against John's comments, and that afternoon reports about a coming assassination attempt had begun to make the rounds. In perhaps the tensest moment during the Jesus Christ tour, the Beatles were startled by a firecracker that was tossed onstage and had exploded near Ringo's drums during "If I Needed Someone." For a split second, the bandmates thought that they were under attack, that one of them had, in fact, been killed. As Lennon remembered, "There had been threats to shoot us, the Klan were burning Beatle records outside, and a lot of the crew-cut kids were joining in with them. Somebody let off a firecracker and every one of us—I think it's on film—look at each other, because each thought it was the other that had been shot. It was that bad." For a moment, it seemed like Martin's fear about their vulnerability had come true, but then, having realized that they were still alive, the bandmates played on as if nothing had happened. Not surprisingly, over the next few days—as the normal rigors of a big-time stadium tour set in—the bandmates began to come to a decision that the current American jaunt would be their last concert tour.[27]

If the Jesus Christ tour had a high point for the Beatles, it was unquestionably their two-day stopover in Los Angeles after a pair of shows in Seattle. As they relaxed in their rented Hollywood home, Beatles associate and current Beach Boys publicist Derek Taylor arranged for McCartney and Harrison to meet Brian Wilson and his brother Carl Wilson. With the release of *Pet Sounds*, the Beach Boys had enjoyed remarkable critical success, the likes of which they hadn't previously experienced with their earlier, less-sophisticated efforts. In July 1966, they had even taken out an advertisement for *Pet Sounds* in *Billboard* in order to thank the music industry and their fans for the unprecedented response to the long-player. "We're moved over the fact that our *Pet Sounds* brought on nothing but Good Vibrations," the ad copy proclaimed, hinting, rather obliquely, at even greater things to come. As the party at Taylor's house got underway, it was McCartney who spoke up first, saying, "Well, you're Brian Wilson and I'm Paul McCartney, so let's get that out of the way and have a good time." Over the next several hours, the men listened to music and shared stories together. And eventually, Brian, unable to contain himself any longer, played a new Beach Boys recording for Paul and George.[28]

With his new track "Good Vibrations," Brian confessed that he'd been working almost nonstop on developing the composition over the past eight months. A complex amalgam of musical layers and vivid Technicolor, "Good Vibrations" had required some ninety hours to record, with Wilson even working in four different studios to bring the track home. Amazingly, "Good Vibrations" had already racked up more expenses than the entire *Pet Sounds* album, and it wouldn't even be released until October. With a final cost estimated to be somewhere in the vicinity of $50,000, the song's Electro-Theremin segment alone had clocked in at $15,000. Years later, Martin would admit that he hadn't been surprised by Wilson's achievement with "Good Vibrations," that Wilson had even greater things up his sleeve beyond *Pet Sounds*. The Beatles' producer had observed as the Beach Boy, buoyed by the sounds and innovation of *Rubber Soul*, had begun changing his industry in pioneering ways. "Good Vibrations" was the culmination of Wilson's trajectory to Martin's mind. "One of the great things about Brian's music is its marvelous unpredictability," said George. "He avoided clichés, giving his melodies changes of direction that amaze and charm the listener. And Brian's sounds take us into a new and beautiful countryside." By this point, "the recording studio had become his [Wilson's] workshop," said George, "the place where he painted his masterpieces, and in doing so, he changed the very concept of record production. The studio became rock's most powerful instrument." It was almost as if, in praising Wilson, Martin wasn't speaking about Lennon and McCartney but rather himself.[29]

On Sunday, August 28, the Beatles were back at it, performing an evening show at Dodger Stadium in Los Angeles. The next day, Monday, August 29, the group performed at San Francisco's Candlestick Park before some twenty-five thousand fans. Like numerous other venues on the dreadful "Jesus Christ" tour, Candlestick Park hadn't sold out—in fact, there were some ten thousand conspicuously empty seats that day. Having now decided among themselves that Candlestick Park would be the scene of their last concert, the Beatles good-naturedly photographed each other in order to commemorate the occasion. Meanwhile, Paul instructed Tony Barrow to make a cassette recording of their final set. It was a blustery evening—complete with a full moon, no less—and the Beatles took the stage at 9:27 PM, having been escorted onto the baseball diamond in an armored car with a security detail of some two hundred police officers in tow. The stage itself was five feet tall, with a six-foot-high wire fence around the perimeter as an extra precautionary measure. The Beatles opened the concert with a searing rendition of "Rock and Roll Music," while Barrow held his cassette player aloft in front of the stage and recorded the show for posterity. Barrow's tape of the Beatles' thirty-three-minute performance ran out of space less than a minute into "Long Tall Sally," the group's final number before a paying audience. As for Epstein, the Beatles' manager had intentionally opted not to attend the band's swan song, hoping against hope that they would change their minds. He spent the afternoon of August 29 swimming in the Beverly Hills Hotel pool with John "Dizz" Gillespie, a sometime boyfriend and full-time hustler. As the Beatles jetted away from San Francisco that night, Harrison remarked to Barrow, "That's it. I'm not a Beatle anymore." At that moment, he later added, "We knew—this is it. We're not going to do this again. We'd done about 1,400 live shows, and I certainly felt that was it."[30]

And for a time at least—in the eyes of the outside world certainly, possibly even to Martin at times—it seemed as if the Beatles were done. Perhaps the trials and tribulations of Beatlemania—not to mention the horrors of the Jesus Christ tour—had taken too great a toll on the four lads from Liverpool, who no longer seemed quite so innocent to their legions of fans and detractors alike.

8

FLOATING ON AIR

I F MARTIN HAD HARBORED any doubts about the Beatles' immediate future in the autumn of 1966, he didn't show it. With an open calendar and without any upcoming Beatles sessions for the first time in years—indeed, for the foreseeable future—he began filling up his time by attending to his neglected AIR clients. For George, first up were David and Jonathan, the duo who had reached into the upper echelons of the UK charts earlier in the year on the strength of their cover version of the Beatles' "Michelle" and their own "Lovers of the World Unite." As with his strategy with the Beatles four years earlier, in which he produced a long-player with the relatively unknown band on the strength of the "Love Me Do" single and the promise of "Please Please Me," George brought David and Jonathan back to Abbey Road to make an album and, hopefully, capitalize on their momentum. For Roger Cook (Jonathan), this was a sound plan of action, and if the duo could benefit from the Beatles' coattails yet again, then all the better. "I don't think that there is a musician in England who didn't learn something from the Beatles records," he later remarked. "How do you do 'reverse echo'? We learnt a lot of tricks from the Beatles, especially as we had their engineer, Geoff Emerick, but you can't say enough about the Beatles. They led the way. Would we have had our first hit in America as David and Jonathan if the Beatles had not already established English artists as being stars? They should have all been Lords for what they did for British music."[1]

In addition to their single, David and Jonathan had been in the spotlight for having performed the theme song for *Modesty Blaise*, Joseph Losey's spy-fi comedy starring Monica Vitti as the title character, along with Terence Stamp and Dirk Bogarde. The "*Modesty Blaise* Theme" paired David and Jonathan with composer Johnny Dankworth, a longtime client and close friend of George's. Performed with Dankworth's orchestra, the theme song was produced by Martin and later released as a single. With *Revolver* behind him and the Beatles apparently on hiatus, Martin set about producing the duo's first long-player, which was subsequently titled *David and Jonathan*. In addition to "Michelle," the album also included a cover version of the Lennon-McCartney song "Yesterday." *David and Jonathan* enjoyed yet another Beatles connection in Leslie Bryce, the photographer behind the imaginative cover art for the long-player. Bryce's photo of David and Jonathan echoed Robert Freeman's work on *Rubber Soul*, although the Beatles connection didn't end there. For many years, Bryce had served as the house photographer for *Beatles Book Monthly*, and by this time, she had carried out some forty photo sessions with the bandmates. With fourteen tracks, as was Martin's usual practice, *David and Jonathan* was released on EMI's Columbia label. But any momentum that the duo had established with "Michelle" and "Lovers of the World Unite" had clearly dissipated, as *David and Jonathan* failed to chart. For the time being, Roger Greenaway and Roger Cook would busy themselves composing songs for other artists, including AIR's Engelbert Humperdinck, Cilla Black, and the Hollies, among others.

As George pondered what to do next with David and Jonathan's flagging career, Gerry and the Pacemakers—one of the mainstays that he had counted among his perennials when he founded AIR—were at a crossroads. Outside of the Beatles and Cilla Black, Gerry and the Pacemakers were easily George's best-selling act. In just three years, they had landed nine top-forty hits on the UK charts, with their first three singles—"How Do You Do It," "I Like It," and "You'll Never Walk Alone"—topping the charts. In 1964, they even seemed, for a time at least, as if they would be genuine rivals for the Beatles as the Mersey beat's most revered act. Inspired by his band's success, Gerry Marsden had begun making his name as a songwriter with such compositions as "It's All Right," "I'm the One," "Don't Let the Sun Catch You Cryin'," and "Ferry Cross the Mersey." In 1965, George and the group were dealt a major blow when the Brian Epstein–produced *Ferry Cross the Mersey* rock musical was widely panned for being a pale imitation of the Beatles' *A Hard Day's Night* film. For Gerry and the Pacemakers, the movie's highly public failure had been difficult to overcome. "Walk Hand in Hand" backed with "Dreams," the band's most recent single in the United Kingdom, had been released way back in November 1965 and barely made it into the top thirty.

A cover version of a 1956 composition by Johnny Cowell and popularized by Andy Williams, "Walk Hand in Hand" was an even bigger failure stateside, where it failed to crack *Billboard*'s Hot 100. Throughout 1966, George had recorded a spate of material with Gerry and the Pacemakers. Their February release, "La La La" backed with "Without You," registered yet another flop, becoming the group's first single that failed to make the UK charts.

For George, Gerry and the Pacemakers had proven to be enigmatic as far as generating sustained record sales was concerned. In the United Kingdom, they had generally made their name on the back of their singles releases. While their first album, *How Do You Like It?*, notched a number-two showing back in November 1963—unable to unseat *With the Beatles* from the top slot—they had since been unable to land a hit long-player in their home country. At one point, when Martin and Epstein's Mersey acts were ruling over the charts, Martin was forced to stagger the latest releases by Gerry and the Pacemakers, Billy J. Kramer and the Dakotas, and Cilla Black, which may have hampered Gerry and the Pacemakers from accruing the kind of momentum that they needed in order to consolidate their fame. In the United States, the group had managed a number of singles and LP successes, but they were likely impeded by the limited reach of Laurie Records, the tiny label that acted as their American distributor.

In September 1966, George convened Gerry and the Pacemakers at Abbey Road to take one last stab at capturing the energy and excitement of their heyday. With George in the control booth, they recorded "Girl on a Swing," a cover version of a composition by jazz bassist Robert Miranda. Martin was also preparing a new album for release on the Laurie Records label. Titled *Girl on a Swing*, the long-player was released stateside in November and included the title track, which had been identified as the band's next singles release, along with a raft of songs that they had recorded during that long year of soul-searching for Marsden and his bandmates. The strangest of the lot, a cover version of Simon and Garfunkel's "The Big Bright Green Pleasure Machine," seemed to take Gerry and the Pacemakers far afield from their original, beat-band comfort zone. Paul Simon's lyrics sounded positively bizarre emanating from Gerry Marsden's lips as he sang,

> people have a tendency to dump on you?
> Does your group have more cavities than theirs?
> Do all the hippies seem to get the jump on you?
> Do you sleep alone when others sleep in pairs?

In its own way, "The Big Bright Green Pleasure Machine" encapsulated Gerry and the Pacemakers' slow demise as they sampled yet another musical style, dilettante like, having roamed from beat music ("How Do You Do It") and symphonic bombast ("You'll Never Walk Alone") to balladry ("Ferry Cross the Mersey"), jazz ("Girl on a Swing"), and now a mid-1960s American satire of consumerism.

In many ways, George had only himself to blame. Perhaps he had been more concerned with guiding the Beatles' career, as earlier acts like Shirley Bassey and the Fourmost had once complained, than with tending to the likes of Gerry and the Pacemakers, who had been allowed to sprawl away from the genre that had made their name. When it was released on October 22, 1966, "Girl on a Swing" notched a number-twenty-eight showing in the United States, while failing, as with "La La La," to crack the British charts. Adorned with bizarre, quasi-psychedelic cover art, *Girl on a Swing* didn't even chart. But by then, it hardly mattered, as Gerry and the Pacemakers had disbanded, calling it quits before the "Girl on a Swing" single even made it to the manufacturing plant.

As September gathered steam, Martin watched as the Beatles, fresh from their sojourn to America for the Jesus Christ tour, dispersed in an array of different directions. While he was always hankering to go into the studio with the bandmates, the Beatles' producer lauded this much-needed four-headed respite. "There was no doubt that the year 1966 had been a disaster for the Beatles," he later observed. "The world was caving in on them. Newton's First Law, that for any given action there is an equal and opposite reaction, had come into play. The universal hysteria was producing its inevitable kickback." Up first was John Lennon, who flew out to Hanover, West Germany, to begin principal photography on Richard Lester's *How I Won the War*. On the set of Lester's film, John would take up the role of Private Gripweed, a part for which the Beatle began wearing steel-rimmed spectacles. After completing work in West Germany, the production shifted to Almería in southern Spain. Lennon quickly discovered that a movie set without the other Beatles in tow could be a spectacularly monotonous place to be. "It was pretty damn boring to me," he later recalled. "I didn't find it at all very fulfilling." Eventually, he began spending the hours, sometimes days, between takes by working out a new composition on his acoustic guitar. As his costar and housemate Michael Crawford later remembered, John "used to sit cross-legged on the beach or on the bed, working out a melody. I heard him playing the same bar over and over again until he got the right sequence." With a dreamlike mood, John's new composition featured deep, impressionistic lyrics: "Living is easy with eyes closed, misunderstanding all you see."[2]

In mid-September, George Harrison and Pattie Boyd traveled to Bombay for an extended visit to India, where the quiet Beatle would continue his sitar study under Ravi Shankar's tutelage. Fresh off the stimulating experience of working on *Revolver*—with his unprecedented three original compositions in "Taxman," "Love You To," and "I Want to Tell You"—Harrison had been inspired to further his knowledge of Indian instrumentation. "The first time I heard Indian music," he later recalled, "I felt as though I knew it. It was everything, everything I could think of. It was like every music I had ever heard, but twenty times better than everything all put together. It was just so strong, so overwhelmingly positive, it buzzed me right out of my brain." He soon discovered that mastering the sitar was a considerable challenge, not merely in terms of learning its intricate tonalities but also in regard to learning how to properly hold the instrument. Harrison's studies with Shankar quickly morphed into a budding friendship founded upon their shared love of Indian music, as well as the Beatle's growing interest in the study of Hinduism and Eastern philosophy. For Harrison, visiting India had emerged as a point of departure into new ways of living and thinking. "Ravi and the sitar were excuses," he later admitted. "Although they were a very important part of it, it was a search for a spiritual connection."[3]

For his part, Ringo enjoyed his extended time away from the Beatles' life on the road. When he wasn't in the bosom of his young family with Maureen, he sought out the company of his friends, even visiting John for a time in Spain. As usual, the most active Beatle was Paul, who spent the first portion of Martin and the Beatles' unscheduled sabbatical in France, where he donned disguises, milled about with the other tourists, and experimented with photography. In November, Paul would travel with Mal Evans to Kenya, where the pair would go on safari. But the big moment came at the end of the trip, as the Beatle and the roadie flew home from Nairobi on November 19. Sitting with Mal in first class, Paul began imagining a concept for a new Beatles album in which the bandmates would assume alter egos and step outside of the constricting world of Beatlemania. "I thought, 'Let's not be ourselves.'" To Paul's mind, they could "put some distance between the Beatles and the public." Mal quickly got into the spirit of Paul's idea, especially when the Beatle happened upon the notion that they take on the personae of an entirely different band. And that's when Mal began absentmindedly playing with tiny packets marked "S" and "P," before asking Paul what they meant. "Salt and Pepper," he replied. And then it came to him: "Sergeant Pepper."[4]

Not surprisingly, as the weeks rolled by with scant news about the Fab Four, the media had begun to register the Beatles' extended absence from their broadcasts and their pages. In a September 20 issue of the *Daily Express*, Judith Simons finally penned the words that fans across the world had feared: "Teenagers may be dismayed at the way the Beatles are splitting off in all directions in pursuit of their separate careers." Across town, whiling away the lonely hours in his Belgravia home, Epstein began to wonder, understandably, if there would be a place for him in the Beatles' post-touring universe. Even more gravely, he was on the verge of losing Cilla Black as a client. During that same period, Cilla came within moments of severing their professional relationship, only to be thwarted by Brian's impassioned plea: "Please don't leave me," he begged. "There are only five people in the world I care about other than my family: the Beatles and you. *Please* don't leave me, Cilla." She quickly relented, later remarking, "How could I leave a fellow who said that? He said he was on top of everything at his work. We decided to give it another go."[5]

Things became even more precarious after Brian was subjected to a succession of blackmail attempts by Dizz Gillespie, who had absconded with the manager's briefcase while Brian dined at the Beverly Hills Hotel with Nat Weiss instead of attending the Beatles' Candlestick Park finale. Unfortunately for Brian, the briefcase contained $20,000 in cash, the Beatles' touring contracts, and, most damaging of all, a parcel of illegal barbiturates. Knowing the power of bad publicity in the wake of the Jesus Christ tour, Gillespie had bartered for hush money from Epstein in exchange for the briefcase. The situation was resolved when Weiss came to the rescue, recovered the briefcase in a sting operation, and had Gillespie arrested. But for Epstein, it was all too much. In late September, Brian's increasingly dire existence came to a head when his assistant Peter Brown discovered the Beatles' manager unconscious in his bedroom. Brown hastily arranged for Epstein's emergency visit to a private hospital, where his stomach was pumped. After he regained consciousness, Brian dismissed the episode as "a foolish accident." But the next day, when Brown returned to Epstein's home, he discovered an empty vial of Nembutal, along with a note, written in Epstein's hand, reading "I can't deal with this anymore. It's beyond me, and I just can't go on." At that point, Brown realized the gravity of the situation and checked Epstein in for a fortnight's stay at a private sanitarium so that he could wean himself off of what had become a steady diet of pills and alcohol. Brian's brother Clive would later attempt to minimize the situation, commenting that "Brian was not distressed, but he was sorry that the touring days were over. He felt that he couldn't make the same contributions to the Beatles' everyday life as he had done. Obviously there were going to be new singles and new albums but that didn't absorb as much of Brian's time as touring. Also, many of NEMS Enterprises' other bands were not featuring as frequently in the charts."[6]

But for Brian—and, to a certain extent, George—there were yet other issues looming on the horizon, including rumors that two of the Beatles may have held a secret meeting with Allen Klein, the crude American business manager who had recently taken up with the Rolling Stones, for whom he earned a huge advance on their standing contract with Decca. For his part, George recognized the gravity in Brian's rapidly deteriorating psychology, later writing that, at the core of things, "Brian was forced to face up to something he had never dreamed he would have to confront: that the Beatles would refuse to perform live again. He had signed them for five years, in 1962, to do just that." Suddenly, the Beatles' manager could no longer glean a sense of purpose in his professional life. "They just said 'no' to his concert dates, and went on saying it," George later wrote. "Going by the received wisdom of the day, this amounted to commercial suicide. Many groups at the time did no recordings at all, relying entirely on live performances for their success. The idea that the Beatles wanted to stop performing and spend months recording an album . . . shook Brian terribly. He thought it was the end."[7]

In October, George and Brian were confronted with the reality that the Beatles would not be providing EMI with a new long-player for the holiday season, as they had done for three straight years in the form of *With the Beatles*, *Beatles for Sale*, and *Rubber Soul*. In fact, it was looking increasingly like the Beatles wouldn't be providing EMI—and, in terms of George's interest, AIR—with a new single either. In the United Kingdom, that meant that the sum total of the band's 1966 output would include the "Paperback Writer" backed with "Rain" and "Yellow Submarine" backed with "Eleanor Rigby" singles and the *Revolver* long-player. For EMI, this state of affairs simply wouldn't stand. With seemingly no other choice, George agreed to compile a greatest hits package in order to keep EMI's coffers sated while also attending to the ravenous consumer demand for more Beatles product. As the band's first greatest hits package, the compilation was titled *A Collection of Beatles Oldies (but Goldies!)*. Preparing the long-player in time for the holiday sales rush required Martin to put in several hours of studio time with Geoff Emerick in order to ensure that the compilation was in stores by December 10, the release date set by EMI. On October 31, Martin and Emerick created a stereo remix in the Studio 1 control room for "Paperback Writer." In contrast with *Revolver*, none of the bandmates attended the sessions associated with *A Collection of Beatles Oldies*. Martin and Emerick had originally planned to remix "Paperback Writer," "I Want to Hold Your Hand," and "She Loves

You" for stereo, but the complexity of the former's stereo remix forced them to reconvene on Monday, November 7, when they completed the stereo remix for "I Want to Hold Your Hand." Once again, Martin was surprised by the time it took to remix the band's earlier output. The lion's share of the singles releases had never been mixed for stereo. To accomplish the remixes, Martin and Emerick worked from the original twin- or four-track recordings, generally relegating the rhythm track to the left channel and vocals to the right.

The next day, November 8, Emerick was left alone to contend with "She Loves You." The original twin-track recordings had been destroyed, leaving only the single's mono master with which to work. To remedy an otherwise impossible situation, Emerick devoted some ninety minutes in Abbey Road's Room 53 to fashion a "mock stereo" version. He fabricated a new version of "She Loves You" by deleting the high frequencies on the left channel, which created a low bass sound. At the same time, he deleted the low frequencies from the right channel to create a treble sound. In this way, they combined to create a faux-stereo version of the song. Martin's team had also intended to create a stereo remix for "From Me to You," although no one, it seems, ever got around to it. Instead, the original twin-track recording was deployed, with the instruments relegated to the left channel and the vocals pushed to the right. On Thursday, November 10, the remainder of the work on the forthcoming compilation was completed, albeit with neither Martin nor Emerick—and certainly none of the Beatles themselves—in evidence. Clearly, *A Collection of Beatles Oldies* was the sole priority of EMI by this juncture. Peter Bown served as engineer for the session, with Graham Kirkby standing by as his second engineer. Bown had worked with Martin for years, particularly during his pre-Beatles days as Parlophone A&R head. Bown and Kirkby created stereo remixes for "Day Tripper" and "We Can Work It Out" before taking up work on a stereo mix for "This Boy."

As it turned out, the latter remix had been a mistake. A miscommunication had occurred between the staff in EMI's Manchester Square offices and the folks at Abbey Road, and "This Boy" had been confused with "Bad Boy," the Larry Williams composition that Martin and the Beatles had recorded back in May 1965. The confusion wouldn't be discovered until the compilation made it to the cutting room. With no time to spare, the existing mix of "Bad Boy" was deployed in place of "This Boy." EMI had lobbied for the inclusion of "Bad Boy"—which hadn't previously been released in the United Kingdom, having been expressly recorded to round out the contents of *Beatles VI,* one of Capitol's repackaging projects for the American marketplace—in order to provide British consumers with a reason for buying *A Collection of*

Beatles Oldies. An embarrassment of riches composed of thirteen UK chart-toppers along with "Yesterday" and "Michelle," the album's sixteen cuts, save one, were already available in British shops. The completists among Beatles collectors would presumably purchase the compilation in order to get their hands on "Bad Boy." The album's cover art featured a painting by David Christian, who was also tapped by EMI to prepare artwork for the cover of the group's annual Christmas message; Christian's work for the holiday Flexidisc was later relegated to ad copy after McCartney submitted a design of his own. For *A Collection of Beatles Oldies,* Christian's cover art depicted a young man donning his Carnaby Street finery, while the back cover of the album sleeve featured a photograph of the Beatles in Tokyo, taken by Robert Whitaker during the band's Far East tour.

As Martin and his team completed the stereo remixes for *A Collection of Beatles Oldies*—or most of them, that is—the first weeks of November were characterized by a confluence of events in the personal and professional lives of the producer and the bandmates. The same week that the remixes were completed for the compilation, John attended an art exhibit at the Indica Gallery. Only the exhibit hadn't opened quite yet. The occasion was an upcoming show by Yoko Ono, a Japanese performance artist who had immigrated to England by way of America, where she had studied with the likes of John Cage and other experimental, avant-garde artists of the day. Ono was loath for anyone to see the exhibition before it opened, but John Dunbar, McCartney and Peter Asher's partner in the Indica Gallery and Bookshop venture, thought Lennon should be an exception. "He's a Beatle. He's got lots of money. He might buy something," Dunbar pointed out. With nothing to lose, Ono's filmmaker husband, Tony Cox, telephoned Lennon, who had only recently returned from Lester's movie shoot in Spain, and invited him for a private showing of Ono's exhibit.

On Wednesday, November 9, Lennon made his private visit to the gallery, where he followed the tiny Japanese woman around the exhibition. At one point, John happened upon a ladder, above which hung Yoko's *Ceiling Painting.* "It looked like a black canvas with a chain with a spyglass hanging on the end of it," Lennon later recalled. At the top of the ladder, John peered through the magnifying glass at the canvas, which sported a single word: *yes.* Lennon suddenly found himself inspired by the spirit behind Ono's art. One of the final works in the exhibition encouraged visitors to hammer a nail into a piece of white plasterboard. But Yoko would have none of it. It was all right for John to preview the exhibit, but the plasterboard should remain unspoiled for the opening. Dunbar pulled the artist aside: "I argued strongly in favor of Lennon's hammering in the first nail," he recalled. "He had a lot of loot—chances are, he would buy the damn thing." Ono finally relented, given the wealth and stature of her distinguished guest. "Okay, you can hammer a nail in for five shillings," she told him. "I'll give you an imaginary five shillings, if you let me hammer in an imaginary nail," Lennon replied, a sly grin growing across his face. It was the defining moment of the artist's life. "My God," Yoko thought to herself. "He's playing the same game I'm playing." Ono now saw Lennon as a potential patron, and she began pursuing him over the next several months, sending countless notes and letters, even sharing a copy of her book *Grapefruit*, which was half autobiography, half artistic philosophy. Lennon was duly impressed with the book's Zen-like instructions, especially *Cloud Piece*, in which she entreated her readers to "imagine the clouds dripping. Dig a hole in your garden to put them in."[8]

Meanwhile, the issue of the Beatles' status as a working rock 'n' roll band had continued to pick up steam in the media. The day after John met Yoko, the *Daily Mail*'s Don Short published an article in which he depicted the Beatles as being "at the crossroads" and reported on "mounting predictions of a split-up of the world's most famous foursome." In their interview with Short for the article, Lennon and Harrison denied that a breakup was imminent, stating that it was their intent to spend more time in the studio and devote less time to the road. But like much of the world, Short wasn't buying it. And he wasn't the only one. During the previous weekend, some two hundred angry fans had picketed outside of Epstein's townhouse, demanding that their idols embark on another tour. By this point, it had become clear that, like the previous December, the Beatles would not be performing their annual spate of Christmas concerts to ring in the new year. In an interview after the protesters had dispersed from outside of his Belgravia home, Epstein attempted to temper any prevailing fears about the Beatles' possible disbandment as best as he could, stating that "I don't think they will split up because I'm certain that they will want to do things together for a long time."[9]

As it turned out, Epstein's effort to quell the rumors fell decidedly flat. With the headline BEATLES GETTING BORED: DRIFT TOWARD BREAKUP, a syndicated United Press International (UPI) story flooded newspapers across the globe with the notion that the group's disbandment was a fait accompli. According to the article, which was published on November 10, "The signs are that the Beatles, over the loyal opposition of thousands of fans, are moving toward an oft-voiced ambition: to develop their individual talents individually." Citing Lennon's appearance in *How I Won the War*, along with Harrison and McCartney's extended foreign travels, the UPI report observed that "the obvious conclusion, supported by the Beatles' own words and actions in the past months, is that they are bored with being the Beatles." Having spent much of the fall months with his wife, Maureen, and their infant son, Zak, Ringo was the only Beatle available for comment. While Brian might have hoped for a much better showing from the Beatles' affable drummer, Ringo went with the truth, telling the UPI reporter, in a moment of unvarnished sincerity, "I have no idea what our future plans are." And the truth was, at that very moment, Ringo was in the dark about George and the bandmates' immediate future as a working musical team. Within a fortnight, Brian's fears would be allayed, and Ringo would have his answer.[10]

The increasing rumors about an impending Beatles breakup were also stoked by an October 14 *NME* story reporting that McCartney had been commissioned to compose a film score for a movie to be titled *Wedlocked, or All in Good Time* starring Hayley Mills. The opportunity had come McCartney's way after he asked Epstein to solicit soundtrack commissions for his consideration. Filmmakers Roy and John Boulting offered *Wedlocked,* and Paul jumped at the chance. Based on the 1963 play *All in Good Time* by Bill Naughton, the screenwriter behind *Alfie,* the film was eventually retitled *The Family Way.* Originally, Lennon had been under the impression that the songwriting partners would be sharing the commission. As he remarked from the film set of *How I Won the War,* "I know we've got music to write as soon as we get back. Paul's just signed us up to write music for a film. I suppose it's—off the plane, into bed, and then 'Knock! Knock! Knock! Get up and write some songs.'" Shortly thereafter, John reported that Paul would be working with legendary songwriter Johnny Mercer of "That Old Black Magic" and "Moon River" fame on the project, and he dutifully stepped aside. Suddenly, Paul was alone at the helm, having only planned to compose a movie theme and not an entire film score.[11]

Realizing that his first solo project might be more than he could handle, McCartney naturally turned to Martin, the man who had so deftly provided solutions for all of the Beatles' musical dilemmas over the years. With only a brief piano motif in hand, Paul turned to George to expand his idea into a full-blown score. To his credit, Martin enhanced the kernel of a concept that McCartney had provided into some twenty-five minutes of incidental music. He accomplished this end by orchestrating Paul's theme and then subjecting it to numerous variations in order to fill out the score. With McCartney receiving credit for composing the soundtrack, the Beatles' producer invited a quartet of George Martin Orchestra regulars to perform the score. With Neville Marriner and Raymond Keenlyside on violin, John Underwood on viola, and Joy Hall on cello, Martin produced and conducted the score in a pair of sessions at CTS Studios, the London shop where he had kicked off the new year, on December 15 and, for the purposes of the soundtrack LP, February 1, 1967. Roy Boulting had originally planned for Martin to conduct the sessions associated with the soundtrack at Shepperton Studios, the massive soundstage and recording facility some twenty miles to the southwest of London. Martin managed to talk the Boulting brothers out of working at Shepperton, given the bureaucratic entanglements of mid-1960s union shops. As George later recalled, "Shepperton Studios at that time was not an ideal place for such novelties, however. Trade unions ruled the roost, and I would have been thrown out of the place if I had dared to touch a microphone. The first session there ended in disaster, and eventually I persuaded Roy that it would be more efficient and cheaper if we recorded the score in a normal recording studio."[12]

The lateness of the recording sessions was necessitated by McCartney's recalcitrance. While he had been hungry for the commission several months earlier, he now seemed devoid of inspiration, much less the requisite inclination to finish out the work. While Martin had been miffed with McCartney at times, the experience of working on *The Family Way* had generally been a pleasant one. As Martin later recalled, "I enjoyed working with Roy Boulting, and he seemed to appreciate the new ideas we were giving him: using a brass band to give a Northern feel to the film, having a small section of strings and woodwind to convey the love themes." But as work on *The Family Way* wore on, George found himself increasingly in the unusual position of having to cajole the cute Beatle into action. For his part, Paul saw their work on *The Family Way* as being akin to their Beatles efforts and his inability to finish the score as a form of writer's block. As he told the *Sunday Times*: Martin "is the interpreter. I play themes and chords on piano and guitar, he gets it down on paper. I talk about the idea I have for instrumentation. Then he works out the arrangement. I tried to learn music once with a fellow who's a great teacher. But it got too much like homework. I have some block about seeing it in little black dots on paper. It's like Braille to me." For George, it was becoming clear that Paul was simply not getting his "homework" done and, worse yet, that he was barely even trying. Martin found himself resorting to the schoolteacherly guise that he had adopted during his very first sessions with the Beatles, long before *Revolver*, during which they had seemed, for the moment at least, to have matured as professional, well-rounded musicians well beyond their years. As the Boulting brothers' principal photography for *The Family Way* trudged forward, the need for a love theme emerged.[13]

With Paul failing to deliver the goods, George was forced to hover over Paul, who sat at the piano in his Cavendish Avenue home, and entreat the Beatle to produce so much as a thread of another musical motif that the producer could expand into a full-blown composition. "I need a wistful little tune," George exclaimed in a moment of frustration with Paul. "You're supposed to be writing the music for this thing, and I'm supposed to be orchestrating it. But to do that I need a tune, and you've got to give me one." Eventually, Paul came through with what George admitted was the germ of "a sweet little fragment of a waltz tune" titled "Love in the Open Air," and he was off to the races. "If it sounds like it was done in a hurry," Martin later pointed out, "it's because it was done in a hurry." Ironically, it would be McCartney who would earn an Ivor Novello Award for Best Instrumental Theme for his work on *The Family Way*. Knowing that McCartney and the Beatles were AIR's most important clients—his rainmakers, in truth—Martin bit his tongue, as he had done many times before. But while George seemed, to the outside world, to be generous to a fault—the kindly tall fellow with the posh accent and a winning smile—he had his limits. Over the years, his colleagues rarely glimpsed the ego at play behind the producer's regal comportment. But occasionally, his feelings of resentment got the better of him. Years later, Abbey Road engineer Ken Scott remembered a moment at the height of Beatlemania when he was waiting on the front stoop of EMI Studios for George to arrive. When he finally showed up, George joined Ken on the studio steps. Together they observed Epstein signing autographs for the phalanx of girls standing vigil just outside the studio gates. "That should be me," said George, as he stared at Brian reveling in the glory of his celebrity.[14]

It was during this same period—as the autumn of 1966 gave way to winter—that the "arms race" at the heart of the contemporary rock scene perceptibly grew even more competitive than it had already been. Like Martin, Lennon had felt tremors in the record business in recent months, remarking to *Beatles Book Monthly* that "I think that within the next couple of years there will be someone very big, perhaps even bigger than us. It might be another group or it might be a solo artist." For his part, George had felt a shift in the industry over the past several months, and he astutely traced it back to Brian Wilson, the Beach Boys, and *Pet Sounds*. As he later remarked, *Pet Sounds* "became the criterion of excellence in our world. His [Wilson's] genius seemingly encompassed everything." With *Pet Sounds*, Martin later observed, Wilson "gave the Beatles and myself quite a good deal to think about in trying to keep up with him." And the Beach Boys weren't the only competition on the horizon. Eric Clapton had formed the rock supergroup

Cream with Jack Bruce and Ginger Baker, while industry stalwarts like the Rolling Stones, the Kinks, and the Who were continuing to up their game. And there were new faces in the mix, including Jimi Hendrix, the American guitar virtuoso who had arrived in London in late September. On November 25, Lennon and McCartney took in Hendrix's lunchtime performance at the Bag O'Nails club. As he showcased such tunes as "Foxey Lady" and "Hey Joe," the two Beatles were blown away by the guitar player's energy and style. When the set concluded, they were the first to congratulate the new kid in town. As Noel Redding later recalled, "Afterwards, in the dressing room, which was like a closet, John Lennon walked in. He said, 'That's grand lads.' Then McCartney walked in and that freaked me out even more." They may have been the first to wish Hendrix well, but they were also clearly on hand to scope out the competition. For Hendrix, the impromptu meeting was the thrill of a lifetime. Like seventy-three million other Americans, he had watched the Beatles' bravura February 1964 performance on *The Ed Sullivan Show*—only in Jimi's case, it had been in the company of the Isley Brothers, for whom he was auditioning to play guitar.[15]

But while they were clearly wowed by the American whiz-kid guitarist, Lennon and McCartney didn't perceive him as a threat. Throughout the production of *Revolver* and beyond, Martin had recognized that "Brian [Wilson] was the musician who challenged them most of all," who beckoned Lennon and McCartney especially to raise the already high level of their artistry and to venture into previously unexplored vistas of creativity. By November 1966, "no one made a bigger impact on the Beatles than Brian," in George's estimation, not even the likes of Elvis Presley, Chuck Berry, or Bob Dylan. By November, the Beach Boys' "Good Vibrations" had finally come home to roost. Released in the United Kingdom back on October 10, the innovative single had risen to the top of the charts in England and America alike. When he first heard the song, Martin knew that in Wilson the Beatles had met their match, and for the moment—as "Good Vibrations" ruled over the airwaves—they may have even been bested by the Californian. After all, Wilson was accomplishing exactly what Martin and the Beatles aspired to do in the studio. To Martin, "Good Vibrations" depicted Wilson in the act of "pushing forward the frontiers of popular music." In the single's grooves, George registered a heightened sense of "instrumental color" merged with "a profound understanding of record production." Years later, Martin would pronounce "Good Vibrations" to be "the greatest single of its day. One of the most remarkable recordings ever. In making it, he [Wilson] developed a brand new style of production. A song in which he stitched together independently recorded themes to make one masterwork." For Martin, even the song's title was a source of inspiration, serving as Wilson's musical imprimatur and defining the essential "spirit behind all his music."[16]

The ramifications of *Pet Sounds* and "Good Vibrations" were felt most acutely by George and the bandmates toward the end of 1966, when the music trade magazines began parceling out their annual awards. *NME* was up first, announcing that "show business will vibrate with the sensational news that the Beatles have been outvoted by the Beach Boys as the World's Outstanding Vocal Group." For his part, Ringo didn't miss a beat, remarking soon thereafter that "we're all four fans of the Beach Boys, maybe we voted for them." Worse yet, Lennon had been unseated as Best British Vocal Personality by none other than Cliff Richard, the one-time beat-music phenom whom Martin and the Beatles had vastly overshadowed for the past several years. In its December issue, *Hit Parader* took things a step further. Having previewed *Smile*, the unfinished, much-ballyhooed follow-up to *Pet Sounds*, the magazine's editors threw down the gauntlet, proclaiming that the Beach Boys were poised not only to eclipse the artistic heights of *Revolver* but to assert their dominion—Wilson's, really—over the whole of the pop world: "The Beach Boys' album *Smile* and single 'Heroes and Villains' will make them the greatest group in the world. We predict they'll take over where the Beatles left off." Back in the United States, *Billboard* took things a step further, proclaiming that the Beach Boys' recent success should be "taken as a portent that the popularity of the top British groups of the last three years is past its peak."[17]

By this point, the Beatles' epitaph had been writ large in entertainment magazines and trade journals across the Western world. In the December 3, 1966, issue of *KRLA Beat*, the question of the Beatles' future seemed to have been rendered moot: "Three years after instigating an entire era, the Beatles are breaking up. At least, that's the consensus among London music observers and those close to the princes of pop. The word came as a whisper at first, but subsequent statements by Brian Epstein and the Beatles themselves have given the speculation certainty."[18]

In those pre-Internet, pre–mass communication days, the insiders among the industry who had foretold the band's demise might have been surprised by the goings on at 3 Abbey Road on the evening of Thursday, November 24, the day that George and the Beatles quietly reconvened after a five-month absence. The idea, at first, was that they would be recording tracks for an as-of-yet untitled new long-player. According to Harrison, the bandmates had privately chosen the session date several weeks earlier but strategically had shared it with no one outside of their inner circle. But now it was time to get back to work. While they were no doubt cognizant of "Good Vibrations" and the Beach Boys' apotheosis as their heir apparent, Martin and the bandmates were never lacking the confidence to plow forward. And they were competitive to a fault, seeing "Good Vibrations" as a direct challenge. The greatest single of its day, huh? The Beatles would have a thing or two to say about that.

9

A WISTFUL LITTLE TUNE

YEARS LATER, MARTIN WOULD CAST the November 24, 1966, session as a turning point for his work with the Beatles, as a moment in which they took full advantage of the considerable goodwill that they had earned from EMI and transformed the studio into the magical workshop of which George had long dreamed. As Martin later observed, "The time had come for experiment. The Beatles knew it, and I knew it. By November 1966, we had had an enormous string of hits, and we had the confidence, even arrogance, to know that we could try anything we wanted. The sales we had achieved would have justified our recording rubbish, if we had wanted to. But then, we wouldn't have got away with foisting rubbish on the public for long." With their latest single and album having been issued in August, George felt that the time was nigh. "It was several months since we had been in the studio, and time for us to think about a new album. 'New' was certainly how it was to turn out," said George. In retrospect, he later recalled, "I suppose the indications were already there. 'Eleanor Rigby' and 'Tomorrow Never Knows,' from *Revolver*, had been strong hints for those with ears to hear what was to come. They were forerunners of a complete change of style." And of course, there was the looming matter of the Beach Boys' evolving arms race with the Beatles. It was, in George's words, "a curious transatlantic slugging match, a rivalry conducted by means of song-writing and recording genius." As he later recalled, "The Beatles thought *Pet Sounds*, its vocal harmonies in particular, was a fantastic album. I thought it was great, too. 'Could we do as well as that?' they asked me, in the run-up to their own new long-player. 'No,' I replied. 'We can do better.'"[1]

But George and the Beatles' stylistic paradigm shift didn't simply commence with one session. As with their work since their earliest days together, it began with a single composition—in this instance, the dreamlike tune that John had begun composing back in Almería. Now going by the title of "Strawberry Fields Forever," the fragment had grown from John's crude structure back in Spain into a series of progressively more structured demo recordings. The November 24 session began at seven that evening with the Beatles, Martin, Geoff Emerick, and Phil McDonald huddled around the Studio 2 console. Years later, Emerick recalled the sight of the Beatles, having changed utterly, as they sauntered into the control room. "It had been five months since I'd last seen the group, but it might as well have been five years. For one thing, they all looked so different. Garbed in colorful clothes and sporting trendy mustaches—George Harrison even had a beard—they were utterly hip, the epitome of swinging London." But it was John who really caught Geoff's eye: "John was the one who had changed the most: having shed the excess weight he'd put on during the *Revolver* sessions, he was trim, almost gaunt, and he was wearing granny glasses instead of the thick horn-rimmed National Health spectacles I was used to seeing. He also had very short, distinctly non-Beatlish hair."[2]

But before Martin could go about the business of "routining" any new compositions that the bandmates had ready that evening, Lennon interrupted the proceedings. It was not only clear that John had something to say but that the Beatles had had a number of private conversations about the band's future—and if there was going to be one, what kind of band they wanted to be. In Geoff's memory, John seemed "agitated" as he took the floor. Even after all these years, when push came to shove, it was John who took the lead. "Look," he said to the Beatles' producer, "it's really quite simple. We're fed up with making soft music for soft people, and we're fed up with playing for them, too. But it's given us a fresh start, don't you see?" As George looked on, Geoff could tell that he was surprised by John's unexpected torrent of passion. "We can't hear ourselves onstage anymore for all the screaming," Paul added, "so what's the point? We did try performing some songs off the last album, but there are so many complicated overdubs we can't do them justice. Now we can record anything we want, and it won't matter. And what we want is to raise the bar a notch, to make our best album ever." Now George was beginning to understand. "What we're saying is, if we don't have to tour, then we can record music that we won't ever have to play live, and that means we can create something that's never been heard before: a new kind of record with new kinds of sounds."[3]

From George's perspective, the November 24 session was already a veritable dream come true. He had long feared that touring would, quite literally, be the death of the band, realizing how vulnerable they were on a tiny stage amid a sea of people. He knew that they suffered from "hotel fatigue" on the road, that their celebrity had become nothing more than a "prison of fame." And the notion that they wanted to continue pushing the boundaries, fearless about the consequences and willing to go wherever their music might take them—well, that was music to George's ears. "When I first started in the music business the ultimate aim for everybody was to try and re-create, on record, a live performance as accurately as possible," Martin later recalled. "But then, we realized that we could do something other than that. In other words, the film doesn't just re-create the stage play. So, without being too pompous, we decided to go into another kind of art form, where we are devising something that couldn't be done any other way. We were putting something down on tape that could only be done on tape." With Lennon's words still ringing in his ears, Martin was ready and willing to take this newfangled and refreshingly arrogant Beatles out for a spin.[4]

And with that, the producer delivered his usual call to action with the Beatles in the studio: "Right, then, let's get to work. What have you got for me?" As Emerick later recalled, McCartney seemed to be on the verge of piping up, when Lennon shouted, "I've got a good one, for a starter!" As Emerick and McDonald readied themselves up in the control booth, the others took their place below in Studio 2. Martin took his customary perch on a tall stool in front of Lennon, who began singing "Strawberry Fields Forever" for the very first time at Abbey Road. "John was standing in front of me, his acoustic guitar at the ready," George later wrote. "This was his usual way of showing me a new song—another of my extremely privileged private performances. 'It goes something like this, George,' he said, with a nonchalance that concealed his ingrained diffidence about his voice. Then he began strumming gently. That wonderfully distinctive voice had a slight tremor, a unique nasal quality that gave his song poignancy, almost a feeling of luminescence." Martin was thunderstruck. "It was a very gentle song when I first heard it," he later recalled. "It was spellbinding. His lyrics painted a hazy, impressionistic world. I was in love with what I heard. All I had to do was record it." If only it would be so simple. Any notion of producing the song with John singing solo along with his guitar, à la Paul's "Yesterday," was out the window almost immediately. For his part, McCartney was just as smitten as Martin, breathlessly telling his songwriting partner, "That is absolutely brilliant." As Emerick later recalled, Lennon was keen to share his demo recording, although his efforts fell on deaf ears: "'I've brought a demo tape of the song with me, too,' John said, offering to play it, but everyone agreed there was no need—they wanted to get straight into recording. The energy in the room was staggering: it was almost as if the band's creative energies had been bottled up for too long."[5]

Drawing its name from an aging Salvation Army home near Lennon's boyhood haunts back in Liverpool, "Strawberry Fields Forever" began shaping up very quickly, with Martin and the bandmates already devising an arrangement for the song as Emerick and McDonald waited in the control room upstairs. As was their practice, they began compiling a basic rhythm track, which featured Paul playing the Mellotron Mark II with the flute stop deployed. Mal Evans had helpfully brought the keyboard instrument to Abbey Road from John's Weybridge estate. The Mellotron had already figured prominently in the composition of two Lennon-McCartney songs, "In My Life" and "Tomorrow Never Knows."

The Beatles rounded out the basic track for "Strawberry Fields Forever" with Harrison and Lennon on their guitars. With Lennon playing rhythm guitar on his Gibson Jumbo, Harrison provided lead guitar accents on his Sonic Blue Fender Stratocaster. Meanwhile, Starr got into the act of experimenting with new sounds by arranging tea towels over the drum heads on his snare and tom-toms. With the towels in place, his drumming took on a distinctive muffled tonality. After recording the first take of the basic track with this arrangement, Martin captured Lennon's first pass at the lead vocals, which was later treated with ADT, along with Harrison and McCartney providing harmonies. For John's vocal, George instructed Geoff to roll the tape fast at fifty-three cycles per second in order to create the illusion of a faster tempo on replay. By the time the session ended at 2:30 AM, Martin and the bandmates had created an exquisite first attempt at the song. Indeed, George felt they already captured the best possible recording in a single, magical take. "That first take is brilliant, especially John's vocal: clear, pure, and riveting," Martin later wrote. "As he sang it that night, the song became hypnotic, gentle and wistful, but very strong too, his sparse vocal standing in sharp contrast to the full sound of George's electric guitar, Paul's imaginative Mellotron, and Ringo's magnificent drums."[6]

But Lennon felt differently, believing that more work had to be done, that "Strawberry Fields Forever" wasn't quite there yet. Even years later, George struggled to understand how the bandmates' very first recording of "Strawberry Fields Forever" had succeeded so powerfully in capturing his own imagination yet at the same time failing to seize John's in even remotely the same way. As George later wrote, the mystery at the heart of any work of art exists at an elemental level for each of us: "I am not sure how much cold-blooded analysis has to do with one's passion for a work of art. It is a bit like falling in love. Do we really care if there is the odd wrinkle here or there? The power to move people, to tears or laughter, to violence or sympathy, is the strongest attribute that any art can have. In this respect, music is the prime mover: its call on the emotions is the most direct of all the arts."[7]

Martin recognized that "Strawberry Fields Forever" was not merely situating the Beatles on the precipice of new soundscapes but on whole new vistas of composition. "It was the beginning of the imaginative, some say psychedelic, way of writing," he later remarked. "I prefer to think of it as being complete tone poem imagery, and it's more like a modern Debussy." By invoking Claude Debussy—the "heavenly" composer who had left a powerful imprint on fifteen-year-old George's schoolboy mind—the producer had granted "Strawberry Fields Forever" the highest possible compliment that he could muster. Indeed, it is difficult to imagine finer praise coming from George.[8]

But as it turned out, additional work on the exciting new song would have to wait until the following week. The next day, Friday, November 25, the Beatles had been booked to record their annual Christmas message. With George in tow, the bandmates traveled across town to Dick James's office on New Oxford Street. Working in the music publisher's basement studio, they hammered things up, recording a series of skits. As Ringo later recalled, they concocted their 1966 Christmas narrative on the spot: "We worked it out between us. Paul did most of the work on it. He thought up the *Pantomime* title and the two song things." Prepared for later distribution to members of the UK Beatles fan club, the disc would be adorned with cover art by McCartney and titled as *Pantomime: Everywhere It's Christmas*. With Martin and Epstein in the control room, the Beatles performed a series of skits, including "Podgy the Bear and Jasper" and "Felpin Mansions." With McCartney on piano accompaniment and Mal Evans and Neil Aspinall providing additional voices, the group sings such hastily improvised compositions as "Everywhere It's Christmas," "Orowainya," and "Please Don't Bring Your Banjo Back." On December 2, *Pantomime: Everywhere It's Christmas* was mixed for released in EMI Studios' Room 53, with Tony Barrow sitting in for Martin and Emerick serving as balance engineer. The recording was distributed to UK fans on December 16.[9]

With their annual holiday chore out of the way for another year, George and the bandmates returned to Studio 2 on Monday, November 28, for another overnight session. Realizing that they were badly in need of a new Beatles release, EMI was happy to grant the Beatles all the time and space the band felt they needed. As Ringo observed at the time, "We're big with EMI at the moment. They don't argue if we take the time we want." For his part, George was all too familiar with the breakneck pace of their past projects. If they really were abandoning the road—if he no longer had to book sessions in the nooks and crannies that Brian Epstein allotted him between concert dates and public appearances—then he intended to take full advantage of the bandmates' availability. When George and the Beatles got to work that evening, they remade "Strawberry Fields Forever" with a slightly different arrangement, notable for a telling shift into the lower key of A major. The shift in key signature would prove to have significant implications for the ultimate direction of the song. With Paul again working the Mellotron with the flute stop toggled, take two saw the Beatles beginning to establish a proper rhythm track. With the same instrumentation in play—save for the addition of maracas—take two collapsed under the weight of several guitar misfires on Harrison's part. Take three stalled after John complained that Paul's Mellotron introduction was too loud. For the moment at least, take four was selected as the best. Including Harrison's guitar work, the basic rhythm track featured a newly recorded slowed-down vocal from Lennon and McCartney's overdubbed bass part. As Martin later recalled, "Typically, John asked me for a speed change on his vocal recording. I thought his voice was one of the all-time greats, but he was always asking me to distort or bend it in some way, to 'improve' it as he thought. So when we overdubbed his vocal, we pumped up the tape frequency to 53 hertz instead of the normal 50 hertz. On playback at normal speed, the adjustment lowered his voice by a semitone, making it sound warmer and huskier." At the session's conclusion, Martin and Emerick prepared three mono mixes for the purpose of creating acetates so that the Beatles could reflect on their progress at home. But by this point, George and the bandmates knew that "Strawberry Fields Forever" was not quite there. And to John's mind, it wasn't even close.[10]

On Tuesday, November 29, Martin and the group worked an afternoon session in Studio 2 that sprawled until eight that evening during which the band remade the rhythm track yet again. By this point, they were satisfied with the arrangement and the instrumentation; they simply hadn't captured the best performance yet. "I thought our baby was perfect," George later recalled, but "over that weekend, however, fertile imaginations went to work, and by the time we arrived for that session on Monday, it was obvious that John and Paul had come up with plenty of ideas on how to improve 'Strawberry Fields Forever.'" In the same vein as the producer's suggestion in earlier years that they begin songs like "She Loves You" and "Can't Buy Me Love" with the chorus, Lennon and McCartney had reconfigured the beginning of "Strawberry Fields Forever." "It was a good move," Martin later wrote, "because the lyric now immediately grabbed you by the throat. The song made you share an intriguing journey." After several hours of rehearsal, take six seemed to be the answer, including a lengthy coda, to which Lennon appended an ADT-treated vocal and McCartney adorned a bass line on his Rickenbacker. After enacting vocal and Mellotron overdubs, Martin and Emerick created three mono mixes—again, for acetate purposes. But as things began to wind down that evening, Geoff could tell that John was still far from happy with their results, that the song still wasn't quite where he wanted it to be. As he later wrote, "John seemed to be having a lot of trouble making up his mind about how he wanted the song recorded."[11]

As it happened, Lennon would have nearly ten days to mull things over and reconsider the direction of "Strawberry Fields Forever." When Martin and the group reconvened for what turned out to be an overnight session on Tuesday, December 6, they tackled yet another new composition—although in this case, it was a song that McCartney had begun back in 1958. With his father, Jim, having turned sixty-four on July 2, 1966, Paul may have revisited the composition titled "When I'm Sixty-Four" in his honor. The tune had occasionally featured in the Beatles' prefame days playing lunchtime concerts in Liverpool's Cavern Club—and often when they suffered from amplifier breakdowns or other equipment failures. As George later wrote, "The song had been lurking around in Paul's mind for a long, long time, ever since I first knew him." He was especially fond of the lyrics: "When I heard 'When I'm Sixty-Four' for the first time, I chuckled at the cleverness of the lyrics," Martin wrote. "It was an affectionate satire regarding old age from a young man's point of view."[12]

Before they tried their hand at recording "When I'm Sixty-Four," George led the bandmates through the production of Christmas greetings recorded expressly for the United Kingdom's pirate radio set. As an alternative to the BBC's broadcast monopoly—not to mention the network's demure programming—pirate radio stations like Radio Caroline and Radio London broadcast across Great Britain from their moorings beyond the coastline. With Martin and his production team in the Studio 2 control room supervising the recording of dozens of messages for the listeners and staffs of Radio Caroline and

Radio London, the group—McCartney, in particular—began experimenting with various instruments and sound effects. Eventually, McCartney asked the Beatles' producer to overlay their messages with tape echo, to which Martin sarcastically replied, "Do you want to make a production out of it?" Harrison continued the joke, saying "Yeah, let's double-track everything!" As if mocking Martin and the bandmates' increasing penchant for treating their vocals and instrumentation with studio effects, Lennon piped up next, remarking that Martin "can double-splange them. That'd be great!"[13]

For "When I'm Sixty-Four," George led the bandmates—namely, Paul—through their standard rehearsal with the tape running. As they attempted to capture the basic rhythm track, Paul worked on piano and bass parts, with Ringo playing brushes on his snare. Two takes were completed, with take two being selected as the best. Two days later, during an afternoon session on Thursday, December 8, work continued on "When I'm Sixty-Four" without the other Beatles present. With Martin and Emerick up in the booth, McCartney continued working on take two as he tried his hand at recording a lead vocal for the snappy vaudeville number. As the dinner hour approached, Martin and Emerick took their leave. Hence, when Paul and the other Beatles arrived at seven that evening for another one of their famous overnight sessions, George and Geoff were no longer in evidence. As technical engineer Dave Harries later recalled, Martin and Emerick "had tickets for the premiere of Cliff Richard's film *Finders Keepers* and didn't arrive back until about 11 o'clock." After having ensured that the group's microphones and instruments were lined up properly, Harries was surprised when "the Beatles arrived, hot to record." With no other choice—and a quartet of EMI's most valuable clients at the ready—Harries supervised the bandmates as they took another go at establishing the rhythm track for "Strawberry Fields Forever." "There was nobody else there but me so I became producer/engineer," Harries remembered. "We recorded Ringo's cymbals, played them backwards, Paul and George were on timps [timpani] and bongos, Mal Evans played tambourine, we overdubbed the guitars, everything. It sounded great. When George and Geoff came back, I scuttled upstairs because I shouldn't really have been recording them." But of course, he never really had any other viable option. By this point in their career, the Beatles weren't waiting for anyone. Not even Martin.[14]

For his part, Emerick had been bothered that Martin wanted to attend the premiere in the first place. "George was quite adamant that we go, which really annoyed me," he later wrote. "I felt our place was with the Beatles, and I felt certain that they were going to be unhappy about us taking time off so early into an album project. In retrospect, I think it may have been a psychological ploy on George's part to show them who was in charge." If it had indeed been a psychological ploy—rather than Martin simply wanting to be seen at a major industry event, especially given the new startup he was spearheading—it failed miserably. If Martin had wanted to attend simply to enjoy the film, he was likely severely disappointed. Directed by Sidney Hayers, *Finders Keepers* was roundly panned. Like Gerry and the Pacemakers' big-screen bomb, *Ferry Cross the Mersey*, back in 1965, *Finders Keepers* proved that rock musicals in the wake of the Beatles' *A Hard Day's Night* feature film almost inevitably seemed like pale imitations of the Fab Four's natural wit and incomparable sound. Still, *A Hard Day's Night*—which had premiered some eighteen months earlier—seemed like a distant memory in comparison with the Beatles of December 1966, who scarcely resembled their former selves both outwardly and artistically.

After the movie, the producer and his engineer returned to Studio 2, "only to find the four Beatles still hard at work with maintenance engineer Dave Harries," Emerick wrote, "who had been recruited to start the session in our absence. In the end, only part of what he recorded ever made its way onto the final release version; George and I stayed on until nearly dawn and ended up redoing most of it." For his part, Martin had been stunned by the scene that greeted him that night:

> When Geoff and I strolled in, Studio 2 was in the grip of a controlled riot. The boys had decided it would be fun to lay down an "unusual" rhythm track for "Strawberry Fields Forever" on their own, with anyone and everyone available simply banging away on whatever came to hand. The racket as we walked in was like something from a very bad Tarzan movie. John and Paul were bashing bongo drums, George was on huge kettledrums, joined sporadically by Paul; Neil Aspinall was playing a gourd scraper, Mal Evans a tambourine, and George's friend Terry Doran was shaking maracas. Somebody else was tinkling away on finger cymbals. Above it all, Ringo was struggling manfully to keep the cacophony together with his regular drum-kit.[15]

In fact, during the producer's absence, the bandmates had worked out a number of issues with the structure associated with "Strawberry Fields Forever." It was John who piped up first, eager to share what they had learned—and seemingly oblivious to George and Geoff's absence. While the heart of the band's production team had been away in Central London, Harries led the Beatles through fifteen additional takes—takes nine through twenty-four—as they continued to refine the rhythm track. At this point, Lennon and his mates selected fifteen and twenty-four—two different, incomplete versions of the song—as the best.

As he and Emerick cleaned up shop in the wee hours of Friday, December 9, Martin replayed the recordings from that evening's "controlled riot." He discovered that he was particularly keen on a section "towards the end of this rogue track," he later wrote, where "everyone was whooping or yelling, and John can clearly be heard chanting very slowly, and in time to the rough-and-ready beat: 'Cranberry sauce, cranberry sauce . . .' Why cranberry sauce? *Why* not? It was coming up to Christmas!" Perhaps this aspect of that "wild and wacky recording" would be of use at some later juncture.[16]

By 2:30 that same afternoon, Martin and the Beatles were already back at work in Studio 2. With "Strawberry Fields Forever" continuing to chew up plenty of real estate, Martin and Emerick dealt with the inherent limitations of four-track recording by mixing down the edit of takes fifteen and twenty-four and reducing them to a single track, which was dubbed as take twenty-five. With three empty tracks at their disposal, Martin and the bandmates provided a series of overdubs. Track two was composed of Starr playing various percussion, along with Harrison playing a swarmandal. After preparing a mono mix to facilitate new acetates, additional overdubs were carried out, including the recording of backward cymbals. Not unlike the backward guitar solos on *Revolver*'s "I'm Only Sleeping," capturing the cymbals on tape was fraught with difficulty. Breaking out pencil and paper, Martin and Emerick worked out the song's structural pattern so as to ensure that the backward cymbals were synchronized in the appropriate instances.

In the intervening days before the next session for "Strawberry Fields Forever" commenced, Lennon sought out Martin to express his disappointment over the song's progress at this juncture. For his part, George was astounded, having felt that the song had already been exquisite back on November 24. With Emerick waiting in the wings, Lennon told the Beatles' producer that "he still wasn't entirely happy with what we had done," Martin later wrote. "The song kept eluding him: he could hear what he wanted, in his head, but he couldn't make it real." As the others attempted to reassure him, John "kept mumbling, 'I don't know; I just think it should somehow be heavier,'" according to Geoff. As Martin questioned the Beatle about his concept of heaviness, Lennon replied, "I dunno, just kind of, y'know . . . heavier." At this point, McCartney interceded. Observing how pleased John had been with the

Mellotron flute stops, Paul suggested that orchestral ornamentation might be an option for beefing up the sound of "Strawberry Fields Forever." Quite suddenly, John's enthusiasm had returned. He was particularly taken with the idea of cello and trumpet accompaniment for the song. All the producer had to do was come up with the appropriate score. "Do a good job, George," John instructed as he left the control room. "Just make sure it's heavy."[17]

With only a few days to spare, Martin went about the business of organizing the instrumental accompaniment for "Strawberry Fields Forever." As usual, George booked a powerhouse of session aces when it came to securing studio musicians for the Beatles. For the purposes of his trumpet quartet, George selected Greg Bowen, Tony Fisher, and Stanley Roderick, the players who had made their name as the "007" trumpet section for the early James Bond films. Rounding out the brass was Derek Watkins, late of Billy Ternent's London Palladium orchestra. Martin's trio of cellists was composed of John Hall, Norman Jones, and Derek Simpson, a long-standing member of the renowned Aeolian Quartet. Knowing that he needed to concoct something "heavy," Martin set straight to work. "I believe in economy in music," he later wrote, "to get a clarity that using too many instruments will sometimes cloud. I had less than a week to write the score that John was looking for. I knew he wanted the brass to be bright and punchy, but I felt the chords needed a bit of reinforcement on some of the changes." As he worked at the piano at the home he shared with Judy on Manchester Square, George consulted the latest "Strawberry Fields Forever" acetates. As he later recalled, "Having a basic recorded track to write to was a great advantage. It meant I could see where to put the flesh on the bones. I decided the cellos should speak with one voice, in unison, forming a bass counterpoint to the melody. The trumpets I wrote either in simple triad (i.e., three-finger) chords, or with a unison staccato emphasis, blasting away on one note."[18]

For the purposes of inspiration, George drew from the quintessentially American sound that had stirred the Beatles so vividly prior to beginning work on *Revolver*. In addition to concocting a punchy brass score, he found himself confounded by the backward cymbals that he and the bandmates had appended to the latest version of the song. With his own penchant for experimentation on full display, George decided to score the cellos in contrast with Ringo's percussion: "I confess I had heard a lot of American records with very groovy horn sections by this time, and lifted one or two ideas from them," he later wrote. "As the song developed further it seemed natural to use the trumpets as a harmony behind the voice, sounding the same phrase as in our lovely intro. Then came the only section I had qualms about. At this particular point, the tempo is held together by a fast rhythm from a cymbal that Ringo recorded backwards—never an easy sound to latch on to. The cellos worked against this urgent beat with a slower, triplet tie motif, and I was not at all sure that it was going to work." As he completed work on his orchestration for "Strawberry Fields Forever," George was forced to contend with a long-standing issue that he had observed throughout the song's labyrinthine production: the Mellotron's tape-replay system had proven to be idiosyncratic in terms of maintaining a steady pace, so much so, in fact, that with "Strawberry Fields Forever," "our rhythm track would vary even from one bar to another!" This presented a problem, of course, when it came to studio musicians, who understandably "take it for granted that if they are overdubbing, their basic track never varies its tempo." For this reason, George "felt that Ringo's drumming on this song is some of his best. His quirky figures accented it in exactly the right way from the outset, complementing John's phrases beautifully throughout all the changes the song underwent."[19]

When George and the bandmates reconvened on December 15, they were joined by the trumpeters and cellists for an afternoon session in Studio 2. Scored in the key of C major, Martin's orchestration was captured in short order and superimposed on the available third and fourth tracks. At this point, Emerick conducted another tape reduction mix, with take twenty-five becoming take twenty-six. For the remainder of the session, which finally broke up around midnight, additional overdubs were undertaken, including Lennon's double-tracked lead vocal and Harrison performing descending arpeggios on the swarmandal. The remnant of Lennon muttering "cranberry sauce" from the madcap December 8 session was in evidence, having been earlier spliced onto the end of take twenty-four. The latest remake of "Strawberry Fields Forever," with the "heavy" orchestration, Ringo's powerful, rhythmic drums, and Lennon's newly minted lead vocals, offered a dramatic contrast to the original, gentler November 24 version of the song. For the time being at least, "Strawberry Fields Forever" seemed to be on the verge of completion.

For the next few days, the studio went dark for George and the Beatles. Martin and McCartney were attending to business involving *The Family Way*, which premiered on the evening of Sunday, December 18, at London's Warner Theatre. The film enjoyed generally strong notices for being "sincere" and "sympathetic"—especially in comparison with the Boulting brothers' earlier movies, including the satirical *I'm All Right, Jack* starring Peter Sellers, which were known for their irreverence. McCartney and Martin's soundtrack received praise for contributing to the film's "understated" tone. On December 23, United Artists released the single "Love in the Open Air" backed with

"Theme from *The Family Way*." Credited to the George Martin Orchestra, the record didn't chart. Earlier that day, Lennon and McCartney had been shocked to learn that their friend Tara Browne, the twenty-one-year-old heir to the Guinness fortune, had succumbed to injuries that he had suffered the previous evening in an Earl's Court automobile accident. With his girlfriend, Suki Potier, by his side, Browne had been speeding in his Lotus Elan through the narrow streets of the city when he swerved to avoid an oncoming car and collided with a parked truck. The next day, December 19, saw a swathe of posters being affixed around the city advertising the upcoming *Million Volt Light and Sound Rave*. Scheduled for January 28, 1967, the festival's centerpiece would be a psychedelic light show by Ray Anderson and music by Unit Delta Plus, a freelance outfit associated with the BBC's Radiophonic Workshop, the same folks who had worked with George (using the pseudonym Ray Cathode) to produce his 1962 electronic concoction "Time Beat." The poster for the *Million Volt Light and Sound Rave* made note of a special musical piece composed by none other than Paul McCartney.

On Tuesday, December 20, George and the Beatles returned to the friendly confines of Studio 2, where they resumed working on "When I'm Sixty-Four," which had been abandoned since December 6. With the Beach Boys' avant-garde hit "Good Vibrations" nearing the end of its thirteen-week assault on the British charts, the Beatles began putting the finishing touches on the vaudeville-throwback number. During the overnight session, McCartney, Harrison, and Lennon superimposed harmony vocals onto "When I'm Sixty-Four," with Starr providing bell sounds to accent the verses. Afterward, Martin and his regular production team of Emerick and McDonald carried out two reduction mixes from take two, with the second being selected as the best. The next day, Wednesday, December 21, George made great strides toward the completion of "When I'm Sixty-Four" with a woodwind overdub courtesy of a trio of studio musicians. Working a two-hour session in Studio 1 that evening, Martin had prepared a score for two clarinets and one bass clarinet. The idea for the clarinet arrangement had apparently been McCartney's brainchild as an effort to mitigate the possibility that "When I'm Sixty-Four" would be taken as an unwelcome departure into corniness. As George later observed, "Paul got some way round the lurking schmaltz factor by suggesting we use clarinets on the recording 'in a classical way.'" With Paul's recommendation in hand, George set about the business of composing the score. He took McCartney's dictum seriously, appropriating his orchestration as a means for shaping the composition's larger thematic impetus. As Martin later observed, "The classical treatment gave added bite to the song, a formality that pushed it firmly towards satire. Without that, the song could have been misinterpreted—it was very tongue-in-cheek."[20]

Drawing upon his many years of experience as an arranger—not to mention his formal training at the Guildhall School—"When I'm Sixty-Four" offers a primer for understanding the manner in which Martin approached the art of crafting a score: "The arrangement of this song is deceptively simple, but in a way it underlines my constant belief in simplicity in orchestration," George later wrote. "By restricting ourselves to three instruments only," he pointed out, "we could hardly be lush. Every note played had to be there for a purpose." With his score complete, George once again recruited London's finest to perform on a Beatles record. As with his work throughout *Revolver*, George never slacked when it came to providing the Beatles with the best available talent. As he later wrote, "We overdubbed two clarinets and a bass clarinet on to track 2, played by the best clarinet players you could get in the business then: Robert Burns, Henry MacKenzie, and Frank Reidy." Years later, Martin recalled recording the woodwind overdub in the "cavernous Number One studio at Abbey Road and thinking how the three clarinet players looked as lost as a referee and two linesmen alone in the middle of Wembley Stadium." After the studio players departed, George supervised three mono mixes of "When I'm Sixty-Four." At this point, the third attempt was considered the best, although merely for acetate purposes. But in terms of George and the Beatles' standards, the song wasn't quite there yet.[21]

They could easily have said the same about "Strawberry Fields Forever," which had dominated the Beatles' return to the studio since November. During the December 21 session, Lennon recorded his lead vocal yet again while also superimposing another piano track. It was sometime during this period—with only a few days before Martin and the bandmates briefly closed up shop for the holidays—that Lennon dropped a veritable bomb on the producer and his production team. Apparently, he had been listening to the acetates in heavy rotation, and a eureka moment had occurred. As George later wrote, "John could not make up his mind which of our performances he preferred. He had long since dismissed the original statement of the song on take 7, and was now torn between the slow, contemplative version and the frantic, percussive powerhouse cello and brass arrangement of take 20." From his position at the mixing desk, Emerick watched the conversation as it unfolded. As he looked on, John announced, "I've decided that I still prefer the beginning of the original version." The Beatles' engineer could hardly believe what he was hearing: "My jaw dropped. Out of the corner of my eye, I could see George Martin blinking slowly. I could almost detect his blood pressure rising." And that's when John said it, turning to George and remarking, "I like them both. Why don't we join them together? You could start with take 7 and move to take 20 halfway through to get the grandstand finish." Years later, Martin would remember his response with an unusual clarity, not to mention the mocking tone with which he delivered it. "Brilliant!" he retorted. "There are only two things wrong with that: the takes are in completely different keys, a whole tone apart, and they have wildly different tempos. Other than that, there should be no problem!" For his part, Lennon was hardly put off in the slightest. As George later recalled, "John smiled at my sarcasm like a grownup placating a child." And then he stared up at the Beatles' producer with a twinkle in his eye: "Well, George, I'm sure you can fix it, can't you?"[22]

And so it was that on the evening of Thursday, December 22, Martin, Emerick, and McDonald conducted an editing session in Studio 2 in an effort, impossible as it may have seemed at the time, to meet the extraordinary challenge inherent in Lennon's demands. "Every time I go on about the primitive state of recording technology in the mid-sixties," George later wrote, "I feel like Baron von Richthofen describing the Fokker Triplane to a group of Concorde pilots. But it must be said that nothing on the technology front existed, at EMI's Abbey Road studios anyways, that could help us out of this fix." Martin and his team definitely had their work cut out for them: "There was no way those two performances could be matched," Martin lamented. But then he realized "that because take 20, the frenetic take, was faster—much faster—I could try slowing the tape right down. This would not only bring down the tempo, it would lower the pitch. Would it work? A whole tone was one hell of a drop—almost 12 percent—but it had to be worth trying." With little genuine hope of actually making Lennon's dream a reality, Martin turned to Ken Townsend, the ingenious father of ADT, to see what might be possible:

> We called up our magnificent band of backroom boys, who wheeled in a Diplodocus-sized washing machine lookalike: the "frequency changer." This valve-powered monster—a lash-up devised by Ken Townsend, our Chief Engineer, and his merry men—took the main electricity supply, and bent the alternating current up and down on either side of the normal 50 cycles per second. Don't ask me how they did it, I haven't a clue. What I can tell you is that it used to get very hot, and would explode in a shower of sparks if you stretched it too far. But it was all we had. We

hooked it up. We were looking for a point in the song where there was a sound change, which would help us disguise the edit of the century.

To their great relief, Martin and his team managed to expose the one moment in "Strawberry Fields Forever" that might just do it.[23]

And there it was. "We found it precisely one minute in," George later observed, the surprise and relief still evident in his voice even decades later. But when it came to effecting the actual edit itself, Geoff realized that "there was still one last hurdle to overcome. I found that I couldn't cut the tape at a normal 45-degree angle because the sound just kind of jumped—I was, after all, joining together two totally different performances. As a result, I had to make the cut at a very shallow angle so that it was more like a crossfade than a splice." With the edit having been completed, the team turned their attention to the coda, including the "cranberry sauce" bit that the Beatles had recorded outside of Martin and Emerick's earshot back on December 8. Not wanting to lose the magnificent cacophony that the bandmates had created during that zany evening, George instructed Geoff to fade out "Strawberry Fields Forever" before it all went berserk, the moment when the structure collapses in on itself and falls to pieces. The producer was equally intent on preserving the waning instances of orchestration that they had captured back on December 15. "The obvious answer," Martin later wrote, "would have been to fade out the take before the beat goes haywire. But that would have meant discarding one of my favorite bits, which included some great trumpet and guitar playing, as well as the magical random Mellotronic note-waterfall John had come up with. It was a section brimming with energy, and I was determined to keep it." But in the end, George did just that: he asked Geoff to begin the fade-out at the last possible moment, and in so doing, he managed to preserve the unique moments of orchestration, sizzling musicianship, and impromptu zaniness. But just as suddenly, George instructed Geoff to abruptly reverse the fade-out and usher "Strawberry Fields Forever" back from the dead. It was George's sonic head-fake: just when listeners believe that the song is over, it comes roaring back to life again, "bringing back our glorious finale," "one final exotic touch of color" before the whole thing fades into oblivion once more. With the edit complete and the coda alive and well in all its madcap splendor, "Strawberry Fields Forever" was, for the first time, relatively complete. With the edited piece now in place, George had seen to it that John's seemingly impossible wish had been granted. And as for that miraculous edit itself, Golden Ears had done it again.[24]

In production circles, of course, the proof is in the playback. And for John, "Strawberry Fields Forever" was an unqualified success. Indeed, he was ecstatic with the result, having finally heard his vision captured on tape, for the most part, as it had evolved over the past month. George had performed precisely as the Beatle had expected, so John wasn't really all that surprised at how it had materialized so effectively. "With the grace of God, and a bit of luck, we did it," Martin later observed. They were able to effect the join between the two versions by gradually increasing the speed of take seven in order to create the illusion of a seamless transition. In fact, most listeners find themselves unable to distinguish the moment where the join occurs. For Martin, this bit of studio trickery never ceased to amaze him in terms of capturing the illusion. "That's funny," he later remarked. "I can hear it every time. It sticks out like a sore thumb to me." The most curious students of the Beatles will find themselves wanting to listen carefully to this moment in the song—some sixty seconds in, right after John sings "let me take you down"—to hear the magic moment that forever joined the two sections. "But seek it out at your peril," Beatles historian Mark Lewisohn cautions, "if you hear it once you might never hear the song the same way again."[25]

For George, John's satisfaction made the glaring edit piece worth it. And while the producer had felt that the magic inherent in "Strawberry Fields Forever" had been fully realized on November 24, the final product was something to behold. "We were all very proud of our new baby," he later wrote. "For my money, it was the most original and inventive track to date in pop music." *To date*, that is. In any event, it was becoming increasingly clear to Martin and his team that the *Revolver*-era Beatles were already morphing into something new and different in these rapidly unfolding post-touring days. The freedom to do what they liked in the studio—and for as long as they wanted—was liberating their collective creative instincts. And not merely for the bandmates, who were relieved to no longer be contending with the often unchecked, unexpected rigors of life on the road. That very same sense of freedom had transformed George and Geoff's approach to their sessions: at this point, they could allow an idea to unfold and flower at its pace, as opposed to rushing from one session to another to satisfy the demands of EMI or, worse yet, to cram in as many recording dates as possible in the face of a looming tour schedule. As he was wont to do, George compared their latest studio practices to the act of painting—particularly in terms of the ways in which artists very deliberately bring their work alive through layers of time, effort, and creative fusion. As George later observed:

The way we worked, the creative process we always went through, reminds me of a film I once saw of Picasso at work, painting on a ground-glass screen. A camera photographed his brushwork from behind the screen, so that the paint appeared as if by magic. Using time-lapse photography you could see first his original construction, then complete change as he applied the next layer of paint, then the whole thing revitalized again as he added here, took away there. It reached a point where you thought, "That's wonderful, for heaven's sake stop!" But he didn't, he went on, and on. Eventually, he laid down his brush, satisfied. Or was he? I wondered how many of his paintings he would have wanted to do again. It was a fascinating film of a great artist, of a brilliant creative mind at work. And I have often thought how similar his method of painting was to our way of recording. We, too, would add and subtract, overlaying and underscoring within the limitations of our primitive four-track tape.[26]

For George, the comparison between sound recording and making fine art had been festering for nearly as long as he had been in the record business. Way back in 1952, when he was still Oscar Preuss's assistant A&R man, he had recorded "Mock Mozart," a three-minute mini-opera, with actor Peter Ustinov overdubbing a four-part vocal ensemble. George had felt like it was "pretty adventurous" at the time, recognizing that the music marketplace may not have been ready for his brand of sound journeys. But if nothing else, "Strawberry Fields Forever" had confirmed George's long-held belief that the recording studio was capable of being a wondrous magic workshop and that producers such as himself were only just beginning to scratch the surface of its capabilities.[27]

As it happened, George wouldn't have to wait very long to see if this evolving method of painting "sound pictures" would be the Beatles' prevailing creative methodology. With "Strawberry Fields Forever" mostly in a state of completion—and "When I'm Sixty-Four" not lagging very far behind—the bandmates were ready to try out new compositions. Up next was a relatively new confection from McCartney titled "Penny Lane," an ebullient tune about "blue suburban skies" and a pretty nurse "selling poppies from a tray." George and the Beatles reconvened after the holidays on Thursday, December 29. With Emerick and McDonald in tow, Martin created mono and stereo remixes of "Strawberry Fields Forever," as well as mono mixes for "When I'm Sixty-Four." Meanwhile, an overnight session would be devoted to working out the signature piano foundation for "Penny Lane," which remained untitled at this juncture in spite of the fact that a year earlier McCartney had informed a journalist that he wanted to compose a song called "Penny Lane" because he liked the poetic cadence of the title. A bus roundabout located a few miles to the west of the Strawberry Field Salvation Army home of John's childhood haunts, Penny Lane and its attendant memories had clearly inspired Paul to compose a rejoinder to John's song about the place where "nothing is real."

For the past few years, Lennon and McCartney had discussed the concept of writing a quasi-musical about their salad days in Liverpool. As John told *Rave* magazine in February 1964, "Paul and I want to write a stage musical. That's a must. Maybe about Liverpool." In December 1965, Paul commented to *Flip* magazine, "I like some of the things the Animals try to do, like the song Eric Burdon wrote about places in Newcastle on the flip of one of their hits. I still want to write a song about the places in Liverpool where I was brought up. Places like the Docker's Umbrella which is a long tunnel through which the dockers go to work on Merseyside, and Penny Lane near my old home." In another light, McCartney's composition of "Penny Lane" on the heels of Lennon's "Strawberry Fields Forever" typified a new phase in their collaboration, which had been brewing since Lennon moved out to Weybridge. For his part, George was acutely aware of the ways in which the songwriters' partnership had evolved. But to his mind, the intensity of their collaboration had slowly but surely become integral to the bandmates'—and his own—collective success:

> John Lennon and Paul McCartney in particular were extremely good friends; they loved one another, really. They shared a spirit of adventure, and a modest little childhood ambition: they were going to go out and conquer the world. You could, though, almost touch the rivalry between them, it was so intense and so real, despite the overriding warmth. No sooner would John come up with an outstanding song evoking, say, his own early childhood, like "Strawberry Fields Forever," than Paul answered him straight back with a winner in the same vein: "Penny Lane." It was typical of the way they worked as a songwriting duo. Creative rivalry kept them climbing their individual ladders—and kept the Beatles on top.

Indeed, as their songwriting practices developed during this period, the Lennon-McCartney partnership might more accurately be understood as a competition. Many of their songs were now written separately, rather than together in the same physical space, before their debut to George and the bandmates. And as time passed, the rites of competition would become increasingly fierce.[28]

From that very first evening, "Penny Lane" was accorded the same patience and care that "Strawberry Fields Forever" had enjoyed across the past month. For his latest composition, Paul had a very strong sense of what he wanted to hear on the finished recording, telling George, "I want a very clean recording." He would later recall that during that period "I was into clean sounds—maybe a Beach Boys influence at that point." With the tape rolling, Paul began working out the basic rhythm track for "Penny Lane," which was dominated by an assortment of keyboard parts. After selecting take six as the best, Martin and the Beatles—McCartney, for the most part—began superimposing additional instrumentation. For track one, Paul performed the basic piano rhythm that characterizes the song, with track two featuring a second piano part that Paul appended to the conclusion of each of the song's verses. Track three offered yet another piano part, along with Starr on tambourine. To afford the piano with a different feel, Emerick fed the signal through a Vox guitar amp and then sweetened the result with added reverb. Track four was composed of a host of sound effects—with many of them treated to varispeed—including additional percussion, two-tone harmonium whistles, and elongated cymbal stylings. As Emerick later recalled, the slow evolution of "Penny Lane" proved to be trying at times for the other Beatles. "For days, the others sat at the back of the studio watching Paul layer keyboard after keyboard, working completely on his own," the engineer later wrote. "As always, his sense of timing was absolutely superb: the main piano part that everything was built on was rock solid despite the fact that there were no electronic metronomes to lay down click tracks in those days." But the real issue at this point—in addition to the others' sense of boredom settling in—involved the problematics of four-track recording. With McCartney creating one layer of piano and sound effects after another, Martin and Emerick were forced to carry out numerous tape reductions, which meant that the vagaries of generational tape loss were not only a risk but an increasing reality.[29]

On the evening of December 30, George and the Beatles—one Beatle, for the most part—returned to "Penny Lane," for which Geoff promptly conducted a tape reduction in order to provide much-needed recording space for the additional overdubs that Paul had in mind. But first, McCartney suggested that they return to "When I'm Sixty-Four." During the eight-hour session in Studio 2, Paul began the workday by suggesting that George and his production team scuttle the December 29 remix and start over. In particular, Paul wanted George to raise his vocal by a semitone to afford it with a more youthful feel. After Emerick's tape reduction, the current version of "When I'm Sixty-Four" was deemed as take seven. Wiping out the existing track four, Martin recorded a new vocal performance from McCartney, with backing vocals from Lennon: "We originally recorded him in the key of C major; but when it came to mixing, Paul wanted to sound younger," George later wrote. "Could he be a teenager again? So we racked up his vocal to D flat by speeding the tape up. His vocal sounded thinner and higher: not quite a seven-stone weakling, but nearly." By the time that work concluded in the wee hours of New Year's Eve, additional overdubs to track three included Starr on chimes, as well as vocal harmonies from McCartney, Harrison, and Lennon. The only thing left to do was to ring in the new year, but not without acknowledging how magnificent 1966 had been for George and the Beatles, the Jesus Christ tour notwithstanding. They hadn't merely grown artistically—they had progressed at a paradigm-shifting rate. After *Revolver, Rubber Soul* seemed like a distant memory. And "Strawberry Fields Forever" promised to render its memory dimmer still.[30]

10

CARNIVALS OF LIGHT

W HEN MARTIN AND HIS STEADY PRODUCTION TEAM of Geoff Emerick and Phil McDonald reconvened on Monday, January 2, 1967, they conducted an afternoon session in the Studio 2 control room in order to create new mono remixes for "When I'm Sixty-Four" and "Strawberry Fields Forever." By this point, there hadn't been any new Beatles product since the "Yellow Submarine" backed with "Eleanor Rigby" single, save for their recent UK compilation. Released just in time for the holiday shopping rush, *A Collection of Beatles Oldies* would mark the final time that EMI would release an album under the Beatles' name without the band's permission. As it was, the long-player registered a paltry number-seven showing on the UK album charts. Perhaps the inclusion of "Bad Boy" had made a difference, shielding George and the bandmates from an even less impressive result. As Beatles records went, barely cracking the top ten made for a mediocre outcome, especially since their previous seven album releases had ruled over the charts—and often for several consecutive weeks at a time. In spite of the self-isolation and substance abuse that had plagued his existence over the past several months, Brian Epstein had succeeded in negotiating a nine-year contract extension with EMI, ensuring that the Beatles would be able to call the shots with the record conglomerate regarding their creative future until 1976. Signed on January 27, 1967, and negotiated between Epstein and Len Wood—Martin's old nemesis during his waning years in EMI's employ—the new contract's terms also dictated that the bandmates would control both the contents and the presentation of their albums. For his part, Wood was discouraged at times by how long it took to negotiate the terms with the Beatles' manager. "You could never pin him down and he always had to go back to the boys to get their agreement on the things we discussed," Wood later remarked. "It all took so long that the new contract did not begin until January 1967, so technically the Beatles were out of contract for over six months from June 1966." For the Beatles—and George, for as long as he remained their producer—the contract called for seventy sides, composed of both 45 rpm singles and long-players. But the payoff was very lucrative indeed, with the contract stipulating that the Beatles would receive 10 percent of their records' retail price, the highest royalty rate—at that time, at least—ever afforded to a recording artist. As for EMI's subsidiary Capitol, it spelled the end of the repackagings and compilations that had been released under the Beatles' name in the United States. For Martin, the new contract suggested that the bandmates would be a going concern for many more years to come. And if he were really fortunate, his services on their behalf would continue unabated, mitigating the sizeable risk that he and his partners had assumed with AIR nearly sixteen months earlier.[1]

By January 1967, the record-company brass on both sides of the Atlantic were clamoring for new Beatles product posthaste. And their concerns naturally cascaded around Epstein, who turned to Martin for a progress report. What Epstein really wanted, of course, was a dynamite single to usher in the new year—a means for reasserting the Beatles' presence with a firecracker-like bang. "We need a single out, George, fast. What have you got?" Brian asked. "I want the best thing you've got." As George later recalled, Brian "was determined to make up any lost ground" across the autumn and winter months of 1966, and, in the manager's words, "to keep the Beatles firmly in the limelight's brilliant blaze." No problem, Martin had assured him. By this juncture, he knew that he was in possession of "a small collection of gems" in "Strawberry Fields Forever," "When I'm Sixty-Four," and the still-unfinished "Penny Lane." "Realizing how desperate Brian was feeling," George later recalled, "I decided to give him a super-strong combination, a double-punch that could not fail, an unbeatable linking of two all-time great songs: 'Strawberry Fields Forever' and 'Penny Lane.'" By Martin's standing prescription for Beatles releases, the new single meant that "Strawberry Fields Forever" and "Penny Lane" wouldn't be included on their next long-player, given his penchant for affording the record-buying public with greater value for their money. He shared this ethic with Epstein, who had been raised to adhere to the business motto of Epstein and Sons, a prominent Liverpool furniture dealership who proudly proclaimed that "the fair deal is the right deal." Martin was so confident about the Beatles' latest work that he went out on a limb, predicting unprecedented success for the upcoming release: "These songs would, I told him [Epstein], make a fantastic double-A-sided disc—better even than our other double-A-sided triumphs, 'Day Tripper' b/w 'We Can Work It Out,' and 'Eleanor Rigby' b/w 'Yellow Submarine.'"[2]

With the pressure building for them to complete "Penny Lane" for a mid-February release, George and the bandmates were racing headlong toward a hard deadline for the first time since bringing *Revolver* to fruition in madcap style back in June 1966. On Wednesday, January 4, George supervised yet another overnight session in Studio 2 for the express purpose of conducting more overdubs for "Penny Lane." As George later recalled, "Penny Lane" had "started life as a fairly simple song. But Paul decided he wanted a special sound on it." Working on the existing take seven, Lennon overdubbed an additional piano part to a song that was, by this point, brimming with a wall of piano sound. Harrison appended a lead guitar part to track two. Meanwhile, McCartney performed additional lead vocals on track three. The next evening, Thursday, January 5, would prove to be one of the strangest happenings in George and the Beatles' career together. The proceedings got underway with McCartney, ever the perfectionist, recording yet another lead vocal in place of the previous night's work. The rest of the evening was devoted to a bizarre, avant-garde recording slated for inclusion at the upcoming *Million Volt Light and Sound Rave*. Scheduled for January 28 at London's Roundhouse Theatre, the event had originated with artist and designer David Vaughan, who had decorated a piano for McCartney with psychedelic imagery. To Vaughan's great surprise, the Beatle offered to contribute a track to the upcoming electronic music and light show.[3]

During the January 5 session, McCartney took charge of the proceedings, while Martin and his team observed the zany events unfold from their perch in the control room above the studio floor. As Paul later recalled, "I said 'all I want you to do is just wander around all the stuff, bang it, shout, play it, it doesn't need to make any sense. Hit a drum, then wander onto the piano, hit a few notes and just wander around.'" And so the Beatles did just that, roaming around Studio 2 from instrument to instrument and occasionally shouting out semi-amusing non sequiturs. Over the years, scant few people—outside of George and the Beatles' inner circle—have actually heard the track, which came to be known as "Carnival of Light." According to Mark Lewisohn, the song is composed of "distorted, hypnotic drum and organ sounds, a distorted lead guitar, the sound of a church organ, various effects (water gargling was one) and, perhaps most intimidating of all, Lennon and McCartney screaming dementedly and bawling aloud random phrases like 'Are you all right?' and 'Barcelona!'" In terms of establishing a basic rhythm track for the song, it seems that the Beatles scarcely even bothered to create an elemental foundation for "Carnival of Light." As McCartney's biographer Barry Miles later pointed out, the song had "no rhythm, although a beat is sometimes established for a few bars by the percussion or a rhythmic pounding piano. There is no melody, although snatches of a tune sometimes threaten to break through."[4]

At McCartney's instruction, Emerick treated the voices and instrumentation for "Carnival of Light" to considerable reverb. Starr's drums were recorded fast in order to afford them with a deeper sound on playback. Meanwhile, Lennon and McCartney provided a variety of vocal inflections, including Native American war cries, the sounds of coughing and gasping, and other assorted vocal fragments. The instrumentation for the song, such as it was, consisted of guitar feedback, organ, drums, percussion, and jangle-box piano. The longest uninterrupted Beatles track to date at nearly fourteen minutes, "Carnival of Light" ended with Paul asking, his voice awash in echo, "Can we hear it back now?" At that point, Martin and his production team created a mono remix of "Carnival of Light," which McCartney dutifully turned over to Vaughan for inclusion in the upcoming rave. At this point in the session, Martin said, "This is ridiculous, we've got to get our teeth into something a little more constructive." For his part, Emerick recalled the recording as "a bit of nonsense, really, but everyone had fun doing it. Whenever the Beatles tried something really outrageous, George Martin would roll his eyes and mutter a clipped 'Oh my God' under his breath. Looking back, I guess that everyone was tripping his brains out that night, but we didn't know it then. When John started shouting 'Barcelona' repeatedly in one of his Goon-like voices, Phil and I were doubled over in laughter." Two decades later, Martin was asked if he remembered the session, replying "No, and it sounds like I don't want to either!"[5]

The next day, Friday, January 6, George and the Beatles got back down to business, toiling away at "Penny Lane" in order to ready their new single for the marketplace. The session began with a spate of new instrumentation—all heavily limited and recorded by Emerick at a slower speed to quicken the pace upon playback. McCartney turned in a bass guitar part on his Rickenbacker, with Lennon playing rhythm guitar on his Jumbo acoustic and Starr on his Ludwigs. An additional overdub found Lennon playing the congas. The latest round of instrumentation left Martin in need of new real estate, which prompted him to supervise a tape reduction to free up more space. At this point, Lennon and Martin piano tracks were thrown into the mix, along with a series of handclaps, as well as Lennon, McCartney, and Harrison providing scat vocals as placeholders for future adornments by studio musicians; at some point over the past few days, McCartney had concocted the idea for brass and woodwind ornamentation. Before the session concluded, Emerick carried out yet another tape reduction to free up two more tracks. And with that, the bandmates closed up shop for the weekend, leaving Martin only a few precious days to concoct a score for "Penny Lane."

That Monday, George strode into a 7:00 PM session in Studio 2. He was joined by the Beatles, of course, along with control room fixtures Geoff and Phil. Also on hand was a sextet of studio musicians. Yet another group of top-flight London players handpicked by George, the visitors included flautists Ray Swinfield, P. Goody, Manny Winters, and Dennis Walton, along with trumpeters Leon Calvert and Freddy Clayton. With his score in hand, Martin made quick work of the session. After making the requisite introduction, the producer turned the session over to McCartney, who played a quick run-through of "Penny Lane" on a piano. At one point, Paul told the musicians that it's "kinda confusing to what key it's in" before offering some impromptu recommendations to the brass players. With the studio musicians at the ready, Martin rehearsed the flautists' performance of the song's chorus, followed by the trumpeters. While listening to the playback, George complained that the tuning didn't seem quite right. After things were sorted out, he conducted the musicians as Emerick captured their performance on track three. In addition to the flute and trumpet parts, three of the six musicians also turned in two piccolo performances and a flügelhorn performance, respectively. After the musicians departed, George and his team carried out two mono remixes.[6]

Another overnight session on Tuesday, January 10, found George and the Beatles working in Studio 3, where they recorded more overdubs onto take nine of "Penny Lane." Much of the evening was devoted to working with an array of harmonies and sound effects, the most notable of which was the superimposition of a handbell. Scavenged from the studio trap room, Ringo rang the handbell at key junctures in the song when the fireman and his fire engine are referenced. For George and the Beatles, the studio was dark on the evening of January 11. With the bandmates taking a rare day off, Paul stayed home at Cavendish Avenue, where he watched BBC Two's *Masterworks* television series. The second of a five-part program, that evening's episode featured a performance of Johann Sebastian Bach's Brandenburg Concerto no. 2 in F Major by the Chamber Orchestra of Guildford Cathedral. The episode featured trumpeter David Mason, the principal player with London's New Philharmonia and an internationally renowned musician. Watching Mason as he performed one of the most difficult trumpet pieces in Bach's repertoire, McCartney was dazzled. When he reconvened with Martin and the other bandmates the next day, the Beatle was still gushing about Mason's exploits. "What was that tiny little trumpet that fellow was playing? I couldn't believe the sound he was making!" said McCartney. "That's called a piccolo trumpet," Martin replied, "and the chap playing it was David Mason, who happens to be a friend of mine." With space for a solo still available at the heart of "Penny Lane," McCartney was ecstatic. "Fantastic!" he told the producer. "Let's get him in here and have him overdub it." And Martin did just that, booking the distinguished player for a session less than a week later in Studio 2.[7]

Meanwhile, George and the Beatles pressed forward with the Thursday, January 12, session. Working in Studio 3, George conducted a second set of classical superimpositions. The session musicians that afternoon included two trumpets, two oboes, two cor anglais, and a double bass. The trumpeters were Bert Courtley and Duncan Campbell. The oboists, who also performed the cor anglais parts, included Dick Morgan and Mike Winfield, along with bassist Frank Clarke, who later recalled that "they wanted me to play one note over and over, for hours." After the musicians had departed, Martin and the bandmates hit upon the idea of recording a backward mélange from the classical adornments for "Penny Lane," although the ornamentation would later be scuttled. Before the day's work concluded, Martin and his team prepared two mono mixes. For his part, Emerick felt confident that "Penny Lane" had finally come into its own. "Combined with Paul's stellar bass playing and superb vocals," he later wrote, "the track was beginning to sound full, polished, and quite finished to me."[8]

The recording sessions associated with "Penny Lane" would finally reach their fruition on Tuesday, January 17. Working an evening session in Studio 2, George and the bandmates welcomed David Mason into their midst in order to provide the song's finishing touches courtesy of an exquisite piccolo trumpet solo. While he was delighted at being able to meet McCartney's expectations and book Mason for the session, Martin approached the evening with a degree of uncertainty, later to be superseded by genuine trepidation. As he later observed, "The normal trumpet is in B-flat. But there is also the D trumpet, which is what Bach mostly used, and the F trumpet. In this case, I decided to use a B-flat piccolo trumpet, an octave above the normal." But as George noted, "It was a difficult session for two reasons. First, that little trumpet is a devil to play in tune, because it isn't really in tune with itself, so that in order to achieve pure notes the player has to 'lip' each one. Secondly, we had no music prepared. We just knew that we wanted little piping interjections. We had had experience of professional musicians saying, 'If the Beatles were real musicians, they'd know what they wanted us to play before we came into the studio.'" To Martin's great relief, Mason "wasn't like that at all. By then the Beatles were very big news anyway, and I think he was intrigued to be playing on one of their records, quite apart from being well paid for his trouble." For the January 17 session, George had managed to secure the special Musicians' Union fee of nearly twenty-eight pounds. This meant that Mason would receive nearly double the going rate for session musicians during that era.[9]

As Mason later recalled, "I took nine trumpets along, and we tried various things, by a process of elimination settling on the B-flat piccolo trumpet." When it came to the solo itself, "We spent three hours working it out. Paul sang the parts he wanted, George Martin wrote them out, I tried them." As for the actual recording process, Mason remembers that it "was done quite quickly." With McCartney retreating to the control room, Mason performed two overdubs, including the solo and a concluding flourish. "They were jolly high notes, quite taxing," said Mason, "but with the tapes rolling we did two takes as overdubs on top of the existing song." But as Emerick later observed, the session proved to be dramatic in more ways than one:

> True professional that he was, Mason played it perfectly the first time through, including the extraordinarily demanding solo which ended on a note that was almost impossibly high. It was, quite simply, the performance of his life. And everyone knew it—except, obviously, Paul. As the final note faded to silence, he reached for the talkback mic. "Nice one, David," Paul said matter-of-factly. "Can we try another pass?" There was a long moment of silence. "Another pass?" The trumpeter looked up at the control room helplessly. He seemed lost for words. Finally, he said softly, "Look, I'm sorry. I'm afraid I just can't do it any better." Mason knew that he had nailed it, that he had played everything note perfect and that it was a prodigious feat that he could not possibly top.

But it was Martin who quickly saved the day, turning to McCartney and saying, "Good God, you can't possibly ask the man to do that again. It's fantastic!" To his credit, McCartney quickly recovered, saying to Mason over the talkback, "Okay, thank you, David. You're free to go now, released on your own recognizance."[10]

For his part, Mason would never forget his first brush with the Beatles that evening. "Although Paul seemed to be in charge, and I was the only one playing," he later recalled, "the other three Beatles were there too. They all had funny clothes on, candy-striped trousers, floppy yellow bow ties, etc. I asked Paul if they'd been filming because it really looked like they had just come off a film set. John Lennon interjected, 'Oh no, mate, we always dress like this!'" As with Alan Civil on *Revolver*'s "For No One," Mason's career would be largely defined by his work with the Fab Four. As he remarked years later, "I've spent a lifetime playing with top orchestras yet I'm most famous for playing on 'Penny Lane!'" With Mason's work complete, Martin was thrilled with the results, later writing that the piccolo trumpet solo "was unique, something that had never been done in rock music before, and it gave 'Penny Lane' a very distinct character." With Mason having departed Abbey Road, Martin and his team carried out three mono mixes, with remix eleven being considered the best. After making a copy of the mix, Martin dutifully dispatched the recording to Capitol Records for the American release of the "Strawberry Fields Forever" backed with "Penny Lane" single, which had been slated for release on February 13.[11]

But as it happened, work on "Penny Lane" hadn't concluded just yet. A week later, during a Wednesday, January 25, session in the Studio 1 control room, George soured on the trumpet flourish at the conclusion of the song. Feeling that it was superfluous, he instructed Emerick to delete Mason's coda from the January 17 mono remix. The problem, of course, was that the January 17 version had already been shipped to California. With Emerick and McDonald in tow, Martin carried out three more mono mixes, with the final version, remix fourteen, being selected to replace the previous one. Unfortunately, by this juncture Capitol had already pressed several promotional discs, which had been distributed to American radio stations forthwith. In so doing, Capitol had inadvertently created some of the most sought-after discs among Beatles collectors to the present day.

Released in the United Kingdom on February 17, "Strawberry Fields Forever" backed with "Penny Lane" proved to be an iconic, paradigm-shifting moment for Martin and the Beatles—just as George had predicted it would be. *NME*'s Derek Johnson described "Strawberry Fields Forever" as "certainly the most unusual and way-out single the Beatles have yet produced—both in lyrical content and scoring. Quite honestly, I don't really know what to make of it." Johnson lauded the song's "complex backing," "weird effects," and "constantly changing tempos, including a startling glissando that sounds as if the disc's slowing down." Johnson concludes by praising "Strawberry

Fields Forever" as being "completely fascinating, a record that becomes more spellbinding with every play." While he makes a special point of describing "Penny Lane" as "by far the more commercial sounding of the two sides," Johnson gushes appropriately about McCartney's contribution, extolling the song for its "jaunty jogging rhythm, a catchy tune, some of the familiar Beatle falsettos, and a colorful lyric." Meanwhile, *Time* magazine heralded the double A-sided single's release in the United States as "the latest sample of the Beatles' astonishing inventiveness." *Time*'s reviewer described "Strawberry Fields Forever" as being "full of dissonances and eerie space-age sounds, achieved in part by playing tapes backward and at various speeds. This is nothing new to electronic composers, but employing such methods in a pop song is electrifying." For *Time*'s reviewer, the verdict of the "Strawberry Fields Forever" backed with "Penny Lane" single was ineluctably clear: "From the first mewings of 'I Want to Hold Your Hand,' the Beatles have developed into the single most creative force in pop music. Wherever they go, the pack follows. And where they have gone in recent months, not even their most ardent supporters would ever have dreamed of. They have bridged the heretofore impassable gap between rock and classical, mixing elements of Bach, Oriental, and electronic music with vintage twang to achieve the most compellingly original sounds ever heard in pop music."[12]

For George and the Beatles, "Strawberry Fields Forever" backed with "Penny Lane" proved to be a blockbuster in almost every sense of the word. *Almost.* After its mid-February release, the single racked up sales of more than 2.5 million copies and dominated the airwaves in the United Kingdom and the United States alike. And the critics loved it, too. In the *Village Voice*, Robert Christgau described "Strawberry Fields Forever" backed with "Penny Lane" as "maybe the finest two-sided record in history." But the single's staggering critical and commercial success didn't translate into a number-one British hit for George and the bandmates. "It broke the roll," George later wrote. For the first time since "Please Please Me" backed with "Ask Me Why" topped the charts in early 1963, the Beatles had been denied the top spot on the UK singles charts. After twelve straight number-one singles, unlucky number thirteen had come up short. The culprit behind George and the Beatles' inability to capture the top spot was twofold: first, "Strawberry Fields Forever" backed with "Penny Lane" had been victimized by its own double A-sided status. In the United Kingdom, sales figures were computed separately for each song as if they were, in fact, two different singles. In a sense, each side canceled out the other. And then there was the matter of balladeer Engelbert Humperdinck, who had come out of nowhere to deny the Beatles their thirteenth straight UK chart-topper.[13]

Released in early 1967, Humperdinck's "Release Me (and Let Me Love Again)" backed with "10 Guitars" had languished for several weeks before the crooner made a fortuitous appearance on Val Parnell's *Sunday Night at the London Palladium*, the very same ATV program that launched British Beatlemania in October 1963. Humperdinck had been a last-minute guest on the popular live television variety show after singer Dickie Valentine had fallen ill. The boost that Humperdinck enjoyed after his television appearance made all the difference. On March 2, "Release Me (and Let Me Love Again)" captured the top spot on the UK charts, marooning the Beatles' latest single at number two, even though "Strawberry Fields Forever" backed with "Penny Lane" had outsold Humperdinck's record by a nearly two-to-one margin. While the Beatles' single failed to top the official UK charts, *Melody Maker* credited "Strawberry Fields Forever" backed with "Penny Lane" with a combined number-one showing for three straight weeks. In the United States, "Penny Lane" captured the number-one spot on *Billboard*'s Hot 100 for a week before being supplanted by the Turtles' "Happy Together."

While the Beatles seemed largely indifferent to their most recent showing on the UK charts, Martin was severely disappointed. For their part, Lennon and McCartney responded to the strange fate of their new single with a sense of mild amusement, although Harrison later admitted that it was "a bit of a shock being number two, but then again, there were always so many different charts that you could be number two in one chart and number one in another." Humperdinck was elated, of course, at his surprisingly strong showing in the face of the Beatles' latest 45 rpm juggernaut: "I don't feel bad about it at all and, indeed, I feel proud that I kept the Beatles from being number one," he later remarked. "To be in front of them in the charts was totally amazing." As they returned to work on their new longplayer—now without the benefit of "Strawberry Fields Forever" and "Penny Lane" as potential album tracks—John and Paul shared their nonchalance with the music press:

> John: The charts? I read them all. There's room for everything. I don't mind Humperbert Engeldinck. They're the cats. It's their scene.
>
> Paul: It's fine if you're kept from being number one by a record like "Release Me" because you're not trying to do the same kind of thing. That's a completely different scene altogether.

John: When [singles] first come out, we follow how much the initial sales were. Not for the money reason, just to see how it's doing compared to the last one; just because we made it. We need that satisfaction, not the glory of number one.

Lennon and McCartney's shared detachment was a sharp contrast to Martin, who blamed himself for not recognizing the problematic nature of pairing two powerhouse songs like "Strawberry Fields Forever" and "Penny Lane." Martin was stunned by the single's performance, second-guessing himself for foisting "Strawberry Fields Forever" backed with "Penny Lane" upon Brian Epstein and the bandmates as an unbeatable combination. "It was a smashing single," Martin later remarked, "but it was also a dreadful mistake." Not mincing words, he later characterized his decision to pair the songs as "the biggest mistake of my professional life. Releasing either song coupled with 'When I'm Sixty-Four' would have been by far the better decision, but at the same time I couldn't see it." Still, Martin knew full well the nature of their accomplishment and its portents for the Beatles' creative future. In later years, he proudly took to describing "Strawberry Fields Forever" backed with "Penny Lane"—in spite of the single's second-place showing—as "the best record we ever made."[14]

George may have been disappointed, but Brian was surprisingly untroubled by the result. The sales receipts spoke for themselves, and besides, the Beatles' manager saw the single as a way for the Beatles (and himself) to worm their way back into the good graces of their northern brethren, a great many of whom now saw the Beatles' collective move to London as a regional betrayal. As he wrote in a letter to Derek Taylor in February 1967, the Beatles' manager couldn't help wondering aloud, "Do you think it'll help our image in Liverpool?" Brian's indifference may also have been fueled by his ongoing business flirtation with Australian financier Robert Stigwood, whose Robert Stigwood Organization had merged with Epstein's NEMS in the new year. With talent like the Beatles and Cilla Black on his roster, Epstein's stable was now augmented by the likes of Cream and the Bee Gees. Known in pop-music circles as "Eppy" and "Stig," Epstein and Stigwood were shaping up, at least publicly, to be a managerial juggernaut. In truth, Brian had brought the Australian on board for a complex of reasons—namely, that the rigors of music management were clearly taking a toll on the thirty-two-year-old Liverpudlian. Privately, Brian feared that the merger was a necessity, given that his contract with the Beatles was set to expire in September 1967. He was fearful that they would reduce his stake from 25 percent to 10—if they even opted to retain him at all in their post-touring years.[15]

George's own disappointment—entirely in himself, as opposed to the Beatles or Epstein—paled in comparison to Brian Wilson, who was absolutely crestfallen at the sound of "Strawberry Fields Forever." The same man whom George himself would later extol as the "one living genius of pop music" first experienced "Strawberry Fields Forever" like many other music lovers of his day: on his car radio. Thunderstruck by the song's groundbreaking production and ethereal sound, he reportedly pulled over, collapsed into tears, and said, "They got there first." After the remarkable commercial and critical success of "Good Vibrations"—not to mention the spate of awards that Brian and the Beach Boys had earned at the tail end of 1966—Brian should rightly have been on top of the world. But as it turned out, he had become irretrievably lodged in the production of *Smile*, the planned and much-ballyhooed follow-up to *Pet Sounds*. By some accounts, Wilson felt that the Beatles' landmark single would leave *Smile* sounding passé in the face of the Brits' arresting newfangled sound. But it was worse than that. Wilson's wavering psychological state made it difficult for him to work as regularly as he would have liked—and with the consistency of thought necessary to bring *Smile* to fruition. In his mind, Wilson conceived of *Smile* in much the same way that he had first imagined "Good Vibrations": as a sea of fragmented vignettes gloriously merged into a seamless whole. To advance his work on what he once dubbed his "teen-age symphony to God," Wilson had formed a partnership with lyricist Van Dyke Parks in order to create order out of the would-be album's mélange of competing styles and genres, ranging from psychedelia and barbershop to ragtime and avant-garde pop.[16]

By the advent of the "Strawberry Fields Forever" backed with "Penny Lane" single's release, Brian had made scant progress on *Smile*, having already missed a January 1967 deadline for the album's completion. As the months wore on, Parks began to distance himself from the project, while the song-writer's fellow Beach Boys were becoming more and more bewildered by his increasingly erratic behavior. As the Beach Boys' Mike Love later remarked, the dream that Brian had wanted to fulfill—"validation from the mainstream media and the alternative press, recognition that he was in the cultural van-guard"—seemed to be just beyond his reach. His only goal had been to "fin-ish *Smile* and bask in the glory." And when that didn't happen, he began to slide into oblivion.[17]

Meanwhile, back in London George and the Beatles didn't have any time to bask in their own glory. They had a long-player of their own to make, and with their latest single selling like hotcakes in record shops, they only had one song, "When I'm Sixty-Four," waiting in the wings. Before things got underway, though, there was the small matter of producing promotional films for "Strawberry Fields Forever" and "Penny Lane." The band's new single was, by any measure, an unusual happening in the annals of popular music. In the United Kingdom, "Strawberry Fields Forever" backed with "Penny Lane" had been accompanied by a full-color picture sleeve, marking the first instance in which the Beatles had been marketed in such a conspicuous fashion. For fans who hadn't seen them since the Jesus Christ tour, the mustached Beatles in their Carnaby wear might very well have registered a shock. Directed by Swedish filmmaker Peter Goldman, the promotional videos were equally colorful, if not more so, with psychedelic images of the bandmates variously riding on horseback and frolicking around a dead oak tree. Principal photography for the videos began on January 30 at Angel Lane, Stratford, before shifting to bucolic Knole Park near Sevenoaks, Kent. On the second day of the four-day shoot—which was scheduled to be completed in early February—John strolled into an antiques shop, where he happened upon a nineteenth-century broadside. An advertisement for a circus near Rochdale, Lancashire, in February 1843, the broadside would come to serve as an inspirational found object for Lennon.

As it happened, yet another pair of found objects in John's imaginary universe had already exerted a profound effect upon the direction of George and the Beatles' creative lives. And they made their presence known in Studio 2 on Thursday, January 19, which proved to be a turning point in the production of the new long-player. Both found objects originated from newspaper headlines, including a December 19, 1966, issue of the *Daily Sketch*, which published a photo of Tara Browne's grisly car crash, along with a January 17, 1967, article in the *Daily Mail* on THE HOLES IN OUR ROADS. As Lennon later recalled, it "was a story about 4,000 potholes in Blackburn, Lancashire, that needed to be filled." John's most recent composition, less than two days old at this point, was borne out of these seemingly incongruous events. Going under the working title of "In the Life Of . . . ," the song was debuted during another one of the bandmates' patented overnight affairs. Years later, Martin recalled hearing the first strains of the composition that would come to be known as "A Day in the Life." He was spellbound as John began singing and softly strumming his acoustic guitar: "Even in this early take, he has a voice which sends shivers down the spine." Sitting up in the control booth with Martin, Geoff Emerick was equally rapt, recalling that this new song "was in a similar vein to 'Strawberry Fields Forever'—light and dreamy—but it was somehow even more compelling. I was in awe; I distinctly remember thinking, '*Christ, John's topped himself!*'" Like George, Geoff was gripped by John's first pass at the vocal. "Once he started singing, we were all stunned into silence," Emerick later wrote. "The raw emotion in his voice made the hairs on the back of my neck stand up."[18]

With the tape running, George supervised the first take, in which the bandmates began to routine the song in an effort to suss out the instrumentation. For take one, the Beatles established a basic rhythm track with John's acoustic guitar, Paul on piano, Ringo on bongos, and George on maracas. John counted off the song by muttering "sugar-plum fairy, sugar-plum fairy" to set the rhythm for his guitar cadence. As Martin later recalled, "The first stab at recording 'A Day in the Life' concentrated on the bare bones of the song, which so far had no middle section." For his part, George thought that "John's voice on the first run-through was marvelous." But as usual, Lennon despised the sound of his own voice. Martin and Emerick attempted to address the Beatle's concerns by overloading his vocals with "stupendous amounts of echo." As George later wrote, "John always hated his voice, always wanted something done to it. In this case, he said he wanted to 'sound like Elvis Presley on "Heartbreak Hotel."' So we put the image of the voice about 90 milliseconds behind the actual voice itself. As the voice goes past the record head, it obviously records. The playback head is situated after the record head, so you hear the voice later. In the old days, we used to do tape echo that way: take the voice off the playback head and feed as much as you wanted of it back into the record head." The resulting effect exceeded Lennon's expectations. "John was listening to this in his cans," George wrote, "and hearing so much distortion on his voice made him feel really happy."[19]

After debuting the first few verses, John admitted to George, "I don't know where to go from here." But John knew he wanted a middle eight, and Paul amiably offered up a solution: "Well, I've got this other song I've been working on." To accommodate the buildup to the future McCartney section, Martin instructed Beatles roadie Mal Evans to count off twenty-four bars during the first take for a potential middle eight. As George later wrote, Mal's "job was to count down the 24 bars in the middle of 'A Day in the Life' that were still blank. Why 24 bars? *Why not?*" As with John's vocal, Mal's counting was overladen with echo, increasing as he counted ever higher until the climax of the twenty-fourth bar, which Mal accentuated with the sound of an alarm clock. As Emerick later wrote, there "happened to be a windup alarm clock set on top of the piano—Lennon had brought it in as a gag one day, saying that it would come in handy for waking up Ringo when he was needed for an overdub." For his part, Martin concentrated on McCartney's piano part. "Paul was carrying the backing of the song on the piano. During that 24-bar gap, all you could hear was his piano banging away, with a lot of wrong notes, some of them deliberate, the dissonance increasing as his playing got more frenzied towards the end." After take four of the song was selected as the best, John began overdubbing his vocals on the available tracks, with each one treated with heavy doses of tape echo. As Geoff later recalled, each new recording of John's vocal was "more amazing than the one before. His vocal performance that night was an absolute *tour de force*, and it was all George Martin, Phil, and I could talk about long after the session ended." For his part, Geoff was impressed by the manner in which John's singing progressed in relation to the sound he was hearing through his headphones. "He used his own echo as a rhythmic feel," said Emerick, "phrasing his voice around the echo in his cans."[20]

Even as that first session for "A Day in the Life" concluded during the wee hours of January 20, George and his production team could tell that they were in the presence of something remarkable. But it was already different even than their recent experience with "Strawberry Fields Forever," a song with more concrete structure in evidence during its debut than the current number. The germ of the idea for this latest song would necessitate even more layering to bring the crude track off. At this point, "A Day in the Life" consisted, for the most part, of John's beautiful, echo-laden verses, Paul's piano flourishes, and Mal's blustery counting. But it was an evolving work of art nonetheless. By the time that George and the bandmates reconvened in Studio 2 some seventeen hours later, they were itching to get back to work. Martin's first task at hand involved leading the Beatles—Lennon, mainly—through an extensive review of the previous evening's lead vocals. As Geoff later recalled, "Our job was to decide which of John's lead vocals was the 'keeper.' We didn't have to necessarily use the entire performance, though. Because we had the luxury of working in four-track, I could copy over ('bounce') the best lines from each take into one track—a process known as 'comping.' . . . All we were really listening for when we were comping John's vocal was phrasing and inflection; he never had trouble hitting the notes spot on. Lennon sat behind the mixing console with George Martin and me, picking out the bits he liked. Paul was up in the control room, too, expressing his opinions."[21]

With the comping process complete, the folks up in the control room had to carry out some important studio housekeeping, with George instructing Geoff to create a reduction mix for take four into three separate mixes—takes five, six, and seven, each with different console settings. After selecting take six as the best, the Beatles added overdubs of yet another vocal from John, Paul's bass, and Ringo's drums. With the basic rhythm track and other adornments for "A Day in the Life" now in place, George and his production team turned their attention to Paul's lead vocal for the middle eight. As George later recalled, "Paul had written a scrap of a song, which John liked." Paul's middle eight found its origins in a passage from Dorothy Fields's 1930 hit "On the Sunny Side of the Street." McCartney had also supplied the phrase "I'd love to turn you on" for the purposes of the song's one-line chorus, which Lennon described as a "damn good piece of work." As it happened, Mal's ringing alarm clock served as an unintentional but well-timed introduction to the first line of Paul's middle eight, "Woke up, fell out of bed." At this point, George flagged Paul's performance as a guide vocal, given the expletive that he uttered after flubbing one of the lines.[22]

For George and the Beatles, Abbey Road would be dark for the next ten days, largely due to the four-day film shoot associated with the "Strawberry Fields Forever" and "Penny Lane" promotional videos. Meanwhile, Martin convened his production team, which included the always reliable Emerick along with Richard Lush—making his first appearance working a Beatles recording since way back on April 13, 1966—for a control room session in Studio 3 on Monday, January 30. The ninety-minute session found George supervising a mono remix of "A Day in the Life" for demo purposes. At this point, he realized that the Beatles' song needed more time to percolate, to develop into something that they hadn't quite imagined just yet. As he later wrote, "I loved the song: John's dry, deadpan voice, Paul's bouncy middle segment acting as a foil to that, and I really liked the chords that got us back to John's section, which was in a different key. We were not sure then what else we wanted to do to it, so we left it for a bit, to think. We often worked in this way, starting something new to give us more time on another song in progress. It was the painter laying aside the canvas, starting a new work, then coming back to the first work afresh, able to see at once what was good or bad about it, and what needed to be done by way of improvement."[23]

With this notion in mind, the bandmates rejoined George in Studio 2 on Wednesday, February 1, and set "A Day in the Life" aside in favor of the concept that Paul had concocted on the flight home from Nairobi back on November 19 and transformed into a song back home at Cavendish Avenue on January 27. Titled "Sgt. Pepper's Lonely Hearts Club Band," the song had quickly emerged as the title track for their new album, which now counted three songs to its name, along with "When I'm Sixty-Four" and "A Day in the

Life." With "Sgt. Pepper's Lonely Hearts Club Band," Paul had discovered a means for the bandmates to adopt new identities in their post-touring years:

> We were fed up with being the Beatles. We really hated that fucking four little Mop-Top boys approach. We were not boys, we were men. It was all gone, all that boy shit, all that screaming, we didn't want any more, plus, we'd now got turned on to pot and thought of ourselves as artists rather than just performers. There was now more to it; not only had John and I been writing, George had been writing, we'd been in films, John had written books, so it was natural that we should become artists. Then suddenly on the plane I got this idea. I thought, "Let's not be ourselves. Let's develop alter egos so we're not having to project an image which we know." It would be much more free. What would really be interesting would be to actually take on the personas of this different band. We could say, "How would somebody else sing this? He might approach it a bit more sarcastically, perhaps." So I had this idea of giving the Beatles alter egos simply to get a different approach; then when John came up to the microphone or I did, it wouldn't be John or Paul singing, it would be the members of this band. It would be a freeing element. I thought we can run this philosophy through the whole album: with this alter-ego band, it won't be us making all that sound, it won't be the Beatles, it'll be this other band, so we'll be able to lose our identities in this.

For Martin, McCartney's concept was a revelation. For years, he had been observing as the bandmates had seen their personalities become subsumed by their media-constructed identities. Perhaps being a member of Sgt. Pepper's band would allow them to recapture their own senses of self in Beatlemania's prodigious wake.[24]

For his part, George particularly admired the concept of Sgt. Pepper and his Lonely Hearts Club Band serving as stand-ins for the Beatles themselves. But he also recognized that Paul's notion of the album as a liberating mechanism was loaded with risk. Sure, it afforded them with a means for feeding mass culture's demand for more and ceaseless Beatles product; and perhaps more importantly for their purposes, it also allowed them to abandon life on the road in favor of the friendly confines of the recording studio. But would the Beatles' gambit actually work? The music business had become set in its ways, with artists earning the lion's share of their income as road warriors, while record companies typically reaped the profits associated with music retail. For his part, George could pinpoint the genesis of "Sgt. Pepper's Lonely Hearts Club Band" to a very specific inspiration:

> In a bizarre way, it may have been the king himself, Elvis Presley, who had inspired the idea. Apparently, he once sent his Cadillac on tour without accompanying it. This crazy ploy was something the Beatles marveled at and often joked about, so an idea was spawned which grew in all their minds: "Why don't we make an album that is a show, and send *that* on tour instead of ourselves?" This was a radical, even fanciful idea at that time, but the Beatles could immediately see the possibilities and potential in it. It might just be a way round the problem of their not touring any more.

For George, the issues associated with this strategy were legion. He harbored significant concerns about its commercial viability, and, while he was confident in the Beatles' musical gifts, he was uncertain about whether their multitude of fans the world over would continue to support them without the promise of live performance: "Could an album, however good, be an effective substitute for a live tour?"[25]

During the overnight session on February 1, George supervised nine takes as the Beatles refined the song's rhythm track, which consisted of two electric guitars, played by Harrison and McCartney, Starr on drums, and Lennon on bass. As Martin later recalled, "I did not have much to do with the musical arrangement of the 'Sgt. Pepper' track. The boys took to the simple tune like the proverbial ducks to water and made up the arrangement as they went along. You could tell how much they enjoyed playing a straight-forward rocker because it fairly hummed along." The difference in the bandmates' standard instrumentation came at the behest of McCartney, who said to his songwriting partner, "Let me do the rhythm on this; I know exactly what I want." Without a word of protest, Lennon simply picked up a bass guitar, and with that, Martin commenced the recording session for "Sgt. Pepper's Lonely Hearts Club Band." The track's high energy was evident from the outset; at one crucial juncture in the middle of the basic track, McCartney can be heard letting out a whoop of pure joy, egging his friends on in the process. Given that Lennon's bass part was considered to be a placeholder, Martin suggested that they record Lennon's fret work on a separate track using direct injection so that it could more easily be replaced later by McCartney. Direct injection, the process of recording the instrumentation directly into the recording console without the necessity of using an amplifier and a microphone, afforded George with a means for skirting the issue of suffering any sound bleed or microphone leakage from John's bass onto the other instruments.[26]

Direct injection had been deployed in other studios by other audio personnel in the past—most notably, by Joe Meek in London and by Motown engineers since the early 1960s. Meek had crafted his own homemade "black boxes" out of tobacco tins, which he strapped together with cellophane tape. At Abbey Road, the ever-reliable Ken Townsend had recently been experimenting with fashioning his own direction-injection boxes for use at EMI Studios. At least part of the maintenance engineer's inspiration came from the inherent difficulties in recording low-end sounds. "One of the most difficult instruments to record was the bass guitar," said Townsend. "No matter which type of high-quality microphone we placed in front of the bass speaker, it never sounded back in the control room as good as in the studio." With take nine having been selected as the best—and with the instrumentation, excepting Lennon's bass part—recorded on track one, McCartney picked up his Rickenbacker to replace Lennon's guide piece with a new bass overdub. With Townsend's direction-injection box at the ready, McCartney fashioned a new bass part, with the signal being fed directly from his guitar into the recording desk. As Townsend explained the function of the direction-injection box to the bandmates, Lennon was suddenly intrigued by the notion of having access to yet another one of Townsend's famous shortcuts. As with ADT, direct injection seemed to be a new avenue for transforming his vocals with veritable ease. After learning about the mechanics of direct injection, Lennon informed "George Martin that he'd like to have his voice recorded that way, too," Emerick later recalled. "Tongue planted firmly in cheek, George explained why we couldn't do that: 'For one thing, John, you'd have to have an operation first so we could implant a jack socket in your throat.' Even then, Lennon couldn't quite grasp why it wasn't possible. He simply didn't like taking no for an answer."[27]

The next evening, Thursday, February 2, George and the Beatles' work on "Sgt. Pepper's Lonely Hearts Club Band" continued. The overnight session commenced with the superimposition of McCartney's lead vocals and the bandmates' harmony vocals onto tracks three and four, respectively. This same evening, the brief song's structure and instrumentation evolved even further to include brass ornamentation. For this reason, Martin and his team carried out a tape-to-tape reduction in order to free up a pair of tracks for additional overdubs at a later date. An acetate was also prepared for the producer's benefit in order to score the brass parts. By this juncture, George was coming to realize that his role in the Beatles' artistry had made yet another shift. Even as recently as the *Revolver* sessions, George was working around the Beatles' schedule and providing as much—or as little—input as they desired. But now,

> they were becoming even more demanding. They would ring up and say, "We want to come in tonight at eight o'clock," and everybody had to be there—whatever else they might have on. I had reconciled myself to the fact that they would be my number-one priority. The long hours were more a problem for me with regard to other recording artists than they were in terms of a personal life. Judy accepted it; so did I. But quite often Neil Aspinall would ring up in his role as the Beatles' road manager and say, "Look, George, we've got to have the studio at seven tonight," and I would have to try to rearrange a session booked with somebody else who was quite important—but not as important as the Fab Four. Then the Beatles would turn up at ten! When it came right down to it, we were all their minions.[28]

And while George may have performed a subsidiary role with the band— as did Brian, Neil, and Mal at times—he had also come to recognize his privileged, even essential place in their creative ecosystem. "By the time of *Pepper*," he later wrote, "the Beatles had immense power at Abbey Road. So did I. They used to ask for the impossible, and sometimes they would get it. At the beginning of their recording career, I used to boss them about—especially for the first year or so. By the time we got to *Pepper*, though, that had all changed: I was very much the collaborator. Their ideas were coming through thick and fast, and they were brilliant. All I did was help make them real." At the same time, he understood that his role dissipated very quickly once the Fab Four roamed beyond the hallowed hallways of Abbey Road. "In the studio," he later wrote, "I was very much part of them; every voice was heard equally. But once they left the studio, out into the night, they closed themselves off again, reverting to their hermetically-sealed unit. Even Brian Epstein didn't get inside that shell. As for the way they viewed me, I was very 'twelve-inch,' in Ringo's memorable phrase. (Back in the fifties we used to issue ten-inch and twelve-inch vinyl records. The ten-inch records were the 'rhythm-style series,' what we now call pop, and the twelve-inch were the cantatas and symphonies: the classical. Ten-inch was common; but twelve-inch—that was a cut above!)" Tony King, a close friend of John's and AIR's publicity agent, echoed Ringo's sentiments, describing Beatles sessions as something akin to experiencing "all the fun of the fair. Everybody would have these funny sort of sixties smiles on their faces; and among all this madness was the Duke of Edinburgh, as we used to call George Martin." The Beatles' producer valued the inherently complimentary nature of such characterizations—and in truth, he was more than a little fond of being referred to in such a "classical" manner—but he also shrewdly recognized, at this relatively early moment in the life of this new phase of the Beatles, that *Sgt. Pepper's Lonely Hearts Club Band* was shaping up to be very different from their previous efforts.[29]

That difference, as Martin came to understand it, was the simple but all-important matter of time. It was something that he and the bandmates so rarely had during their years together. Even *Revolver* felt rushed in spite of the artistic and sonic strides that they had accomplished. George had to hand it to the Beatles: they had earned their place in the industry through well-honed talent and toil, and they were determined to make the most of the very moment in which they could call their own shots, determine their destiny as recording artists. As Martin later wrote, "It was their dreams we were realizing, nothing more or less. Music requires mechanics, people banging, or blowing, or scraping, or strumming; but in the end, it is intangible, it is dreams. You can't get hold of music, you cannot look at it. You may think you can look at it by picking up a score, but that is just a piece of paper. Music does not exist without a pair of serviceable ears, and time. That is why I think it is the most wonderful art of all—why I get so ecstatic about it. Above all other things, music needs time." In addition to the bandmates themselves, the members of George's production team were buoyed by their extended time in the studio. "One of the benefits of working with the Beatles," Richard Lush later recalled, "was that, unlike other artists, they had the luxury of time. As a result, we'd spend hour after hour recording them, which would give Geoff and I the opportunity to work out exactly what sounded good and what didn't. Same for mixing—we were able to rehearse our moves over and over again and get them just right."[30]

But the issue of time, as George well knew, inevitably requires a financial commitment, as well as a show of faith. And he had been working for—or, in terms of his AIR partnership, *with*—EMI for long enough to understand that the record conglomerate wouldn't be giving an inch as far as the bottom line was concerned. Not for the Beatles, not for anybody. And certainly not for George.

11

HOME AND DRY

WITH WORK SET to resume on "A Day in the Life," George was especially mindful about the expenses that he had already accrued in producing *Sgt. Pepper*, as well as the "Strawberry Fields Forever" backed with "Penny Lane" single, which wouldn't officially make its way into record shops until mid-February. As it turned out, Ringo's observation back in November 1966 about EMI allowing the Beatles to gobble up all of the studio time that they wanted was only half true. What Ringo likely didn't realize at the time was that, for all of the millions upon millions of pounds that the Beatles had generated through record sales by that point, they were kept on a strict studio budget by the EMI brass. George and the Beatles had immense power with EMI, but power inevitably has its limits. In many ways, it was no different from George's days as Parlophone A&R head. But with the Beatles' new avant-garde sound already advancing beyond the frontiers that they had explored with *Revolver*, George had been forced to meet with Len Wood in order to placate EMI's managing director about the band's rapidly shifting creative direction. "My own view is and always has been that artists should be able to grow, to blossom," George later wrote. "They should not have to stand still for reasons of simple profit. When the Beatles announced that they were going into the studio for an indefinite period, before *Pepper*, I had some interesting and fairly taut discussions with the powers that be at EMI, who were understandably nervous about what would come of it all." But to his great credit—and ever since the bandmates had heeded his suggestions and amped up "Please Please Me" back in September 1962—George was brimming with confidence about the group's short- and long-term prospects for continuing to be able to mine rock gold. "Luckily for me, the Beatles never let me down," he later recalled. "Whenever I said, 'Give them their heads, let them do different things,' they came up with things that were as good as, if not better than, the material they had been doing before. And it always sold. One of my main jobs with the Beatles, as I saw it by 1967, was to give them as much freedom as possible in the studio, but to make sure that they did not come off the rails in the process."[1]

George's philosophy about affording the Beatles with maximum artistic freedom—but at the same time, preventing them from going "off the rails"—was shortly put to the test when they revisited "A Day in the Life" on the evening of Friday, February 3, in Studio 2. But there was a pall over the proceedings that evening, and it understandably found its roots in the terrible news out of North London. The white-coated personnel at Abbey Road were shocked to learn that Joe Meek had died at age thirty-seven from a self-inflicted gunshot wound. Before turning the shotgun on himself, he had killed his landlord, Violet Shenton, in a fit of rage. Even as recently as the previous week, Sir Joseph Lockwood had met with Meek at EMI House in a last-ditch attempt to bring him on at Parlophone. For Meek, Martin's old job would have been a lifesaver—at least, financially speaking. He had been mired in a protracted lawsuit with French composer Jean Ledrut, who alleged that Meek had borrowed the melody for "Telstar" from Ledrut's "La Marche d'Austerlitz," a standout composition from the composer's score for the 1960 film *Austerlitz*. Incredibly, in spite of all of the renown that he had enjoyed from "Telstar," the lawsuit, which was settled posthumously in Meek's favor, prevented him from earning any royalties from his most acclaimed recording. But even Lockwood's offer—an incredible risk on the chairman's part, given Meek's troubled state—wasn't enough to rouse the beleaguered producer from his depression and make a new start.

As the February 3 session proceeded, George and the Beatles worked from take six as they began to rerecord several key aspects of "A Day in the Life." Having listened to acetates over the intervening days, they were particularly disappointed in the rhythm section. For his part, McCartney overdubbed a new bass part along with a new lead vocal for the middle section. Before recording the new vocal, McCartney had a long discussion with Emerick. "He explained that he wanted his voice to sound all muzzy," Geoff later recalled, "as if he had just woken up from a deep sleep and hadn't yet gotten his bearings, because that was what the lyric was trying to convey. My way of achieving that was to deliberately remove a lot of the treble from his voice and heavily compress it to make him sound muffled. When the song goes into the next section, the dreamy section that John sings, the full fidelity is restored."[2]

But when it came time to superimpose Paul's new vocal onto the existing take, George and his production team ran into trouble. As second engineer, Richard Lush was tasked with editing the vocal into the track. As Geoff later recalled, Paul's vocal "was being dropped into the same track that contained John's lead vocal, and there was a very tight drop-out point between the two—between Paul's singing 'and I went into a dream' and John's 'ahhh' that starts the next section. Richard was quite paranoid about it—with good reason—and I remember him asking me to get on the talkback mic to explain the situation to Paul and ask him not to deviate from the phrasing that he had used on the guide vocal." Years later, Geoff admired Richard's initiative in this instance. "I thought it showed great maturity to be proactive that way," he later wrote. "John's vocal, after all, had such great emotion, and it also had tape echo on it. The thought of having to do it again and re-create the atmosphere was daunting—not to mention what John's reaction would have been! Someone's head would have been bitten off, and it most likely would have been mine. But Paul, ever professional, did heed the warning, and he made certain to end the last word distinctly in order to give Richard sufficient time to drop out before John's vocal came back in."[3]

But the big story that day was Starr's second attempt at fashioning a drum part for the evolving song. One of the track's finest aspects, Starr's drum fills for "A Day in the Life" were performed in sharp contrast to his typically understated approach to working his kit. At Paul's urging, Ringo agreed to try out a more aggressive style for the recording. "Come on, Paul, you know how much I hate flashy drumming," he replied. With Lennon and McCartney cheering him on, Starr turned in a remarkable overdub during the February 3 session, characterized by a host of inventive and at times quirky drum fills. To accommodate Starr's incredible overdub, Emerick made several sonic adjustments up in the booth with Martin, as well as on the studio floor below with Starr's kit. "We were looking for a thicker, more tonal quality," Geoff later recalled, "so I suggested that Ringo tune his toms really low, making the skins really slack, and I also added a lot of low end at the mixing console. That made them sound almost like timpani, but I still felt there was more I could do to make his playing stand out. During the making of *Revolver*, I had removed the front skin from Ringo's bass drum and everyone was pleased with the resultant sound, so I decided to extend that principle and take off the bottom heads from the tom-toms as well, miking them from underneath." In order to accomplish this last feat, Emerick was forced to improvise: "We had no boom stands that could extend underneath the floor tom, so I simply wrapped the mic in a towel and placed it in a glass jug on the floor. For the icing on the cake, I decided to overly limit the drum premix, which made the cymbals sound huge. It took a lot of work and effort, but that's one drum sound I was extremely proud of, and Ringo, who was always meticulous about his sounds, loved it, too."[4]

For his part, George was chuffed, as he so often was, with Ringo's steadiness behind the kit, later remarking that "Ringo has a tremendous feel for a song, and he always helped us hit the right tempo first time. He was rock solid, and this made the recording of all the Beatles' songs so much easier." As the session wound down in the wee hours of February 4, Lennon and McCartney hatched their plans to effect what they hoped would be a stunning climax for "A Day in the Life." As George later recalled, "The question was, how were we going to fill those twenty-four bars of emptiness? After all, it was pretty boring! So I asked John for his ideas. As always, it was a matter of my trying to get inside his mind, discover what pictures he wanted to paint, and then try to realize them for him. John said, 'I want it to be like a musical orgasm. What I'd like to hear is a tremendous build-up, from nothing up to something absolutely like the end of the world. I'd like it to be from extreme quietness to extreme loudness, not only in volume, but also for the sound to expand as well. I'd like to use a symphony orchestra for it. Tell you what, George, you book a symphony orchestra, and we'll get them in a studio and tell them what to do.'" As it turned out, McCartney may have been the culprit behind Lennon's sudden desire to hire out an entire orchestra. "I sat John down and suggested it to him, and he liked it a lot," Paul later recalled. "I said, 'Look, all these composers are doing really weird avant-garde things and what I'd like to do here is give the orchestra some really strange instructions. We could tell them to sit there and be quiet, but that's been done, or we could have our own ideas based on this school of thought. This is what's going on now; this is what the movement's about.'"[5]

While he admired the concept of recording the sound of apocalypse, Martin also recognized that Lennon's approach to recording an orchestra would only serve to irritate the studio musicians as opposed to inspiring any creativity. Years later, George recalled his reply to John's preposterous suggestion: "'Come *on*, John,' I said, 'there's no way you can get a symphony orchestra sitting around and say to them, "Look fellers, this is what you're going to do." Because you won't get them to do what you want them to do. You've got to write something down for them.' 'Why?,' asked John, with his typically wide-eyed approach to such matters. 'Because they're all playing different instruments, and unless you've got time to go round each of them individually and see exactly what they do, it just won't work.'" And then there was the matter of the expense associated with hiring a symphony orchestra and booking time for some ninety session players. George knew that with *Sgt. Pepper* they were already well over their typical budget for producing a long-player. Emerick later recalled the conversation in the booth with Martin and the Beatles, observing that "George Martin liked the idea, but, mindful of the cost, was adamant that there was no way he could justify charging EMI for a full 90-piece orchestra just to play 24 bars of music." George was beside himself with anxiety over the idea. "You cannot, *cannot* have a symphony orchestra just for a few chords," he complained. "Waste of money. I mean you're talking about 90 musicians! This is EMI, not Rockefeller!'" For Martin, the issue over booking a full orchestra offered a stark reminder of the precarious position in which he and the Beatles found themselves. On the one hand, studio time was cheap for the EMI Group, which owned the studios at Abbey Road outright. Hence, the Beatles' inordinately long hours in the studio were never an issue for the record conglomerate but rather an internal accounting transaction. "They didn't bilk at our spending all that time," George observed at the time. "They knew that we were doing something worthwhile." On the other hand, expenses associated with hiring session players came under a very different kind of scrutiny of which George was all too keenly aware, having toiled at EMI Studios since 1950.[6]

Years later, Martin couldn't help dressing himself down for being so cheap, EMI's miserly ways be damned, when it came to the Beatles. "Thus spake the well-trained corporate lackey still lurking somewhere inside me," he later wrote, even going so far as to deride himself as a "cheeseparer!" According to Geoff, "It was Ringo, of all people, who came up with the solution. 'Well, then,' he joked, 'let's just hire half an orchestra and have them play it twice.' Everyone did a double take, stunned by the simplicity—or was it simple-mindedness?—of the suggestion. 'You know, Ring, that's not a bad idea,' Paul said. 'But still, boys, think of the cost,' George Martin stammered. Lennon put an end to the discussion, 'Right, Henry,' he said [to George], his voice carrying the tone of an emperor issuing a decree. 'Enough chitchat, let's do it.'"[7]

And that's exactly what they did. With the Beatles completing their four-day video shoot in Sevenoaks, Kent, on February 5 and 7, George would have the next several days at his leisure in order to put the finishing touches on the score for "A Day in the Life." In spite of his protestations back in the

Studio 2 control room, George was intrigued by the idea of an orchestra of session players backing "A Day in the Life." "I thought very hard," he later wrote. "The song did need a grand flourish of some sort. This crazy idea might just work. We had never used a symphony orchestra before; we'd used a string quartet, an octet, the odd trumpet or sax section, so the notion of a great leap forward into a full-sized orchestra was very appealing—and kind of logical. It is one of the biggest toys you can play with." At the same time, George knew that top symphonic studio musicians would never deign to work in the freewheeling way that John had described. When it came to the musicians, George wrote, "I knew it was of little use telling them to improvise. They were used to working from written parts, no matter how strange. I suppose it was difficult for the Beatles to fully understand that. They had never needed a note of written music in their lives. Why should anyone else? Of course, if we had approached the symphony musicians in those days without a prepared score they would have laughed us out of court."[8]

And so George set to work on the piano at his home near Manchester Square. Working painstakingly from the acetate, George counted on his earlier conversations with John in order to concoct the orchestration. "When I sat down to write the score," George later recalled, "I realized that John had not come up with anything for the first few notes the orchestra would have to play, after he stops singing, 'I'd love to turn you on.' He sings this line in a very characteristic manner, the tune wavering between semitones. This, I thought, would be a great phrase to echo, so I wrote a very slow semitone trill for the strings, bowing with a gentle *portamento* and increasing gradually in frequency and intensity. This gives a suitably mysterious effect, making a good introduction or bridge to the now famous dissonant orchestral climb that is unique to this song." Martin's consultation with McCartney also helped frame the score's musical style. "Paul had been listening to a lot of *avant-garde* music by the likes of John Cage, Stockhausen, and Luciano Berio," George wrote. "He had told John he would like to include an instrumental passage with this *avant-garde* feel. He had the idea to create a spiraling ascent of sound, suggesting we start the passage with all instruments on their lowest note and climbing to the highest in their own time."[9]

But creating the sound of "the end of the world"—the searing climax to "A Day in the Life"—was another matter altogether. "That climax was something else again," George recalled. "What I did there was to write, at the beginning of the 24 bars, the lowest possible note for each of the instruments in the orchestra. At the end of the 24 bars, I wrote the highest note each instrument could reach that was near a chord of E-major. Then I put a squiggly line right through the 24 bars, with reference points to tell them roughly what note they should have reached during each bar. I marked the music 'pianissimo' at the beginning and 'fortissimo' at the end. Everyone was to start as quietly as possible, almost inaudibly, and end in a (metaphorically) lung-bursting tumult." Having scored the song's climactic orchestral ascent, George turned his attentions to the section immediately following Paul's line, "somebody spoke, and I went into a dream." For this portion of his score, George "wrote out the music for the part where the orchestra had proper chords to do." Working to establish a sense of foreboding after Paul's "bouncy" interior section, George composed a preface for John's concluding verse—the moment where "big pure chords come in," in George's words, and prepare the listener for the Beatles' final onslaught of sound and mayhem.[10]

During the incredible lead-up that week to the orchestral session for "A Day in the Life," George and the Beatles tried out two new compositions for *Sgt. Pepper's Lonely Hearts Club Band*. At the outset of the overnight session in Studio 2 on Wednesday, February 8, John debuted "Good Morning, Good Morning," a song that had been inspired by a Kellogg's Corn Flakes cereal commercial. With the tape running, the bandmates recorded eight takes in order to capture the basic rhythm track, which intrigued Martin, given the song's unusual structural qualities. "'Good Morning, Good Morning' has a strange form. It starts off conventionally enough with an eight-bar introduction," George later recalled, "followed by a raucous chant of the title from the boys. But the first verse has only 10 beats in it. . . . In a 10-beat phrase, there has to be an uneven bar somewhere, or else two bars of 5/4—rare enough in pop music today and unheard of in 1967." In addition to Lennon providing a guide vocal, the song featured drums, tambourine, and rhythm guitar. By this early juncture, Lennon made it known to Martin that he wanted to beef up the sound; hence, when the session ended, Emerick and Lush prepared an acetate for Martin to take with him for scoring purposes. "The basic tune was quite simple," he later wrote, "but John wanted a very hard-driving sound to punch it along. This is where the horns came in. I thought the way to do it would be to have a mixture of saxophones, trumpets, and trombones playing either in unison or in octaves, and sometimes on spread chords." As it happened, the eventual horn parts would only be the beginning of the overdubs that would transform "Good Morning, Good Morning" before George and his production team brought the song to fruition.[11]

The very next evening, Thursday, February 9, George and the Beatles were back at it again. Paul was ready to debut a new confection titled "Fixing a Hole," and he was itching to get something down on tape. The new compositions were coming fast and furious by this point—so fast, in fact, that George was unable to secure any space at Abbey Road to conduct the session. With nothing available at EMI Studios—and Paul working "on heat"—George rounded up space on short notice at Regent Sound's Tottenham Court Road location. For George and the bandmates, it would mark the first time they had logged any studio hours outside of Abbey Road since Pathé Marconi in Paris in January 1964 and CTS in London two years later. For his part, George was nonplussed by the thought of working at Regent Sound, which "was little more than a demonstration studio, in the heart of Tin Pan Alley. It was a low-ceilinged, boxy little room with a low-ceilinged boxy little sound to it." But the venue wouldn't be the only issue that they encountered that evening. Writing "on heat" came with its attendant issues beyond a mere change of venue. Working there also meant a change of personnel. As George later recalled, "We weren't allowed to take our engineers with us: Geoff Emerick was employed by Abbey Road in those days and that contractually prevented him from recording elsewhere."[12]

To remedy the matter, Regent Sound's Adrian Ibbetson served as engineer on the recording. For George, it was yet another source of irritation—a reminder, in his own words, that "frustration has many fathers." It was but one more example of the ways in which the mid-1960s British recording industry was systemically unable to understand the nature of the paradigm shift that the Beatles had wrought. And it was a seismic shift that necessitated systemic change, or at the very least special treatment, rather than forcing George to work outside of his standing production team. But as it turned out, Ibbetson wasn't the only stranger in evidence that evening. Also observing the Beatles at Regent Sound was none other than Jesus Christ himself. Earlier that afternoon, a man identifying himself as Jesus had met Paul at the gate to the Beatle's Cavendish Avenue home. Naturally, Paul had his doubts about the veracity of the would-be Lord's identity. As McCartney later recalled:

> I thought, "Well, it probably isn't [Jesus]. But if he is, I'm not going to be the one to turn him away." So I gave him a cup of tea and we just chatted and I asked, "Why do you think you are Jesus?" There were a lot of casualties about then. We used to get a lot of people who were maybe insecure or going through emotional breakdowns or whatever. So I said, "I've got to go to a session, but if you promise to be very quiet and just sit in a corner, you can come." So he did, he came to the session and he did sit very quietly, and I never saw him after that. I introduced him

to the guys. They said, "Who's this?" I said, "He's Jesus Christ." We had
a bit of a giggle over that.

With Christ and Ibbetson in tow, George and the Beatles began rehearsing
the rhythm track for "Fixing a Hole." Track one featured McCartney on bass,
Starr on drums, and none other than Martin playing harpsichord. As George
later wrote, "It's a very simply constructed song, built around a harpsichord
as the mainstay of his rhythm; even so, the bass line is more important than
the harpsichord line. Paul had to play bass guitar on it because nobody could
(or can) play that instrument quite like him. That meant someone else was
going to have to play keyboards. This was unusual because Paul always liked
to play his own keyboards on his own compositions. The part of honorary
stand-in keyboard player to the greatest group in the world was offered to
me. It wasn't too difficult, and didn't seem likely to tax my non-virtuoso
technique too much."[13]

For George, playing the harpsichord part was a delight: "'Fixing a Hole' is
very recognizably a keyboard song. You can see the three-finger piano chords
underpinning its structure. Those basic triads are the platform on which the
lead voice, Paul's voice, and the bass guitar, were overlaid." With track one
for "Fixing a Hole" in the books, Martin recorded McCartney's guide vocal
and Lennon's rhythm guitar on track three, with backing vocals overdubbed
onto track four. The evening was rounded out with George Harrison's nifty
Sonic Blue Fender Stratocaster guitar solo on track two. But for Martin, the
highlight that evening—Jesus Christ's curious presence notwithstanding—was
McCartney's superb bass work. "Paul let rip with a superb and melodic bass
line," George recalled, "something that was rapidly becoming a characteristic
of his songwriting style. He used the instrument like a voice: he was never
content just to use the dominant and tonic—the normal plodding sequence
of a bass—as many others did. He wanted to make that bass sing. Whenever
he had something to say, he said it most eloquently using the instrument
he loved the best." A few days later, Emerick listened to the Regent Sound
recordings, "and while they were a bit disappointing sonically, I was impressed
with the vibe: all four Beatles played together on the backing track, just like
in the old days."[14]

Meanwhile, thousands of miles away in the United States, George enjoyed
an accomplishment of a slightly different sort at Van Gelder Studio, a Frank
Lloyd Wright–inspired structure in Englewood Cliffs, New Jersey. On February 2, jazz trombonist Kai Winding recorded two songs that owed their

genesis, in large measure, to Martin's efforts both as producer and composer. The Danish-born Winding had enjoyed a celebrated career as a member of Benny Goodman's and Stan Kenton's orchestras, and he was in town to record his twenty-fifth album as bandleader. Up first was Winding's cover version of "Penny Lane," which hadn't even been released in the music marketplace as of yet. In a bravura tribute to Martin and the Beatles, Winding and his fellow players recorded a rousing arrangement of "Penny Lane," followed by the jazz instrumental "Time," cowritten by Martin and his former EMI counterpart, Columbia A&R head Norman Newell. Martin had previously been impressed with Winding's rendition of "Yesterday" on the jazzman's 1965 album *The In Instrumentals*, and he was happy to share his original composition for Winding's consideration—not to mention an advance copy of the Beatles' upcoming single. By the time that Winding and his bandmates had wrapped up their new long-player—which the trombonist dubbed *Penny Lane and Time*—he had added two more cover versions to the album's running order, including the standout Lennon-McCartney compositions "Here, There, and Everywhere" and "Eleanor Rigby." But for his part, Martin was downright chuffed, finally beginning to find a home for his original compositions beyond the auspices of his usual duties as arranger and orchestrator for the works of other artists.

When George and the Beatles reconvened in cavernous Studio 1 on Friday, February 10, they spearheaded one of the most transformative sessions in the history of recording artistry. By their current standards, the session was relatively short, clocking in at five hours on the dot. But for George, his day-long prep for the February 10 session, not to mention his well-honed and strategic orchestration, had been essential to the evening's success. Indeed, it depended on it. George had begun making preparations long before the Beatles arrived at Abbey Road at eight o'clock that evening. As it happened, George had reckoned that the only way to get the sound the bandmates desired—the awe-inspiring sound of a symphony orchestra but with only half of its typical personnel in evidence—he would need to develop one of his patented workarounds. This meant that, given the existing rhythm track and sundry overdubs that they'd already carried out, George's standard four-track recording efforts would have to be doubled in order to capture the sound he had in mind. As Ken Townsend later recalled, "George Martin came up to me that morning and said to me, 'Oh Ken, I've got a poser for you. I want to run two four-track tape machines together this evening. I know it's never been done before, can you do it?' So I went away and came up with a method whereby we fed a 50-cycle tone from the track of one machine then raised its voltage to drive the capstan motor of the second, thus running the two in sync. Like all these things, the ideas either work first time or not at all." The proof would be in the pudding during the actual session, of course, but George needed Ken's makeshift, synchronized machines to work if he wanted to pull off the sound in his head and the omnipresent power that "A Day in the Life" merited. George reasoned that with forty musicians booked that evening instead of ninety, he could build his own wall of sound by recording his half orchestra four times on all four tracks of the tape and then mixing them down to one. This would essentially afford the producer with access to the sonic equivalent of 160 musicians![15]

George's gambit not only presented technical challenges for Townsend but also required a bit of chicanery on behalf of himself and his production team. As Emerick later wrote, "Ever conscious of cost, George Martin had warned Richard and me not to let the musicians know we would be recording them multiple times on separate tracks, because doing so would result in massive extra charges. Instead, we were under strict instructions to make them think that each time around we were wiping the previous take and recording over it." As night fell over the studio, the players began to arrive. In advance of the session, the Beatles had asked for the members of the half orchestra to wear their evening finery—coats and tails, the whole shebang. As usual, George had assembled many of London's most respected musicians, not to mention a number of veterans of Beatles sessions past. Alan Civil, the horn player behind "For No One," was there, as was David Mason of "Penny Lane" fame. Several standout string players were there, too, including Jürgen Hess, John Underwood, and, perhaps most notably, Sidney Sax, who had played on the June 1965 "Yesterday" session that George had considered to be his breakthrough with the Beatles in terms of evolving their sound beyond a mere beat band. And while it may not have been a full orchestra, it was easily the largest group to perform on a Beatles session to date. All told, forty studio musicians participated in the session that evening, with their instrumentation composed of twelve violins, four violas, four cellos, three trumpets, three trombones, two double-basses, two clarinets, two bassoons, two flutes, two horns, a harp, an oboe, a tuba, and a percussionist. The total cost rang up to nearly £370, a considerable sum at the time—and certainly one that left George concerned about bringing in *Sgt. Pepper* within EMI's budget strictures. But it was a far cry, of course, from the nearly £1,500 that booking 160 session players would have necessitated.[16]

With George's preparations complete—and with the half orchestra ready and waiting in their evening dress—the Beatles took the stage in Studio 1, with their own presession prep having taken a rather different form. When the Beatles had promised to wear their formal finery, too, George should have known better: "They wore their version of it," he later wrote, "courageously flamboyant floral costumes" that were "very flower power." For Martin, the strangest of the lot was McCartney, hands down. "For reasons known only to himself," George recalled, Paul "arrived wearing a full-length red cook's apron, which clashed horribly with his purple-and-black sub-Paisley pattern shirt!" For his part, John had donned a pair of upside down spectacles. And the Beatles had brought along plenty of novelty items to share. The idea for handing out party favors found its origins with John, who reportedly said, "If we put them in silly party hats and rubber noses, maybe then they'll understand what it is we want. That will loosen up those tight-asses!" Lennon dutifully sent roadie Mal Evans to the nearest novelty store, where he purchased an assortment of silly hats, rubber noses, clown wigs, bald head pates, gorilla paws—and lots of clip-on nipples. During the session, George was startled by the transformation of his regal symphonic session men into a ragtag troupe of zany British partygoers. As the producer later recalled, "I left the studio at one point and came back to find one of the musicians, David McCallum, wearing a red clown's nose and Erich Gruenberg, leader of the violins, wearing a gorilla's paw on his bow hand. Everyone was wearing funny hats and carnival novelties. I just fell around laughing!" Sidney Sax remembered that the Beatles had "stuck balloons onto the ends of the two bassoons. They went up and down as the instruments were played and they filled with air!" Like several members of the Abbey Road staff, engineer Peter Vince sat in on the legend-making session and was amazed by what he observed that evening: "Only the Beatles could have assembled a studio full of musicians, many from the Royal Philharmonic or the London Symphony orchestras, all wearing funny hats, red noses, balloons on their bows and putting up with headphones clipped around their Stradivari violins acting as microphones."[17]

But for the Beatles, the evening wouldn't have been complete without rock's reigning glitterati in attendance. "They were determined to have a party," George recalled, "so they invited along a few of their mates—only about 40 or so, including Mick Jagger, Marianne Faithfull, Pattie Boyd, Brian Jones, Simon Posthuma and Marijke Koger of the design team the Fool, Graham Nash, all of them wearing long, multicolored flowing robes, stripy 'loon' beads, bangles, baubles, badges, and bells." Not to be outdone, George's bride was there, too: "Mingling discreetly in amongst all this unisex hippy flamboyance was Judy," George recalled, "wearing, of all things, a tweed suit—very fashionable!" With everyone in their places inside the studio proper, including

Martin and McCartney serving as conductors—and with Emerick and Lush standing by in the control booth—that incredible session was set to begin. But there was one thing left to do. George later wrote that before the recording got underway, "I told the flower-children to sit around the walls and behave themselves; and, just like good children, they did!"[18]

As George and the Beatles prepared to call the orchestra into action, even Studio 1 itself had emerged as a participant in the production of "A Day in the Life." A fifty-three-hundred-square-foot room with towering forty-foot ceilings, Studio 1 had opened during a gala November 1931 ceremony hosted by Sir Adrian Boult, the very same maestro who would blow fifteen-year-old George Martin away with the BBC Symphony Orchestra's rendition of Debussy's *Prélude à l'après-midi d'un faune* at the Bromley County School in 1941. EMI Studios required nearly two years of construction, and the November 1931 event featured Sir Edward Elgar conducting the London Symphony Orchestra's performance of his own *Land of Hope and Glory*—including the famous *Pomp and Circumstance* march, before which Sir Edward joked to the musicians that they should "play this tune as though you've never heard it before." In 1965, the thirty-four-year-old studio received a much-deserved facelift, including the installment of a state-of-the-art ambiophonics system. The brainchild of Gilbert Dutton, the head of EMI's research labs, the ambiophonics system was designed to increase Studio 1's short reverb time, which typically clocked in around two seconds. The idea behind Dutton's innovation was to afford the spacious studio with the sound and feel of a concert hall.[19]

The ambiophonic process, as Dutton devised it, was relatively simple. The microphones in the studio sent a slightly delayed signal that would be played back through a series of loudspeakers installed on the walls of the mammoth room. The new signal would be picked up, in turn, by the original set of microphones and recorded. In Dutton's design, an increase in reverb would be realized by virtue of the length of the delay and the distance between the speakers and the mics. Dutton's ambiophonic system required ninety-six loudspeakers in order to create the necessary sound diffusion. Historian Howard Massey has described ambiophonics as "the Grand Experiment that never quite worked." And in truth, the whole apparatus fell somewhat short of Dutton's original ambition for creating a kind of midcentury forerunner of contemporary surround sound. Given the limitations of 1960s-era technology, the system maxed out after six signal delays—a process that was made possible by the installation of a "delay drum," which consisted of a rotating metal platter, its outer edge having been treated with ferric oxide, with seven magnetic heads (one for recording, six for playback) randomly interspersed around its perimeter. Each of the playback heads directed its signal to a pre-amplifier, which returned the signal to sixteen of the loudspeakers installed on the walls of Studio 1. As Massey explained, "The whole system was essentially a large feedback loop, and therein lay the rub: It only functioned best when on the verge of howling, which made it largely uncontrollable." For his part, Townsend concurred, feeling that ambiophonics "was too artificial. The results sounded a little phony." In many ways, Dutton's system was just another one of the several discrete elements that needed to come together on that magical evening to bring George and the Beatles' vision for "A Day in the Life" into reality.[20]

With Martin and McCartney poised in front of the half orchestra, Emerick finally set the whole business into motion. Before taking his place in front of the musicians, Martin had given the players a series of vague instructions. "Having given them the score," he later wrote, "I had to tell them how to play it. The instructions given, though, shook them rigid. Here was a top-flight orchestra, who had been taught all their lives by maestros that they must play as one coherent unit. I told them that the essential thing in this case was *not* to play like the fellow next to them! 'If you do listen to the guy next to you,' I told them, 'and you find you're playing the same note, you're playing the wrong note. I want you to go your own way, and just ignore everything else; just make your own sound.' They laughed; half of them thought we were completely insane, and the others thought that was a great hoot." From his place in the booth, Emerick could sense Martin's mounting frustration. "Do what?? What the bloody hell?" Emerick heard through the studio mics as Martin attempted to ease Erich Gruenberg's dismay with the sound of balloons, helpfully supplied by the bandmates, which kept popping in the background. "Just trust me. Please," Martin pleaded with the violinist. "Just trust me." Meanwhile, Alan Civil observed the strange festivities from his place in the brass section, later remarking that "it was such a chaotic session. Such a big orchestra, playing with very little music. And the Beatle chaps were wandering around with rather expensive cameras, like new toys, photographing everything."[21]

As Martin and McCartney took up their batons, the half orchestra finally kicked into gear, performing the producer's strange cacophony of a score, with his even more bizarre, presession instructions to the players blaring in full effect. Of course, the musicians falsely believed that they were rehearsing the passages. But Emerick and Lush were already recording the sounds reverberating in Studio 1. As Emerick later recalled, "At the session, we ran the Beatles' rhythm track on one machine, put an orchestral track on the second machine, ran it back, did it again, and again, and again." As Emerick admitted years later, "We were doing something naughty. Over the remaining two and a half hours of the session, we actually recorded them playing that passage eight separate times, on two clean sections of four-track tape." In so doing, Emerick and Lush had captured the equivalent of four orchestral recordings—exactly as Martin had planned it. But the unsung hero in the process was Emerick, whose quick thinking at the mixing desk ensured that the half orchestra's crescendo had been recorded to Martin and the band-mates' specifications. "It was only by careful fader manipulation that I was able to get the crescendo of the orchestra at the right time," he later wrote. "I was gradually bringing it up, my technique being slightly psychological in that I'd bring it up to a point and then slightly fade it back in level without the listener being able to discern this was happening, and then I'd have about 4 dBs in hand at the end. It wouldn't have worked if I'd just shoved the level up to start with."[22]

And then, before the clock struck eleven on that fateful night, George put down his baton and said, "Thank you, gentlemen, that's a wrap." As Emerick looked on from the booth, "everyone in the entire studio—orchestra members, Beatles, and Beatles friends alike—broke into spontaneous applause. It was a hell of a moment." Looking on from his position beside Emerick, Lush couldn't hide his ebullience, saying, "Wow, I can't wait for people to hear this!" For his part, George was elated. "When we'd finished doing the orchestral bit," he later remarked, "one part of me said, 'We're being a bit self-indulgent here.' The other part of me said, 'It's bloody marvelous!'" To everyone's great relief, Townsend's gambit had paid off, and the synchronized tape machines had done their work. The sounds of the orchestra—four of them, to be precise—now played alongside the words and music of the Beatles in exquisite harmony. And for one night at least, ambiophonics hadn't been all that phony at all. Dutton's brainchild had ensured that the orchestral reverb enjoyed an arresting, artificial echo that served to heighten the song's dramatic intent. For George and the Beatles, the stars had truly aligned on the night of February 10. On that rarest of occasions in Studio 1, the system had worked like a charm—and exactly as Dutton had imagined it would. By 1971, studio personnel, frustrated by ambiophonics' hit-or-miss nature, gave up on Dutton's design and removed the system from Abbey Road altogether.[23]

After the studio musicians packed up and left for the night, Paul ushered the Beatles and their friends around the microphones for one last recording that evening. At this juncture, George's score called for the half orchestra to conclude with an E major chord, which they had duly recorded that evening.

George knew that the Beatles wanted to create an arresting conclusion for "A Day in the Life," and for the moment at least, the orchestral flourish brought the recording to a close. As George later recalled, "It was Paul's idea to do something really tumultuous on the song, something that would whack the person listening right between the ears and leave them gasping with shock. He didn't know quite what it was he wanted, but he did want to try for something extremely startling." Lennon and McCartney had already decided that the orchestral coda was a place-saver. As Geoff remembered, "Paul asked the other Beatles and their guests to stick around and try out an idea he had just gotten for an ending, something he wanted to overdub on after the final orchestral climax. Everyone was weary—the studio was starting to smell suspiciously of pot, and there was lots of wine floating around—but they were keen to have a go. Paul's concept was to have everyone hum the same note in unison; it was the kind of *avant-garde* thinking he was doing a lot of in those days. It was absurd, really—the biggest gathering of pop stars in the world, gathered around a microphone, humming, with Paul conducting the choir. It was a fun way to cap off a fine party."[24]

As mid-1960s concepts go, McCartney's notion of having the assembled glitterati chant *om* represented the emerging counterculture's nod to Eastern philosophy. In the tradition of Transcendental Meditation, om is the primordial sound—the sound that we know from the womb, as well as the sound of nothingness and everything all at once. The om connotes that part of humanity that is stardust, that is the sound of the universe. In this sense, the gigantic om that Paul had in mind made for a potentially powerful conclusion to the Beatles' magnum opus. As they gathered around the studio microphones, the bandmates and their guests attempted several takes. "Eight beats, remember," Paul instructed them. A few of the takes collapsed, understandably, into fits of laughter. Finally, take eleven was selected as the best, and the Beatles and their friends recorded three overdubs to create a massive sound. But George was unimpressed, later describing the om chant as "one of those bright ideas that just didn't work. We thought of all the ideas of Buddhist monks chanting. We thought it'd be a great idea to have everybody messed in the studio doing 'Ommmm,' hanging onto it, and multiply it many times. And the result was—pathetic!" A proper coda, it seemed, would have to wait for another day.[25]

Before the session concluded around one o'clock in the morning, George, the bandmates, and their remaining guests crowded into the control room to listen to the playback from the day's efforts. Everyone was curious about how the recording had turned out, and for the folks who were fortunate to be there in the wee hours of Saturday, February 11, the results were mesmerizing. Many people listened from the hallway, with the Beatles' friends spilling out of the tiny control booth. Disc-cutter Tony Clark stood just outside the door. "I was speechless, the tempo changes—everything in that song—was just so dramatic and complete," he later recalled. "I felt so privileged to be there. I walked out of the Abbey Road that night thinking, 'What am I going to do now?' It really did affect me." George's partner Ron Richards was there—just as he had been at the Beatles' legend-making first session with George back on June 6, 1962. "I just can't believe it," Richards exclaimed. "That's it, I think I'll give up and retire now." EMI mastering engineer Malcolm Davies later observed that Richards was no slouch himself, producing the Hollies at the time and working with a number of top acts. "I think he knew that the Beatles were just untouchable," said Davies. "It blew him away."[26]

But as it invariably happened, the Beatles and their brain trust didn't take a break from working on their latest project to ponder what they'd just accomplished. By Monday, February 13, work continued unabated in Studio 2, where George and his production team created a mono remix of "A Day in the Life" for demo purposes. But the main event that evening was a new Harrison composition going under the unsubtle working title of "Not Known." For his part, Harrison had been uncommonly distant during the early sessions for the Beatles' new long-player. As he later recalled, "I'd just got back from India, and my heart was still out there. After what had happened in 1966, everything else seemed like hard work. It was a job, like doing something I didn't really want to do, and I was losing interest in being 'fab' at that point." While Harrison recognized that "there was a more profound ambience to the band," he also felt that the Beatles were back on the record industry's treadmill, that "we were just in the studio to make the next record, and Paul was going on about this idea of some fictitious band. That side of it didn't really interest me." As his contribution to *Sgt. Pepper*, "Not Known" was composed by Harrison as a "joke relating to Liverpool, the Holy City in the North of England. In addition, the song was copyrighted Northern Songs, Ltd., which I don't own, so it doesn't really matter what chords I play, as it's only a Northern Song."[27]

But for Martin, Emerick, and the other Beatles, working on *Sgt. Pepper* was hardly a joke. Rather, it was shaping up to be a moment of intense artistic engagement. That evening, the Beatles finally got around to creating a basic rhythm track around midnight. The group attempted nine takes during the session, with Harrison plying the Hammond organ, McCartney on bass, and Starr behind the drum kit. With take three selected as the best, the band closed up shop for the night. But Martin and Emerick stayed behind in the control room, perturbed at Harrison's seeming nonchalance about his contribution to *Sgt. Pepper*. To Emerick's mind, "Not Known," which later morphed into "Only a Northern Song," "seemed like such an inappropriate song to be bringing to what was generally a happy, upbeat album." Martin chose his words carefully, telling Emerick, "I'm disappointed that George didn't come up with something better." Geoff understood George's frustration, but he also understood why the producer had to be cautious about his remarks: "He was always on his guard because he didn't ever want disparaging comments to be reported back. The other Beatles were clearly underwhelmed, too. John was so uninspired, in fact, that he decided not to participate in the backing track at all."[28]

Martin had long been concerned about Harrison's subordinate place in the band's calculus. "George Harrison was what you might call the Beatles' Third Man—always there, yet somehow elusive," Martin later wrote. "The electricity that crackled between Paul and John, and that led to such great music, rather left George out in the cold. He had only himself to collaborate with. If he needed help from the other two, they gave it, but often rather grudgingly. It was not so much that Lennon and McCartney did not believe in Harrison; more that their overwhelming belief in themselves left very little room for anything—or anybody—else." But in retrospect, Martin knew that he, too, had contributed to Harrison's junior status among the Beatles' songwriters. "As for my own role, I am so sorry to say that I did not help George much with his songwriting, either. His early attempts didn't show enormous promise. Being a very pragmatic person, therefore, I tended to go with the blokes who were delivering the goods. I never cold-shouldered George. I did, though, look at his new material with a slightly jaundiced eye."[29]

The very next evening, Tuesday, February 14, Martin and the Beatles continued working on "Only a Northern Song" with similar and pointedly less than spectacular results. The session began with a tape-to-tape reduction of take three in order to free up additional recording space. Much of the lengthy session was devoted to the superimposition of two Harrison vocals onto the track. As the other Beatles—namely, Lennon and McCartney—were keenly aware, "Only a Northern Song" originated from Harrison's overt dissatisfaction with the band's financial state of affairs vis-à-vis Northern Songs. The publishing enterprise that Martin's friend and business associate Dick James had established in February 1963 with the release of the band's third single, "From Me to You" backed with "Thank You Girl," Northern Songs provided for a fifty-fifty split between Dick James Music and NEMS, which had generated astounding profits for Brian Epstein along with Lennon and McCartney as the band's primary composers. The February 14 session came to a sudden end around 12:30 AM—early by Martin and the Beatles' standards—when a dejected McCartney exclaimed, "Look, let's knock it on the head for the night." By this point in the brief recording history of "Only a Northern Song," the writing was already clearly on the wall. Required to play the heavy in his role as the band's producer, Martin pulled Harrison aside for the purposes of a difficult, albeit highly necessary, conversation. "I had to tell George that as far as *Pepper* was concerned, I did not think his song would be good enough for what was shaping up as a really strong album," Martin later wrote. "I suggested he come up with something a bit better. George was a bit bruised: it is never pleasant being rejected, even if you are friendly with the person who is doing the rejecting."[30]

On Thursday, February 16, Martin and the Beatles returned to "Good Morning, Good Morning." Working with the basic track from February 8, Lennon recorded a lead vocal while McCartney provided a bass guitar overdub. During a rough remix, John's vocal was treated with ADT, and a tape-to-tape reduction mix was carried out to free up additional space for future overdubs. The next day, Friday, February 17, made for another Beatles milestone, with the release of the "Strawberry Fields Forever" backed with "Penny Lane" single. But it was also the day when Lennon's old circus poster came into play in Martin and the Beatles' universe. "Lennon always had a precise title for each of his songs, and woe betold any of us who didn't get it correct," Emerick later recalled. "I learned that the hard way one night when I slated a take in a hurry and mistakenly shortened the title to 'For the Benefit of Mr. Kite.' John immediately corrected me in an irritated tone of voice: 'No, that's 'Being for the Benefit of Mr. Kite!'" As it happened, John's lyrics were borrowed, nearly verbatim, from the Victorian advertisement. "The song is pure," he later remarked, "like a painting, a pure watercolor." For John, recording the song would only be possible with the correct ambience. As Martin later wrote, Lennon told him, "I'd love to be able to get across the effects of a really colorful circus. The acrobats in their tights, the smell of the animals, the merry-go-rounds. I want to smell the sawdust, George."[31]

Martin saw "Being for the Benefit of Mr. Kite!" as yet another opportunity to experiment. For George, any chance to try out something new was welcome—and in many ways, it was no different from his early days at EMI as Oscar Preuss's assistant. An opportunity to push the boundaries of the technology, just as he had done all those years ago in the company of Peter Ustinov with "Mock Mozart." But like in the old days, George didn't waste any time grasping for ideas. With the Beatles, "very rarely did we waste time groping in the dark. We were always looking to bring something new to the music, but it had to be focused experimentation, and be very deliberate." For "Being for the Benefit of Mr. Kite!" Martin imagined a "kind of hurdy-gurdy sound." When they pooled their ideas, John said, "I've always loved the sound of the music on that children's program *The Magic Roundabout*." Suddenly, George realized that they were on the same wavelength. "Funny you should say that," he replied. "I had in mind the little organ in Disney's *Snow White*, the one the dwarfs had: a very pipy sound. The real equivalent, though, would be a steam organ, a calliope—what they have on carousels."[32]

With their new concept in mind, George and the bandmates recorded a basic rhythm track for "Being for the Benefit of Mr. Kite!" consisting of Lennon's guide vocal, McCartney on bass, Starr on drums, Harrison on tambourine, and Martin playing the studio's harmonium, "the big beast that was part of the furniture at Abbey Road." For the Beatles' producer, pumping the instrument proved to be an unusual physical challenge, as the group played through one take after another in order to capture the backing track:

> I remember only too well pumping away with my feet at that bloody harmonium for hour after hour, trying to get it right, and being absolutely knackered, heart going at about 130 beats to the minute. It was like climbing up a steep flight of stairs non-stop. We would complete a take, I'd heave a sigh of relief, mop my sweaty brow, and then a dreaded call would come from John: "I wouldn't mind doing that again, George. You all right there?" The harmonium was a good idea, though, because it established a vaguely circus atmosphere to the song straight off.

Eventually, Martin's exertions got the best of him. As Emerick later recalled, the song's basic track necessitated several takes. "It did take quite a few tries to nail it down," Geoff wrote, "which caused problems for George, because the harmonium required pedaling to get air through its bellows, kind of like riding a bicycle. After playing it nonstop for hours on end, he finally collapsed in exhaustion, sprawled out on the floor like a snow angel—a sight that gave us all great amusement." For Lush, the sight of Martin splayed on the studio floor was a revelation, with the usually staid producer having eclipsed his usual bounds of gentlemanly comportment. As the engineer later recalled, "George Martin looked especially straight, he always had a tie and shirt and suit. Every now and again he'd take his tie off and we'd go like 'Wow! Gosh! What's going on here?'"[33]

Before the session wrapped up that evening, Martin received an unexpected blast from the past courtesy of Lennon, who was eager to continue discussing how they might establish the song's circus-like atmosphere. John can be heard suggesting that they bring the Massed Alberts in for an overdub, referring to an obscure novelty act that George had recorded back in the 1950s. Working with Spike Milligan and Eric Sykes, George had produced the eccentric brass band on the zany track "You Gotta Go Oww!" For his part, George seemed to feel the sting of John's barb—"Oh, honestly!" George can be heard replying to the Beatle—but in truth, the producer was having the time of his life. The *Sgt. Pepper* project saw George and the Beatles taking the producer's long-held ambition for making sound pictures to a new level, and he was absolutely loving it. On Monday, February 20, George stretched the Beatles' creativity even further still. He was determined to acquire a calliope in order to achieve the "swirly" sound that John desired. But to his great disappointment, George was unable to locate one of the old steam organs for the recording session. And he quickly realized that "manufacturing our own calliope for a single track just wasn't on"—and it certainly wasn't cost-effective.[34]

And that's when George hit upon the idea of creating the artifice of a circus instead. To establish the illusion, George opted to layer a series of organ sounds. "What we shall do is to create a special backing track with organs and mouth-organs—a pumping kind of sound," the producer told Lennon. With the existing harmonium track already in place, "we had to overlay the special effects using a Hammond and a Lowry organ, together with our well-beloved roadie Mal Evans playing a massive bass harmonica. John and I had great fun," George later recalled, "giggling helplessly as we tried to sort out the organ runs and interrupting one another." For the song's maniacal "Henry the Horse" waltz interlude, George imagined a "tremendous chromatic run up on an organ" in order to mimic the sound of a whinnying horse. Realizing that he couldn't play the sequence in tempo, George resorted to his windup piano technique. "The only way I could do it was to slow the tape down to half speed, which allowed me to play the notes nice and slowly, at a pace I could manage." But as George also reckoned, "It is a fact of physics that if you slow the tape down to half speed, then the frequencies are halved, and the sound drops down an octave lower exactly. I duly played the notes an octave down, recording them at that speed, then on playback speeded the tape back up to normal." And to his great relief, "Eureka! It worked!"[35]

But to George's mind, "Being for the Benefit of Mr. Kite!" still lacked the calliope sound that he had originally envisioned. At this juncture, he turned to Emerick, "who by this stage was more than my engineer on our extraordinary album, he was my co-conspirator," and they reasoned that they could simulate the circus ambience via artificial means. Having scoured the EMI archives for recordings of calliopes and organs, Martin and his production team selected a series of musical snatches from the sound-effects records, which Emerick dutifully transferred to tape. "We're going to try something here," Martin explained to his engineer. "I want you to cut that tape there up into sections that are roughly 15-inches long." Soon, Martin, Emerick, and Lush had "a small pyramid of worm-like tape fragments piled up on the floor at our feet. 'Now,' I said, 'pick them all up and fling them into the air!'" As George later recalled, "It was a wonderful moment—it snowed pieces of tape all over the control room. I had an instant flashback to the day I was demobbed out of the Fleet Air Arm in 1947. The last thing the Navy gave me was my gratuity of £260, all in single pound notes. It was the largest amount of money I had ever had. When I arrived home, the first thing I did was to take out that wodge of massive old pound notes, fling them all over the room, and rush about trying to catch them. Wonderful!"[36]

Selecting the pieces of tape at random, George and his team spliced the pieces of tape together. "Strangely enough," George recalled, "Sod's Law being what it is, some of the pieces of tape went back together almost where they'd started. We got round that by turning anything that sounded like it might be in the correct sequence around and splicing it in back to front." The result was a "chaotic mass of sound: it was impossible to identify the tunes they had come from, but it was unmistakably a steam organ. Perfect! There was the fairground atmosphere we had been looking for. John was thrilled to bits with it." Later, on March 29, Martin superimposed the tape loop, which consisted of nineteen separate organ snatches, onto the basic rhythm track for "Being for the Benefit for Mr. Kite!" and the madcap song had finally been captured. On Tuesday, February 21, George and the bandmates returned to "Fixing a Hole," picking up where they'd left off at Regent Sound back on February 9. After carrying out a reduction mix, Martin recorded a new lead vocal by McCartney, which the Beatle subsequently double-tracked.[37]

At this point, George and the bandmates were completing new tracks at an impressive clip. The next evening, Wednesday, February 22, saw the most important finishing touch superimposed onto "A Day in the Life." Working in Studio 2, George instructed Abbey Road personnel to gather up as many pianos as they possibly could. The assembled keyboards included two Steinway grand pianos, a Steinway upright—slightly out of tune in order to produce a honky-tonk effect—a "blond-wood spinet," and Martin's harmonium, which was screened off in the rear of the studio given the ambient sound produced by the instrument's bellows. All of the Beatles participated in the overdub—save for Harrison, who was late in arriving that evening—along with Mal Evans and Martin. Having agreed with their producer that the gigantic om was "pathetic," the Beatles wanted to replace the hummed E major chord with something far more powerful and arresting. A thundering piano crash seemed like it might just do the trick. "To get as strong an attack as possible, everyone decided to play standing up instead of sitting down," Geoff later recalled. "John, Mal, and George Martin each stood behind a different piano, while Ringo and Paul shared the out-of-tune Steinway upright." With McCartney taking charge of the proceedings, the Beatle counted the players in for take one:

McCartney: "Have you got your loud pedal down, Mal?"
Evans: "Which one's that?"
McCartney: "The right hand one, far right. It keeps the echo going."
Lennon: "Keep it down the whole time."
McCartney: "Right. On four then. One, two, three. . . ."

Given the inherent difficulty of four players attempting to achieve absolute synchronicity, the bandmates required nine takes to carry out the E major crash. While take seven made for the longest of the iterations at fifty-nine seconds, take nine was selected as the best. Martin overdubbed the harmonium part to beef up the coda, which clocked in at nearly fifty-four seconds. The only blemish occurred when Ringo shifted his body on the piano bench, emitting a slight squeak as the massive sound decayed into oblivion.[38]

Up in the control room, Emerick struggled to capture the deafening chord at the mixing desk. "It seemed clear to me that the solution lay in keeping the sound at maximum volume for as long as possible," he later wrote, "and I had two weapons that could accomplish this: a compressor, cranked up full, and the very faders themselves on the mixing console. Logically, if I set the gain of each input to maximum but started with the fader at its lowest point, I could then slowly raise the faders as the sound died away, thus compensating for the loss in volume: in effect, I could counteract the chord getting softer, at least to some degree." With the breathtaking piano chord having been recorded, Harrison finally strode into the session, accompanied by the Byrds' David Crosby. "Nice of you to turn up, George," John remarked. "You only missed the most important overdub we've ever done!" With the superimposition complete, Martin supervised the mono mixing session for "A Day in the Life." Townsend was on hand to assist Emerick and Lush in synchronizing the two four-track machines that had been deployed for the orchestral overdub. Even still, maintaining the machines' synchronization proved to be a source of great difficulty throughout the session. As Emerick later recalled, "Often, by the time we got to the orchestral bit, they would drift noticeably out of time with one another. Everyone dealt with the problem in good humor, though. . . . In the end, we were all actually laying down bets as to whether the machines were going to stay in sync or not; we'd be thrilled on the few occasions when it worked perfectly."[39]

But with Martin looking on, Emerick wasn't finished with "A Day in the Life" just yet: "To enhance things further still, I lowered the volume level of the orchestra at the very beginning of the passage, thus making the mix much more dynamic than the original performance was. No one sitting in that control room with us could believe how much bigger I was able to make everything sound by doing that." For his part, Martin was astounded by the sound of the mixes of "A Day in the Life"—and especially by the awe-inspiring power of the chord that punctuated its conclusion and the unerring silence that followed in its wake. "By the end, the attenuation was enormous," he later remarked. "You could have heard a pin drop." But while he understood that the Beatles were exploring revolutionary vistas of sound in those relatively early days during the production of *Sgt. Pepper*, George was still nervous about what was happening at Abbey Road, about whether or not they were the purveyors of a newfangled art or merely self-indulgent poseurs. Were the Beatles and their producer taking their senses of experimentation and whimsy too far? Would they risk losing their massive audience, as Paul had wondered aloud during the *Revolver* sessions? "I suppose I had been worried that we might be leaving our public behind," Martin later wrote, that we were "getting a bit too fast in front."[40]

For George, sweet relief from these anxieties arrived in the usual guise of Alan Livingston, the Capitol Records president whose organization had rejected the Beatles' American release on several occasions back in 1963, only to eat their words with the trailblazing success of "I Want to Hold Your Hand" and *Meet the Beatles* in the first weeks of 1964. But *Sgt. Pepper* was a creative universe away from the nature of George and the bandmates' work together during the heady days of Beatlemania. "What helped me have confidence in the album was that the imperious Alan Livingston flew over to London to find out what we were up to," George later wrote. "This was just after we had finished recording 'A Day in the Life.'" In earlier times, Brian Epstein might have served as his sounding board. But after the fallout from the Jesus Christ tour, and given Epstein's increasingly brittle psychological state, those days were gone. And the producer certainly wasn't turning to EMI's Len Wood for succor. As far as George was concerned, Livingston would do just fine as a test audience. Sitting alone in the studio with the American record man, George played the newly mixed "A Day in the Life" for him, and not surprisingly "it knocked him sideways. He was flabbergasted by it." But for Martin, the best aspect of Livingston's response was revealed by what he *didn't* say. "He was in no way perturbed by any aspect of the song, by its relatively bizarre lyrics, or its *avant-garde* production," George later wrote, "only speechless in admiration. I knew then that we were home and dry."[41]

12

THE SONG THAT GOT AWAY

————

WHEN GEORGE AND THE BANDMATES convened for a Thursday, February 23, session in Studio 2, they tried their hand at a new composition, Paul's "Lovely Rita," a bouncy, colorful number about a comely meter maid. With the tape running, the Beatles worked out a basic rhythm track consisting of Harrison and Lennon playing their acoustic guitars on tracks one and two, Starr's drums on track three, and McCartney's piano on track four. After having selected take eight as the best version, Martin carried out a tape reduction, and McCartney recorded a bass guitar part, which would mark the evening's only overdub. By this point, Paul had developed a practice of working out his bass parts, meticulously crafting their progression from one note to the next. As Emerick later recalled, "He would do those overdubs in the wee hours, long after everyone else had gone home. It would be just Richard [Lush] and me up in the control room, with Paul sitting on a chair out in the middle of the studio, away from his usual corner, working assiduously to perfect his lines, giving all he had to the task at hand. Richard would painstakingly drop the multitrack in and out of record, one section at a time, until every note was articulated perfectly and Paul was satisfied with the result."[1]

The next evening, Friday, February 24, saw McCartney overdubbing his lead vocals for "Lovely Rita," which Martin recorded at forty-six and a half cycles per second in order to afford McCartney's voice with a faster, brighter sound on playback. After taking a long weekend, George and the Beatles were back at Abbey Road on Tuesday, February 28, when John unveiled a new composition, "Lucy in the Sky with Diamonds," which the bandmates rehearsed for nearly the entirety of the eight-hour session. John's inspiration for the song found its origins in his three-year-old son Julian's description of his painting of a classmate—"it's Lucy, in the sky, with diamonds," he told his father. In John's creation, the song presented a magical netherworld of "plasticine porters and looking-glass ties." Lennon would later tell Martin's old friend Spike Milligan that such zany moments in the song's lyrics found their inspiration in old *Goon Show* dialogue. On the same evening that the Beatles debuted "Lucy in the Sky with Diamonds," *Life* magazine reporter Thomas Thompson observed the proceedings as they unfolded in Studio 2, later quoting Martin, who remarked that "we are light years away from anything tonight. They know it is awful now, and they're trying to straighten it out. It may be a week before they're pleased, if ever. They're always coming up with something new they've just learned, something I wouldn't dream of. They never cease to amaze me."[2]

Years later, EMI Studios' Peter Vane described the frustration that would inevitably set in as the Beatles spent hour upon hour struggling with the act of creation:

Although they'd use the studio as a rehearsal room you couldn't just clear off because they might be trying something out—just piano or bass or drums—and they'd want to come up and listen to the thing before carrying on. So you couldn't just disappear or nod off, you had to be around all the time. The nights were so long when you had nothing to do. While they were actually working on the records, wonderful—all those great sounds, wonderful—but what people don't realize is the boredom factor. *Sgt. Pepper's Lonely Hearts Club Band* took four months to record and for probably more than half that time all the engineers were doing was sitting around waiting for them to get their ideas together.[3]

By the very next evening, Wednesday, March 1, George and the bandmates had clearly worked things out to their satisfaction and then some when it came to "Lucy in the Sky with Diamonds." That night, they recorded a basic rhythm track with Harrison's acoustic guitar and occasional piano from Martin on track one, McCartney's Lowrey organ on track two, Starr's drums on track three, and Lennon's guide vocal and maracas on track four. By the time that they reached take seven, Martin's piano had disappeared from the arrangement and Harrison's tamboura drone had emerged instead. But George didn't miss his piano part in the slightest, feeling that the Lowrey created the perfect ambience for John's magical song. "It was more like a modern synthesizer than a conventional organ," he later wrote. "The great thing about the Lowrey was that, whereas with the Hammond it was almost impossible to get any decay, with the Lowrey it was easy." For George, Paul's prefatory piece and John's melody were the making of the composition: "The beginning of 'Lucy,' that hesitant, lilting introductory phrase, is crucial to the staying power of the song. It is also a marvelous piece of composition, based around five notes only, and so simple that virtually anyone can play it. Schubert would have been proud of it. Nothing in the world is more difficult than to write a first-class melody—especially one that uses as few notes of the scale as we find in 'Lucy.' It is the mark of a great composer: and something that both Lennon and McCartney could do—and did often."[4]

The next evening, Thursday, March 2, George and the Beatles completed work on "Lucy in the Sky with Diamonds," making it the quickest production of any song thus far for *Sgt. Pepper*. With the rhythm track in hand from the previous night's work, they set up creating a series of overdubs for the song, which was easily one of the album's most complex arrangements. As George later wrote, "'Lucy in the Sky with Diamonds' is like 'A Day in the Life' in that it is virtually two separate songs. The middle section is a completely different tempo and has a completely different time signature to the opening. John had us jump, quite suddenly, from the opening 3/4 into a big 4/4 rhythm. There was no possibility of making a smooth transition at this point in the song. The big change of tempo had to kick in with a great big bang, a bit like making a clutchless gear change in a car: it crunches, but it keeps you moving forward. The blaring worked and was the most effective way of doing the song." Knowing that the tempo shifts would be invariably abrupt, George ensured that the Beatles' overdubs afforded the song with plenty of ambience, heavily treating the vocal contributions with varispeed. "The vocals on 'Lucy' weren't recorded at normal speed," he later recalled. "The first track was recorded at a frequency of 45 cycles, our normal frequency being 50 cycles. In other words, we slowed the tape down, so that when we played it back the voice sounded 10 percent higher: back in the correct key, but thinner-sounding, which suited the song. It gave a slight Mickey Mouse quality to the vocals. In fact, Paul was also singing on two tracks, lending John a spot of harmony. I also added the odd bit of tape echo to the voices. The second voice track was recorded at 48½ cycles per second to see what that sounded like. 'Lucy' has more variations of tape speed in it than any other track on the album." To compound the atmosphere, Martin recorded McCartney's bass and Harrison's fuzz-box lead guitar at normal speed. In so doing, Martin ensured that "Lucy in the Sky with Diamonds" worked from a host of competing sounds and rhythms in keeping with the magical world that Lennon wanted to simulate in the studio.[5]

The next evening, Friday, March 3, George and the Beatles returned to "Sgt. Pepper's Lonely Hearts Club Band" for the first time since February 2. Up first that night was a brass overdub to account for the mythical Sgt. Pepper's band of lonely hearted players. Without having prepared a score in advance, George rounded up a quartet of horn players, including James W. Buck, John Burden, Tony Randall, and Neil Sanders. As the session men looked on, McCartney shared his vision for the horn interludes, which would be superimposed on track three. "They didn't really know what they wanted," Burden later recalled, so "I wrote out phrases for them based on what Paul McCartney was humming to us and George Martin. All four Beatles were there, but only Paul took an active interest in our overdub." After obtaining Beatles autographs, which had become a regular practice among visiting session men, the players left Abbey Road and the spotlight turned to McCartney, who turned in a sizzling lead guitar on track three. Paul's grungy guitar licks vividly recalled the sound of Jimi Hendrix's debut at the Bag O'Nails back in November 1966. It wouldn't be the last time that the American guitar hero's influence would be heard on the *Sgt. Pepper* album. Before they closed up shop for the evening, Martin and his production team revisited "Lucy in the Sky with Diamonds," which was treated to a significant dose of ADT during the creation of the song's mono mixes.[6]

With the weekend behind them, George and the bandmates reconvened on Monday, March 6, in Studio 2, where Paul experienced a eureka moment. "It was about three or four weeks before the final session when they started thinking about the running order of the songs," Geoff later recalled. "The concept of it being Sgt. Pepper's band was already there when Paul said, 'Wouldn't it be good if we get the atmosphere? Get the band warming up, hear the audience settle into their seats, have the songs as different acts on the stage?'" With this notion in mind, Emerick rifled through the orchestral overdubs that they had conducted back on February 10. Four outtakes from the earlier session had already been duly stored in EMI's tape library. In short order, Emerick spliced a segment of the half orchestra warming up and dropped it into track three as a musical preface for "Sgt. Pepper's Lonely Hearts Club Band." For the song's remaining sound effects, Martin and Emerick drew upon an extract from *Volume 28: Audience Applause and Atmosphere, Royal Albert Hall and Queen Elizabeth Hall* to simulate the murmuring audience during the orchestral warm-up. The song's canned laughter and audience applause arrived courtesy of the satirical British stage revue *Beyond the Fringe*, which had been borrowed from the EMI tape library's *Volume 6: Applause and Laughter*. The latter found its origins in Martin's live recordings of the comedy troupe at London's Fortune Theatre back in 1961.[7]

During the next session on Tuesday, March 7, George and the Beatles moved quickly apace, returning to "Lovely Rita" for a series of overdubs onto take eleven. Much of the work was devoted to a series of backing vocals, spearheaded by Lennon, and other assorted studio chatter. With Geoff as his confederate, John requested that the engineer treat his vocals, which included a running fusillade of screams, moans, and even an occasional "cha-cha-cha," with heavy tape echo. There was also the lingering issue of an empty middle eight that, for the time being at least, would remain unresolved by McCartney, who couldn't decide about which instrument (or instrumentalist) to highlight in a solo section. But even more importantly, the March 7 session in Studio 2 would go down in the annals of rock history for the peculiar instrumentation that the bandmates fashioned for the song's play-out section. Several members of Pink Floyd were working in Studio 3 that same evening under the supervision of Norman Smith, who was producing the band's debut album, *The Piper at the Gates of Dawn*, for Parlophone. A group of former architecture students at London Polytechnic, Pink Floyd had made their name of late as the house band at the UFO Club. Years later, they claimed to have observed, gobsmacked, as Mal Evans gathered up rolls of toilet paper from the Abbey Road restroom for the Beatles' mysterious deployment. "There was a lot of off-the-cuff fooling around," Martin wrote, "and we even resorted to a choir of paper and combs, as a mock brass section. They all blew through combs covered with regulation-issue EMI toilet paper to create a bizarre, kazoo-like sound." As it happened, the quality of the EMI toilet paper had been a long-standing issue among the Beatles, especially Harrison. As Martin later recalled, the band's lead guitarist "complained frequently to the EMI management about the horrible slippery hardness of its loo paper. (Each sheet had the legend 'Property of EMI' stamped across it!) He said it was okay for wrapping round a comb and blowing through, but as to using it for what it was intended, you could forget it!"[8]

For George and the Beatles, Studio 2 was dark on March 8, when the bandmates took a brief sabbatical to prepare new material for the long-player. Meanwhile, Martin took the opportunity to provide Emerick and Lush with a couple of much-needed days off. As Geoff later recalled, "George Martin decided that Richard and I were being overworked and gave us an evening off. It's true that we had been burning the candles at both ends—we still continued to do sessions for other artists on the days when the Beatles were not booked in—and we were now often staying behind long after George Martin would go home." When the bandmates and their producer regrouped on the evening of Thursday, March 9, Emerick and Lush had been conspicuously replaced by a pair of EMI temporary stand-ins, balance engineer Malcolm Addey and the indefatigable Ken Townsend. Addey had been one of Abbey Road's mainstay engineers since the late 1950s, when he recorded Cliff Richard's debut hit "Move It," with Norrie Paramor sitting in the producer's chair. As Addey later recalled, the Beatles were very late in arriving to the studio on March 9. "They eventually straggled in one by one," Addey reported. "Ringo came in about 11 and ordered fish and chips. The others arrived later, they all hung around and finally started work at about one in the morning. The ego trip of the big-time artists had started to set in." For his part, Martin agreed with Addey's assessment, writing that the Beatles "were beginning to take the people at Abbey Road a bit for granted." Even still, Martin's selection of Addey, even as a temporary replacement for his regular production team, made for a strange choice. It was no secret among the corridors of EMI Studios that Addey wasn't very fond of Martin, claiming that he had a tendency to "inject himself into everything." Believing that the producer felt socially "superior to everybody," Addey took particular issue with Martin's affected accent, which Addey derided as the result of personal reinvention—a kind of "mess-hall posh" in which young men like Martin join the service only to be discharged as "something quite different" from their earlier, homegrown selves. Given their interpersonal clashes, Martin and Addey pointedly avoided sharing the control room together. When he returned from his brief respite, Emerick had been surprised by Addey's participation in a Beatles session. Describing Addey as "he of the cigar and never-ending chatter," Emerick thought he was "an odd choice, since I knew that George Martin didn't like working with him."[9]

When the Beatles and their makeshift production team finally settled down to business in the wee hours of March 10, McCartney presented a brand-new composition titled "Getting Better" for Martin and the bandmates' consideration. The song originated during one of Paul's frequent strolls around St. John's Wood. With his sheepdog, Martha, in tow, along with *Sunday Times* reporter Hunter Davies, Paul took note of the springlike weather in the air, remarking to Davies that "it's getting better!" Shortly thereafter, he remembered the words of Jimmie Nicol, Ringo's June 1964 stand-in during his bout with tonsillitis, who often answered "oh, it's getting better all the time" when people asked how he was doing. With the new song in hand, the Beatles fashioned a basic rhythm track, which Martin captured in seven takes. The first track featured McCartney's rhythm guitar and Starr's drums, with McCartney's guide vocal on track two. Meanwhile, Martin played a pianette on track three, with Starr rounding out track four with additional percussion. George worked the pianette by striking its strings in order to provide an innovative sound effect on the mini–electric keyboard. Before he concluded the long session that morning, George carried out a tape reduction after deleting the guide vocal, which would be replaced during the evening session. By the time they closed up shop, that evening session was set to begin in just under sixteen hours.[10]

And when the March 10 session ensued in Studio 2 that night, George and the Beatles were understandably dead tired. The nine-hour session began at seven in the evening, and Martin led the Beatles through a series of overdubs for "Getting Better," including Harrison's tamboura drone, McCartney's bass, and Starr's drums. After taking a breather over the weekend, they were back at it on Monday, March 13, when they resumed work on "Good Morning, Good Morning," which had been on the back burner for the past three weeks. At Lennon's request, Martin had booked Sounds Incorporated for the session. They had played on sessions for a number of top-flight artists over the years, and they had even shared the bill with the Beatles on several occasions—most famously serving as one of the opening acts for the Fab Four's Shea Stadium concert in August 1965. As George later recalled, "It so happened that Brian Epstein managed a group called Sounds Incorporated, who were good pals, if a bit crazy, so we brought them in to give us our horn sound. They worked with us all day on it—and they had a very hard time. John's rhythms, so natural to his ear, were the very devil for the six players to deliver in perfect time. They had to count like mad to know exactly when to do the 'stabs.' It was very easy for them to miss cues, and very hard indeed to hit them as one, bang on." George saw the song as a particular challenge for the Beatles' drummer. "Think of poor Ringo," he later wrote. "His drumming had to be super-accurate, with all the walloping accents spot on. Lucky he was so good, really." As for Sounds Incorporated, sax player Alan Holmes later recalled that the session men were "there for about six hours. The first three hours we had refreshments and the Beatles played us the completed songs for the new LP." Richard Lush's memories cohere with Holmes's. "They spent a long time doing the overdub, about three hours or maybe longer," the Beatles' tape operator recalled, "but John Lennon thought it sounded too straight." As with the swirly sound on "Being for the Benefit of Mr. Kite!" and other recent tracks, "he just wanted it to sound weird." As usual, Emerick was on hand to make that sense of weirdness possible. "To satisfy Lennon's demand that I take a different sonic approach," Emerick later wrote, "I shoved the mics right down the bells of the saxes and screwed the sound up with limiters and a healthy dose of effects like flanging and ADT; we pretty much used every piece of equipment at hand."[11]

On Wednesday, March 15, Harrison heeded Martin's earlier advice and presented "Within You, Without You," untitled at this juncture, as a new composition in place of "Only a Northern Song." While his original contribution to *Sgt. Pepper* may have been out of place on the Beatles' latest long-player, the angst that Harrison revealed in "Only a Northern Song" was very genuine indeed. The quiet Beatle was all too conscious of his place in the band's pecking order and what that placement meant in terms of recording his compositions. "Sometimes I had songs that were better than some of their songs," he later remarked, "and we'd have to record maybe eight of theirs before they'd listen to one of mine." But on March 15, Harrison had come through with a veritable triumph. Written earlier in the year at the home of longtime Beatles compadre Klaus Voormann, "Within You, Without You" proved to be Harrison's Indian tour de force. To make sense of the complex composition, Martin arranged the song into three distinctive parts. As he listened to Harrison debut the piece, he sat mesmerized on his usual high stool in the studio. To Martin's eyes and ears, Harrison was "like a carpet weaver—meticulous with a needle and thread." He later observed that "George understood that in any song written according to the Vedic tradition the voice and the dilruba should accompany one another in unison. This was true even of what was basically a Western pop tune. It was the instrumentation, not the melody, that made it sound Indian."[12]

As with his earlier Indian effusions, Harrison had recruited top players from the Asian Music Circle to perform on "Within You, Without You." Emerick took special care to ensure that the recording environment was welcoming for the Indian musicians. "Studio Two had a hardwood floor," he later wrote, "so in order to dampen the sound, I normally put down carpeting underneath Ringo's drums and in the area where Beatles vocals were recorded. But this time Richard and I got out a bunch of throw rugs and spread them all around the floor for the musicians to sit on, all in an effort to make them more comfortable and make the studio a bit more homey. Mind you, the Abbey Road rugs were completely moth-eaten and dilapidated—but it was the thought that counted." With Harrison working the tamboura, Martin and his production team captured a range of different sounds emanating from the studio musicians' tabla, swarmandal, and sitar-like dilruba. Even Beatles roadie Neil Aspinall chipped in for the occasion. As Emerick later remarked, "The tabla had never been recorded the way we did it. Everyone was amazed when they first heard a tabla recorded that closely, with the texture and the lovely low resonances." Martin was especially pleased with Harrison's penchant for atmospherics, later writing that "George, as usual, set joss sticks smoldering in the corners. He looked a bit like the Lone Ranger with his Indian friends. Although the other Beatles were there, they stuck around for the fun of it. None of them played or sang a note. In order to get them to play what he wanted, George would simply sing to the Indian musicians, or occasionally pick a few notes on the sitar." The evening was also noteworthy for the appearance of pop artist Peter Blake, who had recently been commissioned, along with his wife Jann Haworth, to design the cover art for *Sgt. Pepper*. "George [Harrison] was very sweet," Blake later recalled, "and he got up and welcomed us in and offered us tea." Martin later recalled the artist's sense of fascination, writing that "Peter had never seen a Beatles session, and he was amazed. He thought it was a very gentle, very easy way of working. But it was all the music, really: it was George's hypnotic music that induced that strange air of peace."[13]

As it happened, Martin's own sense of peace was interrupted during this same week when McCartney, working "on heat" with a new composition titled "She's Leaving Home," sought out the assistance of another arranger when the Beatles' producer had been unavailable. As Paul later recalled, "I rang him and I said, 'I need you to arrange it.' He said, 'I'm sorry, Paul, I've got a Cilla session.' And I thought, 'Fucking hell! After all this time working together, he ought to put himself out.' It was probably unreasonable to expect him to. Anyway, I said, 'Well, fine, thanks George,' but I was so hot to trot that I called Mike Leander, another arranger. I got him to come over to Cavendish Avenue, and I showed him what I wanted, strings, and he said, 'Leave it with me.'" Meanwhile, George had been working vigilantly on Cilla's behalf and, in the process, attempting to placate her over what she believed to be Brian Epstein's ongoing neglect—even after he had begged her to remain in his stable the previous autumn. Her latest single, "A Fool Am I" backed with a cover version of the Beatles' "For No One," had failed to crack the top ten, and she was determined to make her way back to the top of the pops. To this end, George recorded Cilla's new single "What Good Am I?" backed with "Over My Head," which ultimately fared even worse than its predecessor, clocking in at number twenty-four on the UK charts later that year.[14]

For his part, George later described the episode involving "She's Leaving Home" as "one of the biggest hurts of my life," noting that Paul should have understood that "at that time I was still having to record all my other artists." To George's mind, Paul simply should have waited. "I couldn't understand why he was so impatient all of a sudden. It obviously hadn't occurred to him that I would be upset." When it had become clear that George would be unavailable, Paul had dispatched Neil Aspinall to ferret out an arranger, which led him to Mike Leander. Later describing "She's Leaving Home" as "the song that got away," George recalled that on the day after the Cilla Black session, "Paul presented me with it and said, 'Here we are. I've got a score. We can record it now.'" And that's exactly what George, ever the professional, did: "I recorded it, with a few alterations to make it work better, but I was hurt." The Friday, March 17, session for "She's Leaving Home" began at seven in the evening, with Martin having rounded up four violinists, two violas, two cellists, a double bassist, and a harpist to accommodate Leander's score. There were a number of familiar faces on hand, including John Underwood and Steve Shingles, who had previously shared their talents on "Eleanor Rigby," as well as lead violinist Erich Gruenberg from the orchestral overdub for "A Day in the Life."[15]

As the first woman to play on a Beatles recording, harpist Sheila Bromberg had already played on a number of pop sessions. As she later recalled, recording "She's Leaving Home" proved to be a challenge for Martin's hastily arranged ensemble: "I got to the studio early to tune the instrument. I walked in and there was Paul McCartney, but I didn't recognize him at first. I was concentrating on what was written on the manuscript, then I turned around, heard the Liverpool accent and realized it was him. I hadn't got a clue, I had just talked to the other musicians and waited. In actual fact, he was quite difficult to work with because he wasn't too sure what he actually wanted. He said, 'no, I don't want that, I want something . . . ,' but he couldn't describe what he wanted, and I tried it all every which way." In the end, George acted as conductor and managed to capture six takes of the song's instrumental backing track, with the harp arranged on track one, the double bass on track two, the violins on track three, and the violas and cellos on track four. Before the evening session concluded, the first and sixth takes had been selected as being the best of the lot.

On Monday, March 20, Martin and the bandmates resumed work on "She's Leaving Home," ultimately selecting take one and subsequently carrying out a tape reduction in order to create space for McCartney and Lennon's vocals. Ultimately, George recorded their voices twice over in order to establish a vivid layer of sound. In so doing, he captured one of their finest vocal duets on record. At one point, George and his production team experimented with the song's introductory harp passage by applying a dose of ADT in order to distort the sound ever so slightly, although the idea was quickly scrapped. While Martin had edited out some of Leander's cello ornamentation, he kept the arranger's score largely intact. When he supervised the mixing session, George applied varispeed to raise the pitch of the singers' voices from E to F major. The song's mono mix reflected the sonic shift, although strangely the alteration was neglected during the preparation of the stereo version of "She's Leaving Home." Despite having felt the sting of McCartney's impatience, Martin was thrilled with the results: "It's almost like a little opera," he later wrote, "and it's one of the best constructed songs they ever did. The lyrics are particularly telling. I am amazed that they could do this at their age because they could see the conflict between the young and the old." During that same session, George created a spoken-word recording titled "Beatle Talk." He took the tape box home with him during the wee hours of the morning, and, rather mysteriously, it was never returned to Abbey Road.[16]

But the whereabouts of "Beatle Talk" seem a rather minor issue in retrospect—and certainly in comparison with what transpired in Studio 2 on the very next evening. As it happened, George and the Beatles' Tuesday, March 21, session was one for the books. The nearly eight-hour affair began at seven that evening, and the studio was chock-full of visitors, including Ivan Vaughan, Paul's childhood friend who had first introduced him to John back in July 1957; Hunter Davies, who had begun working on the band's authorized biography; and Dick James, George and the Beatles' maverick music publisher. James had been a central member of the Beatles' brain trust since their earliest days with Martin at the helm—in fact, it was due to his longtime relationship with the band's producer that he had been invited into the fold in the first place. Under his direction, James had watched Northern Songs quickly transform into an industry juggernaut during the heady days of Beatlemania. Back in January, when EMI announced the Beatles' contract extension, James remarked, "We have some of the greatest assets of any business in the word today—copyrights. You can keep your factories, plant and production lines—give me copyrights." James also boasted about Lennon and McCartney's staying power as composers: "This is no nine-day wonder," said James. "I expect a third of their songs still to be played in A.D. 2000."[17]

Also on hand that evening were members of Norman Smith's new signing, Pink Floyd, who were still toiling away on their debut album in nearby Studio 3. As Hunter Davies later recalled, "Very politely, [Smith] asked George Martin if his boys could possibly pop in to see the Beatles at work. George smiled, unhelpfully. Norman said perhaps he should ask John personally, as a favor. George Martin said no, that wouldn't work. But if by chance he and his boys popped in about 11 o'clock, he might just be able to see what he could do." At the appointed hour, the younger bandmates strolled into Studio 2. "They [the Beatles] were God-like figures to us," drummer Nick Mason later recalled. "They all seemed extremely nice, but they were in a strata so far beyond us that they were out of our league." After exchanging their "half-hearted hellos" with the Beatles, the rapt members of Pink Floyd observed the session from the control room. "The music sounded wonderful, and incredibly professional," Mason later recalled. "There was little if any banter with the Beatles. We sat humbly and humbled, at the back of the control room while they worked on the mix, and after a suitable (and embarrassing) period of time had elapsed, we were ushered out again."[18]

Years later, Martin would remember the March 21 session for a very different reason altogether. As Davies and Vaughan looked on, Martin pressed forward with the session, which featured Lennon, McCartney, and Harrison working out the vocals for "Getting Better." Not long afterward, the bandmates took a break. As George later recalled, "I was standing next to John, discussing some finer point of the arrangement to 'Getting Better' when he suddenly looked up at me. 'George,' he said slowly, 'I'm not feeling too good. I'm not focusing on me.'" And that's when the strangeness of the moment hit the Beatles' producer:

This was a pretty odd thing to say, even for John. I studied him. I'd been oblivious to it until then, but he did look pretty awful—not sick, but twitchy and strange. "Do you want someone to take you home?" I asked.

"No," he replied.

"Come on, John," I said. "What you need is a breath of fresh air. I know the way up on to the roof." When we had clambered out on to the flat roof of Studio No. 2, we found it was a beautiful clear night. John took a deep breath, and, with a bit of a lurch, took a couple of steps towards the edge of the building. I grabbed hold of his arm: it was a good 50 feet to the ground. We stood there for a minute or two, with John swaying gently against my arm. "I'm feeling better," he announced. Then he looked up at the stars. "Wow," he intoned. "Look at that! Isn't that amazing?"

I followed his gaze. The stars did look good, and there seemed to be a good many of them—but they didn't look *that* good. It was very unlike John to be over the top in that way. I stared at him. He was wired—pin-sharp and quivering, resonating away like a human tuning-fork.

At this point, George didn't feel terribly alarmed by the situation, bizarre as it may have been, and returned to the control room to prepare for another stab at "Getting Better." And that's when Paul called up to the booth, "How's John?" he asked. "He's on the roof, looking at the stars," George answered. "You mean Vince Hill?" Paul joked, in reference to the British singer who was currently riding atop the hit parade. Not missing a beat, Harrison began singing "Edelweiss," Hill's latest single. Suddenly realizing why John had felt so sick in the first place, McCartney and Harrison raced to the roof to rescue their friend before it was too late. "They knew why John was feeling unwell," Martin later surmised. "Maybe everyone else did, too—everyone except for father-figure George Martin here! It was very simple. John was tripping on LSD. He had taken it by mistake, they said—he had meant to take an amphetamine tablet."[19]

During that same evening, Martin resolved the prolonged issue of the empty solo section in the middle of "Lovely Rita." With McCartney's grudging assent, he recorded a barrelhouse piano solo to give the song a honky-tonk ambience. Using his windup piano technique, George recorded his solo at half speed so that it could be played back at full speed in order to imbue the sound with greater impact, not to mention a staccato feel. Emerick further manipulated the sound by wrapping a piece of adhesive tape around the capstan, the motor-driven spindle on the studio's tape recorder. In so doing, the capstan would vacillate ever so slightly, affording the solo with even greater sonic textures and nuance. As Martin later remarked, "I used to try out funny things in odd moments and I discovered that by putting sticky tape over the capstan of a tape machine you could wobble the tape on the echo machine, because we used to delay the feed into the echo chamber by tape. So I suggested we do this using a piano sound. The Beatles themselves couldn't think what should go into the song's middle-eight, and they didn't really like my idea at first, but it turned out fine in the end because of the effect." With the windup piano solo complete, Martin "dropped in" the overdub into the existing mix for "Lovely Rita."

While the March 21 session had been a hive of activity, the Beatles didn't miss a beat. On the very next evening, they were back in Studio 2 for another seven-hour affair. In their own way, Martin and the other bandmates were very much like McCartney—also having grown used to working "on heat" with an inexorable drive to bring their latest work to fruition. In this case, that work was *Sgt. Pepper*, and they were working at breakneck speed to bring it home—"home and dry," in Martin's words. The Wednesday, March 22, session witnessed additional overdubs associated with "Within You, Without

You." That evening, George and his production team superimposed two more dilruba performances, courtesy of personnel booked, as always, through the good offices of the Asian Music Circle. George recorded the parts at fifty-two and a half cycles per second in order to afford the overdub with the sound of being slowed down on playback. After completing the dilruba overdub, George conducted a reduction mix in order to free up real estate for additional work. He also prepared a demo mono remix in order to compose a score to accompany Harrison's exotic effusion. Before the day's work concluded, tape operator Graham Kirkby, who had previously shared his expertise in the compilation of *A Collection of Beatles Oldies*, held a listening session at George's request in the Studio 1 control room. During the ninety-minute playback, Kirkby cued up the completed recordings for "A Day in the Life," "Sgt. Pepper's Lonely Hearts Club Band," "Fixing a Hole," "Being for the Benefit of Mr. Kite!," "Lovely Rita," "Lucy in the Sky with Diamonds," and "Getting Better." With "Good Morning, Good Morning," "Within You, Without You," and "She's Leaving Home" nearing fruition, George and the bandmates had the makings of an unusual long-player on their hands, with space for two more compositions that had yet to be debuted in the friendly confines of Abbey Road.

Work continued on "Getting Better" on March 23—fortunately, with Martin and Lennon avoiding any further rooftop excursions. On this occasion, Emerick and Lush were scheduled to work another session at EMI Studios, leaving Peter Vince in the engineer's seat and Ken Scott sitting in as tape operator. Given John's uncertain state during the previous session, George rerecorded the vocal track, with Ringo also providing an overdub on the bongos. With "Getting Better" in a state of completion, George and the band returned to "Good Morning, Good Morning" on Tuesday, March 28. John finally recorded his lead vocal, which was given additional texture during the remixing session with a heavy dose of ADT. After George and his production team carried out a tape reduction, the bandmates began piling on overdubs during the nearly ten-hour session. Paul turned in a sizzling lead guitar solo on his Fender Esquire, and after John and Paul superimposed their backing vocals, John hit upon an idea. As Geoff recalled, "John said to me during one of the breaks that he wanted to have the sound of animals escaping and that each successive animal should be capable of frightening or devouring its predecessor." As it turned out, John's idea wasn't entirely original. Not surprisingly, *Pet Sounds* had struck again, with the animal sounds apparently having been inspired by the Beach Boys' coda for "Caroline, No." The sound effects in "Good Morning, Good Morning" were courtesy of the EMI tape library's *Volume 35: Animals and Bees* and *Volume 57: Fox-Hunt*. Before the long night concluded, the Beatles returned to "Being for the Benefit of Mr. Kite!" With Harrison, Starr, Mal Evans, and Neil Aspinall pitching in as a harmonica quartet, Lennon added an organ overdub, while McCartney superimposed a lead guitar part.[20]

By this point, a self-imposed deadline for delivering the master tape for *Sgt. Pepper* to EMI had emerged. Paul had made it be known that he intended to travel to the United States on April 3 for the purposes of surprising Jane Asher on the occasion of her twenty-first birthday. At the time, Asher was touring the United States with the Old Vic's traveling company for *Romeo and Juliet*. With the date of April 12 slated for the Beatle's return, Martin had promised his former employers that the album would be in EMI's hands before McCartney was back on British soil. So when George and the group gathered in Studio 2 on Wednesday, March 29, they had less than a week to take advantage of McCartney's presence in the studio. First up was "Good Morning, Good Morning," for which Martin and Emerick overdubbed the animal sounds in order to finish off the track. With "Good Morning, Good Morning" in the can, they turned their attentions to "Being for the Benefit of Mr. Kite!" Martin's team superimposed the elaborate sound effects recorded on February 20 onto the track, while George himself provided the "swirly" organ sounds to bring the song to fruition at long last. The March 29 session also witnessed the debut of a new song that went under the working title of "Bad Finger Boogie," a Lennon-McCartney composition written expressly for Ringo to sing. As George later observed, "The tradition that Ringo always had a song to sing on an album was nothing to do with the others being kind to him. Perched up behind his drums at the back of the stage, Ringo occupied a special place in the hearts of many Beatles fans. The most common adjectives you heard about him were 'cute' and 'cuddly.' Having him sing something on every album, then, was extremely good marketing—simple as that."[21]

By the time that John and Paul arrived in Studio 2 on that evening of March 29, they had decided to segue "Sgt. Pepper's Lonely Hearts Club Band" directly into this new song, which would shortly come to be known as "With a Little Help from My Friends." As George later wrote, "With this song, Paul and John had really come up with the goods. Ringo's voice is extremely distinctive, warm and memorable—but he would be the last person to claim that it has much range. So Paul wrote a beautiful simple melody for him, again based around no more than five notes. All Ringo's voice had to carry was one little phrase. Terribly simple, terribly effective. Economy is the mark of genius." Lennon and McCartney had also imagined a fictive character, Billy

Shears, for Ringo to play, believing that building a sense of character and setting would help them in bringing the *Sgt. Pepper* concept off—if only for a couple of songs on the long-player. On that first evening, George and the Beatles devoted ten takes to laying down a basic rhythm track that featured McCartney's piano, Harrison's rhythm guitar, Starr's drums, and Lennon's cowbell. The introduction for "With a Little Help from My Friends"—designed to accommodate the musical transition from the title track—was undergirded by Martin hammering away at the Hammond organ.[22]

Before finishing up that evening's work, George turned to Ringo, who was preparing to perform his lead vocal. After carrying out a tape reduction of take ten, Ringo stood in front of the Studio 2 microphone, ready to capture his vocal, albeit very nervous. As George later recalled, "John could be insecure about his voice; but Ringo made John look brazenly confident." Worse yet, Ringo saw "With a Little Help from My Friends" as a major piece of work, which made him even more nervous still. To George's mind, Ringo's sense of uncertainty was rooted in his personal anxiety about his vocal abilities, as well as in his perceived place in the band's interpersonal calculus. "If George [Harrison] had a slight burden to carry in being the Third Man within the group," Martin observed, "Ringo had the burden, initially at least, of being the 'replacement' man." But by the time he stepped up to the mic in the wee hours of March 30, Pete Best was long gone, having faded into history. Recognizing their bandmate's reticence, Lennon and McCartney joined the Beatles' drummer on the studio floor. "Paul and John coaxed him and cajoled him," George later wrote, "and in the end, they sang along with him when he did his stuff. It was a brilliant three-way live performance, that recording. In the last seconds of 'With a Little Help from My Friends,' when he had to hit the last, dangerously high note, Ringo did it wonderfully well. It is one of the best performances he ever turned in, perhaps the best track he has ever sung." For Ringo, "With a Little Help from My Friends" was a great triumph indeed. As George later concluded, Ringo "came up trumps. He really was Billy Shears."[23]

The very next evening, Thursday, March 30, the Beatles were late in arriving at Abbey Road, having spent the day at Chelsea Manor Studios with Michael Cooper posing for the photographs that would eventually adorn the *Sgt. Pepper* album cover. When they finally turned up at eleven that evening, George and the group went right back to work on "With a Little Help from My Friends," determined to put another *Sgt. Pepper* track to bed. And after overdubbing Harrison's lead guitar, McCartney's splendid bass part, Starr's tambourine, and the call-and-response backing vocals from Lennon and McCartney, the group did just that. A six-hour session in Studio 2 was conducted on Friday, March 31, in order to carry out additional cleanup on "With a Little Help from My Friends," which was doused with ADT. And then, ever the perfectionists, George and the bandmates turned their attentions back to "Being for the Benefit of Mr. Kite!" Before carrying out a remix, organ and glockenspiel parts were added to the song's mix. The next day, April 1, George and the Beatles were in residence at Abbey Road for a rare Saturday session, an eleven-hour affair that wouldn't conclude until six o'clock on Sunday morning. With Paul jetting out to America with Mal Evans on Monday, their backs were against the wall to record the long-player's thirteenth track. In the end, it was one of the Beatles' roadies who came up with the idea of recording a reprise for "Sgt. Pepper's Lonely Hearts Club Band." According to George, "The reprise of 'Sgt. Pepper's Lonely Hearts Club Band' was another Neil Aspinall brainwave. 'You've given a concert,' he commented. 'Why don't you wrap up the concert with another version of 'Sgt. Pepper'?'"[24]

And that's exactly what they did.

13

THE CHICKEN
BECAME THE GUITAR

For the "Sgt. Pepper's Lonely Hearts Club Band" reprise, the Beatles intentionally designed the song to be punchier and more straightforward than its namesake—with no frills and no overdubs diluting its rock 'n' roll mien. "We were in the big studio at Abbey Road, No. 1, for this one," George later recalled, "and the natural acoustics of this vast, cavernous room lent something to the live, bright quality of that recording. Geoff Emerick had a problem sorting out the balance between the various vocal and instrumental inputs, but he fixed it, and the electrifying, football stadium atmosphere comes through." Even still, George added, "We had to use an isolation booth for the heavy stuff—that is, we had to shut away the drums in a sort of portable, sound-absorbing cabinet. Had we not done that, the recording would have been a cacophony, the instruments spilling into one another as though being played in a cathedral." With the acoustics sorted out, the reprise was captured in nine takes, with Harrison and Lennon on electric guitar, McCartney playing bass, and Ringo on the drums. During each take of the rhythm track, Paul had provided a guide vocal. After selecting take nine as the best, the bandmates shared spirited lead vocals on the reprise. "This time, we really went hammer and tongs for a live performance," Martin later wrote. "This version of the song is much better—up-tempo, faster, pulsating with energy, much livelier. The Beatles knew the song inside out by now, and there was a sort of end-of-term feeling in the studio. We never made a second recording of a song on an album before, and that was exciting in itself. We finished the whole recording—vocals, solos, the lot—in one overnight session of 11 hours' straight work."[1]

Amazingly, George and the Beatles had captured the song on a single four-track tape without the necessity of any overdubs—just a single, magical, inordinately live recording. And when they were done, George knew that *Sgt. Pepper* had arrived at last. With a full complement of material in hand for the long-player, he later wrote, "We had an album." By Monday evening, April 3, they were back at work yet again—sans McCartney, of course. Working in Studio 1, they put the finishing touches on "Within You, Without You," the last track to be completed for *Sgt. Pepper*—or so they thought at the time. George had booked eleven musicians for the occasion—eight violinists and three cellists. Led once again by the redoubtable Erich Gruenberg, the session musicians were on hand to record George's orchestral score. As with his earlier work on "A Day in the Life," Martin had composed his string arrangement based upon Harrison's existing melody for "Within You, Without You." Composing the score had proven to be difficult. "What was difficult," Martin later recalled, "was writing a score for the cellos and violins that the English players would be able to play like the Indians. The dilruba player, for example, was doing all kinds of swoops and so I actually had to score that for strings and instruct the players to follow." One challenge, in particular, involved the "sliding techniques" inherent in the Eastern instruments that had been recorded earlier. For Martin, "This meant that in scoring for that track, I had to make the string players play very much like Indian musicians, bending the notes, and with slurs between one note and the next."[2]

For their trouble, the musicians—save for Gruenberg, who, as leader, was paid eleven pounds—received a one-time fee of nine pounds for their performances that evening. Using the available track three for "Within You, Without You," Martin recorded several takes of the orchestral score until Harrison was satisfied with the adornment. As it happened, achieving the right sound was no easy feat. Just as Martin had expected, the Western musicians ran into considerable difficulty in mimicking the Eastern players' style. As Emerick later wrote, "George Martin was conducting the same top-flight orchestral players that worked on most of the rest of *Pepper*, but despite their expertise, the musicians took a long time to get it right; I clearly remember the look of deep concentration on their faces as they struggled to master the complex score. It was painstaking, and it certainly was a challenge to the musicians, many of whom seemed to be getting a bit frustrated as the session wore on." From his vantage point in the control room, Geoff could tell that it "was a really hard session for George Martin—by the end of the night he was absolutely knackered. Thankfully, he had the help of George Harrison, who acted as a bridge between the Indian tonalities and rhythms, which he understood quite well, and the Western sensibilities of George Martin and the classical musicians. I was never more impressed with both Georges than I was on that very special, almost spiritual night."

With the orchestral work completed, the Beatles' producer turned to Harrison's lead vocal, which the Beatle delivered in impressive style, befitting the song's deeply philosophical lyrics. After overdubbing sitar and acoustic guitar flourishes from Harrison, Martin was finally ready to put "Within You, Without You" to bed. And in so doing, the recording sessions for *Sgt. Pepper*—which clocked in at some seven hundred hours in the studio—had reached their end. While the Beatles, especially McCartney, had taken a greater interest in nearly every aspect of their work's production, they tasked Martin with concocting a draft of the LP's running order. Meanwhile, the producer and his production team conducted a control room session on Tuesday, April 4, to carry out mono and stereo remixes for "Within You, Without You," which had been transformed from three discrete parts into a seamless whole. During the mixing session, they had also applied a heavy dose of ADT to the song, and, at Harrison's request, appended "Within You, Without You" with a few seconds of laughter in order to temper the serious mood established by his Eastern-oriented composition. As usual, the sound effects were ferreted out of the EMI tape library—in this instance, courtesy of *Volume 6: Applause and Laughter*.

George's production team continued their work on the evening of Thursday, April 6, when they began carrying out a series of cross-fades in order to blend the contents of *Sgt. Pepper* into a largely continuous work of art. And in George's vision, they did so without benefit of the traditional lines of demarcation, or rills, that had characterized the vast majority of albums during that era. But first, they completed the mono and stereo mixes for "Good Morning, Good Morning." As Emerick later recalled, "During the mix, I enjoyed whacking the faders all the way up for Ringo's huge tom hit during the stop-time—so much so that the limiters nearly overloaded, but it definitely gets the listener's attention! Add in the flanged brass, miked in an unorthodox way, and it's all icing on the cake; take those effects off and the recording doesn't have the same magic. That song serves as a good example of how simple manipulation can improve a track sonically." Martin and Emerick took a similar approach to mixing the contents of *Sgt. Pepper*, painstakingly attempting to bring out the musical color in what was shaping up to be far more than a mere experiment in pop music. As the dazzling contents of *Sgt. Pepper* took shape during the mixing sessions, they were on the precipice of compiling and banding a groundbreaking work of recording artistry.[4]

By the time he arrived at the studio that evening, Martin had succeeded in drafting the long-player's running order. As had been his practice for many years, George worked from a long-standing philosophy about how to best position the product for the marketplace. Martin always felt that the best strategy was to organize a strong first side in order to maximize an album's commercial potential. Given McCartney's original concept, "Sgt. Pepper's Lonely Hearts Club Band" had "to be the first track, naturally. The reprise of the song, for the same reason, had to go last—except that the final chord of 'A Day in the Life' was so final that it was obvious nothing else could follow it. So the reprise of 'Sgt. Pepper's Lonely Hearts Club Band' was put back to second to last." By this point, the bandmates had determined that the title track would segue into "With a Little Help from My Friends," which meant that Martin had already accounted for four of the album's thirteen tracks. In his original draft, George rounded out side one as follows: "Sgt. Pepper's Lonely Hearts Club Band," "With a Little Help from My Friends," "Being for the Benefit of Mr. Kite!," "Fixing a Hole," "Lucy in the Sky with Diamonds," "Getting Better," and "She's Leaving Home."[5]

For Martin, side two emerged fairly quickly once he decided how to deploy "Within You, Without You," easily *Sgt. Pepper*'s most challenging selection—which was saying something, given the long-player's overt avant-garde ambience. "When it came to 'Within You, Without You,'" he later recalled, "I could not for the life of me think of anywhere to put it at all. It was so alien, mystical, and long. There was no way it could end a side, nor did it sit comfortably next to anything else on the album. The self-deprecating laugh George had added at the end of his song gave me a bizarre idea: it could start a side, and I could follow it with a jokey track: 'When I'm Sixty-Four.'" Under this reasoning, side two shaped up very quickly, especially after Martin happened upon one of the most important sonic discoveries in the entirety of his career. As he attempted to figure out the placement of "Good Morning, Good Morning," he listened to the sounds of animalia during the song's play-out section. And that's when it hit him. "I suddenly realized as I was pulling it together," he later wrote, "that the chicken noise we had dubbed on sounded really like the little bit before the reprise of 'Sgt. Pepper's Lonely Hearts Club Band,' when the boys are tuning their guitars. So when I edited it together I turned the cluck-cluck of the chicken into the sound of a guitar string coming under tension as it is tuned, trying to mimic that twang, as near as I could. The chicken became the guitar." Sitting in the Studio 2 control room, George found himself thunderstruck by such an incredible moment of creative caprice. "It sounded great," he wrote. "It really welded the songs together. I couldn't congratulate myself too much on it, though, because it arrived all by itself—a stroke of luck. It just happened."[6]

With the balance of the album's contents in place, George simply slipped "Lovely Rita" between "When I'm Sixty-Four" and "Good Morning, Good Morning," and his running order was complete—for the moment, at least. During the April 6 mixing session, Emerick carried out cross-fades between "Sgt. Pepper's Lonely Hearts Club Band" and "With a Little Help from My Friends" and, to close out the album, between the reprise and "A Day in the Life." In order to mask the edit that morphs the title track into "With a Little Help from My Friends," George reached way back to the Beatles' August 30, 1965, appearance at the Hollywood Bowl, which he had originally recorded for a potential live album. George had scrapped the project because of the inferior sound quality of the music, overwhelmed as it was by the screaming hordes of Beatlemania. But suddenly the band's ear-piercing multitudes served a greater purpose, with the sudden upsurge of their screams punctuating McCartney's boisterous introduction of the fictive Billy Shears in the guise of Ringo. When it came to the album's master reel, George tasked EMI engineer Malcolm Davies with preparing Sgt. Pepper without rills.

On Friday, April 7, Martin and his production team continued working on mixing the long-player in the Studio 2 control room. In contrast with the heady days of Beatlemania, when the bandmates recorded their tracks and left everything else to George's discretion, the group attended all of the mono mixing sessions for Sgt. Pepper. With stereo having not yet come fully into vogue in the UK marketplace, mono reigned supreme, and stereo recordings were considered an afterthought. As Richard Lush later recalled, "After the album was finished, George Martin, Geoff, and I did the stereo in a few days, just the three of us, without a Beatle in sight." Hence, with the Beatles present and providing their input, "there are all sorts of things on the mono, little effects here and there, which the stereo doesn't have." In those days, they only worked from a single loudspeaker in the booth, given mono's primacy. As Emerick later observed, "We did have two speakers but everything was put through the right hand one. We weren't allowed to monitor on both because they were saved for stereo orchestral recordings!"[7]

For his part, George considered the mixing and editing processes associated with the album to be essential aspects of the band's recording artistry. And in the case of Sgt. Pepper, he discovered that much of the album's shape was defined during the postproduction process, as opposed to his early years with the Beatles, when he was able to mix their recordings for release with relative ease—and quickly, at that. But things were markedly different with *Sgt. Pepper*. "When it came to compiling the album," he later wrote, "I tried to edit it together in a very tight format, and in a funny kind of way when I was editing it, it almost grew by itself; it took on a life of its own."[8]

As with *Revolver*, the Beatles' latest album featured a wide range of styles and genres, and both records' strengths were rooted in their mind-blowing diversity. But with such a vast panoply of sonic experiences at his fingertips, George slowly began to recognize that he needed to celebrate the album's rapidly shifting musical palette at every possible turn. For this reason, as *Pepper* evolved during the mixing process, George came to realize that his original running order for side one was problematic—particularly in terms of closing the side with "She's Leaving Home." So with the bandmates' approval, he began to reshuffle the album's sequencing for side one. As he later wrote, "'She's Leaving Home' was a lovely song, but it was a bit downbeat—it didn't exactly shout its optimism—so I decided to place it after the more upbeat but less worthy songs" such as, in George's estimation, "Getting Better" and "Fixing a Hole." With this new gambit in mind, George was left to ponder the placement of "Being for the Benefit of Mr. Kite!" and "Lucy in the Sky with Diamonds." In the latter case, he felt that "Lucy" was "a great song" that "could hardly be more different in atmosphere and mood from 'With a Little Help from My Friends,' so why place it after that? Well, it was because it was so different. It was a complete change of musical color, which was welcome." Having decided that he wanted to end side one "with a bang," the madcap "Being for the Benefit of Mr. Kite!" emerged as the obvious closer.[9]

With *Sgt. Pepper* seemingly in a state of completion, George and the bandmates took a much-deserved two-week break. But for the Beatles' producer, the time off was devoted almost entirely to handling a growing backlog of AIR business. The Beatles' considerable demands upon his time meant that he had little room in his schedule for his existing stable of acts, several of whom were beginning to find themselves at career crossroads. David and Jonathan had been faltering since the release of their "Lovers of the World Unite" single, and George already had a plan up his sleeve to jump-start their flagging career. Knowing that the Beatles had no intention of releasing *Sgt. Pepper*'s tracks as singles, George had selected "She's Leaving Home" as David and Jonathan's next release. Perhaps lightning would strike yet again for David and Jonathan in the form of a Lennon-McCartney composition as it had done back in 1966 with "Michelle." Meanwhile, Cilla Black had all but lost the momentum she had gathered in previous years. Her latest release, "I Only Live to Love You" backed with "From Now On," saw her flailing yet again. Like "What Good Am I?," her previous single, "I Only Live to Love You" had stalled on the charts, going no higher than the midtwenties.

While George's acts were faltering, his partner Ron Richards was tearing up the charts with the Hollies AIR's most reliable hitmakers—outside of the Beatles, of course. In 1966, the Hollies had hit their stride with a lineup that included Allan Clarke, Tony Hicks, Graham Nash, Bobby Elliott, and Bernie Calvert. Richards had discovered the Manchester band in the Cavern Club in 1963, and over the ensuing years they had honed their style as three-part vocalists, with the voices of Clarke, Hicks, and Nash blending in perfect harmony. By 1966, they had developed into one of AIR's headlining acts, with a trio of top-five singles in "I Can't Let Go," "Bus Stop," and "Stop Stop Stop." Richards predicted big things from the Hollies in 1967, and they had already come through with a pair of top-five singles in "On a Carousel" and "Carrie Anne." Attempting to capitalize on the strength of the band's flurry of hit singles, Richards had been working sporadically with the Hollies all spring on their latest album. In fact, they had been recording at Abbey Road during the same period in which the Beatles had been toiling away at *Sgt. Pepper*. But in contrast with the Fab Four, who had spent virtually every possible day attempting to refine their sound, the Hollies had devoted just six days across three months to recording their new long-player, with Richards at the helm. The Hollies planned to call their record *Evolution*, and EMI had scheduled it for release on June 1, the very same day that the record conglomerate had slated for loosing *Sgt. Pepper's Lonely Hearts Club Band* upon a waiting world.

On Monday, April 17, Martin was back in the Studio 2 control room, where he remixed several *Sgt. Pepper* tracks, including "Getting Better," "She's Leaving Home," and "When I'm Sixty-Four," with Emerick and Lush in tow. That Wednesday, George and his production team had to create a new mono remix for "Good Morning, Good Morning" in order to perfect the cross-fade between the animal sounds and the "Sgt. Pepper" reprise. They carried out fourteen remixes until they were able to capture the sound of the hen's final cluck transforming into the lead guitar at the beginning of the reprise, just as George had envisioned it. But for Emerick, it was no easy feat. While the Beatles' engineer admitted it was "one of the cleverest bits of matching a sound effect with an instrument ever done," it wasn't as simple as George had previously imagined it would be to transform the sound of a chicken into a guitar lick. "It wasn't a perfect match," Geoff later recalled, "so we shifted the cluck up in time to match correctly."[10]

Knowing that the Beatles would be back in the studio on April 20 in order to resume work on "Only a Northern Song," which they had left unfinished back on February 14, George had acetates of the song prepared for the bandmates' review. Having been scuttled from *Sgt. Pepper*, "Only a Northern Song" held a new purpose for George and the Beatles, who still had a third film to complete in order to fulfill the deal that Brian Epstein had negotiated with United Artists. By this point, they had agreed to prepare music for an animated feature film to be titled *Yellow Submarine* and produced by Al Brodax, the man behind the Beatles cartoon shorts. Canadian director George Dunning had been tasked with directing the film.

But getting to the point where the Beatles would finally be able fulfill the deal with United Artists had been no easy feat for Epstein, who was still battling the depression that had hobbled him after the Jesus Christ tour. While George and the bandmates had been working on *Sgt. Pepper* at Abbey Road, Brian plotted their follow-up film to *Help!* Over the ensuing months, Epstein and the Beatles had turned down one script after another. At one point, Brodax had even tapped Joseph Heller, the celebrated author of *Catch-22*, to write a screenplay expressly for the Fab Four, although Epstein rejected the author's efforts out of hand. Meanwhile, in the early months of 1967, Epstein had gone so far as to contract British playwright Joe Orton to come up with a script, which resulted in *Up Against It*, a screenplay that left the Beatles' manager aghast. In fact, he was so disgusted by Orton's depiction of the Fab Four that he wouldn't even return the writer's calls. For his part, Orton wasn't surprised about the manager's nonresponse, writing in his diary at the time that "the boys, in my script, have been caught *in-flagrante*, become involved in dubious political activity, dressed as women, committed murder, been put in prison, and committed adultery."[11]

With Orton's side effort having failed miserably, Brodax finally succeeded in capturing Brian's attention with a screenplay titled *Yellow Submarine* by Erich Segal. The Beatles felt that the project was daft, particularly given that King Features, Brodax's company, had been responsible for such cartoon fodder as *Popeye*. In desperation, Epstein had first turned to Brodax, the American television producer behind the successful Beatles cartoons, which were broadcast on ABC for four seasons after debuting in September 1965. In order to facilitate the cartoons, Martin had helped out by providing Brodax and King Features with Beatles masters in order to facilitate each episode's sing-along.

After Brian inked the deal for *Yellow Submarine*, the Beatles openly displayed their disdain for the feature-length cartoon, deliberately planning to

commit their weakest songs to fulfill the four tracks that they were contractually obligated to deliver for the soundtrack. As George later recalled, "If they
had any rubbish, as they considered it, at the end of the session, that would
be one of the songs. There used to be a standing joke: 'Ah, good enough for
Yellow Submarine . . . let them have that one.'" But for his part, George was
confident that King Features could bring home the goods, later remarking
that "the Beatles feared the worst, but in truth the project was in the hands of
very good artists. If Brian hadn't stuck to his guns, that classic would never
have happened."[12]

On Thursday, April 20, George and the Beatles reunited in Studio 2 to
pick up where they had left off with "Only a Northern Song," the first of the
four new songs that they were obligated to provide for the *Yellow Submarine* soundtrack. As they worked the session, Brodax and Dunning visited
the studio—at one point, even pausing to observe as the Beatles refined the
rhythm track for "Only a Northern Song." The production team's visit was
hardly routine at this point. With *Yellow Submarine* slated for a summer 1968
release, they had their work cut out for them in order to prepare the requisite
cartoon cels, on the one hand, and organize the Beatles songs and incidental
film music, which George had been tapped to compose, on the other.

After McCartney provided a new bass part for "Only a Northern Song"
that evening, the bandmates decided to overdub a bizarre arrangement of
intentionally discordant sounds, with Lennon playing the glockenspiel while
McCartney tried his hand at the trumpet. As it happened, the trumpet had
been Paul's first instrument, having received a nickel-plated version of the
brass instrument for his fourteenth birthday. But McCartney's attempt at
picking up the trumpet for the first time in eleven years fared badly. As he
later recalled, "The film producers were wandering around the studio and they
had to sort of go along with this—I saw some very sad faces while I'm playing
this trumpet." At this juncture, Martin needed to make room for additional
vocal overdubs from Harrison. Over the years, his typical maneuver had been
to carry out a tape reduction in order to create more recording space. But
taking a page out of his own book, Martin decided to synchronize a second
tape machine in order to simulate eight-track recording, just as he had done
a few months back, with Ken Townsend's able assistance, on behalf of "A
Day in the Life." In so doing, Martin could add yet more overdubs to take
eleven, an unused reduction from February 14, to which Harrison superimposed two lead vocals, with more instrumental shenanigans from Lennon and
McCartney, who added piano and Mellotron, along with the sound of the
Beatles clearing their throats, to the mix. At one point, Harrison can be heard

jeering at McCartney's trumpet antics, saying "Take it, Eddie!" in reference to the Blue Flames' Eddie Thornton, who had played trumpet on *Revolver's* "Got to Get You into My Life."[13]

During the April 21 session, Martin and his production team synchronized the machines in Studio 2 and successfully merged the two four-track tapes associated with "Only a Northern Song." But for his part, George resented having had to go to so much trouble to simulate eight-track recording—namely, because the technology had been available on a wide scale since the previous year; however, EMI's technical staff hadn't even been authorized to purchase one of the newfangled machines as of yet. But as it happened, the April 21 session was dominated by conversation among George and the bandmates about how to conclude the *Sgt. Pepper* album. Apparently, their latest long-player wasn't quite as complete as they had first believed. The issue, it seemed, was how to punctuate the profound silence following the fifty-four-second piano chord that brought "A Day in the Life" to its thunderous close. "It was just a silly in-joke," Martin later recalled, the idea of "having a little noise just for fun." It was Paul, in particular, who was taken with the concept of undercutting the seeming finality of the deafening piano sound. And at the same time, Paul reasoned, why not play a little prank on the Beatles' listeners by placing a kind of sonic Easter egg in the concentric run-out grooves of their phonographs? Back in those days, music fans with automatic players would be treated to a sudden torrent of sound before the pickup arms on their phonographs returned to their bases. While the owners of expensive phonographic equipment might be startled by such an unexpected burst of sound in the wake of the crashing piano chord at the end of "A Day in the Life," consumers with cheaper equipment were more apt to be irritated by the run-out groove's discordant noise—a seemingly endless influx of sound that could only be terminated by manually returning the pickup arm to its base. "We always said," Martin later wrote, "that when the needle gets to the end and starts swithering around and lifts off, well those people who don't have automatic players should be able to hear something."[14]

For George and the bandmates, the idea of manipulating the long-player's run-out groove—and playing a harmless joke on their listeners—seemed too good to pass up. But it wouldn't necessarily be an easy process, as EMI's ace disc-cutter Harry Moss pointed out to George. "I was told by chaps who'd been in the business a long time that cutting things into the run-out grooves was an old idea that they used to do on 78s," Moss later reported. Even still, Moss would have to wait for the masters themselves to be pressed in order to see if his work in the run-out grooves had been successful. But Moss was never one to shy away from a technological challenge. "It's gonna be bloody awkward, George, but I'll give it a go!" he told the Beatles' producer. Now all the bandmates had to do was record the requisite nonsense to bring their sonic prank to fruition. As Emerick recalled, "They were all there discussing how to end the LP, but the decision to throw in a bit of nonsense gibberish came together in about 10 minutes. They ran down to the studio floor and we recorded them twice—on each track of a two-track tape. They made funny noises, said random things; just nonsense. We chopped up the tape, put it back together, played it backwards and threw it in." In Barry Miles's memory, the work that went into recording approximately two seconds' worth of sound that evening was considerably more involved than Emerick's remarks might suggest. "It was a triple session—three three-hour sessions—which ended around 4 AM. The Beatles stood around two microphones muttering, singing snatches of songs, and yelling for what seemed like hours, with the rest of us standing round them, joining in. Mal [Evans] carried in cases of Coke and bottles of Scotch. Ringo was out of it. 'I'm so stoned,' he said, 'I think I'm going to fall over!' As he slowly toppled, Mal caught him and popped him neatly in a chair without a murmur. In the control room, no one seemed to notice. A loop was made from the tape of the muttering and was mixed."[15]

With the assorted nonsense having been captured on tape, Lennon suggested to Martin that the Beatles' gibberish should be preceded by one more in-joke. In this case, the prank wasn't aimed at the bandmates' legions of listeners but rather at their pets. At Lennon's instigation, Martin later recalled, "we added a special dog whistle which is an 18 kilocycle note that you won't be able to hear. We thought it would be nice to include something especially for dogs." At this point, the producer turned the whole shebang over to Moss, who prepared the mono and stereo masters for *Sgt. Pepper*. As it turned out, adding the dog whistle was remarkably simple for the experienced disc-cutter, who recorded the high-pitched tone at the same frequency as a standard police dog whistle. And sure enough, dogs all over the world would soon be perking up as the Beatles' new long-player came to its rapturous conclusion. But they wouldn't be the only ones able to register the high-pitched tone. Not long after the April 21 session, George presented a prerelease copy of *Sgt. Pepper* to his ten-year-old son Gregory, who told his father that he could hear the dog whistle that graced the end of the album. "Nonsense," his father replied. "No human can hear a note that high-pitched." Perhaps George, like most people, didn't realize that the frequency of a dog whistle often falls within the hearing range of children, whose auditory senses haven't begun deteriorating with age.[16]

But no matter. With "Sgt. Pepper's Inner Groove" nestled into its final resting place at the end of the master reel, the long-player was once and truly finished. But even still, George couldn't help wondering what would happen come June 1, when *Sgt. Pepper's Lonely Hearts Club Band* was simultaneously released on British and American shores. Would George and the Beatles really be "home and dry," to borrow Alan Livingston's turn of phrase, in the wake of such a bizarrely experimental, unprecedented work of aural art?

14

GOOD NIGHT, SWEET PRINCE

IN MANY WAYS, May 1967 served as the calm before the storm for George and the bandmates—which, in the Beatles' ever-shifting universe, was saying something. Pausing to reflect on what they had just accomplished, George chalked up *Sgt. Pepper* as the express result of the Beatles no longer having "the millstone of madcap live performance tours around their necks. Now that they had some time and space, they were spreading their musical wings. They were showing us what they could really do." Commenting at the time, John saw the soon-to-be-released long-player as "one of the most important steps in this group's career. It had to be just right. We tried and I think succeeded in achieving what we set out to do." Harrison was equally thoughtful, remarking, "You just have to keep striving for perfection. This LP, I think, is the best we've done, but only the best we could do at that time. The next one ought to be better. That's always got to be the goal." But perhaps the most peculiar observation in advance of the album's release belonged to Brian Epstein, who had been waiting in the wings since falling into a depression during the previous fall. During an American radio interview, Brian proclaimed that *Sgt. Pepper* would "prove more than a thing or two," adding, "I don't like to be particularly swanky about it, but it is going to be great."[1]

For Brian, *Sgt. Pepper*'s imminent release represented an opportunity to return to the world stage, not to mention a strategic moment to get the Beatles' business affairs in order before what promised to be a media onslaught. After all, the group had been whiling away the hours at Abbey Road, save for the brief interregnum back in February with the release of the "Strawberry Fields

Forever" backed with "Penny Lane" single and its attendant promotional video images of the mustached, Carnaby-dressed Beatles looking very different from the figures that they cut during the heady days of Beatlemania. In recent years, Brian had assembled the finest minds in London economic circles to address the bandmates' labyrinthine business interests. Recognizing that the Beatles were about to suffer the financial penalties associated with falling within the United Kingdom's highest income bracket, Brian's advisers warned of an imminent tax bill that they estimated to be in the vicinity of £3 million. In order to offset their exorbitant income tax, Brian's team of advisers recommended that the Beatles invest in businesses that were most closely aligned with their ongoing work. To this end, Brian launched Apple Music, Limited, on the bandmates' behalf in May 1967. Although Apple was founded initially as a holding company, the Beatles already saw their new venture as a means for seeking out and supporting new songwriting talent, just as Dick James had hoped to do by expanding the reach of Northern Songs. While Epstein helped make the bandmates' nascent Apple dream a reality, the group members—particularly John and Paul—were enamored with the idea of going into business for themselves, of taking the reins of their financial future. For his part, Paul McCartney had already begun developing an idea for the new company's logo. As with so many of his aesthetic impulses during this period, McCartney had been influenced by Robert Fraser. "One day he brought this painting to my house," Paul later recalled. "It just had written across it 'Au revoir,' on this beautiful green apple." The painting in question—Belgian artist René Magritte's *Le Jeu de Mourre*, a slick pop-art depiction of a Granny Smith apple—was precisely the image that McCartney had been seeking: simple and mysterious but at the same time sophisticated and surreal. Just like the Beatles themselves.[2]

For Brian, the bandmates' "swanky" new release also signaled the opportunity for a bravura press launch—the likes of which the record industry had never seen. And on Friday, May 19, Brian did just that, inviting the Beatles to turn up at his home at 24 Chapel Street for one of the most incredible coming-out parties of all time. With the June 1 release date for *Sgt. Pepper's Lonely Hearts Club Band* looming, the Beatles' manager pulled out all of the stops for the occasion, serving a sumptuous spread of champagne, poached salmon, and caviar to his guests. As the launch party progressed, the bandmates posed for photographs in Epstein's drawing room, as well as on the front stoop of their manager's regal townhouse, which was just a stone's throw away from Buckingham Palace.

Not surprisingly, the event made for a who's who among the glitterati of music journalism, including Norrie Drummond of the *NME*, who implicitly understood the auspicious nature of the occasion. The Beatles had ceased touring back in August 1966, and, save for the release of the "Strawberry Fields Forever" backed with "Penny Lane" single, they had largely been out of the spotlight in the ensuing months. And yet here they were, unveiling their groundbreaking new album under an air of mystery as if they were Willy Wonka finally opening up his magical dream factory for the eyes of a waiting world. Even the Beatles' entrance took on a sense of grandeur and great expectation on that illustrious evening. As Drummond wrote, "John Lennon walked into the room first. Then came George Harrison and Paul McCartney, followed closely by Ringo Starr and road managers Neil Aspinall and Mal Evans. The Beatles had arrived at a small dinner party in Brian Epstein's Belgravia home, to talk to journalists and disc jockeys for the first time in many months." And there they were: mustached (save for a clean-shaven Paul) and decked out in their hippie finery. Their carefree Bohemian image was a far cry indeed from the suited bandmates of days gone by. One of the guests that night was none other than American rock photographer Linda Eastman, who had first met Paul four nights earlier at the trendy Bag O'Nails club, where Georgie Fame and the Blue Flames were topping the bill. Linda later remembered that they "flirted a bit" before heading out to yet another club and then concluding the evening at Paul's home at Cavendish Avenue, where Linda recalled being "impressed" to see her future husband's prized trio of Magritte paintings.[3]

If Epstein's other guests were awestruck by the pioneering soundscapes that they heard during the initial May 19 *Sgt. Pepper* listening session, their impressions would be drowned out soon enough by a plenitude of other voices. The first one, as it turned out, proved to be more than a bit unsettling, as BBC director of sound broadcasting Frank Gillard informed Sir Joseph Lockwood in a May 23 letter that the media corporation would be banning "A Day in the Life" because of the refrain "I'd love to turn you on," which Gillard interpreted as having a "sinister meaning." He allowed that the "recording may have been made in innocence and good faith, but we must take account of the interpretation that many young people would inevitably put upon it. 'Turned on' is a phrase which can be used in many different circumstances, but it is currently much in vogue in the jargon of the drug-addicts. We do not feel that we can take the responsibility of appearing to favor or encourage those unfortunate habits, and that is why we shall not be playing the recording in any of our programs, Radio or Television." For his part, Martin was disgusted by the shortsightedness of the ban, especially in terms of "A Day in the Life," which he already perceived as being on an artistic plane at a significant remove from the Beatles' previous achievements. While Gillard's decision proved to be not only unfortunate but an embarrassment for the BBC, which came off looking very stodgy in the face of contemporary mores, his would be one of the very few dissenting voices. Within a matter of days of the album's release, the revolutionary long-player's reviews came in swiftly and were overwhelmingly positive. Writing in the London *Times*, William Mann proclaimed *Sgt. Pepper* to be "a pop music master-class," while his colleague Kenneth Tynan went even further, calling the LP "a decisive moment in the history of Western civilization." In the United States, the cultural elite at the *New York Times Book Review* proclaimed *Sgt. Pepper* as beckoning the commencement of a "golden Renaissance of Song." And while he wasn't entirely sure about the album's overall aesthetic impression, which he faulted for its "obsession with production," the *New York Times*'s Richard Goldstein singled out "A Day in the Life," which he described in moving terms as a "deadly earnest excursion in emotive music with a chilling lyric. Its orchestration is dissonant but sparse, and its mood is not whimsical nostalgia but irony. With it, the Beatles have produced a glimpse of modern city life that is terrifying. It stands as one of the most important Lennon-McCartney compositions, and it is a historic Pop event."[4]

While Brian's launch party had proven to be a spectacular success, it was merely subterfuge. For Brian, the past several months had gone from bad to worse. After rousing himself out of his post-touring depression, he had succumbed to his inner demons yet again. With his psyche in disarray, Brian increasingly turned to drugs and alcohol to salve his aching heart. On May 17, his psychiatrist, John Flood, encouraged Brian to admit himself to the Priory Hospital in Roehampton. On May 19, he left the sanitarium for the *Sgt. Pepper* launch party, only to return to the mental health facility immediately afterward. As if his psychiatric problems weren't enough, Brian had spent much of the past several months in turmoil over his business relationship with the band. For Brian, the creation of Apple Music was nothing short of a death knell. "He'd decided this was the Beatles' first real step toward ending their relationship with him," Peter Brown remarked. But nothing was further from the truth. The group had established Apple Music expressly as a tax dodge—as Brian well knew—and they had done so at his urging, no less.[5]

Meanwhile, Allen Klein had recently strong-armed Decca Records into rewarding the Rolling Stones with a lucrative signing bonus. Known for his crude mannerisms and tough-guy demeanor, he had similarly approached

Brian about restructuring the Beatles' EMI contract. Epstein had become deathly afraid of the American interloper, particularly after McCartney inquired about Klein's recent success on the Rolling Stones' behalf. "What about us?" he asked Brian. For months, the manager had been attempting to convince the Beatles to tour again but to no avail. Even after he successfully negotiated the contract extension with EMI back in January, he felt that his days with the group were numbered—a situation that he did nothing to improve by offering a controlling interest in NEMS to Robert Stigwood, who had recently begun grooming an Australian group known as the Bee Gees for the big time. When Epstein balked at signing the Australians, Stigwood inked them to a contract with Atlantic Records. With his keen eye for talent and the smooth verbal gifts to match, Stigwood set his sights on the Beatles. For a paltry £500,000—considerably undervaluing the company in the process— he bought his way into NEMS, with the option of obtaining a controlling interest in the corporation after six months. In short order, Stigwood had begun handling the daily operations of NEMS, although Epstein had already decided, if only in his mind, to decline Stigwood's option. As the days wore on, the Beatles' manager became ever more paranoid about his progressively tenuous relationship with the band.[6]

For his part, Martin had never been more confident about his place in the Beatles' universe. What had once been a teacher-pupil relationship had evolved into a genuine creative partnership. But as it happened, George was nowhere to be found during those heady, pre-*Pepper* release days. He wasn't even in the city on the night of Brian's fabled launch party, having opted to make himself scarce for the first time since he had begun working with the bandmates back in 1962. George could feel the winds of change in the air. In fact, by his own reckoning they had already begun to swirl around the Beatles. In just one session, he could sense that the group's creative heat was dissipating, losing its focus. "Only a Northern Song" had been a mere prelude to the less concerted, often lackadaisical work that they would carry out during that most unusual summer. The May 12 session for "All Together Now," which occurred outside of George's control, had been one of the strangest since "Yellow Submarine" the previous May, when George had been absent with food poisoning and Judy had attended the session in his stead. Years later, Geoff Emerick remembered the "All Together Now" session with a shrug, recalling that "the Beatles nonetheless soldiered on without him [Martin], and I was officially listed on the tape box as both producer and engineer."[7]

From Emerick's perspective, Martin's sudden yen for a holiday didn't make any sense. "Frankly, George going on vacation in the middle of these sessions did not go down well in anybody's book. We were all tired, yet he was the only one taking time off." Worse yet, "things were definitely more relaxed when George Martin wasn't around. There was always a certain protocol when he was at a session: we in the control room felt that we had to be on our best behavior, and even the Beatles seemed slightly constrained by his presence at times. When he wasn't there, we'd all let our hair down and have a bit of fun. There was just a different dynamic." But along with the loose atmosphere that George's absence created in the studio was a sense of aimlessness and a lack of direction. As Emerick remembered, it was a general feeling that "now that the schoolmaster's out, we kids finally get a chance to play." George had sensed the growing unease among the bandmates and his production team—and not merely regarding their preternatural need to let their personalities roam free and buck George's desire to establish organization and a purposeful drive. There was an even more pressing and larger question related to how the band would move forward after willing the likes of *Sgt. Pepper* into existence. George could feel the bandmates' unsettled nature during their first few sessions after putting the finishing touches on the album.[8]

For Martin it had all begun to spiral out of control back on Tuesday, April 25, although in truth, he should have sensed the coming disarray during the "Getting Better" session back in March, when Lennon might very well have tumbled off of the studio rooftop had it not been for the well-timed intervention of his eminently more sober friends. During the nearly nine-hour session on the twenty-fifth, George and the bandmates had tried their hand at a brand-new McCartney composition titled "Magical Mystery Tour." The song had found its origins during Paul's American trip with Mal Evans after the Beatles had recorded the "Sgt. Pepper" reprise. Flying back to the United Kingdom on April 11, Paul hatched the idea for a Beatles television movie about riding about the countryside on a mystery coach tour. As Paul later remembered, "The *Mystery* show was conceived way back in Los Angeles. On the plane. You know they give you those big menus, and I had a pen and everything and started drawing on this menu and I had this idea. In England, they have these things called mystery tours. And you go on them and you pay so much and you don't know where you're going. So the idea was to have this little thing advertised in the shop windows somewhere called *Magical Mystery Tours*."[9]

As it happened, the Beatles had also considered other projects in mid-1967. For several months, they pondered the concept of making a television movie based on *Sgt. Pepper's Lonely Hearts Club Band*. They had even gone so far as scheduling the principal photography for the would-be production for October and November 1967, with a screenplay by Ian Dallas under the direction of Keith Green. In addition to a mammoth "A Day in the Life" segment, the film was slated to feature 115 extras—including a troupe of motorcycle-riding "rockers" and a dozen "Model Rita Maids." But with the idea for *Magical Mystery Tour* now brewing in his synapses, McCartney was working "on heat," which meant, as it usually did, that he would stop at nothing to bring his vision to life.

After rehearsing "Magical Mystery Tour," Martin and the Beatles settled down to the creation of a basic rhythm track on April 27, which included Harrison and Lennon's guitars, McCartney's piano, and Starr's drums. By this point, they had already decided that "Magical Mystery Tour" would require a fusillade of trumpets, as well as plenty of ambient sound effects—especially of the highways and byways variety, this being a song about a bus and all. After recording three takes of the rhythm track—with the third being selected as the best—the bandmates sent Emerick to the EMI tape library to ferret out the appropriate sound effects. In this case, *Volume 36: Traffic Noise Stereo* fit the bill, with the sound of cars and trucks roaring along England's highways. As it turned out, Martin's longtime colleague Stuart Eltham had originally recorded the sounds, later recalling, "I did that leaning over a bridge on the M1 motorway. It was a quiet day, a Sunday, because that was the only way one could capture the sound of individual vehicles. On any other day, all I would have had was a mass of traffic noise."[10]

Over the next few days, George and the Beatles made quick work of "Magical Mystery Tour." On Wednesday evening, April 26, George carried out a tape reduction and they overdubbed Paul's bass guitar, along with a spate of percussion—maracas, cowbell, tambourine, and the like—played by all four Beatles. At this point, the band concocted a series of playful shouts and other attendant frivolity—including John ad-libbing, "Step right this way!" By Thursday, they were overdubbing McCartney's lead vocal, with Lennon and Harrison providing harmonies. Martin recorded Lennon ad-libbing "Roll up, roll up for the Magical Mystery Tour!" at half speed to quicken the intensity on playback. As Richard Lush later recalled, "They really wanted those voices to sound different." The session ended with Emerick and Lush cutting acetates, presumably for Martin to use as a reference when scoring the trumpet section. At that point, George booked studio musicians for the following week, including the ubiquitous David Mason, only to learn that Geoff would be unavailable for the upcoming session. Along with Ken Townsend, he was booked for a mobile recording of the Wurzels, a "Scrumpy and Western" comedy act from Somerset. When the Beatles learned that Emerick would be

130 miles away in Royal Oak, they were aghast. With no other choice, Martin was forced to impress Malcolm Addey into service as Emerick's stand-in.[11]

By the time that the Beatles and their producer reconvened on Wednesday, May 3, George apparently hadn't found his way clear to scoring the trumpet parts. And this unusual lack of preparation on George's part didn't escape notice. In addition to Mason, trumpeters Elgar "Gary" Howarth, Roy Copestake, and John Wilbraham were also on hand for the session. Without a score from which to work, Martin and McCartney attempted to improvise. As Addey observed from his place in the control room, "Paul McCartney was humming to the musicians the notes that he wanted, trying for a long time to get his thoughts across to them. In the end, we had to send the trumpet players off for tea while Paul and George [Martin] worked things out on the Studio 3 piano." In the end, Howarth became understandably irritated by the situation and hastily composed trumpet parts for himself and the other players. By the time that the session concluded some five hours later, the brass overdubs were complete, with Mason leading the way and delivering a volley of high-velocity sixteenth notes. The next evening, with Emerick back in the fold, Martin conducted a mixing session for the new song. Amazingly, the title track for the bandmates' next project was already nearing a state of completion, and *Sgt. Pepper* hadn't even been released yet.[12]

But any momentum that George and the Beatles enjoyed at this point began to dissipate precipitously the following week. During the Tuesday, May 9, session in Studio 2, for instance, George and the bandmates toiled until six o'clock in the morning while only committing sixteen minutes of a malingering instrumental jam to tape. The music consisted of the Beatles plying their electric guitars, woefully out of tune, along with drums and harmonium. Two days later, they convened in suburban Barnes at Olympic Sound Studios, one of the United Kingdom's most esteemed independent recording venues and a regular haunt of the Rolling Stones, who had been recording *Their Satanic Majesties Request*—the follow-up long-player to the strong-selling *Between the Buttons*—at the studio since February. Martin and the Beatles convened that evening at nine o'clock—once again, without Emerick and Lush, who were not permitted to work in non-EMI facilities. Sitting in their places were Keith Grant, Olympic's manager, and Eddie Kramer. That night, the Beatles tried out a new composition titled "Baby, You're a Rich Man," another number under consideration for the soundtrack for the *Yellow Submarine* animated film, which would be announced during a June 7 press conference. During the session for "Baby, You're a Rich Man," John played the studio's handy Clavioline, the same space-aged instrument that Joe Meek had used to propel "Telstar" to international fame back in 1962. With the Stones' Mick Jagger and Brian Jones in attendance, they made fairly short work of the new tune, McCartney overdubbing bass and piano parts, along with Harrison on lead guitar and Starr on drums. At one point, Kramer even pitched in with a turn at the studio's vibraphone. In the wee hours of the morning, as John and the other Beatles sang the play-out for "Baby, You're a Rich Man," John can be heard aiming a satiric barb at the Beatles' manager, ad-libbing, "Baby, you're a rich fag Jew." By this period, Brian had shrewdly made himself scarce in the studio, having been rebuffed on several occasions when he attempted to make suggestions about the band's musical direction. In addition to overseeing the *Sgt. Pepper* launch, Brian was growing increasingly paranoid about the band's drug use—and whether its public disclosure might result in some future PR disaster—while also privately hoping that Harrison would tone down his infatuation with Eastern music. As he confided in Nat Weiss at the time, "I wish George would stop making such a big issue of the sitar and just *use* it instead of getting it out of context."[13]

By the very next evening, the bandmates were back in the studio working on a new composition—this one slated explicitly for *Yellow Submarine*—titled "All Together Now." An upbeat children's song from Lennon and McCartney in the same whimsical vein as "Yellow Submarine," Lennon played a harmonica part on a Beatles song for the first time in two years. The song concluded with a lighthearted sing-along that slowly gathers up speed before galloping into a sudden climax. But in contrast with their experiences back at Olympic earlier that same morning, Martin was absent from the producer's chair, with Emerick sitting in for him. For his part, George was already making his way toward the English Channel, bound for a three-week jaunt in France. As George later recalled, "I knew as *Pepper* was coming to a close that it was the end of a chapter in our lives. Judy, my wife, who had been pregnant all this time, needed a holiday as much as I did. We left Britain on 12 May, despite the fact that the Beatles wanted to, and did, record 'All Together Now' with Geoff Emerick looking after them in my absence. We set off in our little Triumph Herald for France and Italy, and had a lovely holiday buzzing about by the sea. We were a day late getting back, coming home to all the furor of the album's release on 1 June."[14]

And what a furor it was. With his heavily pregnant wife by his side, George found himself in the eye of a very different storm than the one he had left only a few weeks earlier. In fact, the long-player had already hit the shops by the time George and Judy had rolled back into London from their holiday abroad. Released early, on May 26, in the United Kingdom after pirate radio had already begun playing it nonstop, and without bothering with the niceties of commercial interruption, *Sgt. Pepper* had been an instant blockbuster. The long-player debuted at number one on the UK charts, selling 250,000 copies during its first seven days of release and holding down the top spot for twenty-two consecutive weeks. Stateside, *Sgt. Pepper* quickly ruled the pop-music roost, lording over the *Billboard* charts for fifteen uninterrupted weeks and selling 2.5 million units during the summer months alone. Like their British counterparts, American radio stations kept the LP in heavy rotation. Writing in 1968, *Rolling Stone* magazine's Langdon Winner described the album's release as a great moment of cultural unification—rivaling, if not exceeding, the night the Beatles made their American debut on *The Ed Sullivan Show*:

> The closest Western Civilization has come to unity since the Congress of Vienna in 1815 was the week the *Sgt. Pepper* album was released. In every city in Europe and America the stereo systems and the radio played, "What would you think if I sang out of tune . . . Woke up, got out of bed . . . looked much older, and the bag across her shoulder . . . in the sky with diamonds, Lucy in the . . ." and everyone listened. At the time, I happened to be driving across the country on Interstate 80. In each city where I stopped for gas or food—Laramie, Ogallala, Moline, South Bend—the melodies wafted in from some far-off transistor radio or portable hi-fi. It was the most amazing thing I've ever heard. For a brief while, the irreparable fragmented consciousness of the West was unified, at least in the minds of the young.

For McCartney, *Sgt. Pepper*'s resounding impact would become clear much closer to home and only a few days into its release. On June 4, the Jimi Hendrix Experience played London's Saville Theatre, the old vaudeville house on Shaftesbury Avenue that Epstein had taken over back in April 1965. McCartney and Harrison were in attendance that night as the American guitar hero blew the audience away with a sizzling rendition of "Sgt. Pepper's Lonely Hearts Club Band," a song that bore Hendrix's unmistakable influence and that, amazingly, had only just been released.[15]

As striking as *Sgt. Pepper*'s sales figures and critical acclaim were, the impact of the LP's revolutionary music had been matched for many consumers of the day by the album's stunning cover art. Peter Blake, Jann Haworth, Michael Cooper, and their team had clearly accomplished their objective, creating an artistic design wholly appropriate for the long-player's avant-garde aspirations. The center of the unusual cover art featured the Beatles themselves, decked out in psychedelic military regalia as Sgt. Pepper's mythical troupe. To their right stand the bandmates' Beatlemania-era selves as wax figures, along with nearly sixty of their cultural and countercultural "friends" from the annals of history, religion, Hollywood, music, sports, and literature. In addition to the high literary presence of Lewis Carroll, Edgar Allan Poe, and Oscar Wilde, the cover montage ranges from Marlon Brando's steely visage in *On the Waterfront* and Bob Dylan in thoughtful repose to the stereotypically one-dimensional portrait of boxer Sonny Liston and the lost, penetrating gaze of Stuart Sutcliffe, the Beatles' original bassist who had died of a brain hemorrhage in April 1962, two months before they first met Martin at Abbey Road. At one point, Epstein had been so concerned about the potential controversy associated with the mustached Beatles posing in front of a grave adorned with cannabis leaves that he considered releasing the album in a plain brown wrapper. As it was, the cover design had cost nearly £3,000, a considerable sum for that era in the British record industry. But it proved to be a pittance in comparison with the LP's overall production costs, with the final tally of expenses associated with *Sgt. Pepper* totaling approximately £25,000. As a point of comparison, their first album, *Please Please Me*, had cost some £400 to produce. But ultimately, *Sgt. Pepper's* cover art, like the long-player itself, would show its mettle. As with Klaus Voormann's *Revolver* design the previous year, Blake and Haworth would be rewarded with a Grammy Award for Best Album Cover, Graphic Arts. Indeed, *Sgt. Pepper* would capture a number of the coveted statuettes at the Tenth Annual Grammy Awards in 1968, including awards for Best Engineered Recording, Non-Classical; Best Contemporary Album; and, perhaps most impressively, Album of the Year, marking the first time that a rock LP had bested that category. EMI may have been known for its penny-pinching ways, but *Sgt. Pepper* was an investment that, even at that early date, had already paid for itself many times over.

For Martin, *Sgt. Pepper* was, without question, the highlight of his production career, a hallmark that would be difficult to equal, much less surpass. Writing twenty years later, George was still lost in the moment, describing *Sgt. Pepper* as "a musical fragmentation grenade, exploding with a force that is still being felt. It grabbed the world of pop music by the scruff of the neck, shook it hard, and left it to wander off, dizzy but wagging its tail. As well as changing the way pop music was viewed, it changed the entire nature of the recording game—for keeps. Nothing even remotely like *Pepper* had been heard before. It came at a time when people were thirsty for something new, but still its newness caught them by surprise." But for George, *Sgt. Pepper's* cultural apotheosis wasn't all pomp and circumstance. For the Beatles' producer, it would ultimately come at a price. A few months after the LP's release, *Time* magazine devoted a cover story to herald the Beatles' "New Incarnation." In the accompanying article titled "The Messengers," Christopher Porterfield accords the bandmates with a host of platitudes, describing them as "creating the most original, expressive and musically interesting sounds being heard in pop music. They are leading an evolution in which the best of current post-rock sounds are becoming something that pop music has never been before: an art form. 'Serious musicians' are listening to them and marking their work as a historic departure in the progress of music—any music." But when he finally arrived at the heart of the matter, Porterfield reserved some of his greatest accolades for the older man with the posh voice: "With the help of their engineer, arranger and record producer, George Martin, they plugged into a galaxy of space-age electronic effects, achieved partly through a mixture of tapes run backward and at various speeds." Later describing Martin as "the producer whose technical midwifery" made *Sgt. Pepper* possible, Porterfield unknowingly set off a brushfire that would trail the producer for years and be echoed across the record industry by musicians and techies alike. Like other music consumers of the day, Rick Wakeman, the keyboard-playing virtuoso of the progressive rock band Yes, recalled hearing *Sgt. Pepper* for the first time in June 1967 and being "gobsmacked. It was pushing the bounds of technology. It really showed you what George Martin could do." In this way, the Beatles' producer was suddenly emerging as a much-vaunted auteur in his own right. Interpreted in a less-than-favorable light, he might even have been seen as competing with, if not overshadowing, the bandmates themselves. And he would later discover, much to his own chagrin, that such accolades hadn't escaped their notice.[16]

While George and the bandmates reveled in adulation at the beginning of what would come to be known as the Summer of Love, not all of their listeners had been buoyed by the aural experience of *Sgt. Pepper*. For Brian Wilson, the Beatles' world-beating long-player punctuated months of professional and personal setbacks as he attempted to put the finishing touches on the Beach Boys' *Smile*, the album that *Hit Parader* had heralded as the next great pop masterwork during the previous December. Only by this point, Wilson hadn't even come close to fulfilling the rock magazine's great expectations, much less his own. For Brian, *Sgt. Pepper* had proven to be heartbreaking in more ways than one. In a sense, he found the album to be a heartrending revelation. Back in April, Paul had previewed "She's Leaving Home" for the Beach Boy and his wife Marilyn during his West Coast jaunt. As Brian later recalled, "We both just cried. It was beautiful." But in another sense, *Sgt. Pepper* had proven to be heartbreaking for Brian in a highly personal fashion. Its release and subsequent fanfare had left him shattered, having exposed his inability to bring *Smile* to fruition. "Time can be spent in the studio to the point where you get so next to it," Brian later observed, that "you don't know where you are with it, [and] you decide to just chuck it for a while." Within days of *Sgt. Pepper*'s release, the other Beach Boys gathered at Brian's Bel Air estate, where they began a series of harried recording sessions to complete a stripped-down version of *Smile* in order to meet their contractual obligations with Capitol Records. By that point, Van Dyke Parks was long gone, having begun recording his solo debut *Song Cycle*.[17]

With a July deadline looming, the Beach Boys didn't have the option of chucking the project, which was rechristened as *Smiley Smile* and released in mid-September. But by then, Brian's mystique, so carefully cultivated with the twin masterstrokes of *Pet Sounds* and "Good Vibrations," had vanished. *Smiley Smile* topped out at number forty-one in *Billboard* while still managing to eke out a top-ten showing in the United Kingdom, where an *NME* reviewer panned the album, writing that "by the standards which this group has set itself, it's more than a grade disappointing." For Brian, *Smiley Smile* was a hollow version of his original vision for the group's successor for *Pet Sounds*. But even still, he recognized that *Sgt. Pepper* was in a class all its own. Years later, when he was asked how his original conception of *Smile* compared with the Beatles' long-player, Brian didn't mince words. "It wouldn't have come close," he exclaimed. "*Sgt. Pepper* would have kicked our ass."[18]

By the time that Martin reunited with the Beatles on the evening of Thursday, June 1—the official date of *Sgt. Pepper*'s much-anticipated release, no less—he was itching to get back to work. During his absence, the group had not only tackled "All Together Now" but had made inroads into a comedy number titled "You Know My Name (Look Up the Number)" and a new Harrison composition that went under the working title of "Too Much." For the latter song, they had been working at De Lane Lea Music Recording Studio, a somewhat clinical facility housed in a Kingsway-area office building where Jimi Hendrix had recently recorded significant portions of his debut album, *Are You Experienced?* Like Regent Sound and Olympic Sound Studios, De Lane Lea was an independent shop, which meant that Emerick and Lush were prohibited from working the sessions. But Martin and the Beatles trudged on without them, anxious to capture their latest ideas on tape without benefit of EMI Studios, which was booked with other artists at the time. De Lane Lea's Dave Siddle and Mike Weighell served as George's makeshift production team. In a similar vein to the May 9 session, when the band produced a virtually unusable, meandering instrumental jam, the June 1 affair was an even more unfocused mess. Once again, the Beatles produced a tortuous, even slipshod and unprofessional at times, muddle of a session, with the bandmates overloading their instruments with reverb and mindlessly scraping their guitar strings. As Mark Lewisohn has astutely observed, "The single-minded channeling of their great talent so evident on *Sgt. Pepper's Lonely Hearts Club Band* did seem, for the moment, to have disappeared."[19]

The very next evening, Friday, June 2, Martin and the group had returned to De Lane Lea, where the producer supervised an overdubbing session for Harrison's "Too Much," which had now been elongated as "It's All Too Much." The song's brass and woodwind superimposition included four trumpets and a bass clarinet. On hand that evening was David Mason, who was frustrated with Harrison, who didn't seem to know what he wanted in terms of the session musicians' participation. Without benefit of a score, the musicians were left to their own devices. For his part, Mason lifted a section of baroque composer Jeremiah Clarke's *Prince of Denmark's March* (commonly known as the *Trumpet Voluntary*), which afforded Harrison's composition with a robust flavor of Englishness. As usual when working outside of Abbey Road, Martin and the Beatles were also without benefit of Emerick. By this point, Emerick had begun engineering a new project at EMI Studios, a long-player by the Zombies that would come to be known as *Odessey and Oracle*. Geoff was assisted by John Kurlander, a newly minted Abbey Road tape operator. As for Martin, the rest of the June 2 session was dominated by yet more of the same unfocused jamming that had permeated the previous one. For his part, George could only watch from his place in the control booth, hoping against hope that the Beatles would find their way. This was uncharted territory for the bandmates in the studio, where they had so often found solace and a sense of artistic drive. In earlier years, George had made tactical withdrawals, at times, in order to support their ideas and creative energies. But these kinds of mindless, directionless sessions were very different.

Fortunately, things took a turn for the better on Wednesday night, May 17, when George and the Beatles returned to Studio 2 and the familiar faces of Emerick and Lush. That evening, the band picked up where they had left off with "You Know My Name (Look Up the Number)." Perhaps the bandmates' sudden concentration had as much to do with the friendly confines of Abbey Road as is it did with the material, which was truly up Martin's street. Chock-full of the very kinds of comedic elements that George had mined back in his Parlophone days with the likes of Peter Sellers and

Spike Milligan, "You Know My Name (Look Up the Number)" was a vehicle around which everyone, the production team included, could rally. Even the song's origins were zany, having emerged after Lennon happened to glance at a London telephone book that was embossed with the words "You know the name, look up the number." That evening, the Beatles established a rhythm track consisting of electric guitar, drums, and tambourine, along with some shoddy flute adornment. The next night, June 7, George and the bandmates' efforts became even more concentrated after they selected take nine as the best realization of the rhythm track. At this juncture, they began a series of overdubs, including piano, drums, lead guitar, bass, and vibraphone tracks. The great highlight of the evening involved an appearance by the Rolling Stones' Brian Jones, who provided a bluesy alto sax solo. The session came to a close with several additional superimpositions, including harmonica, bongos, piano, and, absurd as it may seem, a bird whistle, which they had presumably lifted from the studio's trap room. For the time being, the band's work on "You Know My Name (Look Up the Number)" reached its conclusion that Friday night, when George conducted a control room session to create a mono mix for the song, which at this point was an instrumental. While the song's purpose seemed entirely unclear at this juncture—and it was difficult to imagine that it would have any place on the impending *Yellow Submarine* soundtrack—"You Know My Name (Look Up the Number)" had been a concerted effort, in contrast with "It's All Too Much," which the band seemed to have been making up as they went along. And it was certainly better than the earlier, tortuous jam sessions that had inaugurated their post-*Pepper* effusions. What the Beatles really needed, at this point, was a project around which to coalesce their considerable talents.

Fortunately, in the Beatles' mid-1960s universe, events and opportunities always seemed to turn on a dime, and June 1967 was no different. A few months earlier, Epstein had made one of his rare appearances at Abbey Road, although it had scarcely registered a blip on their radar at the time. "Boys," he announced, "I have the most fantastic news to report. You have been selected to represent England in a television program which, for the first time ever, will be transmitted live around the world via satellite. The BBC shall actually be filming you making your next record." As Emerick later recalled, the bandmates barely reacted to their manager's news, and, after sensing Epstein's dismay at their nonchalance, chided him for not including them in the decision. "Well, Brian, that's what you get for committing us to doing something without asking us first," said Lennon. For the next several weeks, George and the Beatles seemed to have all but forgotten about the BBC program, working intensely to complete *Sgt. Pepper* at the time. During George's post-*Pepper* holiday, the issue came up again during the session for "You Know My Name (Look Up the Number)," with Paul nonchalantly asking John, "How are you getting on with that song for the television broadcast? Isn't it coming up fairly soon?" Once again, the matter was neglected—even after signing their formal performance contract on May 18—until after their producer's return. Exasperated by the Beatles' continuing inertia, Brian dropped into the studio yet again to make another pass at stoking the passions of his jaded clients. As George later recalled, "Brian suddenly whirled in and said that we were to represent Britain in a round-the-world hook-up, and we'd got to write a song. It was a challenge. We had less than two weeks to get it together, and then we learnt there were going to be over 300 million people watching."[20]

By this point, George recognized the precariousness of their position, especially given their seeming inability to generate the requisite enthusiasm for the event. Titled *Our World*, the program was the brainchild of BBC producer Aubrey Singer and had been some ten months in the making. As George later recalled, the Beatles initially planned to come up with something at the last minute: "'But you can't just go off the cuff,' I pleaded with them. 'We've got to prepare *something*.' So they went away to get something together, and John came up with 'All You Need Is Love.' It had to be kept terribly secret, because the general idea was that the television viewers would actually see the Beatles at work recording their new single." With the chips down and the bandmates in desperate need of new material, they had come through in the nick of time with a composition that, in Martin's words, "seemed to fit with the overall concept of the program." Years later, he would describe the song as an "ideal, lovely" composition, but when John first debuted "All You Need Is Love," the composer reportedly sat at the piano and performed it in a "dirge-like" fashion. At one point, Martin turned to McCartney and muttered, "Well, it's certainly repetitive." But for George, the real issue was whether or not the Beatles could even succeed in performing the song in a live setting—particularly one that would be further complicated by the pressure of being a global simulcast. If George knew anything after the Beatles' latest bout of studio disarray, he understood implicitly that there was virtually no way that they could simulate the act of recording for a live audience—let alone, several hundred million viewers. He and his production team would have to be fully prepared for any hitches that might emerge in the process. What the Beatles needed, George reasoned, was a foolproof backing track with which to play along during the simulcast. "I was still worried about the idea of going out totally live," Martin later wrote. "So I told the boys:

'We're going to hedge our bets. This is how we'll do it. I'll have a four-track machine standing by, and when we go on the air I'll play you the rhythm track, which you'll pretend to be playing. But your voices and the orchestra will really be live and we'll mix the whole thing together and transmit it to the waiting world like that.'"[21]

And it was with this mind-set, on Wednesday, June 14, that they finally settled down to work on "All You Need Is Love." With Abbey Road unavailable on such short notice, George and the band returned to Olympic, with Eddie Kramer serving as engineer and George Chkiantz sitting in as tape operator. With the musical flavor for "All You Need Is Love" still in a state of evolution, John asked to sing his guide vocal from the control room, where he could converse with George. To accomplish this end, Kramer had to think quickly on his feet: "We rigged the talkback mike so that it could be used for vocals," Kramer later recalled, "and he sang through that." As John performed his vocal, the Beatles went about the business of establishing a basic rhythm track. Lennon took his seat behind the studio's harpsichord, where he led the group through the basic chord structure. Meanwhile, with Starr behind the drum kit, Harrison took up a violin and McCartney played a double bass, both of which had been left over from a previous orchestral session at Olympic. After the session, Martin was left with an invoice for ten guineas for the use of the harpsichord, although he was more concerned with Harrison's impromptu attempt at playing the violin. "I remember that one of the minor problems was that George [Harrison] had got hold of a violin, which he wanted to try to play, even though he couldn't!"[22]

From the outset, Martin and the Beatles had concocted the idea of deploying "La Marseillaise," the French national anthem, as the instrumental motto for "All You Need Is Love." And with that, the idea of orchestral backing was born. As John observed at the time, "So then we thought, 'Ah, well, we'll have some more orchestra around this little three-piece with a drum.'" While their original intention had been to conclude the song with some kind of chaotic demonstration—they had "wanted to freak out at the end and just go mad," in Martin's words—the bandmates ultimately gave him free rein to compose the score in any way that he saw fit.[23]

But in keeping with the frenzied timetable of that incredible week, they had waited until the eleventh hour in order to make their intentions known to their producer. As Geoff later recalled, "Adding to the chaos was John's insistence on making a last-minute change to the arrangement, which sent George Martin into a tizzy—he was doing the orchestral score and had to rapidly come up with new sheet music for the musicians, who milled around impatiently waiting for him. To his credit, George came up with a spectacular arrangement, especially considering the very limited time he had to do it in and the odd meters that characterized the song." Years later, Martin would remember things more charitably, as was his typical wont, writing that the Beatles told him to "write absolutely anything you like, George. Put together any tunes you fancy, and just play it out like that." In addition to "La Marseillaise," Martin culled the play-out section of his score from "a Bach two-part invention, 'Greensleeves,' and the little lick from 'In the Mood.' I wove them all together, at slightly different tempos so that they all still worked as separate entities." In so doing, George created one of pop music's first mash-ups.[24]

With Harrison and McCartney still plying the strings with varying degrees of success, along with Lennon's harpsichord and Starr's drums, Martin conducted thirty-three takes of "All You Need Is Love." The group carried out each new performance with rapid-fire precision, with John counting off a new take in the same instant in which the previous one had concluded—or, in some cases, had collapsed in a false start or some other sort of instrumental breakdown. Before leaving Olympic that night, acetates were created, with Martin taking the long weekend to begin concocting a score. On Monday, June 19, George and the Beatles were back in the friendly confines of EMI Studios, where things quickly became more businesslike—as well they should: they had just six short days to get their act together for a global audience. After selecting take ten as the best of their motley bunch of attempts back at Olympic, they began adding overdubs to "All You Need Is Love." After the requisite tape reduction, track two consisted of Martin's piano and Lennon's banjo. Lead and backing vocals—including the song's seminal "love, love, love" chorus—were adorned on tracks three and four.

With the makings of a backing track in hand, George and the bandmates planned to continue refining "All You Need Is Love" on the evenings of June 20 and 21 in Studio 2. But those sessions would be abruptly canceled when the specter of real life interrupted George's breakneck effort to bring the Beatles to the finish line for the *Our World* telecast. With George and Judy expecting their first child later that summer, they had also chosen that very week to relocate from their tiny flat on Manchester Street to a house of their own off of Hyde Park Crescent. Reflecting on that period, George later wrote that "most of us look back on 1967 as a great vintage year, the year of *Sgt. Pepper*. It was more than that for me, as it had great highs, it is true, but also it had a dark side." For George, that dark side first revealed itself, only faintly at first, on Friday, June 16, when his father Harry took ill and was hospitalized in Wimbledon with chest pains. Visiting his father that weekend, George recalled that "he certainly looked strong to me. We chatted, and he joked about getting better." With reassurances from the duty nurse that his father would shortly recover, George went so far as to reassure his sister Irene, who was on vacation, that she needn't rush back to London on their father's account; he was going to be just fine. Before heading off to Abbey Road to resume work on "All You Need Is Love" on Monday, June 20, George recalled telling his father, "'I'll see you tomorrow morning.' But when I arrived on the Tuesday morning, the nurse stopped me. 'Your father died in the middle of the night,' she said." Felled by a myocardial infarction, Harry had died in his sleep on the eve of what would have been his eighty-third birthday. For George, "it was a desperate shock. He had seemed so well." But even still, George soon realized that "he did manage to have the last laugh on me." When George returned to Wimbledon to retrieve his father's effects, "the nurse handed me his watch and some personal belongings, including his Post Office savings book." And that's when he took a closer look at his father's savings account: "Looking through it, I noticed there was an entry every week for all the money that I'd given him as an allowance, and it was all still there, untouched. I was so overcome I just burst into tears. I thought, 'You old devil!'"[25]

While Martin was away on family business, Emerick and Lush worked in the Studio 3 control room, where they prepared remixes of the Olympic Sound rhythm track for "All You Need Is Love." An acetate of the second remix was delivered to BBC broadcast director Derek Burrell-Davis in advance of the June 25 telecast. By the evening of Friday, June 23, all hands were on deck in Studio 1 to rehearse "All You Need Is Love" for the simulcast, which was now fewer than forty-eight hours away. In addition to the bandmates and George's production team, a thirteen-member orchestra was in evidence. Years later, George would remember that he "did a score for the song, a fairly arbitrary sort of arrangement since it was at such short notice." As with the Beatles themselves, George wasn't leaving anything to chance in terms of the orchestra, who were on hand to record their own backing track. The players included four violinists, two cellists, two saxophonists, two trombonists, two trumpeters, a flügelhornist, and an accordionist. Beatles session veteran Sidney Sax served as leader, while David Mason made his fourth appearance at Abbey Road on the Fab Four's behalf. For his performance on "All You Need Is Love," he played the same trumpet that he had used back in January for "Penny Lane." During the three-hour session, George led the players through ten performances of the score, which was captured in a series of four-track-to-four-track tape reductions for reference purposes.[26]

In the middle of the Friday evening rehearsal, Brian interrupted the proceedings to hold an impromptu meeting with George and the bandmates in the Studio 1 control room. Brian was taken with the idea of releasing "All You Need Is Love" as a single to take advantage of *Our World*'s status as a truly global event, to cash in on what could be the greatest and most visible pop-song debut in the history of the record business. As Geoff later recalled, "John, of course, was keen—it was his song, after all—and it didn't take much effort to talk Paul into it, either, since he knew the value of the massive publicity they would be receiving by virtue of the broadcast, thereby guaranteeing huge record sales." As always, Brian was keen on promoting new Beatles product at every possible juncture. For George, the idea of releasing "All You Need Is Love" as a single was a no-brainer. But his overriding concern at this point was ensuring that they didn't fall flat on their faces in front of a worldwide television audience. He had spent the balance of the past month observing the Beatles loafing their way through one drug-addled session after another. For his part, he could never understand why they felt the need to give themselves over to any of their drug inducements of the moment, whether they be amphetamines, marijuana, or acid. To George's way of thinking, the Beatles were the most ingenious recording artists he had ever met, and they simply didn't need psychotropic or other enhancements to heighten their creativity.[27]

On the eve of the simulcast, George and the Beatles convened at Abbey Road at two in the afternoon for a press call in which more than one hundred journalists and photographers flooded Studio 1. It was an unprecedented moment in Martin and the Beatles' five-year collaboration, which had taken place almost entirely behind closed doors. In the early afternoon, the BBC technical personnel conducted a rehearsal, blocking their camera angles for the Beatles and the session players. By this juncture, George had decided to remain in the control room in order to ensure that the backing track went off without a hitch, so he recruited Mike Vickers to serve as conductor. During the rehearsal, Burrell-Davis announced that he would be mounting a TV camera in the control room to capture George and his production team at work during the Beatles' performance. As Emerick later recalled, "An obviously pleased George Martin turned to Richard and me and said, 'You two had better smarten yourselves up—you're about to become international TV stars,' which had the effect of making me even more nervous! But we were both into clothes at that point, and during a break, Richard and I excitedly discussed what we were going to wear. He owned a loud, stripey jacket that he thought would strobe in the cameras, so he planned on donning that, just for a joke. In the end, though, he was only seen in the broadcast for the briefest of moments. I opted for a simple white shirt and tie. I knew that it would simply be too hot in that control room, especially on a warm summer night, to consider wearing a jacket." After the BBC team concluded their business that afternoon, the band and the orchestra held a three-hour session in which they recorded four additional takes of "All You Need Is Love."[28]

When the moment of truth arrived on Sunday, June 25, George and the bandmates were as ready as they could possibly be under the circumstances. Another round of rehearsals got underway at two o'clock that afternoon in Studio 1, with George supervising several rehearsal takes with the Beatles and the orchestra poised in front of the BBC cameras, which were ready and waiting for the big event scheduled to begin in just under eight hours. George Martin was joined in the booth by his usual production team of Emerick and Lush, along with the BBC's Martin Benge. During the rehearsals, John and Paul broke into giggles on more than one occasion. During the play-out section, John had begun trying out a series of non sequiturs, variously singing bits from "She Loves You," "Yesterday," and, strangest of all, "She'll Be Coming 'Round the Mountain." At one point, McCartney got into the act, ad-libbing "I believe you, Johnny!" as Lennon practiced the first verse of "All You Need Is Love" for the cameras, which, like the audio, was linked by a series of cables with a mobile broadcasting unit in the Abbey Road parking lot. From there, the signal would beam across five continents through the auspices of the Early Bird "space booster" and Lana Bird and ATS/B satellites. The *Our World* program itself was conceived as a goodwill mission to unite a troubled world gripped, as it was, by geopolitical strife in those Cold War days. And for one evening at least, it would largely succeed, with *Our World* enjoying an audience of some four hundred million people—even without the participation of the Soviet Union, which dropped out, predictably, at the last possible moment.

During the rehearsals, the BBC took a page out of Martin's book and prerecorded the sequence in which the Beatles engage in a mock recording session. The preamble clocked in at roughly two minutes, with BBC host Steve Race narrating the events inside the studio, including images of Martin pretending to supervise the recording of a vocal track. With the orchestra seated in Studio 1, Race observed that "the Beatles get on best with symphony men." Meanwhile, Lush simulated the act of rewinding the rhythm track, while Lennon and McCartney engage in studio banter, including Lennon singing the Kinks' "Waterloo Sunset" as McCartney jokes with their producer, whom he refers to as "Uncle George." But it was all a charade for the cameras, of course.

Through Martin's careful planning, the only authentic aspects of the evening would be Lennon's lead vocal, McCartney's bass, Harrison's guitar solo, and the orchestral accompaniment. Starr's drums had been prerecorded as part of the basic rhythm track. Ringo was perfectly capable of keeping time that evening, but George knew that the Beatle's drums would inevitably spoil the sound via leakage. Everyone was dressed to the nines, with Martin donning a white linen jacket for the occasion, the orchestra adorned in formal evening wear, and the Beatles done up in their hippie finery. Even though the band's performance would be broadcast in black and white, the room was brimming with colorful streamers and placards. The only thing more colorful was the audience of friends and relations, including such rock 'n' roll glitterati as Mick Jagger, Marianne Faithfull, Keith Richards, Eric Clapton, Keith Moon, Pattie Boyd, Mike McGear, Jane Asher, and Graham Nash, among others.

As if everyone's nerves weren't already on high alert, the Beatles' *Our World* segment actually commenced about forty seconds earlier than planned. At 9:36 PM, the BBC transmitted the pretaped Beatles "recording" session, and at 9:38 the live feed was launched, startling George and Geoff, who were downing much-needed shots of Scotch whisky. "There was a big panic to hide the bottle and the glasses," Emerick later recalled. "We were shoving them under the mixing console!" For Martin, the tussle with the shot glasses was quickly overshadowed by an unexpected technical glitch:

> To cap it all, at the last minute, just before we were due to go on the air, there was a panic call from the producer, sitting outside in the control van. "George, I've lost contact with the cameras in the studio. They can't hear me. Can you relay my instructions to them?" So, apart from worrying about the vast audience who were going to be watching me, and worrying about the sound we would produce, and worrying about the orchestra in the studio, which Mike Vickers was conducting, I had, at the moment of truth, to worry about linking the TV cameramen to their producer. It became so complicated that I was on the verge of hysterical laughter. I remember thinking: "If we're going to do something wrong, we might as well do it in style in front of 200 million people."

And with that frame of mind, Martin called the session to order, Vickers took up the baton, and the whole shebang finally got underway for better or worse. But any fears that George and his production team held were decidedly short lived. Incredibly, the Beatles' (mostly) live performance of "All

You Need Is Love" went off without any further hitches, with the assembled friends and family merrily singing along with the chorus. When Burrell-Davis yelled "cut!" a member of the assembled glitterati gleefully shouted, "Happy new year, everybody," as Harrison attempted, futilely, to pick out the notes of "La Marseillaise" on his guitar.[29]

Before they went home that evening, George and the Beatles put the finishing touches on the "All You Need Is Love" single. By the time that the studio had cleared out, with BBC personnel and the bandmates' guests having departed, John was raring to go. From his place in the studio, he called up to his producer in the booth, "I'm ready to sing for the world, George, if you can just give me the backing." After Lennon corrected a few flubs during his lead vocal, Ringo also replaced the tambourine part that he played during "La Marseillaise" with a stirring snare roll. That same day, Epstein telephoned his old friend and business partner Nat Weiss in New York City and proclaimed, "All you need is love. Love is all you need. Tell Capitol Records Monday morning, that's the single. That says it all." On Monday evening, George supervised a mono mixing session for "All You Need Is Love" in the Studio 2 control room. In the process, he treated Lennon's vocal with a dose of ADT to give it more texture. With "Baby, You're a Rich Man" having been selected as the B-side, the Beatles' first singles release since February was ready to go into production. On July 7—Ringo's twenty-seventh birthday—the "All You Need Is Love" backed with "Baby, You're a Rich Man" single was in the hands of British consumers. "Funnily enough," George later remarked, few listeners among the Beatles' massive fan base ever "realized the single was any different to the TV version of the song." Within a fortnight, "All You Need Is Love" topped the UK charts, and "the roll," which had been short-circuited by Humperdinck's "Release Me" earlier in the year, was back on with a vengeance. Meanwhile, back in the United States, "All You Need Is Love" conquered *Billboard*'s Hot 100 within a matter of weeks.[30]

For George, "All You Need Is Love" and the Beatles' *Our World* performance had made for another career milestone, not to mention a makeshift anthem for the Summer of Love. As his old friend Lionel Bart later remarked, "One knew that the whole world was seeing things together for the first time ever. The Beatles sang a song of love and it was *good*." Marking the band's fifteenth UK single, "All You Need Is Love" was the first time, oddly enough, that George received a production credit on one of the Beatles' seven-inch discs. In those days, producers and engineers were rarely acknowledged on LP sleeves and liner notes, much less the records themselves. But George's experience with "All You Need Is Love" wasn't all sunny optimism and smooth sailing. "Unfortunately, there was a sting in the tail for me," he later wrote. "I was being paid the princely sum of £15 for arranging the music and writing the bits for the beginning and ending, and I had chosen the tunes for the mixture in the belief that they were all out of copyright. More fool me. It turned out that although 'In the Mood' itself was out of copyright, the Glenn Miller arrangement of it was not." In short order, EMI was asked for a royalty by Miller's estate. "The Beatles, quite rightly I suppose, said: 'We're not going to give up our copyright royalty,'" George later recalled. "So Ken East, the man who had by then become managing director of EMI Records, came to me and said: 'Look here, George, you did the arrangement on this. They're expecting money for it.'" Martin was understandably aghast when East announced that EMI expected the Beatles' producer to pay the royalty out of his £15 fee. But in contrast with early 1964, when he stood by, sour-faced, as EMI denied him his holiday bonus, George wasn't giving in to the record conglomerate's miserly ways. With the producer not giving an inch, EMI ultimately settled with the Miller estate, leaving Martin with yet another bitter taste in his mouth after dealing with the company for whom his records had netted a king's ransom and then some.[31]

With the manifold anxieties of *Our World* fading into George and the bandmates' rearview mirror—and the sheer exhaustion of recording *Sgt. Pepper* only just beginning to ebb—the group and the brain trust agreed to take a much-deserved holiday for the rest of July and much of August. After all, they planned to conduct principal photography for the *Magical Mystery Tour* television movie in the fall, and with "All Together Now," "It's All Too Much," and "Only a Northern Song" in the can, they were ahead on compiling their new recordings for the *Yellow Submarine* cartoon feature. For George, the break was a blessing, affording him with more time to spend with Judy, who expected to give birth to their first child in August, as well as to catch up on the backlog of AIR recordings that he desperately needed to produce.

David and Jonathan, the duo for which George held such high hopes, faltered yet again with their "She's Leaving Home" backed with "One Born Every Minute" single. With Martin having produced the A-side, Vickers chipped in for "One Born Every Minute." But in spite of the duo's obvious talent—and a cover version of a tune from *Sgt. Pepper*, no less—David and Jonathan had clearly begun to lose their way. Vickers produced their follow-up single for AIR, "Softly Whispering I Love You" backed with "Such a Peaceful Day." Like its predecessor, "Softly Whispering I Love You" failed to crack the UK charts. Indeed, the only place that David and Jonathan seemed to be able to muster an audience was Australia, where "She's Leaving Home" and "Softly

Whispering I Love You" charted at numbers ninety-three and twenty-three, respectively. A final single released in June 1968, "You Ought to Meet My Baby" backed with "I've Got That Girl on My Mind," failed to chart in any marketplace, proving the sobering truth that David and Jonathan had truly run their course. As the decade wore on, Roger Cook and Roger Greenaway would try their hand as a newly minted act, the Congregation, before settling into a world-beating career as the composers behind "I'd Like to Teach the World to Sing (in Perfect Harmony)" and "Long Cool Woman in a Black Dress," which were both massive international hits and cemented the duo's name as Ivor Novello Award–winning songwriters.

While David and Jonathan had reached their nadir, George's mainstay Matt Monro managed to find a new audience in 1967 via the North American adult-contemporary market. For years, Monro had been making inroads into that audience, but with rock 'n' roll dominating the industry, he had begun to enjoy more regular success as a crooner on the adult contemporary charts. Back in March, his single "Where in the World" backed with "The Lady Smiles" had notched a number-eleven showing stateside, and Martin achieved similar results with Monro's "What to Do" backed with "These Years," which clocked in at number twenty-two the summer of 1967. Although Monro was hardly a chart-topping evergreen in the same league as the Beatles, he possessed a loyal audience, and in the highly competitive mid-1960s pop world, he was more than holding his own.

Never straying too far from his origins as a producer of comedy records, George continued his work with Lance Percival, with whom he had recorded a top-forty novelty hit, the calypso-styled "Shame and Scandal in the Family," back in October 1965. More recently, Percival had lent his talents as the voices of Paul and Ringo for Al Brodax's Beatles cartoons. But Percival's follow-up single, "The Maharajah of Brum" backed with "Taking the Maharajah Apart," failed to chart. Produced by Martin with Vickers providing the arrangement, "The Maharajah of Brum" was cowritten by Percival and Martin. Based on Cat Stevens's 1966 song "Matthew and Son," Martin's lyrics take aim at Birmingham, the West Midlands metropolis that locals and Londoners alike disparage as Brummagem. With Percival deploying a mock Indian accent—like Peter Sellers's work in early Martin productions such as "Wouldn't It Be Loverly?"—"The Maharajah of Brum" offers an intentional skewering of mid-1960s pop's infatuation with Indian music, a trend that found its origins in Harrison's Eastern sensibilities. Had Martin grown tired of Harrison's penchant for adorning his songs with Indian instrumentation?

Or was he simply maligning the ersatz imitators who were following in the Beatle's trailblazing wake?

As George attended to AIR business during the Summer of Love, not to mention awaiting the birth of his first child with Judy, the Beatles made increasingly bizarre use of their time away from the studio. For Martin, the summer, and especially August, passed in a kind of blur. "After working during June on 'Magical Mystery Tour' and 'All You Need Is Love,'" he later wrote, "we had the blessed relief of a break in Beatles recordings during July. 'Relief' because I could give a bit more time and energy to further drastic upheavals in my personal life. Our first child, Lucie, was born on 9 August. Judy was fine, and was back home within a week. Little Lucie, however, being slightly premature, had to remain in hospital for a while. So in August my time was spent rushing between St. Thomas's and Abbey Road studios, where I was doing bits and bobs on 'Your Mother Should Know.' After a couple of weeks of this, we were allowed to take Lucie home."[32]

On the evening of Tuesday, August 22, George and the Beatles convened for the first time in nearly two months. With Abbey Road fully booked and McCartney aching to get back to work, they held the session at Chappell Recording Studios, a frequent haunt of Martin's in the service of his AIR clientele. After its most recent incarnation on Bond Street had burned to the ground in a 1965 fire, Chappell reopened on Maddox Street in Central London. The owners spared no expense in building out the new facility and in so doing had created one of the city's foremost state-of-the-art recording studios. With John Timperley sitting in the engineer's chair and John Iles serving as tape operator, Martin supervised eight takes of McCartney's "Your Mother Should Know," a contestant for the *Magical Mystery Tour* project and, by many accounts, the runner-up to "All You Need Is Love" in the Lennon-McCartney sweepstakes for the *Our World* performance. The basic rhythm track for "Your Mother Should Know" featured Paul on piano with Ringo on drums. Before wrapping up for the evening, Paul recorded a pair of lead vocals. On Wednesday, George and the bandmates were back at Chappell to continue working. That same night, Brian made another rare appearance at a Beatles session, observing as George conducted playbacks of their recent, post-*Pepper* output. Before the night was out, the bandmates added backing vocals and rhythm guitar flourishes to accent the song's choruses. From his place in the engineer's seat, Timperley recalled that Epstein "came in to hear the playbacks looking extremely down and in a bad mood. He just stood at the back of the room listening, not saying much."[33]

With McCartney's yen to get back into the studio momentarily quenched with the "Your Mother Should Know" sessions under their belt, Harrison wasted little time in continuing his quest for spiritual awakening, which he had begun through his study of Eastern music and philosophy. With John and Paul in tow, he attended a lecture given by the Maharishi Mahesh Yogi at the Hyde Park Hilton on Thursday, August 24. At fifty years old, the maharishi had been on a journey of spiritual regeneration for much of his life. In 1945, he began a personal program of solitary meditation in the Himalayas, which lasted for more than a decade. When he literally came down from the mountain, the maharishi devoted himself to spreading traditional Indian teachings to the masses, a project that he started in 1957 with the founding of the Spiritual Regeneration Movement, the crusade that would eventually bring him to London during the Summer of Love. His timing couldn't have been better. Of particular interest to the Beatles was the maharishi's development of an increasingly popular technique known as Transcendental Meditation. The maharishi urged his followers to engage in a pair of twenty-minute daily sessions in which they focus on their mantra, the simple phrase whose repetition promises to open new vistas of spirituality, inner calm, and human consciousness. Swept up in their latest euphoria, the Beatles trundled off to Euston Station on August 25, where they boarded the train for University College in Bangor, Wales, the site of the maharishi's upcoming Transcendental Meditation seminar. The usual rock retinue was in tow, including Mick Jagger, Marianne Faithfull, and Donovan. Brian Epstein had been invited to attend the seminar by John, but the manager refused, having already decided to go out on the town with Peter Brown. In the wake of his father's death in July, Brian's mother, Queenie, had moved in with him at his Chapel Street home ten days earlier, and he was desperate to rejoin the London nightlife that had once been the staple of his existence.

Years later, Martin would recall the last days of the Summer of Love with a certain wistfulness. Along with the Beatles, he had succeeded in weathering the post-*Pepper* malaise, not to mention the death of his father during the *Our World* whirlwind. Having finally been able to bring Lucie home from the hospital, George and Judy were eager to hide out for a while, to let the world roll on without them for a change. "I knew the boys were off to Wales, to meet up with the Maharishi," he later wrote. "So it was with great joy that we found ourselves able to go to the country, with Lucie in our arms for the first time, that weekend, 25 August. It was a marvelous place, far from the madding crowd but not exactly overflowing with mod cons. We had no phone in our cottage." It was precisely with this carefree mind-set that George and Judy stepped out for a Sunday morning drink in the village pub. As they strolled into the tavern, the room suddenly fell silent. "We knew straight away that something was wrong. The proprietor leaned over to me: 'Your friend's dead,' he murmured." As he realized the awful truth, that the barman was referring, impossible as it may have seemed, to Brian, George couldn't believe what he was hearing. "I couldn't understand why he should be dead," George later recalled. "He had been pretty much alive the last time I had seen him, and he was quite a young man. It was inexplicable."[34]

15

"WE'VE FUCKIN' HAD IT"

EORGE WAS HEARTBROKEN. Brian Epstein, the man who was the architect of
Beatlemania, who brought the Beatles to his doorstep back in 1962, was
only thirty-two years old. The authorities shortly determined that Brian had
died from an overdose of Carbitral, a barbiturate that he had taken to battle
his insomnia. After George and Judy had absorbed the awful news, they made
their way back to London, still stunned by their sadness and grief. "When
Judy and I arrived back at our London flat," George wrote, "there was a
poignant reminder of Brian awaiting us. He had been delighted to hear of
our daughter's safe birth and with typical generosity had sent Judy a really
huge bouquet of flowers. When he had received no reply from our flat, the
messenger had simply left the flowers on the doorstep. Now, like Brian, they
were dead."[1]

As with George, the Beatles were understandably shocked to learn of
Brian's death. Their exhilaration over their spiritual excursion to Wales in
the maharishi's company was quickly replaced by an overriding sense of
shock. Newsreel footage from Bangor found John, like the other Beatles, in
a state of disbelief. But in spite of his internal trauma, it was John—just as it
had been during their second session with George back in September 1962,
when he fought for the producer's consideration of "Please Please Me"—who
acted as the band's spokesman. "We've only just heard," John announced to
the press pool, "and it's hard to think of things to say. But he was just—he
was a warm fellow, you know, and it's terrible." As he began to gather his
thoughts, he cited the maharishi, who recommended the bandmates "not to

get overwhelmed by grief. And whatever thoughts we have of Brian to keep them happy, because any thoughts we have of him will travel to him wherever he is." John concluded his remarks by paying Brian the highest compliment that a Beatle could bestow upon anyone from among their inner circle: "We loved him," said John. "He was one of us."[2]

Like many of Brian's closest friends, George attended the funeral, which was held in Liverpool on Tuesday, August 29. But the Beatles had purposefully stayed away, realizing that their appearance would cause a media circus, which the Epstein family desperately wanted to avoid. Knowing that they couldn't be present, Harrison presented Nat Weiss with a chrysanthemum, discreetly wrapped in newspaper, as a remembrance from the Beatles. He asked that Nat place the flower atop Brian's coffin. Attending Brian's internment at Long Lane Jewish Cemetery with NEMS executive Geoffrey Ellis, Weiss suddenly found himself in the horns of a dilemma. Knowing that flowers are verboten at Jewish funeral and burial services, Weiss made a last-second decision as he observed gravediggers shoveling dirt over the coffin. As Ellis later recalled, "Nat, who himself was Jewish, cast the newspaper package unopened onto Brian's coffin, where it was swiftly covered by earth." As for the burial service itself, the event had proven to be traumatic for the attendees, thunderstruck in their grief, as the attention-grabbing Rabbi Dr. Norman Solomon decried Brian, who had died just two days earlier, as "a symbol of the malaise of our generation." At the time, many in Brian's inner circle dismissed the official ruling that his death was the result of an accidental overdose. But George knew better, confident that his friend hadn't committed suicide, which had been the prevailing rumor at the time. "I am still convinced that Brian did not intend to take his own life," George wrote. "If he had, I think he would have done it with more of a flourish. As it was, he went out not with a bang but with a whimper. Brian was a showman. Had he designed his own death, it would not have been done in that timid, hole-in-the-corner way."[3]

The Beatles would finally get the opportunity to pay their respects to their fallen manager during a memorial service held on October 17 at the New London Synagogue, located at 33 Abbey Road, just a few doors down from the recording studio where they had made their name. It was the very place where the bandmates had made good on Brian's boast, improbable as it seemed at the time, that they would be bigger than Elvis Presley. Martin still recalled that very first day, way back in February 1962, when he first met the Beatles' manager: "I laughed at him, on first meeting, because what he played me on the demonstration tape was not very good," George recalled. "I laughed, but his faith in them never wavered. He was in love with them. So was I." For George, the memorial service proved to be even more devastating than the funeral back in August. Other present and former NEMS and AIR artists were on hand, including Cilla Black, Gerry Marsden, Billy J. Kramer, and members of the Fourmost. Rabbi Louis Jacobs officiated, lauding Brian for "encouraging young people to sing of love and peace rather than war and hatred." Years later, George remembered seeing "the Beatles coming into the synagogue, their faces white and pinched still with shock. Out of respect for Brian, they were all wearing yarmulkes. They had all washed their hair for the occasion, and the little round caps kept slipping off, falling to the floor. Wendy Hanson [Brian's former assistant], who was standing behind the Beatles, had to keep picking their yarmulkes up and fixing back on to their mop-tops. Somehow, that made me feel so sad, sadder than anything."[4]

But George also recognized Brian's untimely death in terms of its larger implications for his professional life with the Beatles, as well as the bandmates' capacity to endure as a working unit. "Brian's death really was the end of an era," the producer later wrote. "*Sgt. Pepper* had been our best work to date, the most thoughtful, among the best musically, and the most successful. Brian had steered them from the dark early days of struggle and hardship to this triumph." At the same time, George could read the writing on the wall, having watched Brian's slow collapse in the wake of the Jesus Christ tour and its attendant fallout. With the advent of *Sgt. Pepper*—possibly even beforehand, really—George had begun to glimpse a clear shift in the group's calculus:

One of the awful things is that, if Brian had lived, he would have lost the Beatles. He wouldn't have survived as their manager. . . . They would probably have sought their own, younger, different people to look after their affairs. Brian, by his own design, had become too fragmented and the Beatles were too selfish to ever have someone like that. They wanted someone who did nothing else but the Beatles. Even more than that: by that time, Paul wanted someone who did nothing but Paul, John wanted someone exclusively, and so on. So it would have become an impossible situation. I cannot see that Brian could have retained managership of the Beatles. One hesitates to know how the future might have gone if Brian had not died.

Clearly, George could sense the winds of change in the air. In many ways, Brian's recent gambit with Robert Stigwood had been symptomatic of the loosening of his hold on "the boys." In short order, the Beatles would buy out the Aussie entrepreneur and send him on his way. As for Martin, he understood, rather intuitively, how the bandmates were beginning to see the world, with McCartney and Lennon increasingly desirous of individual, even exclusive attention.[5]

But as for Lennon, the founding Beatle's own shock eventually gave way to a very different emotion, a feeling of fear over the Beatles' capacity to survive in a post-Epstein world. "I knew that we were in trouble then," he later recalled. "I didn't really have any misconceptions about our ability to do anything other than play music and I was scared. I thought, 'We've fuckin' had it.'" As it happened, Paul was frightened, too. Before the bandmates had left the maharishi back in Wales, they had accepted the holy man's invitation to visit his ashram for an extended retreat in India, where they would study Transcendental Meditation. But on September 1, McCartney gathered the other Beatles at his Cavendish Avenue home with a different objective in mind. During the meeting, he unveiled his plan for making the *Magical Mystery Tour* television film a reality. Paul's outline for the movie entailed a circle representing sixty minutes of screen time, with eight pie-shaped segments apportioned into sketches and musical numbers:

1. Commercial introduction. Get on the coach. Courier introduces.
2. Coach people meet each other / (Song, Fool on the Hill)
3. marathon—laboratory sequence.
4. smiling face. LUNCH. Mangoes, tropical (magician)
5. and 6: Dreams.
7. Stripper & band.
8. Song.

END.

Paul had previously unveiled his concept for filming a mystery tour back in April. But now he had a far different motive in mind, given the uncertainty that had plagued the band in the wake of Brian's death. "If the others clear off to India again now on another meditation trip," he confided in Tony Barrow, "I think there's a very real danger that we'll never come back together again as a working group. On the other hand, if I can persuade them today that we should go straight into shooting this film, it could save the Beatles."[6]

McCartney had clearly succeeded in convincing his friends to postpone their plans for visiting the maharishi. In short order, they agreed to begin principal photography for the television movie during the week of

Released in 1966 and credited to George Martin and His Orchestra, *George Martin Instrumentally Salutes The Beatle Girls* was the producer's third collection of pop instrumental arrangements. *Publicity Photo/United Artists*

Released on February 17, 1967, the Beatles' groundbreaking "Strawberry Fields Forever" backed with "Penny Lane" single was considered by Martin to be "the best record we ever made." *Publicity Photo/EMI*

Martin and the Beatles rehearsing "All You Need Is Love" in advance of their June 25, 1967, *Our World* global simulcast performance. The Beatles are, from left to right, Paul McCartney, John Lennon, Ringo Starr, and George Harrison. *Getty Images*

LEFT: Brian Epstein (left), Martin, and Geoff Emerick (right) in the control booth at EMI Studios during the *Our World* global simulcast. *AP Images*

RIGHT: On March 6, 1968, Martin and Starr posed with Emerick (center), who had earned a Grammy Award for "Best Engineered Recording, Non-Classical, Best Contemporary Album" for *Sgt. Pepper's Lonely Hearts Club Band. Alamy, Inc.*

LEFT: Released in 1968 and credited to George Martin and His Orchestra, *British Maid* marked the producer's fourth collection of pop instrumental arrangements. The LP was released in the United States and retitled as *London by George*. *Publicity Photo/United Artists*

RIGHT: George and Judy Martin at the January 1969 wedding of Cilla Black (center) and her manager, Bobby Willis. *Scope Features*

George Martin, Yoko Ono, and the Beatles in the Apple Studios control booth during the January 1969 sessions for the *Get Back* project. *Everett Collection*

Martin and his colleagues at AIR (Associated Independent Recording) posing around the twenty-four-track console at their Oxford Street studios for a 1970s print advertisement. Pictured, from left to right, are Bill Price (seated), Keith Slaughter, Peter Sullivan, Martin, and John Burgess (seated). *Publicity photo/AIR*

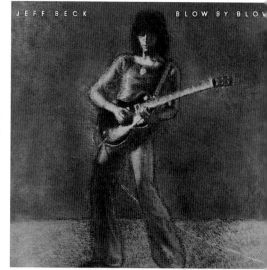

Scored by Martin, the *Live and Let Die* soundtrack album was released in July 1973. Martin later earned a Grammy Award for "Best Arrangement, Accompanying Vocalist(s)" for his work on Paul McCartney and Wings' "Live and Let Die" theme. *Publicity photo/United Artists*

Released in March 1975, Jeff Beck's *Blow by Blow* netted a platinum album for Martin and the guitar virtuoso. *Publicity photo/Epic Records*

Martin, photographed in 1976, with the folk rock band America on the beach of Kauai, Hawaii. From left to right, Gerry Beckley, Dewey Bunnell, and Dan Peek. *Getty Images*

Released in October 1980, Cheap Trick's *All Shook UP* features deft musical references to the Beatles, as well as Martin's turn at spoken-word performance on "Love Comes a-Tumblin' Down." *Publicity photo/ Epic Records*

McCartney and Martin working the boards during the 1980s, when their collaboration produced thre
LPs, including *Tug of War, Pipes of Peace,* and *Give My Regards to Broad Street. Alamy, Inc.*

Martin and the "Threetles" pictured at Abbey Road Studios in 1995 during the production of the Beatle
Anthology project. *AP Images*

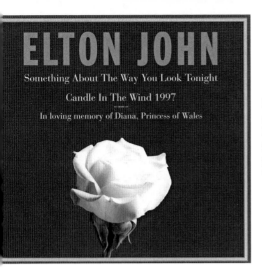

Released on September 13, 1997, Elton John's "Candle in the Wind 1997" single commemorated the life of Diana, Princess of Wales. Martin's production became the bestselling song in UK history and, in the United States, second only to Bing Crosby's "White Christmas." *Publicity photo/Rocket*

March 2004, Sir George was recognized with a commemorative ield from the College of Arms. For his arms and crest, he selected e image of three beetles along with a house martin clutching a corder. For his Latin motto, Sir George selected the words *"amore lum opus est"*—all you need is love. *College of Arms*

Sir George and his son Giles at the fiftieth annual Grammy Awards on February 10, 2008. Together, they earned statuettes for "Best Compilation Soundtrack Album for Motion Picture, Television, or Other Visual Media" and "Best Surround-Sound Album." *Alamy, Inc.*

Sir George, pictured with his eldest son, Gregory Paul Martin, celebrates Father's Day in June 2015 at the Old Rectory in Coleshill, Oxfordshire. *Photo courtesy of Gregory Paul Martin*

On March 14, 2016, Sir George was interred at the King's Hill cemetery after a private funeral at the All Saints parish church in Coleshill, Oxfordshire. *Photo courtesy of Kenneth Womack*

September 11, which meant that they needed to begin compiling new material for the holiday-flavored lark—and fast. As it happened, Lennon had a new composition up his sleeve, a surreal, Lewis Carroll–inspired number called "I Am the Walrus." From their places up in the control booth, Martin and Geoff Emerick found the concept of the *Magical Mystery Tour* project relatively difficult to grasp. "I tended to lay back on *Magical Mystery Tour* and let them have their head," George later observed. "Some of the sounds weren't very good. Some were brilliant, but some were bloody awful." Emerick shared Martin's misgivings, later remarking that "there was something lacking about *Magical Mystery Tour*. It wasn't going to be another album, or another single, it was probably going to be a film. It was a funny period." For his part, George, at least initially, had great difficulty in coming to grips with "I Am the Walrus." To his mind, "It was organized chaos. I'm proud of that." This was in contrast with the "disorganized chaos" that he had experienced during the summer, when the Beatles couldn't seem to find their mettle.[7]

Years later, Emerick would attribute Martin and the Beatles' September 1967 malaise to Epstein's untimely loss. "There was a pallor across the session that day—we were all distracted, thinking about Brian—but there was a song to be recorded, too." The bandmates were out of sorts, to be certain, but so was Martin, who had counted Epstein as one of his closest friends during that era. When John finished debuting his strange new tune, "there was a moment of silence," Geoff recalled, "then Lennon looked up at George Martin expectantly. 'That one was called "I Am the Walrus,"' John said. 'So . . . what do you think?'" In Geoff's memory, George looked "flummoxed" and, oddly for him, speechless. Eventually, the producer spoke up, saying, "Well, John, to be honest, I have only one question: What the hell do you expect me to do with that?"[8]

For Martin—the same man who had welcomed the opportunity to try his hand at "Tomorrow Never Knows"—his reaction to "I Am the Walrus," which was no less peculiar, was out of character. The room was permeated by "a round of nervous laughter" in the wake of George's pronouncement, and John was clearly irritated by his producer's response. As the Beatles began to make preparations for recording a basic rhythm track, George continued to fret about the song up in the booth. In Geoff's observation, George "simply couldn't get past the limited musical content and outrageous lyrics; he flat out didn't like the song." For the backing track for "I Am the Walrus," the instrumentation featured Lennon on electric piano, Harrison on rhythm guitar, Starr on drums, and McCartney on bass. During the bandmates' initial attempts at capturing the track, Lennon can be heard faintly singing a guide vocal. By the time that they reached take sixteen, Paul had switched from bass to tambourine in order to assist Ringo in maintaining the cadence. "Not to worry," Paul said to the drummer. "I'll keep you locked in." And with that, the Beatles finally captured the song, with Martin still stewing up in the booth—no doubt distracted by the very same thoughts that plagued the group. "I distinctly remember the look of emptiness on all their faces," Emerick later recalled. "It's one of the saddest memories I have of my time with the Beatles."[9]

The very next evening, Wednesday, September 6, George and the Beatles began to rebound rather precipitously. As always, once they had their hooks in a new track—or in the case of that night's session, *three* relatively new tracks—their passion and verve inevitably took over. At such times—with the chips down and the Beatles seemingly out of commission—they had begun to develop a knack for pulling victory out of the jaws of defeat. The eight-hour session ensued with a tape reduction of "I Am the Walrus," followed by McCartney overdubbing a bass guitar part on his Rickenbacker and Starr augmenting his snare drum. The highlight of the evening was Lennon's superlative lead vocal, which he sang over and over again until he got it right. London DJ Kenny Everett visited the studio that night, later recalling an interaction between Martin and Lennon: "George Martin, their producer, was working with John on the vocal track and he said: 'Look, you've been singing now for about seven hours, you're beginning to sound hoarse, why don't we do it tomorrow?' John wanted to get it done that day and that's why he sounds so raucous on that track." To further enhance the Beatle's lead vocal, Emerick filtered the signal from Lennon's mic in order to afford his vocal with a raspy, intentionally nasty sneer. That same night, the bandmates kept the compositions coming, with McCartney debuting "The Fool on the Hill," a ballad that he had begun back in March, and Harrison's eerie "Blue Jay Way," a composition that the quiet Beatle had penned during a California sojourn in August. While "The Fool on the Hill" featured McCartney playing a solo piano along with delivering a guide vocal, "Blue Jay Way" was considerably more evolved, with Harrison working Studio 2's Hammond organ, along with Lennon playing a second organ, McCartney on bass, and Starr on drums.[10]

By this point, Martin was just beginning to find his sea legs with the *Magical Mystery Tour* project. During the Thursday evening session in Studio 2 on September 7, work on Harrison's "Blue Jay Way" continued, with Martin and his production team, which included Peter Vince and Ken Scott sitting in for Emerick and Lush, treating Harrison's lead vocal to a heavy dose of ADT and all manner of backward studio manipulations. But by Friday night, the bandmates were back to their post-*Pepper* tricks as they worked on incidental music for their upcoming television movie soundtrack. Originally titled "Aerial Tour Instrumental," the song would later come to be known as "Flying." In addition to being the first song attributed to the songwriting team of Harrison-Lennon-McCartney-Starkey, "Flying" would mark the Beatles' first instrumental since the unreleased, *Rubber Soul*–era "12-Bar Original." "Flying" consisted of Lennon's organ, McCartney's bass, and Starr's drums on the backing trick, which Martin captured in six takes. A trio of backward organ tracks was then overdubbed, in addition to all four Beatles scat-singing along with the melody. The Beatles were clearly in an experimental mood, with John trying out a Mellotron part with the trumpet stop toggled and, at the song's nadir, a saxophone part lifted directly from a jazz record. For George, sessions like this one were proving to be insufferable. As he later recalled, the *Magical Mystery Tour* project was "terribly badly organized, and it's amazing that anything ever came out of it. They were into their random period—they said, 'If Laurence Olivier walks in this room, we'll record it and it'll be great.' All that sort of thing, the John Cage influence." To George's mind, it was, in a word, "chaotic"—perhaps the worst possible epithet that the venerable producer could bestow upon a Beatles session.[11]

For the next few weeks, the Beatles and their entourage traveled about the western English countryside in a not-so-subtle nod to Ken Kesey's Merry Pranksters, who conducted "Acid Tests" while trolling America's highways in a multicolored school bus. In addition to exterior shots of their giant yellow coach zooming across the English byways, the bandmates conducted principal photography at the Royal Air Force's West Malling base, a key military outpost that had once served as the United Kingdom's aerial front line against the Luftwaffe. With its aircraft hangars and runways, the base afforded the Beatles, who had very little direction beyond Paul's crude circular storyboard, with a variety of different settings to stage their *Magical Mystery Tour*. With a new baby at home, George relished his time away from the Beatles' maelstrom. Besides, he had heard through the grapevine that "the [coach] tour itself was dreadful, apparently," which left George feeling fortunate to have sat the bandmates' latest venture out. In addition to scoring the orchestration for "I Am the Walrus," he devoted his energies to his other clients—namely, Cilla Black, who, like George and the Beatles, was having great difficulty rebounding from the terrible news about Brian. As she later recalled, "When somebody close to you dies, memories float in and out of the mind at the most unexpected, inappropriate times. I could be singing a song on a live TV program and suddenly I would see Brian's face as clear as day, and remember moments we had shared together—a laugh here, a giggle there." Brian's dream of making Cilla into a television star was beginning to come to fruition. BBC One was preparing to broadcast the *Cilla* variety show beginning in January 1968. The network had ordered nine prime-time, fifty-minute episodes. To capitalize on Cilla's upcoming television premiere, George began routining songs with the singer for a new long-player. George astutely planned to synchronize Cilla's new album with the series' first season. And with any luck, he might turn her fading recording career around in time to make hay with her television debut.[12]

During this same period, George was invited to compose the signature jingle for the BBC's new Radio One, which was set to make its debut on the British airwaves on September 30. The radio station's controller, Robin Scott, had originally approached Northern Songs' Dick James in an effort to entice McCartney to take the commission. After Paul demurred, Dick turned to his old friend George to "write a piece of impressive, almost heraldic, British music that had classical overtones but still had its feet firmly in the rock 'n' roll repertoire, so it appealed to young people." To Dick's mind, George more than fit the bill. When he accepted the commission, Martin joked that if Scott "wants Paul McCartney and gets me, that's a poor substitute." In short order, the Beatles' producer concocted "Theme One." As George later recalled, "I wanted to use a cathedral organ to open it with, so, having done the main part of the recording, I did the introduction at the Central Hall, Westminster, where there is a large pipe organ, and cut that into the beginning of the record. That was quite an experience in itself, because I played the organ myself and found that the sound came out a good quarter of a second after I had placed my fingers on the keys. Playing in rhythm was really quite difficult, because it takes such a long time for the sound to go through the pipes." For the next few years, Martin's tune served as the station's flagship theme, introducing its programming first thing in the morning and closing it down every night. Anna Instone, the BBC's classical music head, joked that George's composition sounded like "William Walton on speed" in an irreverent reference to the British composer, known for his melancholic, old-fashioned works, who had earned a knighthood in 1951.[13]

But as it happened, George's respite from the Beatles' universe came to a sudden halt on Saturday, September 16, when the bandmates took a break from their moveable *Magical Mystery Tour* set and made their way back to London. That evening, they reconvened with George in Studio 3 for a nearly nine-hour session for the express purpose of making headway on the television movie's impending soundtrack. But when the bandmates trundled into the studio that night, Emerick was nowhere to be found, having taken a long-overdue vacation in the Norfolk Broads, not far from Great Yarmouth on England's easterly coast. For his part, Geoff was loath to miss any Beatles sessions, but EMI was adamant, as was George, who recognized how exhausted his chief engineer had become and encouraged him to take a much-deserved holiday. Taking his place in the control booth was Ken Scott, who had recently been promoted to balance engineer at EMI Studios. Before Geoff left for his vacation, Ken asked him "a lot of questions about what it was like working with the Beatles and he was quite nervous at first, but he quickly struck up a good rapport with the group—George Harrison, in particular—despite the bittersweet vibe that hung over us like a cloud." Martin's production team was rounded out by Jeff Jarratt, who served as tape operator in Lush's place. That night, George and the Beatles remade "Your Mother Should Know," with McCartney leading his bandmates through eleven takes of the song, which was now slated to close the film. By this juncture, the composition had taken on a military flavor, complete with snare drum accompaniment courtesy of Ringo. Meanwhile, George prepared a reel-to-reel tape copy of "I Am the Walrus" for *Magical Mystery Tour* producer Denis O'Dell to begin staging the Beatles' mimed performance of the song in the movie. After his first night as balance engineer, Scott was struck by how mercurial the Beatles had become. "They half knew what they wanted and half didn't know, not until they'd tried everything," he later remarked. "The only specific thought they seemed to have in their mind was to be different, but how a song might reach that point was down to their own interpretation and by throwing in as many ideas as possible, some of which would work and some wouldn't."[14]

On Monday, September 25, the Beatles were once again back in London, having wrapped up principal photography for *Magical Mystery Tour*, which, at this point, consisted of some ten hours of improvised, oddly disconnected scenes. For the most part, the novice-filmmaking Beatles left the raw footage in the hands of editor Roy Benson, part of the editorial team behind Richard Lester's *A Hard Day's Night*. During the day, the group—McCartney, mainly—worked with Benson at Norman's Film Productions across town in Soho. With principal photography (mostly) behind them, the bandmates returned to Abbey Road to concentrate on the only thing at which they truly excelled. Martin already held his own misgivings about the project. He knew full well that the Beatles had been hot and cold, creatively speaking, since *Sgt. Pepper*, and he privately doubted that they could pull off a cohesive televisual narrative. But the music was slowly but surely beginning to come around, as they demonstrated during the eight-hour session that evening, which was devoted to "The Fool on the Hill." As the Beatles toiled away at Paul's composition, they were observed by Yoko Ono, who was visiting Studio 2 that evening as John's guest. By this point, "The Fool on the Hill" was evolving into a first-rate ballad. With his production team, composed of Scott and Lush, Martin led the Beatles through three takes of the basic rhythm track. Using McCartney's demo from September 6, Martin recorded Lennon and Harrison's innovative harmonica accents. During a fourth take, McCartney added a recorder part, along with Starr's percussion and McCartney's lead vocal.

The very next evening, the bandmates worked without Martin, who was tending to AIR business. With Scott sitting in the producer's chair, they remade "The Fool on the Hill," creating numerous overdubs, including new piano, percussion, and lead vocals. Martin's absence left Scott in a lurch. As Lush later recalled, "He was, understandably, a little flustered. He was so nervous that it was just unbelievable. He was saying, 'What lights do I use?' and 'What do I do?' I really felt for him that day. The Beatles always put a bit of pressure on their engineers; they expected you to be there doing your job, but there wasn't a lot of thanks." By the next evening, Scott was safely ensconced in the engineer's seat, with Martin having returned to oversee the orchestral overdubs for "I Am the Walrus." While he may have initially seemed lukewarm about John's bizarre composition, George's score was a masterwork of style and control. His orchestration accented Lennon's lyrics, often establishing nuances of complementary color and irony that render the original song even more playful and disturbing. Scott later recalled being "scared to death" after being "thrown into the fire" of another session with Martin and the Beatles. But once he had settled down, Scott was able to observe Martin's superb orchestration and arrangement practices, which the young sound man chalked up to "overwriting." As Scott later recalled, "I learned something from those sessions that later became invaluable to me as a producer. I discovered that the best way to work with an orchestra is to have the arranger overwrite. The reason is that it's always easier to get rid of material than to put something in during a session. That's what George Martin used to do on his arrangements for Beatles songs." Overwriting allowed Martin to work around the criticisms and concerns of his artist—in this case, Lennon, who would frequently interrupt the orchestral overdubs, offering interjections such as "I don't like that bit. Keep this bit. Can you change that a little?" For the Wednesday afternoon session in Studio 1, George had assembled yet another parcel of top-drawer London session men for the occasion. The sixteen-member ensemble was composed of eight violins, led by the redoubtable Sidney Sax, late of "Yesterday" and "All You Need Is Love," along with four cellos, a contrabass clarinet, and three horns. With thematic input from John, George's score deftly emphasizes the song's wacky march from one strange admixture of lyrical images to another. George's orchestration of the strings is particularly adept, with chilling musical stabs from the violins and cellos accenting the score. The string glissandi were an inspired touch and clearly reminiscent of Martin's recent work with Eastern musicians, particularly on "Within You, Without You." When he finally heard the mix, Emerick was blown away by Martin's creative approach to "I Am the Walrus." "I was quite impressed with the complex score he wrote," Geoff later wrote, "especially given George Martin's initial distaste for the song."[15]

For George, the recording sessions associated with "I Am the Walrus" were indicative of the steady shift that had been occurring in his professional relationship with the Beatles. As he later recalled, "By the time we got to a song like 'Walrus,' or any of John or Paul's later songs, they would have very definite ideas on what they wanted to do, which they hadn't to begin with. It was a gradual drift so that they became the teachers." Which meant that George, in essence, had evolved into becoming their pupil. And with "I Am the Walrus," a song with which he had initially been perplexed, he had found his way into the composition through his score. In so doing, he had learned to privilege their ideas over his own—a sea change from their early days together, when George's head arrangements for the Beatles' songs ruled the roost.[16]

On the same day that he debuted his score for "I Am the Walrus," George supervised a separate overdubbing session in which he conducted a sixteen-person choir—with eight male and eight female voices tasked with singing a host of vocal absurdities by Lennon, including, most notably, "Oompah, oompah, stick it up your jumper!" For George, John's ribald non sequitur was an obvious reference to the Two Leslies, a prewar novelty act composed of Leslie Sarony and Leslie Holmes. Recorded back in 1935, the Two Leslies' "Umpa, Umpa (Stick It Up Your Jumper)" enjoyed an unexpected burst in popularity during the 1950s, especially among snickering teenagers—a group that undoubtedly included Liverpool's own John Lennon. As with his inventive score, George was taken with the idea of adding a bizarre choral layer to John's extraordinary composition. "The idea of using voices was a good one," George later remarked. "We got in the Mike Sammes Singers, very commercial people and so alien to John that it wasn't true. But in the score I simply orchestrated the laughs and noises, the *whooooooah* kind of thing. John was delighted with it." For his part, Paul saw "I Am the Walrus" as one of the finest collaborations between John and their producer. Together, they "did some very exciting things with the Mike Sammes Singers, the likes of which they've never done before or since, like getting them to chant, 'Everybody's got one, everybody's got one,' which they loved. It was a session to be remembered. Most of the time they got asked to do 'Sing Something Simple' and all the old songs, but John got them doing all sorts of swoops and phonetic noises." For the Mike Sammes Singers, "I Am the Walrus" was just another day on the job for the hardworking vocal troupe. As Sammes himself later recalled, "The next day we did a Kathy Kirby session at Pye Studios, then *The Benny Hill Show* for ATV, and we had some men doing recordings for *The Gang Show* at Chappell!"[17]

With the orchestral and choral overdubs complete, George and his production team joined the Beatles over in Studio 2, where they conducted remixing sessions for "I Am the Walrus" before returning to "Flying," which was overly long at nearly ten minutes, and "The Fool on the Hill," for which Paul tried his hand at yet another lead vocal. While the next session on Thursday, September 28, was dominated by additional refinements to the bandmates' current *Magical Mystery Tour* repertoire, the real story occurred during the following Friday evening session in Studio 2, the site of yet another innovative moment in George's career with the Beatles. In addition to putting the finishing touches on "Your Mother Should Know," Martin and his control booth team of Scott and Graham Kirkby began remixing "I Am the Walrus." And that's when Lennon had a eureka moment. It all started when McCartney shared some of the footage from the *Magical Mystery Tour* editing sessions. As Martin looked on, McCartney demonstrated how visual images frequently dovetailed, even when selected at random, with the soundtrack, creating unintentional yet eye-popping synergies. Later, as John listened to playbacks of "I Am the Walrus," the Beatle felt a sudden pang of inspiration: "You know, I think it would be great if I could put some random radio noise on the end of it," he said, "just twiddling the dial, tuning into various stations to see what we get and how it fits with the music."[18]

Brian Epstein's longtime assistant Alistair Taylor was visiting the studio that evening, and he later recalled the chain of events: "We were in Abbey Road and John suddenly disappeared and he came back and he said, 'George, I'm looking for a radio.' We all looked at him and said, 'What do you mean, you're looking for a radio?' George Martin said, 'I'm sure there's got to be a radio somewhere in the building.' So, John went off again and he found a radio on the floor above and he put it on short wave, because that was what John wanted. George Martin had to figure out how to get the radio from above down into the studio where they were recording." The problem was solved after a radio tuner had been provided by EMI's maintenance office for George and the bandmates' experimentation. To make the contraption work, the cumbersome rack-mounted tuner had to be patched into the mixing console, which John found to be doubly frustrating. "Bloody EMI," he exclaimed, "can't even get a radio organized!" Eventually, the studio technicians succeeded in rewiring the console, and suddenly John found himself able to "twiddle" the radio dial, randomly selecting stations as he listened to playbacks of "I Am the Walrus." As the song's play-out section unspooled, John happened upon the BBC's Third Programme, which was broadcasting a radio production of *King Lear*. Working the dial, John had landed upon the sycophantic scoundrel Oswald's death scene in act 4, scene 6:

> *Oswald:* Slave, thou hast slain me. Villain, take my purse.
> If ever thou wilt thrive, bury my body,
> And give the letters which thou find'st about me
> To Edmund, Earl of Gloucester; seek him out
> Upon the British party. O, untimely Death!
> *Edgar:* I know thee well: a serviceable villain;
> As duteous to the vices of thy mistress
> As badness would desire.
> *Gloucester:* What, is he dead?
> *Edgar:* Sit you down father, rest you.

George managed to capture the dialogue, which featured the voices of John Bryning (Oswald), Mark Dignam (Gloucester), and Philip Guard (Edgar), by feeding the live radio signal directly into the console as he and his team conducted the mono mixing session. In so doing, George was able to supervise a unique instance in Beatles recording history, one that can never be reproduced. As Emerick later explained it, "'I Am the Walrus' can never be remixed: the radio wasn't recorded on the multitrack. Instead, it was flown into the two-track, live, as the mix was occurring."[19]

By Monday, October 2, George and the Beatles were entering the home stretch of the *Magical Mystery Tour* soundtrack, although editing the film itself was still several weeks away from fruition. That night, McCartney debuted a new tune in Studio 2, a catchy new composition that went under the working title of "Hello Hello." As was his typical practice with the Beatles during this era, Martin was pushing for a new single's release to capitalize on the upcoming holiday shopping season. With its infectious, commercial qualities at the fore, "Hello Hello," later retitled as "Hello, Goodbye," seemed like the ideal candidate for the single's A-side. Indeed, Martin and McCartney were confident that "Hello, Goodbye" was a surefire hit, that it would keep "the roll" that they had reinvigorated with "All You Need Is Love" intact. But for his part, Lennon was taken with the idea of releasing "I Am the Walrus" as the A-side. In the wake of *Sgt. Pepper* and *Our World*, the bandmates were privy to a massive global audience, and they were penetrating almost every conceivable demographic, from children ("Yellow Submarine") all the way through pensioners ("When I'm Sixty-Four"). Surely, John reasoned, they could challenge their audience to keep up with their penchant for experimentation and give "I Am the Walrus" a listen. But by the time that George and the bandmates concluded their work that evening, the case had been settled, with McCartney and his producer having pressed and won their case on the grounds of commercialism. "Hello, Goodbye" would be the Beatles' next single all right.

Martin was joined in the control room that same evening by Emerick and Lush, marking Golden Ears' first Beatles session since his enforced holiday at the hands of EMI Studios management. That night, the bandmates recorded the basic rhythm track for "Hello, Goodbye," which was composed of McCartney's piano, Lennon's Hammond organ, Harrison's maracas, and Starr's drums. In addition to capturing the rhythm track in fourteen takes, the bandmates improvised a free-spirited coda. "The best bit was the end," John later recalled, "which we ad-libbed in the studio, where I played the piano. Like one of my favorite bits on 'Ticket to Ride,' where we just threw something in at the end." Later that week, George and the Beatles put the finishing touches on "Blue Jay Way," with cello and tambourine overdubs. On Thursday, October 12, Martin was back at De Lane Lea, with Dave Siddle and Mike Weighell assisting, in order to carry out mono remixes for "It's All Too Much." By this juncture, the Beatles were at the mercy of two different projects: on the one hand, Al Brodax and his production team were hungry for new Fab Four material to synchronize with animated cels; on the other, the Beatles themselves were running headlong into a set of dual deadlines involving the *Magical Mystery Tour* soundtrack release, slated for early December, as well as the late December broadcast of the television movie. Meanwhile, across town at Abbey Road, Lennon sat in as the producer of record, with Scott serving as his engineer and Lush as tape operator. That evening, Lennon supervised the recording of "Shirley's Wild Accordion," incidental music for the television movie. The bandmates conducted eight takes, which featured session player Shirley Evans—she of the "wild accordion"—along with Reg

Wale, her accompanist, on percussion. Evans had been featured in *Magical Mystery Tour*, where she played the accordion during a sing-along in the fabled yellow coach. "Shirley's Wild Accordion" also featured Ringo on drums and Paul playing the maracas and providing intermittent shouts of encouragement.

With Lennon and McCartney working "on heat"—and with several rapidly encroaching deadlines on their radar—they once again sought out Mike Leander, who, as with "She's Leaving Home," managed to bang out an arrangement in short order for "Shirley's Wild Accordion." While he had been incensed at Leander's role in "She's Leaving Home," this time around Martin didn't seem to care in the slightest. From what he could tell at this juncture, the Beatles seemed to be making some sort of elaborate home movie. For Martin's part, he was simply trying to keep it all together—to ensure that the Beatles and their producer succeeded in hitting their marks. The most pressing issue at this point was to make certain that "Hello, Goodbye" was ready to ship off to the manufacturing plant. On Thursday, October 19, Martin and the bandmates worked a long session in Studio 1, recording guitar overdubs from Harrison and Lennon, as well as imbuing McCartney's vocal with tape echo at key junctures. The next evening, Martin supervised orchestral overdubs from two groups of studio musicians in Studio 3 for "The Fool on the Hill" and "Hello, Goodbye," respectively. For the former, George had engaged the services of three flautists—Christopher Taylor, Richard Taylor, and Jack Ellory—to accent the song's chorus. Like the session men who played on "Hello, Goodbye" later that evening, the flautists worked from George's hastily prepared score. For the latter overdub, George had booked two viola players—Ken Essex and Leo Birnbaum—to afford McCartney's buoyant composition with a little classical zest. Birnbaum later narrated a scene that many Beatles session men had experienced over the years. As Birnbaum recalled, "Paul McCartney was doodling at the piano, and George Martin was sitting next to him, writing down what Paul was playing." Essex remembered seeing all of the Beatles there. "One of them was sitting on the floor in what looked like a pajama suit, drawing with crayons on a piece of paper."[20]

When George and the bandmates reconvened on October 25, in Studio 2, they put the finishing touches on "Hello, Goodbye," with Paul overdubbing a bass part to bring the song to fruition. But apparently, the Beatle wasn't done just yet. The following Thursday, Paul superimposed a new bass overdub, a masterful performance that included spirited bursts of sixteenth notes to accent the chorus. And with that, Martin and Emerick began carrying out mono remixing sessions for the A-side of the Beatles' sixteenth UK single.

Released on November 24, "Hello, Goodbye" backed with "I Am the Walrus" debuted at number three and topped the British charts the following week. If nothing else, George would enjoy the satisfaction of seeing "the roll" back in full swing. For his part, John might have felt vindicated by the reviews, with the *Melody Maker*'s Nick Jones describing "Hello, Goodbye" as "super-ficially . . . a very 'ordinary' Beatles record without cascading sitars, and the involved, weaving hallucinogenic sounds that we've grown to love so much." Writing stateside, where "Hello, Goodbye" quickly ascended the US charts, the *New York Times*' Richard Goldstein observed that McCartney's composi-tion "sounds like a B-side" that is "interesting, but subordinate." Lennon had been irritated by Martin and McCartney's relegation of "I Am the Walrus" to play second fiddle to "Hello, Goodbye"—and at least for the time being, he would look the other way.[21]

As it happened, there was very little spare time for George and the band-mates to get annoyed by much of anything. With the "Hello, Goodbye" backed with "I Am the Walrus" behind them, they still had two soundtracks to fill out, not to mention the film that McCartney was editing with Benson every day in Soho. On Wednesday, November 1, Martin and his production team of Emerick and Lush carried out mono remixing sessions of "All You Need Is Love" and "Lucy in the Sky with Diamonds" for *Yellow Submarine*, as well as a stereo remix of "The Fool on the Hill" for *Magical Mystery Tour*. On November 7, George carried out mono and stereo mixing sessions in the Studio 2 control room for "Blue Jay Way," "Flying," and "Magical Mystery Tour." But the real challenge occurred when Martin and his production team were mixing "Blue Jay Way" for stereo. Harrison had requested that backward effects be added to the song. With the mono remixes having already been completed, Martin eventually solved the problem by virtue of an ingenious solution: by playing a recording of the song backward, he was able to pan the backward sounds into the stereo remix. That same evening, Martin received a visit from Capitol Records' Voyle Gilmore, whom the Beatles' producer had first met a decade earlier during a Frank Sinatra session. With EMI's subsidiary hungry for new Beatles product, Gilmore left Abbey Road that evening with a full complement of tracks for a forthcoming *Magical Mystery Tour* LP for the American marketplace.

As November wore on, work continued apace as George and his team worked on behalf of the soundtrack for *Yellow Submarine*. On November 15, Emerick and Lush created mono tape copies for "All Together Now," "It's All Too Much," and "Only a Northern Song" for Brodax and his production crew, leaving Martin and the Beatles one song shy of the four songs that they had promised for the upcoming animated feature film. That same day, they also created a new mono remix for "Hello, Goodbye," with the violas helpfully eliminated for the purposes of a promotional video that the Beatles had filmed in the Saville Theatre a few days earlier on November 10. The film, which depicted the bandmates miming the song in their *Sgt. Pepper* costumery, would later be broadcast on *The Ed Sullivan Show* on November 26. But the real issue was the British marketplace, which was governed by the Musicians' Union, which had banned miming in promotional films. George and the Beatles' brain trust had reasoned that the "Hello, Goodbye" promotional video, with the violas having been silenced from the soundtrack, could be broadcast in the United Kingdom without violating the Musicians' Union ban. But it was all for naught, as the Beatles themselves were clearly simulating their performance of "Hello, Goodbye," thus undermining their efforts at subterfuge and rendering the video useless for broadcast in their homeland.

As George attempted to put the finishing touches on the *Magical Mystery Tour* and *Yellow Submarine* projects—even as he was in the midst of composing the film score for the latter—he returned to Cilla Black, who was determined to complete a new long-player for release in the new year. As that breakneck month proceeded, George convened a session for Cilla at Chappell Recording Studios to routine a new Lennon-McCartney number titled "Step Inside Love." The song was written by Paul as the potential theme for Cilla's upcoming television series after he had been approached by the singer and producer Michael Hurll, who later recalled that "all [McCartney] had given us was one verse and a chorus with him playing on guitar. We played it that way for the first couple of weeks and then decided that we needed a second verse. Paul came over to the BBC Theatre in Shepherd's Bush and sat with me and Cilla and worked on a second verse. It started off with the line, 'You look tired, love,' because Cilla was tired after a lot of rehearsing and most of what he wrote related to what was going on that day." During the November 21 session, George rehearsed the song with Cilla and Paul. As the session progressed, Paul played "Step Inside Love" on his acoustic guitar as Cilla practiced phrasing the lyrics. At one point, George supervised a demo recording, while noting that the composition would require a key change given Cilla's higher vocal range. Eventually, George joined in on piano, with occasional interruptions by Paul, who coached the producer through the chord changes, while Cilla refined her vocal. Years later, Cilla recalled the November 21 session, writing that "although Paul and I didn't talk about Brian that day, he was in my thoughts, and I know he'd have been over the moon that Paul came up with the idea for the song. Later on," Cilla added, "the song was banned from the radio in South Africa—they thought it sounded like a prostitute inviting her client into her house, which was totally out of character for me!"[22]

On Tuesday, November 28, George and the Beatles convened in Studio 3 to record holiday greetings in the form of a Flexidisc for their fan club. As the fifth iteration of their annual seasonal message, the Beatles' 1967 Christmas record, *Christmas Time (Is Here Again)*, was arguably their finest holiday moment, as well as being one of the very few songs, along with *Magical Mystery Tour*'s "Flying," to be credited to all four Beatles as composers. The six-minute Christmas record centered around a narrative in which various groups audition for a BBC radio show, with "Christmas Time (Is Here Again)" serving as the track's periodic refrain. The four Beatles voice various characters, ranging from game-show contestants and musicians (the Ravellers) to actors in a fictive radio program titled *Theatre Hour*. For the recording, the bandmates were joined by the voices of Martin and actor Victor Spinetti, who had featured in three Beatles films—*A Hard Day's Night, Help!*, and of late as a drill sergeant in *Magical Mystery Tour*. With "Auld Lang Syne" as his accompaniment, Lennon brings "Christmas Time (Is Here Again)" to a close with a reading of his Joycean, nonsensical poem titled "When Christmas Time Is Over," concluding with the line, "Happy breastling to you people all our best from me to you." As 1967 raced to a close, it was exactly the kind of ribald sentiment, borne out of good humor, that George and the bandmates had shared since their very first meeting back in June 1962.

With the annual Christmas record behind them for another year, Martin and the Beatles had finally closed up shop on 1967, one of the most remarkable years in the career of any artistic fusion *ever*. And if things had ended right there, the bandmates might have been spared one of the most embarrassing episodes in their professional lives. But first: the good news. On Friday, December 8, Parlophone released the *Magical Mystery Tour* extended-player (EP). To accommodate the soundtrack's six new songs—"Magical Mystery Tour," "Your Mother Should Know," "I Am the Walrus," "The Fool on the Hill," "Flying," and "Blue Jay Way"—EMI released *Magical Mystery Tour* as a double-EP set, complete with a colorful gatefold sleeve and a twenty-eight-page booklet. In the United Kingdom, the record was an unqualified success, topping the official EP charts and climbing as high as number two on the singles charts, where it was denied the top spot by none other than the "Hello, Goodbye" backed with "I Am the Walrus" single. Writing in *NME*, Nick Logan praised the Beatles for "stretching pop music to its limits. The four musician-magicians take us by the hand and lead us happily tripping through the clouds, past Lucy in the sky with diamonds and the fool on the hill, into the sun-speckled glades along Blue Jay Way and into the world of Alice in Wonderland." As Logan concluded, "This is the Beatles out there in front and the rest of us in their wake."[23]

Meanwhile, back in the United States, Capitol had released *Magical Mystery Tour* on November 27 as a long-player, filling out the nonsoundtrack cuts with "Hello, Goodbye," "Strawberry Fields Forever," "Penny Lane," "Baby, You're a Rich Man," and "All You Need Is Love." As on previous US releases, Capitol's production folks saw fit to tamper with Martin's work, treating the latter three tracks with the simulated stereo of Duophonic sound. The *Magical Mystery Tour* LP enjoyed an eight-week run at the top of *Billboard*'s album charts, sold some 1.5 million copies before Christmas, and earned rave reviews from the likes of *Hit Parader*, which proclaimed that "the beautiful Beatles do it again, widening the gap between them and 80 scillion other groups." In a nod to George, *Hit Parader* lauded the LP as "a supreme example of teamwork." The newly minted *Rolling Stone* magazine, which featured a film still of Lennon in *How I Won the War* as the cover of its inaugural issue in October 1967, offered a one-sentence review, quoting Lennon's August 1966 remark to *NME*'s Keith Altham: "There are only about a hundred people in the world who really understand what our music is all about." The American *Magical Mystery Tour* long-player was so popular among fans that it managed to notch a number-thirty-one showing on the UK album charts as an import.[24]

On December 21, the Beatles held their annual holiday party, which John had helpfully themed as a *Magical Mystery Tour* costume ball in order to celebrate the recently completed television movie. Not surprisingly, the bandmates and their entourage, including George and Judy, were costumed to the nines. As George later recalled, it was a party that Brian, had he lived, would have adored, given his well-known penchant for high-styled revelry. Held at the Royal Lancaster Hotel on Bayswater Road, the lavish affair began with pomp and circumstance only to end in a scene of drunken embarrassment. Given the exclusivity of the soiree, security was tight, with elaborate psychedelic invitations serving as the sole means of admittance. The Bonzo Dog Doo-Dah Band provided the entertainment. As George later wrote, "Judy and I went as the Queen and Prince Philip, which was an 'in' joke. The boys always thought she sounded just like the Monarch, and whenever they saw her would ask: 'How's your husband and you?'" For his part, George "acquired an Admiral of the Fleet's uniform from one of the naval outfitters; since they wouldn't let me have a sword, I put my old observer's wings on the sleeve, out of sheer cussedness. Judy had a lovely tiara and silk ball dress, a blue sash with some star-and-garter type of apparatus draped across her bosom, and a handbag a-dangle from her left wrist." George and Judy played the scene to the hilt, making a grand entrance into the hotel ballroom and briefly stealing the show from the Fab Four. "People formed themselves into a line, bowing and curtseying," George recalled, "while Judy and I gave limp handshakes to one and all. In the background, someone said loudly: 'My God! I didn't think they'd get *them*.'"[25]

As it happened, the Beatles didn't disappoint in the costume department. Lennon dressed as an Elvis-styled rock 'n' roller, while Cynthia Lennon fashioned herself as a Victorian lady. Paul and Jane Asher adorned matching regal outfits, and Ringo played the part of a regency gentleman while his wife Maureen affected the look of an Indian maiden. Harrison dressed as a swashbuckling Errol Flynn type, with his wife Pattie donning a slinky belly dancer getup. Press officer Derek Taylor was costumed as Adolf Hitler, complete with Nazi uniform, while Peter Brown dressed as King Louis XIV. They were joined by nineteen-year-old Lulu, the AIR recording artist who had recently landed an international hit with "To Sir with Love." Dressed as Shirley Temple in a blond wig, Lulu's costume was complemented with a giant lollipop, which she eagerly clutched throughout the affair. Meanwhile, Cilla was costumed as a Cockney laborer, with her fiancé, Bobby Willis, dressed as a nun. For all of the good-natured merrymaking and frivolity that night at the Royal Lancaster Hotel, the party came to an unhappy end when a drunken John pointedly ignored his wife and openly leered at Pattie Boyd, arrayed as she was in her sexy costume. Never one to shrink from a scene, Lulu came to Cynthia's rescue, loudly calling out the inebriated John on the carpet in front of his guests. Scolding him loudly in the ballroom, she gestured wildly with her lollipop prop, which she waved back and forth in rhythm with her harangue. For his part, John stood quietly and accepted Lulu's rebuke. As Cynthia later wrote, "It was such a lovely sight, Lulu cornering John and giving him what for. John was much taken aback by Shirley Temple's serious lecture on how to treat his wife."[26]

After the party, George wasted little time in getting back to work. As he packed in a few more sessions with Cilla before settling in for a much-deserved holiday rest, the Beatles forged ahead with the upcoming broadcast of the *Magical Mystery Tour* television movie. George had purposefully distanced himself from the film project, preferring to concentrate on producing the soundtrack. But other members had seen the writing on the wall. Having viewed the finished product and sensing imminent disaster, Peter Brown recommended that the Beatles mothball the *Magical Mystery Tour* movie and cut their losses. "I tried to suggest writing off the £40,000 [in production expenses] and moving on," Brown later remarked. "But Paul didn't know it was a mess and insisted on making the deal" with the BBC. Had McCartney simply become far too enamored with the bandmates' home movie, which he had been editing for the past several months? Or had he fallen victim to exactly what Lennon had feared—the seemingly inevitable "misconceptions about our ability to do anything other than play music"? In any event, it was an artistic gamble, however well intentioned, that failed miserably. As perhaps the Beatles' single greatest artistic failure, the *Magical Mystery Tour* television movie depicted the band members in a beguiling series of burlesques that are memorable solely for their utter disarray. The film reaches its ridiculous nadir in a variety of nonsensical skits—set in, of all places, an army recruiter's office and a strip club—that attempt to recall the zany vignettes inherent in *A Hard Day's Night* and *Help!* To make matters worse, the BBC premiered the film on Boxing Day (December 26) in black and white, thus depriving the movie of its multicolored virtues. NBC Television, which owned the rights to broadcast *Magical Mystery Tour* in the United States, opted not to air the film at all.[27]

Like so many other Britons, George watched *Magical Mystery Tour* at home, and he knew that the Beatles were in for it. "*Magical Mystery Tour* was not really a success—in fact, that's putting it mildly," he later recalled. "It looked awful and it was a disaster. Everyone said it was pretentious and overblown, but it was a kind of *avant-garde* video, if you like." As it turned out, George was far more generous in his assessment of *Magical Mystery Tour* than the reviews, which were swift and merciless. "The bigger they are, the harder they fall. And what a fall it was," James Thomas wrote in the *Daily Express*. "The whole boring saga confirmed a long held suspicion of mine that the Beatles are four pleasant young men who have made so much money that they can apparently afford to be contemptuous of the public." Meanwhile, the *Daily Sketch* couldn't help poking fun at the Beatles' recent forays into Eastern mysticism: "Whoever authorized the showing of the film on BBC1 should be condemned to a year squatting at the feet of the Maharishi Mahesh Yogi." For its part, the *Daily Mirror* condemned *Magical Mystery Tour* as "rubbish . . . Piffle . . . Nonsense!"[28]

For the Beatles, it was a critical drubbing that had proved difficult to stomach—especially after enjoying the artistic heights of *Sgt. Pepper.* As Hunter Davies, the band's authorized biographer, commented, *Magical Mystery Tour* marked "the first time in memory that an artist felt obliged to make a public apology for his work." Indeed, McCartney later remarked, "We don't say it was a good film. It was our first attempt. If we goofed, then we goofed. It was a challenge and it didn't come off. We'll know better next time." Paul added, perhaps unadvisedly, "I mean, you couldn't call the Queen's speech a gas, either, could you?" While Martin could rightly see himself as being blameless in the awful chain of events that played into the production of the *Magical Mystery Tour* television movie, the Beatles were undeniably *his* artists—a reality that he had come to know all too well in the months since Epstein's untimely demise. He had also begun to understand the root of their malaise, recognizing that Brian had been "the fulcrum of the Beatles' existence, and suddenly he was no longer there. Quite out of the blue, the boys no longer had anyone to tell them what to do, and there was a vacuum. Paul tried to organize things and get them all working together, and that unfortunately created the beginning of some resentment within the group." George had weathered the Beatles' highs and lows before, and he reasoned, with a certain degree of confidence, that he could weather these latest setbacks as well. After all, *Magical Mystery Tour* wasn't merely a humiliating "disaster" of a film production; it had also been a blockbuster soundtrack. And George could work with that. As 1967 rolled into the new year and his memories of the Beatles' very public flop began to fade, George started to gain a more measured perspective, later writing that "the basic idea of the film was a bit thin, but the music was jolly good." In this way, the Beatles' producer began to see his way clear toward righting the band's increasingly unsteady ship. "They were at a major crossroads," he observed. "It was time to take stock, time to go back to their first love: making music."[29]

16

ALL THAT AND
A BAR OF CHOCOLATE

O N TUESDAY, JANUARY 30, 1968, the *Cilla* variety show finally made its debut, fulfilling Brian Epstein's long-held dream of making the Liverpool chanteuse a bona fide TV star. He hadn't lived to see it, of course, but even the manager's lofty expectations had been exceeded by the show's success. During the show's first series, *Cilla* attracted some thirteen million viewers per episode. For Cilla Black, it was a bittersweet triumph. As she later wrote, "The first time I saw the mug-shot of myself on the cover of the *Radio Times*, accompanied by the words 'Cilla Black in her own show on BBC1,' was one of these Brian moments." For his part, George was ecstatic. The *Cilla* show represented a key opportunity to change the singer's professional fortunes for the better. By this juncture, Cilla's 1964 consecutive number-one songs with "Anyone Who Had a Heart" and "You're My World" were beginning to seem like a distant memory, and George was determined to change her fortunes for the better. George's fingerprints were all over the show, with Cilla's guests ranging from the likes of Ringo Starr and Spike Milligan to Dudley Moore and Roger Cook and Roger Greenaway. The show's theme, the Lennon-McCartney number "Step Inside Love," was released in March to take advantage of the regular face time that Cilla was enjoying on BBC One. While it didn't attain the heights of her mid-1960s efforts, "Step Inside Love" backed with "I Couldn't Take My Eyes Off of You" registered a top-ten

UK hit, setting the table for the long-player that George had been preparing since autumn.[1]

Under George's supervision, the ensuing album, titled *Sher-oo!*, was carefully marketed to take advantage of Cilla's newfound TV fame. In addition to "Step Inside Love," Martin produced a number of tracks penned by Cilla's favorite composers, including Bacharach and David's "What the World Needs Now Is Love," which had originally been popularized by Jackie DeShannon in 1965, and "This Is the First Time." For *Sher-oo!*, George was pulling out all of the stops, even going so far as to record an Italian-language version of "Step Inside Love" with Cilla. Produced from a translation by Mogol (Giulio Rapetti), "Step Inside Love" was targeted to the Italian marketplace, where Cilla had enjoyed a substantial audience dating back to the global success of "You're My World." The album also afforded George with the opportunity to work with Mike Vickers, who arranged and conducted the orchestration. For the cover, the long-player featured a photograph by John Kelly. "I was sporting a hairstyle I had never had before," Cilla later wrote. "I was transformed by a perm that produced masses of big sausage-like curls. It lasted all of a week." When *Sher-oo!* was released on April 6, 1968, the long-player quickly did its work, netting a top-ten showing for Black on the UK charts. With a hit single and album in the record shops, Cilla's dry spell was clearly over.[2]

In addition to the success that he and Cilla enjoyed with *Sher-oo!*, George was delighted to see a certain degree of professional order returning to the singer's life. In the days following Brian's death, Cilla had been at sea. But in recent months, her fiancé, Bobby Willis, had assumed a managerial role, and his guidance and devotion to her career were already paying off. As far as George was concerned, working with Bobby suited him just fine. Martin had been friendly with Willis since 1965, even cowriting a song with him at one point. By this juncture, George and Judy had even begun socializing with Cilla and Bobby. As George later recalled, "We hit it off pretty well and liked each other from the word go. I've always been friends with the people I record with, and some people you get more friendly with than others. The age difference—about 17 years—never meant anything. As for the great cultural divide, Britain is Britain and I get on fine with people no matter where they come from. Quite often after a recording session, Judy and Bobby would join us and we'd go and have a bite to eat. It became a social thing. Then we started going on skiing holidays together; we had riotous fun. We went to Lech in Austria for quite a few years running."[3]

During this same period, George had also begun preparing a new long-player of his own to fulfill his standing contract with United Artists. Working under the moniker of George Martin and His Orchestra, he recorded the follow-up album to *George Martin Instrumentally Salutes The Beatle Girls*. The resulting album was titled *British Maid*, a punning title on the "British-made" nature of the LP's regular helping of instrumental cover versions, including Procol Harum's "A Whiter Shade of Pale," the New Vaudeville Band's "Winchester Cathedral," and the Small Faces' "Itchycoo Park," among others. As usual, George included a healthy dose of Beatles covers, including "Sgt. Pepper's Lonely Hearts Club Band" and "I Am the Walrus," the song that he had originally loathed, only to see it in a different light after composing its orchestration. Not to be outdone, he also featured "Theme One," his jingle for the BBC's Radio One. Like *George Martin Instrumentally Salutes The Beatle Girls*, *British Maid* was targeted at consumers of easy-listening music. But also like its predecessor, *British Maid* accented sex and youth as the core of its media campaign, with the LP's cover art depicting a comely model swathed in a Union Jack bathing suit and clutching a sitar.

In the new year, George also caught up with the Scaffold. The producer had been truly taken with the novelty act's "crazy songs" like "2 Day's Monday" and "Goodbat Nightman," but he couldn't seem to find a vehicle to drive them up the charts. In the case of the latter composition, George had been disappointed that the comedy number failed to find an audience, especially since "Goodbat Nightman" cleverly appropriated the current superhero craze. With McGear, McGough, and Gorman singing the hyperbolic lyrics—"God bless all policemen and fighters of crime. / The thieves go to jail for a very long time"—the Scaffold reels off a litany of superhero couples before hitting upon the whereabouts of Batwoman, who seems to be missing in action. The song's spoken-word middle section, in which the bandmates speculate about Batwoman's demise, is vintage Martin in his comedy heyday by way of the Scaffold. But as for the bandmates, the Scaffold—and McGear in particular—were in a furor over what they considered to be their maltreatment by Epstein, whom they blamed for the failure of "Goodbat Nightman" to climb the charts. In the months before his death, the bandmates felt that Epstein had been stalling in terms of releasing the single, when in fact Epstein's ineffectiveness during that period might reasonably be attributed to his post-touring malaise after the Beatles' Jesus Christ tour. But as far as McGear was concerned, the only thing that mattered was that "Goodbat Nightman" was "released too late. Died a death. We got disillusioned with Brian after that. I went out with him in Wheeler's in London and said, 'Brian, it's like a race-track and we're on the outside. All your heavyweights, the Beatles and Cilla and Gerry, are on the inside. It's just not working for us.' He says, 'Oh, I

quite agree, Michael.' I felt like hitting him, to tell you the truth. So we left."
In many ways, the Scaffold's interactions with Brian were very much like
Cilla's during the fall of 1966, when the manager had to lure her back into
the fold. In another sense, the Scaffold's disillusionment was not unlike the
experiences of other NEMS and Parlophone artists during the early years of
Beatlemania. Like Shirley Bassey and the Fourmost in years past, the Scaffold
felt neglected by George and Brian, who understandably—at least from their
point of view—tended to the premier artists in their stable.[4]

After "Goodbat Nightman," George and the novelty troupe had regrouped
to record "Thank U Very Much," which proved to be their breakthrough
number. Released in November 1967, "Thank U Very Much" backed with
"Ide Be the First" had been McGear's brainchild. As he later recalled, "There
was this other song I'd written where we'd thank the audience for coming
along: 'Thank you very much for keepin' the seats warm,' and so on, just to
close our show. So we recorded 'Thank U Very Much,' a good strong track.
We had a hit there—it was Harold Wilson's favorite record, and it got us
on the telly in a major way. *Top of the Pops!*" While "Thank U Very Much"
notched a number-seven showing on the UK charts, it was also, alas, the end
of the Scaffold's association with George. During the summer of 1967, as the
Beatles' producer had been taking a breather and trying to make sense of the
Yellow Submarine and *Magical Mystery Tour* projects, Gorman stood aside
while McGear and McGough toiled away on a long-player of their own—
and often in the company of McGear's older brother, Paul McCartney, who
had been on hand during the recording session for "Thank U Very Much."
With McCartney sharing his instrumental talents and occasionally standing
in as producer, along with McGear and the Yardbirds' Paul Samwell-Smith,
the comedy duo were joined by the likes of Jimi Hendrix and Dave Mason
acting as their session men. By the time that the Scaffold reunited to record
their follow-up to "Thank U Very Much," George was out of the picture.
Their next single, "Lily the Pink," produced by none other than George's
old nemesis Norrie Paramor, landed the Scaffold's only UK number-one hit
in December 1968.[5]

Years earlier, when he was still slugging it out with the other EMI A&R
men as Parlophone's label head, George would almost certainly have been
galled by such a turn of events. But by the time that Paramor settled down
to record "Lily the Pink," Martin would be embroiled in far more pressing
matters involving the most important act in his stable. On Saturday, February 3, 1968, George reconvened with the Beatles for a quick spate of sessions
before their long-planned visit to India to study Transcendental Meditation

under the tutelage of the Maharishi Mahesh Yogi. With Lennon and Harrison scheduled to depart on February 15—and the Transcendental Meditation retreat to keep the Beatles at bay until April—time was of the essence. As always, EMI was hungry for new Beatles product to ring in the new year, and as luck would have it, McCartney had been working "on heat" and was eager to get back to Abbey Road. As with so many of the Beatles' singles releases in the past, Paul was ready to vie with John for the A-side.

During the February 3 afternoon session in Studio 3, George supervised the bandmates' rehearsal for a new number from Paul called "Lady Madonna." McCartney's piano-boogie introduction owed a clear debt to Humphrey Lyttelton's British trad-jazz hit, "Bad Penny Blues," which had been produced by the late Joe Meek for Parlophone back in 1956. With Martin working up in the booth with Ken Scott and Richard Lush, the group refined a basic track in three takes, featuring McCartney's piano and Starr's drums. As Ringo later recalled, "We said to George Martin, 'How did they do it on 'Bad Penny Blues'? And he said, 'They used brushes.' So, we put an off-beat" on "Lady Madonna." As the band pressed forward with the session, McCartney added a bass overdub, along with Lennon and Harrison's fuzzed guitars. For the vocal tracks, McCartney sang lead using his "Elvis voice," accompanied by Lennon and Harrison's scat harmonies.[6]

The next day, John presented his entry in the single sweepstakes, a haunting acoustic number titled "Across the Universe." During that rare Beatles Sunday session, Martin and the bandmates spent nearly ten hours working on the song. For John, "Across the Universe" arrived as another found object in his songwriterly life, emerging after a late-evening tiff with his wife Cynthia. After she fell asleep, he "kept hearing these words over and over, flowing like an endless stream. I went downstairs and it turned into sort of a cosmic song." But for John, capturing the song in the studio proved to be difficult, even as the Beatles attempted to refine a basic rhythm track over six takes. In the song's first iteration, the instrumentation included Lennon's acoustic guitar, Star's tom-toms, and Harrison's tamboura, with Emerick filtering the signal through a Leslie speaker to give it more texture. For take two, Martin recorded Lennon's lead vocal with his own acoustic guitar accompaniment and Harrison's sitar. By the time they reached fruition with the rhythm track, Lennon recorded a new version of his lead vocal, with Martin running the tape machine slow to afford the Beatle's voice with a brighter sound on playback.[7]

Yet Lennon and McCartney were still shaking their heads, feeling as if the song was missing some essential element. And that's when they hit upon the idea of falsetto harmonies. Needing to round up female background singers on a Sunday night in St. John's Wood was a relatively minor matter for the Beatles, whose fans regularly congregated outside the studio gates. In short order, McCartney dispatched Martin Benge, who was subbing for an ill Ken Scott, to the streetscape. Scanning the dozens of girls waiting outside for their heroes to emerge, Benge selected sixteen-year-old Lizzie Bravo, visiting the United Kingdom from Brazil, and seventeen-year-old Gayleen Pease, a Londoner, to join him back in Studio 3. As Benge later recalled, "They were so excited. They couldn't believe they'd actually been invited by Paul not just inside the building but into the studio itself, to sing with the Beatles." After they recorded their harmony vocals, singing "nothing gonna change our world," they were escorted back outside so that George and the bandmates could superimpose a backward bass and drum track. But to John's mind, the song still wasn't quite right.[8]

With time running out in advance of the group's Indian jaunt, Martin and the bandmates turned to Harrison's "The Inner Light," which the Beatles' lead guitarist had begun recording back in mid-January at EMI's Bombay studio. Harrison had been working in India on his recently commissioned soundtrack for *Wonderwall*, a psychedelic film by first-time director Joe Massot. With Harrison sitting in the producer's seat, the Beatle refined an instrumental track for "The Inner Light" while working with a host of Indian musicians. During a Tuesday, February 6, session in Studio 1, Martin and the Beatles—sans Starr, who was doing a guest spot on *Cilla*—focused their attentions on "The Inner Light," with Harrison superimposing his lead vocals onto the existing instrumental track. As tape operator Jerry Boys later recalled, "George [Harrison] had this big thing about not wanting to sing it because he didn't feel confident that he could do the song justice. I remember Paul saying 'You must have a go, don't worry about it, it's good.'"

With Harrison's composition nearing fruition, Martin turned to "Lady Madonna," for which he supervised yet another McCartney lead vocal, as well as backing vocals from Lennon, McCartney, and Harrison, singing, "See how they run." While the three Beatles had attempted an imitation brass solo by cupping their hands around their mouths, McCartney wanted the real thing. Without missing a beat, Martin rang up Laurie Gold, EMI's session organizer, to arrange for a quartet of saxophonists. Up first was Harry Klein, a baritone sax player whom Gold roused from his bath for the session at Abbey Road that evening. Klein suggested that Gold hire Ronnie Scott, the London jazz club owner, to play tenor sax.[9]

When Klein arrived at the studio, Martin's sax quartet was set with Scott and Klein, along with baritone and tenor sax players Bill Jackman and Bill

Povey, respectively. With George and the Beatles working "on heat," the sax men were treated to the sight of empty music stands. As Klein recalled, "There was no written music but we played around with a few riffs until Paul liked what he heard. And then we recorded it—101 times! I remember there was a big pile of meditation books in the corner of the studio, like the back room of a publisher's office, and I also recall that they asked if we wanted a bite to eat. We were expecting a terrific meal but a few minutes later someone returned with pie and chips!" As Martin looked on, McCartney took the lead. "There was not only no prepared music for us to follow," Povey later reported, "but when Paul called out some chords at us our first reaction was to look at each other and say, 'Well, who plays what?'" The days when session play-ers could expect to arrive to the sight of a carefully crafted score by Martin were no longer in vogue. And on this day, as had become an increasingly regular practice, the musicians were left to their own devices. As Jackman recalled, "Paul went through the song on the piano and we were each given a scrap of manuscript paper and a pencil to write out some notes. Had there been music we would have been in and out in about ten minutes. As it was, it took most of the evening, recording it in A-major pitch with the rhythm track playing in our headphones."[10]

With his eye on the calendar, Martin and his production team carried out a mono remixing session for Harrison's "The Inner Light" during the February 8 session before turning back to Lennon's "Across the Universe." As for John, he was still at sea about the song's instrumentation. For their next attempt, Martin chipped in with an organ part and Lennon played the Mellotron. But when Lennon proved dissatisfied with the new instrumentation for "Across the Universe," the Beatle started anew with a tone pedal guitar part, Harrison's maracas, and McCartney's piano. With the next instrumenta-tion worked out, Martin erased the backward bass and drum track, which he replaced with harmony vocals from Lennon, McCartney, and Harrison. But the real highlight for Martin and Emerick was Lennon's remarkable vocal performance, one of the finest that he had ever committed to tape. As Emerick later recalled, "'Across the Universe' was such a superb performance from John. He put so much feeling into the song, and his vocal was just incred-ible." But to John's mind, "Across the Universe" remained unfinished, so he dropped out of the single sweepstakes. As it happened, George's old friend Spike Milligan was visiting the studio that night, and he made a pitch to John that the Beatles offer "Across the Universe" for an upcoming charity album for the World Wildlife Fund that the former Goon was spearheading. John accepted Spike's entreaty with a simple "yeah, whatever." Meanwhile, with no other credible choice in the offing, Martin went with McCartney's "Lady Madonna" backed with Harrison's "The Inner Light" for the upcoming single.[11] Incredibly, this marked the first occasion in which a Harrison composition had appeared on a Beatles single, albeit as a B-side.

On Sunday, February 11, Martin and the Beatles rode their latest burst of creativity to the hilt, recording a brand-new composition, Lennon's "Hey Bulldog," from start to finish in a single session in Studio 3. In so doing, they completed their quota of original material for the *Yellow Submarine* soundtrack. Led by Tony Bramwell, a camera crew was on hand in the studio that day—a rarity in George and the bandmates' professional universe—to capture images of the Fab Four at work. The resulting footage was slated to serve as a promotional video for the "Lady Madonna" single. With Emerick and Phil McDonald joining him up in the booth, Martin recorded "Hey Bulldog" on four tracks without the necessity of a tape reduction. As the session began, John issued a single instruction to George, "Just tell us when we get a good one," before launching into ten takes of the basic rhythm track. With Lennon's piano, McCartney's tambourine, Harrison's rhythm guitar, and Starr's drums, the basic track for "Hey Bulldog" found the bandmates at their searing, electric best. Clearly, they had turned a corner from the psychedelic impulses that had consumed their artistry in the months following the Jesus Christ tour. During the subsequent overdubs, Martin supervised the recording of McCartney's fuzz bass line, along with guitar doubling from Harrison and Starr adding a snare drum part to the beat. Up next were John and Paul singing the vocal track, with John belting out his lead vocals with a powerful, unflinching rasp. The track ended with John and Paul clowning around, barking and howling into the fade-out. The final overdub found Lennon borrowing Harrison's Gibson SG Standard and breaking off a scorching guitar solo. During the remixing session later that evening, George afforded "Hey Bulldog" with a healthy dose of ADT, and the Beatles' contribution was all but complete.[12]

Martin carried out a mono mixing session for "Lady Madonna" on February 15, the day on which Lennon and Harrison, anxious to begin their sojourn, embarked for India, and the Beatles' latest UK single was ready for the marketplace. Released on March 15, "Lady Madonna" backed with "The Inner Light" topped the charts, extending the bandmates' post–"Strawberry Fields Forever" backed with "Penny Lane" roll yet again. The reviews for "Lady Madonna" were oddly mixed, with *Melody Maker*'s Chris Welch reporting that the "best bit is the piano intro, then you can have fun wondering why Paul sounds like Ringo." Ultimately, Welch wrote, "I can't really see this being a hit." Stateside, where the single topped out at number four, *Billboard* proclaimed "Lady Madonna" as a "powerful blues rocker." Clearly, Welch had underestimated the Beatles' lingering appeal. For his part, George knew that the Beatles had plenty upside left in terms of creativity—the recent setback with the *Magical Mystery Tour* television movie notwithstanding. George, like Brian, recognized the potential that the *Yellow Submarine* feature film portended in terms of widening the Beatles' demographic even further.[13]

With the Beatles out of the picture for the next few months, George settled into scoring the *Yellow Submarine* orchestral soundtrack. The bandmates continued to be indifferent to the animated film, only acknowledging that they were contractually bound to participate in its soundtrack. And while they may have seemed dismayed by the whole business, they good-naturedly filmed a live-action, one-minute cameo back on January 25 at Twickenham Studios. In the footage, the Beatles can be seen cheerfully leading a movie-ending sing-along to "All Together Now." But in the recording studio, they had been anything but delighted. As producer Al Brodax later reported, "Apparently, they would say, 'this is a lousy song, let's give it to Brodax.'" For Brodax, the saving grace of the project was Martin, particularly after Epstein's untimely death. "George is a prince of a man," Brodax later wrote, "unflappable, charming, the ultimate in English gentlemanliness." Brodax saw their kinship as being rooted in "a fraternity of humble beginnings. George is a carpenter's son from one of London's less affluent boroughs. I'm the son of an immigrant tailor, out of a rough Brooklyn neighborhood. Beyond these similarities, our life experiences have shaped us differently. George matures undeniably upper-class in manner and speech; I remain a product of Brooklyn's mean streets."[14]

In this way, Brodax and Martin became natural allies. For his part, George was painfully honest with the film's producer about the band's musical contributions, which, in Martin's words, amounted to "the dregs of their inventory. Pieces they would in any case jettison: junk, file-and-forget pieces. John in particular damns the TV series, thinks *Submarine* will just be an embarrassing extension of that." Martin could see the writing on the wall in terms of the precariousness of their situation. "So you broke your ass to get them their third picture solution," he told Brodax, "and they throw a bunch of junk your way in gratitude. A good deed never goes unpunished, especially in our world." Fortunately for Brodax, Martin was determined to be part of the solution. With director George Dunning working at a breakneck pace to complete the animation and voice overlays—the Scaffold's Roger McGough was hired to provide Scouse-like dialogue and assorted in-jokes for the screenplay—Martin threw himself into the score. But it was not as though he had any other choice. As he later wrote, "It was done so quickly that George Dunning, the director, actually said to me, 'We haven't got time for you to write the music after the film is finished. You've got to write it as we make it.' He gave me a movieola (an editing device through which you can view professional film) which I set up in the drawing room of my house in London, and from that I would make my own timings."[15]

George had scored soundtracks before, but *Yellow Submarine* was clearly going to be different. Animated films typically required years to make. By contrast, *Yellow Submarine* was completed, from start to finish, in the space of a single year. And the film was produced on a shoestring budget, courtesy of United Artists, of £250,000, a paltry sum for a film that featured the biggest act on the planet. But George didn't have time to consider such details. "Once again, I was on a sharp learning curve," he later wrote. "Not only did I have to decide (along with George Dunning) where the songs that the Beatles had supplied would go into the film, I also had to write something like an hour's worth of original music for the background score. And for that he said, 'I can't really direct you on this because I am so damn busy. What I suggest is you write as much as you think is appropriate, if you don't mind losing some of it when we come to the dub.'" As each reel of the film came off the production line, most often out of sequence, it was shipped to Martin. As he pondered each new reel, George wrote, "My job was to look through it and say, 'Well, this scene needs some music here,' and I would just write what I thought was appropriate. Poor George Dunning didn't know what I was writing until the editing stage."[16]

For Martin, concocting the score for *Yellow Submarine* forced him to grow as a film composer in innumerable ways—not merely in terms of working under pressure but also regarding the manifold opportunities to be groundbreaking and inventive, just as he had done in his finest moments with the Beatles. As Martin later recalled, "Everything had to be tailor-made for the picture. If a door opened or a funny face appeared at a window, and those moments needed to be pointed-up, it was the musical score that had to do the job." During the composition process, he added, "you plan whatever tempo your rhythm is going to be, and then you lay down what is called a 'click track.' That is, a separate track which simply contains a click sound which appears every so many frames of film. You know that 35mm film runs at 24 frames per second, so knowing what tempo you want, you simply ask the film editor to put on a click at whatever interval you want. Then while conducting the orchestra, you wear headphones through which you can hear the clicks, and by keeping to that particular beat you 'lock in' the orchestra to the film. In that way you can write your score knowing that, even if something happens a third of the way or halfway through a bar, you can safely put in whatever musical effect you want, with absolute certainty that it will match the picture—that is how I did it with *Yellow Submarine*."[17]

In spite of the fact that scoring the animated feature was a work for hire as far as George was concerned, he pointedly drew his inspiration from Maurice Ravel, "the musician I admire most," he later wrote. While his youth had been characterized by his early love for Claude Debussy, Martin had cleaved ever closer to Ravel throughout his Guildhall days and beyond. For Martin, Ravel "was one of the greatest orchestrators of all time." In many ways, Martin's score for *Yellow Submarine* acted as a long-playing form of homage to Ravel, whose influence can be heard in the nooks and crannies of the film's incidental music. To George's mind, "the astonishing man was Ravel, of whom we always think in terms of lush orchestrations. He was a very fine pianist, and—with the exception, I think, of his *Piano Concerto*—he always wrote his compositions as piano pieces first of all. Then he orchestrated them. I find this very curious. If I'm writing an orchestral piece, I write straight for orchestra." As Martin discovered during the composition process for *Yellow Submarine*, fashioning his orchestration after Ravel provided him with a sense of liberation in the face of his looming deadline, the opportunity to take chances that he might normally have avoided.[18]

The score afforded the producer with the opportunity to push the previously traditional boundaries of his work as a composer. As Martin later wrote: "*Yellow Submarine* saw some pretty strange experiments, too. In one sequence, in the 'Sea of Monsters,' the yellow submarine is wandering around and all kinds of weird little things are crawling along the sea floor, some with three legs. One monster is enormous, without arms but with two long legs with wellington boots on, and in place of a nose there is a kind of long trumpet. This is a sucking-up monster—when it sees the other little monsters, it uses its trumpet to suck them up. Eventually it sucks up the yellow submarine, and finally gets hold of the corner of the [movie] screen and sucks that up too, until it all goes white. I felt, naturally, that scene required special 'sucking-up' music—the question was how to do it with an orchestra!" Eventually, Martin came up with a solution that had been a go-to maneuver for the Beatles since their days recording *Revolver*: backward music. As George later observed, "Music played backwards sounds very odd anyway, and a trombone or cymbal played backwards sounds just like a sucking-in noise. So I scored about 45 seconds for the orchestra to play, in such a way that the music would fit the picture when we played it backwards. The engineer working at CTS at that time was a great character named Jack Clegg, and when I explained the idea to him he said, 'Lovely! Great idea! I'll get the film turned round, and you record the music to the backward film. Then, when we turn the film round the right way, your music will be backwards.' It sounded like something from a Goon script."[19]

As it happened, almost all of the music that Martin composed was used by Dunning in the final cut. As the months wound down, Martin conducted the London Symphony Orchestra during the production of the film's incidental music, which was recorded at Olympic Sound Studios that spring with Keith Grant and George Chkiantz serving as Martin's engineering team. Time was clearly of the essence, given the movie's anticipated July 1968 premiere, along with a UK general release in late summer and an American release later that fall. And while he had been working at a breakneck pace, George had proven yet again that he could come through in a pinch. For their part, Dunning and Brodax were astounded by the results. During *Yellow Submarine*'s "Sea of Monsters" sequence, for example, George included a sly reference to J. S. Bach's *Air on the G String*. In other instances, George quoted works by Wolfgang Amadeus Mozart and Igor Stravinsky and even the Beatles themselves. "Sea of Time" featured an Indian-themed reference to "Within You, Without You," while "Yellow Submarine in Pepperland" included a deft reprise of the title track.

In early March, George took a break from his work on the *Yellow Submarine* soundtrack to pose with Geoff and Ringo for photographs of the Beatles' production team receiving their Grammy statuettes for *Sgt. Pepper*. The awards had been announced, with Martin, Emerick, and the Beatles in absentia, back on February 29 at a dinner ceremony in Los Angeles hosted by comedian Stan Freberg. During EMI's makeshift ceremony in Studio 3 on March 6, Ringo hadn't made the trip out to India yet, and he can be seen presenting the awards to George and Geoff, then good-naturedly pretending to speak into the funnel-shaped horn of the miniature phonograph.

Within a matter of days, all four Beatles would be ensconced at the maharishi's ashram in Rishikesh, the holy city that rests on the banks of the Ganges. Despite its remote location, the maharishi's six-acre compound was replete with creature comforts, including a swimming pool, a laundry, a post office, and a lecture hall from which the holy man would deliver his teachings to his assembled guests. Not surprisingly, each of the Beatles responded to their experience in the ashram in radically different ways. Complaining about the spicy cuisine, Ringo left after only ten days, having exhausted his secret supply of Heinz Baked Beans. For Paul, life in Rishikesh offered a sublime opportunity to cleanse his mind and replenish his writerly muse. When he and Jane Asher left after six weeks in the compound, he graciously thanked their host, telling the holy man that "you will never fathom what these days have meant to us. To have the unbroken peace and quiet and all your loving attention—only a Beatle could know the value of this." For Harrison, the privilege of pondering the maharishi's lectures and practicing Transcendental Meditation in the ashram had been one of life's great blessings. For Lennon, the Rishikesh sojourn had also started out as an ebullient journey, only to collapse in a moment of crisis when he declared that he and Harrison were leaving the compound immediately. Rumors had begun circulating in the encampment that the holy man had made sexual advances toward women in the encampment, and for John the hypocrisy was simply too much to bear. When questioned by one of the maharishi's followers about his decision to break camp, Lennon angrily replied, "If you want to know why, ask your fuckin' precious guru." Quite suddenly, eight weeks of serenity had evaporated into thin air by mid-April, and the Harrisons and the Lennons began making their way back to London.[20]

For George and the Beatles, May 1968 would prove to be a pivotal month in more ways than one. For their part, the bandmates returned from India with dozens of new compositions in their arsenal. In many ways, their sojourn in Rishikesh—its unhappy finale notwithstanding—had proven to be arguably their most productive and concentrated creative moment in years, possibly ever. During the last week of May, the Beatles gathered at Kinfauns, Harrison's recording studio at his home in suburban Esher. At Kinfauns, they created twenty-three demos in preparation for recording the songs that would comprise their next long-player. With such a bounty of material, there was already talk among the bandmates that the new LP would be a double album. In contrast with their painstaking efforts in the studio, the Esher tapes witness the Beatles working in unison and exalting in the pure joy of their music. With its splendid acoustic introduction, the demo for "Revolution" offers a perfect case in point. The band had rarely, if ever, sounded more uninhibited and free. With its enthusiastic handclaps, ad-libs, and lighthearted harmonies, it makes for one of the Beatles' most convivial recordings. Yet for all of their geniality, the Esher tapes were calculated rough drafts—coherent blueprints for the upcoming project. Simply put, the group had seldom exhibited such a self-conscious and highly organized approach to their art. For Martin, it was a creative boon that he was determined to exploit.[21]

But first there was Apple. The tax dodge that the Beatles had concocted a year earlier had transmogrified into a full-fledged enterprise. Reflecting a pun devised by Paul, Apple Music was rechristened as Apple Corps in an explicit effort by the Beatles to wrest hold of their business affairs and control their own destiny after months of uncertainty in the wake of Brian's death. "We're just going to do—everything!" John announced to Pete Shotton. "We'll have electronics, we'll have clothes, we'll have publishing, we'll have music. We're going to be talent spotters and have new talent." But the corporation had gone awry almost from the very start. Back in December 1967, they had opened the Apple Boutique at 94 Baker Street. To mark the occasion, the Fool created a brilliantly arrayed psychedelic mural that enveloped the building—that is, until legal entanglements from the City of Westminster led to its removal after only a few weeks. By midsummer, the bandmates, not very surprisingly, had lost interest in operating the boutique, famously giving away its wares to an eager public after first ransacking its racks and aisles for themselves. On May 11, John and Paul traveled to the United States in an effort to promote Apple's musical interests on an international stage. On May 14, they held a press conference at New York City's Americana Hotel, where Paul announced that "we really want to help people, but without doing it like a charity or seeming like ordinary patrons of the arts. We're in the happy position of not really needing any more money. So for the first time, the bosses aren't in it for profit. If you come and see me and say, 'I've had such and such a dream,' I'll say, 'Here's so much money. Go away and do it.' We've already bought all our dreams. So now we want to share that possibility with others." Paul's idealism was one thing. But after the *Magical Mystery Tour* debacle, John's was inexplicable. Apparently, Lennon simply couldn't see the irony that establishing Apple Corps was not so different from the bandmates' experience with directing the *Magical Mystery Tour* film, another venture that fell well outside their expertise. During that same visit, McCartney rekindled his romance with Linda Eastman, who made arrangements to join him back in the United Kingdom later that year.[22]

The risks associated with establishing the Beatles' own media corporation were not lost on George, who understood implicitly that their creative energies were best realized making music in the recording studio. To George's mind, Apple looked like a "complete fiasco" in the making. "From the start," he later wrote, "I took a jaundiced view of the whole proceedings because I could see the awful way it was going, and that it was doomed from the outset." With Brian out of the picture, the Beatles were left to their own devices, George reasoned, and that meant that Apple "was being run by four idealists, with nobody really in control." With the bandmates' lack of expertise in relation to their new business venture, George could clearly see the writing on the wall, especially given his many years in the record industry. But at the same time, he admitted to finding the concept of Apple Corps to be an appealing concept. "The tragedy was that it was an extremely praiseworthy idea," he wrote. "They wanted to put to a good use all the monies which were coming in. The motivation was, roughly: With these resources we can do anything. We can employ people to build things for us, develop new arts and new sciences, encourage scientific people to develop new inventions, encourage new writers. . . . And so on. It was a marvelous Utopian idea. If it had been handled properly it would have been a great boon to the music business."[23]

As Apple Corps evolved, the bandmates and their inner circle began establishing divisions, including a planned electronics unit to be helmed by Alexis Mardas, a Greek émigré. Since the Summer of Love, Lennon had been under the spell of Mardas, a self-styled inventor whom the Beatle rechristened as "Magic Alex" because of his penchant for imagining new forms of electronic gadgetry. For his part, George didn't care if the Beatles allowed the eccentric inventor to gambol about as part of their growing entourage, but things had come to a head in recent months as Magic Alex, with John's apparent blessing, had begun to assert himself in George's domain—the recording studio. The Beatles' producer had come to see Apple Corps as attracting a veritable "army of hangers-on," and "the one I recall most vividly, because he impinged on my work and my musical relationship with the boys, was Magic Alex." In George's mind, Magic Alex "was so preposterous that it would have been funny had he not caused so much embarrassment and difficulty with me in the recording studio." By this point, George had experienced firsthand the would-be inventor's shenanigans on several occasions. As George later wrote, Magic Alex

was one of a group of sycophants who were forever making mischief, telling the boys they weren't getting the best treatment, telling them they deserved better than the rotten old equipment that everyone else was using. I didn't need that. I knew better than anyone that we lacked certain facilities which were available in independent American studios. I was still working on four-track machines when I knew that eight-track was already common in America, and that 16-track was just around the corner. It annoyed me as much as it did the boys. But I could do without Magic Alex turning up one day and announcing in a supercilious voice: "Well, of course, I'm designing a 72-track machine."

To George's mind, this was an outrageous thing to say, a truly ludicrous suggestion to make to the Beatles, of all people, who could be gullible when it came to technical matters.[24]

On occasion, George would go so far as to admit that Magic Alex could be "clever," even a "good electronic technician." But in their naïveté, the Beatles would pander to his most far-fetched ideas. Years later, George would remember the day that Magic Alex presented John with "a little machine about half the size of a cassette, powered by a microcell battery. When it was switched on, it made a series of random bleeps." As George looked on, John became mesmerized by the useless gadget. Seeing that John had taken the inventor's bait, Magic Alex launched into his sales pitch: "That's just to give an idea of the sort of thing we can do," he told John. "Now, I've had an idea for a new invention. It's a paint that, when I spray it on the wall, and connect it up to two anodes, will make the whole wall glow. You won't need lights." All Magic Alex required, of course, was a little start-up money, which the Beatles freely supplied. After a while, George found himself laughing at the mere mention of the inventor's silly name. But to George's mind, Magic Alex's "prize idea" was a scam involving a sonic force field that would mitigate the need for sound screens in the studio—namely, the screens that separated Ringo and his drum kit from the rest of the bandmates in order to prevent sound bleed. Flush with Magic Alex's latest brainchild, George could only hold his tongue and listen as the bandmates reveled in the inventor's vision: "Alex has got a brilliant idea! He's come up with something really great: a sonic screen! He's going to place these ultra-high-frequency beams round Ringo, and when they're switched on he won't be able to hear anything because the beams will form a wall of silence." For his part, George could only listen in horror as the Beatles regaled him with yet another one of Magic Alex's harebrained ideas. "Words, I fully admit, failed me," he wrote. But George also remained silent because he had come to realize that the bandmates' infatuation with Magic Alex—and George's contrasting disgust with the inventor—was beginning to cause a "minor schism" to develop in his own relationship with the Beatles. And George was not about to let that happen.[25]

On Thursday, May 30, George and the Beatles finally reconvened in Studio 2 to work on their next long-player, the much-anticipated and as-of-yet untitled follow-up album to *Sgt. Pepper*. They clearly planned to attack the new LP with a vengeance, having prebooked Abbey Road studio time, every weekday from 2:30 PM to midnight, through late July. And while the bandmates were armed to the teeth with new compositions, pretested and demoed at Kinfauns only a few days earlier, they weren't alone. They were joined by Yoko Ono, only this time things were decidedly different from the Japanese artist's visit to Abbey Road during "The Fool on the Hill" sessions back in September. On May 19—with Cynthia away on holiday in Greece—John had invited Yoko to his Weybridge estate, where they stayed up all night improvising recordings on his Brenell reel-to-reel tape recorders as Yoko shrieked a series of wordless, discordant vocals into the growing cacophony. At dawn, they consummated their new relationship. A few days later, Cynthia returned from her Grecian holiday just in time to discover Yoko wearing her bathrobe and sitting cross-legged on the floor of her Kenwood kitchen with John. In short order, Cynthia's marriage to John had fallen into shambles as the Beatle pondered a new life with Yoko beyond Cynthia and his five-year-old son, Julian.

And now, Yoko had insinuated herself into the lives of George and the Beatles as well. The professional sanctum of the studio, which had long been the bandmates' sanctuary from the ever-encroaching outside world, had suddenly been upended by Yoko's presence. With the exceptions of Sheila Bromberg's harp work on "She's Leaving Home" and the Mike Sammes Singers' turn on "I Am the Walrus," George and the Beatles' collaboration had largely been a masculine one. They had each hailed, in their own ways, from Old World mores in which men and women followed highly gendered norms—George from working-class North London and the Beatles, who shared traditional northern upbringings. By drawing Yoko into their workaday world, John had turned their universe on its head.

It was Emerick who felt the winds of change first. When John arrived at the studio that day, he deposited Yoko in the control booth before shuttling into the studio. As Geoff later wrote, "For the next couple of hours Yoko just sat quietly with us in the control room. It had to have been even more uncomfortable for her than it was for any of us. She had been put in an embarrassing situation, plunked right by the window so that George Martin and I had to crane our heads around her to see the others out in the studio and communicate with them. As a result, she kept thinking we were staring at her. She'd give us a polite, shy smile whenever she'd see us looking in her direction, but she never actually said anything."[26]

But Yoko wasn't the only new face in the control room that day. George had invited a guest of his own named Chris Thomas, the producer's twenty-one-year-old protégé from AIR, who was learning the ropes of record production. Thomas had first caught Martin's eye after he wrote a letter to the Beatles' producer seeking work. In 1967, George had hired him as a production assistant at AIR, and he had recently cut his teeth attending sessions at Abbey Road with Ron Richards and the Hollies.

As the May 30 session got underway, John debuted a new song that would come to be known as "Revolution 1," a standout composition from the Esher demos. With Martin and a whole array of people up in the booth, the Beatles perfected a rhythm track in eighteen takes, including Lennon's lead vocal, McCartney's piano, Harrison's acoustic guitar, and Starr's drums. As the longest performance of "Revolution 1," the eighteenth and best take clocked in at more than ten minutes. Emerick can be heard announcing "take 18" when the song rolls into being, with the bandmates eventually concluding "Revolution 1" with an extensive jam before Lennon shouts, "Okay, I've had enough!" During the song's final, chaotic six minutes, John and Yoko, who had succeeded in making her way down to the studio proper, dropped a series of non sequiturs into the sonic bedlam on May 31. In addition to John's moaning and other nonverbal ministrations, Yoko can be heard deadpanning "if you become naked." While such random effects would be reserved for later deployment on the new album, George and the Beatles were forced to contend, in the short run, with the take's gargantuan length, especially as they were already considering "Revolution 1" as a candidate for the next single. As for Yoko, once she had cleared a path to her boyfriend working down in the studio, she would almost never leave his side.

But for Emerick, the May 30 session would be memorable for reasons well beyond the unexpected appearances of Ono and Thomas. As the session got underway, Geoff could tell that the Beatles were playing louder than ever before, with John's amp turned up to "an ear-splitting level." As George looked on in silence, Geoff was especially concerned because of the sonic leakage from John's amp into the other microphones. After politely suggesting that John lower the volume so that he could adequately capture the recording, Geoff was stunned by the Beatle's response over the talkback: "I've got something to say to you," John caustically replied. "It's your job to control it, so just do your bloody job." At that point, George and Geoff exchanged knowing glances. And that's when the Beatles' producer told Geoff, "I think you'd better go talk to him." Moments later, Emerick had joined Lennon down in the studio. "Look," John calmly explained, "the reason I've got my amp turned up so high is that I'm trying to distort the shit out of it. If you need me to turn it down, I will, but you have to do something to get my guitar to sound a lot more nasty. That's what I'm after for this song." As Geoff began to make his way back to the booth, already imagining a solution to John's dilemma, he was thunderstruck when the Beatle sneered, "Come on, get with it, Geoff. I think it's about bloody time you got your act together."[27]

When Geoff returned to the booth, he was met by George, who asked, impassively, "What's he on about?" But for his part, Geoff was speechless in the face of John's bluster. "I was so mad I couldn't even answer," the engineer later recalled. "After taking a few minutes to regain my composure, I decided to overload the mic preamp that was carrying John's guitar signal." Geoff was essentially drawing on the same remedy that had been devised to afford John's voice with additional texture during the sessions devoted to "I Am the Walrus." As the "Revolution 1" session progressed, with John's guitar resonance having been rendered to his liking, Geoff had become transfixed by the evening's unsettling ambience. "That first night's session was uncontrolled chaos, pure and simple," he wrote, "and George Martin had looked puzzled and concerned from start to finish. He and I knew that something was not quite right here."

For his part, George had also registered the difference in the Beatles' atmosphere, and he strategically fell back on the calculated approach that had served him well in previous years. He self-consciously enacted a "tactical withdrawal," just as he had done during the production of the *Help!* long-player and, more recently, during the post-*Pepper* era. To his mind, this approach allowed him to be available as a resource for the Beatles while carefully navigating his way among their understandably towering egos after years of unparalleled success. But in the ensuing days and weeks, he began adopting a different guise in the studio, arriving early, as he had always done, but purposefully carrying a thick stack of daily London newspapers along with a large Cadbury bar. Outfitted in this fashion, he would recline in the control booth, occupying his mind until he was needed. Withdrawn and catching up on the news of the world, to be sure, but also eminently ready to answer the Beatles' every beck and call.[28]

On Friday, May 31, Martin and the bandmates returned to "Revolution 1," which grew further still as McCartney and Harrison provided intentionally disconcerting "shooby doo-wop" backing vocals to the raucous tune. They were joined by twenty-three-year-old American Francie Schwartz, yet another new face in the studio that week. Introduced as Paul's new girlfriend, Francie was a budding screenwriter and one of the legion of would-be artists who had descended upon Apple Corps after John and Paul's open-ended offer of patronage to the world. In short order, Francie made her way into Apple's offices, where she met Paul and found her way into the Beatle's heart. In a matter of days, McCartney's engagement and long-standing relationship with Jane Asher was effectively over. During the May 31 session, Paul added a bass part and John double-tracked his lead vocal. Before George and his production team closed up shop for the night, John and Yoko had begun assembling a sound collage during the six-minute coda for "Revolution 1."

During the next session, held on Tuesday, June 4, Martin reconvened the recording of "Revolution 1," with Peter Bown instead of Emerick sitting in the engineer's chair. George was absolutely livid. Alan Stagge, Abbey Road's new studio head, had recently adopted a practice in which he planned to regularly shuttle different engineers among the studios' sessions and recurrent acts as if they were interchangeable. Stagge believed that the only thing that mattered in the world of recording artistry was technical expertise. With the appropriate training and experience, Stagge reasoned, anyone could work a session. In terms of Emerick, the practice would be decidedly short lived after Martin went over Stagge's head, complained to his superiors, and had Emerick reinstated to all Beatles sessions thenceforward.

During the Emerick-free June 4 session, as technical engineer Brian Gibson recalled, Lennon opted to rerecord his lead vocal for "Revolution 1" in a most unusual fashion. "John decided he would feel more comfortable on the floor," Brian recalled, "so I had to rig up a microphone which would be suspended on a boom above his mouth. It struck me as somewhat odd, a little eccentric, but they were always looking for a different sound, something new." That same evening, Bown took special note of an offhanded remark by Lennon when the Fairchild limiter, which was often deployed to modulate Lennon's vocals, was on the fritz. "The fucking machine has broken down again?" Lennon asked, aghast at the state of EMI's equipment. "It won't be the same when we get our own studio down at Apple." Meanwhile, the bandmates continued adding more overdubs to the song, with McCartney providing an organ part, Harrison and McCartney adorning the coda with yet more harmonies—including a bizarre call-and-response cadence of "mama, dada"—and Harrison turning in raunchy electric guitar work on a heavily distorted Fender Stratocaster.[29]

For the next session, June 5, Emerick was back in his familiar place in the booth, courtesy of Martin's tirade earlier that same day with Stagge's EMI superiors. That evening, Starr debuted a new composition that went under various working titles—"Ringo's Tune" and "This Is Some Friendly"—before settling on "Don't Pass Me By." At this juncture, Ringo had been working on the song for nearly five years. After capturing the basic rhythm track in three attempts, Ringo gleefully shouted up to the control booth, saying, "I think we've got something there, George!" At this point, the bandmates began adding overdubs, including perhaps most strangely a holiday sleigh bell. The next evening, Paul superimposed a bass part onto "Don't Pass Me By," while Ringo provided various bits of percussion. As work proceeded apace, Ringo and Paul's piano turns were recorded through a Leslie speaker in order to afford them with greater texture. Meanwhile, John had begun reshaping the collage that served as the coda for "Revolution 1" into a freestanding work of *musique concrète* that came to be known as "Revolution 9." With assistance from Yoko, he supplemented the experimental recording with tape loops, bits of conversation, tinkling piano sounds, and assorted vignettes from the EMI tape library's fabled green cabinet. By the week of June 10—with John occasionally working alone in the studio with Yoko by his side—the collage was now composed of twelve different sound effects, several of which were labeled as "Various," with the other seven being identified by John as "Vicars Poems," "Queen's Mess," "Come Dancing Combo," "Organ Last Will Test," "Neville Club," "Theatre Outing," and "Applause/TV Jingle." All the while, George thumbed through the daily papers and quietly munched on his chocolate. During one outtake, he can even be heard absentmindedly singing Chubby Checker's 1962 hit "Let's Twist Again."[30]

On the evening of Tuesday, June 11—with Starr and Harrison traveling abroad in the United States—Martin and his production team shuttled between Studio 3, where Lennon was toiling away at "Revolution 9," and Studio 2, where McCartney debuted a new composition titled "Blackbird." For the most part, John was left to his own devices, occasionally dispatching Chris Thomas or Phil McDonald to ferret out new sound effects from the tape library, while George and Geoff attended to Paul's gentle ballad. Playing his Martin D-28 dreadnought-style acoustic guitar, McCartney made thirty-two attempts at recording "Blackbird." To augment the recording, Geoff helpfully placed a microphone near Paul's tapping foot on the floor of Studio 2 in order to capture the sound of the Beatle keeping time. After recording the song's basic rhythm, Paul double-tracked his lead vocal. George and Geoff finished the song off with the sound of a chirping blackbird, which they had culled from the EMI tape library's *Volume 7: Birds of a Feather.* As yet another effect compiled by Stuart Eltham, the sound of the blackbird had been recorded in the engineer's garden back in 1965. For Emerick, the session had been a joy. Working alone with Martin and McCartney "came as a blessed relief to me after all the stress of the preceding sessions," he later remarked. "It always was a lot easier to deal with one Beatle."[31]

Thursday, June 20, proved to be an unprecedented day in the life of Martin and the Beatles. With McCartney traveling stateside, Lennon worked alone with Ono on "Revolution 9," save for occasional non sequiturs from Harrison. In fact, John had commandeered every available space in the complex—Studios 1, 2, and 3—for the purposes of completing the basic soundscape for the

experimental sound collage. With Yoko by his side, John worked at the recording console, fading the tape loops in and out of the mix in order to bring the
collage to fruition. In the final version of the pastiche, Martin's heavily echoed
voice can be heard saying, "Geoff, put the red light on." Also in evidence was
an extract from the February 10, 1967, orchestral overdub for "A Day in the
Life." During the June 20 "Revolution 9" session, John also happened upon
the collage's distinctive "number nine, number nine" introduction, which
had been culled from an examination recording for the Royal Academy of
Music in the EMI tape library. As Richard Lush later recalled, when John
discovered the "number nine" voice, he "thought that was a real hoot. He
made a loop of just that bit and had it playing constantly on one machine,
fading it in or out when he wanted it, along with the backwards orchestral
stuff and everything else." As the session came to an end that night, Martin
and Emerick imbued "Revolution 9" with a heavy dose of STEED (single tape
echo and echo delay) in order to afford the pastiche with a live-sounding
echo effect, just as they had done three years earlier with tracks like *Beatles
for Sale*'s "Rock and Roll Music" and "Everybody's Trying to Be My Baby."[32]

The very next afternoon, Martin and Emerick observed as Lennon overdubbed one last batch of sound effects on the "Revolution 9" montage. As
Emerick later recalled, "Every once in a while, Lennon would shoot a glance
at George Martin and me to see if we approved of what he was doing. Personally, I thought the track was interesting, but it seemed as though it was
as much Yoko's as it was John's. Certainly, it wasn't Beatles music." Later
that evening, George assembled a group of session players to perform a brass
arrangement for "Revolution 1." Working from Martin's score, the instrumentation consisted of two trumpets and four trombones. Before the session concluded, Harrison superimposed a sizzling lead guitar part on "Revolution 1,"
adding further zest to the song's cacophony of competing styles and genres.

As the month of June came to a close, Martin supervised several additional sessions in which Lennon's songs held sway. Like McCartney for much
of 1967, Lennon was clearly working on heat. The next week, John debuted
yet another new composition, eventually titled "Everybody's Got Something
to Hide Except Me and My Monkey." By this point in the production of the
new long-player, George and the bandmates had evolved a different means of
approaching new songs. In contrast with their most recent efforts on *Revolver*
and *Sgt. Pepper*, this new approach involved not only rehearsing their songs
with the tape running but treating the rehearsals themselves as actual recordings, complete with individual take numbers. It was an indulgent and time-
consuming method to be sure, especially in contrast with the comparatively

economical *Sgt. Pepper*, but it illustrates the pains to which the bandmates were willing to go to capture their sonic visions. For Emerick, it meant hours upon hours of close attention to the Beatles' every move. But for George, it spelled one session after another in which he studied the London news and feasted on Cadbury chocolate bars.[33]

With July looming on the horizon, "Everybody's Got Something to Hide Except Me and My Monkey" began as a hulking mess of a song on June 26, only to be transformed, via the bandmates' new rehearsal/recording practice, into a taut and rhythmic basic track. With Lennon and Harrison's distorted electric guitars, McCartney's thundering bass, and Starr's highly compressed drum sound, courtesy of Emerick, "Everybody's Got Something to Hide Except Me and My Monkey" took shape over the next several sessions. Eventually, the Beatles added a host of percussion, including a fire bell and a chocalho, the metal shaker that they had previously deployed on "She's a Woman."

On June 28, John unveiled yet another new composition, a gentle serenade titled "Good Night." Working in Studio 2 with Emerick up in the booth, Martin took the bench in front of Abbey Road's Steinway grand and delivered a deft accompaniment for Lennon's beautiful lullaby for his estranged son, Julian. Astutely turning the lead vocals over to Starr, whose baritone was pitch perfect for the tune, Lennon strummed his Gibson Jumbo along with Martin's smooth piano glide. As the session progressed, Ringo charmingly donned his fatherly guise and tried out a range of spoken introductions, at one point saying, "Come on children! It's time to toddle off to bed. We've had a lovely day at the park and now it's time for sleep." As the song evolved even further, John hit upon the idea of accompanying Ringo's warm vocal effusions with a lush orchestral score—"corny" even, in John's vision. That same night, the producer dutifully prepared an acetate, which he took home with him in order to begin concocting the score for "Good Night." Perhaps George would finally succeed in making inroads into the Beatles' new long-player after all.[34]

17

THE GREAT TAPE
RECORDER ROBBERY

O N WEDNESDAY, JULY 17, 1968, the *Yellow Submarine* animated feature film premiered at the London Pavilion. As with *A Hard Day's Night* and *Help!*, it was an evening redolent with the fanaticism of Beatlemania's great onslaught in its early days. The scene around Piccadilly Circus was appropriately raucous, with the Beatles having traded in their psychedelic finery for the upscale Carnaby wear that was coming into vogue. And George and Judy were there, too, looking out of place as usual, dressed to the nines as if they were at a Hollywood opening circa 1955, with the Beatles' producer wearing a sleek tuxedo and his wife donning a fancy gown.

For Martin and Al Brodax, *Yellow Submarine* proved to be a vindication in every sense of the word. The film enjoyed rave reviews both at home and abroad, and even the Beatles warmed to the occasion, having come to realize that the animated feature was a far cry from the King Features cartoons that they claimed to despise. After the premiere, the bandmates stopped distancing themselves from *Yellow Submarine* and actually began to embrace it. Writing for the *New York Times* later that year, Renata Adler captured the magic of the animated feature, as well as the Beatles' uncanny portability across nearly every genre and demographic: "*Yellow Submarine* is a family movie in the truest sense," Adler wrote, "something for the little kids who watch the same sort of punning stories, infinitely less nonviolent and refined, on television; something for the older kids, whose musical contribution to the arts and longings for love and gentleness and color could hardly present a better case; something for parents, who can see the best of what being newly young is all about. *Hard Day's Night* and *Help!* were more serious, and more truly Beatle saturated. But *Yellow Submarine*, with its memories of Saturday morning at the movies, and its lovely Oswald the Rabbit in Candyland graphics, makes the hooking up and otherwise commingling very possible. When invited to, the whole audience picks up the 'all together now' refrain and sings."[1]

In the space of a single compact paragraph, Adler had managed to capture the essence of what Martin and Brian Epstein had achieved with the Beatles. Riding on the backs of the bandmates' enormous songwriting talent and musicianship, the group's brain trust had shrewdly sought out a range of vehicles for showcasing their otherworldly gifts to new and increasingly diverse audiences at every turn. And as Harrison, one of the most vocal critics of the project back in 1967, later observed, "That film works for every generation—every baby, three or four years old, goes through *Yellow Submarine*."[2]

In spite of the movie's astounding success—it turned over millions of pounds in ticket sales on a relatively meager budget—the *Yellow Submarine* soundtrack album would be delayed until January 1969. First, there was the issue of the Beatles' new long-player, which would require the balance of 1968 to complete. But there was also the matter of the soundtrack itself, which Martin wanted to rerecord for posterity. On October 22 and 23, the Beatles' producer convened his forty-one-piece George Martin Orchestra in Abbey Road's Studio 1 to record the *Yellow Submarine* score in a pair of three-hour sessions, with his AIR colleagues John Burgess and Ron Richards on hand as coproducers, Geoff Emerick working as engineer, and Nick Webb serving as tape operator.

When the soundtrack was finally released on January 17, 1969, in the United Kingdom, Martin's score comprised half of the album, with the remainder of the long-player consisting of "Yellow Submarine," "Only a Northern Song," "All Together Now," "Hey Bulldog," "It's All Too Much," and "All You Need Is Love." Not surprisingly, fans and critics alike were suitably miffed with the release, which included several songs that were already available and the score for a film that was, by that point, already six months old. With cover art by Heinz Edelman, the *Yellow Submarine* soundtrack nevertheless registered top-five showings in both the UK and US marketplaces, where consumer enthusiasm for new Beatles product continued to reign supreme. Indeed, the soundtrack might have even topped the charts had there not been another newly minted Beatles release in heavy rotation the world over. In March 1969, the bandmates considered releasing a five-song EP, which was slated to include the still-unreleased "Across the Universe" as a bonus track in order to afford their fans with better value for their money. EMI even went so far as to instruct Edward Gadsby-Toni to create a master tape for the EP, which was composed of "Only a Northern Song," "Hey Bulldog," "Across the Universe," "All Together Now," and "It's All Too Much." But the project was scrapped not long afterward. It was a tricky proposition in any event, given Martin's contractual rights regarding the *Yellow Submarine* project, which called for his score to be showcased with the Beatles' original songs.

As it happened, the full *Yellow Submarine* soundtrack album proved to be one of the biggest paydays in George's career. Orchestrating the film score, he later admitted, was "very rewarding, both artistically and financially." With *Yellow Submarine*, he was finally fulfilling his dream of earning residuals for his contributions to his artists' success—the very same case that he had attempted to prosecute, albeit to no avail, with EMI's Len Wood back in 1965—and a best-selling international LP ensured that he was a financial participant in the Beatles' commercial attainments with *Yellow Submarine*. In 1970, he was rewarded yet again with a nomination at the Twelfth Annual Grammy Awards for Best Original Score Written for a Motion Picture or a Television Special.[3]

Meanwhile, as July progressed, George and the bandmates logged increasingly long hours in the studio. Back on July 3, McCartney had debuted a new, playful composition called "Ob-La-Di, Ob-La-Da." Of all the songs that they would attempt that summer, "Ob-La-Di, Ob-La-Da" revealed the inherent limitations of the group's painstaking rehearsal/recording practice. Over the ensuing days, the new song would be the subject of successive remakes as McCartney and the other Beatles made marginal strides toward capturing his vision for the song. By July 5, Paul attempted a reggae version of the song, with George hastily recruiting a trio of saxophonists and a bongo player for the session. Seemingly mad for effect, Paul asked for a piccolo superimposition later that same evening, only to wipe it from the mix shortly thereafter. Before the session was out, the Beatle had replaced the woodwind instrument with a guitar overdub. But to Chris Thomas's mind, the guitar superimposition made little sense, as "Paul was deliberately overloading the sound through the desk so that it sounded like a bass." By the following Monday, McCartney arrived in Studio 2 ready to remake "Ob-La-Di, Ob-La-Da" once again. In short order, the work of Martin's session men was scrapped in favor of a new basic track featuring McCartney's fuzz bass, Starr's drums, Harrison's acoustic guitar, and Lennon's piano. By this point, the morale among Martin's production team—not to mention his own—was decidedly low. As Richard Lush later recalled, "They spent so much time doing each song that I can remember sitting in the control room before a session dying to hear them start a new one. They must have done 'Ob-La-Di, Ob-La-Da' five nights running and it's not exactly the most melodic piece of music. They'd do it one night and you'd think, 'That's it.' But then they'd come in the next day and do it again in a different key or with a different feel. Poor Ringo would be playing from about three in the afternoon until one in the morning, with few breaks in between, and then have to do it all over again the next night."[4]

Before the Monday night session mercifully concluded, McCartney had revised his vision for "Ob-La-Di, Ob-La-Da" yet again—this time, opting for a Latin American feel in place of the track's earlier reggae sound. Amazingly, the next evening the song finally began to come together, with the bandmates enjoying a convivial session, complete with pervasive laughter and inside jokes. With "Ob-La-Di, Ob-La-Da" holding steady for a change, George and the Beatles turned back to "Revolution 1"—only John had something else in mind for his composition. Since early June, he had maintained that "Revolution 1" should be the band's next single. But Harrison and McCartney, in particular, vetoed the idea. "They said it wasn't good enough," Lennon later recalled. To his mind, they "were resentful and said it wasn't fast enough." And Martin, perhaps inadvisably, had taken Harrison and McCartney's side in the ongoing squabble. As Emerick later recalled, "In the early days, George Martin had picked the songs that would comprise the A-side and B-side of a Beatles single. But by this point in their career, it would be the group's decision; George might offer some input or suggestions, but it was their final call." John's solution to the dilemma was obvious to his way of thinking—call their bluff, speed up the song, and release it as the next Beatles single posthaste. With the Maoist revolution in full flower and the Vietnam conflict raging overseas, Lennon felt that the Beatles were duty bound to join the political fray, to take advantage of their bully pulpit and comment on the international malaise.[5]

During a July 9 session, Lennon led the other Beatles on a new recording of "Revolution 1," with the faster, hard-rocking version to be titled simply "Revolution." Lyrically, the compositions were almost identical but for a single word. As John later recalled, "There were two versions of that song, but the underground left only picked up on the one [the faster version] that said, 'count me out.' The original version, which ends up on the LP, said, 'count me in,' too; I put in both because I wasn't sure." After rehearsing a basic track featuring Harrison and Lennon's electric guitars, McCartney's bass, and Starr's drums, they remade the song on July 10. That evening, Martin produced a searing version of "Revolution" for the ages. As the producer later remembered, "We got into distortion on that, which we had a lot of complaints from the technical people about. But that was the idea: it was John's song and the idea was to push it right to the limit. Well, we went to the limit and beyond." As Phil McDonald later noted, George captured the blistering sound by feeding the guitar signals through the recording console. "It completely overloaded the channel and produced the fuzz sound," McDonald reported. "Fortunately the technical people didn't find out. They didn't approve of 'abuse of equipment.'" After capturing "Revolution" in ten takes, the bandmates applied overdubs to the recording, including a series of handclaps and a sizzling, double-tracked lead vocal from John. The next evening, Thursday, July 11, witnessed an additional overdub courtesy of keyboard session man Nicky Hopkins, who superimposed a magnificent electric piano solo onto the track. And with that, Lennon's "Revolution" was complete. He had met, if not exceeded, his self-imposed burden of imagining a faster version of the song, and in so doing he had duly presented "Revolution" as the lead contender for the next Beatles single.[6]

In many ways, the ball was now in Martin's court. While the Beatles had clearly taken ownership of their artistic direction, even assuming a greater role in the production of their music from ideation through remixing, the band's producer was often forced to weigh in with his own perspective in order to settle their differences of opinion. And "Revolution"—a song to which George himself was clearly partial—was setting up the Beatles and their inner circle for a showdown. As mid-July came and went, George and the bandmates completed several more tracks, including Ringo's "Don't Pass Me By," which had been waiting in the wings. On July 12, George booked fiddle-playing Jack Fallon to superimpose a string adornment for the song. As Fallon later recalled, "George Martin had jotted down a 12-bar blues for me. A lot of country fiddle playing is double-stop but Paul and George Martin—they were doing the arranging—suggested I play it single note. So it wasn't really the country sound they originally wanted. But they seemed pleased. Ringo was around too, keeping an eye on his song." At the end of the recording, Fallon can be heard improvising a free-form coda. "I thought that they had had enough so I just busked around a bit," he recalled. "When I heard it played back at the end of the session I was hoping they'd scrub that bit out, but they didn't, so there I am on record, scraping away!"[7]

During the week of July 15, the tensions that had been brewing among the bandmates and their production team finally came to a head. The Monday night session in Studio 2 began, ominously enough, with McCartney returning yet again to "Ob-La-Di, Ob-La-Da," for which he recorded a new lead vocal, eating up considerable studio time in the process. Working until three o'clock in the morning, the Beatles then devoted more than two hours to rehearsing a new Lennon composition titled "Cry Baby Cry," with its nursery-rhyme lyrics and somber tones. But earlier that same evening, all hell had broken loose during McCartney's efforts to perfect his vocal. Only this time, the fireworks weren't emanating from among the Beatles, with Yoko in tow, as always, down in the studio. Strangely, the blowup occurred upstairs in the control booth, and the central player was Geoff, the timid and unfailingly respectful sound engineer for the Beatles' most innovative recordings. And perhaps more importantly, he was Martin's right-hand man throughout the ups and downs along his journey with the group.

It all started, innocently enough, as Emerick and Lush engineered McCartney's latest stab at singing "Ob-La-Di, Ob-La-Da." As Geoff later recalled, "Richard and I began the long, tedious process of rolling and rerolling the tape as he [Paul] experimented endlessly, making minute changes to the lead vocal, in search of some kind of elusive perfection that only he could hear in his head." And that's when George chimed in, offering advice to the Beatle about rephrasing his vocals. "Paul, can you try rephrasing the last line of each verse?" George asked. To Geoff's ears, the Beatles' producer was adopting the same "gentle, slightly aristocratic voice" that he had always deployed in his dealings with the Beatles. Geoff couldn't help admiring the older man, later lauding him for "still trying to do his job, still trying to steer his charges toward increased musical sophistication and help push them to their best performances." But Emerick wasn't prepared for McCartney's curt response: "If you think you can do it better, why don't you fucking come down here and sing it yourself?" The engineer sat there in the booth, dumbstruck by Paul's tone. "What happened next shocked me to the core," Emerick later wrote. "In sheer frustration, quiet, low-key George Martin actually began shouting back at Paul. 'Then bloody sing it again!' he yelled over the talkback, causing me to wince. 'I give up. I just don't know any better how to help you.' It was the first time I had ever heard George Martin raise his voice in a session. The silence following the outburst was equally deafening." For Geoff, George had suddenly crossed a line. While his colleagues at Abbey Road often referred to him affectionately as "Golden Ears" or "Ernie," others called him "Emeroids" in a crude reference to his tendency, during extreme occasions, to be overwhelmed by his anxiety. And in this moment, after witnessing George going toe-to-toe with his clients, the engineer's disquiet had reached a fever pitch. Emerick knew, in his heart, "that was it for me. I sat at the mixing console and continued to man the controls, even though every fiber in my body was screaming, 'Get out! Now!'"[8]

The next afternoon, as George was making preparations for the upcoming session, the engineer made his intentions known. After having tossed and turned the night before, a sleepless and dejected Emerick walked into the control room. "I took a deep breath," Geoff later wrote, "and at last the words came out. 'That's it, George,' I announced. 'I've decided I can't take it anymore. I'm leaving.'" For his part, Martin was thunderstruck. "You can't leave in the middle of an album," he told the engineer, who replied, "I can, George, and I am." With Martin hot on his heels, Emerick made his way to Alan Stagge's office to announce his decision to quit working Beatles sessions. With George openly sympathizing with Geoff's frustrations, the studio head asked Geoff to finish out the week before rotating to another artist. But Geoff wouldn't hear of it. With no other choice, Stagge gave him the rest of the week off and pressed Ken Scott into service as his replacement. For Geoff, the mere notion that he had been liberated from the toxic atmosphere with the Beatles was sweet relief. But for George, as he made his way back to Studio 2, the situation had suddenly been rendered even more bleak than it had been before Geoff's desertion. Until that point, Martin had been able to hide behind his newspapers and allow the moveable feast of the Beatles' discontent to roll on without him. But now, with Emerick gone, he was suddenly very much alone up in the booth. When he made his way down into the studio after Emerick had bade farewell to the band, Martin supervised ten takes of "Cry Baby Cry" and even pitched in with a nifty harmonium part.[9]

If George felt a sense of hollowness in the wake of Geoff's sudden absence in his life with the Beatles, it may have been—in retrospect—decidedly short lived. For his part, Scott acted as a kind of emollient for the tension that had overwhelmed the bandmates' atmosphere. Easygoing and unflappable in contrast with the bashful, high-strung Emerick, Scott may have been just what Martin and the Beatles needed to finish off their new long-player. "I was much more of a basic rock and roll type engineer than Geoff was," Ken later recalled. To his mind, it was clear that "they wanted more of a rock and roll album. With me coming in at that point, it worked out perfectly." There were still "moments of tension" with Scott in the engineer's chair, to be certain, "but the majority of the time we had a blast. It was such good fun!" Scott added, suggesting that his participation "gave them what they were looking for at that point, so they could relax and have more fun."[10]

George certainly wasn't averse to having more fun with the Beatles in the studio. By this point, the heady days of *Sgt. Pepper* seemed like a distant memory—not only for Martin but for McCartney, who was being considerably outpaced by Lennon in terms of the new long-player. In addition to slaving over "Ob-La-Di, Ob-La-Da," McCartney had been burning the candle at both ends, with Beatles sessions at all hours of the night and production work with Mary Hopkin during the day. As one of Apple's inaugural signees, the Welsh folk singer had been recommended to McCartney by Twiggy (Lesley Lawson). Working with arranger Richard Hewson, McCartney had been hard at work producing Hopkin's debut single, "Those Were the Days," a cover version of the romantic Russian ballad originally composed by Boris Fomin. With McCartney and Hopkin working their acoustic guitars along with a hammered dulcimer accompaniment, "Those Were the Days" took shape that July. Hewson's arrangement called for a balalaika, banjo, and a children's chorus, which afforded the song with an old-world feel. With "Those Were the Days" slated for a late August release on Apple Records, McCartney had begun routining new material for Hopkin's debut album, *Postcard*. One of those songs was one of George's original compositions titled "The Game," a haunting song with a plaintive piano, played by George, and recorder accompaniment. The lyrics bespeak a melancholic existence, a narrative about love and a sense of inevitable loss: "I wondered why / All the good things happen to pass me by," Hopkin sings. "Life was the game we played." In "The Game," George writes about a forlorn world where "your love would slip away from me," a darkling place where "the good things happened to turn out wrong."

By this juncture in George and the Beatles' career, the producer had grown much friendlier with Paul than with John, who clearly had been George's closest ally during the bandmates' early years. McCartney shared Martin's affinity for production, and like the producer, he believed in the recording studio as a kind of dream factory where artists can make their visions come true. For Paul, those visions weren't always the playful, upbeat terrain of "Penny Lane" and "Ob-La-Di, Ob-La-Da." On Thursday, July 18, the day after the *Yellow Submarine* premiere, he unveiled a new composition made up of raw, abject terror. McCartney had been inspired to author the song out of sheer competitive energy. He had recently seen an interview with the Who's Pete Townshend in *Melody Maker* in which the guitarist boasted of having created "the loudest, most raucous rock 'n' roll, the dirtiest thing they've ever done." With Martin up in the booth along with Scott and Lush, "Helter Skelter" began to slowly take form—first, as an elongated blues effusion. Recorded over three takes, the song eventually grew to more than twenty-seven minutes in length. Played live by the Beatles in the studio, with a powerful vocal and lead guitar from McCartney, Harrison's rhythm guitar, Lennon's bass, and Starr's heavy drum delivery, "Helter Skelter" was overloaded with tape echo by Martin's production team, affording the song, in its present state at least, with a chaotic, circular ambience.

Not to be outdone, Lennon returned the next evening with a scorching new composition of his own titled "Sexy Sadie," a bitter paean about his unsettling experiences with the maharishi in Rishikesh. As with "Helter Skelter" the night before, the bandmates continued their rehearsal/recording practice by allowing "Sexy Sadie" to develop organically in the studio. Along the way, John made forays in a variety of directions, at one point leading a lengthy instrumental jam devoted to George Gershwin's "Summertime." During that same session, he pushed the boundaries of good taste when he broke off a little ditty about the Beatles' late manager. "What about Brian Epstein?" John sang, before taking aim at Brian's brother Clive—"he's a dirty old man"—and his mother, "dirty Queenie, well she's the queen of them all." Later, during a break in the session, Harrison seemed to call Martin out for his sullen attitude in the days since Emerick's departure:

Scott: Sorry George, what did you say?
Harrison: I said it's no point in Mr. Martin being uptight.
McCartney: Right.
Harrison: You know, we're all here to do this, and if you want to be uptight—
Martin: I don't know what to say to you, George.
Harrison: I mean, you're very negative!

By this juncture, Martin was clearly not immune to the growing tensions in the studio. Blessed relief eventually came when the band regrouped long enough to attempt another stab at "Sexy Sadie," with the unusually good-humored Lennon shouting up to the control booth, "See if we're all in tune, George!" before launching into twenty-one passes at the still-unfinished song. When the session finally came to a close, Lennon can be heard remarking, "I don't like the sound very much for a kickoff. Does anybody?"[11]

As work on the long-player moved inexorably forward, Martin found himself back in his element during a Monday, July 22, session in cavernous Studio 1. That evening, George conducted his score for "Good Night" with a raft of top-flight London session players. George's stirring orchestration called for twelve violins, three violas, three cellos, a harp, three flutes, a clarinet, a horn, a vibraphone, and a string bass. After capturing the score in twelve takes, the producer bade goodbye to the musicians and welcomed the Mike Sammes Singers back to Abbey Road. After recording the choir of four male and four female voices, George turned to Ringo, who recorded his lead vocal with charm and grace aplenty. In between takes, the Beatles' drummer can be heard cracking jokes and chatting good-naturedly with Martin and Scott. All in all, it was a convivial session in contrast with the "Sexy Sadie" affair during the previous week, and for their part Lennon and McCartney were satisfied with the results. "The arrangement was done by George Martin," Paul remarked during a 1968 interview, "because he's very good at that kind of arrangement, you know, a very lush, sweet arrangement."[12]

Over the next several days, George and the Beatles seemed, for the time being at least, to be gathering a much-needed sense of momentum. They finally completed work on "Everybody's Got Something to Hide Except Me and My Monkey," with Lennon making the inevitable request that his vocals be refashioned with studio trickery. As Richard Lush recalled, "As usual, John was wanting his voice to sound different. He would say, 'I want to sound like somebody from the moon or anything different. Make it different!'" In the end, John opted to double-track his lead vocal, later overdubbing a raucous layer of backing vocals with Paul. Together, they chanted "come on" ad nauseam in order to accent the cacophony. That same week, Martin and the group made great progress on "Sexy Sadie" before turning to the first Harrison composition of that summer. Indeed, it was Thursday, July 25—nearly two months into the sessions for their new album—when they finally got around to "While My Guitar Gently Weeps." Inspired by the *I Ching*—namely, "The Book of Changes"—"While My Guitar Gently Weeps" explores the Eastern notion about life's interconnectedness. As Harrison later recalled, "I always had to do about ten of Paul and John's songs before they'd give me the break." As he would later admit, Martin was just as guilty as Lennon and McCartney for shunting Harrison aside as a kind of junior member of the Beatles' partnership. While they may have diminished Harrison's role in the group at times, Martin recognized something greater in the quiet Beatle. To Martin's mind, Harrison had "something stronger than power. He had influence. Witness the fact that all of the boys followed him to India to sit at the feet of the Maharishi." And that night in the studio, Martin began to see the guitarist in a different light, just as he had begun to do with *Sgt. Pepper*'s "Within You, Without You." With Harrison singing his lead vocal with his acoustic guitar as his sole accompaniment, Martin was enchanted by the new composition. When Harrison completed work on the brief recording, he shouted up to Martin in the control booth, "Let's hear that back!" to which the Beatles' producer eagerly obliged.[13]

For Martin and the Beatles, the studio was dark the next day, as Lennon and McCartney worked at the latter's Cavendish Avenue home, putting the finishing touches on a new composition titled "Hey Jude." The bandmates and their producer may have had their trials and tribulations during the summer of 1968, but as Ringo observed years later, nothing excited the group more than working on a great new track. Inspired by Paul's recent visit with John's son Julian, "Hey Jude" had *single* written all over it. On Monday, July 29, with Martin taking a rare night off, McCartney debuted the song in Studio 2 with Ken Scott and new tape operator John Smith working up in the booth. The band recorded six takes of the song during the ensuing rehearsal, with McCartney on piano and lead vocals and Lennon's acoustic guitar, Harrison's electric guitar, and Starr's drums. By the time that Martin joined them at Abbey Road the next evening, "Hey Jude" was quickly taking shape as a Beatles song of inordinate length. "In the case of 'Hey Jude,'" George later recalled, "when we were recording the track, I thought that we had made it too long. It was very much a Paul song, and I couldn't understand what he was on about by just going round and round the same thing. And of course, it does become hypnotic." But even still, George could see the song's obvious hitmaking potential. The session itself was a muddled affair in spite of the Lennon-McCartney masterwork unfolding in Studio 2. For one thing, there was a film crew present from the National Music Council. They were on hand to film the Beatles for a documentary to be titled *Music!* As Ken Scott later recalled, "The film crew was supposed to work in such a way that no one would realize they were there, but of course they were getting in everyone's way and everyone was getting uptight about it." In the surviving footage, Harrison can be seen up in the booth with Martin and Scott. The quiet Beatle had sought refuge in the control room after McCartney rebuffed his suggestion that his lead guitar part echo McCartney's lyrics in a call-and-response fashion. For his part, Harrison felt the sting of McCartney's rejection. "Personally, I'd found that for the last couple of albums," Harrison later observed, "the freedom to be able to play as a musician was being curtailed, mainly by Paul." In situations such as the "Hey Jude" session, said Harrison, "Paul had fixed an idea in his brain as to how to record one of his songs. He wasn't open to anybody else's suggestions." When the session came to an end in the wee hours of the morning, Martin took home a rough stereo mix of "Hey Jude" for the purposes of scoring an orchestral arrangement.[14]

By this point, Martin had booked a half orchestra for an August 1 session at Trident Studios, a brand-new, five-month-old facility in London's St. Anne's Court. The studio was the brainchild of Norman Sheffield. "I'd opened the studio thinking it could be something very different to the antiseptic, almost laboratory atmosphere of Abbey Road and the other big studios," he later wrote. "People there wore white coats and behaved like boffins. It sucked the creative life out of artists. From the outset I'd wanted Trident to be a place where musicians could be free to express themselves. I wanted a different vibe." For McCartney and Harrison, Trident was already familiar territory, given the former's recent sessions there with Mary Hopkin and Harrison's work with newly minted Apple artist Jackie Lomax. But for Martin and the Beatles, Trident's real attraction was its Ampex eight-track recording capabilities.[15]

As it happened, EMI Studios had had three 3M eight-track recorders in its possession since May, although the machines were still in the hands of Abbey Road's maintenance personnel, who were putting the recorders through their paces and making various adjustments. "Whenever we got in a new piece of equipment at Abbey Road it went to Francis Thompson, our resident expert on tape machines, and he would spend about a year working on it," Ken Townsend later recalled. "The joke was always that when he'd finished with it he'd let the studios use it! He was unhappy with the overdub facility, it didn't come directly off the sync head as it did with the Studer four-track, and there was no facility for running the capstan motor varispeed from frequency control. Francis had to make some major modifications." For his part, George had known about the studio's 3M machines, but had kept it to himself. For Martin and the Beatles, the studio's recalcitrance had been an ongoing source of frustration, especially when they seemed disinterested in ramping the studio's technology up to contemporary standards. As Townsend recalled, "I remember George Harrison asking why we hadn't got one—'When are you going to get an eight-track, Ken?'—and we had a wooden replica of the new desk EMI was making to go with it. He said, 'When are you going to get a real one, not a wooden one?'"[16]

On the evening of Wednesday, July 31, Martin and the Beatles acclimated themselves to Trident. Working outside of EMI Studios meant that Ken Scott was unable to participate. Barry Sheffield, one of Trident's co-owners, worked the boards instead. With the tape running, the bandmates remade "Hey Jude" and began working on a carefully layered basic rhythm track featuring McCartney playing the studio's magnificent Bechstein grand piano and singing a guide vocal, Harrison on electric guitar, Lennon playing his

Jumbo acoustic, and Starr on drums. After recording four takes, Martin and the bandmates selected take one as the best before calling it a night. When they reconvened the next afternoon at Trident, the Beatles superimposed a number of overdubs to "Hey Jude," including McCartney's lead vocal and bass part, as well as three-part backing vocals from Lennon, McCartney, and Harrison. At that point, they were joined by Martin's thirty-six-piece orchestra, with the players including ten violinists, three violas, three cellists, two flautists, a bassoon, a contra bassoon, two clarinets, a contrabass clarinet, four trumpets, four trombones, two horns, two string basses, and a percussionist. By this juncture, Martin had come to see his score as an antidote to the song's extraordinary length, especially given the lengthy play-out chorus that concludes it. As George later recalled, "I realized that by putting an orchestra on you could add lots of weight to the riff by counter chords on the bottom end and bringing in trombones, and strings, and so on until it became a really big tumultuous thing. So that was my only real contribution to that. The real credit goes to Paul for thinking up the song in the first place, and the riff, and the way it extended." But still, "even when we'd finished, I was terrified because it was so darn long."[17]

With the orchestra tuned up and ready to play, Martin recorded the session players during an evening session from eight to eleven that night. As Chris Thomas later recalled, "The studio at Trident was long and narrow. When we did the orchestral overdub, we had to put the trombones at the very front so that they didn't poke anyone in the back!" With the eight-track machine providing twice the usual real estate, the producer wiped Paul's bass part, consigning the newly liberated track to afford the string section with more separation. Bill Jackman, one of the flautists and one of the sax players on "Lady Madonna," remembered playing the "refrain over and over—the repeated riff which plays in the long fadeout." After recording Martin's score, the session players were invited to provide backing vocals and handclaps to the song's play-out section. For the most part, the musicians good-naturedly joined in; as with previous Beatles session players, they were keen on gaining the bragging rights associated with one of the Fab Four's recordings. But better still, the chance to provide backing vocals on "Hey Jude" doubled their session fees. However, not everyone was thrilled at the opportunity, with one of the players walking out of Trident in a huff, saying, "I'm not going to clap my hands and sing Paul McCartney's bloody song!"[18]

Over the next several days, George conducted mono and stereo mixing sessions for "Hey Jude" at Trident, with Barry Sheffield assisting. As Martin worked to adjust the track to the Beatles' specifications, their producer repeated his concerns about the song's length, which clocked in at more than seven minutes. The bandmates immediately countered with the example of Richard Harris's "MacArthur Park," which had notched a top-five US and UK hit that June. Composed by Oklahoma-born songwriter Jimmy Webb, who had made his name in the mid-1960s with "Up, Up, and Away" and "By the Time I Get to Phoenix," "MacArthur Park" had enjoyed massive airplay and international sales with a length of seven minutes and twenty-one seconds. But George remained unconvinced, given that "Hey Jude" had a substantial length, for a Beatles track at least, of seven minutes and eleven seconds. "It was a long song," he later observed. "In fact, after I timed it, I actually said, 'You can't make a single that long.' I was shouted down by the boys—not for the first time in my life—and John asked, 'Why not?' I couldn't think of a good answer, really, except the pathetic one that disc jockeys wouldn't play it." And that's when John played his trump card: "They will if it's us," he told the producer. There was also the matter of manufacturing a 45 rpm record with the appropriate fidelity for a song of such length. Clearly, the folks at Harris's label—ABC Records' Dunhill subsidiary—had managed to handle the unusual length posed by "MacArthur Park." But for his part, McCartney wasn't worried. EMI's technical team had already overcome a number of manufacturing challenges in the past. "It was longer than any single had been," Paul observed, "but we had a good bunch of engineers. We asked how long a 45 could be. They said that four minutes was about all you could squeeze into the grooves before it seriously started to lose volume and everyone had to turn the sound up. But they did some very clever stuff, squeezing the bit that didn't have to be loud, then allowing the rest more room. Somehow, they got seven minutes on there, which was quite an engineering feat."[19]

But when it came to "Hey Jude," George and the Beatles weren't quite out of the woods just yet. On Thursday, August 8, Ken Scott began listening to the Trident mix in the Studio 2 control room. "Back at Abbey Road," Scott recalled, "I got in well before the group. Acetates were being cut and I went up to hear one. On different equipment, with different EQ [equalization] levels and different monitor settings, it sounded awful, nothing like it had at Trident," where he had observed the Beatles working during the previous week. When George arrived shortly afterward, he asked Ken about the Trident mix, and the engineer didn't mince his words. "Well, when I was at Trident," Scott replied, "I was blown away, but listening to it here, it sounds like shit." And that's when John stepped into the control room, and George drolly informed the Beatle that "Ken thinks the mix sounds like shit." In short order, the other Beatles joined George and Ken in the booth in order to play back the Trident mixes, which, sure enough, sounded murky. Not long afterward, George happened to bump into Geoff Emerick in the corridor outside the control room. Sensing an opportunity, George invited Geoff into the booth to listen to the problematic mix from Trident. Emerick could tell right away that "Hey Jude" was "a great, catchy melody, but the recording quality was poor, with no top end whatsoever." For their part, the Beatles were elated to see their estranged engineer. "Ah, the prodigal son returns!" Lennon exclaimed. Sitting in front of the console, Geoff worked the controls on a Beatles session for the first time in a month. "Eventually we got it to sound pretty good," he later recalled, "although the track still didn't have the kind of in-your-face presence that characterizes most Beatles recordings done at Abbey Road." A few moments later, standing with Geoff in the studio corridor, George asked him to reconsider his decision to abandon his work with the Beatles, which Geoff politely declined. But he could see the disappointment on the producer's face. "I understand, Geoff, I understand," he replied, with a hint of sadness in his voice.[20]

With "Hey Jude" on the straight and narrow, sonically speaking, the Beatles' eighteenth UK single—and inaugural Apple Records release—was finally ready for the music marketplace. For his part, McCartney, like Martin, was slightly concerned about the song's length. A few days before the single's release, the Beatle gathered feedback about "Hey Jude" from none other than the Rolling Stones' front man. "I remember taking an acetate down to the Vesuvio," he later recalled, "a three-in-the-morning-dossing-round-on-beanbags type club in Tottenham Court Road. As it was a suitable time in the evening, I got the DJ to put it on. I remember Mick Jagger coming up to me and saying, 'It's like two songs, man. It's got the song and then the whole na, na, na at the end.'" As it turned out, Lennon's brash confidence about "Hey Jude" was right on the money. Not only did DJs play the song in heavy rotation, but consumers bought it in droves. Released in the United Kingdom on August 30, the "Hey Jude" backed with "Revolution" single proved to be the band's strongest commercial release to date. By September 14, "Hey Jude" sat atop the UK charts, where it was supplanted a few weeks later by Hopkin's "Those Were the Days." Needless to say, Martin was elated to learn that "the roll" would remain unabated. By mid-September, *NME* reported UK sales of more than two million copies. Stateside, "Hey Jude" backed with "Revolution" proved to be a veritable blockbuster, where it held *Billboard*'s number-one spot for an incredible nine straight weeks. For his part, John was thrilled to see his boast validated by the single's runaway success, but he was still miffed about George and the bandmates' dismissal of "Revolution" as a potential

A-side. As he later remarked, "I wanted to put it out as a single, but they said it wasn't good enough. We put out 'Hey Jude,' which was worthy—but we could have had both."[21]

As it happened, John had ensured that the "Hey Jude" single left the manufacturing plant with a little something extra nestled inside its grooves—and having escaped George's detection, no less. That *something*—an undeleted expletive that occurred at 2:58 in "Hey Jude"—originated when Paul shouted "fucking hell!" after playing a wrong note. As balance engineer Ken Scott later remarked: "I was told about it at the time but could never hear it. But once I had it pointed out I can't miss it now. I have a sneaking suspicion they knew all along." While their producer may not have registered McCartney's invective, the bandmates were well aware of the accursed moment in the mix. Indeed, tape operator John Smith remembered Lennon gleefully pointing out the expletive during playback. "Paul hit a clunker on the piano and said a naughty word," John later reported, "but I insisted we leave it in, buried just low enough so that it can barely be heard. Most people won't ever spot it—but we'll know it's there." It was a moment of sophomoric, postadolescent humor to be sure—a reminder that the Beatles were still twentysomethings with a lot of growing up left to do. But the incident with "Hey Jude" was also reminiscent of similar moments across the group's corpus, including the ribald "tit tit" chorus in *Rubber Soul*'s "Girl" or, more recently, Lennon's vulgar reference to Epstein in the waning strains of "Baby, You're a Rich Man."[22]

As August gathered steam, George and the Beatles' efforts on the new long-player increased precipitously. The bandmates' incredible pace was rendered even more impressive by the fact that they devoted several sessions and some hundred takes to a single composition—Harrison's "Not Guilty"—that wouldn't even make the album's final cut. Begun back on August 7, "Not Guilty" racked up forty-six takes, most of them false starts, during the very first session. With a basic rhythm track composed of Harrison's electric guitar and guide vocal, Lennon's electric piano, McCartney's bass, and Starr's drums, the tongue-in-cheek, self-referential "Not Guilty" proved to be difficult to capture given the song's shifting time signatures and elliptical introduction. As "Not Guilty" progressed, Lennon shifted from electric piano to the studio's harpsichord. Meanwhile, Harrison worked painstakingly on a lead guitar over-dub that had the studio techs working all hours of the night. As Brian Gibson later recalled, "George [Harrison] asked us to put his guitar amplifier at one end of one of the echo chambers, with a microphone at the other end to pick up the output. He sat playing the guitar in the studio control room with a line plugged through to the chamber." That same evening, Friday, August 9, found McCartney toiling on a new composition, "Mother Nature's Son," in the wee hours of the morning—and pointedly after the other Beatles had gone home for the night. As with "Blackbird," "Mother Nature's Son" was a stirring acoustic ballad. But like Harrison earlier that same evening, McCartney had ventured out on his own, working individually to bring his latest song to fruition without benefit of, or artistic input from, the other Beatles. It was a practice that would have long-running implications—especially for Martin. That same evening, Paul hit upon the idea of adorning "Mother Nature's Son" with a brass accompaniment. Dutifully preparing to concoct a score, George took home an acetate of the song for reference purposes.[23]

In contrast with "Mother Nature's Son," Lennon's "Yer Blues," which he debuted in Studio 2 in mid-August, was a group effort that had begun as Lennon's pointed response to the British blues boom and ended with the bandmates working together in arguably the closest quarters of their recording career. The idea of recording "Yer Blues" in the cozy Studio 2 annex had actually emerged during a recent session for "Not Guilty," which by mid-August still hadn't been captured to Harrison's satisfaction. The Beatles set up their gear in the tiny room in order to rehearse a basic rhythm track for their fiery fusion of blues and rock 'n' roll. As Ken Scott later recalled, "With the instruments that close together, there was so much leakage of all the instruments into all of the mics that it was just a question of doing the best you could to blend it all together to get the sound, because you couldn't pull up the drums without increasing the level of the guitars as well. That said, I loved the drum sound we got, and it was one of the best drum sounds on the album as far as I'm concerned." After perfecting "Yer Blues" over fourteen takes, McCartney took a break, leaving the others to lapse into the kind of protracted instrumental jam that had characterized their post-*Pepper* malaise. Martin made no secret of his distaste for such unfocused studio meanderings. That same week in mid-August, George and the bandmates took up another one of the Esher demos, a peculiar Lennon concoction titled "What's the New Mary Jane." McCartney and Starr declined to participate in the song's rehearsal, leaving Harrison and Ono, along with Mal Evans, to provide the instrumentation. Over four takes, the makeshift Beatles, with Lennon on piano and Harrison on acoustic guitar, improvised a melody in concert with the composition's bizarre lyrics and repetitive chorus: "What a shame Mary Jane had a pain at the party." Take four came to a sudden conclusion with John shouting up to the booth, "Let's hear it, before we get taken away!"[24]

Fortunately for George, as the month wore on, the bandmates briefly righted their ship for "Rocky Raccoon," McCartney's tongue-in-cheek country and western number. Rehearsing the song during nine takes on Thursday, August 15, the Beatles' instrumentation included McCartney's acoustic guitar and guide vocal, Lennon's bass, and Starr's drums. In a rare moment in the studio, the two Georges exchanged places, with Harrison up in the booth with Ken Scott and John Smith, while Martin contributed a honky-tonk piano down below. As "Rocky Raccoon" quickly took shape, Lennon, McCartney, and Harrison provided backing vocals, with Lennon also overdubbing a harmonica part. The next day, August 16, Harrison pressed his case for "While My Guitar Gently Weeps" by convening his colleagues to perform a full-band version of the searing rock song. As they rehearsed a basic rhythm track over fourteen takes, the Beatles' instrumentation included Harrison's electric guitar, McCartney's bass, Lennon's organ, and Starr's drums. As it happened, Martin was very likely not in attendance on August 16. The official studio documentation listed "While My Guitar Gently Weeps" as being "produced by the Beatles." Martin's whereabouts were unclear. He was preparing a new album of instrumental cover versions to fulfill his contractual obligation to United Artists, and, as would shortly become known, he had plans of his own in the works. As technical engineer Brian Gibson later recalled, during this period "George Martin was starting to relinquish control over the group. There were a number of occasions—holidays, and when he had other recording commitments—when he wasn't available for sessions, and they would just get on and produce it themselves."[25]

Meanwhile, George was back in the control booth on Tuesday, August 20, in order to lead the brass overdub for "Mother Nature's Son." That same evening, the growing tensions among the bandmates were revealed in stark fashion. Sitting up in the booth, Ken Scott observed as McCartney and Martin discussed the brass arrangement with the session players down below in Studio 2. "Everything was great, everyone was in great spirits," Scott recalled. "It felt really good. Suddenly, halfway through, John and Ringo walked in and you could cut the atmosphere with a knife. An instant change. It was like that for 10 minutes and then as soon as they left it felt great again. It was very bizarre."[26]

By this point, Martin was becoming increasingly aware of the band's fragmentation. But he didn't merely attribute it to growing emotional tensions. Since the beginning of the recording sessions for the new long-player, George had been troubled by the sheer amount of material—some thirty new compositions—that they had gleaned during their Indian sojourn. "I was a bit overwhelmed by them," he later recalled, "and yet underwhelmed at the same time because some of them weren't great." A case in point emerged during the same evening as the "Mother Nature's Son" brass overdub, when McCartney recorded the slapdash "Wild Honey Pie," a relatively weak song in comparison to the contemplative, well-wrought "Mother Nature's Son." The wide range of different compositions necessitated a multipronged strategy that forced Martin to act as a kind of executive producer. "For the first time I had to split myself three ways because at any one time we were recording in different studios. It became very fragmented, and that was where my assistant Chris Thomas did a lot of work." To make matters even more complicated, EMI had recently imposed a deadline, asking that George deliver the LP by the end of October in order to target its release with the holiday shopping season, a looming target that rendered the producer's way of thinking, which he was shortly to reveal, even more suspect.[27]

As for the bandmates and their growing interpersonal anxieties, things came to a head on Thursday, August 22, when McCartney unveiled a new upbeat rocker called "Back in the USSR," a Cold War parody with affectionate nods to the Beach Boys' "California Girls" and Chuck Berry's "Back in the USA." It was also the day when Ringo quit the Beatles. As it happened, the drummer barely attended the session at all. Ron Richards, George's partner with AIR, recalled the genesis of the incident: "Ringo was always sitting in the reception area waiting, just sitting there or reading a newspaper. He used to sit there for hours waiting for the others to turn up. One night he couldn't stand it any longer, got fed up, and left." For his part, George had seen it coming, had recognized Ringo's growing frustrations with his friends. Confronted with Ringo's glaring absence and purported plans to leave the band, the Beatles and their brain trust agreed to a veil of secrecy. Like George, Richard Lush had observed Ringo's malaise growing steadily worse since *Sgt. Pepper*, when he often acted as an on-call player. "Ringo probably had the hardest job in the band, playing for hours and hours," Lush recalled, "and he probably shared the same view that we occasionally had, 'I played that last night for nine hours. Do I have to do it again?' He had a hard job trying to please them." In this instance, Ringo was especially frustrated by Paul's insistence on coaching him about how to play the drums on "Back in the USSR." It wasn't the first time that someone had departed the Beatles' universe. McCartney had walked out during the "She Said She Said" sessions at the tail-end of *Revolver*, and Emerick had conspicuously made his exit only the month before Starr's departure.[28]

With Starr having left the other Beatles to their own devices, Martin watched as Lennon, McCartney, and Harrison shrugged the incident off for the moment and proceeded with a basic track for "Back in the USSR," with

McCartney on the drums, Lennon playing bass, and Harrison on lead guitar. The next evening, additional bass and lead guitar parts were adorned on the track, along with soaring Beach Boys–styled harmonies and a rocking piano. The song's signature jet plane introduction was supplied courtesy of the EMI tape library's *Volume 17: Jet and Piston Aeroplane*.

On Wednesday, August 28, George and the Ringo-less bandmates relocated to Trident to take advantage yet again of the studio's eight-track capabilities. That evening, Lennon unveiled the elegant "Dear Prudence." The song's basic track featured Lennon and Harrison's exquisitely layered acoustic guitars, and, as dictated by the Beatles' new circumstances, McCartney on drums. Over the next few days, the group superimposed a variety of different overdubs, including Paul's inventive piano and flügelhorn tracks. By this juncture, the looming issue of Abbey Road's failure to embrace eight-track technology had clearly reached its breaking point as far as the Beatles and their production team were concerned.

But any confrontation with Stagge and the obstinate, conservative members of EMI's technical staff would have to wait for the moment. On September 4, the Beatles were scheduled to record performances of "Hey Jude" and "Revolution" at Twickenham under the direction of Michael Lindsay-Hogg and with the newly appointed director of Apple Films, Denis O'Dell, in attendance. With David Frost serving as host, the promotional films were destined for broadcast on Frost's popular British talk show, *Frost on Sunday*, and on the American variety show *The Smothers Brothers Comedy Hour*. To everyone's relief, Starr had returned to the fold only the day before, his reappearance heralded by Harrison with bouquets of flowers festooned about Studio 2. For his part, George understood exactly how Ringo had felt at the time, later observing, "I think they were all feeling a little paranoid. When you have a rift between people—if you go to a party and the husband and wife have been having a row—there's a tension, an atmosphere. And you wonder whether you are making things worse by being there. I think that was the kind of situation we found with Ringo. He was probably feeling a little bit odd because of the mental strangeness with John and Yoko and Paul, and none of them having quite the buddiness they used to have. He might have said to himself, 'Am I the cause?'" At some level, George may have even wondered the same thing himself. In the end, Ringo had been summoned back to the fold via a well-timed telegram from his friends: "You're the best rock 'n' roll drummer in the world. Come on home, we love you." For Ringo, that was reason enough to make his return. "And so I came back," he said, reasoning that "we all needed that little shake-up."[29]

At Twickenham, the Beatles reveled in the act of performing in front of a studio audience for the first time in two years. As it was, they were actually miming their performances of "Hey Jude" and "Revolution," and as for the audience, the assembled throng had been helpfully rounded up in the city earlier in the day by Mal Evans. In addition to noting that the group hadn't appeared live "for goodness knows how long," Frost playfully introduced the Beatles as "the greatest tea-room orchestra in the world." Moments earlier, the bandmates couldn't help taking advantage of Frost and Martin's combined presence and tried their hand at playing "By George! It's *The David Frost Theme*." And with that, the group began miming "Hey Jude" for the cameras, save for the vocals, which were recorded live. During the famous coda, the spectators mobbed the bandmates on stage for a spirited sing-along. It was a bravura moment indeed, and the excellent vibe on stage didn't escape the notice of the Beatles, who were thrilled to be playing in front of an audience. Long after Mal's audience slipped back into the night, the bandmates hung out at Twickenham, drinking scotch and Cokes and reminiscing about performing in front of an audience again. "They were jamming and having a good time and having a better time than they thought they were going to have," Lindsay-Hogg remembered. "So they sort of thought maybe there is some way they can do something again in some sort of performance way." To the Beatles, it seemed like a splendid idea, albeit one that would have to wait at least until the new year, when the long-player had hopefully been completed.[30]

While they were willing to wait a few more months before contemplating a live performance, time had run out, as far as the Beatles were concerned, for eight-track recording to be at their beck and call at EMI Studios. On September 3, the Beatles finally took matters into their own hands. That same day, they had learned what George already knew: namely, that EMI's maintenance engineers had been in possession of 3M recorders since May. Having learned that there were eight-track machines in Francis Thompson's office, they decided to "liberate" one of them for their immediate use. "When you've got four innovative lads from Liverpool who want to make better recordings, and they've got a smell of the machine, matters can take a different course," technical engineer Dave Harries later recalled. With Scott and Harries as their willing confederates, the bandmates removed one of the 3M machines from Thompson's office and installed it in Studio 2, where they resumed work on "While My Guitar Gently Weeps." For the Beatles, commandeering the 3M machine must have felt like a victory in the face of EMI's arcane ways, an opportunity to flex their muscles as the biggest artists on the record conglomerate's roster—on the planet, really. For his part, Martin was no stranger to EMI's old-school ways. Indeed, he had long crowed about the lack of the availability of contemporary technology at Abbey Road.[31]

But in the great moment of emancipation, when the Beatles' engineering team had finally succeeded in prying loose the eight-track recorder from the white-coated personnel upstairs, George was silent, having not come out to the studio that night. Nor was he on the scene when the group taped their performance for *Frost on Sunday*. In fact, by this point, George wasn't even in England. As the Beatles would shortly learn, George had devised a "little shake-up" of his own.

18

UP ON THE ROOF

O N THURSDAY, SEPTEMBER 12, George mailed a postcard addressed to Ken Scott and the bandmates at 3 Abbey Road, London. At the time, he was writing from the northern coast of Sicily, not too far from the vicinity of Villa Blanca, a rustic resort town. "I have found the perfect spot for a recording studio," he wrote. "Only hang up is that there is no electricity. Heavenly weather and swimming, completely cut off—no papers or radio. We chalk the days on the wall and cross them off one by one. Sorry I am not with you while you are working hard." By then, Chris Thomas had shared the news with the other members of the Beatles' production team that George had taken a breather, leaving his AIR protégé with a simple instruction: "I'm going on holiday. You take over the Beatles for a while." Over the years, George had begun to perfect the art of tactical withdrawals in terms of his role with the band, but this may have been his boldest move yet. Other than his terse instruction to Chris, he hadn't bothered to inform the group about his plans. Still a virtual outsider to the Beatles' circle, Chris was about to undergo a trial by fire. When Paul McCartney encountered him at the first session after George's unexpected departure, Chris explained that George had suggested he assist the Beatles with production during his absence, to which Paul replied, "Well, if you want to produce us, you can produce us. If you don't, we might just tell you to fuck off."[1]

For George, his Italian holiday was laden with risk. For six breathtaking years, he had done everything he possibly could to consolidate his place in the Beatles' world—to bring their musical aspirations to life in the studio but also, just as surely, to enrich himself, both artistically and financially. Like the Beatles, he had desired an opulent lifestyle. He had made no bones about it years earlier, when he set his sights on finding a beat band to ride to the top of the hit parade. His goal, plain and simple, had been to lay his hands on a new E-Type Jaguar like the one owned by Norrie Paramor, his archrival at EMI. And in recent years, with the success or failure of AIR in the balance, the stakes had grown even higher. There were his partners to think about, of course. On a personal level, George knew that his decisions held larger implications beyond himself. He had an ex-wife and two children in the suburbs who depended on him and a growing family with Judy in the city. But still, George took a leap of faith in his relationship with the Beatles. That long summer of despair had left him in a state of doubt about his place in the band's chemistry—and about whether they even needed him at all at this juncture outside of the occasional orchestration or some such musical arrangement.

When George finally rolled back into London on September 26, with Judy and baby Lucie safely ensconced at home, he was met with a set of acetates for the songs that Chris and the Beatles had completed during his absence. The bandmates had clearly been working on heat, George discovered. "Cry Baby Cry" and "Helter Skelter" had progressed considerably during his absence, and "While My Guitar Gently Weeps" had seen a tremendous transformation, with its latest incarnation sporting a searing guitar solo from Eric Clapton. Meanwhile, Lennon's impressive pace had continued, with a strange, satirical effusion called "Glass Onion" nearing completion, along with an intricate, multilayered song that had been inspired back in the summer after George had presented John with a magazine, its cover emblazoned with the unsettling words HAPPINESS IS A WARM GUN. And then there was "I Will," a romantic acoustic ballad from Paul, and "Piggies," an acerbic political critique from Harrison. Thomas and the Beatles' efforts during Martin's absence were rounded out by "Birthday," a high-octane number that they had improvised in the studio. But most importantly, what George discovered upon rejoining the Beatles at Trident Studios on Tuesday, October 1, 1968, was that they were acting like a band again.

As he played the acetates, George was ecstatic, telephoning Chris to congratulate him on a job well done. His protégé, it seemed, had been exactly the caretaker that George hoped he would be—and more. "George Martin couldn't believe it. He phoned me up so excited and happy," Thomas later recalled. "When George came back from holiday the whole thing gathered more and more momentum. We were working in different studios with different guys and it all became sort of a factory." Ken Scott later chalked up the Beatles' reversal of fortunes to Ringo's return to the fold. "Once Ringo left, suddenly they realized that they couldn't quite take this all so much for granted," Ken later remarked. "When he returned, that was really the sort of high spot when they became a band again. All four would be down in the studio working hard. We got more done during that period of time when George Martin was on holiday and Chris Thomas took over for him. It was phenomenal." But Scott also recognized what Martin had observed amid the group's calculus over the past year. With the Beatles' most recent studio practices, "once the basic was put down, the songwriter was the one that would be in charge for the rest of the recording, and the others might not even show up for days on end until the song was finished," Scott wrote. "If Paul had to come in to put a bass track on one of George's songs, Paul would come in that day, do his thing, and then leave. Every song was very much like that. The individual songwriter took control of the process."[2]

George was absolutely blown away. The Beatles may not be a working unit, yet they had found a way to work together, even if their approach meant elevating the desires of the individual over the group. But at the same time, as George played the acetates yet again, he could hear a space, just as he had done in years gone by, where he could make the bandmates' latest batch of songs even better. When he arrived at Trident on October 1, George was presented with a new number from Paul, a jazzy throwback called "Honey Pie." That evening, the bandmates rehearsed a basic rhythm track with McCartney's piano and guide vocal, Harrison's bass, Starr's drums, and Lennon's electric guitar. By the end of the session, McCartney had begun to imagine a brass and woodwind arrangement. And Martin was all too happy to oblige, taking home an acetate of "Honey Pie" in order to concoct a score. But as it happened, the Beatles wanted to welcome him back to the studio in fine style. Only for George, the celebration wouldn't involve flowers but rather a prank. That night, Jimmy Webb, the budding songwriter behind "MacArthur Park," was also working at Trident. Spotting Webb, McCartney took a break from rehearsing "Honey Pie" and invited the American into the studio, where he introduced Webb to Martin as "Tom Dowd from Atlantic Records." As Jimmy later recalled, "I was so terrified and so overawed by where I was that I did not correct this impression, and they proceeded to treat me as though I were Tom Dowd. They were asking me what I thought of this guitar solo and that guitar solo, and I was doing the best I could. I didn't want to disappoint them by telling them that I was only Jimmy Webb! Finally, after what I thought was entirely too much of it, George Harrison tapped me on the shoulder and said, 'By the way, man, I loved those strings on "MacArthur Park."'" Realizing that they'd been had—that the Liverpudlians had had a laugh at their expense—Martin and Webb joined in on the merriment. During that same period, a young Birmingham musician named Jeff Lynne also found himself in the bandmates' orbit when he was performing with the Idle Race. "To be in the same room as the four of them caused me not to sleep for, like, three days," Lynne later recalled.[3]

A few days after work had convened on "Honey Pie," Harrison presented a new composition titled "Savoy Truffle," a hard-driving confection that found its roots in Mackintosh's Good News chocolates, his friend Eric Clapton's favorite dietary vice. With Harrison imagining a "beefy" sax sound to accompany his song, Martin dutifully began preparing a score, just as he would begin doing the following week after McCartney debuted a piano ballad, "Martha My Dear," which had been inspired by his sheepdog. That same evening, Friday, October 4, Martin recorded his score for "Honey Pie," which called for seven session players, including a raft of saxophones and clarinet. And with Paul working on heat with "Martha My Dear," George readily obliged the songwriter's wishes, conducting fourteen musicians for his hastily prepared brass and string arrangement. At the end of the night, George even managed to engage in the kind of sound trickery that he adored. Given the Jazz Age feel of "Honey Pie," they had decided to record the sound of an old phonograph record being cued up at the start of the song. With McCartney singing "now she's hit the big time in the USA!" Martin clipped the high and low ends of the frequency range associated with the Beatle's vocal and recorded the sound of a scratch 78 rpm record to complete the sonic picture.

As mid-October approached, the songs were coming in a deluge. In short order, Martin supervised lengthy sessions devoted to Harrison's somber "Long, Long, Long," as well as to Lennon's breezy "I'm So Tired" and yet another number from Rishikesh, the crowd-pleasing "The Continuing Story of Bungalow Bill." For the latter, everyone got in on the act, with Chris Thomas contributing an elegant Mellotron part and Yoko Ono making her Beatles singing debut. Meanwhile, McCartney continued working in the margins—this time, as he made progress on a bluesy rocker titled "Why Don't We Do It in the Road." In short order, Martin's orchestral work had returned with a vengeance. Up first was "Glass Onion," which, in Thomas and the Beatles' production, featured an avant-garde outro involving the sound of breaking glass and the voice of football commentator Kenneth Wolstenholme screaming, "It's a goal!" Martin replaced the song's bizarre ending with an understated string arrangement played by an octet of studio musicians, which imbued the coda with a much-needed sense of irony. With the same players in tow, Martin turned to Harrison's "Piggies," with his score affording the song a buoyant dose of English pomp and circumstance. That same week, the producer completed work on Harrison's "Savoy Truffle" with a heavy sax overdub. As Brian Gibson later recalled, "The session men were playing really well—there's nothing like a good brass section letting rip—and it sounded fantastic. But having got this really nice sound, George [Harrison] turned to Ken Scott and said, 'Right, I want to distort it.' After Scott complied and doused the track with ADT, Harrison announced to the sax players, 'Before you listen, I've got to apologize for what I've done to your beautiful sound. Please forgive me—but it's the way I want it!'"[4]

By the week of October 15, Martin and the Beatles were entering the home stretch. In the days since George's return, his production team had been carrying out mono remixing sessions even as he supervised new material with the Beatles, including "Julia," John's heartrending ballad memorializing his late mother, who had died in July 1958. And with that, the long-player was all but complete, save for a few housekeeping duties such as Chris Thomas's work on "While My Guitar Gently Weeps" to ensure that, at Eric Clapton's request, the guitar solo was appropriately modulated to sound more "Beatley." "I was given the grand job of waggling the oscillator on the 'Gently Weeps' mixes," Thomas later recalled. "So we did this flanging thing, really wobbling the oscillator in the mix. I did that for hours. What a boring job!" Meanwhile, Ken Scott often worked closely with the bandmates, usually McCartney, in order to carry out the mono and stereo remixing sessions. With Paul shifting the faders up and down, Ken observed as the Beatle pointedly mixed two different versions of "Helter Skelter." For the stereo remix, Paul included Ringo screaming "I've got blisters on my fingers!" during the coda. Yet for the mono version, he purposefully omitted the non sequitur. When Scott asked McCartney about his decision, he told the engineer that Beatles fans were listening for the different versions of songs, so Martin and the Beatles had begun trying to make mono and stereo different. That way, die-hard fans would buy both the stereo and mono versions of the album. At this juncture, all that was left were the attendant sequencing activities for the voluminous and often-enigmatic collection of songs. But as it happened, only two Beatles would be available to see the album through to fruition. That very week, Ringo had gone abroad for a family vacation in Sardinia, where he lounged on Peter Sellers's yacht. On one occasion, the yacht's captain spoke movingly about octopuses. "He told me that they hang out in their caves," Ringo later remarked, "and they go around the seabed finding shiny stones and tin cans and bottles to put in front of their cave like a garden. I thought this was fabulous." A few days later, Harrison flew out to Los Angeles, leaving Lennon and McCartney alone with Martin at Abbey Road to bring the long-player in for a landing.[5]

At five o'clock in the evening on Wednesday, October 16, Martin, Lennon, and McCartney, along with a production team that included Ken Scott and John Smith, assembled at Abbey Road for the most remarkable mixing and sequencing session of the Beatles' career—perhaps of *any* career. Commandeering Studios 1, 2, and 3, along with Rooms 41 and 42 in EMI's complex, George held a twenty-four-hour session in order to sequence, band, and cross-fade thirty-one Beatles tracks, including the McCartney snippet "Can You Take Me Back?" recorded in mid-September but omitting "Not Guilty" and "What's the New Mary Jane," which were no longer in contention for the album. Not surprisingly, assembling the long-player's running order took some figuring out, given the motley assorted songs' wide-ranging genres and styles. Eventually, they settled on a thematic approach in order to remedy the situation while still attempting to adhere to Martin's long-held notion that the best approach is to begin each long-playing side with a stirring, upbeat track. In order to accent the LP's sense of variety, Harrison's songs were spread out across all four sides of the double album. With "Back in the USSR" launching the record into action with a rock 'n' roll punch, side B was devoted to the numerous animal songs that had been accrued—namely, "Blackbird," "Piggies," and "Rocky Raccoon"—with side C serving as the site of the album's heavier rock numbers, including "Birthday," "Yer Blues," "Everybody's Got Something to Hide Except Me and My Monkey," and "Helter Skelter." In perhaps the LP's brashest move, they opted to conclude the album with the eerie snippet "Can You Take Me Back?" and the experimental, apocalyptic "Revolution 9," followed closely on its heels by the intentionally syrupy closer "Good Night." Even stranger still, "Revolution 9" now sported a spoken-word introduction in the form of a conversation between Martin and Apple office manager Alistair Taylor, who begs the producer's forgiveness for some unknown slight:

> Taylor: . . . bottle of claret for you if I'd realized. I'd forgotten all about
> it, George. I'm sorry.
> Martin: Well, *do* next time.
> Taylor: Will you forgive me?
> Martin: Mm, yes.
> Taylor: Cheeky bitch.

With the running order having been decided, George took a page out of his own book and began sequencing the songs together using a series of cross-fades, just as he had done on *Sgt. Pepper*. Working as a team, Martin, Lennon, and McCartney identified key moments between songs in order to weave them together—and often in highly innovative fashion, such as the manner in which "The Continuing Story of Bungalow Bill" explodes into "While My Guitar Gently Weeps" or later when Jack Fallon's meandering fiddle collides with the blues power of "Why Don't We Do It in the Road?"

Years later, audio tech Alan Brown recalled the sight that welcomed him to EMI Studios on the morning of Thursday, October 17. "I remember arriving at the studios to find the Beatles still there," said Brown, "They had been there all night, finalizing the master tapes. . . . They were all over the place, room 41, the front listening room—anywhere—almost every room they could get. It was a frantic last-minute job." Martin, too, must have felt that the effort was slapdash, that it paled in comparison to the painstaking work that had concluded *Sgt. Pepper*. At some point, he took Ken Scott aside and "did something that will endear him to me forever," the engineer later wrote. "Ken, I have to be honest," said Martin, standing alone with Scott in the studio corridor. "I don't want you to feel bad about this, and I don't want you to take this personally, but I don't think that this album is going to win a Grammy," Martin said, before adding that "it's no reflection on you." To Scott's mind, Martin "meant it in all kindness because the Beatles were expected to do something even greater than *Sgt. Pepper* and keep on winning Grammys. It was obvious that this one wouldn't because it was such a different album from what they'd done previously. George was looking after me in a fatherly way." Scott would never forget that moment when the most celebrated record producer in the world took a few minutes to reassure a young engineer. "Just the fact that he made the effort blew me away," he wrote.[6]

By the time that Martin, Lennon, and McCartney wrapped things up that night, the album was ready to be mastered and shipped off to the manufacturing plant. As frantic and chaotic as things had seemed at times, they had succeeded in completing the long-player with plenty of time to spare in order to ensure a holiday release. For several months, the group considered naming the album *A Doll's House* at the suggestion of Lennon, who wanted to pay homage to Norwegian playwright Henrik Ibsen. They even went so far as to commission a cover illustration by Scottish artist Patrick (John Byrne). But with the July 1968 release of Family's *Music in a Doll's House*, the Beatles were forced to go back to the drawing board. At the suggestion of Robert Fraser, McCartney met with pop-art designer Richard Hamilton, who proposed that the cover effect a dramatic contrast with the colorful albums of the band's recent psychedelic past. Hamilton recommended a plain white cover imprinted with individual numbers in order to assume the exclusive quality of a limited edition—although in this case it was a limited edition composed, quite ironically, of some five million copies. At Hamilton's urging, the bandmates decided to name the album *The Beatles*, a deliberately simple title in relation to *Sgt. Pepper's Lonely Hearts Club Band*. But as the album's title, *The Beatles* never really stood a chance. With its stark white cover art, the two-record set became known as *The White Album* within scant days of its release. *The White Album*'s packaging included four individual color shots of the Beatles taken by John Kelly, the photographer behind Cilla Black's recent album *Sher-oo!*, along with a poster-sized lyric sheet adorned with a collage of additional photographs.

Released on November 22—exactly five years after *With the Beatles*—*The White Album* quickly ruled the charts. With eighteen months having passed since the Beatles' last studio album, the new LP was easily the most anticipated rock release of the year. In the United Kingdom, *The White Album* debuted in the top spot, eventually lording over the charts for eight weeks. Stateside, the long-player was even more successful, with Capitol turning over receipts for 3.3 million copies in the album's first four days of release. All told, the album held *Billboard*'s top spot for nine weeks. The critical response nearly, but not quite, matched the records' overwhelming commercial success. Writing in the *Sunday Times*, Derek Jewell observed that "of course, the new Beatles double LP is the best thing in pop since *Sgt. Pepper*. Their sounds, for those open in ear and mind, should long ago have established their supremacy. . . . They have misses, but there aren't many. It's a world map of contemporary music, drawn with unique flair. Musically, there is beauty, horror, surprise, chaos, order. And that is the world; and that is what the Beatles are about. Created by, creating for, their age." Meanwhile, the *Times*' William Mann was less generous, writing that "the poetic standard varies from inspired ('Blackbird') through allusive ('Glass Onion') and obscure ('Happiness Is a Warm Gun') to jokey, trite, and deliberately meaningless. There are too many private jokes and too much pastiche to convince me that Lennon and McCartney are still pressing forward," he argued, but at the same time, "these 30 tracks contain plenty to be studied, enjoyed, and gradually appreciated more fully in the coming months." Writing in *Rolling Stone*, which had just celebrated its first anniversary, Jann Wenner hailed *The White Album* as the Beatles' best work to date, as well as a portrait of "the history and synthesis of pop music." Intuitively understanding the Beatles' aesthetics vis-à-vis 1968, Wenner added that the group's multigenre, hybridized approach to rock music is "so strong that they make it uniquely theirs, and uniquely the Beatles. They are so good that they not only expand the idiom, but they are also able to penetrate it and take it further."[7]

For his part, Martin remain unconvinced, even years later, about the overarching quality of *The White Album*. Perhaps his recollections found their origins in the emotional highs and lows that he experienced along with the bandmates and their crew during the record's production, although rather pointedly he opted to attribute the album's relative merits to a host of other factors. "I didn't like *The White Album* very much," he later remarked. "They'd turned up with 36 songs after their Indian trip and they were pretty insistent that every song was to be included. I wanted to make it a single album, and I stressed to the boys that whilst they could record whatever they liked, we should weed out the stuff that wasn't up to scratch and make a really super single album." Over the years, George contended that there may have been a more calculated reason for the double album's release involving the Beatles' long-term contract, which held them under contract with EMI until January 1976. "I didn't learn until later the reason why they were so insistent," George remarked, but "it was a contractual one. By this time, the contractual negotiations were above my head and I didn't know that their current contract with EMI stipulated a number of years or a number of titles, whichever was the earlier. So the boys, in an effort to get rid of the contract, were shoving out titles as quickly as they could. This was on the advice of the people governing them and there was a sinister motive behind that album."[8]

But with the new year looming ahead, George was clearly in the minority opinion about the experience that they had just shared. For his part, Ringo felt very differently than his producer, believing the record to be a sign of a new Beatles artistic renaissance: "As a band member, I've always felt *The White Album* was better than *Sgt. Pepper* because by the end it was more like a real group again. There weren't so many overdubs like on *Pepper*. With all those orchestras and whatnot, we were virtually a session group on our own album." From his vantage point, Harrison seconded Starr's position, observing that *The White Album* "felt more like a band recording together. There were a lot of tracks where we just played live."[9]

As it happened, Harrison and Starr were about to get their opportunity to feel like they were part of a working rock band again. On the morning of Thursday, January 2, 1969, the bandmates convened at Twickenham Studios' massive soundstage to begin working on what would come to be known as the *Get Back* project. Originally, the band had planned to conduct rehearsals at Abbey Road, but they were unable to book space on such short notice. When they arrived at Twickenham that morning, they were rehearsing on the very same soundstage where Richard Lester had shot *A Hard Day's Night* some five years earlier.

For George, the idea of "getting back" to the Beatles' roots and taking a new approach to their recording practices was an idea worth pursuing. "The boys were seeking ideas for a new project," George wrote. "We all talked about it, and someone came up with an idea to put on a live show of new songs which had never been heard before. Live recordings always featured hits that people knew, but this idea was to rehearse and develop a number of new songs and then perform them for the first time live—and make that performance the album. I thought it was a terrific idea." But even from the outset, George could glimpse the challenges inherent in the band's latest gambit: "The problem was that indoor venues in Britain were all too small for them by then," he later wrote. "They also wanted to make the album in January and February, and you could not do an outside show in Britain when it was freezing cold." But at the same time, they didn't have many options outside of the United Kingdom either. "If they had gone to the States," George reasoned, "they would have lost one half percent of their royalties and they didn't want to do that. So we had some absurd ideas, like going to Tunisia and taking a lot of fans with us."[10]

As for the album itself, Martin was excited about the novel opportunity to produce a live album of original material. Lennon, in particular, was enamored with the idea of presenting the Beatles in their rawest form in comparison to albums like *Sgt. Pepper*, which was the express result of layers of painstaking production. As George later recalled, "John was still very determined that it should be a live album. He said that there were to be no echoes, no overdubs, and none of my 'jiggery-pokery,'" and "if they didn't get the song right the first time, they'd record it again and again until they did." As if to drive his point home, John explained his perspective in the starkest possible terms, telling George, "I don't want any of your production shit. We want this to be an honest album," by which the Beatle meant "I don't want any editing. I don't want any overdubbing. It's got to be like it is. We just record the song and that's it." For his part, Martin was perplexed by Lennon's notion of honesty, later remarking, "I assumed all their albums had been honest." With the Beatles working outside of EMI Studios, their regular production team was unavailable. McCartney suggested that the Beatles hire twenty-six-year-old Glyn Johns to serve as balance engineer. Having worked on records by the Rolling Stones, the Small Faces, Traffic, and the Steve Miller Band, Johns had already accrued an impressive resume. Not surprisingly, Johns didn't hesitate to accept the Beatles' offer. "When you have a hit group like the Beatles," wrote George, you "jump at the chance. Glyn Johns was a very good engineer and producer, and he was very helpful and he got on well with the boys."[11]

For George, the idea of working with Michael Lindsay-Hogg and Glyn Johns seemed like a welcome change from his recent bout producing *The White Album*. With a film crew on hand to document the band's preparation for the planned concert, Lindsay-Hogg developed a rough concept, which Martin and the director variously described as *cinéma vérité* and *audio vérité* in reference to the notion of capturing the truth behind the Beatles' video and audio representations. While Martin embraced the concept of filming the band's rehearsals as they unfolded, Lindsay-Hogg had something even more extreme in mind. Hoping to capture the brute, gritty truth of the authenticity of the Beatles preparing for the live concert, he deployed a pair of Nagra tape recorders and two cameramen in order to document, through audio and video means, nearly every nuance of the group's experience at Twickenham. In order to propel his subjects into action, Lindsay-Hogg acted as a shameless participant in the proceedings, provoking the group into a series of exchanges about their plans for the live performance and the evolving nature of the songs being rehearsed.

Martin thought that the concept was "brilliant" and that in many ways the new album might energize the band and challenge them to explore new frontiers of recording artistry. And at first, even Lennon's jabs about "jiggery-pokery" and Martin's "production shit" didn't seem to bother the Beatles' producer, who was eager to learn how the new long-player would unfold under such conditions, as well as after many years of working at EMI Studios. But for George, it wasn't meant to be—at least not in the way that he expected things to unfold. Years later, he would claim that, given the Beatles' stated wish to minimize the amount of production on their new project, he purposefully stayed away for several of the sessions, which was a surprise to Johns, who was with the group on their very first day of production at Twickenham. "After they had finally run through the first song a couple of times," Glyn later recalled, "Paul turned to me and asked what I thought they should do for an intro. I nearly fell over in shock. I thought I had been employed to just engineer and here I am in the first hour of rehearsals being asked for my input into the arrangement." And that's when it hit him: "It was only then that I realized that George Martin was not to be involved. I assumed that was because it was a live recording and did not require the normal studio production associated with their records." For Johns, not working with the producer who had made the Beatles' name was a source of embarrassment. "A couple of days into the project I asked Paul where George Martin was, only to be told that they had decided not to use him."[12]

For Martin, this new normal in the Beatles' world was a terrible blow. But he was also troubled by their apparent inability to find and sustain their mettle in the film studio's environs. During his sporadic visits to Twickenham, George could tell that something wasn't quite right with the new project. Things started out well enough, with the Beatles rehearsing rudimentary versions of Lennon's bluesy new composition "Don't Let Me Down," Harrison's meditative "All Things Must Pass," and a fresh pair of rock 'n' roll tunes by McCartney, the bluesy "I've Got a Feeling" and the up-tempo "Two of Us," which went under the working title of "On Our Way Home." While the bevy of new tunes clearly demonstrated the seemingly unquenchable songwriting talent at the Beatles' disposal, the bandmates themselves were complaining about Twickenham's sterile recording atmosphere from the very first day. Like nearly all of the rehearsals during the Beatles' fortnight at the soundstage, the proceedings were determined by the sporadic arrival of the bandmates, especially Lennon, who, along with Ono, would often be the last member to arrive on the scene. Lennon was particularly incensed about having to work under the watchful eyes and ears of Lindsay-Hogg's production unit: "We couldn't get into it," he later remarked. "It was just a dreadful, dreadful feeling in Twickenham Studio, being filmed all the time. I just wanted them [the film crew] to go away. You couldn't make music at eight in the morning or ten or whatever it was, in a strange place with people filming you and colored lights."[13]

In retrospect, John's unhappy response to the conditions at Twickenham shouldn't have been surprising given that the group had become used to working evening sessions at EMI Studios, and the sudden shift to daylight must have been understandably jarring. But as with *The White Album*, perception was everything in terms of characterizing the atmosphere associated with the *Get Back* project. For the former, Martin's and Scott's recollections were starkly different, with the engineer considering *The White Album* to be a joyous occasion. Similarly, Johns felt dramatically different than Martin about the *Get Back* session, which he remembered with a special fondness: "The whole mood was wonderful," he later remarked. "There was all this nonsense going on at the time about the problems surrounding the group. . . . In fact, they were having a wonderful time and being incredibly funny. I didn't stop laughing for six weeks."[14]

While Johns may have enjoyed the Beatles' vibe at the *Get Back* sessions, Martin was experiencing something very different when he made his periodic visits to the Twickenham soundstage. As the days wore on, the bandmates had trouble focusing on the work at hand. Their malaise didn't escape George's notice. By the end of that first week, the producer realized that the sessions were "awful to do. We did take after take after take, and John would be asking me if take 67 was better than take 39." To George's mind, it was becoming increasingly clear that John was very "druggy," that the hallucinogenic roller coaster that the Beatles had been riding since the spring of 1965 had taken a darker turn with John and Yoko. While Martin had generally kept his feelings about drug abuse to himself—working, as he had, for nearly twenty years in an industry that was rife with excess—he couldn't help believing that artists like the Beatles "were creative enough without the drugs." As the sessions continued, conversation was dominated by discussion about the location for the upcoming live performance, which the band planned to undertake, impractical as it may seem, by mid-January. Referring to the chaos and fanaticism of Beatlemania, Paul suggested that they could control their audience's fanaticism by simply making a rule that no one could approach the stage. "Barbed wire might do the trick," Martin joked. As for the performance itself, the bandmates initially considered a lavish concert at the Royal Albert Hall, with Apple recording artists Mary Hopkin and James Taylor on the bill, before settling, for a short while, on the comparatively intimate Roundhouse Theatre, the unofficial headquarters for London's underground music scene. Other ideas included performing in a Roman amphitheater in North Africa or perhaps onboard a ship at sea or even by torchlight in the middle of the Sahara Desert. At one point, Lennon suggested, half jokingly, that a concert in an insane asylum might be more appropriate given the band's recent spate of interpersonal problems. Ringo made it known on several occasions that he refused to go abroad, prompting Paul to tease the drummer that they would be forced to replace him with Jimmie Nicol. While Denis O'Dell suggested that they film the concert with the band performing in the middle of one of London's renowned art museums, Yoko had become particularly intrigued by the avant-garde concept of the Beatles playing a concert before twenty thousand empty seats in order to signify "the invisible nameless everybody in the world." In one instance, she even suggested that they reorient the documentary so as to film the Beatles' personal activities, reality-television style, from dusk to dawn in their private homes. As Martin looked on, the group's increasingly outrageous concert ideas began to wane rather precipitously, however, when Ono pointed out that "after 100,000 people in Shea Stadium, everything else sucks."[15]

George had to admit that Yoko had a point. And besides, in his view the innovative aspect of the live performance had almost nothing to do with the event's outlandish circumstances but rather with the idea of recording a live album wholly composed of brand-new material. And at this point, they weren't having very much luck in the songwriting department—the one element of their chemistry that had seemingly never failed them. In increasing fits of creative frustration, the Beatles began taking stabs at their prefame rock 'n' roll repertoire—and often poorly at that, as they suffered through one false start after another in their attempt to recall the old songs. In this way, the *Get Back* sessions increasingly found the Beatles manically improvising one song after another, including a wide range of classic rock 'n' roll numbers like "Shake, Rattle, and Roll," "Johnny B. Goode," "Lawdy Miss Clawdy," "Lucille," "You Really Got a Hold on Me," "Mailman, Bring Me No More Blues," "Little Queenie," "Rock and Roll Music," "Blue Suede Shoes," and "Be-Bop-a-Lula," among a host of others. For his part, Martin could only look on in dismay, occasionally breaking into snickers of exasperation as the bandmates meandered through spates of old chestnuts under Johns's supervision while failing to generate anything in the way of new material. Worse yet, at other junctures, the Beatles fell back on their own catalog, at one point playing a ragtag version of "Ob-La-Di, Ob-La-Da," with Martin lending a dispirited tambourine in accompaniment. By this juncture, George was beginning to realize that his only move was to retreat further and further into the background. During *The White Album* sessions, he had maintained his composure, with his daily newspapers and his chocolate as his signal diversion. But with the *Get Back* project, "I kind of withdrew more and more," he later wrote. "I was getting fed up."[16]

As for the Beatles themselves, as January rolled along, they seemed increasingly unable to concentrate on the project at hand, with John and Paul reeling off occasional guitar riffs or mindlessly playing fragments of songs, mostly oldies from their days in Hamburg. Johns may have felt elated to be producing the biggest band in the world, but Martin recognized the bandmates' current state for what it was, a growing interpersonal and chemically induced nightmare. At this point, they were even having trouble coming up with new material—the Beatles' superpower if ever there were one. Fed up with being the band's solitary cheerleader, the normally well-mannered Paul became unhinged during the January 7 session: "We've been very negative since Mr. Epstein passed away," he remarked. "I don't see why any of you, if you're not interested, get yourselves into this. What's it for? It can't be for the money. Why are you here?" Worse yet, he attributed the band's inability to move forward creatively as the ruinous work of their own suffocating nostalgia: "When we do get together, we just talk about the fucking past. We're like OAPs [old-age pensioners], saying, 'Do you remember the days when we used to rock?' Well, we're here now, we can still do it." If nothing else, Paul's angry words of wisdom served to revive his flagging songwriting partner, who seemed to be unable to rouse the necessary creative energy to generate new material. When Paul finally confronted him about his inability to produce new compositions beyond "Don't Let Me Down," John responded with his classic defensive posture, a combination of sarcasm and petulance:

> Paul: Haven't you written anything?
> John: No.
> Paul: We're going to be facing a crisis.
> John: When I'm up against the wall, Paul, you'll find that I'm at my best.
> Paul: I wish you'd come up with the goods.
> John: I think I've got Sunday off.
> Paul: I hope you can deliver.
> John: I'm hoping for a little rock-and-roller.

Lennon's lethargy was understandable given the band's considerable output and activity during the previous year, not to mention his escapades with Ono and the personal tragedy of her October 1968 miscarriage. As George had surmised at the onset of the project, John and Yoko's protracted heroin abuse, which dated back to the previous summer, may have been taking its toll—at one juncture during the Twickenham sessions, Yoko joked about shooting heroin as the couple's form of exercise.[17]

Whatever the cause for his malaise, for his lack of productivity, Lennon began increasingly to focus his wrath upon Harrison. Indeed, the two Beatles' disintegrating relationship was beginning to exert a troubling effect on the bandmates' efforts at Twickenham. The annals of Beatles history tend to blame McCartney's controlling behavior for the group's interpersonal dilemmas during the *Get Back* sessions, a conclusion that seems to be buttressed by a January 6 quarrel in which McCartney and Harrison resumed their rancor from the previous summer involving "Hey Jude." Apparently still smarting over McCartney's rebuke of his creative suggestion, Harrison reacted to McCartney's patronizing attitude about his guitar arrangement for "Two of Us": "I'll play whatever you want me to play or I won't play at all if you don't want me to play," he told Paul. "Whatever it is that will please you, I'll do it." There is no denying McCartney's increasingly proscriptive songwriterly behavior, and if nothing else the *Get Back* project demonstrated Harrison's—not to mention Starr's—second-class citizenship in the band, an aspect of their communal makeup that had been growing in intensity in recent years as the guitarist's songwriting abilities began to improve radically. "The problem for me was that John and Paul had been writing the songs for so long," Harrison pointed out. "It was difficult. They had such a lot of tunes, and they automatically thought that theirs should be the priority, so I'd always have to wait through 10 of their songs before they'd even listen to one of mine. It was silly. It was very selfish, actually." As a means of blowing off steam, Harrison took to singing impromptu Bob Dylan tunes during the rehearsals, including the symbolic "I Shall Be Released" and "All Along the Watchtower," with its prophetic opening lyric, "There must be some way out of here." Martin, for one, was sympathetic to Harrison's plight, although he ascribed the guitarist's lower artistic stratum in the Beatles to a kind of natural creative order: "He'd been awfully poor up to then. Some of the stuff he'd written was very boring. The impression is sometimes given that we put him down," Martin recalled. "I don't think we ever did that, but possibly we didn't encourage him enough. He'd write, but we wouldn't say, 'What've you got then, George?' We'd say, 'Oh, you've got some more, have you?' I must say that looking back, it was a bit hard on him. It was always slightly condescending. But it was natural, because the others were so talented."[18]

Unfortunately, as the sessions trudged onward, Lennon even seemed to be baiting Harrison. During a rehearsal of Harrison's new composition "I Me Mine," Lennon "jokes that a collection of freaks can dance along with George's waltz," before telling the guitarist "to get lost—that the Beatles only play rock and roll and there's no place in the group's playlist for a Spanish waltz." As if on cue, Paul later took to singing "I Me Mine" while feigning a Spanish accent. The trio's behavior tellingly reminds us that the stakes of authorship—and the divisions that it creates—had never really ebbed. They had merely been redistributed among three Beatles instead of two. Although Lennon may have been equally annoyed by Harrison's obvious surfeit of new material, there is little question that their growing feud involved Harrison's exasperation with Ono's constant presence in the studio, particularly when she spoke up for Lennon while her silent boyfriend nervously plucked at his guitar. On Friday, January 10, Harrison had reached a breaking point, no longer able to hide his vexation with Ono's unremitting presence. After enduring a morning session in which Paul goaded him about how to perform his guitar part and a heated argument with John during lunch, the quiet Beatle abruptly quit the group, making a hasty exit and uttering, "See you 'round the clubs," as he left the soundstage. Either out of spite or ennui—or both—Lennon began improvising the Who's "A Quick One While He's Away" within minutes of Harrison's departure. At one point, he sarcastically called for an absent Harrison to play the guitar solo.[19]

At it happened, Martin hadn't yet arrived at Twickenham that day. Walking into the studio, Martin was beside himself, frantically looking for Harrison as he made his way inside. And that's when he ran headlong into Harrison, who was walking brusquely towards the exit. As it turned out, Martin had every reason to be frazzled. "I remember that George Martin had just backed across the car park in his Triumph Herald and knocked a dent in the door of George Harrison's Mercedes," Dave Harries later recalled, "and he didn't have time to tell him he'd dented his car before George walked out in a huff and drove off." For his part, Martin was hardly surprised by the turn of events. He had long recognized Harrison's subordinate place in the pecking order—a hierarchy that he himself had helped to maintain at times—and the latest episode was symptomatic of the larger malaise. "For one thing," Martin reasoned, "there was no manager, and it was very difficult to get anybody to give a decision. They were just floundering, and I had to deal with this." But moreover, "John would often be very late for sessions or not turn up at all," George later wrote. "It was a very unhappy time." While the bandmates would later claim that Lennon and Harrison had fought a war of words rather than engaging in fisticuffs that day, Martin knew otherwise, maintaining that "there was actually a punch-up."[20]

When he joined the bandmates in the studio that afternoon, Martin discovered how quickly things had deteriorated since Harrison's departure. Lennon had already begun calling for the group to replace the quiet Beatle with Eric Clapton, a caustic suggestion given Harrison's close friendship with the renowned guitarist, whom Lennon described as "just as good and not such a headache." As Martin looked on, the songwriter advanced his impromptu plan even further. "The point is: if George leaves, do we want to carry on the Beatles? I do," John told Paul and Ringo. "We should just get other members and carry on." The day's session ended with a spate of improvised jamming, including a rendition of "Martha My Dear" in which Yoko provided a screeching solo, screaming John's name over and over. Meanwhile, Paul played on, seemingly unfazed by the chaos around him.[21]

For Martin, who had already been exasperated by the Beatles' behavior and inability to produce new material at Twickenham—not to mention his own diminished status with the group—things appeared to look up, if only briefly, when the bandmates succeeded in calling a truce with Harrison. A weekend meeting on Sunday, January 12, with Harrison and the others at Starr's estate had collapsed after the guitarist pointedly refused to return to Twickenham. Realizing that Harrison meant business, on Wednesday, January 15, they held an afternoon meeting in which the quiet Beatle laid out his terms for restoring peace to the group. The truce involved at least two considerations: first, they would abandon Twickenham's dour atmosphere immediately in favor of Apple's newfangled basement studio; and second, they would dispense with the concept of a live performance, instead staging a concert for Lindsay-Hogg's cameras without benefit of an audience. The shift from Twickenham to Apple effectively spelled the end for the television production, with the Beatles now supposedly setting their sights on recording a new album and a concomitant documentary. Although their fantasy of making a spectacular return to the stage had perished, the idea for a new studio album had been born—and if Martin and the Beatles knew nothing else, they understood implicitly how to make an LP. What the bandmates were clearly beginning to understand at this juncture was the extent to which their misspent dream of Apple Corps was transforming into a financial nightmare, just as Martin had feared it would. In an interview published in the January 17 edition of *Disc and Music Echo*, Lennon admitted that "Apple is losing money. If it carries on like this, we'll be broke in six months."[22]

The *Get Back* sessions would have resumed on the following Monday had it not been for Magic Alex, who had promised back in July to build a seventy-two-track recording studio for the group in the basement of the Apple building at 3 Savile Row in Soho. When George arrived at the studio, he was shocked to discover sixteen speakers arrayed along the basement walls, with Magic Alex's multitrack system nowhere in evidence. The facilities, from Martin's perspective, "were hopeless." As Harrison later recalled, "Alex's recording studio was the biggest disaster of all time. He was walking around with a white coat on like some sort of chemist, but he didn't have a clue what he was doing. It was a 16-track system, and he had 16 tiny little speakers all around the walls. You only need two speakers for stereo sound. It was awful. The whole thing was a disaster, and it had to be ripped out." It was at this point, Johns later recalled, that "George Martin came to the rescue." Realizing that Magic Alex's handiwork couldn't be easily remedied with a soldering iron and a few stray cables, George called Abbey Road in desperation. "For God's sake," he implored EMI's studio techs, "get some decent equipment down here!" In short order, EMI engineers Dave Harries and Keith Slaughter were hurriedly dispatched to Apple with the requisite equipment. They were joined by a twenty-year-old tape operator named Alan Parsons. "I couldn't believe it," Parsons later remarked. "There I was. One day I was making tea at Abbey Road, and the next day I was working with the Beatles at their studio."[23]

The first thing Alan noticed was Magic Alex's ostensibly state-of-the-art mixing desk, which "looked like it had been built with a hammer and chisel. None of the switches fitted properly, and you could almost see the metal filings. It was rough, all right, and it was all very embarrassing, because it just didn't do anything." Consequently, Martin and Glyn Johns spent the next two days turning Apple's basement into a respectable recording studio by bringing in two mobile four-track mixing consoles from EMI, as well as overhauling the basement's amateurish soundproofing. And then there was the troubling matter of the building's noisy heating system. "The heating plant for the entire building was situated in a little room just off the studio," Martin later wrote. "And since the sound insulation was not exactly magical," he quipped, in sly reference to the Beatles' would-be inventor, "every now and then in the middle of recording there came a sound like a diesel engine starting up."[24]

For his part, Johns was impressed with Martin's easygoing demeanor and willingness to help out after being shunted aside by the band that he had driven to the top of the hit parade. As Glyn later wrote, "By the time we moved to Savile Row, George, realizing I was in an awkward position, was kind enough to take me to lunch in order to put my mind at rest, saying I was doing a great job, everything was fine, and I was not stepping on his toes in any way. What a gentleman he is." By Wednesday, January 22, when Martin and Johns had finally managed to knock Apple Studios into semi-acceptable shape, production-wise, Harrison officially returned to the fold, performing a duet of "You Are My Sunshine" with Lennon in order to signify their renewed camaraderie. Later that day, Harrison decided to alter the band's chemistry, as he had done so successfully with Clapton back in September 1968, by inviting ace keyboard player Billy Preston to lend his talents to the Beatles. As luck would have it, Harrison and Clapton had seen Preston performing in Ray Charles's band on January 19. The Beatles had first met Preston back in Hamburg in 1962 when he was a member of Little Richard's backup band. "I pulled in Billy Preston" for the *Get Back* sessions, Harrison later recalled. "It helped because the others would have to control themselves a bit more. John and Paul mainly, because they had to, you know, act more handsomely," he continued. "It's interesting to see how people behave nicely when you bring a guest in because they don't want everyone to know that they're so bitchy." When Preston began playing the Fender Rhodes electric piano, "straightaway there was 100% improvement in the vibe in the room." Harrison's gambit had clearly worked its magic. Martin later described Preston's appearance at Apple Studios as a much-needed "emollient" that altered the band's calculus in just the nick of time. Even Lennon was impressed, lobbying hard almost immediately for Preston to become a permanent member of the group, although McCartney demurred at the thought of five Beatles: "It's bad enough with four!" he exclaimed.[25]

For the next several days, Martin, Johns, and the five musicians rehearsed with a vengeance. Time was clearly of the essence, as Ringo was due to star in *The Magic Christian* with Peter Sellers in early February. Meanwhile, Johns was scheduled to record an album with the Steve Miller Band in the United States, and Preston was about to embark upon a concert tour back in his native Texas. If the Beatles were going to salvage the *Get Back* project, something had to happen—and soon. With George having managed to regain a toehold in the studio, the group began to rally perceptibly. From January 23 through the end of the month, Martin and Johns would supervise the production of no fewer than seven outstanding Beatles songs. With Preston working alongside the Beatles on their first full day of recording sessions at Apple Studios, they continued working on "Get Back," which had evolved over a series of false starts and improvisations back at Twickenham. In one instance, Martin spoke to McCartney over the talkback, inquiring about the song's title. "What are you calling this, Paul?" he asked. "Shit," McCartney replied. Without missing a beat, George deadpanned, "Shit, take one."[26]

At another point, Johns offhandedly interrupted one of the "Get Back" takes to converse with Parsons, for which the engineer was rewarded with a curt "fuckface!" from Lennon and McCartney. With "Get Back" beginning to coalesce with the affable Preston working his Fender Rhodes, Martin, Johns, and the quintet turned to McCartney's "Two of Us," which had been refashioned by this point into a nostalgic, acoustic guitar oriented tune. In a moment of unscripted gusto, the band took a stab at "Maggie Mae," the traditional Liverpool ditty about a cheeky prostitute that George had recorded with the Vipers back in the late 1950s. That same day, they also took a stab at John's "Dig It," a lengthy, free-form, improvisational rant in which Lennon name-checked the FBI, CIA, BBC, singer B. B. King, actress Doris Day, and Manchester football coach Matt Busby. The day concluded with the quintet recording basic rhythm tracks for "I've Got a Feeling" and an evolving Lennon number, "Dig a Pony," which went under the working title of "All I Want Is You."

Working a rare weekend, Martin, Johns, and the Beatles convened at Apple Studios on Saturday, January 25, for work on a pair of new compositions, including Harrison's "For You Blue," which went under the working title of "George's Blues," and McCartney's "Let It Be," a piano ballad that the songwriter had been rehearsing in the morning hours at Twickenham before the others, Martin included, arrived. Before making his way to Savile Row, George and Judy drove to the Marylebone Registry Office, where Cilla Black married her manager, Bobby Willis, with the Martins as their witnesses. Afterward, they joined the happy couple and their guests for a wedding luncheon at the Ritz. That afternoon, Martin made his way to Apple Studios, where Johns and the quintet were already in full swing. While the group was finally getting down to business by this point, they were unable to resist their penchant, which was rapidly becoming commonplace during this period, for unfocused jamming. As the distractions continued, they even recorded an impromptu cover of the Everly Brothers' "Bye Bye Love," for which Lennon and McCartney shared lead vocals. While "Let It Be" would continue to evolve over the next few days, "For You Blue" was completed by the end of the session. With McCartney playing a note-perfect honky-tonk piano, Harrison's twelve-bar blues effusion featured Lennon's nifty slide guitar solo—played with a Höfner 5140 Hawaiian Standard lap steel guitar resting on his knees. Buoyed by a spirited ad-lib from Harrison—"Go, Johnny, go!"—Lennon seemed to lose himself in the pure joy of his solo.

The weekend concluded with a Sunday session in which work continued on "Let It Be" and "Dig It," which at one point featured John in an unlikely duet with six-year-old Heather, the daughter of Paul's new fiancée Linda Eastman. Martin good-naturedly played a shaker part on the tune. Another seemingly inevitable bout of jamming ensued, with the Beatles quintet working through a medley of such chestnuts as "Shake, Rattle, and Roll," "Kansas City," "Miss Ann," "Lawdy Miss Clawdy," "Blue Suede Shoes," and "You Really Got a Hold on Me," followed by Harrison's delivery of Smokey Robinson and the Miracles' "Tracks of My Tears." When the bandmates finally regained their focus, they tried their hand at a new McCartney ballad, "The Long and Winding Road," which he had debuted back at Twickenham during his solo morning rehearsals, and Harrison's evocative "Isn't It a Pity?"

During the Sunday session, Martin, Johns, and the bandmates—spurred on, no doubt, by Michael Lindsay-Hogg, who was searching in vain for an ending to his planned documentary—hit upon the idea of performing a concert on the rooftop of the Apple building. "At the moment, this documentary's like *No Exit*," Lindsay-Hogg complained. "There's a lot of good footage, but no pay-off." Like the characters in Jean-Paul Sartre's 1944 existentialist drama, a play in which the characters torture each other endlessly, residing in a kind of living hell from which they are free to leave yet unable to escape, the Beatles' latest filmic adventure seemed interminable. But on Saturday afternoon, the "payoff" appeared to have presented itself when Lindsay-Hogg, with McCartney and Mal Evans in tow, stepped out onto the rooftop above Savile Row. While Harrison would later cringe at the notion of performing about the "chimneys," the rooftop's enviable place atop the cityscape, with the whole of the Mayfair district revealing itself before them, seemed like as good a spot as any to bring the Beatles' *Get Back* chapter, and Lindsay-Hogg's film, to a close.[27]

Arguably the most triumphant week of their recording career—as the improbable moment when they wrenched victory from the jaws of defeat—George and the Beatles' week began somewhat dismally with yet more unfocused studio jamming, as well as a loose progress through a working repertoire that now included "Get Back" and "I've Got a Feeling." They also attempted a new McCartney tune titled "Oh! Darling." With Johns and Parsons working alongside Martin in the booth, "Get Back" began to shape up considerably across eighteen takes. At one point, Lennon parodied the song with a lighthearted bit of studio chatter, singing "Sweet Loretta Fart she thought she was a cleaner, / But she was a frying pan." At the conclusion of "Oh! Darling," John enjoyed a moment of unrestrained delight, announcing, "I've just heard that Yoko's divorce has just gone through. Free at last!" On Tuesday, the Beatles finally seemed to rediscover their mettle, recording serviceable versions of "Get Back" and "Don't Let Me Down." Still caught up in the notion of getting back to their roots, the bandmates performed a ragged version of their first single, "Love Me Do," the song that had started it all with Martin back in June 1962. They also tried their hand at their old Skiffle number, "The One After 909," which they had last attempted in George's company back on March 5, 1963. In addition to working on two demos featuring Preston, they rehearsed McCartney's "Teddy Boy," a midtempo composition that the songwriter had begun back in India. As George looked on, the Beatles engaged in studio chatter about the direction of their project, which still seemed to be uncertain. Was it, in fact, a documentary in advance of a concert or a new long-player, which raised the obvious question, should they be rehearsing or recording? All the while, Lindsay-Hogg's crew kept filming away, strolling among the bandmates with their handheld cameras running. "We got used to it after a time," George later wrote, "but all the rows that went on were filmed as well."[28]

The next day, Martin, Johns, and the bandmates continued their unlikely progress toward unexpected greatness, with Lennon trying out a new composition titled "I Want You," which would later sport the subtitle "She's So Heavy." But as was their wont during this period, the recording devolved into yet another oldies jam, with the quintet lumbering their way through Buddy Holly's "Not Fade Away" and "Mailman, Bring Me No More Blues," as well as "Bésame Mucho," another throwback to their first session with Martin back in 1962. Things took a decidedly different turn on Thursday, January 30, when the quintet made good on Lindsay-Hogg's concept of a rooftop finale, with Martin and the group making their way upstairs on a wintry, windy day to deliver the live performance that they had been pondering, in several different forms, since taping "Hey Jude" for *Frost on Sunday* back in September 1968. Even at that late moment, with Mal Evans and Neil Aspinall already having set up their gear up on the roof, the bandmates considered scuttling their director's plans at the last minute. As Lindsay-Hogg later recalled, "We planned to do it about 12:30 to get the lunchtime crowds. They didn't agree to do it as a group until about twenty to one. Paul wanted to do it and George [Harrison] didn't. Ringo would go either way. Then John said, 'Oh fuck, let's do it,' and they went up and did it."[29]

As Martin later recalled, "At the end of the day, they said, 'Let's go and give a performance after all. Let's go do one on the roof.' So they set up the equipment one very cold winter's day, and at lunchtime started this tremendous noise from the roof in Savile Row. All the neighbors and passersby were asking what the hell was going on, and it was the Beatles broadcasting to London." With nearly a dozen cameramen working on the roof, Johns observed the proceedings on the roof, leaving Martin six floors below in the basement studio, where he manned the converted eight-track equipment courtesy of Abbey Road. The Beatles themselves were quite a sight. With Preston working his Fender Rhodes electric piano, a bearded McCartney strapped on his Höfner violin bass for the occasion, while Lennon, having donned Ono's fur coat to fight off the wind, played his Casino. While Harrison worked his Rosewood Telecaster, an orange rain-coated Ringo played his new drum kit, a set of Ludwig Hollywoods with a maple finish. While the rooftop concert was by no means perfect—it suffered from the same stops and starts that had plagued the band throughout the month—they managed to storm their way through five splendid numbers that day, including "Get Back," "Don't Let Me Down," "I've Got a Feeling," "One After 909," and "Dig a Pony." Finally, after some forty-two minutes above the streetscape, they concluded the show with a spirited reprise of "Get Back," followed by John's parting words to the assembled crowd below: "I'd like to say thank you on behalf of the group and ourselves," he remarked. "I hope we passed the audition."[30]

While the Beatles' performance proved to be a triumph given its seeming unlikeliness and the band's January malaise, the rooftop concert hadn't passed without any hiccups. For George, the most pressing dilemma had been the ominous arrival of a squad of London bobbies, who rode down Savile Row in one of Scotland Yard's conspicuous Black Maria vans. When the police had been called to quell the noise, George was convinced "we'd all end up in jail, myself included." Dave Harries remembered the moment when the Beatles' producer learned about the arrival of the Black Maria van. "George Martin went as white as a sheet," he recalled, "which I thought was hilarious." From Lindsay-Hogg's perspective, the bobbies' appearance was no laughing matter. "We all thought we would probably be arrested up on the roof," Lindsay-Hogg recalled. "I was more nervous than the Beatles were because I was an American and I thought I'd be deported or something." For his part, Ringo was elated, later remarking, "I always felt let down about the police. I was playing away and I thought, 'Oh, great! I hope they drag me off!' I *wanted* the cops to drag me off—'Get off those drums!'—because we were being filmed and it would have looked really great, kicking the cymbals and everything." But it was not to be. Although Beatles lore and Lindsay-Hogg's eventual documentary depicted the police officers as being determined to end the concert prematurely, the truth was far less dramatic and eminently predictable. As Harries recalled, one of the bobbies agreed to allow the concert to continue as long as they could watch: "When they found out who it was," said Harries, "they didn't want to stop it."[31]

After the concert, George and the bandmates were ecstatic, feeling the adrenaline rush of the moment. "They played wonderfully," George later wrote, clearly relieved by the Beatles' high-energy performance and most especially by their ability to rebound from their unsettling month at Twickenham and Apple Studios only to produce a concert for the ages. "That was one of the greatest and most exciting days of my life," recalled Alan Parsons. "It was just unbelievable." As they rejoined Martin in the basement down below, the bandmates and their producer can be heard reveling in the excitement of the moment, with Martin imagining a "whole squadron" of speaker-laden helicopters broadcasting their output to the city and Harrison fantasizing about the Beatles uniting London's rock bands in the spirit of a singular, communal purpose:

Martin: It's come off actually much better than I thought it would.

Lennon: Yes, just the whole scene is fantastic!

Martin: As Michael was saying, this is a very good dry run for something else too, apart from the value of its own as it stands.

Harrison: Yeah, I think for taking over London.

Lennon: Try the Hilton tomorrow.

Martin: The idea is, we'll have a whole squadron of helicopters flying over London with loud, mounted speakers underneath them, you see.

Lennon: That's fantastic, yeah.

Harrison: And every rock group in the world, in London, all on top of the buildings playing the same tunes.

In many ways, the rooftop concert performed a similar function for George and the Beatles. As they made their way downstairs, with January 1969 rapidly fading into their rearview mirror, they felt, if only for the moment, as if they could do anything.[32]

19

COME TOGETHER

AND FOR ANOTHER DAY at least, the magic of the rooftop concert held sway. On January 31, George Martin, Glyn Johns, and the bandmates effectively concluded the principal recording sessions for the project with the production of a trio of first-rate McCartney compositions, including "Two of Us," "Let It Be," and "The Long and Winding Road," three numbers that had been left off of the rooftop set list. While the session produced outstanding performances vis-à-vis the relatively new compositions, it also demonstrated that the Beatles were still susceptible to aimless jamming, as witnessed by an unruly, ragtag version of "Lady Madonna." In spite of their occasional lack of focus, the bandmates managed to capture "Two of Us" in an economical three takes, "The Long and Winding Road" in seven takes, and "Let It Be" in nine takes. For the latter song, the Beatles finally gave up on ridding the project of any of Martin's "production shit." After selecting the best take of "Let It Be," McCartney begrudgingly assented to overdubbing his lead vocal, with Lennon exclaiming to Johns, "Okay, let's track it. You bounder! You cheat!"[1]

With several new songs in advanced states of production—including "Dig a Pony," "Dig It," "Don't Let Me Down," "For You Blue," "Get Back," "I've Got a Feeling," "Let It Be," "The Long and Winding Road," "Maggie Mae," "The One After 909," and "Two of Us"—the Beatles had the makings of a new long-player on their hands. But any further progress on the *Get Back* project would need to be delayed, if only briefly, while Ringo took a break to join Peter Sellers on the set of *The Magic Christian*. Meanwhile, Johns and Billy Preston were traveling stateside. During this same period, Harrison was

felled by a bout of tonsillitis, which left him in need of surgery along with a
requisite hospital stay and recuperation.

On Saturday, February 22, the bandmates reconvened to work on their
new project at Trident Studios with Johns. But then it happened again that
Martin was the odd man out and far more ignominiously than at the beginning of January. In spite of everything George had done to help bring the
Get Back project to fruition, especially in terms of outfitting Apple Studios to
professional recording standards, he had been "included out," to borrow his
own words from 1965 when describing his treatment at the hands of director
Richard Lester during the composition of the soundtrack for *Help!* For the
veteran producer and the Beatles' elder statesman, it was mind-boggling. Martin had honorably ceded Johns the requisite space to work with the Beatles,
had modulated his own self-interest in an effort to elevate the needs of his
clients over his own, and now he was back at square one as far as the Fab
Four were concerned. For Martin, it would have been understandable to
conclude that the Beatles were simply done with him at this point. Perhaps
they simply didn't have the courage to tell him that they no longer wanted
to retain him as their producer.

But fortunately for George, there was plenty of AIR business to occupy his
time. For the past few years, he and his partners had been raising capital to
build a recording studio of their own. The idea of owning their own production made perfect sense for a variety of reasons. First, an AIR facility would
greatly mitigate their expenses associated with recording, and second—and
perhaps most importantly—studio fees would represent a potentially lucrative and regular revenue stream to supplement their income. For the past
several years, Martin and his partners had been working out of the Park
Street offices and shuttling among London's premier studios—Abbey Road,
Trident, Olympic, Decca, and Chappell, among others—where they bought
recording time for their clients. From George's perspective, this was simply
no way to do business—and certainly not for the long run as far as AIR was
concerned: "We had to rent whatever studio was available and suitable for the
particular recording," George later wrote. "The more work we got, the more
money was being spent on other people's studios. It didn't take a genius to
work out that if we had our own studios the trend would be reversed—not
only would that money not have to be paid out, but some might even start
coming in. In addition, the company was enjoying an ever-increasing income
from royalties, which was likely only to be fodder for the taxman. So it made
sense for us to keep our belts tightened, not pay ourselves very high salaries,
and plough back the money into our own company, quite legitimately, to

finance the building of our own studios." Having been stashing away a portion of their collective royalties since 1967, George and his colleagues were
ready to break ground on their own facilities by early 1969.[2]

In addition to raising the necessary capital, the biggest challenge was
finding a suitable location. Given London's historically vexing real-estate
market, it wasn't easy, especially when factoring in George's desire to land a
spot in Central London. "Finally, I heard about the top of the Peter Robinson
building at Oxford Circus," he later wrote. "You certainly couldn't get more
central than that. Peter Robinson is one of the big old London multi-purpose
department stores. Like many of them, it had at the top a huge restaurant—a
banqueting-hall, in fact—in which the gentry had been wont to take their
china tea, cucumber sandwiches and cakes after making their purchases. The
gentry having been whittled away, or absorbed into a world of T-shirts and
hamburgers, it had fallen into disuse, and for two years the store, which still
occupies the building, had been trying to let the floor as offices. Lack of success in this enterprise was hardly surprising, as conversion would have cost
a fortune. To walk into that place was to step back half a century into the
high Edwardian era. It had a huge vaulted ceiling with neo-classical frescoes,
marble columns, and kitchens at each end. It was enormous, and very tall."[3]

To their good fortune, George and his partners were able to strike a
sweet rental deal. But properly fitting out the studio presented a number of
difficulties on its own. First up, George later recalled, was "the fact that we
were looking directly down on one of the world's busier traffic junctions. In
addition, we were in a steel-framed building directly above three Underground
railway lines (which today have become four, with the new Victoria Line).
There were clearly going to be acoustic problems!" To remedy the attendant
matters presented by their new space, George and his partners assembled a
top-flight team, including their architects, Bill Rossell Orme and Jack Parsons, as well George's old friends from EMI Studios, Keith Slaughter and
Dave Harries, who had the enviable job of designing a cutting-edge recording
studio with all of the latest gear. "After all," said George, "we didn't want
to be obsolete before we started." But the real coup, Martin later observed,
was AIR's hiring of Kenneth Shearer, the United Kingdom's most revered
acoustics expert. "He is the man who designed all those 'flying saucers' in
the Albert Hall. The answer to the rumble up through the building from
the Underground was drastic, and dramatic. The whole works—studios and
control rooms—would be made completely independent of the main building. Essentially, a huge box was to be built inside the banqueting-hall, and
mounted on acoustic mounts."[4]

With Shearer having dealt with Oxford Street's noise and ventilation challenges in one fell swoop, Orme presented a bid of £66,000 to bring the project home, estimating that the studio could be completed in a year. It was a steep price tag, to be sure, but one that George and his partners felt that they could accommodate, albeit with a little more belt-tightening. But "unfortunately, it didn't end there," George later recalled. "A few weeks later Bill Orme rang me to say: 'I want you to come to a meeting. I'm afraid I've got some bad news for you.' As I entered, all the experts were sitting round a table—14 of them: quantity surveyors, sub-contractors, architects, air-conditioning people and the rest. 'You'd better sit down first,' said Bill, 'because I don't want you to take the shock standing up.'" And what a shock it was. Orme's revised estimate had come in at £110,000. Suddenly, George later joked, "I felt as if I were on the set of the film *Mr. Standings Builds His Dream House*; we had been trying to build AIR on a shoestring—and it seemed the string had just snapped. The whole business shook me to the core." After rounding up his partners for an emergency meeting later that same day, George laid bare the awful truth. But to his great relief, they shrugged their shoulders in grudging acceptance. The bigger risk had been going out on their own back in 1965 and leaving their record company homes behind. Why stop now? Throwing caution to the wind, as he had done so many times before, the always competitive Martin was ready and raring to go. Still, he recognized that it would be an enormous undertaking to stave off bankruptcy and build out the studio at the same time. "We had to strip our company to the bone, and were in what the jargon calls a 'serious cash-flow situation' for a while," he later wrote. And he knew one thing for sure: as they finally broke ground on AIR Oxford Street, "the money was going out far more quickly than it was coming in."[5]

Ironically, it was during this same period that EMI offered George his old job back. For Martin, there was never a real possibility that he would give up his independence and return to Parlophone, the subsidiary that he had slaved over to fight off its extinction and render it profitable. He was proud of how the once-disparaged "third label" had gone from also-ran status to one of the most successful brands in the world—and largely on the back of George and the Beatles' unparalleled success. But still, when the offer came from managing director Len Wood, George enjoyed a laugh of recognition as he caught a glimpse of the salary, which came in at £25,000—more than double the amount that he had rejected back in 1965 before leaving EMI and founding AIR. And to think that his only mission in the mid-1960s had been to force the record conglomerate to provide him with a few paltry residuals for his world-class efforts. In 1965, an offer of £25,000 might very well have kept him in EMI's employ. But four years later, he barely gave it a second thought. Clearly, Wood and EMI would always remain tone deaf in terms of understanding the ways in which Martin ticked, about the role of profit sharing and individual accomplishment in his professional makeup. That February, George arrived at another crossroads when he and United Artists ended their long-term deal by mutual agreement. The British Invasion boon that had resulted in steady sales for George's easy-listening recordings was no longer in vogue. But all of that was behind him now—EMI, United Artists, an entire era, really—and it was increasingly apparent that the Beatles were behind him, too. They had been working sporadically of late with Glyn Johns at Trident, where they were recording numerous takes for Lennon's "I Want You (She's So Heavy)," one of the songs that they had debuted at Apple Studios.[6]

By early March, Lennon and McCartney had set their sights on completing and releasing a *Get Back* long-player. As Glyn later recalled, "I got a call from John and Paul asking me to meet them at Abbey Road. I walked into the control room and was confronted by a large pile of multitrack tapes. They told me that they had reconsidered my concept for the album that I had presented to them in January and had decided to let me go ahead and mix and put it together from all the recording that we had done at Savile Row. I was thrilled at the idea and asked when they would be available to start. They replied that they were quite happy for me to do it on my own as it was my idea. I left feeling elated that they would trust me to put the album together without them, but soon realized that the real reason had to be that they had lost interest in the project. I went straight into the mix room at Olympic and spent the next three nights mixing and editing the album and, having finished, presented it to the band at the session we had at Olympic the following day."[7]

When Johns played back his new creation for the group's inspection, it was soundly rejected. In all likelihood, Johns had taken Lennon and McCartney's notion of "getting back" to the raw rock 'n' roll sound of their roots far too literally. Brimming with studio banter and false starts, Johns's version of the album was clearly designed to seem rough and spontaneous in contrast with the band's previous LPs. If nothing else, Johns had succeeded in adhering to Lennon's dictum against the slick "jiggery-pokery" of professional studio production.

As if to compound Martin's pain, the Beatles released their follow-up single to "Hey Jude" on April 11 in the form of "Get Back" backed with "Don't

Let Me Down." For EMI, it was difficult to account for who had produced the record—was it Martin or Johns or *both*?—so the release pointedly didn't include a production credit. Attributed to "the Beatles with Billy Preston," the single may not have featured George's usual byline, but it succeeded in continuing "the roll," which was alive and well at five consecutive number-one singles on its way to a global commercial onslaught. Likely referencing the bandmates' desire for a raw sound, the "Get Back" backed with "Don't Let Me Down" single was advertised, borrowing a phrase from McCartney, as "The Beatles as Nature Intended."

As if George needed any further cues, the group's latest record served as an obvious reminder that he was no longer on the Beatles' radar in quite the same fashion that he had been as recently as the *Magical Mystery Tour* project and, on a good day, *The White Album*. Still trying to meet Lennon and McCartney's vague expectations for the new LP, Johns had shared his *Get Back* mixes with Martin, and the elder producer assisted him with compiling yet another version of the record. Working with Johns at Olympic, Martin tried to "put together an album which captured this documentary approach and included their [the Beatles'] mistakes and interjections." But still, George knew that even though "the sessions were over, not one of those titles was perfect. They needed more work on them, but John wouldn't have that at all. So in the end because EMI wanted something, Glyn Johns and I put together a kind of *cinéma vérité* album," just as they had conceived back in early January. Having adopted the title *Get Back, Don't Let Me Down, and 12 Other Songs*, the Beatles went so far as to commission Angus McBean to shoot a cover photograph for the album. On May 13, the group convened at EMI House, where McBean positioned the bandmates in the same fashion as they had appeared six years earlier for the cover of *Please Please Me*. In retrospect, it was a clever idea—a means of bookending their career, as well as underscoring their intent to return to the unadulterated rock 'n' roll sound that brought them fame and fortune in the first place. And in many ways, that was Johns's error back in March, and Johns and Martin's misinterpretation of the Beatles—namely, Lennon's and McCartney's motives—in much the same fashion in May. Perhaps they weren't so disdainful of George's glossy production after all.[8]

For his part, George wasn't surprised by the group's inability to embrace *Get Back* and release another album. As with its predecessor, Martin and Johns's latest mix was "warts and all, with the mistakes and count-ins and breakdowns and so on. That was the album. I thought it was a write-off. I didn't hear any more, and I thought that was the end of our days. I thought,

'Well, that's the finish of the Beatles. What a shame.'" As it happened, George wasn't very far off the mark. First there was Allen Klein, who had made good on his boast to Johns back in 1968 that he would one day manage the Beatles. At the time, Johns flatly informed Klein that he was "bonkers." But within a matter of months, the brash American businessman had succeeded in wooing Lennon, Harrison, and Starr to the fold, only to be thwarted temporarily by McCartney, who wanted his new in-laws, father and son attorneys Lee and John Eastman, to handle his affairs. Outvoted by the other Beatles, McCartney had little choice but to ultimately assent to Klein's management, even as he refused to sign their new contract. During this same period, Apple Corps' woes had begun to spiral further out of control, only to be compounded by Lennon and McCartney's powerlessness to purchase Northern Songs when Dick James placed it on the open market. As historian Brian Southall has observed, the Beatles were confronted with a perfect storm in the form of Apple's financial turmoil coupled with the Beatles being cash poor at the worst possible moment. "Dick James was of the old school and had had enough of it," Southall wrote. "He saw the Lennon and McCartney partnership falling apart and he and his partner Charles Silver, who founded the company with him, decided to sell their stake in Northern Songs. They sold their shares to Lord Grade at ATV. Dick James didn't tell the Beatles what he was doing. He felt that they would never bid themselves as they were in disarray."[9]

While Klein structured a new deal that would have allowed Lennon and McCartney to maintain their holdings in Northern Songs, it eventually began to collapse when Lennon learned that McCartney had been secretly buying up shares of their publishing behind his back. At the same time, they recognized that their artistic freedom would be mitigated by faceless businessmen in suits, as opposed to the homegrown organization that Brian Epstein had created with NEMS. "John Lennon wasn't going to be told what to do by 'fat arses,'" Southall later observed. John "walked out of the room and that was the end of their bid." The business consortium that Epstein and Martin had established back in 1963 with James, one of Martin's oldest friends, was suddenly in tatters, leaving the Beatles' own partnership in the direst of straits.[10]

And so it was a genuine surprise for Martin when McCartney called him later that spring and announced that the Beatles were going to make another record. "Would you like to produce it?" he asked George. "Only if you let me produce it the way we used to," Martin countered. "We do want to do that," said Paul. "John included?" asked George. "Yes," Paul replied. "*Honestly.*" That was all the assurance that George needed. In truth, there was very little that he wouldn't do for them. The Beatles had been the making of him, and he knew it. But he had been the making of them, too, and that meant he was emotionally involved in their destiny, just as he had been back in November 1962 when he threw his lot in with them behind the strength of their first single and the great promise of "Please Please Me," the composition that they had reconfigured to his specifications. As for this new Beatles album, George knew that it would require a bit of juggling to pull off the scheduling; his commitments were stacked up for the next several weeks. But as it turned out, the Beatles were ready and eager to regain the mettle that they had revealed during their heyday. They would show George Martin yet.[11]

As if to make good on their new energy and commitment, in short order Lennon and McCartney also talked Geoff Emerick back into the fold, via Peter Brown, as they made preparations for recording a new composition titled "The Ballad of John and Yoko." A song about the notorious couple's international escapades, much of the tune concerned the hijinks surrounding their recent marriage; just as Paul and Linda Eastman did, John and Yoko Ono had enjoyed a March 1969 wedding. Recorded under the working subtitle of "They're Gonna Crucify Me," the song's production was supervised by George on Monday, April 14, in EMI's Studio 3. With Harrison traveling abroad in the United States and Ringo still working on the set of *The Magic Christian*, the Beatles' personnel was limited to John and Paul. While Lennon handled the lead and rhythm guitar parts, McCartney provided the song's rhythm section. In addition to his pounding bass lines and assorted piano flourishes, Paul kept a steady beat on Ringo's Ludwig Hollywoods. McCartney achieved a distinctive cracking drum sound courtesy of Emerick, who placed microphones both above and below the snare. In contrast with their recent, lengthy bouts in the studio, Lennon and McCartney recorded the song in eleven workmanlike takes. For his part, Emerick was overwhelmed with relief: "The two Beatles seemed remarkably relaxed, despite the horror stories I had heard about the rows and bad feelings engendered by the [*Get Back*] sessions," he later wrote. "On this one day, they reverted to being two old school chums, all the nastiness of recent months swept under the rug and replaced by the sheer joy of making music together."[12]

For Emerick, the whole experience had been a whirlwind. Only days before, he had been offered the opportunity to oversee the renovation of Apple Studios in the wake of Magic Alex's shenanigans. Geoff had jumped at the chance to leave EMI and Alan Stagge behind. As it happened, he was part of a mass engineer exodus that also included Ken Scott, who took a job at Trident, and Peter Vince, who went to work for Norrie Paramor, George Martin's old rival. In a moment that surely resonated with Martin, Emerick later recalled the day he walked out of EMI Studios with Vince. "Despite the fact that we had worked on some of the biggest-selling albums of all time," he wrote, "no one said thank you, no one said goodbye. No one said anything, in fact."[13]

A few days later, Martin was back in Studio 3, where he recorded Harrison's bouncing, electric "Old Brown Shoe," a composition that the quiet Beatle had demoed back in February with Johns in the producer's seat. Having captured a series of overdubs for "Old Brown Shoe" on Wednesday, April 16, complete with a nifty jangly part from McCartney, Martin turned to another Harrison composition from February, a romantic ballad titled "Something," which Harrison had debuted for Chris Thomas during *The White Album* sessions. "It took my breath away," said Martin, "mainly because I never thought that George could do it—it was a tremendous work and so simple." Rehearsed with the tape running, the bandmates recorded a basic track for "Something" that included Harrison's electric guitar, McCartney's bass, Starr's drums, and Martin's piano. For the producer, it was a revelation to be playing on a Beatles track again when just scant days earlier he had all but given up on the notion of working with them in any capacity.[14]

On Friday of that same week, Chris Thomas stood in for Martin, completing work with the bandmates on "Old Brown Shoe" before turning back to Lennon's "I Want You (She's So Heavy)," one of the February Trident recordings with Glyn Johns. As it turned out, "I Want You (She's So Heavy)" would be the first track recorded for the new Beatles' long-player. Later that same evening, Thomas supervised a session, with Jeff Jarratt and John Kurlander working as engineers, in which Harrison and Lennon recorded layer after layer of lacerating electric guitars for the song's Wagnerian finale. "John and George went into the far left-hand corner of Number 2 to overdub those guitars," Jarratt recalled. "They wanted a massive sound so they kept tracking and tracking, over and over." By this point, the Beatles had rebounded from their winter funk with a vengeance. For the balance of April 1969, they worked several more dates with Thomas in which they continued working on the loose ends of the new compositions that they had debuted in recent months, including McCartney's "Oh! Darling" and Starr's "Octopus's Garden."[15]

As Martin continued working to disentangle his schedule from other projects in advance of producing the new Beatles long-player, Thomas carried out yeoman's duty on his AIR colleague's behalf. During the Saturday, April 26, session, he recalled being "thrown into the deep end. George Martin informed me that he wouldn't be available. I can't remember word for word what he said, but it was something like 'There will be one Beatle there, fine.

Two Beatles, great. Three Beatles, fantastic. But the minute the four of them are there that is when the inexplicable charismatic thing happens, the special magic no one has been able to explain.'" Sure enough, Thomas later recalled, that inexplicable thing was present and accounted for—and arguably for the first time in nearly two years. Later that same evening, Richard Langham worked a Beatles session for the first time since the early 1960s, when he had departed Abbey Road to work abroad. With Kurlander assisting, Langham conducted a remix for "The Ballad of John and Yoko" in advance of the song's release as the next Beatles single.[16]

Meanwhile, Martin was working at breakneck speed with Cilla Black, whose career had continued at full throttle since the debut of her blockbuster television series. Together, George and Cilla were making good on the opportunity to further consolidate her fame, recording a pair of hit singles and putting the finishing touches on a new album in a matter of only a few months. The first single, "Surround Yourself with Sorrow" backed with "London Bridge," had catapulted into the number-three spot on the UK charts first, following closely by "Conversations" backed with "Liverpool Lullaby," which also scored a top-ten hit. As for the long-player, George and Cilla had been plying away at the new album, to be titled *Surround Yourself with Cilla*, since late 1968, with George routing songs and scoring the orchestrations along the way. With EMI having scheduled a firm release date for the LP in late May, George had no time to lose.

With Glyn Johns in tow, Martin rejoined the Beatles at Olympic Studios on Monday, May 5, when they took up Harrison's exquisite "Something" for additional overdubs, including Harrison's electric guitar, which he filtered through a Leslie speaker, and McCartney's fluid bass work. By Tuesday, May 6, a framework had begun to emerge in terms of the new album's structure, with many of the early tracks already slated for side one of the LP, a distinction that was necessitated by the musical suite that had been conceived for side two of the record. The notion of a pop opera was very much in vogue during this period in popular-music history, as evidenced by works from the Who ("A Quick One While He's Away"), Frank Zappa and the Mothers of Invention (*Absolutely Free*), Keith West ("Excerpt from a Teenage Opera"), and the Small Faces ("Happiness Stan"), among others. That same month, as the Beatles began working on an extended suite of their own, the Who released *Tommy*, the album that would come to define the rock opera as a musical form. Hence, George and the Beatles were not acting as trendsetters, which was typically their wont, but rather as trendfollowers. But given that Martin and McCartney were highly competitive—witness McCartney's clear motive to one-up the Who's "I Can See for Miles" with the even more raucous, explosive "Helter Skelter"—the idea of besting the field with their own "huge medley" or "the long one," as it came to be known among EMI staffers, was temptation enough.

As always, Martin welcomed the opportunity to expand the Beatles' generic considerations. "I wanted to get John and Paul to think more seriously about their music," said George. "There would be nothing wrong with making a complete movement of several songs, and having quotes back from other songs in different keys. And even running one song into another contrapuntally, but thinking of those songs in a formal classical way." To this end, George pointedly "tried to instruct them in the art of classical music, and explain to them what sonata form was. Paul was all for experimenting like that." And at the time, apparently so was John. As the Beatles began working in earnest to accrue new material, Lennon could barely contain his excitement during an interview with *NME*. "Paul and I are now working on a kind of song montage that we might do as one piece on one side," he remarked. "We've got about two weeks to finish the whole thing, so we're really working on it." During the May 6 session, Martin supervised thirty-six takes of a complex new composition called "You Never Give Me Your Money," an obvious reference to the bandmates' ongoing financial and legal woes associated with Apple Corps. With take thirty having been selected as the best, the song's instrumentation featured McCartney's piano and guide vocal, Lennon's distorted Casino, Harrison's chiming electric guitar filtered through a Leslie speaker, and Starr's drums.[17]

On May 30, the bandmates released "The Ballad of John and Yoko" backed with "Old Brown Shoe." To mark the occasion, Lennon and Ono celebrated the release in Room 1742 of Montreal's Hôtel Reine-Elizabeth with one of their notorious "bed-ins" in which they deployed their celebrity as a vehicle for promoting world peace. That same weekend, John met with Timothy Leary, who asked the Beatle to compose a song based on the slogan for Leary's 1970 California gubernatorial campaign, COME TOGETHER—JOIN THE PARTY! On June 1, John and Yoko famously recorded "Give Peace a Chance" in their bedclothes. Strumming his Jumbo, Lennon was joined on vocals by Leary, Allen Ginsberg, Murray the K, and Derek Taylor, among others. The embryo for the song had been born the day before, when Lennon told a reporter that "all we are saying is give peace a chance." Meanwhile, with "The Ballad of John and Yoko" unseating the group's own "Get Back" atop the UK charts, "the roll" now stood at six consecutive number ones, for a total of seventeen Beatles chart-toppers since 1963, an incredible feat that left Martin understandably chuffed—and certainly putting to rest any doubts about who held the upper hand in his rivalry with Norrie Paramor. Notably, "The Ballad of John and Yoko" was the first Beatles single released solely in stereo without the availability of a simultaneously released mono mix. Stereo's domination among consumers had been on the rise since the early 1960s—with stereophonic sound being widely marketed to music fans as a richer, more satisfying aural experience. But in 1968, the tables began rapidly turning against monaural sound. In January of that year, a banner *Billboard* magazine headline trumpeted the format's death, which it attributed to the major record manufacturers working in collusion to bring mono to its knees. For his part, George wasn't bothered in the slightest. Despite being admittedly very "twelve-inch" in his thinking, he had long preferred the stereo format to monaural sound's lack of definition. As he later recalled, "I like to sit right in front of the desk, right *within* the triangle of the optimum stereo. So that you get the real feeling of sitting in a theatre or cinema, then shutting your eyes and hearing things. One of the fascinating things I used to find was when you panned something from left to right, it didn't just go straight across, it goes up in an arc *above* you. It was like going through a proscenium arch in a theatre. And you could then see—very vividly in your mind—what the sounds were doing as a stereo picture."[18]

With July rapidly approaching, Lennon and McCartney worked feverishly at Cavendish Avenue to amass new material. Martin had block-booked the majority of Abbey Road's studio time during the 2:30 to 10:00 PM time slot from July 1 through August 29. To corral two months' worth of studio time was a considerable feat at the time, although George had no problem throwing his weight around when it came to the Fab Four. "One of the things about being the Beatle producer in those days: it didn't give me a great deal of money, but it did give me a great deal of clout," he later remarked. "I was able to say, 'Well, look, we want to do this.' And everybody would say, 'Yes, sir! Yes, sir! Three bags full, sir!' Or almost." Meanwhile, for John and Paul, the medley was high among their priorities. As McCartney later remarked, "I wanted to do something bigger, a kind of operatic moment." For his part, John was especially eager to begin working on the project: "If I could only get the time to myself, I think I could probably write about 30 songs a day," he observed in an interview with *Disc* magazine. "As it is, I probably average about 12 a night. Paul, too: he's mad on it. As soon as I leave here, I'm going 'round to Paul's place and we'll sit down and start work. The way we're writing at the moment," he added, "it's straightforward and there's nothing weird. The songs are like 'Get Back,' and a lot of that we did in one take."

Unfortunately, John's great rush of excitement would be decidedly quelled on July 1, less than twenty-four hours before work on the album was formally set to begin. Some six hundred miles to the north of EMI Studios, John had been tooling around the narrow roads of Scotland with Yoko by his side and their children—John's six-year-old son, Julian, and Yoko's five-year-old daughter, Kyoko—in the rear of their Austin Maxi. The newly married couple had been visiting Lennon's relatives in the far north when the Beatle lost control of the car and drove off of a steep embankment near Golspie. Yoko, who was two months pregnant, crushed several vertebrae and received a concussion in the accident, while all four suffered cuts and bruises. As it was, the couple spent five days in the hospital. In truth, they were lucky to have escaped with their lives. Given his injuries, which required seventeen stitches in his face, John would be forced to miss several of the Beatles' upcoming sessions.[19]

On Wednesday, July 2, Martin and the bandmates, sans Lennon, got down to business in Studio 2. Working alone that afternoon, Paul recorded three takes of "Her Majesty," which was under consideration for the medley. After Harrison and Starr arrived at the studio later that day, they tried their hand at "Golden Slumbers," with lyrics based on a sixteenth-century poem by British playwright Thomas Dekker, and "Carry That Weight." Martin super-vised fifteen takes of the songs, which were recorded as a single track with McCartney on piano and guide vocal, Starr on drums, and Harrison playing bass. For the rest of the week, the bandmates carried out overdubs for "Golden Slumbers" and "Carry That Weight." For the latter, Harrison and McCartney superimposed electric guitar parts, followed by lead vocals from McCartney and a stirring vocal passage performed in unison by Harrison, McCartney, and Starr for the middle eight. The songs' connective tissue consisted of a drum figure by Ringo, who was still gushing over the sound of his Ludwig Hollywoods. Recording the album "was tom-tom madness," he later remarked. "I had gotten this new kit made of wood, and calfskins, and the toms had so much depth. I went nuts on the toms. Talk about changes in my drum style— the kit made me change because I changed my kit." In addition to Ringo's impassioned drumming, the album's sound would benefit from the studio's eight-track recording technology—now the standard technology at Abbey Road—and particularly in terms of its solid-state electronics, as opposed to the vacuum tube–driven equipment that had served the band throughout their career. Hence, the latest Beatles tracks revealed a perceptibly different sound, a "mellower" flavor and tonality, according to Emerick, who was set to resume his role as the band's balance engineer and Martin's right-hand man on a full-time basis in late July.[20]

The following Monday, with Phil McDonald and John Kurlander serving as his engineers, Martin supervised the recording of "Here Comes the Sun," the splendid new song that Harrison had composed that spring while strolling in Eric Clapton's garden. Recorded in thirteen takes, with the last one being selected as the best, the instrumentation for "Here Comes the Sun" consisted of Harrison's acoustic guitar and guide vocal, McCartney's bass, and Starr's drums. From Martin's perspective, "Here Comes the Sun" marked a turning point for Harrison. "I think there was a great deal of invention," said Martin. "I mean, George's 'Here Comes the Sun' was the first time he'd really come through with a brilliant composition, and musical ideas, you know, the multiple odd rhythms that came through. They really became commercial for the first time on that one." On the afternoon of Wednesday, July 9, the three Beatles once again became four, with Lennon and Ono, still bruised and clearly the worse for wear, having made their return from Scotland. As McDonald later recalled, "We were all waiting for them to arrive, Paul, George [Harrison], and Ringo downstairs and us upstairs. They didn't know what state he [Lennon] would be in. There was a definite 'vibe': they were almost afraid of Lennon before he arrived, because they didn't know what he would be like. I got the feeling that the three of them were a little bit scared of him. When he did come in it was a relief, and they got together fairly well. John was a powerful figure, especially with Yoko—a double strength."[21]

For George and the bandmates, it must have been quite a sight, with Yoko wearing a tiara in order to hide the scar on her forehead that she had received from the car wreck. Given her high-risk pregnancy, Yoko was under her physician's orders for constant bed rest, so John had a double bed shipped into EMI Studios from Harrods and a microphone positioned within easy reach so as to allow her to be in continuous communication with him. For his part, Martin's partner Ron Richards was flabbergasted by the sight of seeing Yoko lounging in "the bed," as it came to be known. "I popped into one of the later sessions in Number 3," he later recalled, "and there was Yoko in this blooming double-bed. I couldn't believe it! John was sitting at an organ, playing, and I went up to him and said, 'What the bloody hell is all this?' and he was very touchy about it, so I kept quiet and walked out."[22]

Up first during Lennon's first session back was McCartney's "Maxwell's Silver Hammer," which the Beatles had last taken up during their scattershot rehearsals at Twickenham Studios. With Martin up in the booth, the bandmates recorded more than a dozen takes of the song. The next evening, they superimposed a number of overdubs, including McCartney's piano and Martin's Hammond organ. The highlight that day was a blacksmith's anvil, which Martin had rented from a theatrical agency especially for Starr to periodically strike with a hammer during the song's chorus.

By this point, John had begun to find "Maxwell's Silver Hammer" particularly loathsome. Years later, he admitted, "I hate it. 'Cuz all I remember is the track—he made us do it a hundred million times. He did *everything* he could to make it a hit single and it never was and it never could've been." By week's end, they had put aside "Maxwell's Silver Hammer" in order to return to "Something," for which Harrison superimposed a new lead vocal, and "You Never Give Me Your Money," which received a new bass guitar line from McCartney.[23]

By this juncture in the production of their new album, the Beatles' manic energy to complete the LP led to them working simultaneously in all three EMI studios, from which they communicated using walkie-talkies in order to coordinate the project's overall production. For his part, George was delighted with the vibe in the studio, which "was really good," although the group's intense new work style meant that he "had to be dashing from one place to another."[24]

By the following week, things were moving briskly, with additional superimpositions for "You Never Give Me Your Money," including new vocals, along with a wind chime overdub to mask the song's closing section. Martin and the bandmates continued to add yet more layers, courtesy of the greater sonic real estate provided by eight-track technology, to Harrison's "Here Comes the Sun" and "Something." For the former, the Beatles superimposed handclaps and a harmonium part. As work moved forward on the new long-player, McCartney developed a routine in which he would come in each day to try his hand at singing the raucous lead vocal for "Oh! Darling." As Alan Parsons later recalled, "My main memory of the Abbey Road sessions is of Paul coming into studio three at two o'clock or 2:30 each afternoon, on his own, to do the vocal," adding that "he only tried it once per day, I suppose he wanted to capture a certain rawness which could only be done once before the voice changed." Indeed, for several days running, McCartney gave it a shot, usually ending his most recent bout with the vocal by saying, "No, that's not it. I'll try it again tomorrow!" During this same period, the bandmates added harmony vocals, McCartney's piano, and various sound effects to Starr's "Octopus's Garden." Many of the effects were created by McCartney and Harrison, who made gargling sounds while McDonald modulated them with limiters and compressors.[25]

During the Monday, July 21, session, as the world marveled at the previous day's moon landing, Emerick made his full-time return to the Beatles' fold, with McDonald and Kurlander assisting. Taking a break from his work at Apple Studios, Emerick had returned as "the first freelance engineer that had walked into the building." That day, Martin supervised a basic rhythm track for "Come Together," Lennon's first new composition since "The Ballad of John and Yoko" in mid-April, a period spanning more than three months. Rehearsed with the tape running, the mid-tempo, bluesy "Come Together" was captured in six takes, with Lennon's lead vocals, Harrison's electric guitar, McCartney's bass, and Starr's drums, on which the drummer performed his distinctive tom-tom shuffle. That same week, George and the bandmates made further progress on the medley—namely, a new track that went under the title of "Ending," the working title for "The End." Recorded in seven takes, the rhythm track for the song was beginning to take on the proportions of an old-time rock 'n' roll revue, a perfect vehicle for showcasing the band members' musicianship and bringing the medley to a close. With the benefit of eight-track recording, Emerick was able to devote particular attention to Starr's drum solo, which the engineer captured in all its percussive power through the careful placement of a dozen microphones around the drummer's kit.[26]

On Thursday, July 24, Martin produced McCartney's solo demo for "Come and Get It," a song that was slated for a later recording by Badfinger, a Welsh band formerly known as the Iveys, which had recently been signed by Apple Records. Meanwhile, Lennon presented two new compositions, "Sun King" and "Mean Mr. Mustard," for consideration for the medley. With Harrison and Lennon on their electric guitars, McCartney's bass, and Ringo's drums, the session was ripe for an instrumental jam, which is exactly what happened during one of the takes, when Lennon segued into "Ain't She Sweet," the song that they had recorded with Tony "the Teacher" Sheridan way back in June 1961, followed by Gene Vincent's "Who Slapped John?" and "Be-Bop-a-Lula." The bandmates rounded out the week with a whopping thirty-nine takes of Lennon's "Polythene Pam" and McCartney's "She Came in Through the Bathroom Window," which were recorded for the medley—like "Golden Slumbers" and "Carry That Weight"—as a single song. As "Polythene Pam" and "She Came in Through the Bathroom Window" developed, a number of unusual overdubs were attempted, including Lennon's comical studio chatter with Mal Evans ("Oh, look out!") and Starr's cracking whip to punctuate the verses on the latter.

Martin and the bandmates brought the hyperbusy month of July to a close with an extended session on Wednesday, July 30, devoted to compiling a rough draft of the medley. At this point, a number of songs were under consideration, including "Golden Slumbers"/"Carry That Weight," "Her Majesty," "Polythene Pam"/"She Came in Through the Bathroom Window," and "Sun King," with "You Never Give Me Your Money" and "The End" having already been slated to open and close the suite. Although the songs were largely unfinished at this juncture, Martin and the group wanted to hear how the whole shebang sounded and develop a rough mix. Eventually, a working order began to emerge that unfolded with "You Never Give Me Your Money," "Sun King," "Mean Mr. Mustard," "Her Majesty," "Polythene Pam"/"She Came in Through the Bathroom Window," "Golden Slumbers"/"Carry That Weight," and "The End." Clocking in at fifteen minutes and thirty seconds, the medley seemed fairly cohesive, more or less, with a few notable exceptions. According to Dave Harries, this first problematic section of the medley involved the cross-fade between "You Never Give Me Your Money" into "Sun King," which had been accomplished by merging the songs via an organ note, which stuck out like a sore thumb to the bandmates and their production team. And then there was "Her Majesty," which seemed out of place when Martin and the Beatles previewed the mix. As John Kurlander later recalled, "We did all the remixes and crossfades to overlap the songs," and Paul said, "I don't like 'Her Majesty,' throw it away." Kurlander dutifully excised the song, accidentally including the last note, which he neglected to edit out, given that it was only a rough mix, after all.[27]

The very next day, "Her Majesty" experienced a bizarre recommendation when Malcolm Davies prepared a playback lacquer of the medley at Apple Studios, with Mal Evans returning the lacquer to EMI later that same day. Although the young tape operator wanted to adhere to Paul's wishes, he also knew that "I'd been told never to throw anything away, so after he [Paul] left I picked it up off the floor, put about 20 seconds of red leader tape before it, and stuck it onto the end of the edit tape." By the time that Kurlander returned to Abbey Road for his next shift, he was surprised to discover that "Her Majesty" was back in the mix, albeit with a very different placement than when he had gone home the previous evening. When Martin and McCartney heard the lacquer, they clearly liked hearing "Her Majesty" at the end of the medley. "The Beatles always picked up on accidental things," said Kurlander. "It came as a nice little surprise there at the end." On July 31, McCartney decided that "You Never Give Me Your Money" wasn't quite there yet—especially the song's third verse, with its tempo change in contrast with the plaintive early stanzas. To enhance the passage and establish momentum, McCartney planned to superimpose a boogie-woogie piano, only he couldn't play the complex section up to tempo. At this juncture, Martin recorded McCartney performing the solo at half speed using the producer's windup piano technique. In so doing, the section was transformed into a full-tilt piano boogie when played back at full speed.[28]

On Friday, August 1, Lennon presented yet another new composition, titled "Because," which he had been inspired to write after hearing Ono play Beethoven's *Moonlight Sonata* on the piano. He completed his new song after reversing the song's chord structure and adorning it with suitably introspective lyrics. During the Friday evening session, Martin and the Beatles captured the song in twenty-three takes, with Lennon providing a guide vocal and electric guitar, McCartney playing bass, and Martin working a Baldwin spinet electric harpsichord. For the purposes of recording the basic rhythm track, Starr played a gentle beat on his hi-hat, which was projected into the other musicians' headphones to provide a tempo. "Because I'm not renowned as the greatest time-keeper when I'm playing," Martin later recalled, "Ringo was our drum machine." On August 4, the Beatles and their producer returned to "Because," effecting the same kind of three-part harmony that they had perfected with "This Boy" in 1963 and later, in 1965, with "Yes It Is" and *Rubber Soul*'s "Nowhere Man." In many ways, "Because" may stand as the bandmates' most exquisite multipart vocal effort, with a vital assist from eight-track technology, which allowed Martin to spread out the vocals with great separation and hence finer vocal resolution. Designating two tracks for the harmonies, "we put down one set of voices with John, Paul, and George singing in harmony and we then designed two more sets of trios to go on top," Martin remembered. "So we finished up with nine voices, nine sounds, that's all but it worked. It was very simple."[29]

Working with McDonald and Parsons up in the booth that same evening, Harrison carried out rough stereo remixes of "Something" and "Here Comes the Sun." Having decided that both songs would benefit from orchestration, acetates were provided for Martin so that he could compose the scores at home at his leisure. Knowing that he already planned to superimpose orchestral overdubs for "Golden Slumbers"/"Carry That Weight" and "The End," George began working with EMI's Laurie Gold to start lining up the requisite session musicians. With "Something" and "Here Comes the Sun" now also on the docket, it made increasing sense to organize a single, large-scale session in which to carry out the orchestral overdubs. When Martin returned to Abbey Road on Tuesday afternoon, he arrived to find McCartney working in the Studio 3 control room with a plastic bag of tape loops that he had fashioned at his nearby St. John's Wood home on his Brenell tape machine. Working with George and his production team, Paul transferred the mono loops—which included variant sounds of birds, bells, and chirping crickets—onto four-track tape. At this point, Emerick replaced the cross-faded organ note that served as the sonic joint between "You Never Give Me Your Money" and "Sun King" with McCartney's soothing layer of ambient noise.

During the evening session, the bandmates—namely, Harrison—began experimenting with the quiet Beatle's recently purchased Moog Series III synthesizer. Harrison had bought one of the keyboard instruments directly from its inventor, Robert Moog, in advance of working on his solo LP *Electronic Sound* for the short-lived Zapple label. The Moog system worked by generating electronic signals that allowed users to create unique sounds when they depressed the keys and activated a series of modules, which could subsequently be manipulated further still by means of an internal oscillator. In this way, the user could produce unique soundscapes with a Moog synthesizer in contrast with a Mellotron, which only worked with a static series of pre-recorded tape loops. Fortunately for Harrison, Martin had recently bought a Moog Series III for AIR after taking an introductory course in San Francisco offered by Moog's colleagues Bernie Krause and Paul Beaver. Together, the two Georges were able to make good use of the Moog synthesizer. Only days earlier, Harrison had transported his Moog Series III from Kinfauns to Abbey Road. Unlike later, portable versions of the instrument, the Moog synthesizer circa 1969 consisted of an unwieldy two-tiered keyboard setup, complete with a massive bank of wires and other attendant cabinetry. But with the Moog still in its relative infancy, Martin recognized that the best way to approach the instrument was through trial-and-error experimentation. As he later remarked, Moog synthesizers were essentially "sound generators—sine waves, sawtooth, and so on—and you just had to learn how to make sounds with it, which was fascinating stuff." Martin brought in Mike Vickers, who had developed a steep working knowledge of the instrument, to help program the Moog to meet the Beatles' creative needs. As Kurlander later recalled, "The Moog was set up in Room 43, and the sound was fed from there by a mono cable to whichever control room we were in. All four Beatles—but particularly George—expressed great interest in it, trying out different things." The bandmates were quick studies, making shrewd use of the instrument on "Maxwell's Silver Hammer," for example. "On that particular one," Martin later recalled, "I suppose we were still influenced by real sounds and we were still trying to get sounds that were like instruments we knew, more than synthetic sounds but nevertheless, there was a floaty mystical thing about the sound on 'Maxwell's Silver Hammer.'" One of the first Moog overdubs was for "Because," for which Harrison executed a contemplative backdrop that echoed Martin's harpsichord part.[30]

As work on George and the Beatles' new long-player was coming briskly to a close, with the bandmates often working in different studios simultaneously to carry out overdubs and apply an array of finishing touches, tensions were becoming heightened yet again. There was no more powerful example of this aspect of the Beatles' working relationship during this period than the Thursday, August 7, session in Studio 2, which began in the early afternoon and concluded at midnight. The trouble started when the bandmates were sitting in the control booth with Martin, Emerick, and Kurlander, listening to playbacks of "Come Together" during a remixing session. As Kurlander looked on with the others, they could see Ono down in the studio below, where she slowly rose out of bed and tiptoed across the room to Harrison's Leslie speaker cabinet. As they watched, Yoko picked up one of the guitarist's digestive biscuits from where he stored them atop the cabinet and began slowly unwrapping the package. "That bitch!" Harrison yelled. "She's just taken one of my biscuits!" At that point, Emerick recalled, "Lennon began shouting back at him, but there was little he could say to defend his wife (who, oblivious, was happily munching away in the studio), because he shared exactly the same attitude toward food. Actually, I think the argument was not so much about the biscuits," Emerick continued, "but about the bed, which they had all come to deeply resent," even Martin, who always tried to do his level best to stay out of the fray.[31]

But what Kurlander would remember most about that day was the way in which the tempest so quickly blew over. Only a short time later, the feuding Beatles seemed to have forgotten all about the explosion up in the Studio 2 control room. Working in Studio 3, Harrison and Lennon put aside their differences to perform a fusillade of guitar solos for the rock 'n' roll revue that concluded the medley. With McCartney on his Fender Esquire, Harrison on his Gibson Les Paul Standard, and Lennon on his Casino, each guitarist succeeded in improvising a two-bar solo for the ages. As Emerick later recalled, "John, Paul, and George looked like they had gone back in time, like they were kids again, playing together for the sheer enjoyment of it. More than anything, they reminded me of gunslingers, with their guitars strapped on, looks of steely-eyed resolve, determined to outdo one another. Yet there was no animosity, no tension at all—you could tell that they were simply having fun." Like Kurlander, Starr had been thunderstruck by the virtuosic performance. "Out of the ashes of all that madness," said Ringo, "that last section is one of the finest pieces we put together."[32]

The next day, August 8, the Beatles arrived early at the studio to finally resolve the lingering matter of their new album's cover art. Since early summer, the title had been a running issue among the group, with several names being bandied about, including *Four in the Bar, All Good Children Go to Heaven*, and the absurd *Billy's Left Foot*. One of the strongest contenders had been to name the album *Everest* in honor of the brand of cigarettes that Emerick smoked. "We were stuck for an album title," McCartney later recalled, "and the album didn't appear to have any obvious concept, except that it had all been done in the studio and it had been done by us. And Geoff Emerick used to have these packets of Everest cigarettes always sitting by him, and we thought, 'That's good. It's big and it's expansive.'" The bandmates ultimately balked at the idea when they realized that they didn't want to go to the enormous trouble of journeying to Tibet to shoot the album's cover art. Besides, Paul added, "You can't name an album after a ciggie packet!" Suddenly out of options, they turned to the studio from whence they had made their name. "Fuck it," Ringo reportedly said. "Let's just step outside and name it *Abbey Road*." And that's exactly what they did. At the appointed time, the Beatles gathered outside the stately gates of 3 Abbey Road for the photo shoot. While the London Metropolitan Police helpfully cleared the area of traffic, photographer Iain MacMillan stood atop a ladder and took the famous cover shot of the bandmates walking single file across the crosswalk only a few yards from the main entrance to EMI Studios.[33]

A few days later, George conducted the monumental orchestration session for *Abbey Road*, second only in size and scope to the February 1967 session in Studio 1 for "A Day in the Life." Working in that very same studio on Friday, August 15, Martin conducted the session musicians, whose music and images were transmitted by closed-circuit television to the Studio 2 control room, where Emerick, McDonald, and Parsons monitored the proceedings. As Alan Brown later recalled, "It was a mammoth session. We had a large number of lines linking the studios, and we were all walking around the building with walkie-talkies trying to communicate with each other." Up first that day was "Golden Slumbers"/"Carry That Weight," for which Martin had scored arrangements for twelve violins, four violas, four cellos, a string bass, four horns, three trumpets, a trombone, and a bass trombone. By this juncture, Martin had perfected the art of orchestration as a means for complementing not only the Beatles' compositions but also the production style that he deployed in order to bring their creativity to life. "Production and arranging are two different jobs, even though they go hand in hand," he later remarked. "If you can score, if you can orchestrate, it's obviously a tremendous help to realize the production ideas that you have. You know what to write in order to get the right sound in the studio. Similarly, if your production end tells you what you need to write, you're working hand-in-glove with yourself so to speak. And that's where your orchestrating style affects your production style."[34]

With "Golden Slumbers"/"Carry That Weight" under his belt, Martin turned to "The End," which, in terms of sheer cost per second, was the most exorbitant recording on the day. With the same musicians working in Studio 1, Martin conducted the powerful coda for "The End." As the medley thundered to a close, a series of guitar flourishes coalesce with George's orchestration, establishing a sense of an ending amid the warmth of the musicians' harmonics. In contrast with "A Day in the Life," which climaxes in a darker hue—with the inherent tension and uncertainty of an E major chord—Martin's score for "The End" reached the finish line with the comparative serenity of C major. As Brown later observed, "The orchestral overdub for 'The End' was the most elaborate I have ever heard: a 30-piece playing for not too many seconds—and mixed about 40 dBs down. It cost a lot of money: all the musicians have to be paid, fed, and watered; I screw every pound note out of it whenever I play the record!"[35]

After taking a break to arrange the new configurations of musicians and prepare the next set of scores, Martin turned to "Something" and "Here Comes the Sun." The Beatles' producer had concocted a pair of exquisite orchestrations for Harrison's contributions to *Abbey Road*. His arrangement for "Something" called for twelve violins, four violas, four cellos, and a string bass. As the most complex recording on the day, the session for "Something" found the composer sharing the podium with Martin, as well as taking up his electric guitar to record, live in the studio with the players arrayed nearby, his sublime solo for the middle eight. As Emerick later recalled, "The problem was that there was only one track available, and we needed to use that for the orchestra. The only solution was for him to play it live, right along with the orchestra, so we could record them simultaneously on the same track. I was enormously impressed when he nonchalantly said, 'Okay, let's do that'—it took a lot of nerve and self-confidence to be willing to put himself under that kind of pressure. George had to play the solo correctly all the way through, without punch-ins, because the sound coming from his guitar amp would leak onto the other mics, and he wouldn't get a lot of whacks at it, because it was costing quite a lot to have that orchestra there. But he managed to play the intricate solo with ease." Later, for "Here Comes the Sun," Martin's score called for four violas, four cellos, a string bass, two clarinets, two alto flutes, two flutes, and two piccolos. In this instance, Martin's deft arrangement perfectly complemented Harrison's buoyant, optimistic lead vocals, as well as the delicate layers of his acoustic guitar and Moog overdub, the latter of which he would record on the following Tuesday. By the wee hours of Saturday, August 16, the orchestrations for *Abbey Road* were complete.[36]

By Monday, August 18, Martin and the Beatles were nearly there. On that day, the medley had been completed, for the most part, with a final overdub for "The End" that featured McCartney's four-second piano track followed by his final lyrical flourish, "And in the end, the love you take is equal to the love you make." In so doing, McCartney succeeded in concluding the medley with a quasi-Shakespearean couplet—"a cosmic, philosophical line," in Lennon's words. By Wednesday, George and the Beatles were working in Studio 3 in an effort to complete "I Want You (She's So Heavy)," the song that had kicked things off back in February at Trident, when Glyn Johns and Billy Preston were still on the scene. Back on August 8, Lennon had superimposed a layer of white noise that he produced on the Moog Series III. During the August 18 session, Martin supervised the final mixing and editing of "I Want You (She's So Heavy)." For the song's distinctive ending, with its powerful sonic buildup, John offered careful instructions in order to ratchet up the intensity. "Louder! Louder!" Lennon implored Emerick during the mixing process. "I want the track to build and build and build, and then I want the white noise to completely take over and blot out the music altogether." With only twenty-one seconds remaining of the original recording, "all of a sudden he barked out an order" to the Beatles' engineer, "Cut the tape here!"[37]

And with that, "I Want You (She's So Heavy)" was complete, as were all of the tracks for *Abbey Road*. All that was left, as far as George and the Beatles were concerned, was to define the running order, as well as to compile and band the final master tape. Working in the Studio 2 control room from the dinner hour through just past one o'clock the following morning, Martin and the bandmates, joined by Emerick, McDonald, and Parsons, set about formatting each side of the album. They had recently been debating whether to situate the medley on side one or side two—in contrast with their perspective back in early May. In one instance, Lennon had even floated the idea of placing all of his songs on side one and all of McCartney's on the other, McDonald later recalled. But with the medley effecting a potentially dramatic climax for the album, there was little point in reversing their original plans. Besides, they now had the bookended high points of the sudden, startling conclusion of "I Want You (She's So Heavy)" on side one, balanced with the explosive rock 'n' roll revue of "The End" on the other. The only other matter was a relatively minor one, with George and the bandmates debating whether to place "Octopus's Garden" before "Oh! Darling" on side one or vice versa. In the end, they opted to go with "Oh! Darling" first. As for the openers for each side, they followed Martin's long-held precept about starting with the strongest material, which *Abbey Road* had in spades. Side one began with "Come Together" and "Something"—a one-two punch, if ever there were one—while side two opened with Harrison's "Here Comes the Sun," the LP's finest track as far as Martin was concerned.

Although Paul still preferred *Sgt. Pepper*, for George's money, *Abbey Road* was a fine album, indeed—possibly even their best. As the assembled group made their way into the cool summer air of early morning, they could hardly have known that they would never pass that way again—at least collectively, that is. But for his part, George couldn't help feeling that the Beatles seemed to be on their last legs as a working unit. The *Get Back* sessions had taken their toll, and there was no mistaking the bandmates' continuing animus in the studio. From George's perspective, *Abbey Road* had been an uplifting experience, but the bandmates were clearly running on fumes, and there was no denying an inevitable breaking point. He had recognized this fact, as had John, scant days after Brian Epstein's untimely demise. But what their producer couldn't possibly have known—wouldn't have even have believed at the time—was that he was only just getting started as far as the Fab Four were concerned. For George, unlike the bandmates themselves, the end of the Beatles would be a long way off—decades even. And quite possibly for the rest of their producer's life.

20

SENTIMENTAL JOURNEYS

———

WHEN IT WAS RELEASED on September 26, 1969, *Abbey Road* was met with largely rave reviews, although a few critics took issue with what they perceived to be the album's glossy production and sound effects. Writing in the *Times*, William Mann attacked this notion, remarking that "if adverse reviews elsewhere have dissuaded you from buying *Abbey Road*, the Beatles' new LP, do not hesitate any longer. It teems with music invention—mostly by Lennon and McCartney, though all four contribute songs—and the second side, as a piece of musical construction, is altogether remarkable and very exciting indeed," adding that the album will only be "called gimmicky by people who want a record to sound exactly like a live performance." In *Melody Maker*, Chris Welch went even further, proclaiming the Beatles' new album is "just a natural born gas, entirely free of pretension, deep meanings, or symbolism." For Welch, "While production is simple compared to past intricacies, it is still extremely sophisticated and inventive." Stateside, *Abbey Road* was similarly lauded as a masterpiece, demonstrating Martin and the bandmates at the height of their powers. "That the Beatles can unify seemingly countless musical fragments and lyrical doodlings into a uniformly wonderful suite, as they've done on side 2, seems potent testimony that no, they've far from lost it, and no, they haven't stopped trying," observed John Mendelsohn, writing in the November 15 issue of *Rolling Stone*. "No, on the contrary, they've achieved here the closest thing yet to Beatles freeform, fusing more diverse intriguing musical and lyrical ideas into a piece that amounts to far more than the sum of those ideas." By contrast, a minority of American critics such as

Life's Albert Goldman derided the album—and the medley in particular—as seeming "symbolic of the Beatles' latest phase, which might be described as round-the-clock production of disposable music effects."[1]

Abbey Road debuted at number one on the UK charts, eventually holding the top position for a total of seventeen weeks. In June 1970, the Beatles' manager Allen Klein announced that *Abbey Road* had sold five million copies in the United States alone, an incredible feat—even by the Beatles' lofty standards. Even EMI Studios was not immune to the LP's runaway success. Within a matter of months, the facility had become synonymous with the album, and EMI Studios was rechristened as Abbey Road Studios in 1970. As for the album's embarrassment of riches, critics and consumers alike lauded Harrison's "Something" as a standout cut from the album; Martin and the group agreed, uniformly citing it as their favorite *Abbey Road* track. Released on October 6 as a double A-sided 45 rpm record with "Come Together," the single marked Harrison's first and only A-side with the Beatles. Undoubtedly hampered by the album's runaway success, "Something" backed with "Come Together" topped out at number four on the UK charts, with both sides winging their way to the toppermost of the poppermost of *Billboard*'s Hot 100. Alas, this meant that "the roll" had been ended in the United Kingdom once again. But if the single's also-ran status slipped George Martin's notice at the time, it would have been understandable. In the few short months since they had completed work on *Abbey Road*, things had changed very precipitously in George and the bandmates' universe.

Just six days before *Abbey Road*'s release, everything had finally unraveled. During a September 20 meeting at Apple, Allen Klein had secured McCartney's signature, along with the other Beatles', save Harrison's, on a new contract with Capitol. While McCartney had his reservations about Klein's management, the new rate called for the Beatles to take home an incredible 25 percent of their US retail sales per unit. Klein's gambit was simple: if Capitol didn't pony up, the Beatles wouldn't record for them again. But as it turned out, they wouldn't be recording for anyone. Later during that same meeting, Lennon blurted out that he wanted a "divorce" from the band. As McCartney recalled, "I didn't really know what to say. We had to react to him doing it; he had control of the situation. I remember him saying, 'It's weird this, telling you I'm leaving the group, but in a way it's very exciting.' It was like when he told Cynthia he was getting a divorce. He was quite buoyed up by it, so we couldn't really do anything: 'You mean leaving?' So that's the group, then. . . . It was later, as the fact set in, that it got really upsetting." As it happened, Harrison wouldn't sign the contract until a few days later. He was in Cheshire, visiting his ailing mother, so the Apple meeting wouldn't be the last time that all four Beatles were together. As it turned out, that had already happened back on Friday, August 22, at John and Yoko's Tittenhurst Park estate, where the bandmates had gathered for a photo shoot only a few days after working out the running order for *Abbey Road*.[2]

At the end of the Apple meeting, everyone had been sworn to secrecy given the renegotiated American contract in the offing, not to mention the upcoming release of the new long-player. There was simply too much at stake. And anyway, Paul reasoned, why not give John space to change his mind and return to the fold? The Beatles wouldn't really be over if nobody bothered to announce it as a point of fact. For Martin, the only possible solace involved the production of *Abbey Road*. The *Get Back* project "was a very uncomfortable time. I was losing control of the boys and they were losing control of themselves," he later remarked. "I thought it was the end of everything and so I was quite happily surprised when they asked me to make another album with them." To his way of thinking, George's gambit of producing the new LP "like the old days" had made all the difference. "They wanted me to exert control the way I did in the *Pepper* days. So I did, and *Abbey Road* proved to be a very happy album. They'd been disliking each other and having punch-ups, but now they came together and collaborated very well. I was very pleased that the group went out on a note of harmony and not one of discord." And on a personal note, George had been delighted with the symphonic grandeur of the medley. For this reason alone, he later remarked, "There's far more of me on *Abbey Road* than on any of their other albums."[3]

When George got wind of the Beatles' impending "divorce," he was happy to maintain the veil of secrecy. First, it wasn't his story to tell, and second, he was, as usual, working at all hours on a wide range of projects in various states of production. By the autumn months of 1969, one of those projects included *Hey Jude*, a compilation hastily arranged for American release by Capitol in order to take advantage of the new contract that Klein had negotiated in September. Originally to be titled *The Beatles Again*, *Hey Jude* was a ten-song retrospective of the band's singles and B-sides from 1964 through the present. In early December, Martin and Emerick conducted stereo remixing sessions for "Lady Madonna," "Rain," "Hey Jude," and "Revolution" for inclusion on the *Hey Jude* compilation, which had been slated for a February 1970 release, complete with images from the Beatles' last photo session at Tittenhurst Park in August 1969. Years later, this period in George's life would be memorable for the pop-cultural phenomenon that would come to be known as the "Paul Is Dead" controversy. As press officer Tony Barrow later recalled, "There were rumors all through the years that one of the Beatles had been killed in a road crash or fallen off a cliff or whatever. Some of them were from fans ringing up the press so that the press would ring me and thereby find out where the Beatles were. If the press asked me if Paul was in a crash in Edinburgh, I would say, 'No, he's in Paris.' After many unfounded rumors, things came to a head when a lot of people said they could prove that the Beatles themselves were admitting that Paul McCartney had died and had been replaced. It was a fascinating story, but totally without foundation." But as far as Martin was concerned, the "Paul Is Dead" controversy became a personal matter when fans began to track down the Beatles' producer at home. As George later recalled, "I started getting letters about how obvious it was that Paul was dead, and why were we covering it up? Paul was round at my place one afternoon, and we had a good laugh about it, but it wasn't so funny to be woken in the middle of the night by some little girl in Wisconsin wanting to know if he was still alive." Eventually, McCartney was forced to quell the rumors by agreeing to pose with his family for a November 1969 *Life* magazine cover with the headline, PAUL IS STILL WITH US.[4]

On October 3, 1969, Martin was back at Abbey Road, where he carried out the finishing touches for his old friend Spike Milligan's World Wildlife Fund benefit LP. The charity long-player had been slated for a December 12 release date with Regal Starline, an imprint of Regal Zonophone, which dated back to the 1930s and was distributed by Parlophone. Titled *No One's Gonna Change Our World*, the LP's name had been drawn by Milligan from the Beatles' "Across the Universe," which would finally make its debut as the lead track for the benefit record some twenty-two months after it had first been produced by Martin back in February 1968. "Across the Universe" had proven to be a coup for Milligan, all but guaranteeing that the charity album would create a genuine benefit for the World Wildlife Fund, which had been founded in 1961 to preserve the wilderness and address humanity's impact on the natural environment. As it happened, George had been compiling the LP for some time. "There's a lot of work involved in these charity albums," he later wrote. "You have to get permissions from everybody concerned, organize the cover, and so on. In this case, I had to make the record as well." Working with John Kurlander at Abbey Road, George compiled and banded *No One's Gonna Change Our World* for release. He also adorned "Across the Universe" with introductory and concluding sound effects of birds flying and children playing—both of which had been gleaned from EMI's trusty green sound-effects cabinet. Martin rounded out the album with a number of tracks by his stable of artists—both before and after AIR—including Cilla

Black's "What the World Needs Now Is Love" and Rolf Harris's "Cuddly Old Koala." In addition to spoken-word novelty tracks from Milligan and "Land of My Fathers" by fellow Goon Harry Secombe, the LP included the Hollies' "Wings," one of their final tracks with Graham Nash. Other standout selections for the charity compilation included Cliff Richard and the Shadows' "In the Country," originally produced by Norrie Paramor, the Bee Gees' Robert Stigwood–produced "Marley Purt Drive," and the 1966 hit "Bend It" by Dave Dee, Dozy, Beaky, Mick, and Tich.[5]

On October 9, a few scant days after compiling *No One's Gonna Change Our World* for release, George's wife, Judy, gave birth to Giles, the couple's second baby in two years and George's fourth child. John good-naturedly rang George up to mark the occasion and noted that Giles had been born on the Beatle's own twenty-ninth birthday. "Now you know what kind of asshole he's going to be!" Lennon chortled to Martin over the phone. Never one to rest idle, George had continued working throughout this period. Over the past few years, he had begun grooming Edwards Hand, a Welsh psyche-delic pop duo, for AIR. Formerly known as Piccadilly Line, Edwards Hand was composed of keyboard player Rod Edwards and guitarist Roger Hand. George had first heard their music on Piccadilly Line's 1968 LP *The Huge World of Emily Small*, which featured Herbie Flowers on bass and flautist Harold McNair. Having pronounced their music to be "exceptional," George produced Edwards Hand's eponymous debut in 1969.[6]

Recorded at Abbey Road, *Edwards Hand* was released by RCA Victor only to hit the charts with a thud. But George, optimistic to a fault, was not to be deterred. In recent months, he had been producing the duo's second album, to be titled *Stranded*. Martin recorded the long-player at Morgan Sound Studios in northwest London, with assistance from engineer John Miller. With guest artists such as bassist John Wetton and guitarist James Litherland chipping in, Martin pulled out all the stops, even going so far as to commission cover art from Klaus Voormann. In spite of George's enthusiasm for the project, the notices were decidedly mixed, with reviewers often being stumped by the duo's strange admixture of styles and genres. While *Stranded* failed to generate any commercial waves, the album's American release was met with controversy due to Voormann's artwork, which featured a black-and-white drawing of a sheriff, his arms defiantly crossed above a massive belly and his sidearm, in reference to the Edwards Hand song "Sheriff Myras Lincoln." After the album cover was banned in the United States, George was forced to substitute a more benign image of an American flag. The duo's follow-up LP, titled *Rainshine*, was recorded by George for a 1971 release, although it was not to be. Frustrated by the band's inability to generate any consistent sales, RCA Victor rejected the album out of hand, bringing George's partnership with the group to an end.

As 1969 came to a close, George made progress on two very different and far more commercially successful projects than Edwards Hand, which, in many ways, had been a labor of love on George's part. The first production involved an album with legendary American tenor saxophonist Stan Getz, who was known in jazz circles as "the Sound" due to the warm, mellow tones that defined his horn playing. Produced by George with Richard Hewson providing orchestration and arrangements, the LP acted as a jazz homage to recent pop hits, including such compositions as Graham Nash's "Marrakesh Express," Bacharach and David's "Raindrops Keep Fallin' on My Head," Paul Simon's "Cecilia," and even a nod to Lennon and McCartney's *Abbey Road* track "Because." For George, working with the jazz great had been a disheartening experience given the Sound's recent bout with drug addiction. Years later, George would describe Getz's *Marrakesh Express* as "really quite embarrassing," given the jazz man's failure to perform up to his previously high standards. "It was very sad to see him like that." To George's mind, their collaboration had helped Getz to recover. For their follow-up LP, *Dynasty*, Martin and a cleaned-up Getz assembled a tight band—with the Sound's sax, Eddy Louiss's keyboards, René Thomas's electric guitar, and Bernard Lubat's drums. Working with a "rather ancient amp," Martin helped Thomas achieve a kind of "old-fashioned jazz sound" that bridged Getz's earlier successes with Brazilian music into a new period of jazz fusion.

But the big prize for the producer during the autumn months of 1969 was Ringo Starr's debut album, which George had begun producing with the Beatles' drummer in October, only a few weeks after Giles's birth that same month. The project had first come his way after "Ringo decided to sing an album of old songs, and he asked me to produce it," George later wrote. "His stepfather Harry, who he regarded as his father, loved old songs, and Ringo, sentimentally, wanted to make an album to please him." But it was more than that, as Starr later admitted. "I was lost for a little while. Suddenly, the gig's finished that I'd been really involved in for eight years." In September, the same month in which John had asked for a divorce from the band, Ringo checked into London's Middlesex Hospital with severe stomach pains and intestinal blockage. After his release, he hired Neil Aspinall as his personal manager and set out to make a solo album. "I called George Martin and said, 'I'm going to do an album of standards that will get me out of bed, out of the house, and get me back on my feet.'" For the album, George worked from the concept that Ringo would rifle through the songs enjoyed by his mother, Elsie, and stepfather, Harry, all those years ago at family parties. "I was brought up with all those songs, you know, my family used to sing those songs, my mother and my dad, my aunties and uncles," the drummer wrote. "They were my first musical influences on me." After Ringo assembled a roster of potential numbers with his mother back in Liverpool, George hatched a plan in which Ringo would sing an array of standards, with a different arranger for each song and the George Martin Orchestra as his accompaniment.[7]

In December, George took a break from Ringo's solo album to prepare for a Yorkshire Television Christmas special to be titled *With a Little Help from My Friends*. Billed as a tribute to Martin, the show was filmed in Studio 4 of the Leeds Television Centre on December 14. Produced by David Mallet, *With a Little Help from My Friends* was set to be broadcast at seven in the evening on Christmas Eve. A host of celebrated guests from across Martin's career participated in the extravaganza, including Dudley Moore, the Hollies, Lulu, Milligan, and the Pan's People dancers, along with Martin himself conducting a forty-piece incarnation of the George Martin Orchestra. While Ringo performed "Octopus's Garden" in George's honor, the producer's most famous clients were otherwise not in evidence.

As for Ringo's impending solo album, George had completed work on the lion's share of the tracks by the advent of the new year, with a second bout of recording sessions held in February and March 1970. Many of the arrangers were personal friends of George, with the remainder being rounded up by Aspinall. With several of the arrangers joining Martin at Abbey Road for the recordings, McCartney provided orchestration for Starr's cover version of the Hoagy Carmichael classic "Stardust," while Elmer Bernstein delivered a stirring arrangement for "Have I Told You Lately That I Love You?" George's old friend Johnny Dankworth got in on the act with "You Always Hurt the One You Love," as did Bee Gees vocalist Maurice Gibb for "Bye Bye Blackbird." George had been particularly excited about working with celebrated producer Quincy Jones on an arrangement for "Love Is a Many-Splendored Thing," although ironically that experience proved to be one of the LP's low points. "I remember Quincy Jones's reaction being, 'What do I do with this song, George?' He was terribly non-plussed; when he turned up at the studio, he'd written a score which sounded like he really wasn't sure what to do." Released on March 27, 1970, *Sentimental Journey* featured a nostalgic cover photograph of the Empress pub, located in Liverpool just a few blocks away from Ringo's boyhood home on Admiral Grove. In spite of its throwback subject matter, the album enjoyed strong sales—notching a top-ten showing in the United

Kingdom and landing at number twenty-two on *Billboard*'s album charts. But the critics had a field day, with Robert Christgau describing the album in the *Village Voice* as being "for over-50s and Ringomaniacs." Although Harrison reacted charitably, calling *Sentimental Journey* "a great album" and "really nice," Lennon was unable to hold his tongue. In December 1970, he exclaimed to *Rolling Stone* editor Jann Wenner that he was "embarrassed" by Ringo's schmaltzy effort.[8]

But by that point, *Sentimental Journey* had already become a minor footnote in the Beatles' unfinished, ongoing saga. In March 1970, as George conducted his orchestra while Ringo filmed a promotional video for the new album at London's Talk of the Town nightclub, the band's collective vitriol had come roaring back into all of their lives with a vengeance. For George, it had all started, like the Beatles' unexpected *Abbey Road* renaissance a year earlier, with a telephone call: "Paul rang me up one day and said, 'Do you know what's happened? John's taken all of the tapes'" and dropped them in the lap of maverick American producer Phil Spector. The latest bout with the wayward *Get Back* project had actually begun back in December 1969, when Allen Klein had sold the rights to Michael Lindsay-Hogg's documentary to United Artists, who reincarnated the project as a feature film. The Beatles subsequently altered the title of their album from *Get Back* to *Let It Be* in order to synchronize the marketing of its release with the movie of the same name. Angus McBean's EMI House photograph of the band was used in a March 1970 mock-up for *Let It Be*'s cover art, although it was later replaced by American photographer Ethan Russell's January 1969 still photographs of the group in various states of rock 'n' roll performance.[9]

As far as Martin had known at the time, the recording sessions for the Beatles' misbegotten LP had ended a few months earlier, after he had worked with Harrison, McCartney, and Starr in the studio to complete "I Me Mine" and add a bit of polish to "Let It Be" for the documentary's imminent soundtrack release. With the estranged Lennon on a lengthy vacation with Ono in Denmark, Martin supervised Harrison, McCartney, and Starr in a remake of "I Me Mine" at EMI Studios on Saturday, January 3, 1970, the producer's forty-fourth birthday. As they prepared to record "I Me Mine," Harrison acknowledged Lennon's absence with a wry reference to the popular British band Dave Dee, Dozy, Beaky, Mick, and Tich: "You all will have read that Dave Dee is no longer with us, but Mickey and Tich and I have decided to carry on the good work that's always gone down in Number 2." The recording session for "I Me Mine" had been necessitated because of the song's appearance in Lindsay-Hogg's forthcoming documentary. Recorded across sixteen takes, the basic rhythm track featured Harrison's acoustic guitar and guide vocal, McCartney's bass, and Starr's drums. At one point, the trio broke into an instrumental jam that morphed into Buddy Holly's "Peggy Sue Got Married." After selecting take sixteen as the best, the group recorded electric guitar, electric piano, and lead and harmony vocal overdubs to bring the relatively short song, which clocked in at one minute and thirty-four seconds, to fruition.[10]

On Sunday, January 4, George and the Beatles' trio reconvened in Studio 2 to complete work on "Let It Be," which had now been recast as the title track for the documentary, as well as the A-side for a planned March single. With Phil McDonald and Richard Langham assisting, Martin conducted a whirlwind session, nearly fourteen hours long, in which Harrison overdubbed yet another lead guitar solo for the song, with Harrison, McCartney, and Linda McCartney later adding a new harmony vocal to the Beatles' January 31, 1969, performance of the song. At this point, Martin conducted a brass orchestral overdub involving two trumpets, two trombones, and a tenor saxophone. As the night wore on, Martin carried out additional overdubs with percussion from Starr and McCartney, along with another, more sizzling guitar solo from Harrison for the song's middle eight. Working "on heat" of his own that long evening, Martin added a cello score at the end of the recording. As the trio wrapped up work on "Let It Be," Glyn Johns waited in the wings to gather up the latest addition to his wayward project. Working at Olympic Studios the next day, Johns concocted a third and final attempt at mixing the *Get Back* sessions into a cohesive whole, albeit without the recently recorded "I Me Mine," only to be shortly rebuffed yet again. For all of their bluster about getting back to their roots with the original *Get Back* concept, the bandmates—especially John, in a moment of great irony—simply couldn't fathom their sound without a healthy dose of production. Lennon had also blanched when Johns demanded a production credit for his efforts over the past year. Lennon may have known by this point, of course, that he had already planned to engage Phil Spector in just such a capacity, which may explain his reluctance to accede to Johns's request. And then there was also the matter of Martin's participation at key, albeit sporadic instances throughout the production.

Meanwhile, with EMI clamoring for new Beatles product as always, the band and their management had opted to release "Let It Be" as the group's next single. With Lindsay-Hogg's documentary in the offing, it made sense to build up buzz for the film and the soundtrack—however and whenever it would materialize, which was still in jeopardy at this point. Released on Friday,

March 6, the "Let It Be" single's B-side featured the thirty-four-month-old, long-gestating "You Know My Name (Look Up the Number)," which lent a welcome bit of comedy to what would amount to the Beatles' final UK single. Writing in *NME*, Derek Johnson observed that "as ever with the Beatles, this is a record to stop you dead in your tracks and compel you to listen attentively." Stateside, the "Let It Be" backed with "You Know My Name (Look Up the Number)" single easily notched *Billboard*'s top spot. But alas, in the United Kingdom it was simply not to be. The Beatles' twenty-second and final single's release in their homeland would climb no further than number two. Sure enough, "the roll" that Martin had worked so hard to sustain was over and out.[11]

But until McCartney's phone call, Martin had been unaware of Spector's professional involvement on the Beatles' behalf. In late March and early April, Spector had been cloistered away at Abbey Road, often in Room 4, working on remixing the songs slated for the *Let It Be* soundtrack. For his part, Martin could understand Spector's motives in jumping at the opportunity to work with the Beatles in spite of the group's current disarray. "Spector is the kind of person who was in the doldrums for a long time," Martin observed. "He made a tremendous name for himself many years ago as a producer with a particular sound. I mean, he became an original, and a characteristic of his sound was that of a big, spacious work, you know, enormous, putting everything but the kitchen sink in, and which worked frightfully well" with hitmaking acts like the Ronettes and the Righteous Brothers. Spector's postproduction work with *Let It Be* culminated in a massive overdubbing session in Studio 1 on April 1 for "The Long and Winding Road" and "Across the Universe," with orchestrations provided by the ubiquitous Richard Hewson. During the session, Spector applied his famous "wall of sound" echo-laden recording technique to the tracks. In the case of "The Long and Winding Road," Spector overdubbed a thirty-three-piece orchestra, a fourteen-member choir, two studio musicians on guitar, and one drummer—ironically, Starr, the last Beatle to join the band and the last member to play on a Beatles session. At one point, Ringo was forced to step away from his drum kit to quell one of the volatile producer's notorious temper tantrums. Meanwhile, the choral voices belonged to Beatles-session mainstays the Mike Sammes Singers, who had no compunction about working outside of Martin's earshot. As Sammes himself later remarked, "It wasn't our problem. We just went in and did what Phil Spector wanted."[12]

For his part, Martin was infuriated by the results of Spector's intervention, later writing that "through Allen Klein, John had engaged Phil Spector and done everything that he told me I couldn't do: he overdubbed voices, he added choirs and orchestras. I could have done that job easily, but he [John] decided to do it that way, and I was very offended by that. Paul was livid at what was done to 'The Long and Winding Road.'" At one point, McCartney even attempted, albeit unsuccessfully, to block the album's release. "I'm not struck by the violins and ladies' voices on 'The Long and Winding Road,'" he complained. Meanwhile, McCartney's estranged songwriting partner vehemently defended Spector's efforts on the disintegrating band's behalf: "He worked like a pig on it," Lennon recalled. "He'd always wanted to work with the Beatles, and he was given the *shittiest* load of badly recorded shit—and with a lousy feeling to it . . . and he made *something* out of it." Not surprisingly, Glyn Johns, like Martin, didn't see things that way, later writing that "after the group broke up, John gave the tapes to Phil Spector, who puked all over them, turning the album into the most syrupy load of bullshit I have ever heard." But Johns also understood that in his own way, he (and, at times, Martin) had failed to capture the Beatles' vision for the project, however poorly communicated: "My master tape, perhaps quite rightly, ended up on a shelf in the tape store at EMI."[13]

With Martin and McCartney seething in advance of the *Let It Be* soundtrack's release, the cute Beatle took advantage of the moment to announce the band's breakup on April 10, 1970, as well as the upcoming release of his eponymous debut solo album. Rather than make the pronouncement via news conference or press release, Paul concocted a set of questions and answers with Apple's Peter Brown in order to drive home his point about the finality of the Beatles' disbandment:

> Q: Did you miss the other Beatles and George Martin? Was there a moment when you thought, "I wish Ringo were here for this break?"
> A: No.

If Martin felt any sting from McCartney's words, he never revealed it, preferring to understand the end of the Beatles in a more philosophical light. Readily admitting that "it's pretty obvious that without the Beatles I wouldn't be where I am," George felt a momentary glint of sadness after Paul's April 1970 announcement. "I felt a little bit of emptiness, but on the other hand it was almost a relief because I had gained my freedom," the producer later wrote. "I had devoted eight years of my life to them; they were always Number One in my book, and all my other artists had to understand they took second place to the Beatles. After Brian [Epstein] died, I felt some responsibility for their careers, too. I didn't want to fail them; I wanted them always to be successful. Suddenly, that responsibility was removed."[14]

But what really rankled George at the time was what he believed was the shoddy release of *Let It Be*, an album that might have benefited from the producer's allegiance to the high-fidelity sound of the Beatles' legacy. To Martin's mind, Spector's postproduction work fell far short of this dictum. For Martin and Johns, the album's liner notes proved to be especially unsettling, casting *Let It Be* as "a new phase Beatles album. Essential to the content of the film *Let It Be* was that they performed live for many of the tracks; in comes the warmth and the freshness of a live performance as reproduced for disc by Phil Spector." Martin was patently disgusted, later remarking that "the album credit reads 'Produced by Phil Spector,' but I wanted it changed to 'Produced by George Martin. Over-produced by Phil Spector.'" For his part, Spector couldn't help taking pot shots at Martin—especially after the press had panned the American producer for "ruining the Beatles," among a host of other criticisms. "They don't know that it was no favor to me to give me George Martin's job, because I don't consider myself in the same situation or league," Spector remarked at the time. "I don't consider him with me. He's somewhere else. He's an arranger, that's all. As far as *Let It Be*, he had left it in a deplorable condition, and it was not satisfactory to any of them [the Beatles], they did not want it out as it was."[15]

Released on May 8, 1970, the *Let It Be* soundtrack proved to be an international best seller, easily topping the charts in the UK and US marketplaces alike. But in spite of the LP's commercial success, the critics understood the project for what it represented. Writing in *NME*, Alan Smith observed that "if the new Beatles soundtrack is to be their last, then it will stand as a cheapskate epitaph, a cardboard tombstone, a sad and tatty end to a musical fusion which wiped clean and drew again the face of pop." In a moment of utter damnation, Smith concluded that the LP revealed a "contempt for the intelligence of today's record-buyer" and derided the bandmates for having "sold out all the principles for which they ever stood." *Rolling Stone*'s John Mendelsohn was equally acerbic, writing that "musically, boys, you passed the audition. In terms of having the judgment to avoid either over-producing yourselves or casting the fate of your get-back statement to the most notorious of all over-producers, you didn't." Offering a minority opinion among a sea of critical voices, the *Sunday Times*'s Derek Jewell described *Let It Be* as a kind of "last will and testament, from the blackly funereal packaging to the music itself, which sums up so much of what the Beatles as artists have been—unmatchably brilliant at their best, careless and self-indulgent at their least." If nothing else, more than one critic observed, the *Let It Be* soundtrack surpassed the quality of Lindsay-Hogg's documentary, which had been soundly rebuffed.[16]

In contrast with the earlier Beatles film premieres, in which Martin and the bandmates paraded for the press, none of the principals, save for Lindsay-Hogg, appeared at the London Pavilion debut on May 20. That same month, the Beatles' final American single, "The Long and Winding Road" backed with "For You Blue" was released, quickly ascending to *Billboard*'s top spot. In a final note of nostalgic sadness, "The Long and the Winding Road" netted George and the bandmates' record-making twentieth number-one song in the American marketplace. For Martin, it may not have kept "the roll" alive, but the success enjoyed by "The Long and Winding Road," even with Spector's window dressing, amounted to something along the lines of solace during those bewildering post-Beatles times. In spite of all of the attendant critical rancor, *Let It Be* would be remembered fondly during awards season, when the soundtrack took home an Academy Award for Original Song Score, with Quincy Jones accepting the statuette on the absent bandmates' behalf. As it happened, in a great moment of irony, McCartney would be on hand to accept *Let It Be*'s Grammy Award for Best Original Score.

In contrast with the days and weeks following *Abbey Road*'s release, when he felt a sense of relief at having brought the album home under seemingly impossible interpersonal constraints, the finality associated with *Let It Be* gave way to new and much-earned feelings of optimism and goodwill for Martin. "I was unshackled to a certain extent, and that was good," he later wrote. "I was in great demand now because I was a successful and well-known producer, and for the first time in my life I was able to accept work from all over the world without a long-term commitment. If I were asked to produce one album with an artist, I could agree to it provided I didn't have to do any more than that. If I enjoyed it and liked the result, I might want to do another album, but I didn't have to. And that was great." And as George soon discovered, "life after the Beatles was like a series of flirtations after being divorced."[17]

21

THE EMERALD ISLE
OF THE CARIBBEAN

—————

ORTUNATELY FOR GEORGE, one of his very first and most successful flirtations involved the completion of AIR's Oxford Street Studios, which enjoyed a gala send-off in October 1970. In spite of the facility's enormous cost over-runs and architectural challenges, the grand-opening party was held in fine style on October 7, with George and his AIR partners officiating. Delivered in "true showbiz tradition," the event was attended by "all our friends and enemies from EMI," Martin later wrote, "people from other record companies, and—with a certain magnanimity, I thought—the architects, with whom we had had a major falling-out over the spiraling costs." During the two-day party, the AIR team and their guests dispatched with more than four hundred bottles of Bollinger champagne.[1]

But the real story during that memorable week in the life of George's career was the studio itself. In addition to Martin's own dogged perseverance, the new facility had been well served by the contributions of Jack Parsons, who had worked tirelessly for the past few years on bringing the complicated project home, especially given the unusual specifications associated with establishing a working recording facility in the bustling heart of London. "It was one of the noisiest places you could choose to build a recording studio," Dave Harries later recalled. "When Geoff [Emerick] first showed me the pictures at Abbey Road I said that simply can't work. It will never work. But work it did!" As Simaen Skolfield, one of the studio's first tape operators, later recalled, musicians adored working at Oxford Street, which, given its Central London location, was seemingly in the middle of everything. "It was a very, very busy spot," Skolfield later recalled, "but a wonderful spot because you could look out of the windows of Studio 1 and look straight down Oxford Circle. We were actually five floors up, but everybody looked like little people coming in and out of the tube station." At one juncture, the studio had become "so successful that George and John [Burgess] who had built it primarily for themselves couldn't get in there and had to go back to Abbey Road. We were certainly one of the pioneering independent studios—and among the first to go 16-track. When we opened, our studio rates were £35 per hour." Indeed, almost from the beginning AIR Oxford Street emerged as the most successful arm of the partnership. While AIR had begun life with the express intent of producing records by the partners' clients, AIR Oxford Street demonstrated that there was an even more lucrative market for providing top-drawer production space outside of "dependent" studios and their record company overseers like Abbey Road and EMI. Not long after opening its doors, AIR Oxford Street became especially well known for its spacious Studio 1, which had formerly been a banquet hall. "The main studio was actually quite large and had a quite live sound," Harries later remarked. "The idea was originally that we would do film scoring in there, with the smaller No. 2 studio which had a much drier sounding aspect and was built for pop. They both had basically the same equipment in the control room." But in spite of AIR's original intentions, Studio 1 enjoyed wide appeal among artists of all stripes. "As it turned out," said Harries, "the main room for a number of reasons, including its great drum sound, got booked out by bands. It just worked. Film people couldn't get in. We had good equipment and good technicians. We were in the right place at the right time. George once again picked out the right thing. Throughout, he had the Midas touch with artists and with studios, as the hits kept coming on both sides of the Atlantic."[2]

On October 9, 1970, with the debris from the raucous opening gala still in evidence, George supervised the inaugural recording session at AIR Oxford Street, an honor that he accorded to Cilla Black. With the Beatles having been consigned to the history books, she was his longest-standing and most successful client, with the exception of occasional sessions devoted to old friends like Johnny Dankworth and Spike Milligan. While Cilla's television series continued to exceed all expectations, her recording career was in need of a commercial hit. Her latest long-player for Parlophone, *Sweet Inspiration*, had fared poorly, peaking at number forty-two on the UK album charts, and George and Cilla were determined to stem the tide, just as they had done with "Surround Yourself with Sorrow" backed with "London Bridge" back in 1969. And for a while, it appeared as if they might just do exactly that. With "Something Tells Me (Something's Gonna Happen Tonight)" backed with "La La La Lu," Cilla enjoyed a 1971 holiday hit with the A-side, penned by Roger Greenaway and Roger Cook, notching a top-five showing on the UK charts in the bargain. As it turned out, "Something Tells Me (Something's Gonna Happen Tonight)" was easily Cilla's biggest hit since her heyday in the mid-1960s. But in the years since the release of *Sher-oo!* in 1968, her long-players had fallen into a steady decline in terms of her ability to find commercial success. For George and Cilla, this was a continuing source of frustration—particularly given the fact that she enjoyed regular face time with a massive audience courtesy of her variety show. With George in the producer's chair, Cilla's long-players continued to fade, with *Images* (1971) and *Day by Day with Cilla* (1973) failing to find a steady listenership, and the two longtime collaborators decided to go their separate ways. As Cilla later wrote, "Probably as a way of trying to be positive and keep my life moving along, we'd decided it was time for a new beginning on the musical front." Besides, she pointed out, "George Martin was an enormous international artist himself, and it was getting more and more difficult for the two of us to find time when we were both free to work together." Her first Martin-free album, 1974's *In My Life*, found her working with Australian record magnate David Mackay, who had set the world afire with the New Seekers' global hit (and the Hillside Singers' blockbuster Coca-Cola jingle) "I'd Like to Teach the World to Sing (in Perfect Harmony)," coauthored by none other than David and Jonathan themselves—Greenaway and Cook.[3]

Not surprisingly, Cilla's *In My Life* LP prominently featured a cover version of the Lennon-McCartney composition of the same name, but by then George was long gone. Running a world-class studio had proven to be a great boon for AIR, but it was not without its challenges. In one such instance, George and his partners rose to the occasion—and, in so doing, established a niche in spoken-word recording, the very same genre in which George had found success with Parlophone back in the 1950s. AIR Oxford Street's foray into spoken-word recording occurred after Argo Records approached George about becoming the company's regular vendor for spoken-word projects. Argo was particularly interested in learning about the studio's capabilities—namely about the "acoustics of the studio, with its floor 'floating' two feet above the original floor and its walls and ceilings suspended from acoustic mounts." Argo had become flustered by the relative ineffectiveness of Decca Studios during recent sessions devoted to a spoken-word recording of *Julius Caesar* starring Laurence Olivier. During one key passage during the Decca sessions, Olivier's performance had been spoiled after studio mics captured the sound of a jet flying overhead. Now "it's well-known and generally found acceptable that there are certain anachronisms in Shakespeare, such as cannons going off when cannons hadn't even been invented," Martin later joked, "but it was felt that a Boeing 707 was taking things a little too far!" Determined to test the fidelity of AIR studios, Argo's chief engineer visited Oxford Street and put the facility through its paces, variously turning up the gain on all of the amps and listening for ambient sound like air-conditioning or the like. With AIR having passed the test, Argo subsequently shifted the Olivier sessions to Oxford Street. "So they were satisfied," George wrote, "and we gained the first of many customers for recording the spoken word." But "there was only one embarrassment. Their first session with us was to record a jet-less version of *Julius Caesar*. Just as Olivier was delivering a speech from the steps of the Roman Forum, he moved, and we discovered to our horror that we had a squeaky floorboard!"[4]

George spent much of the early 1970s trying his hand with a wide array of artists—with the single proviso, of course, that working with them appealed to his sense of adventure and that he admired their work. This meant that at times George would shuttle from one client to the next as he searched for that same elusive *something* that had eluded him in his pre-Beatles years. Given the growing success of AIR Oxford Street, for the first time in his life, George enjoyed the kind of financial freedom that allowed him to follow his own whimsy wherever it might lead. As Skolfield later remarked, by this juncture "there were four studios operating at AIR Oxford Street—and those studios were operating pretty much 24/7." One of Martin's earliest post-Beatles acts was Seatrain, an American roots-fusion band that ended up drawing the ire of John Lennon, in a backhanded way, when he took issue with Martin's contributions to the Beatles' achievements during his 1970 *Rolling Stone* interview with Jann Wenner. At one point, John began criticizing supporters of the Fab Four like Dick James, whom the former Beatle denigrated as "another one of those people who think they made us. They didn't. I'd like to hear Dick James's music, and I'd like to hear George Martin's music, please, just play me some." In a 1971 interview with *Melody Maker*'s Richard Williams, Martin was asked to respond to Lennon's claims. In a rare moment of unvarnished candor, Martin didn't mince words, saying, "That's silly, of course. I guess I feel sorry for him, because he's obviously schizophrenic in that respect. He must have a split mind—either he doesn't mean it, or if he does mean it he can't be in a normal state of mind at that time. The contrary thing is that in

June of last year I was in the States, and I did the *David Frost Show*, [and] obviously, we talked about the Beatles. . . . Then about six weeks after I got back, I had a postcard from the Beverly Hills Hotel, written by John in his own fair hand, saying that he caught the Frost show, thought it was great, and it was so nice of me to say such nice things about him and how he hoped that my wife and children were well and love from John and Yoko. That was the last time I heard from him, and that's the other side of the coin. He'd probably hate people to know that he was that sentimental."[5]

And that's when John upped the ante, further trivializing George's role in shaping the Beatles' sound. In a 1971 open letter to Martin and Williams published in the pages of *Melody Maker*, Lennon replied with a vengeance:

Here I am again! For a start, I don't see anything "schizoid" in having more than one emotion, though obviously you do. When people ask me questions about "What did George Martin really do for you?" I have only one answer, "What does he do now?" I noticed you had no answer for that! It's not a put down, it's the truth. I sent the postcard about the *David Frost Show* because you did say nice things about "Across the Universe." I reciprocated in kind, okay? Schizoid, my arse. . . . Of course, George Martin was a great help in translating our music technically when we needed it, but for the cameraman to take credit from the director is a bit too much. . . . Don't be so paranoid, George, we still love you.

John (and Yoko, who was there)

P.S. And as for *Let It Be*, just listen to the two versions, the bootleg "original" and the Spector production.

P.P.S. I think Paul and I are the best judges of our partners. Just look at the world charts, and by the way, I hope Seatrain is a good substitute for the Beatles.

For George, the *Melody Maker* exchange was a vivid reminder of the producer's own dictum about working with highly creative musicians and songwriters. "You have to be careful," Martin had once written. "If the artist feels threatened, it can raise a barrier between producer and artist, and make it harder to work together." While Martin and Lennon were obviously no longer working together, the producer's public remarks had clearly left

Lennon feeling threatened about the degree of his own achievements, which, by Martin's every admission, had been superlative. By the early 1970s, George had developed a number of stock phrases for explaining his production efforts with the Beatles. And one of these oft-repeated descriptions about "painting pictures in sound" had clearly gotten under John's skin—so much so, that the former Beatle disparaged such thinking as "pure hallucination." For George, it was the summer of 1967 all over again after *Time* magazine had singled out the producer as the unobtrusive genius behind *Sgt. Pepper.* But even still, George should have known better. The result of the *Melody Maker* squabble was almost exactly the same, with the artist—in this case, Lennon—taking conspicuous issue with any suggestion that the supporting players who made their work possible held a larger stake in the artist's success.[6]

As for Seatrain, George had relished the opportunity to record the American band, even going so far as to temporarily relocate his family to Marblehead, Massachusetts, in 1971 in order to immerse himself in the production of their work. "Working with Seatrain was interesting because it was such a varied group," he later recalled, "a mixture of so many different talents. I loved the homespun, folky feel of the band." With AIR's in-house engineer Bill Price in tow, George traveled to Marblehead, where he "discovered that there were houses to rent in the summer, and I started working on the notion of equipping our own studio in one of them. I soon found the ideal house. It was huge, empty, almost derelict, and stood in its own grounds on Marblehead Neck, which was effectively an island, connected to the town by a causeway. It had a very large sitting-room, about 25 feet by 16, which we could use as a studio, and right next door to that was another room which was suitable for a control room." Not missing a beat, Martin and Price rented a recording desk from 3M's Rhode Island office, along with a sixteen-track machine. With Dolby Laboratories throwing in some hardware and having shipped his own loudspeakers over from London, George was ready to go. For the Martins and their young family, life in Marblehead was idyllic. Living in a rented house near the makeshift studio, they "would spend most mornings on the beach. Then we would start recording at two in the afternoon, with a break at seven, when I would cycle home for supper, returning to work until about two in the morning."[7]

As for Seatrain, George had difficulty getting the group off the ground. He consciously shifted the band's sound from its roots-music origins into a more folk rock–oriented aesthetic. At one point, George and Seatrain even enjoyed a minor hit with "13 Questions" backed with "Oh My Love," which cracked *Billboard*'s top fifty. For *The Marblehead Messenger,* the group's much-anticipated second album with George, he directed them toward an even edgier sound, which the bandmates supplemented with subtle lyrics about the Vietnam conflict and other activist issues like the environment. While Seatrain succeeded in landing a British tour as the supporting act for Traffic, their high mark proved to be "13 Questions," and George bowed out as their producer. But by that point, he had already pivoted to another artist, Paul Winter, whom he had met in Marblehead during his Massachusetts sojourn with Seatrain. With his band, the Paul Winter Consort, Winter had made his name as a top-flight soprano saxophonist with a penchant for "chamber pop," a genre whose classical origins meshed nicely with Martin's background. Wanting to take advantage of his makeshift recording facility, which had come to be known as "Seaweed Studios," Martin suggested that the Paul Winter Consort take advantage of AIR's investment and undertake an album with him during his stay in Marblehead. According to oboist Paul McCandless, the band didn't hesitate to take George up on his offer. "Paul Winter was dying to work with George Martin because Paul was looking to find the most powerful, smartest producer he could to help get his music, and instrumental music in general, out to the wider public," McCandless later remarked. "George's signature was putting all these unique-sounding instrumental breaks on the Beatles records. They weren't the normal guitar solos: sometimes there was a string quartet or a Salvation Army brass band or you name it."[8]

For the band's members, working with George was a revelation. Together with Price, Martin was able to challenge them to expand their soundscapes and take risks. As McCandless later recalled, "I remember there was one piece ['Whole Earth Chant'] for which we were looking for a big tamboura sound. George had the whole band come out, and we held down a chord and the middle pedal of the piano, which effectively creates a harp. Then he had the band strum the piano, and they recorded it but with the tape turned around so they were recording it backwards. So there was this big crescendo, and the engineer, Bill Price, faded it before it actually hit the attack. It had the effect of this swarming, swirling kind of thing." George later described the resulting album, *Icarus*, as "probably one of my favorites of all of the albums I have made," including those with the Beatles. While "sales were nothing special," George wrote, "the title song has the distinction of being the first record to fly around the moon." While it may have been apocryphal, the story went that the band's cellist, David Darling, talked a relative, Apollo 15 astronaut Joe Allen, into taking the recording with him on a NASA mission, during which the astronauts supposedly listened to the song as they circumnavigated the moon. "Part of the mission was to plot the location of unrecorded craters," George wrote. "Joe spotted a particularly fine one and named it Icarus after our record. So we are now part of the history of our planet's nearest neighbor."[9]

With the recording sessions for *Icarus* under his belt, George returned to the United Kingdom in late 1971 to mix the album at AIR Oxford Street. In recent months, he had also accepted a commission for the soundtrack for *Pulp*, a 1972 British comedy starring Michael Caine and directed by Mike Hodges, the filmmaker behind *Get Carter*. Film and TV work had emerged as a regular income source for George, as witnessed by his composition of the theme for *Mister Jerico*, a television series starring Patrick Macnee of *The Avengers* fame. Sung by Lulu, George's catchy number featured lyrics by Don Black, John Barry's frequent collaborator on the popular James Bond soundtracks. George also entered into a new collaboration with the King's Singers, a vocal group founded by six King's College, Cambridge University, choral scholars. As one of the first groups to apply a choral approach to pop tunes, the a cappella vocal ensemble had formed in 1968 and were clearly on the verge of commanding a much larger audience given their growing popularity on the concert circuit. Under George's tutelage, the King's Singers made their first extended forays as recording artists. With Jack Clegg serving as his engineer, George recorded their debut LP, *The King's Singers Collection*, at AIR Oxford Street in 1972, which featured a range of cover versions, including the producer's arrangements of Lennon-McCartney's "She's Leaving Home" and his own composition "The Game." Martin's old friend Ron Goodwin chipped in with lyrics and arrangements for "Watch Me" and "Building a Wall." The producer's association with the choral group continued in 1973 with a follow-up LP, *A French Collection*, an album of French-language tunes, and *Deck the Hall*, a live recording of religious numbers, which George supervised at St. John's Church in Hyde Park Crescent in February 1973. Years later, the King's Singers would evoke their collaboration with George, and their recordings of Lennon-McCartney compositions in particular, with their long player titled *Madrigal History Tour*.

In March 1973, George received an unusual blast from his past with the release of Pink Floyd's blockbuster LP *The Dark Side of the Moon*. In many ways, *The Dark Side of the Moon* was a brilliant extension of the multitrack achievements of Martin and the Beatles at the height of their studio years together. Working at Abbey Road, Pink Floyd enjoyed access to a sixteen-track machine—an incredible technological leap from the Beatles' EMI Studios heyday only a few years earlier. *The Dark Side of the Moon* was helmed by a number of George's associates, including Alan Parsons, who engineered Pink Floyd's masterwork, and Chris Thomas, who was brought in to supervise the album's complex mixing sessions. Over the years, the album would become one of the best-selling LPs of all time, with sales estimated at forty-five million copies. *The Dark Side of the Moon* would spend a record-setting 741 weeks on the *Billboard* album charts from 1973 to 1988. Not surprisingly, audiophiles flocked to the multilayered masterpiece, studying every nook and cranny of the record in much the same fashion as the most zealous Beatlemaniacs do with the intricacies of *Sgt. Pepper* and *The White Album*. Ardent listeners to *The Dark Side of the Moon*'s stirring conclusion—as the song "Eclipse" segues into a beating heart—found themselves treated to a sonic Easter egg in the form of the faint sounds of music lingering deep in the heart of the mix. It was none other than a snippet of George's 1965 orchestral arrangement, as performed by the George Martin Orchestra, of the Beatles' "Ticket to Ride." Back in the predigital days of the early 1970s, tape was often recycled for later use. Had Parsons and his team failed to effectively wipe the tape that was used to record the heartbeat sound effect? Or, more likely, was the George Martin Orchestra's "Ticket to Ride" playing somewhere in the extreme background when the sound of the heartbeat was captured at Abbey Road?

For George, 1973 proved to be a significant turning point in his post-Beatles career, the anomalies of Pink Floyd's legendary LP notwithstanding. After his success with the *Pulp* soundtrack, George landed the opportunity to score an even bigger film, *Live and Let Die*, the latest installment in the James Bond movie franchise. But for George, the soundtrack hadn't fallen into his lap so easily. The opportunity had first come available after the series' stalwart composer John Barry had feuded with Harry Saltzman during the production of the previous Bond film, *Diamonds Are Forever*. Still stinging over his falling out with the producer, Barry decided to go on hiatus for *Live and Let Die*, opting to work on a stage musical instead. In need of a title song for the new film, Albert Broccoli, Saltzman's coproducer, contacted Paul McCartney about composing the theme song. McCartney's star was on the rise, having landed a pair of hit singles with his new band Wings in the form of the top-ten US hit "Hi-Hi-Hi" and, most recently, the number-one single "My Love." As with previous Bond movies, the title track for *Live and Let Die* was a much-sought-after commercial vehicle for pop singers, and McCartney jumped at the chance, inviting Martin to produce and orchestrate the song. For his part, George was delighted to be working with the former Beatle for the first time since the January 1970 sessions in advance of *Let It Be*.

To Paul's mind, George's participation made perfect sense, having previously produced Matt Monro's and Shirley Bassey's hit theme songs for *From Russia with Love* and *Goldfinger*, respectively. After reading Ian Fleming's novel, McCartney made short work of the project. "I read it and thought it was pretty good. That afternoon, I wrote the song and went in the next week and did it," McCartney later recalled. "It was a job of work for me in a way because writing a song around a title like that's not the easiest thing going." During sessions for Wings' *Red Rose Speedway*, George and the band convened at AIR Oxford Street to record what the producer thought would be a demo for the Bond producers' consideration. At Paul's urging, George had booked an orchestra to accompany the band, whose instrumentation included Paul on piano and lead vocals, his wife Linda on keyboards, former Moody Blues member Denny Laine playing bass and singing harmony vocals with Linda, lead guitarist Henry McCullough, and drummer Denny Seiwell. George had secured ace percussionist Ray Cooper to round out the recording. By this point, AIR's London studios were in high demand, emerging as one of the city's preeminent locales, and Paul and his contemporaries were eager to record there. As Simaen Skolfield later recalled, "AIR just took off straight away. It was huge. We had them pulling in big orchestral pieces for films so we had the screen, with projectors and all this kind of stuff. So Studio 1 was busy all the time. It would be Stevie Wonder, and if it wasn't Stevie Wonder it would be Paul McCartney and Wings." When Wings had finished playing "Live and Let Die" in the former banquet hall, with the song's inherent spine-tingling drama on full display, George said to Paul, "We seem to be making a real record, not a demo. Are you sure about that?" he asked, concerned that they were going beyond the producers' request. "The hell with demos," Paul replied. "Let's give it the works!"[10]

At this point, Martin passed the finished track on to Saltzman and Broccoli. Not long afterward, Saltzman invited the producer to a meeting in Jamaica during which, to Martin's surprise, the idea of the producer composing the film score for *Live and Let Die* seemed to be a foregone conclusion, "even though nothing had been agreed," he later wrote, "and no one had yet said anything to me about time or money or arrangements." And that's when the meeting took an even stranger turn, with Saltzman praising Martin's arrangement for the title track and then asking, "Who are we going to get to sing it in the film? What do you think of Thelma Houston?" George was flabbergasted. "But you've got Paul McCartney," he countered. Undeterred, Saltzman suggested Aretha Franklin. "Aretha's very, very good," George answered. "But you've already got Paul McCartney." At this point, with nothing left to lose, Martin delicately explained that Saltzman could only have the song if it was attached to the Wings' recording that he'd recently produced in London. With Saltzman finally coming around to Wings' version of "Live and Let Die," Martin began composing the score. Working with director Guy Hamilton resulted in a great partnership for Martin. Even still, "writing a film score is a race against time," George wrote, "it is hard graft, but it makes it a lot easier when the director is not a musician but trusts you to do the job well." Hamilton "was very articulate in his instructions, and as we went through the film reel by reel, he would give me his thoughts, explaining what my music would do to heighten the tension and effect."[11]

While working with Hamilton had proven to be a tremendous boon for Martin, the *Live and Let Die* project soured precipitously for him when it came to negotiating with EMI. After Paul contacted him about working with Wings, "I was delighted, and at the outset didn't think about the money," George later recalled. "I never do; I get too excited about the prospect of work that interests me." The trouble began after the fact, when George contacted Len Wood, his former supervisor at EMI, to discuss his royalty associated with the forthcoming single, "Live and Let Die" backed with "I Lie Around," which was released in June 1973. George requested a 2 percent royalty, which was below his typical 3 percent rate. "My dear fellow," Wood replied, "you've forgotten that you signed a document saying you would operate on the same terms and conditions for a period of 10 years from 1965, and we're still within that period." For George, the retort was ineluctably simple: "But Len, the Beatles don't exist any more." Wood's rejoinder would stick in Martin's craw for years to come. "You look at the wording on your contract," he answered. "It says that you will be available to record the Beatles or any one of them."[12]

At this rate, George's effective royalty would be 0.15 of a cent per record. Realizing that the B-side, "I Lie Around," would be a McCartney-produced Wings track, Martin's percentage would be halved yet again. Wood ultimately struck a compromise in which he agreed to compensate Martin as if he had produced both sides of the single. "What you mean to say is that you'll pay me double a pittance," George soberly replied. At this rate, AIR would receive $310 for every one hundred thousand copies sold. "It was the last straw," George later wrote. "My relations with EMI were at their lowest ebb." But amazingly, "worse was to come" when George realized that after three years, he hadn't been paid at all for the *Let It Be* LP given his lack of an official production credit. From thenceforward, George had learned his lesson and would never attempt to "negotiate" with Len Wood again. He had resolved in all future disputes to get "bloody-minded" and work through his attorney.

Just as George had predicted, "Live and Let Die" became a worldwide smash, notching a number-two US hit in the process. In short order, the "Live and Let Die" backed with "I Lie Around" single earned a gold record from the Record Industry Association of America for having sold more than a million copies, which meant a paltry $3,100 flowing into the AIR coffers on the back of a legitimate blockbuster. Fortunately for George, the soundtrack proved to be far more lucrative, becoming a best seller, as well as netting him a tidy profit for his *Live and Let Die* score. George had the last laugh of sorts when "Live and Let Die" was nominated for an Academy Award for Best Original Song (only to lose out to "The Way We Were"), marking the first time that a James Bond theme had accrued such an honor. In 1974, George earned a Grammy Award for Best Arrangement, Accompanying Vocalist(s), for his work on "Live and Let Die," marking his first statuette since *Sgt. Pepper*. Buoyed by the success of the soundtrack, he conducted a series of concerts under the punning title of *Beatles to Bond and Bach*, including a December 1974 performance with the Royal Liverpool Philharmonic Orchestra. That same year, he released his first album-length collection of instrumentals since *British Maid*. Distributed by Polydor, *Beatles to Bond and Bach* included selections from *Yellow Submarine*, *Live and Let Die*, and Bach's *Air on the G String*.[13]

For George, the episode with "Live and Let Die" had returned him to the vanguard as one of rock's most preeminent producers. During this period, he would often meet with up-and-coming or established artists who captured his fancy. One of those bands was the American blue-eyed-soul duo Hall and Oates, who had recently released their *Abandoned Luncheonette* LP, which had received strong praise from the British music press. Taking the initiative, George invited the duo to lunch at New York City's Plaza Hotel. He was clearly attracted to the duo's soulful, bluesy ambience, much as he had been with the Beatles' harmonica sound during his first session with the beat band in June 1962 after hearing their performance of "Love Me Do." In their early recordings, Hall and Oates revealed a similar aspect of their evolving sound. "We joined him in the posh, stately, silver-service Edwardian Room," John Oates wrote, "with its massive windows overlooking a wintry, postcard-perfect, Currier and Ives Central Park. Over a reserved and polite conversation without a lot of musical details discussed, the meeting felt more social and more an opportunity to get to know one another. Perhaps it was the style of the luncheon, held in such an imperial, somewhat stuffy venue, which put us off. There was no doubting this master's golden, elegant touch in the studio, but Daryl and I were now infused with the energy, grit, and edge of downtown New York, which I believe led us to thinking that George

Martin simply was not right for us. At least in that moment." And with that, George politely withdrew his offer to produce the duo. Years later, Oates would admit that "it was probably a musically life-changing moment that we let slip through our fingers," but the meeting typified Martin's attempts to grow his roster of artists during that period.[14]

Not long after releasing "Live and Let Die," George tried his hand at producing Stackridge, an up-and-coming Bristol rock band that was riding on the heels of a recent BBC Two television spot and a winter tour. Attempting to build on this momentum, George brought the sextet into Oxford Street to record their third album, *The Man in the Bowler Hat*. George threw himself into the project, assisting the band in reshaping their rock sound into a progressive admixture of chamber pop and baroque musical stylings. George scored the album's lush orchestral arrangements and even chipped in with piano parts for "Humiliation" and "The Indifferent Hedgehog." But the LP's clear highlight was "Fundamentally Yours," a song brimming with rich melodies, a nifty synthesized harpsichord, and a driving beat from Billy "Sparkle" Bent. George tapped a wide range of musicians for the Stackridge project, including the Kinks' Ray Davies, who played trumpet on the album, as well as George's old Beatles compadre Derek Taylor, who laid down a horn solo for "To the Sun and the Moon." While the album may have been a one-off for George, *The Man in the Bowler Hat* proved to be a middling seller for Stackridge after its release in February 1974, clocking in at a respectable number twenty-two on the UK charts. The album cover was devised by John Kosh, the veteran art designer behind *Abbey Road* and *Let It Be*. But George didn't completely leave Stackridge behind. Within a year, Sparkle would retire his drum kit, leave Stackridge, and work as George's personal assistant.

In 1974, George also enjoyed the unexpected opportunity to right one of the most notorious wrongs of his career—a "big goof," in the producer's own words, that saw him passing on the chance to work with Tommy Steele, the musician who would emerge as the United Kingdom's first legitimate rock 'n' roll star. After years of working on the cabaret circuit, Steele had developed a beloved stage persona, and Martin was eager to assist the former teen idol in transforming his career yet again. The result was an LP titled *My Life, My Song* that hit the charts with a thud. It was a "brave attempt" at "an autobiographical experiment," George wrote, "that did not quite work." It was also, alas, an outcome that the producer had encountered throughout his long career in the record business. While acts like the Beatles prove to be commercial evergreens, the majority of George's clientele were victims of circumstance, good or bad, as well as prisoners of the longitude of their own

talent. With Steele—and clients before him like Judy Garland and Ella Fitzgerald—the producer had come to learn that late-career encounters were just
that: glowing opportunities and sometimes desperate efforts to recapture the
contemporary musical consciousness and, more often than not, old glories.[15]

While acts like Hall and Oates couldn't see their way clear to working
with George, one band that didn't decline his entreaties was America, the
Anglo-American folk-rock trio that featured Dewey Bunnell, Dan Peek, and
Gerry Beckley. America had broken onto the music scene in the early 1970s
with their best-selling eponymous debut album, which scored a pair of top-ten
US hits, including the chart-topping "A Horse with No Name." While their
second album, *Homecoming*, had continued the band's success, including
the top-ten hit "Ventura Highway," America's third album, *Hat Trick*, had
barely cracked the top thirty, failing to go gold where the first two LPs had
achieved platinum status. As with *Homecoming*, America had handled their
own production duties for *Hat Trick*, and by the time they met George, they
were understandably in a panic over their recent commercial slide. For his
part, George was delighted to help them try to reverse their "nosedive." "Let's
have a go," the producer told them. "We'll work quickly and efficiently." And
did they ever. The bandmates joined him at AIR Oxford Street, where they
worked for just over a fortnight from April 17 to May 7, 1974. The album,
which was titled *Holiday*, was released in June 1974, in keeping with George's
plan to work expeditiously with the band. But the speed at which he produced
the record belies the intensity of their efforts together. George made a point
of working with America like he would have back in his Parlophone days.
With Geoff Emerick in tow as the project's engineer, George had met with
them in London in mid-April and began routining their latest material. And
for their part, they met George's challenge with a steely resolve. "They were
very well-organized in the studio," he later wrote, which made it easier for
him to score their songs, when necessary, and overdub the instrumentation
with great precision. In addition to featuring America's new drummer Willie
Leacox, *Holiday* also found George providing keyboards on several songs.
The bandmates were thrilled to be working with the legendary producer. As
Bunnell later remarked, it "was great working with George. It was like we
knew each other. We were familiar with the Beatles, of course, and we had
that British sense of humor." Buckley was equally pleased, later describing
Martin as "such a hot arranger," which made their latest tracks even stronger. Their new collaboration proved to be a boon, with *Holiday* generating
a pair of top-five singles in "Tin Man," with Martin chipping in on piano,
and "Lonely People." The latter composition had been composed by Dan

Peek and his wife, Catherine, who self-consciously composed an optimistic rejoinder to the Beatles' "Eleanor Rigby." Instead of resigning itself to the fate of a solitary existence, the Peeks' "Lonely People" pointedly counseled its audience, "Don't give up until you drink from the silver cup, / And ride that highway in the sky."[16]

For George, the mid-1970s had already seen an incredible turnaround in terms of his professional fortunes. With the twin successes of "Live and Let Die" and America's new best-selling album, he was rightly chuffed about the state of his career after the post-Beatles malaise. And for the latter release, he was now enjoying a full producer's cut of 5 percent, which meant that he was being appropriately compensated as a professional, and that meant a great deal to George after dealing with EMI's conservative ways over the years. "For the first time in my life," George later wrote, "I was starting to earn some good money." On a personal front, George was no doubt pleased to learn that John had begun softening his post–*Let It Be* hard-line stance, as communicated in interviews with Jann Wenner and others, in which he diminished the contributions of folks like Martin to the Beatles' success. By 1974, Lennon had been explicitly reframing his commentary about Martin's role. As May Pang, John's girlfriend during his "Lost Honeymoon" period of estrangement from Yoko, later recalled, "John liked and admired George," remarking that the producer challenged John to work "beyond his norm" and helped him to imagine seemingly impossible sounds, which George would capture and make real in the studio. In a March 1975 BBC television interview with Bob Harris, John took great pains to clarify his association with George over the years, going so far as to admit that "it's hard to describe a relationship. They either say that George Martin did everything or the Beatles did everything. It was neither one, you know. We both. . . . George had done little to no rock 'n' roll when we met him, and we'd never been in a studio, so we did a lot of learning together." With a conciliatory perspective in stark contrast with his remarks to Wenner, Lennon observed that Martin "had a very great musical knowledge and background, so he could translate for us and suggest a lot of things, which he did." Lennon concluded that Martin and the Beatles "grew together, and so it's hard to say who did what. He taught us a lot, and I'm sure we taught him a lot by our sort of primitive musical ability, which is all I have still. I still have to have somebody to translate what I'm trying to say all the time. So it was a 'mutual benefit society.'"[17]

During this same period, George made a point of meeting with John during one of the producer's periodic West Coast visits. It marked the first time that he had seen the former Beatle in the flesh since August 1969 at the tail end of the *Abbey Road* sessions. For his part, George didn't mince words when it came to the *Rolling Stone* and *Melody Maker* episodes back in the early 1970s. "You know, you were pretty rough in that interview, John," George remarked. "Oh, Christ," said John, "I was stoned out of my fucking mind," adding "you didn't take any notice of that, did you?" George replied, "Well, I did, and it hurt." But the producer also knew John well enough to understand that this was the closest he would ever get to receiving an apology for John's insensitive remarks. For his part, George understood the source of his friend's malaise, reasoning that John had gone "through a very, very bad period of heavy drugs, and *Rolling Stone* got him during one of those periods. He was completely out of it." In his heart, George knew that "John had a very sweet side to him. He was a very tender person at heart. He could also be very brutal and very cruel. But he went through a very crazy time."[18]

Meanwhile, George had become inspired by the incredible success that AIR was enjoying with its Oxford Street studios. The project had succeeded, as he imagined it might, in becoming the cornerstone of AIR's income. As George later wrote, the partnership had begun to take a multiplicity of functions. "We have our own record label. We have our own artists, whom we record. We record artists for other labels. We hire out our studios to other producers—who may either use our own recording engineers, or bring their own as is current practice in America; and we hire out producers and engineers to others. But most often, because we now have a world-wide reputation, people come to us not only for the studios themselves but also to use our staff, knowing they are backed by AIR's training and high standards. That may sound like a sales pitch, but it happens to be true, to the extent that we have a very live agency which actually exports the talents of AIR's creative people." By this juncture, Emerick had joined Martin and his partners on a full-time basis, with the Apple Studios project having fallen into disarray after the engineer had spent years turning it into a world-class facility. At one point in late 1973, AIR's London studios had become so popular that Emerick couldn't even book studio space to mix Paul McCartney and Wings' *Band on the Run* LP, which he was forced to complete at the comparatively remote Kingsway Recorders. Buoyed by AIR Oxford Street's runaway success, George began hatching a plan for a "total environment" studio. The idea had started percolating after he had recorded America's *Hideaway* LP at Jimmy Guercio's Caribou studio in the Rocky Mountains, some fifty-five miles northwest of Denver. "I loved the creative freedom it gave," George wrote. "You were there to make an album, and the studio was yours for as long as you wanted it, any time of the day or night. It was very comfortable, with individual homely log cabins and a good studio with a Neve console. The only thing wrong was the time of year that I was there. In February, Colorado can be pretty cold, and a macabre sense of humor could easily label it as an expensive labor camp! Our nickname for it was Stalag Luft III."[19]

As Skolfield later observed, the idea of escaping to a "residential studio"—where artists and their production team could "get out of the city, go play tennis, and go horseback-riding"—was becoming fashionable by the mid-1970s. During this same period, Richard Branson had built a pioneering studio that came to be known as "the Manor," a Virgin Records facility in a historic Oxfordshire manor house. Such studios, according to Skolfield, are "more homely, more personal, and, most importantly, more private." For George, even studios like Caribou and the Manor seemed constrictive. He imagined something even more daring, a studio space that would be available wherever and whenever a recording artist desired. "I had the temerity to think of building a studio on a ship," George later admitted. "It could go anywhere— preferably the Mediterranean or the Caribbean—and it would certainly give the groups their get-away-from-it-all feeling." George assigned AIR's Keith Slaughter with the task of locating a suitable vessel—which the producer had taken to calling the "AIR Ship"—and Slaughter finally narrowed down his search to two options: the *Albro*, a spacious and luxuriously appointed 120-foot yacht fashioned out of a converted Scandinavian freighter, or the *Osejeuik*, a 160-foot Yugoslavian passenger ferry. The latter was a twin-engine vessel that offered even more spacious potential recording facilities than the *Albro*, which could only be fitted out by placing the studio in the ship's comparatively cozy hold. But the real issue, as with Oxford Street, concerned the exorbitant expense of converting the space, whether on land or sea, into a state-of-the-art recording studio. "Running costs would obviously be high, power supplies had to be stable, and the acoustic problems presented by a large steel box made the building of AIR London a picnic by comparison," George later wrote. When the specs had been completed, Slaughter predicted that it would cost some £400,000 to convert the *Osejeuik* to meet AIR's needs. With a mid-1970s economic crisis in full swing in the United Kingdom and an oil crisis impacting the world over, George lost his nerve. "So it became an unrealized dream," he wrote, "and I turned my thoughts to a land studio."[20]

With his shipbuilding aspirations having come to naught, George's terrestrial visions immediately turned to a tropical locale. Over the years, he had come to adore Hawaii, valuing the archipelago's relaxed tropical climate. Feeling that Hawaii was too far away from the old United Kingdom, George settled his sights on the Caribbean, which was geographically situated between the

United States and Europe, where the vast majority of AIR's jet-setting clientele was based. "I knew the Caribbean fairly well, but never seriously considered it because of its political instability," George wrote. "There always seemed to be undercurrents in the Bahamas and Virgin Islands, and beautiful Jamaica is sadly an unhappy place." And that's when George discovered beautiful, tranquil Montserrat, the British colony that hailed itself as the Emerald Isle of the Caribbean. "I was struck by the natural friendliness of the place, which I am sure has a lot to do with the lack of progress in 'civilized' developments. I am happy to say Montserrat does not have a casino, high-rise hotels, or concrete sunbathing pads beside huge chlorinated swimming-pools. But it does have a fresh charm of its own." George's problems were finally solved when he found a thirty-acre farm nestled five hundred feet above the Caribbean Sea. As George scanned the landscape, he began to imagine cutting-edge, multitrack studios, with nearby villas where his artists could relax and find inspiration without sacrificing their privacy. For George, Montserrat more than fit the bill. In his eyes, the studio would become nothing short of a tropical paradise.[21]

22

"A SERIES OF ONE-NIGHT STANDS"

BY THE MID-1970S, AIR's success in the recording industry had clearly surpassed George's expectations by a wide margin. Indeed, the partnership's original mission to produce independent recordings had given way to a much larger profit sector associated with booking studio time in state-of-the-art facilities. A few years earlier, Management Agency Music (MAM) founder Gordon Mills offered £2 million to purchase AIR, lock, stock, and barrel. As chairman of the partnership, George's first inclination was to turn down the offer. The company was just short of a decade old. "It's silly, after all the effort to build up our own company," George reasoned. But "on the other hand, none of us had a penny to his name, and it was hard to resist the temptation of a cool half a million pounds each." Negotiations broke down with Gordon after AIR's leadership realized that it wouldn't entirely be a cash deal. Worse yet, "there was a cat's cradle of strings attached, all of which added up to the fact that we wouldn't be our own bosses."[1]

In 1972, Dick James Music made a bid for AIR. In recent years, George's relationship with the music publisher had deteriorated—largely over the tangled web associated with the Beatles' publishing interests. George was well aware that Dick had been the beneficiary of George's goodwill in the group's early years, that Dick was the person to whom he had "given" the Beatles and who had become a multimillionaire in the process. "I think the truth of the matter is that he had never forgiven me for that," George later wrote. "After all, it is a bit of a burden to carry around. He once said to me: 'How many times must a man say "Thank you"?' I never wanted him to say 'Thank you'; I didn't want it to get in the way of our relationship." With AIR in play, James didn't waste any time offering a million pounds in cash to purchase AIR outright. As George later recalled, "Since ours was a private company, the decision to sell had to be unanimous among the four of us. But we were all still penniless, and with a quarter of a million each being dangled in front of our noses we decided to talk. The fact was that, apart from our individual problems, we had no capital assets except for the company itself, into which we had been ploughing back everything we made. We wouldn't have minded selling a bit of the company in order to raise some capital. But that was the problem; a little bit wasn't enough. From Dick James's point of view, it had to be what would eventually become a controlling interest."[2]

For his part, Martin was wary about dealing with James given their long history together. As the years wore on, George and his partners soured on the offer, which finally collapsed in early 1974 in a heated boardroom discussion between the two businessmen. "The truth was that I got extremely annoyed," said George, "because I realized that he was trying to buy not only the company, but also me and my future work." At this point, the negotiations became "acrimonious," with James banging his fists on the table and Martin shouting back in kind over the provenance of AIR. "We went our different ways," said George, and all the producer could think about, even as he argued with his old friend, was "a nagging sense of guilty gratitude which went back to the day I suggested to Brian Epstein, 'Why don't you get Dick James as your publisher?'" While a deal with Dick James was off the table, George and his partners were still liable for their attorneys' fees, which meant that they actually lost money over the whole "non-deal."[3]

In October 1974, George and his partners received a very different kind of offer from Chris Wright and Terry Ellis, the visionary founders behind Chrysalis Records. "It was a different bag of tricks altogether," Martin later recalled, as they only wanted to purchase a small portion of the company. And why not? For Chrysalis Records to have ready access to a world-class London studio was reason enough for Wright and Ellis to make the offer, which promised to afford Martin and his partners with the capital that they so desperately desired. While the deal provided Chrysalis with the option to buy a controlling interest in AIR, Wright and Ellis avowed that they would not interfere in the company's day-to-day operations. "To all intents and purposes," George wrote, "it was to remain ours." For George, the Chrysalis merger portended an "ideal marriage." As far as he was concerned, "the brilliant thing about the deal is that it has not cost me my freedom. I can do exactly what I want. I'm as free as the wind. If I want to write music for a film, I can. If I want to go away and write a symphony, I can."[4]

As it happened, though, the Chrysalis deal wasn't consummated without any casualties for George and his partners. Ron Richards, in particular, felt the sting of the negotiations. Richards had preferred the earlier cash offers, especially the most recent deal with Dick James. As chairman, Martin held sway in spite of his stated belief in pure democracy, leaving Richards, as AIR's managing director, to maintain a sense of unity among the partners. The attendant stress associated with the Chrysalis negotiations left Richards in ill health, and shortly thereafter he left the company. It was an unhappy ending for Martin and Richards's long-standing partnership—an association that went back to the Beatles' first days at Abbey Road and long before that during their Parlophone years together. While Richards had remained a viable producer into the 1970s—he had supervised the Hollies' international hit "The Air That I Breathe" in the spring of 1974—his enthusiasm for the recording industry had waned considerably during his post-AIR years. Richards produced his last long-player, the Hollies' *Five Three One–Double Seven O Four*, in 1979.

In 1976, as George began making plans to launch his ill-fated "AIR Ship," he was dealt another blow from his old nemesis EMI. As it was, AIR had only just begun to chart a new path without Richards in the fold, and John Burgess was still finding his sea legs as AIR's new managing director. The trouble with EMI started when each of AIR's original partners, Richards included, received a registered letter from the record conglomerate announcing that EMI was terminating its original contract with AIR. This was the very same contract that George had negotiated with Len Wood back in 1965 during his earliest days as an independent producer. George described receiving the registered letter as a "shock, the nature of which could truly be described as incredible. Because that's what it was: unbelievable." While EMI was entitled to terminate the original contract, that agreement stated that the company would be liable to pay royalties for twenty-five years, which would take them through 1990. But astoundingly, EMI's letter proclaimed that royalties would cease with the contract's termination date. "We were shattered," George wrote—and especially after AIR's lawyers unearthed an ambiguous clause in the contract.[5]

Apparently, the whole business had started after George and his partners became suspicious that they had been underpaid in terms of their quarterly royalties. When they demanded an audit into EMI's business affairs after having not received royalty statements for some eighteen months, the clause

allowed EMI to terminate the contract without cause. It was pure gamesman-
ship on EMI's part to avoid having to provide the statements, which would,
in turn, presumably demonstrate the deficits. To George's mind, it was but
one more example of the record conglomerate's callous disregard. And for
George, it was the height of incivility. "There was no question of anyone
ringing us up to say: 'Look, old boy, this is what we're doing.' Just a registered letter." In the end, the matter was resolved in AIR's favor, but as far as
George was concerned, he had been duped yet again by the record company.
In spite of the recent past, he hadn't seemed able to learn that attempting to
effect cordial relations with his former employer was a lost cause. Resolving
to redouble his efforts, he decided, once and for all, to no longer find himself
ensnared by Wood.[6]

While he may have been frustrated by the financial challenges that he
and his partners had encountered of late, George had entered a post-Beatles
heyday in which he felt liberated enough (and, after the Chrysalis deal, more
fully capitalized) to take risks and follow his fancy as far as his production
activities were concerned. After the success of America's Martin-produced
comeback with *Holiday*, the producer was eager to get the band back in the
studio for yet another go. Recorded at the Record Plant in Sausalito, California, America's follow-up album, *Hearts*, picked up where *Holiday* had left off,
generating yet another top-five US album, as well as three hit singles, including
the chart-topping "Sister Golden Hair." For George, America's "Sister Golden
Hair" was a milestone that marked his first American number-one hit since
the Beatles' "Let It Be" five years earlier. With America, George had finally
discovered his first bona fide mainstay since the Beatles. While they could
never hope to approach the Fab Four's commercial and critical accomplishments—in truth, who really could?—America afforded Martin with a steady
band to shape and reshape for the music marketplace. In many ways, it was
like the old days, when he would routine an act in his role as A&R head and
take aim at the hit parade in competition with the likes of Norrie Paramor.
Only in the 1970s, Martin found himself on a proving ground with such
production powerhouses as Brian Eno, Quincy Jones, Roy Thomas Baker,
Eddie Kramer, and Tony Visconti.

In addition to Wings and America, George's mid-1970s renaissance would
be founded on a series of sizzling, guitar-oriented long-players with the likes
of classical wizard John Williams, the virtuosic John McLaughlin, and Jeff
Beck, one of rock's preeminent guitar gods. Over the years, Williams had
emerged as one of the world's most celebrated classical guitarists. Working with the Australian prodigy was an opportunity for Martin not only

to produce Williams's latest LP, *The Height Below*, but also to try his own hand at performance, which he truly relished. Williams was joined on the album by a host of luminaries, including Brian Gascoigne and Tristan Fry on percussion; Charlotte Nassim on koto, the traditional Japanese stringed instrument; and George's old friend Dudley Moore on organ.

With John McLaughlin, George was able to assist the talented guitarist in redirecting his career after years of excess. When Martin met him in 1974, McLaughlin had "cut his hair short, renounced drink and drugs, became vegetarian, and took to wearing all white clothes. A complete change of life." Working with McLaughlin's second incarnation of the Mahavishnu Orchestra, which included Jean-Luc Ponty on the electric violin, Martin produced *Apocalypse*, a tour de force that resulted in a top-ten jazz album in the American marketplace. With Geoff Emerick handling the engineering duties, George was dazzled by the music that they captured at AIR's London studios. It was, George wrote, "a flowing lyrical sequence of beautiful sounds bound together with a driving rock sound that almost brutalized the sweetness of the conception." For George, one of the highlights of recording *Apocalypse* occurred when he conducted simultaneous sessions in two different AIR studios, with the Mahavishnu Orchestra in one and the London Symphony Orchestra (LSO) in the other. "The scale of decibels between one and the other was ridiculous," he later recalled. "Michael Waldon's drumming was louder than any instrument in the LSO, much louder. So we had to put them in separate studios. The sections of music that required the bands together, we did that way. We laid down tracks and overdubbed the LSO: we laid down LSO and overdubbed the band, which is a strange way of doing it, but there were long *colla voce* or *legato* sections which the LSO were recording that didn't require a rhythmic emphasis. That could be laced in afterwards. John McLaughlin worked very closely with Mike Gibbs, who was the orchestrator, and he in turn worked very closely with Michael Tilson Thomas, who is a classical conductor. It was really quite complicated, but beautiful music."[7]

With Jeff Beck, George enjoyed one of the most vital collaborations of his post-Beatles career. During his 1960s heyday, the guitarist had experienced an illustrious run with the Yardbirds before forming the Jeff Beck Group, which featured the likes of Rod Stewart, Ron Wood, and Nicky Hopkins. A November 1969 automobile accident in which he fractured his skull had launched Beck on a tortured path that placed his career in a series of fits and starts. His early 1970s malaise eventually led him to AIR Oxford Street, where he began recording instrumentals with George at the helm in late 1974. For Martin, the collaboration didn't seem to make sense, and he was surprised that

Beck wanted to work with him at all. "I think timing is always important," George later commented. "I think that when people start working together, whether you have a sort of mystical thing about it, and you say the gods are looking down on you in the right way, or whether the timing is just right. That you're in the right mood for each other, and your talents do actually complement each other." But still, Martin recognized that he and Beck "were rather unlikely bed partners, in a way. In fact, a lot of people told me that I shouldn't do it, but I loved his guitar work and I did want to work with him. And I was quite flattered and surprised when he asked me to produce a record. So it was a coming together of his wonderful sense of guitar work, the way he can handle a guitar, like nobody else I know of—including the really great ones. He has a style; he has something which is unique to him."[8]

The first album that resulted from Martin's collaboration with Beck was *Blow by Blow*, a masterwork of jazz-rock fusion. Martin produced the album with Denny Bridges as engineer. Martin was confident in Bridges's abilities, although he "hadn't done a tremendous amount of work at the time, but he was very enthusiastic and he wanted to experiment with a clean sound with Jeff. There was really nothing clever about it, just straightforward recording." With George handling scoring duties and Max Middleton turning in a noteworthy keyboard performance, *Blow by Blow* proved to be one of George's most carefully plotted productions. "The subject matter we were recording had to be chosen very carefully," he later remarked. "And I did very much want to make a good modern rhythmic record. In other words, I wanted to take influences from black music, which Jeff was very keen on anyway and had a great affinity to." Generically and philosophically, *Blow by Blow* was vastly different from nearly all of the albums Martin produced across his career. "I wanted to make it very much a foot-tapping party kind of record so I ran a lot of the tracks together except in cases where it wouldn't work," said George. "It was almost like a disc jockey exercise. Jeff really used to paint music with his guitar, too. He thought of it in that way, with sounds as well as notes. And the extraordinary thing was he used to be able to do it with the most primitive of weapons, too. His axes weren't the best in the world sometimes, but he just used to make them sing." George's favorite track on the album was "Diamond Dust": "I scored an accompaniment for strings," he later wrote, "a duologue with Jeff's guitar. To his credit, he agreed, and we both jumped into the deep end, and I loved the result. His amazing guitar sound was the perfect front for a string orchestra."[9]

As for the album's title, it was George who came up with *Blow by Blow*. He devised the title as a means for connoting the notion of "blowing," which was how Beck would describe the evolution of his solos in the studio. But "as it turned out," George wrote, *Blow by Blow* had several meanings, one of which, in my innocence, I had not thought of. I liked the idea of Jeff's blows being his off-the-cuff solos as well as the double-entendre of a boxing match, but I never thought of anyone blowing (or snorting) cocaine. Perversely, this actually helped the sales of the album." Did it ever. *Blow by Blow* enjoyed a top-five showing on the American jazz album charts, proving to be Beck's most successful release of his illustrious career. To George's delight, the platinum-selling LP even included a funky take on the Beatles' "She's a Woman." But even after the album hit the record stores in March 1975, Beck, ever the perfectionist, asked Martin to join him in the studio for further overdubs and other guitar adornments. When he phoned Martin up, the producer didn't know what to say, finally telling him, "I'm sorry, Jeff, but the record is in the shops!"[10]

Sadly for Martin, his collaboration with Beck was short-lived. In spite of the remarkable success of *Blow by Blow*, the producer and guitarist lost their footing on *Wired*, Beck's follow-up LP. From the onset, George felt that the album was taking an unfortunate turn. For one thing, Beck wanted the LP to have a more synthesized feel to it, an aspect that saw him replacing Middleton with famed keyboardist Jan Hammer, late of the Mahavishnu Orchestra. Beck decided to call the album *Wired* in reference to the mechanized, electronic sound that he wanted. A second issue that confronted Martin in recording Beck's album was the guitarist's anxiety-riddled mind-set. For the new record, Jeff "was much more inhibited," said George. "He had much more to lose when we made *Wired*. When we started *Blow by Blow*, he hadn't made a solo album for a long time, and he was starting from scratch, and if it didn't work out, people would say, 'We told you that it wouldn't work with those people anyway,' so it was no real problem for him. But *Blow by Blow* was such a success that everyone was saying, 'Right! What's the next album going to be like?' And in a way, that worried him. He got more inhibited about his solos and about the way he was playing." Martin also felt that Hammer's contributions constrained the previous album's free-floating, jazzy feel, and besides, Martin later remarked, Hammer "really wasn't my cup of tea. I much preferred the cleanliness of the Max Middleton stuff. So it wasn't quite the kind of record that I wanted to make for the second album, and I think the sales reflected that, too." The album managed to break into the top twenty, and it earned platinum status for Beck. But in contrast with *Blow by Blow*, *Wired* didn't approach the critical success of its precursor. Renowned rock critic Robert Christgau took issue with the LP's overreliance on technology, describing *Wired* as "mindless trickery." Engineer Peter Henderson felt some of the sting as well, later calling his own work on the LP into question. "I listened to that a few years later and it sounded like it had been recorded direct to cassette. I don't think it was one of my finer moments."[11]

In 1976, George found himself back in the Beatles' fold—*sort of*—for the first time since *Abbey Road*. In spite of his recent rancor with EMI, he was happy to work with the record conglomerate's American subsidiary, and especially Capitol's president Bhaskar Menon, of whom George had grown quite fond over the years. The project at hand was a compilation of Beatles hits to be titled *Rock 'n' Roll Music*. Menon had called Martin in a desperate attempt to endorse the double album's provenance in advance of the LP's release. As George later recalled, "He [Bhaskar Menon] asked me if I would approve the tapes before they went out, since they couldn't get hold of any of the Beatles, and I was the only other person of whom they could think who had been involved. So I went along to listen—and was appalled." The real issue, as George saw it, was that "EMI were terrified of the Beatles, who had issued an edict that the tapes must not be touched in any way. No one was to 'mutilate' them, and if they were reissued it had to be exactly as they were recorded. EMI had taken this absolutely literally. They had put the tapes on a transfer machine and were going to issue them just as they were—but in stereo! The effect was disastrous."[12]

Rolling up his sleeves, George spent two days working at Capitol to redub the tapes using state-of-the-art recording equipment. He tweaked the recording's equalization and remastered the tapes in order to prepare the album for a June release date. At the end of his Capitol stint, George found that the tracks "really sounded quite tolerable." George had carried out the work as a kind of labor of love, noting that "it wasn't really my job. I'd long since left EMI, and I wasn't getting paid—since they were early records, I was not even receiving any royalties on them; I just wanted to make sure that our work didn't get mutilated." In the end, EMI's executives—fearing a Beatles backlash over the album—expressly refused to release George's new masters in the United Kingdom, although Capitol gladly distributed the updated *Rock 'n' Roll Music* in the American marketplace. The compilation proved to be a shrewd bet on Menon's part, notching a number-two showing on the *Billboard* album charts—and ultimately denied the top spot by Paul McCartney and Wings' *At the Speed of Sound* album, which was currently lording over the charts during the band's triumphant Wings over America summer tour.[13]

Meanwhile, it turned out the EMI execs had been correct all along: the Beatles hadn't liked the *Rock 'n' Roll Music* release in the slightest, although it had little to do with the sound of its music. As Ringo Starr later noted, the more pressing issue was the cover art, which inexplicably trafficked in the 1950s-era nostalgia in promoting the sound and image of the Beatles. "It made us look cheap, and we were never cheap," Ringo crowed to *Rolling Stone* about the cover art. "All that Coca-Cola and cars with big fins was the 50s!"[14]

With *Rock 'n' Roll Music* ensconced in the record shops, Menon approached Martin with yet another opportunity. Capitol's president was eager to counterbalance the upcoming unauthorized release of the low-fidelity *Live! at the Star-Club in Hamburg, Germany; 1962*, a double album's worth of material recorded in December 1962 during the Beatles' final West German residency. Menon's plan involved releasing *The Beatles at the Hollywood Bowl* to coincide with the bootleg LP's distribution, which the band's lawyers were attempting to block through legal means. The Beatles' 1964 performance had been considered for release back in the mid-1960s, when George and Voyle Gilmore, the senior producer at Capitol Records, originally recorded the August 23 concert. But with thousands of screaming fans and other attendant ambient noise corrupting the recording, George found it impossible to prepare a live album for release. As Gilmore noted at the time, "There's not much [George Martin] could do. It was recorded on three-track machines with half-inch tapes. The Hollywood Bowl has a pretty good stereo sound system, so we plugged our mikes right in there. I didn't do an awful lot. There wasn't much we could do. They just played their usual show and we recorded it." In 1965, Capitol repeated the exercise, with Gilmore attempting to capture the Beatles' August 29 and 30 return engagements at the clam-shaped venue, albeit with the same lo-fi results. In 1971, Phil Spector had been given a shot at mixing the Hollywood Bowl concerts for release, but he gave up on the recordings, which lay dormant until a bootleg, *Back in '64 at the Hollywood Bowl*—which had been pilfered from the Capitol vault—began making the rounds among collectors.[15]

Having been tapped by Menon to prepare *The Beatles at the Hollywood Bowl* for a May 1977 release, Martin found himself stymied by the very same sonic issues that had plagued the recordings back in 1964. As George later recalled, "We recorded it on three-track tape, which was standard US format then. You would record the band in stereo on two tracks and keep the voice separated on the third, so that you could bring it up or down in the mix. But at the Hollywood Bowl they didn't use three-track in quite the right way. I didn't have too much say in things because I was a foreigner, but they did some very bizarre mixing. In 1977, when I was asked to make an album from the tapes, I found guitars and voices mixed on the same track. And the recording seemed to concentrate more on the wild screaming of 18,700 kids than on the Beatles on stage." At first, Martin had warned Menon that the project might not be salvageable. "As far as I could remember, the original tapes had a rotten sound," said George. "But when I listened to the Hollywood Bowl tapes, I was amazed at the rawness and vitality of the Beatles' singing. So I told Bhaskar that I'd see if I could bring the tapes into line with today's recordings. I enlisted the technical expertise of Geoff Emerick, and we transferred the recordings from three-track to 24-track tapes. The two tapes combined 22 songs and we whittled these down to 13. Some tracks had to be discarded because the music was obliterated by the screams." Emerick's technical expertise involved deploying a vacuum cleaner to blow air onto the old three-track tape machine in order to prevent it from overheating, which, in turn, melted the magnetic tape during the transfer to the twenty-four-track machine for equalization and remixing.[16]

With the technical aspects of the project having been ironed out, EMI required all four Beatles' approval before moving forward with releasing *The Beatles at the Hollywood Bowl*. McCartney was happy to give his approval, while "the reaction of George [Harrison] and Ringo was much cooler," Martin later recalled, although they ultimately signed off on the long-player's release. With John Lennon still unaccounted for, Martin decided to make a personal plea for the former Beatle's assent. By this point, John and Yoko Ono had ended their separation and were living together at the Dakota, an exclusive New York City apartment building. "I had to go to New York anyway, so I rang John Lennon and told him about the recordings. I told him that I had been very skeptical at first, but now I was very enthusiastic because I thought the album would be a piece of history which should be preserved. I said to John, 'I want you to hear it after I've gone. You can be as rude as you like, but if you don't like it, give me a yell.'" And with that, he dispatched a copy of the album by messenger for John's review. When he spoke to Lennon the next day, Martin discovered that Lennon was "delighted" with the album. For his part, Martin himself had been won over by the 1977 remixes, especially "the electric atmosphere and raw energy" of the Beatles in their touring heyday. "Those of us who were lucky enough to be present at a live Beatle concert—be it in Liverpool, London, New York, Washington, Los Angeles, Tokyo, Sydney or wherever—will know how amazing, how unique those performances were. It was not just the voice of the Beatles: it was expression of the young people of the world. And for the others who wondered what on Earth all the fuss was about, this album may give a little clue. It may be a poor substitute for the reality of those times, but it is now all there is," Martin wrote in the LP's liner notes. "I am very proud to have been part of their story. Thank you John, Paul, George and Ringo."[17]

The Beatles at the Hollywood Bowl proved to be a surprise hit during the late spring and summer of 1977, capturing the top spot on *NME*'s album charts and notching the number-two spot in *Billboard*. Writing in the *Village Voice*, even the typically acerbic Robert Christgau was impressed, describing the LP as "a tribute not only to the Beatles (which figured) but to George Martin and Capitol (which didn't necessarily figure at all). The sound rings clearly and powerfully through the shrieking: the segues are brisk and the punch-ins imperceptible; and the songs capture our heroes at their highest."[18]

During that same period, George recorded albums with another pair of 1960s mainstays, vaunted songwriters Jimmy Webb and Neil Sedaka. During his work on *The Beatles at the Hollywood Bowl*, George had temporarily relocated his family to Los Angeles, where he rented a house on Mulholland Drive in Beverly Hills. With Judy, nine-year-old Lucie, and seven-year-old Giles in tow, George took to Southern California living, tooling about the coastline in his massive Cadillac El Dorado. After years of finding renown through other artists' recordings of his work, Webb was eager to score some hits of his own. And having already produced and recorded six albums, he was ready to turn over the reins to somebody else. To Webb's mind, Martin fit the bill perfectly, and Webb had long admired the other man's work as the Beatles' producer. "*Sgt. Pepper* was only cut on a four-track recorder, and it is a testament to George Martin's genius," Webb later remarked. "The studio became more than just an organ that soaked up and preserved a performance. George Martin and the Beatles were aware of the possibilities, and so the studio came into its own." Eager to see if he could expand his own artistic horizons through a freelance producer, Webb worked with Martin at Hollywood's Cherokee Studios, where they cut the tracks for *El Mirage*. Martin assembled a group of heavy-hitters for the occasion, top-flight West Coast musicians, including the likes of ace keyboard player David Paich, slide guitar master Lowell George, vocalist Kenny Loggins, bassist Larry Knechtel, and a duo of superstar drummers in Nigel Olsson and Jim Gordon. With *El Mirage*, Webb hoped to jumpstart his career in order to recast his image as not merely a songwriter but a performer as well. For his part, Webb showed up, as always, with the goods: a series of powerful, well-wrought, and often-autobiographical gems. Martin answered the call by affording Webb's tunes—the drama-laden "The Highwayman" and "The Moon Is a Harsh Mistress," for example—with lush, awe-inspiring head arrangements and soaring orchestral scores. *El Mirage* offered a powerful demonstration of the resounding impact of George's early forays into writing notation with Sidney Harrison, and his later experiences at the Guildhall School, upon his craft as an arranger and orchestrator. In so doing, Martin assisted Webb in establishing new frontiers as a performer.[19]

Working with Neil Sedaka was another matter altogether. In contrast with Webb, finding time and space to record Sedaka was exceedingly difficult, with the singer-songwriter being invariably on the move, either writing new songs or performing in some far-flung locale. To remedy the situation, George recommended that they complete the album, to be titled *A Song*, in two phases. During the first, they would lay down the tracks with Sedaka's band. This would allow Martin to spend some time with the recordings, provide orchestration where necessary, and reconnect with Sedaka to bring the project to fruition. After the first phase of the project was completed, George and Judy spent a month in Mexico City for tax purposes. Staying as guests of the British ambassador, the Martins stayed in a remote hotel some sixty miles outside of the city. With a piano having been moved into his suite, Martin scored the album, recorded the orchestration at AIR Oxford Street, and reconvened with Sedaka in New York City, where he stitched *A Song* together at the Record Plant. As an added bonus, Sedaka and Martin chartered a plane for a kind of whistle-stop tour in which they debuted the new record and promoted its wares across the United States. The idea had been the brainchild of Elektra Records president Joe Smith, and it certainly impacted the album's reach. But when the project had concluded, George found himself reciting a familiar refrain: *A Song* "wasn't a great hit, but it did sell moderately well, and Neil was still very, very pleased with it. We parted company at the end, having had a good time."[20]

While working at the Record Plant with Sedaka, Martin came into the orbit of Malcolm Addey, the Abbey Road engineer with whom he had frequently clashed during the 1960s. Addey had lived in the United States since 1968, when he moved to New York City and made his name as a much-sought-after freelance engineer. Perhaps out of nostalgia for the old days at Abbey Road, when A&R men and their balance engineers worked several sessions a day and banged out one recording after another in close quarters, Martin invited Addey to dinner at an Italian restaurant on the Upper East Side. As Addey later recalled, sharing a meal with the famed producer gave the two men a chance to catch up on old times, as well as an opportunity to see each other in a different light after their hotly competitive days back at Abbey Road. But things came to a head, as they always seemed to do whenever Martin and Addey got together, when the engineer innocently brought up AIR Oxford Street. For his part, Malcolm remembered asking George how he managed to make a profit in the high-rent district around Oxford Street and its environs. Quite suddenly, Martin became incensed with the engineer for bringing up the studio's profitability. George was fuming mad, as if Malcolm were calling AIR's entire business model into consideration. For Addey, Martin's fury seemed to have come out of nowhere. Clearly, the engineer had touched a nerve when it came to George's business interests. Was the vast expense associated with fitting out AIR Montserrat beginning to take its toll on the normally staid producer? For his part, Addey would never know. In short order, Martin returned to his formerly convivial self, and by the time the check arrived, the two men agreed to let bygones be bygones.[21]

For Martin, working with the likes of Webb and Sedaka found him reflecting upon the strange path that his career had taken across the past few years, when he more often than not worked with music veterans whose professional lives had been established in previous eras, even having been "made" by other producers at very different junctures in their own careers. With the exceptions of America and Jeff Beck, the vast majority of his efforts were one-off projects like *El Mirage* and *A Song*. For George, it was "like a series of one-night stands after being married to the same woman all your life." This point was driven home on October 18, 1977, when he attended the British record industry's Britannia Centenary Awards at London's Wembley Conference Centre. Programmed as part of the year-long celebration associated with Queen Elizabeth II's silver jubilee, as well as a means for marking a century since Thomas Edison invented sound recording, the awards ceremony honored the most significant British musical attainments of the past twenty-five years. The event was embroidered with a variety of performances, including Martin leading a rendition of "A Hard Day's Night," along with Cliff Richard singing "Miss You Nights," Procol Harum playing "A Whiter Shade of Pale," and Simon and Garfunkel reuniting to sing "Old Friends."[22]

For George, the awards ceremony itself was an embarrassment of riches. The Beatles' *Sgt. Pepper's Lonely Hearts Club Band* bested a field that included Elton John's *Goodbye Yellow Brick Road* and Pink Floyd's *The Dark Side of the Moon* in winning the Best Album statuette, while George's former client Shirley Bassey took home the award for Best British Female vocalist. Best British Group honors went to the Beatles, of course, in a category that also included Pink Floyd, the Rolling Stones, and the Who. When it came to the Best Producer award, George took home the statuette, easily besting a field that included Glyn Johns, Gus Dudgeon, and Mickie Most. For George, it was nevertheless a moment laden with irony. As he later recalled, "The award immediately preceding mine was a special one for Outstanding Contribution to the British record industry. The man who mounted the rostrum to receive it was, you've guessed, Len Wood." The comedy was further compounded when George later studied the statuette, which was actually Paul Simon's award for *Bridge Over Troubled Water*. Meanwhile, Simon had Martin's Best Producer statuette. "How typical of the record industry to make a mistake like that," George later remarked. Enjoying the levity of the circumstances, "Paul [Simon] and I agreed to keep each other's award."[23]

As work continued on building AIR's Montserrat studio complex, with a projected grand opening slated for the spring of 1979, George frequently visited the island to keep tabs on construction, eager to see his dream for a residential recording studio come to life in the tropical locale. As he awaited the completion of AIR Montserrat, George busied himself with one of the most complex productions of his post-Beatles career—and one that he had begun to regret almost from its onset. The idea had been the brainchild of Robert Stigwood, the Australian music mogul behind RSO Records and the Bee Gees, and who had flirted with someday managing the Beatles in the waning months of Brian Epstein's life. Armed with a hefty $12 million budget, Stigwood had assembled a star-studded cast to mount a feature film based on *Sgt. Pepper's Lonely Hearts Club Band*. The idea had begun to germinate after the Bee Gees recorded cover versions of "Golden Slumbers"/"Carry That Weight," "She Came in Through the Bathroom Window," and "Sun King" for the recent musical documentary *All This and World War II*. Written by Henry Edwards, the story line behind Stigwood's opus follows one Billy Shears as he tangles with an unfeeling record industry bent on corrupting his music, as well as his beloved hometown of Heartland. Selections from the Beatles' *Sgt. Pepper* and *Abbey Road* albums establish a rock opera, with American comedy legend George Burns providing the narration.

With television and film director Michael Schultz signed on for the project, the casting for Stigwood's film was brilliant in scope, with Peter Frampton playing the lead, having just landed *Frampton Comes Alive!* as the best-selling live album in the history of the record business. Meanwhile, he was flanked by his band—"the Hendersons," in an obvious reference to "Being for the Benefit of Mr. Kite!"—who were composed of the Bee Gees, the central players in the blockbuster *Saturday Night Fever* soundtrack. The cast was rounded out by Steve Martin, the American comedian whose *Wild and Crazy Guy* comedy LP ruled over the airwaves, even notching a number-two showing on *Billboard*'s music charts. Not surprisingly, the buildup to Stigwood's film was incredible by the time it was released in July 1978, with the Bee Gees' Robin Gibb going out on a limb and unadvisedly proclaiming that "there is no such thing as the Beatles now. They don't exist as a band and never performed *Sgt. Pepper* live in any case. When ours comes out, it will be, in effect, as if theirs never existed."[24]

With such inspired casting on the movie's side, Stigwood was confident that RSO Records would enjoy yet another smash-hit LP in the same vein as its *Saturday Night Fever* and *Grease* soundtracks. But George had his druthers from the start. In 1976, Stigwood had approached him to serve in a multifaceted capacity as musical director, conductor, and arranger, not to mention as producer of the eventual double-record soundtrack release. With some twenty-four songs and hundreds of performers shifting in and out of the soundscape, Martin's work was cut out for him, and he sagely enlisted Emerick to act as his engineer and right-hand man throughout the project. At the urging of Judy and with the promise of a sizable fee, George had agreed to the project after becoming inspired by the success of Tom O'Horgan's 1974 off-Broadway production of *Sgt. Pepper's Lonely Hearts Club Band on the Road*. But for George, it was also a matter of professional ego and respect for the legacy that he shared with the Beatles. As the producer later wrote, "I couldn't bear the idea of what someone else might do with the music if I turned it down."

In retrospect, said George, "I shouldn't have done it." For Martin, the central issue involved the movie's all-star lineup of performers. A number of the artists were experienced, top-flight musicians, including the likes of the Bee Gees, Peter Frampton, and Billy Preston, while others, like comedians Steve Martin and Frankie Howerd, didn't have the vocal caliber to which Martin had become accustomed. As the producer later wrote, "I had not realized until after I had agreed to my contract that I would be required to do things musically that I did not approve of. Nor did I have a say in the casting, so I found myself coaching unknowns on songs which frankly did not suit their voices, songs which were sacred to me."[25]

As Martin brought Stigwood's *Sgt. Pepper* in for a landing, he could already see the writing on the wall. Preternaturally confident in the studio, he found himself increasingly bewildered and uncertain about the soundtrack's direction. To make matters worse, many of the sessions had been marked by discord, with Frampton and the Bee Gees not surprisingly developing tensions over their competing generic interests, with the brothers Gibb riding high on the disco wave at the time and Frampton acting the part of a 1970s-era rock god. After he had completed his scoring and orchestration duties, Martin and Emerick carried out their mixing and editing duties at Hollywood's Trident Music, where a certain George A. Martin was assigned as their assistant tape editor. Years later, George A. Martin recalled working with the vaunted producer in the autumn months of 1977. At one point, the younger Martin recorded George as he performed a piano transition for the soundtrack. After they had finished, George A. Martin said, "We make a good team. We should go on the road. We should be George Martin and George Martin." Not missing a beat, George joked, "No, I want top billing!" At one point, George A. Martin observed as the other George and Geoff mixed the score. The assistant editor was surprised and flattered when they asked him to listen to a playback of the instrumental backing track for "A Day in the Life." When the music concluded, Martin and Emerick turned to face the younger man, asking expectantly, "What do you think?" For his part, George A. Martin could only sit there in awe, replying, "Wow. It's just fabulous."[26]

And for one brief shining moment when the soundtrack was released in July 1978, a good portion of the American record-buying public thought that it was fabulous, too. The *Sgt. Pepper* soundtrack came out of the gate with significant airplay, landing a trio of hit singles, including Aerosmith's cover version of "Come Together," produced by Jack Douglas, which notched a number-twenty-three showing on the American charts; Earth, Wind, and Fire's smash-hit version of "Got to Get You into My Life," produced by Maurice White, which topped the rhythm-and-blues charts; and Robin Gibb's "Oh! Darling," which notched a top-twenty hit. Even Billy Preston managed to land a minor hit with the Martin-produced "Get Back," which managed to crack *Billboard*'s Hot 100. While the soundtrack album debuted at number five on the US charts, within a matter of weeks, as the *Sgt. Pepper* movie was met with critical scorn from nearly every quarter, the bad publicity and attendant rancor took their toll. In the *Village Voice*, Robert Christgau awarded the soundtrack with his "must to avoid" warning. "At first I felt relatively positive about this project," he wrote. "I'm not a religious man, I liked the Aerosmith and Earth, Wind, and Fire cuts on the radio, and I figured the Bee Gees qualified as ersatz Beatles if anyone did." But "from the song selection, you wouldn't even know the originals were once a rock 'n' roll band." Later, in *The New Rolling Stone Record Guide*, Dave Marsh called the soundtrack "an utter travesty," adding that "two million people bought this album, which proves that P. T. Barnum was right and that euthanasia may have untapped possibilities." But apparently, not all of the album's potential consumers were suckers, as millions of the copies were returned to the distributor, and RSO Records ultimately destroyed a good number of them. It was an unmitigated disaster for nearly everyone involved: a huge financial loss for Stigwood, not to mention the careers of Frampton and the Bee Gees, which never quite returned to the stardom that they had enjoyed prior to their participation. And then there was George. As the producer behind the corrosive reinterpretation of his own legacy with the Beatles, he was disheartened by the result that he himself had very nearly foretold. For the rest of his life, he never minced words when the episode with the *Sgt. Pepper* soundtrack came up. "It was my own fault," he soberly concluded.[27]

As the 1970s came to a close, George threw himself into AIR Montserrat, determined to see his dreams of a studio paradise become a reality. While he was smitten by the convivial environment that the West Indies promised, he was really jazzed about the technology. He had spent years at EMI Studios longing for the advancements that would make his artists' tracks truly shine, and now that he was his own boss, he wouldn't accept anything less than state of the art. As he noted when the studio opened in 1979, AIR Montserrat was an embarrassment of riches—and potentially too rich, even for his musical imagination. "The studio has both 24- and 32-track machines, but I personally am not over-enthusiastic about 32-track. I can cope quite nicely, thank you, with 24; and, if more are really needed, I prefer to use our locking device to harness two 24-track machines together, giving up to 46 tracks." But while he was willing to spare no expense on his island getaway, he was conscious of the incredible cost of building the studio of his dreams. "Our first console at AIR London, built by Rupert Neve who makes the Rolls-Royce of recording desks, was 16-track, and cost $35,000. At the time, we thought that was a lot of money. The Montserrat console, by contrast, cost $210,000." It was a handmade console, custom-designed to George and his partners' specifications, with an incredible fifty-two inputs, twenty-four or thirty-two outputs, depending on the tracking, and twenty-four separate monitors.[28]

But if George held any doubts about AIR Montserrat's potential for enjoying the same level of success as Oxford Street, his concerns were shortly allayed by the onrush of celebrated clientele clamoring to work on his island retreat. In short order, the studio became the regular stomping grounds of the likes of the Police, Dire Straits, Elton John, Eric Clapton, and Stevie Wonder. And the locals were blown away by the economic impact. As one islander later remarked, AIR's "involvement with the island was such a positive note for Montserrat, as it struggled compared to other Caribbean islands to attract tourists." Yet another said, "I grew up having to explain where the British colony of Montserrat was, yet thanks to George, Montserrat is now known as the home of some of the best music of the 1980s." One of those artists was the Rolling Stones, who thought of AIR Montserrat as a second home. As lead guitarist Keith Richards once remarked, "Everything is there. A great bar, great restaurant, great cook. The studio itself is like a plus. It's the best place to live on the island!"[29]

George wasted little time in making himself feel at home on Montserrat, buying a home there and frequently bringing his family for extended sojourns beside the Caribbean Sea. The first album that George himself recorded at Montserrat was America's *Silent Letter*. George had righted his ship after the *Sgt. Pepper* debacle with Gary Brooker's *No More Fear of Flying*, the inaugural solo album by Procol Harum's former front man. For the title track, George assembled layers of saxophones and brass, creating a hard-driving tapestry in the same vein as the Beatles' "Good Morning, Good Morning." With *Silent Letter*, George was attempting to turn the band's fortunes around after their lackluster LP *Harbor*. Throughout the decade, he had been instrumental in transforming the band, which was now a duo featuring Gerry Beckley and Dewey Bunnell, into a world-class act. He had even remixed pre-Martin tracks such as "A Horse with No Name," "I Need You," and "Ventura Highway" for their greatest hits album, titled *History*. For George, *Silent Letter* was a make-or-break opportunity. When the album failed to crack *Billboard*'s Top 100 albums, the writing was on the wall. George and the bandmates politely parted ways, with America shopping for a new producer to try to change their fortunes yet again.

That same year, George finally put pen to paper and compiled his memoirs. For much of the 1970s, he had been regularly approached by agents and publishers attempting to make their mark on the burgeoning Beatles book trade. Not surprisingly, given his signal role in the bandmates' story, George was a big fish in what, at least at the time, was still a fairly shallow pond. At a relatively youthful fifty-three, George may have even felt somewhat loath to begin a tour down memory lane. But with the promise of a sizable advance, he ultimately landed a deal with London's esteemed Macmillan publishing house. To assist him in the process of capturing his memories, Jeremy Hornsby was commissioned to serve as his coauthor. The University College–trained Londoner had worked in a similar capacity for British actor Pete Murray, whose memoirs were published as *One Day I'll Forget My Trousers* in 1976. Years later, Hornsby would recall the experience of "ghosting" Martin's biography with a special fondness, writing that the producer's "first requirement was that alternate chapters would combine to form a *vade mecum* (handbook) for any aspirant record producers; and so it was. Typically of the man, he wanted his experiences to benefit others." Hornsby also recalled, "I have never met anyone who combined modesty, courtesy and generosity in such measure; the last of these was typified when we came to discuss terms. Unlike any of the other 'ghosting' projects with which I have been involved, he insisted first that my name should be on the cover with his, and secondly that the proceeds should be split 50-50. The many days I spent with him working on the book were among the most enjoyable and instructive in my life."[30]

Given his jaunty style, Hornsby seemed like the perfect voice for telling the story of Martin's incredible career. After conducting a lengthy series of in-depth interviews with his subject, Hornsby captured the contours of Martin's life, from his earliest years in impoverished North London and his days in the Fleet Air Arm through his work as Parlophone A&R head and beyond. Naturally, the lion's share of the resulting book, titled *All You Need Is Ears*, concerned George's life and times with the Beatles. For music fans and scholars alike, his memoir was a revelation. For many readers, *All You Need Is Ears* marked the first occasion when they caught a glimpse of life inside Abbey Road during the Beatles' heyday. Structurally, the book suffered at the hands of Martin's alternating-chapters scheme, which created a jarring lack of chronology as the producer and his ghostwriter abruptly shifted from one anecdote to another, often flitting across the decades between chapters. Buoyed by strong reviews and an insatiable book-buying public hungry to learn more about life in Martin and the Beatles' hit-making factory, *All You Need Is Ears* became a modest best seller for Martin and Hornsby.

As 1979 came to a close, George enjoyed a series of bittersweet moments before ushering in a new, less certain decade. His dreams of creating a tropical studio paradise were coming up aces, already promising to match if not exceed the revenue that AIR enjoyed from Oxford Street. But at the same time, his series of "one-night stands" was starting to take its toll. It had been a full decade since his *Abbey Road* triumph, and while the 1970s had seen a vast number of incredible highs with America, Jeff Beck, and *Live and Let Die*, among others, George was all too conscious of his unhappy experiences with one-off, less fulfilling projects and, most recently, the *Sgt. Pepper* fiasco. Only months away from celebrating his fifty-fourth year, he felt the first pangs of mortality. Always a robust man, still taking his skiing jaunts with Judy and impressively athletic, he took note when his old nemesis Norrie Paramor died at age sixty-five in September 1979. Like Oscar Preuss, Martin's Parlophone mentor, Paramor had barely made it into retirement before an untimely death. It had been seventeen years since Martin had torpedoed the Columbia producer in a secret interview with David Frost that later saw Paramor pilloried on national television as the man who was making pop culture "ordinary" through his collaboration with Cliff Richard. Paramor likely never knew that it was Martin, his opposite number at EMI's Parlophone label, who had done him in. Paramor worked with Cliff Richard until 1972, although by then they were no longer the hit-making machine of their 1960s heyday. In 1977, Paramor had gathered the Shadows, Richard's onetime band, one last time to record "Return to the Alamo," with the producer's orchestra providing accompaniment. When he learned of Paramor's death, Martin was sitting with his eldest son, Gregory, in an English pub. "Well, he'll never be bigger than me now," said George, soberly raising his glass to the man who had fueled his own ambitions and fiery inner competition all those years ago.[31]

And it was only a few months later, in December 1979, when George managed to finally catch up with an old friend, perhaps the most elusive relationship across his many years as a working producer in the record industry. During a holiday visit to New York City, Martin met John Lennon for dinner at the Dakota. Together, the old friends had dinner in the kitchen of John's apartment. "Yoko quite tactfully kept out of the way for the whole evening," said George, "and we just reminisced about the good old times." There they were, "mulling over past glories like a pair of old codgers." At one point, "I tackled him about the *Rolling Stone* interview. I said, 'What was all that shit about, John? Why?' He said, 'I was out of my head, wasn't I?' And that was as much of an apology as I got." But for George, the most incredible aspect of that special evening occurred much later. As George later wrote:

> John suddenly looked up at me. "You know what, George," he said. "If I had the chance, I'd record everything we did again."
>
> "What?" I replied. "Even 'Strawberry Fields Forever'?"
>
> "*Especially* 'Strawberry Fields Forever,'" he said.

George was flabbergasted. "It shocked me," he later recalled. But then, upon reflection, he began to remember John in a fonder light, thinking back about the gifted singer and songwriter who was never quite satisfied with the sound of his own voice, the person who was always striving for something better—something more powerful and more meaningful just beyond the horizon. "For John, the vision was always better than the reality," George wrote. "Everything inside him was greater than its expression in the outside world. That was his life."[32]

23

HERE TODAY, GONE TOMORROW

O N JANUARY 3, 1980, George turned fifty-four years old. It had been nearly
three decades since he'd first tried his hand at the record business as Oscar
Preuss's assistant at Parlophone. He was ready, no doubt, to try something
new, to attempt to set his sights beyond the one-night stands of his recent
musical forays. The opportunity he was looking for had arrived, it seemed,
at the hands of Cheap Trick, a hard-driving rock band out of Rockford, Illinois. Cheap Trick had exploded from a regional band into an international
phenomenon through their *Cheap Trick at Budokan* and *Dream Police* LPs,
both of which were released stateside in 1979. At this point, the band's four
studio albums had been produced by Tom Werman with their live album
having been mixed by Jack Douglas. *Cheap Trick at Budokan* and *Dream
Police* had been massive sellers, registering top-five showings on *Billboard*
and going platinum in the process. The group was clearly poised for even
greater things to come, and by any measure it made sense to continue working with Werman behind the console. And that's when Cheap Trick threw
caution to the wind and invited George into the control booth for their next
album, appropriately titled *All Shook Up*. To a person, the bandmates were
all confirmed Beatlemaniacs, as evinced by *At Budokan*'s "I Want You to
Want Me" and by *Dream Police*'s "Voices," a slow, Lennonesque burn if ever
there were one. For his part, George was happy to oblige the hard-rocking

midwesterners, having recently recorded the gritty *No Place to Run* by British heavy-metal stalwarts UFO with great results.

While Cheap Trick was committed to throwing their lot in with George, their label bosses at Epic Records weren't so sure. "The record company didn't want George Martin," drummer Bun E. Carlos later recalled. "They thought the stuff was working with Werman, so why change it?" But the group—which included Carlos, vocalist Robin Zander, guitarist Rick Nielsen, and bassist Tom Petersson—was determined to experiment with the rocking sound that they had developed over the years, and Martin, the man who had produced their heroes' masterpieces, perfectly fit the bill. Working at AIR Montserrat with Geoff Emerick sitting in as engineer, George took to the bandmates almost instantly. "Cheap Trick were charming people, great fun and good musicians." Just as George had hoped, the band lost themselves in the warmth and remoteness of the Caribbean. "The group loved the island," he later wrote. "Rick Nielsen brought his family with him, and I used to take them up to Rendezvous Beach in my boat for a picnic when we had a day off. One never saw Rick without his trademark baseball cap—I swear he must sleep in it. I have a memory of Rick diving in to the sea, still clutching his baseball cap to his head as he went below the waves."[1]

Taking the group at their word, George pushed them to the limit with every track that they had prepared for *All Shook Up*, challenging them to try new things at every turn. With "Stop This Game," the album smoldered into life with the portentous drone of a piano chord, played by George no less, echoing the sound of apocalypse that concluded the Beatles' "A Day in the Life." With "World's Greatest Lover," Cheap Trick evoked the Fab Four to the *n*th degree. As one of George's favorite tracks from the latter part of his career, "World's Greatest Lover" found Cheap Trick evoking drama at every turn. Described as being "very Lennon-ish" by George, the song's tension was ratcheted up even further still by the producer's heartrending orchestral score. In one of the album's strangest, most avant-garde moments, George provided a spirited, spoken-word accompaniment for the heavy-metal infused "Love Comes a-Tumblin' Down." As Nielsen's thundering guitar soars ever forward, Martin's posh accent fades into view, gleaming above the mix with the sounds of optimism and pure joy:

I'm wishing to live longer aided by the supreme healing force of music. It most definitely overcomes all weakening aspects of the body. I have felt quite lost and distraught without those wonderful vinyl productions. I'm convinced it's an addiction, too. I feel just great again!

In many ways, it makes for George's strangest, most bravura moment on record, a moment of unexpected gusto laid afloat by its speaker's buoyant thirst for living. In addition to "Stop This Game" and "World's Greatest Lover," the long-player was rife with Beatles references, including "Baby Loves to Rock," which finds Zander singing "Not in Russia!" above the sound of a roaring jet airliner à la "Back in the USSR." And then there's "Who D'King?" the album's rousing conclusion. With obvious echoes of Ringo's rumbling drum solo on *Abbey Road*'s "The End," Carlos ends the album by quite figuratively beating the band's listeners into submission.

For Martin and Emerick, *All Shook Up* was one of their favorite productions during their post-Beatles years together. And while the album had proven to be the explicit departure from the group's previous sound that Cheap Trick had envisioned, it didn't necessarily translate in sales. In terms of its commercial success, *All Shook Up* was a far cry from the personal bests that the group had established with *Cheap Trick at Budokan* and *Dream Police*, with their latest LP topping out at number twenty-four in *Billboard* magazine and narrowly earning a gold record for Martin and the bandmates. But the critics raved. Writing in *Rolling Stone*, David Fricke praised "the dense, pseudo-ELO orchestration in the Whostyle 'Stop This Game'; the gonzo, post–*Sgt. Pepper's Lonely Hearts Club Band* psychedelia of 'Go for the Throat (Use Your Own Imagination)'; and vocalist Robin Zander's impassioned singing of a John Lennon–like ballad, 'World's Greatest Lover,' complete with Martin's *Imagine*-style arrangement." As "not just another 'new' Beatles," Fricke concluded, "Cheap Trick are the latest in a long line of spiritual heirs to the Fab Four's Anglo-pop tradition, traceable back through the Move, the Electric Light Orchestra and such hard-rock tangents as the Who and the Yardbirds."[2]

For George, working with Cheap Trick had been an exceedingly joyful collaboration, although by the time they got around to their next album, he was fully ensconced with a not-so-new client in need of his own change of musical scenery. But for Cheap Trick, the thrill of working with Martin didn't quite end with *All Shook Up*. During the summer of 1980, John Lennon had ended his self-imposed retirement to head back into the studio with veteran producer Jack Douglas, with whom the former Beatle was working to produce his new *Double Fantasy* LP with Yoko Ono. Knowing that Cheap Trick was working with Martin at Montserrat, Douglas called him up to see if Nielsen and Carlos might be interested in backing Lennon on a new number titled "I'm Losing You." "I had to call Martin at his island studio to book my players," Douglas later recalled. "I called him and said, 'Can I borrow some of my guys to play with your guy?'" Without missing a beat, Nielsen and Carlos hitched a ride on the next plane to New York City, where they recorded a bone-crunching rendition of "I'm Losing You" with Lennon at the Hit Factory on August 12, 1980. Their version of the song didn't make *Double Fantasy*'s final cut when the LP was released in November, but for Nielsen and Carlos, it was the thrill of a lifetime.[3] For George, working with Cheap Trick had been a much-needed shot in the arm. His robustly delivered words in "Love Comes a-Tumblin' Down" were more than mere window dressing. It was as if George were announcing his manifesto for living, his fondest wish for a new renaissance aided by the pure truth that he could only discover through song. There would be more one-offs in his future, to be sure, but he felt more directed and enthusiastic than he had in years. With two world-class studios in operation and turning over enviable revenue for AIR, his financial life was in fine shape. He and Judy and their young family had left their home in London's Hyde Park Crescent and settled into the Old Rectory, a fifteenth-century church that had been converted into an estate by a pediatrician. Some eighty miles west of London, the sprawling home was nestled in the tiny English village of Coleshill. When the Martins saw the Old Rectory advertised as being for sale in the *Times*, they jumped at the chance to buy the place. "The lovely old house was in a bad way," George later wrote. It was "riddled with dry rot, woodworm, even death-watch beetle and every kind of vermin, but all these things can be eradicated, and buying it was one of the best things we ever did." After living out of suitcases for years, shuttling from one place to another, George was happy to find a place to call home.[4]

While the summer of 1980 had proven to be one of his happiest in years, George's reverie had been tinged with an unexpected sadness after he learned that Peter Sellers had succumbed to a heart attack in London on July 24. Sellers had been in town for a reunion dinner with his old Goon mates Spike Milligan and Harry Secombe. But on the day of their reunion, Sellers was rushed to the hospital, where he died a few days later at age fifty-four. A private funeral was held on July 26 at Golders Green Crematorium, where mourners were treated to the funnyman's final joke as they were serenaded by Glenn Miller's "In the Mood," a song that Sellers deeply detested. George and Judy attended a memorial service for Sellers at St. Martin-in-the-Fields on September 8, which would have marked the comedian's fifty-fifth birthday.

In October 1980, George's life took yet another turn when he was approached by none other than Paul McCartney to try his hand at producing the soundtrack for a short film to be titled *Rupert and the Frog Song*, a pet project of McCartney's based on the popular British cartoon character Rupert Bear. "After the breakup of the Beatles, I saw more of Paul [and Linda] than the others," said George, "but I never thought for a moment we would work together again. Paul had been through his Wings records and proved himself to be an excellent producer, so I was surprised when one evening, after the four of us had enjoyed a good dinner, he asked me to produce him again." Although he had enjoyed producing "Live and Let Die," George was reticent at first about the prospect of working with Paul. Why would the ex-Beatle want to sacrifice his artistic independence after so many years of producing himself? But Paul persisted, and George began to realize that the other man was at a turning point of sorts. In January, Wings' most recent tour had been cancelled after Paul's arrest for cannabis possession. He spent ten days in a Tokyo jail before being deported back to the United Kingdom, where Wings had been languishing ever since. Even in their inactivity, the band had scored a sixth number-one US hit with a live version of "Coming Up" during the spring of 1980.[5]

Concerned about the potential pitfalls of returning to their producer/artist relationship of days gone by, George made a single demand of the former Beatle, saying, "It will only work if you accept what I have to say as being valid, because there's no point in having a yes man, you can get somebody else. If you want somebody to agree with everything you do, that's destructive." At the same time, George was worried about his own psychological challenges in working with Paul again. He was well aware of his own at times porous ego boundaries, later observing that "it's all too easy for the producer to get smart and start disagreeing with the artist so as to look big. That's fatal, too. That's stupid and ridiculous." In short, George reasoned that the only way their new partnership could work would be with unremitting honesty in all of their dealings. "If the producer really thinks the artist's song isn't good enough, he's got to say so unequivocally, and the artist has got to trust him," said George. "If you don't have that relationship, then you're done." But at the heart of it all was George's realization that Paul was no longer the much younger man who struggled to find his way back at Abbey Road nearly two decades earlier. Things had changed precipitously in the ensuing years. "Paul's probably the greatest living songwriter in the world and here I am, a producer who's never written a hit song in his life," George later remarked. "So what temerity do I have to go to the guy and say a song is not good enough? It's a terrible thing to do, but it's absolutely necessary."[6]

After George agreed to try his hand at producing Paul again, the two old friends held recording sessions for "We All Stand Together," the planned theme song for the Rupert Bear animated film, at AIR Oxford Street. Explicitly written for children, "We All Stand Together" featured McCartney on lead vocals and harmonies, along with the King's Singers and the St. Paul's Cathedral Choir providing additional backing vocals. Working from Martin's choral arrangement and Kenneth Sillito's orchestration, the instrumentation featured flautist Elena Durán. With Emerick chipping in as engineer, "We All Stand Together" was recorded in October and November 1980, but not released until 1984 to coincide with the *Rupert and the Frog Song* film debut, charting a top-five UK hit in the process. During this same period, Paul had begun holding rehearsals for a new Wings album involving a raft of new material that he had accumulated since his return from the Far East. As rehearsals moved forward that fall at Finchden Manor in Kent, guitarist Laurence Juber was surprised to learn from McCartney that Martin would be producing the new LP, and that Martin "does not want it to be a Wings album. He wants it to be a McCartney album and use session players, casting it on a per-song basis." For his part, Juber was caught unawares, although "looking back, I think he was passing the buck onto George." At that point, Juber and drummer Steve Holley departed the scene, leaving longtime Wings sideman Denny Laine and Linda McCartney to begin working on Paul's upcoming solo album with Martin.[7]

By the late fall, George and Paul were devoting considerable studio time to the solo LP, which was to be titled *Tug of War*. As it turned out, there may have been a hint of fact to Juber's insight about McCartney's motives. "The idea of working with Wings again," said Paul, "in truth, it would have just been limiting, I thought. And George agreed. I slightly blamed it on him a bit. Only a bit, though." For his part, George felt that Wings had been an unnecessary facade during Paul's post-Beatles career. Throughout the group's successful 1970s run, McCartney had clearly been the star. But Paul had felt he needed the edifice of a working rock group. "I like being in a band, you know?" he once remarked. "I don't like being out of work, and, in a way, when you're just recording, you can get to feel a bit out of work. You like to have a strum and sing. So that's the main reason behind it." In a September 1980 interview, Lennon had made special note of Wings. "I kind of admire the way Paul started back from scratch, forming a new band," he observed. "I kind of admire the way he got off his pedestal," adding that "he did what he wanted to do." For his part, George appreciated the success that Paul had created with Wings while recognizing that Paul no longer needed the structural device of a band in his life. He was Paul McCartney, after all.[8]

By early December 1980, George and Paul were routining new material at AIR Oxford Street, with Geoff in tow. The two old colleagues were working under a single proviso: "We decided not to be as restricted," Paul later commented in the LP's liner notes, "so we started a new era, working with whoever we thought was most suitable for the tune." For Paul, it was like turning over a new leaf in his storied career. "As if it was a film," he added, "once we had decided that this wasn't going to be a Wings album, George and I chose the right performers for every track. I wanted to play with Stevie Wonder and we did two together instead. I wanted Steve Gadd on drums and Stanley Clarke on bass simply because they're the best, and I wanted the best. Why not?" On December 7, they tried out a host of new numbers, including "Ballroom Dancing," a particular favorite of George's, and "Keep Under Cover" before tackling "Rainclouds" and the whimsical "Ode to a Koala Bear" on December 8. But on the morning of December 9, Martin and McCartney were awakened to the tragic news of John Lennon's senseless murder at the hands of twenty-five-year-old Mark David Chapman in the archway of the Dakota the night before. The ex-Beatle was only forty years old, leaving behind Yoko, seventeen-year-old Julian, and five-year-old son Sean.

Making their way to the studio in a state of shock, George and Paul could barely keep it together, too besotted with grief to do much else but apply a few overdubs to "Rainclouds." Emerick was there, too, whiling away that awful day in the control booth. Finally, all three old friends stood together, struggling to come to terms with their despair. "For a few moments," Geoff later wrote, "the three of us stood there numbly, reminiscing about the impact John Winston Ono Lennon had had on our lives, focusing on the positive, the lighthearted, the absurd. We smiled as we conjured up pleasant memories, but there were tears behind our laughter. Somehow none of us could seem to come up with the right words to say. There probably *were* no right words to say." For McCartney, this last aspect would become horribly true as he walked away from the studio that evening. Confronted by reporters, he could barely muster a response to John's untimely death, remarking, "It's a drag, innit?" He was subsequently pilloried in the British press, but for his part, George understood implicitly the sense of shocked detachment that Paul was feeling in that moment. During an interview with the BBC's Gavin Hewitt, George described the rage that was boiling up inside of him. "I feel frightfully sorry for Yoko and Sean," he said, "and all the people who loved him so much. But I also feel very angry that it's such a senseless thing to happen. That one of the great people that happened this century was just wiped out by madness. I'm very angry about it."[9]

For a week, the studio remained dark, with George and Paul huddling with family and friends to take stock of the tragedy. But by Sunday, December 14, they were back at Oxford Street, where they recorded a demo for a new tune titled "Ebony and Ivory," a composition about striving for racial equality. With the image of a piano keyboard in mind, McCartney had been inspired by an old line from Spike Milligan, who was known to say, "Black notes, white notes, and you have to play the two to make harmony, folks!" After the holiday break, Martin and McCartney took their recording sessions to Montserrat, where they were joined by Laine and drummer Dave Mattacks. Over the next several days, Martin supervised rehearsals of new McCartney compositions such as "Average Person," "Dress Me Up as a Robber," and "The Pound Is Sinking." Stanley Clarke and Steve Gadd showed up not long afterward, with Mattacks taking a backseat as the bandmates plowed through several other tunes, including "Somebody Who Cares," "No Values," "Give My Regards to Broad Street," and "Hey Hey." George and Paul's new approach to the studio was elevated further still when Ringo Starr joined his old friends at Montserrat on February 15, 1981. Working alongside Gadd, he played on "Take It Away," with Martin sitting in on electric piano. For the producer, the combination of Starr and Gadd made for a unique, complementary sound: "Steve is a really versatile drummer," George wrote, "and he's meticulous with his timing. On the other hand, Ringo isn't one of those technical drummers, but he has a most distinctive sound, and you always know it's him. He's got a great beat, and flows with the beat, too, which is terribly important. So we had very, very contrasting types of talent, and when they played together you could tell it most acutely. It was a good sound."[10]

Soon, they were joined by rockabilly legend Carl Perkins, with whom McCartney performed a duet titled "Get It," along with "My Old Friend," Perkins's tribute to the ex-Beatle. For Paul, it was one of the great highlights of the *Tug of War* sessions. "I wanted to play with Carl Perkins," he later remarked. "I have loved him since I was a boy. His songs were the first blues I ever listened to. 'Blue Suede Shoes,' for example. We didn't cast him in a track, I just rang him up and asked if he fancied getting involved. He said, 'Why, Paul, I sure do,' and he came down to Montserrat." George was rightly chuffed when Carl woke up on his first day on the island. "This morning, I thought I'd died and gone to heaven," Perkins exclaimed. "It's so pretty here and so beautiful." The Montserrat sessions concluded with Stevie Wonder's arrival on February 26, 1981, to record "Ebony and Ivory" as a duet with McCartney, along with "What's That You're Doing?" an upbeat power-groove that McCartney and Wonder perfected in the studio. For "Ebony and Ivory," they rehearsed with a drum machine that Wonder had brought with him from California but that had broken in transit. For his part, Stevie made short work in fixing the machine: "He was amazing in his ability to ignore his blindness," said Martin, and the erratic drum machine was no match for Wonder's technical smarts. "Stevie said he knew how to fix it, and asked me to get an engineer to take off the cover so he could get to the works. Then he insisted on the current being restored. I was horrified when I saw his fingers wandering over the components. There were 440 volts going through the chassis! He explained that it was the only way to be sure it worked. Of course, he fixed it perfectly. Such blind confidence!"[11]

For George, watching the two veterans record "Ebony and Ivory" was "a tremendous privilege because they are each multi-talented instrumentalists. For the song, McCartney and Wonder played more than a dozen different instruments ranging from a basic track comprised of guitar, bass, piano, and drums through a wide array of overdubs, including McCartney's masterful vocoder, which synthesizes the human voice, and Wonder's innovative percussion and electric piano work. In mid-March, Martin and McCartney returned to Oxford Street, where they worked on *Tug of War* through December 1981. In the process, they recorded more than two albums' worth of material, including the moving, introspective title track and a wistful piano ballad, again with Ringo, titled "Wanderlust." By this point, Laine had exited the production only to be replaced by 10CC mainstay Eric Stewart, who began collaborating with McCartney on a host of new compositions. In May 1982, George and Paul recorded "Say Say Say" with the legendary Michael Jackson, who was riding high after the release of his smash-hit *Off the Wall* and currently recording a follow-up LP with Quincy Jones. The McCartney-Jackson duet came together rather quickly, with McCartney playing guitar, keyboards, and percussion, which he shared with Jackson. The track was rounded out by a posse of top-flight studio musicians, including harmonica player Chris Smith. With Emerick behind the boards, Martin scored a crisp horn quartet that contributed to the song's driving funk sound. Working with Jackson was a revelation for Martin, who said that "he actually does radiate an aura when he comes into the studio, there's no question about it. He's not a musician in the sense that Paul is," George added, "but he does know what he wants in music and he has very firm ideas." During this period, George superimposed a host of orchestral arrangements on the *Tug of War* tracks, including the high-stepping "Ballroom Dancing," for which he scored an unusual, soaring clarinet-trumpet figure. As George later recalled, "There's a clarinet kind of *glissando* which is a bit like Gershwin's 'Rhapsody in Blue,' and the clarinet swoops up from its bottom chalumeau register. It's much wider than the Gershwin one going through two octaves and in fact is almost impossible to do. Jack Brymer played it, but at the very top it isn't a clarinet any more, it's a trumpet which finishes his phrase. It was difficult to get the crossover point so that you couldn't really hear the join, although we did manage it. But that's the kind of thing I love. Again, it's painting isn't it? A little bit of magic."[12]

After they returned from Montserrat, Martin and McCartney took time away from the *Tug of War* sessions to join George Harrison at his Friar Park estate to work on "All Those Years Ago," a song that Harrison had originally intended for Starr. Together, Harrison and Starr had already recorded a version of the track, but the drummer didn't think it made sense given his vocal range. With a new set of lyrics memorializing the bandmates' experiences with Lennon, "All Those Years Ago" began to assume the context of a tribute to their fallen bandmate. "You were the one who imagined it all," George wrote, "all those years ago." Retaining Ringo's drum track, George Harrison invited Paul, Linda McCartney, and Denny Laine to add backing vocals to the song, with George Martin and Geoff chipping in with goodwill and camaraderie. When they had completed the tracking, Martin, McCartney, and Harrison spent hours reminiscing about Lennon and their years together. The Friar Park session marked the first time that the trio had worked together on a recording, along with Ringo's prerecorded drum track, since January 3, 1970, when they produced "I Me Mine." "All Those Years Ago" became an international hit for Harrison, clocking in at number two on the *Billboard* charts.

That summer, Martin and McCartney worked on several additional tracks at "the Mill," McCartney's Sussex home studio. The clear highlight was "Here Today," the ex-Beatle's heartrending tribute to his fallen songwriting partner. With McCartney plucking his acoustic guitar along with a plaintive string quartet arranged by Martin, "Here Today" found McCartney engaged in an imaginary conversation with Lennon. Paul later admitted that part of the song found its origins in the Beatles' 1964 American tour when the songwriters were riding out a hurricane in Key West: "It was during that night, when we'd all stayed up way too late, and we got so pissed that we ended up crying—about, you know, how wonderful we were, and how much we loved each other, even though we'd never said anything. It was a good one: you never say anything like that. Especially if you're a Northern man." For George, adorning "Here Today" with a string quartet initially seemed troubling, especially as it might strike listeners as being a not-so-subtle echo of "Yesterday." But for his part, Paul pressed forward, finally upending their shared concern. "I thought, well, this is stupid, it's like saying because you've used a guitar once in 1980 you should never use a guitar again," he commented in the liner notes. "It's silly condemning the format of a string quartet just cause we'd used it once on a famous record—you know, 'Yesterday.' So I then said to George, 'Look, let's just try a string quartet, let's get it all worked up, let's do it. There's no reason why we shouldn't keep using string quartets till we drop."[13]

With work having been concluded on *Tug of War*, the album was released in April 1982 and became an international blockbuster for the longtime colleagues. Topping the charts in the United States and United Kingdom alike, *Tug of War* spawned two hit singles in the number-one "Ebony and Ivory" and top-ten "Take It Away," with "Say Say Say" being held back for a future release. For McCartney, *Tug of War* was a spectacular return to form as a solo artist. The album earned a Grammy nod for Album of the Year, as well as a host of rave reviews. *Rolling Stone*'s Stephen Holden described the album as "the masterpiece everyone has always known Paul McCartney could make," adding that together, McCartney and Martin created "a record with a sumptuous aural scope that recalls *Sgt. Pepper's Lonely Hearts Club Band* and *Abbey Road*." About "Here Today," Holden writes that "George Martin's string arrangement is, if anything, even more graceful than the one he did for 'Eleanor Rigby.'" Holden attributed the album's overarching success to Martin's painstaking attention to detail. "It's in these seemingly lighter moments," Holden writes, "that George Martin's studio touches illuminate McCartney's wistful hominess with exquisite musical details: a brass ensemble in 'Wanderlust,' pan pipes in the affably shuffling 'Somebody Who Cares' and Beatlesque inner voices in the madcap 'The Pound Is Sinking.'" As the album soared up the charts, the video for "Take It Away" fell into heavy rotation on the fledgling MTV network and featured Starr and Martin on drums and keyboards, respectively, as well as a cameo by John Hurt, the renowned Oscar-nominated actor who had turned heads with his recent turn in *The Elephant Man*. For the video's stage sequence, Martin plays the electric piano while wearing a naval uniform patterned in the style of the producer's old Fleet Air Arm getup from the 1940s.[14]

For George, *Tug of War* had proved to be one of the most rewarding experiences of his career, which was saying something. And working with Paul had been a dream, with the producer and artist working together with unremitting honesty and mutual respect. George's misgivings about being able to challenge Paul in the studio had been met professionally and then some. "To give Paul his due," said George, "he accepted my criticisms with remarkable *bon-homie*, and I guess it's only because we've worked together for so long that he could do it."[15]

Although *Tug of War* had dominated George's studio work during this period, it was hardly his only project. Throughout his life, George had been blessed, for good or ill, with an agile mind, and he thrived when his life was purring along at its busiest possible clip. In 1981 alone, for example, he had scored the soundtrack for *Honky-Tonk Freeway*, while recording albums with a diversity of acts including Little River Band and Ultravox—all of which were produced during his collaboration with McCartney on *Tug of War*.

For George, it was a strange period, indeed. He was working again with Paul, arguably his most successful and talented artist, and trying out a host of new bands from very different generic backgrounds. Yet at the same time, at age fifty-five, he often found himself feted by well-meaning organizations with a nostalgic eye for his otherworldly past achievements. One such opportunity had recently arrived in the form of the popular British television program *This Is Your Life*. He had long worried that the *This Is Your Life* production team would attempt to memorialize him, and he purposefully made a pact with Judy to resist their ministrations. Hence, he was "quite shocked" when he learned that she had made secret arrangements with their old friend Ron Goodwin to lure him into a London television studio to record an episode devoted to his life and work. He knew something was up when the taxi pulled out outside the studio, where the Temperance Seven, the band behind his first number-one single, were playing along the curb, with Gerry Marsden and Billy J. Kramer loitering nearby. As the program unfolded, George was bowled over by seeing so many friends and colleagues, including Cilla Black, Rolf Harris, Dudley Moore, Bernard Cribbins, and Matt Monro, among others. The producers had even rounded up the Four Tune Tellers, George's dance band from his teenage years. George later discovered that Judy had gone ahead with the episode in order to include his older sister, Irene, who was battling cancer at the time. Irene ultimately survived, and George, for his part, understood his wife's motives implicitly. And besides, he later admitted, his bout with *This Is Your Life* made for a truly "wonderful night."[16]

Having written numerous film scores over the years, George was excited to begin work on *Honky-Tonk Freeway*, a surefire hit starring the likes of Beau Bridges, Jessica Tandy, and Hume Cronyn. The story about a small southern town being bypassed by a freeway project that promised to change the burg's fortunes for the better, *Honky-Tonk Freeway* was being directed by Englishman John Schlesinger, who poked gentle fun at American ways in the film, which George scored along with Elmer Bernstein's orchestral work. The film proved to be a box office flop, but by that time George was already on to his next gig, which involved working with Little River Band on their latest LP *Time Exposure*. The Australian bandmates were in a precarious position of sorts, having just released a live album, *Backstage Pass*, that had failed to capitalize on the success of their platinum-selling *First Under the*

Wire album, which included the hit singles "Lonesome Loser" and "Cool Change." Little River Band joined George at AIR Montserrat during one of the producer's breaks from the *Tug of War* sessions, and the Australians, restless and riddled with anxiety, worked doggedly on their new album, often recording round the clock. When Martin and Emerick arrived in the studio most mornings, they discovered the bandmates still hard at work from the night before. "It was tough," George later wrote. "It's not a good way to work at all. We were exhausted by the end." Perfectionists in the studio, the members of Little River Band conducted numerous instrumental overdubs and endlessly double-tracked vocals. "To be honest," said George, "it used to drive me up the wall because it was so inhuman." Released in August 1981, *Time Exposure* righted Little River Band's fortunes with a pair of top-ten US singles in "Take It Easy on Me" and "Night Owls."[17]

Easily the most unusual line on his résumé, George's collaboration with British new wave band Ultravox turned plenty of heads when the respected producer decided to try his hand at producing the mechanistic, electronically oriented band. For George, Ultravox wasn't that strange of an assignment. He was eager to work with a younger, cutting-edge group, and Ultravox perfectly fit the bill. As he once remarked, "Today's market requires something different, and I'm going to come up with instrumental sounds that accent a beat and that highlight the sounds that are now attracting listening interest." George had become friendly with band leader Midge Ure, and together they hatched the idea of him producing Ultravox's 1982 album, *Quartet*. For Ultravox, the collaboration marked a departure from longtime producer Conny Plank, while George couldn't resist working with the band, who was a favorite of his fifteen-year-old daughter, Lucie. "I get on very well with them," George later recalled about the group. Keyboard player "Billy Currie is very good. He thinks kind of orchestrally with his synthesizer work. I didn't find it as alien as people would have thought." For George, the overriding issue involved trying to get the band to think about their music more organically, more humanly. Drummer Warren Cann emerged as a project for the producer, who desperately wanted to liberate the musician from his obsessive reliance on click tracks to maintain a rigid, unrelenting beat. "His beat was metronomic," George later wrote, "to the extent that before recording he used to spend days programming his computer drum machine." At one point, Martin suggested that Cann try playing without benefit of his electronic touchstones, but the drummer simply couldn't do it—"he just fell apart." Martin's favorite aspect of the Ultravox production was the song "Hymn," which required him to score the band's choral work. Propelled by the success of the hit single "Reap the Wild Wind," *Quartet* delivered a strong-selling album for the British band.[18]

During this same period, George revisited his plan, originally hatched back in 1979 with his *All You Need Is Ears* memoir, to provide fledgling producers with a handbook for embarking upon a career in music. Titled *Making Music: The Guide to Writing, Performing, and Recording*, the resulting anthology provided insights into composing popular music, musical performance, and recording techniques and was a primer on the nature of the music industry itself. To accomplish this end, George gathered a diversity of essayists from the music business to try their hand at sharing the fruits of their labors. For his part, George recognized the growing dilemma of making and enjoying music in an age characterized by evolving technologies. "At the present time, music is available to everyone on a scale which would be incredible to anyone living 100 years ago," George wrote. "Indeed, we have such a host of good sounds that we are liable to chronic indigestion unless we are circumspect about our consumption." To navigate the morass, he called on the likes of Paul McCartney and Stephen Sondheim to address the act of writing music; Eric Clapton, Jeff Beck, and Chick Corea to explore music performance; Geoff Emerick, Phil Ramone, and Quincy Jones to share their experiences with sound production; and Richard Branson and Chris Wright to comment on the trials and tribulations of working in the record industry. *Making Music* enjoyed rave reviews, as evinced by Steve Morse's notice in the *Boston Globe*, which praised Martin's anthology as "an extremely informative guide through the labyrinth of the music biz" that "neither insults nor panders to the reader."[19]

Having accomplished his long-standing goal of providing budding musicians and record producers with an introductory guidebook, George returned to the studio with Paul in order to compile the ex-Beatle's next solo effort. With *Tug of War* having proven to be an unprecedented return to form for McCartney, Martin set about the business of culling through the remaining tracks that they had recorded in the early 1980s with an eye toward future projects. Up first was *Pipes of Peace*, the long-player that McCartney saw as the thematic answer to *Tug of War*, with its accent upon the worldly tensions of everyday life. By this point, McCartney was collaborating with Eric Stewart, who had supplanted Laine as the ex-Beatle's artistic partner. With "Say Say Say" already primed and ready for release, Martin and McCartney turned their attention to the new LP's title track, an antiwar number penned as a counterpoint to "Tug of War." As George later recalled, "We wanted to try and convey the sound of as many pipes as possible. The pipe is such a universal folk instrument. From China through Afghanistan through to Ireland, you'll find pipes of one sort or another. So Paul's thought was, 'Can we convey this, that we can actually unite the world with music, with the pipes of peace portraying that?'" To capture the attendant sounds that Paul desired, George even tried his hand at playing the oboe, the slippery "live eel" that he had first attempted back in his Guildhall days. As he later remarked, "A lot of the pipes had to be synthesized, and for that we used a Fairlight. I used to play the oboe, and on one phrase I wanted to use an oboe lick. I haven't played for about 20 years, but I said, 'Rather than get an oboist in, I'll play it.' Arrogance itself. I got the oboe in and I was terribly depressed when I realized what sound I was producing. It was ghastly. My diaphragm was no longer what it was and nor was my lip control. I was able to produce one or two good notes, but only one or two. I didn't have the dexterity, and I suddenly realized how inferior my technique had become." So he remedied the situation by playing the notes on a keyboard.[20]

Enamored with the concept of espousing global unity, George built up several layers during the production process, including a children's choir to imbue the song with a sense of optimism and goodness. In this way, he opted to combine the pipe sounds with "the effect of innocence and children, and in fact, we got the Pestalozzi Children's Choir along to perform, thinking that they might add another dimension to it, and they did." With "Pipes of Peace," the ultimate challenge for George involved capturing Paul's lead vocal. Now forty years old, McCartney was beginning to lose the vocal dexterity that he had enjoyed for most of his singing career. When he originally composed "Pipes of Peace," said George, "he wrote it in C. When I heard him sing it, I said, 'You know, it's in the wrong key for you. You have to sing it awfully low.' When he sang it in another key, part of it sounded awfully high. Then I realized the range was over two octaves. A lot of writers—even the most experienced ones like Paul—don't think about how a song is going to affect their voice. They quite often write their songs so that their fingers feel comfortable with the instrument they're playing, forgetting that it may not be the best key for their voice." George remedied the issue by having Paul sing "Pipes of Peace" in different keys, modulating from E to C and back again. For his part, Paul was pleased with the results, saying, "Oh, that's great. I like it, and it sounds much more interesting."[21]

Released in October 1983, *Pipes of Peace* continued the success of *Tug of War*, albeit on a different trajectory. Where the latter album had been a best seller in its own right, *Pipes of Peace* only rose as high as number fifteen on the American album charts. But like its predecessor, *Pipes of Peace* resulted in a raft of hit singles, including "Say Say Say," which was a megaseller for McCartney and Jackson, notching a number-one single on *Billboard* and clocking in at number two on the rhythm-and-blues charts. While "Pipes of Peace" was relegated to the B-side of "So Bad" in the US marketplace, where it charted a top-thirty single, in the United Kingdom "Pipes of Peace" proved to be a chart-topping single. With a bevy of hit singles under his belt, McCartney was ready to return to acting in the same style that he done in the 1970s with such Beatles fare as *A Hard Day's Night* and *Help!* Having tapped George as his producer, Paul settled on a caper film, to be directed by Peter Webb on a $9 million budget, titled *Give My Regards to Broad Street* as his vehicle. George loved the idea of making another rock musical, but he wasn't so sure about *Give My Regards to Broad Street*, recalling the *Magical Mystery Tour* debacle all too well. As George later described the film, "*Give My Regards to Broad Street* is a slightly dramatic story, a sort of day in the life of McCartney, but it has a twist to it. It's a vehicle for his songs, and from the moment you see him at the beginning of the picture to the end, there are 14 of them—10 are old songs and four are new." For his part, George was enchanted by the soundtrack possibilities, but the problem as he saw it was that "Paul was expecting the music to make the film a success." The plot "was a thin one, but Paul went ahead with it regardless and spent his own money on it. He'd actually talked to quite a few directors who had turned it down—he was a bit headstrong in that respect."[22]

For the soundtrack, George produced a mélange of different songs, including rocking numbers like "No Values" and "Not Such a Bad Boy," as well as a medley of Beatles and McCartney tunes with Ringo chipping in on drums, such as "Yesterday," "Here, There, and Everywhere," and "Wander-lust." In large part, the soundtrack relied on this kind of recycling, with George producing new versions of old hits, including a futuristic, techno version of "Silly Love Songs" and a jazzy take on "The Long and Winding Road." George relished the opportunity to revisit such a variety of old songs, later writing that "'Yesterday' is such a unique record. I prefer the original. But I prefer the new versions of 'Silly Love Songs' and 'The Long and Winding Road,' which I think are both terrific tracks—much better than the originals." He was particularly taken with "The Long and Winding Road," which "starts off with a saxophone played by Dick Morrisey, then it goes into the vocal and we used a black gospel choir, the London Community Gospel Choir." For the track, "we had a live band in the studio with Herbie Flowers on bass, with Paul and Trevor Barstow on keyboards. On 'Silly Love Songs,' we had most of Toto—Jeff Porcaro on drums, Steve Lukather on guitar, and Louis Johnson on bass, and it was terrific, really beautiful."[23]

In the end, George's premonition had been correct about *Give My Regards to Broad Street*, with the movie generating a paltry $1.4 million in receipts after its autumn 1984 debut and closing shortly thereafter. Renowned film critic Roger Ebert described the music as "wonderful" while observing that the cinematic experience had been "about as close as you can get to a non-movie." The soundtrack LP was moderately more successful, mostly riding on the strength of McCartney's "No More Lonely Nights" single, which was the last track to be recorded for the project. The basic track featured McCartney's bass and lead vocal, backing vocals from Linda McCartney and Eric Stewart, Herbie Flowers's bass, Anne Dudley's synthesizer, and Stuart Elliott's drums. But the crowning touch was Pink Floyd mainstay David Gilmour's searing lead guitar solo, which afforded the midtempo love song with a welcome edge. Martin took special care in arranging the backing vocals. As he later remarked, "There are choral sounds that come in on the slow ballad version of 'No More Lonely Nights'—slightly ethereal, floaty, slightly synthetic choral sounds. I built up a lot of backing vocals with Linda, Eric Stewart, and Paul, and created a lot of sort of complex harmonic washes." After it was released as a single in September 1984, "No More Lonely Nights" scored a top-ten showing in the UK and US marketplaces alike, with the *Give My Regards to Broad Street* soundtrack topping the UK album charts while settling in at a lackluster number twenty-one, at least by McCartney's standards, in the United States.[24]

By 1985, George had self-consciously decided to select his production efforts with even greater exclusivity. He still hadn't become immune to the occasional "one-night stand," but he made a point of being more deliberate in his selection of artists after his recent bout of successes with Paul. "I think the most difficult thing, if you are successful," he remarked at the time, "is to stay successful. And to keep coming back and keep doing good things, which I've always tried to do. All I'm saying is it gets harder, it doesn't get any easier. No, I shall just gradually slip away." The notion of gradually slipping away had clearly been on his mind in 1985—and especially as he contemplated his upcoming sixtieth birthday on January 3, 1986. In those days, rock 'n' roll was still considered a young person's game, and George was older than just about anyone else he knew in the industry. Having been feted for much of his adult life, he understood the precarious place that he occupied in his highly competitive and always-evolving business. And perhaps more than ever before, he knew that one day his time would come—just as it had for

Oscar Preuss so very many years ago—to settle into the twilight and leave the record industry to other, younger hands. "You're in competition still, with all these people," said George. But "after being the Fastest Gun in the West," he added, "you've got to learn when to hang up your holster."[25]

24

GROW OLD WITH ME

For the time being at least, George wasn't even remotely considering the idea of hanging up his holster just yet. As 1985 wore on, George took on another highly selective project—this time, with "the Gambler" himself, country megastar Kenny Rogers. Over the years, Martin had done precious little production work with country and western acts, save for the country rock of America, and he likely saw Rogers as a unique challenge. As Rogers prepared to record his thirteenth studio album, he took a chance and asked Martin to produce the long-player. To the singer's surprise, George accepted, and before long they were working at AIR Montserrat on his new record, to be titled *The Heart of the Matter*. "I don't know why he ever bothered to do an album with me," Rogers later remarked, "but I was thrilled and touched that he did." For the album, Martin routined a host of different cover versions at his island retreat with Rogers, including Dave Loggins's "Morning Desire" and Michael Smotherman's "Tomb of the Unknown Love." As they recorded each number, Martin would score the string arrangements, which he completed back in London. For Rogers, working with Martin was "the highlight of my personal career. He brought a whole different touch to my life and my perspective on music." For Martin and Rogers's one-off collaboration, *The Heart of the Matter* proved to be a triple threat, with the album along with the "Morning Desire" and "Tomb of the Unknown Love" singles notching number-one hits on the *Billboard* country charts.[1]

For George, one of the clear highlights of the late 1980s was the much-anticipated release of the Beatles' albums on compact disc. Codeveloped by

Philips and Sony, CD technology had quickly emerged as the successor to vinyl records as the dominant music-delivery format after its introduction to the marketplace in 1982. By 1985, CD technology netted its first million-selling album in Dire Straits' *Brothers in Arms*, which had been recorded in the tropical splendor of AIR Montserrat. While the music industry quickly embraced the format shift from analog to digital mastering, the Beatles had been conspicuously late in joining the CD revolution. This was due in large part to EMI's reluctance to join its industry peers in paying the requisite royalty per disc to Philips and Sony, as well as the multinational record company's lack of manufacturing capacity as it made the shift toward CD production. And worse yet, EMI had been markedly slow in tapping George to supervise the attendant digital mastering associated with preparing the Beatles' CD debut. In fact, by the time that the record conglomerate contacted the producer about working on the project, the first four LPs—*Please Please Me*, *With the Beatles*, *A Hard Day's Night*, and *Beatles for Sale*—were already mastered and scheduled for release as CDs on February 26, 1987. For reasons known only to EMI management, George wasn't contacted about assessing the mixes until December 1986. In a March 1987 interview with Richard Buskin, George suggested that EMI's motive may have been to seek his imprimatur before beginning the cascade of CD releases. But after they brought him into the project, George assumed the mantle of custodianship for the Beatles' music, striving at every turn to ensure authenticity and fidelity to the band's original artistic intentions. In short, he wouldn't simply be rubber-stamping EMI's technical decisions but rather making certain that those decisions were made on solid footing.

In this way, EMI probably received much more than they had originally bargained for; but George made it eminently clear that he wouldn't be going away quietly, that he was in it for the long haul as far as the integrity of the Beatles' musical corpus was concerned. As he remarked during his interview with Buskin, the irony is that he didn't have any complaints about the first batch of CDs—as long as they were released in their original productions, that is—noting that when "I was brought in, I couldn't influence the first four in any way except pass my judgment on them. I actually think they're very good." What concerned George were the subsequent batches of CDs. With the 1987 Beatles CD releases, EMI had concocted a shrewd marketing plan that involved positioning the band's CD debut as an "event," with new batches being released each month. After the February 1987 release, the second batch, including *Help!*, *Rubber Soul*, and *Revolver*, was slated for April; *Sgt. Pepper* was scheduled to be released in June, marking the twentieth anniversary of the album's original distribution; *The White Album* and *Yellow Submarine* in August; the *Magical Mystery Tour* LP in September; *Abbey Road* and *Let It Be* in October; and the Beatles' singles releases and rarities, to be compiled as *Past Masters, Volume 1* and *Past Masters, Volume 2*, in March 1988. Through this protracted scheme, EMI unveiled the Beatles' music as a signature cultural event. As future projects would demonstrate, marketing the Fab Four as a blue-chip brand would pay dividends for EMI time and time again.[2]

When the initial batch of CDs was released that February, Bhaskar Menon announced that the first Beatles LPs "were actually made for mono. In very close discussions with George Martin, the Beatles' producer, we determined that there was no question that we must preserve the original mixes—that the releases really must be in mono because stereo was not the intent of the performers." In 1978, Menon had been appointed as chairman of EMI Music Worldwide, and he was actively taking advantage of the CD revolution as a means for leveraging the record conglomerate's massive back catalog, with the Beatles being the cream of EMI's very fertile crop. During the 1970s, Menon had been the driving force behind Capitol Records' sustained success with Pink Floyd's *The Dark Side of the Moon*, and he was eager to position the Beatles' music for new generations of listeners attracted to digital technology, as well as for first-generation fans of the Fab Four who were interested in authentic engagements with the music of their youth, which was where Martin came in.

During those pre-internet days, Martin's considerable contributions to the Beatles' story were understood most thoroughly by diehard fans, musicians and music insiders, and industry types. In contrast to the present, when literally thousands of books attempt to capture the contours of George and the Beatles' story, there was comparatively little resource material available. That veiled state of affairs began to shift rather perceptibly after the distribution, in 1982, of *The Compleat Beatles*, which started life as a two-hour PBS documentary, enjoyed an MGM-backed theatrical release, and was later released on VHS home video. Until the 1990s, the documentary would serve as one of the central jumping-off points for audiophiles and new generations of fans alike. Directed by Patrick Montgomery and narrated by Malcolm McDowell, *The Compleat Beatles* devoted particular attention to George, who received considerable screen time in order to outline his signal role in the band's achievements. For his part, Menon implicitly understood Martin's central place in Beatles lore. Embarking upon a press tour in advance of the Beatles' CD releases, Menon promised that the band's CDs would be "an absolute replication of the masters approved by the Beatles and George Martin when the records were first put out." Even as the first batch hit the stores, Menon avowed that "any remix that is required on any of these, we will request him [Martin] to undertake them for us."[3]

For Martin, it seemed like an incredible guarantee for Menon to make, especially since the producer had only become involved in the project a few months earlier. Worse yet, Menon's pledge to "preserve the original mixes" held very little validity given that EMI had no intention of releasing any additional mono mixes after the first four Beatles CDs. For George, the latter issue didn't pose any ethical quandaries for him, as he had begun taking great care with both the mono and stereo mixes for Beatles LPs by the advent of 1965. While he had no issue with the quality of the February 1987 CD releases, George was especially concerned about the existing stereo mixes for the second batch, which included *Help!*, *Rubber Soul*, and *Revolver*. As for the latter, George didn't foresee any issues for *Revolver*—or *Sgt. Pepper*, for that matter—because his own production skills during the 1960s were progressively "getting better along with the technology"; hence, the albums from 1966 onward required considerably less attention during the CD format shift. But the original 1965 stereo remixes for *Help!* and *Rubber Soul* were virtually useless, in George's opinion, because they sounded "very woolly, and not at all what I thought should be a good issue." To remedy the situation, George returned to the original four-track tapes and remixed them for stereo. Looking back, "I was beginning to think in terms of stereo by the time *Rubber Soul* came along," said George, but listening to his 1965 remixes left him "somewhat embarrassed" about the results. In keeping with Menon's dictum about maintaining authenticity, Martin resisted any urges to make wholesale balance changes in order to enhance his stereo remixes. Instead, he met EMI's mandate by focusing on cleaning up the individual sounds in the mixes, a feat that he accomplished by going back to the original four-track source tapes. "My intention was not to change anything," he later explained, but "I was able to harden up the sound and cut down on some background noise."[4]

With George having rehabilitated the second CD batch, the rest of the releases proved to be smooth sailing. Menon's plan worked virtually to a tee, with several of the Beatles' long-players zinging back onto the album charts. Not surprisingly, the most notable and vaunted release of the year belonged to *Sgt. Pepper*, which made its appearance as a CD two decades after the LP's original, breathtaking debut. With a national "It was 20 years ago today" campaign reaping dividends, *Sgt. Pepper* enjoyed the highest placement of the lot, notching a number-three appearance that summer of 1987. *Sgt. Pepper* was the pinnacle of EMI's event-driven marketing plan, with the band attracting legions of new listeners via the album's CD release. As for George, he simply couldn't imagine that the Beatles had another resurgence in them after the hoopla associated with the group's digital debut. "I think we're going to see the end of the hype now," he remarked at the time. "This is the last day. This is June the 1st, 1987. Tomorrow, we'll be forgotten for another 20 years. Then you'll have to really dig me up!"[5]

Even still, the walk down memory lane had been an emotional experience at times for George. After listening to the original mixes and attendant studio chatter with the 1960s-era Beatles productions, he found himself transfixed as he made his way through the old tapes. "It is fascinating listening," he observed. "You listen to the outtakes, you listen to the endless tucks and tails, and a lot of times I was in the studio performing with them, and I hear John's voice talking to me, and me talking back, and it's been absolutely fascinating. I've been going back to my youth."[6]

Never one to only reminisce, George wasted little time in busying himself with other projects. That same year, he mixed Paul McCartney's latest single, "Once Upon a Long Ago," for release. Produced by Phil Ramone, "Once Upon a Long Ago" scored a top-ten UK hit and was distributed along with *All the Best!*, a compilation of the ex-Beatle's solo and Wings hits. In 1988, George produced yet another album at Montserrat: *Say Something*, a solo release by Andy Leek, the singer-songwriter front man for Dexys Midnight Runners. For Martin, working with such diverse artists, from Kenny Rogers and Paul McCartney to Andy Leek and others, was a nonissue for him. "I don't go for a conscious style," he observed. "It's just that you do what you do the way that you do it, and I don't know any other way. It's as simple as that really. It's not any desire to achieve a trademark or anything, it's just the way I go about making records." In this way—and like his Beatles days—George's production often "disappeared" into the music, relegating any sense of style to the recording artist, where, to the producer's way of thinking, it rightfully belonged.[7]

In 1988, George undertook one of the most significant non-Beatles projects of his career, a long-held ambition to bring renowned Welsh poet Dylan Thomas's *Under Milk Wood* to life as a musical production. The narrative had originally come to life as a 1954 BBC radio drama starring Richard Burton not long after the poet's untimely death in December 1953. Directed by Andrew Sinclair, a film version was subsequently released in 1972. Working on extant evidence that Thomas planned to append music to his story line, Martin approached Douglas Cleverdon, the producer of the original radio drama, about turning *Under Milk Wood* into a musical production with the

1954 script about the fictional Welsh village of Llareggub (derived from "bugger all" spelled backward). In support of his project, Martin assembled an all-star cast, including renowned Welsh actor Anthony Hopkins, as well as Jonathan Pryce, Bonnie Tyler, and Harry Secombe, one of the original Goons. In April 1988, George conducted a performance of his score for *Under Milk Wood* at the Barbican with the London Symphony Orchestra and, buoyed by the bravura reception, continued to develop the project even further. With additional music provided by Elton John and Mark Knopfler, Martin pushed the project forward, planning to create a full-fledged stage performance of *Under Milk Wood* composed of Thomas's original libretto, Martin's score and the new music from John and Knopfler, and the producer's star-studded cast of voices.

But before George could proceed, a series of circumstances interceded in his professional life that threw AIR into disarray. Since 1970 and the grand opening of AIR Oxford Street, the company had been ascending to greater and greater heights on the strength of its studio-driven revenues, whose growth accelerated with the addition of AIR Montserrat to the company's portfolio nine years later. But in 1989, the edifice of AIR's business model was assaulted, first, by the forthcoming end of the company's twenty-one-year lease on the Oxford Street property, which the owners intended to redevelop. Hence, the lease was set to expire in 1991. George and his partners were at a crossroads, and many of his advisers "thought we should now forget the studio business and concentrate on other aspects of showbiz. I said the choice was a simple one—either we rebuilt somewhere in London or we closed down the whole operation. And if we opted to rebuild, we had two options: either we should get smaller," George reasoned, "or we should aim for the top, going for a studio that would embrace classical music, film scores, and post-production sound facilities." Knowing that the latter option was considerably expensive, George dispatched Dave Harries to find a potential site that might be economical to develop given the city's historically exorbitant real-estate prices. And Harries did just that, discovering a deserted Congregational church in Hampstead, North London, which had fallen into disuse for nearly two decades. Known as Lyndhurst Road Congregational Church, the massive, hexagonal space promised to be a unique environment in which to conduct recordings large and small and with a range of different kinds of acts and projects. Standing in the derelict building not long after Harries made his discovery, Martin fell in love with the concept. In order to test his thinking about the facility's potential, he enlisted several colleagues to visit Lyndhurst Hall with him, including a trio of consultants in the form of John Kurlander,

Haydn Bendall, and Mike Jarrett. Years later, Kurlander, who had risen to the post of chief engineer for EMI Classics, would remember standing in the midst of the dusty and dilapidated church as Martin shared his grand vision for the studio. For his part, Kurlander knew that Martin was relying on his EMI competitors to validate his decision to renovate the old building into a world-class recording facility. But even then, as he stood inside the derelict old church, Kurlander knew that Martin was on to something really special, the kind of production palace that they had all been aspiring to throughout their professional lives.[8]

Working with his advisers, George estimated the build-out costs for the deluxe studios that would come to be known as AIR Lyndhurst at £8 million. After reporting the requisite expenses to his board, George was met with understandable concern over the company's ability to provide the hefty capital to bring his latest dream to fruition. After AIR board member Chris Wright suggested that they bring in an equal partner on the project, George contacted Japanese music industry scion Kazunaga Nitta, who arranged for a partnership with prodigious car and home stereo manufacturer Pioneer Electronics, and the deal was on. Pioneer moved quickly, supplying the necessary capital in short order, but AIR Lyndhurst, with the requisite church redevelopment and George's yen for cutting-edge technology at the fore, would be a complex project. The studio wouldn't be open for business until 1992 at the earliest, and as George himself noted, "building work is always fraught with unknown hazards."[9]

George was in fine fettle in the spring of 1989 when he delivered the Berklee College of Music's commencement address. The esteemed Boston-area institution feted George in fine style, and he even sat in on several production courses. Years later, students would recall the incredible opportunity to work with George during that special week leading up to his commencement address. As the story goes, at one point George visited a production class, pried up a reel of tape, cut it into strips, and laid it out in front of the students. "I'll see you tomorrow," he reportedly told them, leaving them to their own devices to be creative and make something—old school with masking tape—out of the tape loops. For his April 1989 address to the graduates, during which he received an honorary doctorate in music, George noted that in his own professional life he had "had my share of success and failure, rejection, and acceptance," but he also recognized the importance of timing to anyone's fortunes, whether they be for good or ill. "I was lucky enough to join the record industry at a time of change," he remarked. "I took a job at Abbey Road studios to give me a bit more money, and I became hooked on the fascination of recording. I was lucky enough to arrive at the right time, and to become part of a team that was learning as it was developing. It was hardly science in those days. We flew by the seat of our pants, and improvisation was the order of the day. That timing, that luck, is something that we all need. Everyone has opportunities of one sort or another throughout their lives, and one cannot expect to benefit from every one. The trick," he concluded, "is to recognize the break when it comes and to take advantage of it." For George, that aspect was the heart of the matter: to be able to realize, in the moment, that something may be worth pursuing, even as evidence and opinion seem to suggest otherwise.[10]

For George, timing would shortly rear its ugly head in devastating and far-flung ways. As work continued to forge ahead with AIR Lyndhurst in North London, disaster struck thousands of miles away in the Caribbean in the form of Hurricane Hugo. On Sunday, September 17, 1989, the category-four storm battered Montserrat, killing ten residents, destroying nearly every home, and leaving eleven thousand of the island's twelve thousand inhabitants homeless. In the process, the hurricane dealt AIR Montserrat what eventually would amount to a deathblow. At first things seemed to be optimistic for the ten-year-old studio. Shortly after the hurricane struck, studio manager Yvonne Kelly reported that AIR's facilities were some of the few buildings to survive the onslaught, remarking that the studio was "built like a bunker" and adding that "the next band that's got the guts to come out to record, we're ready for them." But as it turned out, Kelly's hopeful outlook was unwarranted. Several weeks later, George visited the site to survey the damage for himself. Standing inside AIR's main studio, he opened a piano keyboard only to discover that the keys were covered in mold. In that moment, George knew that the studio's electronics couldn't possibly have survived. "I realized then we were done," he later recalled. Not long afterward, George released a statement in which he lamented the loss of AIR Montserrat, which he attributed not only to the hurricane's destruction but also to a rapidly shifting business model in the record industry. "After 10 great years of recording there the music business had changed," he proclaimed. "The moguls running the business no longer wanted their artists miles away, outside their control. That coincided with the devastation caused by the hurricane and sadly the studios had to close." Any hope that AIR Montserrat might be resurrected was dashed only a few years later, when the island's Soufrière Hills volcano erupted, burying the colony under a layer of lava and mud. George and Judy were vacationing on the island during the initial eruption. At first, they were mesmerized by the volcanic display: "I saw a ribbon of gold coming down through the clouds,"

George wrote. "'Bloody hell,' I said. 'Come and take a look at this, Judy.' We were only a mile or so away from it, and there was lava coming out of the volcano. We were actually thinking how lovely it looked! Silly idiots that we were." But as the eruptions continued over the next few years, the devastation mounted, leaving the island in a state of ruin. The studios remain there today, rotting and decaying at the hands of the island's elements.[11]

As it happened, one of the last LPs recorded at AIR Montserrat was the Rolling Stones' stellar comeback LP *Steel Wheels*, one of nearly seventy hit albums produced over the years at George's island paradise. In September 1997, George convened a benefit concert, titled *Music for Montserrat*, to raise relief funds for the island's citizenry in the wake of its volcano's eruption. For the event, George assembled an all-star roster of musicians who had recorded on the island over the years, including Paul McCartney, Phil Collins, Jimmy Buffett, Mark Knopfler, Sting, Elton John, Midge Ure, and Eric Clapton, among others. The bravura event also featured Carl Perkins, who died a few months later at age sixty-five. Arranged and produced by George, the concert provided relief funds through DVD sales. The producer also spearheaded plans to establish a cultural center on Montserrat, which opened in 2006. As the concert's grand finale, Martin conducted a full orchestra as McCartney led the assembled glitterati in a performance of the *Abbey Road* medley, followed by an all-star "Hey Jude" sing-along.

If George had any plans to gradually slip into the waiting arms of history at this juncture, they were a secret known only to him. In the spring of 1992, he starred in ITV's television documentary *The Making of Sgt. Pepper* as part of the network's twenty-fifth-anniversary celebration of the landmark LP. Broadcast in the United Kingdom on June 14, 1992, *The Making of Sgt. Pepper* featured Martin playing unreleased outtakes from the original sessions as he narrated his way, song by song, through the story of the album's production. A few years later, Martin made astute use of the documentary's contents, which he commemorated with the book-length publication of *Summer of Love: The Making of Sgt. Pepper*. Retitled as *With a Little Help from My Friends* in the American marketplace, George's latest memoir was ghostwritten by novelist William Pearson, who assisted the producer in compiling his memories of recording *Sgt. Pepper*. Writing in the *Guardian*, Nicholas Lezard praised the book "as an invaluable insight into their creative process, and a riveting description of how [George and the Beatles] rewrote the book about studio recording. Martin can't write for toffee, but if you're keen this shouldn't matter a whit." Although also taking issue with the volume's stylistic shortcomings, Robin Blake lauded *Summer of Love* in the *Independent* for its attention to the recording details and instrumentation associated with *Sgt. Pepper*'s legend-making songs. "The fogeyish George Martin was the Beatles' record producer," Blake remarked, consigning George and his achievements with the Fab Four to some distant yesteryear, "but he was much more—musical arranger, collaborator, a man who could convert the boys' ideas into staves and dots."[12]

During the same month in which *The Making of Sgt. Pepper* debuted on British television, Martin got down to business converting the "staves and dots" of McCartney's latest musical ideas into notation. Working in Abbey Road Studio 2, George conducted orchestral overdubs for Paul's new composition "C'mon People," a peace anthem slated for his upcoming *Off the Ground* album. George had previously scored a string arrangement for "Put It There" on Paul's *Flowers in the Dirt* LP.

In December 1992, George marked AIR Lyndhurst's grand opening with a performance of *Under Milk Wood*. Titled as *An Evening with Dylan Thomas*, the bravura opening was held as part of the Prince's Trust, with Prince Charles in attendance, along with Anthony Hopkins, Jonathan Pryce, and Harry Secombe returning to their original roles, and Catherine Zeta-Jones and Tom Jones lending their voices to the cast. As for the new studio itself, George could barely contain his elation, proclaiming AIR Lyndhurst to be "the biggest and the most expensive and the most complicated, but also the most beautiful studio I've ever had. It's certainly my last one; I won't do any more after this! There are lots of other studios I've worked in I still enjoy, but I like my own one best of all." When the studio officially opened for business a few weeks later, it quickly gained its niche, just as George had predicted, as a premier recording facility for film and orchestral work. Years later, Simaen Skolfield caught up with George at AIR Lyndhurst. To Skolfield's delight, the producer gave him and his young children a grand tour of the facilities, where selections from the Harry Potter films had recently been recorded. As they visited the main hall, with its majestic studio appointments, Martin invited Skolfield's ten-year-old son to try his hand at the grand piano that featured on the latest Harry Potter soundtrack. As Skolfield later recalled, his son was stunned by the experience of sitting with Martin at the piano. But for his part, Skolfield was blown away by the great facility. "It was absolutely beautiful," he later recalled.[13]

With *Under Milk Wood* having finally received a proper debut to George's satisfaction, he began to contemplate the hearing loss that had slowly descended upon him over the past several years, perhaps even longer. He later admitted, "I first noticed a loss of certain high frequency sounds in the mid 1970s." By the early 1990s, his handicap had become much more acute.

"I have to accept the fact that I will never recover my hearing," he lamented. "Music and recording have been my passion, so it's ironic that my progressive deafness has been caused by years and years of listening to music at too high a level." Yet in keeping with his working-class roots, he vowed to continue his production efforts until his impediment fully prevented him from doing so. One of the first productions at AIR Lyndhurst involved George's work with Japanese artist Yoshiki, who recorded his first classical album, *Eternal Melody*, in the main studio in February 1993. With arrangements by Martin, Gavin Greenaway, and Graham Preskett, the music was conducted by Martin and performed by the London Philharmonic Orchestra.[14]

The following month, March 1993, George's rock-musical production of the Who's *Tommy*, directed by Des McAnuff with choreography by Wayne Cilento, opened on Broadway's St. James Theatre for nearly nine hundred performances. Invited by Pete Townshend to undertake production duties, Martin recognized the inherent risks: "It was an ambitious and dangerous project, a real gamble, because Broadway musicals are the most expensive shows to stage and the outcome could be a flop." Fortunately for Martin and Townshend, McAnuff had assembled a top-drawer cast chock-full of talented singer-actors. In a rave review in the *New York Times*, Frank Rich wrote that *Tommy*, "the stunning new stage adaptation of the 1969 rock opera by the British group the Who, is at long last the authentic rock musical that has eluded Broadway for two generations." For the soundtrack, George "booked the big studio at Electric Lady in New York for a weekend. I'd organized it so that we didn't waste a moment because we couldn't interrupt the theatre run." With fewer than two days to capture the original soundtrack recording, George conducted the session as if it were a live show, bringing one performer in after another to maintain a semblance of the Broadway production. George's production of the *Tommy* soundtrack later earned a Grammy Award for Best Musical Show Album, his fourth statuette overall and his first since "Live and Let Die" nearly two decades earlier.[15]

With his hearing continuing to deteriorate, George decided to take advantage of the moment and revive the George Martin Orchestra for a series of one-off concerts for the first time since *From the Beatles to Bond and Bach* in the 1970s. The highlight for George was conducting a concert in Brazil in October 1993 with more than eighty thousand in attendance. As a thunderous deluge came down from the sky, he soldiered on with the concert at an outdoor venue in the Quinta Da Boa Vista national park in Rio, where music lovers braved the elements to enjoy the show, merrily singing along with George's classic scores. For Martin, the most stirring moment of that unforgettable evening occurred when he took the stage alone, sat in front of the grand piano, and played an instrumental version of "Here, There, and Everywhere," only to receive a standing ovation from the rain-soaked audience.

In addition to producing an LP of old standards for *The Glory of Gershwin*, for which the producer scored a top-thirty hit with Kate Bush's "The Man I Love" in July 1994, George's work in the mid-1990s was dominated by one Beatles "event" after another. EMI had come to learn the evergreen power of the Beatles' back catalog by this point—and especially after the success of the 1987 CD releases—and the record conglomerate was eager to jump back into the fray. EMI's latest Beatles foray had been made possible by recent legal settlements between the label and the band, which paved the way for a host of new projects. In contrast with the CD releases, EMI made sure to approach George with plenty of lead time to carry out production work for *Live at the BBC*, a planned compilation devoted to the bandmates' numerous early to mid-1960s performances on the BBC Radio's Light Programme. Working with renowned BBC producer and archivist Kevin Howlett, George described the project as "an assembly job more than anything else" as he made his way through hundreds of hours of performances. Composed of fifty-six songs, the LP offered what George later deemed to be the antithesis of the shoddy Hollywood Bowl concerts, with the Beatles playing clearly and audibly at the top of their game for the Light Programme. Released on November 30, 1994, *Live at the BBC* topped the UK charts and netted a number-three showing on *Billboard*'s album charts. Writing in *Rolling Stone*, Anthony DeCurtis hailed the double album as "an exhilarating portrait of a band in the process of shaping its own voice and vision."[16]

As George later wrote, *Live at the BBC* held a very specific purpose for EMI, acting as a kind of "prelude" for the long-planned Beatles *Anthology* project. Some five years in the making, the Beatles' *Anthology* consisted of a carefully coordinated preparation and release of a book, three albums of unreleased recordings and studio outtakes, and a television miniseries broadcast in the United Kingdom and the United States. Set to commence with the television program and concomitant album release in December 1995, the *Anthology* project found its origins in *The Long and Winding Road*, Apple executive Neil Aspinall's ninety-minute documentary on the history of the band. Completed in 1971, *The Long and Winding Road* project lay dormant throughout the decade, with the bandmates' involvement only beginning around 1980, when, according to Yoko Ono, they had begun making plans for a reunion concert and recording new material. The background for *The*

Long and Winding Road was made public in a 1980 legal deposition related to the Beatles' lawsuit against the *Beatlemania* musical. John Lennon's December 1980 murder put an end to any further work by Aspinall or others on *The Long and Winding Road*, but eventually the surviving Beatles involved themselves in the *Anthology* project in 1990, after the 1989 resolution of a long-standing lawsuit between McCartney and the other surviving Beatles regarding the unequal payment of royalties.

Directed by Geoff Wonfor and Bob Smeaton, the *Anthology* documentary took some five years to compile. Produced by Aspinall and Chips Chipperfield, the *Anthology* television miniseries consisted of six hours of interviews with George and the Beatles, as well as a host of archival footage. Aspinall and Chipperfield, like Menon before them, recognized the value of Martin's input in understanding the Beatles' remarkable musical achievements, and the producers kept Martin front and center throughout the project, affording him with a broad canvas for constructing the three double albums' worth of outtakes and rarities. For the project, George was ably assisted by Geoff Emerick, his loyal AIR colleague and, of course, an eye- and earwitness to the storied recordings back in the 1960s. Working from July 1994 through May 1995, Martin and Emerick culled through thousands of hours of material in compiling the six *Anthology* CDs. In addition to the tapes in EMI's vaults, George searched for rare lacquers that may have eluded the Beatles' grasp over the years, only to discover that the original recording of "Love Me Do" from his first session with the band back in June 1962, complete with Pete Best sitting in on the drums, had been socked away in his attic. Judy had happened upon the lacquer by accident during a bout of spring cleaning more than three decades after the recording had been made.

Working with Geoff was a great boon for George, with the two old friends and colleagues quickly establishing a routine. As Emerick later recalled, "George Martin sat in one control room with Abbey Road archivist Allan Rouse, painstakingly listening to every single Beatles recording all the way through. When George came upon a segment he thought worth including, it would be sent upstairs to me in another control room, where I would pull the multitrack masters from their original boxes and remix it." For George, working on the *Anthology* was a revelation. In previous years, George had often argued that sifting through all those unused takes was a fool's errand, that only the mastered recordings were of significance to the Beatles' incredible story. But the *Anthology* project proved him wrong. "It was an extraordinary experience," he later observed. "I was re-living my life, really, listening to outtakes, compositions worked out on the spot, studio chatter, and so on.

Quite dramatic in a way." He was most gratified when he found something unusual as he rifled through the vaults. In such moments, "the boys got very enthusiastic," he wrote. "Sometimes Ringo [Starr] would come in, sometimes George [Harrison] would come in. Paul would come in more often because he lived around the corner. Sometimes, though very rarely, all three of them would come in at once, and on those occasions a big buzz would go round Abbey Road; the staff would be goggle-eyed to see the four of us reminiscing and chatting about old times."[17]

As part of the *Anthology* project, Yoko had provided four of John's demos for potential completion by the surviving bandmates, who came to be known as the Threetles. Years later, Martin's hearing would be cited as the reason he opted not to produce the demos with Harrison, McCartney, and Starr. But in truth, he wasn't asked. "It's all water under the bridge," he later explained, but "I wasn't too unhappy about not being asked because I was a bit uncomfortable about the idea of John's voice being used that way." Instead, the Threetles tapped Jeff Lynne of ELO fame, as well as the producer of Harrison's best-selling solo album *Cloud 9* and one of the guitarist's Traveling Wilburys bandmates, to handle production duties, with Emerick sitting in as engineer. On the strength of the resulting singles releases, which included "Free as a Bird" and "Real Love," the *Anthology* project proved to be a massive success, with the television miniseries chalking up impressive ratings and the three *Anthology* double albums each topping the US charts and resulting in top-five showings in the Beatles' homeland. In his November 1995 *New York Times* review on the occasion of the release of *Anthology 1*, Jon Pareles got to the heart of George's accomplishments with the band: "Although they were well rehearsed, as the *Anthology*'s outtakes show, the Beatles hid their craftsmanship behind exuberance. Even in songs proclaiming innocuous romantic sentiments, or in a corny novelty 'Bésame Mucho,' the Beatles' rock had a sense of freedom. In the band's first years, it was more the freedom of bending rules than of breaking them. Thirty years later, what comes through is the Beatles' optimism that they could get away with anything if they did it skillfully." In his December 1996 *Rolling Stone* review of *Anthology 3*, Parke Puterbaugh gently takes George to task, writing that "for more than two decades after the Beatles broke up, the band members and their producer, George Martin, insisted that everything of quality that they created in the studio was already a matter of record—that there was nothing left worthy of reconsideration, much less release." If nothing else, Puterbaugh concludes, *Anthology 3* shows "that those who make history are often the least qualified to judge it."[18]

While Martin may have been disappointed about not being invited to produce the Threetles' "Free as a Bird" and "Real Love" singles, he would very shortly get his chance to shine, as well as to reconsider his own reservations about producing Lennon's ghostly sound. In 1998, EMI's Rupert Perry invited Martin, with Ono's blessing, to score an orchestral accompaniment to Lennon's demo for "Grow Old with Me," one of his very last compositions. For George, working with the demo proved to be a challenge given that John frequently recorded his demos by placing his tape recorder on top of his piano at the Dakota, resulting in the instrument being louder than the vocal. "What I did was construct an arrangement where I could take out the whole of John's track when he wasn't singing, rather than leaving the track in throughout and then trying to smother it," George wrote. In the end, "it was strange working with John's dead voice," and as for working with John's demos in such a fashion, "I'm still not sure I approve!" With his twenty-eight-year-old son, Giles, playing bass guitar on "Grow Old with Me," George superimposed an orchestral score onto the track at Abbey Road, and it was released in November 1998 on the *John Lennon Anthology* box set.[19]

In the late 1990s, with his hearing in a continual state of erosion, George still managed to produce a smattering of acts when they caught his fancy. In 1997, he produced Céline Dion's top-twenty UK hit "The Reason," while also working with Paul on several songs for the ex-Beatle's *Flaming Pie* long-player, including the orchestration for "Beautiful Night" and "Somedays." George also coproduced "Calico Skies," which he found to be particularly affecting. At the time, Paul's wife, Linda, was battling valiantly with breast cancer, and the sessions for the song were especially poignant as George prepared a string quartet for a version of the song that would later appear on Paul's *Working Classical* album. "I will hold you for as long as you like," Paul sings. "I'll hold you for the rest of my life." On April 17, 1998, Linda succumbed to her illness at age fifty-six. A few months later, a memorial service was held at the Church of St. Martin-in-the-Fields, with all three surviving Beatles in attendance. George and Judy were there, too, to bid farewell to their friend. In the church that day, a congregation of seven hundred sang "Let It Be," the tender ballad about Paul's mother, Mary, who had lost her own battle with breast cancer in 1956, when Paul was just fourteen years old. The moving service ended with David Bailey's emotional recitation of a poem by Spike Milligan:

It was heaven. You were 7 and I was 8.

And we watched the stars suspended

Walking home down an apple lane
Me and Rosie, a doll, a daisy chain
On an evening that would never come again.[20]

During the previous autumn, George had felt the deep pull of God and country to orchestrate a tribute marking the untimely death of yet another woman of renown. On August 31, 1997, Diana, Princess of Wales, had died at age thirty-six in a Paris automobile accident. The nation had been plunged into a period of national mourning, and Elton John, who had been a close friend of the princess, wanted to pay tribute to her through song. Working with his longtime lyricist Bernie Taupin, Elton swiftly revised his 1973 song "Candle in the Wind," a composition originally written to memorialize the life and loss of Marilyn Monroe, to fit the occasion. At the time, George and Judy were relaxing on their boat near the Turkish coastline when Elton telephoned him and asked him to produce the record, which the musician planned to release as a charity single. For his part, George was no stranger to venerating fallen leaders through song, having produced Millicent Martin's moving tribute to President John F. Kennedy with "In the Summer of His Years" within days of his assassination in November 1963. With no time to spare, George and Judy made their hasty return to the United Kingdom, where, on Saturday, September 6, Elton performed his new version of the song, recast as "Candle in the Wind 1997," at Diana's funeral at Westminster Abbey. For Elton, the experience was heartbreaking and intense. He later described playing the song that day in the packed cathedral—and with some two billion television viewers glued to their screens—as "one of the most difficult things he'd ever done." For George, who watched the live feed a few miles away, it had been nothing short of "beautiful."[21]

With Giles in tow, George waited for Elton to make his entrance at Townhouse Studios in West London that same day. When Elton arrived, George suggested that he record the song exactly as he had played it earlier that day at the funeral. Within three takes, Elton had captured his vocal and piano accompaniment. At first, the pop star had suggested superimposing a synthesizer part onto the composition, but George had something else in mind. With Elton's portion of the recording having been completed, George began writing a score that called for a string quartet and an oboe. By the time that the session players arrived at eight o'clock that evening, the producer was ready to conduct the overdub, which featured a quartet composed of Peter Manning, Keith Pascoe, Levine Andrade, and Andrew Schulman, along with oboist Pippa Davies. By the time the musicians had departed, George had already begun mixing the record for release, and on Saturday, September 13, the single was in the shops. In the UK and US marketplace, "Candle in the Wind 1997" debuted at number one, with Elton's single becoming the biggest seller in UK history and second only to Bing Crosby's "White Christmas" stateside. All told, "Candle in the Wind 1997" sold thirty-three million copies around the globe. But for George, it occupied a very different place in his personal legacy as the last single he would ever produce.

As the twentieth century came to a close, George's life had fallen into a familiar routine of humbling tributes and heartbreaking goodbyes. More often than not, he and Judy would find themselves bidding farewell to life-long friends. Yet on other occasions, they would bear witness to one accolade after another. There were few more affirming moments than George's knighthood on June 29, 1996, when, with a few gentle movements from a sword, Queen Elizabeth II recast the couple as Sir George and, by definition of his stately honor, Lady Judy. Years later, George couldn't help but joke about the perfunctory nature of the experience. After kneeling in front of Her Majesty, he wrote,

> She picks up a sword from a cushion, touches your right shoulder with it, and then describes a huge arc around your head (presumably to avoid cutting it off) and touches the other shoulder. Then she returns the sword to its cushion and you arise as Sir George. She places the insignia around your neck, chats to you and, to finish, funnily enough, she pushes you away. Then you go and have a good lunch. It's nice. It's all very old fashioned. And not without its humor. There was a military band playing in the Minstrel's gallery, and the tune that I heard as I received my accolade from the Queen? "Hi-ho, hi-ho, it's off to work we go. . . ."[22]

When it came to his Rock and Roll Hall of Fame induction in March 1999, George was suitably chuffed to be acknowledged by his peers, proclaiming, "I am very honored to be placed in a galaxy alongside many of my own heroes." For the august organization, feting George was a no-brainer. As his official Rock and Roll Hall of Fame and Museum biography notes, "As a result of his work with the Beatles, George Martin played a major role in changing the face of rock and roll. He was responsible for much of the group's sound, and he introduced many musical elements that were new to rock and roll. He also had tremendous commercial success: he is responsible for 30 Number One singles in the UK and 23 Number One singles in the US." Paul McCartney was inducted as a solo artist during the same ceremony—with the Beatles having been honored for their achievements as a band back in 1988—making the event all the more poignant for Martin.[23]

With the Rock and Roll Hall of Fame having made its pronouncement, seventy-three-year-old Sir George had truly become part of the cultural firmament. In the United States, he was regularly greeted with flashbulbs and autograph requests while being commemorated at nearly every turn and, on occasion, gently lampooned in his homeland. In 1998, the BBC Two comedy troupe Big Train took aim at Sir George, poking fun at his zealous custodianship of the Beatles' legacy, as well as his recognition as their most authoritative and perhaps most visible spokesman over the years. In a sketch devoted to George, comedic actor Kevin Eldon played the august producer as a nonstop chatterbox who can't stop himself from delivering one anecdote after another—even as Middle Eastern terrorists kidnap him and hold him in captivity. At one point, the terrorists removed a duct-taped George from the wheel well of their truck as he prattles on about the recording session for "Can't Buy Me Love." The sketch's final segment depicted a bearded Martin at his postrelease press conference as he sidesteps questions about his imprisonment in order to share a non sequitur about the Beatles smoking pot on the sly while working in the studio with him during the *Sgt. Pepper* years. In so doing, the Big Train team succeeded in mixing the low culture of sketch comedy with the high culture of George and the Beatles' art. It wasn't the first time that Martin had been skewered on British television. Years earlier, he had been depicted as record producer "Sir Archie Macaw" (played by actor Frank Williams) in *All You Need Is Cash*, Eric Idle and Neil Innes's Beatles parody that premiered on BBC2 in March 1978.

When he wasn't being roasted on national television, George was a frequent guest on British talk shows, where he would wax poetic about the Beatles' world-beating accomplishments. To his credit, he made a rule of refusing to take credit for the many ways in which they had so dramatically altered both their musical genre and his industry. And for the occasions when he was called on to share his own thoughts about his life in music, he was unfailingly careful to include the Fab Four's achievements not as his own but as a fortunate happenstance that gave his work meaning and afforded him with a platform for imagining a career beyond his lean, early years with Parlophone. During a November 19, 1995, episode of *Desert Island Discs* with commentator Sue Lawley, for example, George spoke movingly about the music that first lit the fuse of his artistic soul, including such personal touchstones as Maurice Ravel's *Daybreak* from *Daphnis and Chloé* and Wolfgang Amadeus Mozart's Oboe Quartet in F Major. But at the same time, he included his own productions of the Beatles' "I Want to Hold Your Hand" and Peter Cook and Jonathan Miller's "Aftermyth of War" among the discs that he would treasure if he were to be marooned on some uncharted desert isle. When asked to choose a favorite, George Martin, as hapless castaway, chose Pyotr Tchaikovsky's *Fantasy Overture* from *Romeo and Juliet* as his favorite musical confection, suggesting that, as John Lennon had mused so many years before, "all you need is love."

But as tenderhearted and poignant as George's episode of *Desert Island Discs* truly was, he couldn't help finishing his stint on BBC Radio without a wink in his eye and a smile in his heart. What book would he choose to take with him to while away his days in lonely exile, Lawley asked? "A book on how to build a boat to try and escape!" George countered. And as for his luxury item? Of that there was never any doubt, said George. He would be happy with a keyboard, he surmised: "Something I could make music on would be very nice, indeed."[24]

EPILOGUE

SWAN SONGS

A S THE NEW CENTURY UNFOLDED, George Martin found himself spending more and more time at the Old Rectory, the Oxfordshire estate that he shared with his wife, Judy. By this period, he had lapsed into what would pass, for George, at least, as the semblance of retirement. The couple's spacious National Trust home was a far cry from the luxurious manse that one might expect from a pop-music legend, save for the array of gold and platinum discs arrayed in a downstairs bathroom. When he wasn't working in the city at AIR Lyndhurst, more often than not George could be found in his shed behind the Old Rectory, its ceiling pocked with model airplanes hanging from the rafters and a snooker table beckoning nearby. His passion for aeronautics dated back to his teen years and eventually to his years in the Fleet Air Arm. As usual, George's life was never static. In 2000, his renewed zeal for airplanes was even showcased in an episode of *Airshow World* with host Alain de Cadenet, who interviewed the former airman about his experiences with the Royal Navy torpedo bomber the *Fairey Swordfish*.

During that same period, George experienced another recurring blast from his past in the form of those four lads from Liverpool. Indeed, by the summer of 2001, the Beatles were all the rage again. In November 2000, the folks at Apple had released *1*, a compilation album featuring the Beatles' twenty-seven chart-topping UK and US hits, to mark thirty years since the group's disbandment. For his part, George had penned a foreword for the booklet that accompanied the CD's release. Like the 1987 CD releases and the *Anthology* project, *1* was spearheaded by shrewd, event-driven marketing. The

481

compilation wildly exceeded industry expectations—including George's—and topped the charts in thirty-five countries, turning over more than thirty million units in the process. By that point, as always, George was already looking ahead, working away on the next big thing. But those who knew him well weren't really surprised by the speed from which he went from one project to the next. As his son Giles, then thirty-two and a producer in his own right, pointed out, his father "didn't look back. It wasn't really in his nature." For George, the next big thing involved a CD and documentary extravaganza to be titled *Produced by George Martin*, an all-encompassing career retrospective that would see him rifling through the EMI vaults yet again.[1]

By this juncture, the idea of producing new work held discernible pitfalls for George. While he acknowledged his 1999 Rock and Roll Hall of Fame induction as one of the great highlights of his career, he had swiftly come to realize that being installed in that particular institution, with its highly specific focus, made him feel significantly more detached from the music that had comprised the majority of his life's work. "As I got older and older," he remarked, "I realized that I was becoming less and less attuned to being a rock 'n' roll producer," even going so far as to say that "old men shouldn't be in the rock 'n' roll business." This realization was compounded by his rapidly deteriorating hearing loss, which made working with electric guitar–laden sounds even more taxing on his fading senses. For George, admittedly competitive to a fault, the mantle of being the fastest gun in the West simply no longer held its appeal as he approached his midseventies.[2]

With the release of his *In My Life* project back in October 1998, George self-consciously began preparing to bid farewell to the musical stage. It had been nearly fifty years since the day in September 1950 when he rode his bike across the city in his Fleet Air Arm great coat and made his way up the steps of 3 Abbey Road, where Oscar Preuss offered him a job as his assistant A&R man. When it came time to call it a career, George eschewed the familiar confines of St. John's Wood for the sterling new facilities of AIR Lyndhurst. Recorded from March to August 1997, *In My Life* featured a host of present-day celebrities trying their hand at covering Beatles songs, including Robin Williams and Bobby McFerrin singing a duet for "A Hard Day's Night," while Jeff Beck turned in a searing take on "Come Together." Céline Dion chipped in a cover of "Here, There, and Everywhere," while John Williams performed a classical guitar rendition of "Here Comes the Sun." At one point, George even flew out to Austin, Texas, to record Goldie Hawn singing "A Hard Day's Night." He took particular care in producing Phil Collins's performance of the *Abbey Road* medley, including bravura orchestration from the producer's original score. As for his own contribution, George conducted a new arrangement of "The Pepperland Suite" from *Yellow Submarine*. In the album's oddest moments, Jim Carrey performed "I Am the Walrus," with Sean Connery closing out the LP with a spoken-word rendition of "In My Life." The reviews, not surprisingly given the nature of their collaborations, were generally discouraging, with critics often taking issue with the album's inherent sense of whimsy. As *PopMatters*' Sarah Zupko opined, Martin "has chosen to go out with a whimper instead of a bang," adding, "I don't really have to tell you that Goldie Hawn impersonating a chanteuse on 'A Hard Day's Night' or Sean Connery literally reading 'In My Life' is an embarrassing display, do I?"[3]

With *Produced by George Martin*, George would stick to the original music that had made his name before, during, and after the Fab Four. If nothing else, Zupko's commentary was mindful of the high critical bar for Beatles cover versions. Compiled by Beatles historian Mark Lewisohn, the music of *Produced by George Martin* provided a fascinating overview of a career that had been endlessly variegated from the producer's early days through his very last productions. Knowing this, Lewisohn sagely divided up the six-CD box set thematically, with selections devoted to "Crazy Rhythms"; "Transports of Delight"; "That Was the Decade That Was"; "Gold Fingers"; "Smiles of the Beyond"; and "Nice Work." In so doing, the inherently quirky nature of George's musical pursuits came shining through. With more than 150 tracks, *Produced by George Martin* provided a thoroughgoing retrospective of George's unusual, albeit unique, career in the annals of twentieth-century popular music. The project wasn't a whimper in the slightest, and neither was the documentary, which was released in April 2011. Directed by Francis Hanly, *Produced by George Martin* was carefully crafted, featuring cameos from Paul McCartney, Ringo Starr, Giles Martin, and a host of living witnesses, including the likes of Bernard Cribbins, Rolf Harris, Cilla Black, and Jeff Beck, to the remarkable contours of George's life and work. Far more exacting and significant, the *Produced by George Martin* box set and ensuing documentary succeeded where *In My Life* came up short by aiming to capture the sheer volume of George's achievement.

In 2002, George's place as rock music's elder statesman was venerated yet again when he was tapped to serve as creative consultant for the *Party at the Palace*, a gala concert to be held on the grounds of Buckingham Palace on June 3 in honor of Queen Elizabeth II's golden jubilee. With twelve thousand fans having earned their place in the audience through a national lottery, the concert would be broadcast on gigantic television screens to a million visitors gathered around the Mall and the Queen Victoria Memorial, along with some two hundred million viewers watching at home.

For George, it would be a monumental undertaking to stage the event's artists and repertoire. In the end, he managed to gather rock's most vaunted living performers—without benefit of a fee, no less—and keep their egos in check as they marked the queen's longevity. With Michael Kamen having agreed to conduct the Royal Academy of Music Symphony Orchestra, Giles Martin lent a hand by rehearsing the house band, which featured Phil Palmer on guitar, Pino Palladino on bass, Paul "Wix" Wickens on keyboards, Eric Robinson on saxophone, Phil Collins on drums, and Ray Cooper on percussion. Sam Brown, Margo Buchanan, and Claudia Fontaine lent their talents as backing vocals for the makeshift group, which was charged with learning the set list for the bravura event. To his credit, George was able to call in a number of favors in assembling a roster that included the likes of Paul McCartney, Queen, Eric Clapton, Rod Stewart, Cliff Richard, Brian Wilson, Shirley Bassey, and Ozzy Osbourne, among a host of other music luminaries.

In the end, the concert came off without a hitch. Fittingly, George kicked off the event by staging Queen's Brian May perched high above the grounds, where he played a sterling guitar rendition of "God Save the Queen" atop the roof of Buckingham Palace. The three-hour celebration came to a close with McCartney's set, which included all-star performances of "All You Need Is Love," "While My Guitar Gently Weeps," and "Hey Jude." At one point, Paul even chipped in an impromptu version of "Her Majesty." After the grand finale, the queen herself took the stage, escorted by none other than Sir George. For the producer, the *Party at the Palace* was a moment of exquisite validation. He had been called into action by the monarchy, and he had delivered in spades. Standing on the stage that night as the whole joyous celebration came to fruition, George basked in the well-earned glory of a job well done. "It cheered me up no end!" he later recalled, as the fireworks burst overhead on that special night.[4]

While the *Party at the Palace* was a great tribute to George's standing in his industry, he knew full well that many, if not all, of his personal achievements as a music professional would always be eclipsed by his collaboration with the Beatles. It was with this modest spirit that he compiled *Playback*, a limited-edition memoir in which he shared photographs and memories from his interwoven personal and professional lives. Published in a signed edition of two thousand copies by Genesis Publications in 2002, in many ways *Playback: An Illustrated Memoir* came into being as George's last, albeit highly selective, word on his life in music. A genial look back across his eight decades on the planet, Martin's memoir presented a largely sunny depiction of life in the record industry, as well as a fairly sanitized version of his personal life that was, in reality, at times riven by turmoil and intrigue. "I wasn't going to write anymore," George explained to Allan Kozinn, "except I'm at the end of my life now. And do you know what tipped the scales for me? The fact that it would be such a good thing for my family, my children and grandchildren. It would be like a family heirloom, or a photograph album." With this goal firmly in mind, George commissioned his old friend Staffan Olander to act as his amanuensis as the producer took one last amiable stroll down memory lane. Writing in the *Guardian*, Phil Hogan described *Playback* as "an agreeable impression of Martin's adventures with 'the boys' . . . in the form of anecdotes told over a page or so, brevity being relied upon perhaps too much as the soul of wit." Hogan concluded that "anyone looking for dirt will be out of luck." Just as Martin had intended, *Playback* "is a gentle, affectionate memoir, written for the most part without rancor or regret."[5]

For George, the new millennium had already begun with plenty in the way of rancor and regret, including a series of losses on an international and personal scale. On September 12, 2001, he contemplated the horrific events of 9/11 in the company of John Kurlander. In the midst of tragedy, they took time to reminisce about days gone by. For Kurlander, it had been some thirty-three years since his first session with Martin and the bandmates, when the producer asked him to share the first playbacks of "Hey Jude," which he and the Beatles listened to for hours as they marveled at their latest creation. On a personal level, the year continued its awful slide into November, when George Harrison, having suffered from a lengthy battle with cancer, died at age fifty-eight. Martin admired Harrison's spirit in the face of his fate, remarking in late November, only days before the Beatle's death, that "he has an indomitable spirit, but he knows that is going to die soon, and he is accepting that."[6]

With his death on November 29, 2001, Harrison left behind his wife, Olivia, and twenty-four-year-old son, Dhani. And while he admired the younger man's resolve, Martin felt the loss acutely. During the 1990s, Martin had suffered his own battle with cancer. In 1995, he was aghast to discover a lump in his groin. "I became rather ill and had a series of operations which left me low for a while," Martin later wrote. "Hearing I was under the weather, George [Harrison] rang up and suggested he come over one afternoon. He had a huge bunch of flowers and a small, beautifully carved wooden statue of the Hindu god Ganesh. 'Keep him by your side,' he told me. 'He will look after you.' I must say, so far he has. It was typical of George to show he cared. His faith never wavered." In one of his last great moments of inspiration, since 1999 Harrison had been working with his friend Guy Laliberté on the concept of bringing the Beatles' music to life through the interpretive theatrics of Cirque du Soleil, the famed troupe of acrobats and aerial performers. Founded in Montreal in 1984, Cirque du Soleil had been the brainchild of Laliberté and his partner Gilles Ste-Croix, who cut their teeth as street performers.[7]

With Harrison's passing, the project entered a protracted period of negotiations between Cirque du Soleil and Apple Corps, resulting in an agreement to launch the ensuing production, to be titled *Love*, at Las Vegas's Mirage resort and casino in the summer of 2006. With Cirque du Soleil conceiving a host of breathtaking acrobatics as accompaniment to the Beatles' music, the Mirage constructed a custom theatrical space to stage the show. The creation of French artist Jean Rabasse, the *Love* theater cost more than $100 million and was designed to treat more than two thousand patrons to 360-degree views of the production. In order to accommodate the Cirque du Soleil performers, the space was rigged with numerous tracks and pulleys, along with twenty-three digital projections and four translucent screens to partition the theater throughout the production. Most importantly, each of the auditorium's seats was fitted out with a trio of personal speakers, including two in the headrest, in order to maximize the patrons' experience of the Beatles' music, which was the undeniable star of the show. Working with his youngest son—whom he described as "his ears" on the project—George Martin threw himself into the production, which Giles had begun to imagine as a series of innovative "mash-ups" of existing Beatles tracks.

At first, George was loath to work from his son's approach, preferring to sidestep altogether what some listeners might perceive as a kind of sacrilege. After all, during this same period American DJ Danger Mouse had masterminded *The Grey Album*, a controversial mash-up of *The White Album* and rapper Jay-Z's *The Black Album*. For his part, Giles understood his father's concerns, recognizing that a large swath of Beatles audiophiles—"the socks and sandals brigade," in the younger producer's words—were die-hard purists and considered the Beatles' music to be untouchable. Giles finally earned his father's acquiescence for the innovative concept after providing him with a sample of what he had in mind. "At the beginning of the project," said Giles, "I knew that no one would ever hear my mistakes as we'd been secretively shut away, so I thought I'd start by trying to combine a few tracks to see what the result would be. Feeling like I was painting a moustache on *The Mona Lisa*, I started work mixing the bass and drums of 'Tomorrow Never Knows' with

George [Harrison]'s track 'Within You, Without You.'" For his part, George was enchanted by the results, particularly in terms of the elasticity of the Beatles' songs, as the younger producer grafted various tracks together from across the band's career. But like his son, George recognized the gravity of what they were doing in the studio:

> We agonized over the inclusion of "Yesterday" in the show. It is such a famous song, the icon of an era, but had it been heard too much? The story of the addition of the original string quartet is well known, however few people know how limited the recording was technically, and so the case for not including it was strong, but how could anyone ignore such a marvelous work? We introduce it with some of Paul's guitar work from "Blackbird" and hearing it now, I know that I was right to include it. Its simplicity is so direct; it tugs at the heartstrings.

Working at Abbey Road, father and son toiled away at the task, finding intriguing and inventive means of blending the Beatles' tracks together. As Giles explained, they assembled fragments from "the original four tracks, eight tracks and two tracks and used this palette of sounds and music to create a soundbed." In the end, the Martins sampled 120 songs in the creation of twenty-seven discrete musical segments. For Giles, the painstaking process was a joyful, albeit transfixing, one. At one point, he admitted to feeling like his father was actually "producing" him, given that Giles was working from the vantage point of an author of sorts in cahoots with George's original vision and production of the Beatles' tracks.[8]

For George, the production activities associated with *Love* culminated in an emotional spate of sessions in the spring of 2006. In April, he and Giles convened an orchestra at AIR Lyndhurst to record George's orchestral score for "While My Guitar Gently Weeps." For the eighty-year-old producer, it made for an incredible moment, as he recorded a string arrangement for Harrison's original demo that they recorded together back in July 1968. "My responsibility in adding music to it weighed very heavily on me." Working in the cavernous main studio at Lyndhurst, Martin conducted the players as they performed his haunting, tenderhearted score. Knowing that he intended that day at Lyndhurst to be his final orchestral session, the musicians presented him with a bouquet of flowers. George was overcome by the significance of the moment, remarking, "'Yesterday' was the first score I had written for a Beatle song way back in 1965, and this score, 41 years later, is the last. It wraps up an incredible period of my life with those four amazing men who changed the world." Later that day, George joined Giles and David Stark in the control booth to complete their work on "While My Guitar Gently Weeps." Stark would never forget the moment when George gently turned the master fader down and said, "That's it for me." As Stark later recalled, "It was a truly priceless moment."[9]

With production work for *Love* having been completed in London, George and Giles traveled to the Mirage, temporarily ensconcing themselves in Las Vegas in order to carry out postproduction work. Meanwhile, Cirque du Soleil rehearsed in advance of the show's previews, which were scheduled to begin that June. George's reliance on Giles by this point had grown considerably. In 2005, his hearing had eroded dramatically, taking a "nose-dive" and leaving him "profoundly deaf," he later remarked. Together, father and son debuted their *Love* mash-ups in the Mirage theater's revolutionary sound system. During the month-long previews, Cirque du Soleil welcomed a number of guests, including Beatles Brunch personality Joe Johnson. After the show, Johnson saw Martin at an after party in one of the Mirage's nightclubs. Echoing a similar moment nearly thirty years earlier with George A. Martin during the making of Robert Stigwood's *Sgt. Pepper*, the producer promptly asked Johnson what he thought about *Love*. For his part, Johnson was ebullient, telling Martin that it was "spectacular and amazing" and that he "loved the mash-up mixes." To his surprise, George seemed relieved, replying, "I'm so glad. I was worried." Finally, on June 30, the Mirage held a gala premiere for *Love* with George, Judy, and Giles in attendance, along with one of the largest gatherings of the Beatles' extended family in the years since their disbandment. Along with Paul McCartney and Ringo Starr, the friends and family included Yoko Ono, Cynthia Lennon, Julian Lennon, Olivia Harrison, and Dhani Harrison. At the conclusion of the performance, as Cirque du Soleil took their curtain calls, Paul, Ringo, Olivia, Yoko, and George ascended the stage—the surviving Beatles, Harrison's and Lennon's widows, and the producer who never lost faith in the legacy that they had created all those years ago. And that's when Paul, caught up in the spirit of the moment, asked for "just one special round of applause for John and George!"[10]

For his part, Giles would never forget the gala event, especially as he watched his father trade stories with his old friends and their families in a jovial mood on the occasion of the Beatles and Cirque du Soleil's joint triumph. At one point, Yoko walked over beside Giles and said, "It's funny. John's just a voice to me now." With *Love*, George and Giles had succeeded, in their own way, in affording new sounds and textures to the Beatles' timeless music. In November 2006, the *Love* soundtrack was released to great fanfare, notching top-five showings in the UK and US marketplaces alike, proving that the Beatles were evergreen, through and through. Writing in *Pitchfork*, Mark Richardson pointed out that "what seems to consume people most about this record is the sound of the thing, just how beautifully the original material was recorded and how great it comes over on a purely sonic level." For Richardson, the *Love* soundtrack's finest moments occur when it creates a sense of intergenerational community. In so doing, the LP transforms "everyone into an audiophile," Richardson reasoned, in that coming to understand and revel in the Beatles' music makes "young people a little older. And it's also a mash-up remix, which means it's making older people a little younger." Sure, "they were just a pop band," Richardson concluded, "but if anyone can bring all these music fans together under one tent, it's the Beatles. Which is what *Love* is ultimately about."[11]

The Beatles, along with George and Giles, were recognized at the Fiftieth Annual Grammy Awards for Best Compilation Soundtrack Album for Motion Picture, Television, or Other Visual Media and Best Surround-Sound Album. But not everyone was pleased, of course. Geoff Emerick, for one, could scarcely fathom the notion of tampering with the Beatles' recordings, which he considered to be sacrosanct. "I won't listen to it," he later remarked. "Look, the four artists were present when we did the mono mixes of the original records. And the recordings were fresh in our minds when we did the stereo mixes: even if the Beatles weren't present, they were involved. It's their record—and now it's been messed around with. The original records are iconic, they're pieces of art. Would you go and repaint the Sistine Chapel?" If George registered Geoff's disdain for *Love*, he never gave it any credence. As Giles had observed, his father may have had a healthy reverence for history, but he wasn't really the type to look backward. After *Love*, George took on scant few projects, although he spent his last several years completing a documentary on the craft of studio artistry. Titled *Soundbreaking: Stories from the Cutting Edge of Recorded Music*, the TV documentary was conceived in the same vein as *The Rhythm of Life*, George's three-part BBC documentary series, broadcast in the late 1990s, in which he explored concepts associated with musical composition with the likes of Billy Joel, Brian Wilson, and Céline Dion. Produced in collaboration with PBS and directed by veteran filmmakers Jeff Dupre and Maro Chermayeff, *Soundbreaking* explored the history and art of music production and recording.[12]

With *Love*, George had finally seemed to come full circle in the industry that he happened upon, as if by accident, so long ago at the behest of his fairy godfather Sidney Harrison, the beloved mentor who talked him into interviewing for the job as Oscar Preuss's assistant. In their later years, George and Judy socialized with their wide circle of friends, sharing in the trials and tribulations of growing older. In 1999, they were by Cilla Black's side at the funeral of her husband, Bobby Willis. George eulogized him as Cilla's "guardian angel" before reciting Joyce Grenfell's moving poem about human loss and the need for renewal in the face of death:

> If I should go before the rest of you
> Break not a flower nor inscribe a stone,
> Nor when I'm gone speak in a Sunday voice
> But be the usual selves that I have known.
> Weep if you must,
> Parting is hell,
> But life goes on,
> So sing as well.

But George and Judy celebrated, too, marking Cilla's sixtieth birthday a few years later in fine style. For George, it must have seemed like old home week, with the likes of Cynthia Lennon, Mike McCartney, Roger McGough, Pattie Boyd, and the Fourmost's Dave Lovelady in attendance. And they celebrated again in March 2004, when George was granted his own coat of arms by Great Britain's august College of Arms. For the appointments on his shield, George chose the image of three beetles along with a bird—a house martin, no less—clutching a recorder. For his Latin motto, George selected *amore solum opus est*. All you need is love.[13]

In his last years, when George mostly kept to the Old Rectory, he would describe himself as being "in the waiting room." With his hearing having failed him utterly, he often connected with friends and family through email. His eldest son, Gregory, couldn't help but smile when he saw his father's familiar handle appear in his inbox. No stranger to nostalgia, George adopted "Tumpy," the name of his family's Jack Russell terrier, as his email address. By that point, given the wages of living into old age, George had seen plenty of his most cherished friends pass on before him. In 2008, George and the Beatles' first engineer, Norman "Normal" Smith, died at the ripe old age of eighty-five. In the 1970s, he had recast himself as "Hurricane Smith" and tried his hand at the hit parade. In 2009, Capitol president Alan Livingston and AIR's Ron Richards had passed on, as did Sheena, George's first wife, in

2014. That same year, the British tabloids were awhirl with the salacious story of eighty-four-year-old Rolf Harris, who was tried and convicted of indecent exposure. In possibly the strangest moment in the trial, George's 1965 production of "Jake the Peg" was entered into evidence. In two of the more tragic instances in George's final years, Cynthia Lennon died in April 2015 at age seventy-five in Majorca. Just four months later, Cilla perished in August 2015 at age seventy-two after an accident in her Spanish villa. In the wake of her untimely loss, *The Very Best of Cilla Black*, chock-full of Cilla's hits with George, topped the UK charts, marking the singer's first number-one LP.[14]

By the time of his death, at age ninety, on the night of March 8, 2016, George had outlived almost everyone in his circle, save for Judy, now eighty-seven. George died in his sleep at home at the Old Rectory. He had ultimately died from complications associated with stomach cancer. Word went out to the masses via Twitter, courtesy of Ringo Starr. "God bless George Martin," he tweeted. "George will be missed." Paul McCartney followed suit shortly thereafter. "I have so many wonderful memories of this great man that will be with me forever," he wrote. "He was a true gentleman and like a second father to me. He guided the career of the Beatles with such skill and good humor that he became a true friend to me and my family. If anyone earned the title of the Fifth Beatle it was George. From the day that he gave the Beatles our first recording contract to the last time I saw him, he was the most generous, intelligent and musical person I've ever had the pleasure to know."[15]

On March 14, 2016, after a private funeral at the All Saints parish church attended by family and friends, George was interred at the nearby cemetery on King's Hill, a quiet resting place in the village—and mere steps away from the Old Rectory. On May 11, a memorial service was held at St. Martin-in-the-Fields church on the edge of Trafalgar Square. As with the *Love* premiere a decade earlier, the Beatles' extended family and friends were on hand to celebrate his life and work. A congregation of six hundred strong was in attendance, including McCartney, Starr, and their families; Yoko, Sean, and Julian Lennon; Olivia and Dhani Harrison; and such pop luminaries as Elton John and James Bay. So, too, were George's old friends from Abbey Road, including Geoff Emerick, Ken Scott, and Ken Townsend, who came into EMI's employ back in September 1950 during the very same month that George met Judy and assumed his role as Preuss's assistant. For his part, Scott felt transported during the memorial, especially as the hymns in St. Martin-in-the-Fields reached a great swell, washing over the attendees with the sound of music, which possesses the awesome power to inspire—just as it surely felt for fifteen-year-old George Martin as he experienced the first measures of the BBC Symphony Orchestra's rendition of Claude Debussy's *Prélude à l'après-midi d'un faune* in 1941. George fell in love with music that day at the Bromley County School when he discovered the amazing sounds that humans could make. And he never looked back.[16]

Within the year, Lady Judy would take up George and the Beatles' legacy and become a patron of the Strawberry Field Trust, a movement spearheaded by the Salvation Army to transform the site of John Lennon's childhood inspiration into a public cultural space. And in short order, George would be memorialized, time and time again, on McCartney's subsequent concert tours as the ex-Beatle performed "Love Me Do" for stadiums filled with adoring fans, young and old. Brimming with emotion, Paul would rest his hands on his guitar and hearken back to the band's very first, tentative recording of the song with George back in June 1962. But Paul and the other Beatles hadn't been the only ones trying to find their way forward on that fateful day. George may have had more than a decade on them in years, but he was just as green—*greener,* even—than the Beatles when it came to rock 'n' roll. "We taught each other what was required, the Beatles and I," he later wrote. "We groped our way jointly towards an exciting sound." But as for the hoopla, the pomp and circumstance about his central role in their legend, George unfailingly pointed to their gifts as the heart of the matter. "Whatever I did shouldn't be stressed too much," he once remarked. "I was merely the bloke who interpreted their ideas. The fact that they couldn't read or write music, and I could, has absolutely nothing to do with it. Music isn't something which is written down on paper. Music is stuff you hear. It's sound and they thought of those notes. I was purely an interpreter, rather like a Chinese interpreter at the League of Nations. Certainly I taught them all I could in terms of recording techniques and brought an influence of classical music to their work. But the genius was theirs, no doubt about that."[17]

Modest to a fault, George also recognized that the bandmates were always the sum of their parts, that the post-Beatles rancor, the lawsuits, the name-calling, was unrelated to the nature and quality of their achievement. In *Playback,* George observed that "the Beatles themselves all went on working individually, but none of them I think quite achieved the greatness that they achieved when they were together. Someone once said that a fist is stronger than five fingers, and something like that is true with the Beatles. The four of them together were stronger than the four individuals." The same could easily be said for George, who, like the Fab Four, never reached the same heights as he enjoyed during their heady days together during the 1960s. Their collective genius was in working together and sustaining their partnership as long and as far as they possibly could.[18]

For the Beatles, George proved to be the perfect producer to interpret and make manifest their art in the studio because he implicitly understood that the act of production should be invisible. In its finest instances, the act of record production should be so effective and evocative that the artist no longer even remembers that the producer is somewhere in the background of the recording, behind the curtain, bringing the whole effort into tantalizing Technicolor and real life. For all of his accolades, a Phil Spector production was always inalienably by Spector. Whether it involved the Beatles or the Chiffons, the echo chamber was right there, front and center, reminding us who was standing behind the control board. But a George Martin production was both less and more. It was decidedly *less* because George's identity in the music was latent—he had guided the artist to the moment in which the art came to fruition without noise or fanfare. But it was also *more* because he was able to facilitate the release of the magical germ inside the artist's head over and over—so much so, in fact, that George's skills as a producer emerged as a kind of fifth instrument for the Beatles: it was always there for the playing, for making the track brighter and, more often than not, better. And with George Martin and the Beatles, brighter and better invariably translated into a new classic for the ages.

But for George, beyond the music, the fanfare, and an enduring legacy that had already passed among the generations, the Beatles would always be "the boys," a nickname that he had inherited from Brian Epstein. For George, they had been frozen in time as the "four fascinating, impossible, enormously talented, infuriating, adorable young men who changed all our lives." Gifted and frustrating in the same breath, they were still the boys. For the bandmates, he was Big George in the studio. And in John, Paul, George, and Ringo's more mischievous moments—when they would poke fun at the older gentleman with the posh voice and the prim and proper ways—he was the Duke of Edinburgh. But beyond that, in those instances when it really mattered, George Martin was the Beatles' most steadfast and devoted friend.[19]

ACKNOWLEDGMENTS

A **PROJECT OF THIS MAGNITUDE** could not possibly come to fruition without the encouragement and support of a host of friends and colleagues. I owe special debts of thanks to Patrick Alexander, Steven Bachrach, Phil and Eileen Beard, David Bedford, Harry Burton, Lauren Caruso, Al Cattabiani, Eileen Chapman, John Christopher, Lynne Clay, James Collins, Kathryn Cox, Chris DeRosa, Grey Dimenna, Scott Erickson, Mike Farragher, Scott Freiman, Furg, Rob Geurtsen, Katie Kapurch, Karen Keene, Jason Kruppa, Mark Lapidos, Carmel Lee, Helen Lucas, Ed McKenna, Nancy Mezey, Jacob Michael, Laura Moriarty, Kit O'Toole, Michael Plodwick, Judy Ramos, Joe Rapolla, Stu Rosenberg, George and Kathy Severini, Jim Slevin, Joe Studlick, Chris Smith, Jay Sweet, Michael Thomas, Rich Veit, Kurt Wagner, and Rob Winston.

A number of Beatles specialists, music scholars, and firsthand witnesses to George Martin's remarkable story have shared their time and expertise on behalf of this project, including Malcolm Addey, Mitch Axelrod, David Bedford, Jim Berkenstadt, Gerry Buckley, Dewey Bunnell, Richard Buskin, Bun E. Carlos, Chris Carter, John Covach, Geoff Emerick, Walter Everett, Michael Frontani, Joe Goodden, Jerry Hammack, Piers Hemmingsen, Peter Hodgson, Laurence Juber, Donnie Kehr, Jude Southerland Kessler, Allan Kozinn, Howard Kramer, Aaron Krerowicz, John Kurlander, Denny Laine, Richard Langham, Jeff Larson, Spencer Leigh, Steve Marinucci, George A. Martin, Giles Martin, Gregory Paul Martin, Ken Michaels, Staffan Olander, May Pang, Donna Parsons, Bill Quinn, Russ Reising, John Repsch, Tim Riley, Robert Rodriguez, Bob Santelli, Ken Scott, Fred Seaman, Adam Sharp, Simaen Skolfield, Brian Southall, Bruce Spizer, David Stark, Al Sussman, Ken Townsend, Steve Turner, and Peter Vince. I am especially grateful, as always, to Mark

Lewisohn, whose groundbreaking work and painstaking scholarship continue to benefit music historians around the world. As with *Maximum Volume*, this book simply would not have been possible without his lifelong devotion to getting the Beatles' story right.

I am thankful for the steadfast encouragement of my agent, Isabel Atherton, and my indefatigable publicist, Nicole Michael. I am grateful for the efforts of the folks at Chicago Review Press, particularly Yuval Taylor and his top-drawer staff, including Olivia Aguilar, Mary Kravenas, Julia Loy, and Michelle Williams. Special thanks are also due to Josh Rowe of the Independent Publishing Group and most especially to Helen Bowden and Emily Freer, Orphans Publishing's dynamic duo.

Finally, I am thankful, as always, for the love and support of my family—Fred, Jennifer, Andy, Becca, Peter, Tori, Josh, Ryan, Chelsea, Emma, Landon, Justin, and Mellissa—and especially to my wife, Jeanine, who makes all things possible.

NOTES

Prologue: Get Back to Where You Once Belonged

1. George Martin, *All You Need Is Ears*, with Jeremy Hornsby (New York: St. Martin's, 1999), 136, 180.

2. The Beatles, *The Beatles Anthology* (San Francisco: Chronicle, 2000), 337.

1: You Say It's Your Birthday

1. Keith Badman, *The Beatles Off the Record: Outrageous Opinions and Unrehearsed Interviews* (London: Omnibus, 2001), 188; Beatles, *Beatles Anthology*, 194; Kevin Ryan and Brian Kehew, *Recording the Beatles: The Studio Equipment and Techniques Used to Create Their Classic Albums* (Houston, TX: Curvebender, 2006), 402.

2. Bob Spitz, *The Beatles: The Biography* (Boston: Little, Brown, 2005), 591.

3. Martin, *All You Need Is Ears*, 224.

4. Howard Massey, *The Great British Recording Studios* (Milwaukee, WI: Hal Leonard, 2015), chap. 3.

5. "The Beatles at Shea Stadium," *Mix: Professional Audio and Music Production*, January 12, 2017, www.mixonline.com/beatles-shea-stadium/429036.

6. "The Beatles at Shea Stadium."

7. M. Clay Adams to Michael Adams, January 10, 1966, Beatles-History.net, www .beatles-history.net/beatles-shea-stadium.html.

8. M. Clay Adams to Michael Adams.

9. M. Clay Adams to Michael Adams; "Beatles at Shea Stadium."

10. Martin, *All You Need Is Ears*, 184–86.

11. Martin, *All You Need Is Ears*, 140.

12. Dominic Cavendish, "The 10 Worst Musicals of All Time," *Telegraph*, February 13, 2015, www.telegraph.co.uk/culture/theatre/3672844/The-10-worst-musicals-of-all -time.html.

13. Cilla Black, *What's It All About?* (London: Ebury, 2003), 138.

14. Black, *What's It All About?*, 138.

15. "George Martin in US for Material Hunt," *Cash Box*, February 19, 1966, 18; "From the Music Capitals of the World," *Billboard*, March 5, 1966, 37.

16. Paul Du Noyer, *The Illustrated Encyclopedia of Music* (Fulham, UK: Flame Tree Publishing, 2003), 36.

17. Martin, *All You Need Is Ears*, 189; Spencer Leigh, *Love Me Do to Love Me Don't: The Beatles on Record* (Sleaford, UK: McNidder and Grace, 2016), chap. 5.

18. Leigh, *Love Me Do*, chap. 5.

19. Leigh, *Love Me Do*, chap. 5.

20. Black, *What's It All About?*, 136.

21. Mat Snow, *The Who: Fifty Years of My Generation* (New York: Race Point, 2015), 36, 53.

22. Lewisohn, *Tune In: The Beatles—All These Years* (Boston: Little, Brown, 2013), extended ed., 1:641; Snow, *The Who*, 53–54. For Martin's affidavit, see the High Court of Justice Chancery Division, Group A, 1966 0. No.1000 in *Orbit Music Company Limited v. Polydor Records Limited*.

23. George Martin, *With a Little Help from My Friends: The Making of Sgt. Pepper*, with William Pearson (Boston: Little, Brown, 1994), 6.

2: "Why Can't We Cut a Record Like That?"

1. The Beatles, *The Beatles Anthology* (ABC, 1995), television documentary.

2. The Beatles, *The Beatles Anthology*; Steve Turner, *Beatles '66: The Revolutionary Year* (New York: HarperCollins, 2016), 229.

3. Spitz, *The Beatles*, 599; Martin, *With a Little Help*, 16; The Beatles, press conference, Los Angeles, CA, August 24, 1966, The Beatles Interview Database, www.beatles interviews.org.

4. Turner, *Beatles '66*, 127; Spitz, *The Beatles*, 599; Tony Barrow, "Beatle Rumor Half True," *KRLA Beat*, May 7, 1966, 1.

5. Richard Williams, *Phil Spector: Out of His Head* (London: Omnibus, 2009), 142.

6. Turner, *Beatles '66*, 220.

7. Turner, *Beatles '66*, 128.

8. Martin, *With a Little Help*, 46.

9. Martin, *With a Little Help*, 46–47.

10. Spitz, *The Beatles*, 599; Barrow, "Beatle Rumor Half True," 1; Mark Lewisohn, interview with author, June 30, 2017; Geoff Emerick, interview with author, October 20, 2017.

11. Barry Miles, *Paul McCartney: Many Years from Now* (New York: Holt, 1997), 218; Spitz, *The Beatles*, 597.

12. Miles, *Paul McCartney*, 219.

13. Martin, *With a Little Help*, 16, 80.

14. Turner, *Beatles '66*, 52; Spitz, *The Beatles*, 597.

15. John Repsch, *The Legendary Joe Meek: The Telstar Man* (London: Woodford, 1989), chap. 11.

16. Repsch, *The Legendary Joe Meek*, chap. 11.

17. Geoff Emerick and Howard Massey, *Here, There, and Everywhere: My Life Recording the Music of the Beatles* (New York: Gotham, 2006), 110, 367.

18. Emerick and Massey, *Here, There, and Everywhere*, 106–7.

19. Emerick and Massey, *Here, There, and Everywhere*, 109.

20. Turner, *Beatles '66*, 62.

21. Turner, *Beatles '66*, 148.

22. Turner, *Beatles '66*, 141.

23. Turner, *Beatles '66*, 142; Miles, *Paul McCartney*, 291; Beatles, *Beatles Anthology*, 210.

24. Emerick and Massey, *Here, There, and Everywhere*, 112.

3: Every Sound There Is

1. Beatles, *Beatles Anthology*, 206.

2. William J. Dowlding, *Beatlesongs* (New York: Simon and Schuster, 1989), 78; Emerick and Massey, *Here, There, and Everywhere*, 8; Robert Rodriguez, *Revolver: How the Beatles Re-imagined Rock 'n' Roll* (Milwaukee, WI: Hal Leonard, 2012), chap. 5.

3. John C. Winn, *That Magic Feeling: The Beatles' Recorded Legacy*, vol. 2, *1966–1970* (Sharon, VT: Multiplus, 2003), 8.

4. Emerick and Massey, *Here, There, and Everywhere*, 9.

5. Emerick and Massey, *Here, There, and Everywhere*, 10.

6. Emerick and Massey, *Here, There, and Everywhere*, 10.

7. Beatles, *Beatles Anthology*, television documentary.

8. Mark Lewisohn, *The Complete Beatles Recording Sessions: The Official Abbey Road Studio Session Notes, 1962–1970* (New York: Harmony, 1988), 71.

9. Lewisohn, *Recording Sessions*, 71.

10. Lewisohn, *Recording Sessions*, 71.

11. Ian MacDonald, *Revolution in the Head: The Beatles' Records and the Sixties* (New York: Holt, 1994), 169; Emerick and Massey, *Here, There, and Everywhere*, 112.

12. Emerick and Massey, *Here, There, and Everywhere*, 113.

13. Martin, *With a Little Help*, 83.

14. Lewisohn, *Recording Sessions*, 72.

15. Lewisohn, *Recording Sessions*, 72; Emerick and Massey, *Here, There, and Everywhere*, 137.

16. Lewisohn, *Recording Sessions*, 72.

17. George Martin, "Listen to My Story: George Martin Interview with *Melody Maker*," interview with Richard Williams, *Melody Maker*, August 21, 1971, http://beatles number9.com/martininterview1971.html; Martin, *All You Need Is Ears*, 259.

4: A Rube Goldberg Approach to Recording

1. Emerick and Massey, *Here, There, and Everywhere*, 114.

2. Emerick and Massey, *Here, There, and Everywhere*, 114.

3. Emerick and Massey, *Here, There, and Everywhere*, 115.

4. Emerick and Massey, *Here, There, and Everywhere*, 116.

5. Miles, *Paul McCartney*, 279; MacDonald, *Revolution in the Head*, 196; Keith Badman, *The Beach Boys: The Definitive Diary of America's Greatest Band, on Stage and in the Studio* (San Francisco: Backbeat, 2004), 104.

6. Lewisohn, *Recording Sessions*, 74; Emerick and Massey, *Here, There, and Everywhere*, 150.

7. Badman, *The Beatles Off the Record*, 208.

8. Emerick and Massey, *Here, There, and Everywhere*, 116–17.

9. Lewisohn, *Recording Sessions*, 74.

10. Lewisohn, *Recording Sessions*, 13.

11. Turner, *Beatles '66*, 154.

12. Emerick and Massey, *Here, There, and Everywhere*, 111; Spitz, *The Beatles*, 605.

13. Lewisohn, *Recording Sessions*, 74.

14. Beatles, *Beatles Anthology*, 214; Lewisohn, *Recording Sessions*, 75.

15. Lewisohn, *Recording Sessions*, 75.

16. Maureen Cleave, "George Harrison: Avocado with Everything," *London Evening Standard*, March 18, 1966, 8.

17. Walter Everett, *The Beatles as Musicians: Revolver Through the Anthology* (Oxford: Oxford University Press, 1999), 49.

18. Turner, *Beatles '66*, 135.

19. Lewisohn, *Recording Sessions*, 77; Everett, *Beatles as Musicians*, 46.

20. Lewisohn, *Recording Sessions*, 77.

21. George Martin, *Playback: An Illustrated Memoir* (Guildford, UK: Genesis Publications, 2002), 160.

22. Turner, *Beatles '66*, 164; Dowlding, *Beatlesongs*, 135.

23. Badman, *Beatles Off the Record*, 228; Turner, *Beatles '66*, 166.

24. Steve Turner, interview with author, July 4, 2017; Emerick and Massey, *Here, There, and Everywhere*, 127; Lewisohn, *Recording Sessions*, 77.

25. Emerick and Massey, *Here, There, and Everywhere*, 127.

26. Emerick and Massey, *Here, There, and Everywhere*, 127.

27. Lewisohn, *Recording Sessions*, 77; Leigh, *Love Me Do*, chap. 6.

28. Turner, *Beatles '66*, 169.

5: Collective Madness

1. Turner, *Beatles '66*, 170.

2. Turner, *Beatles '66*, 171.

3. Paul Du Noyer, *Liverpool, Wondrous Place: From the Cavern to the Capital of Culture* (London: Virgin Books, 2007), 103; Martin, *All You Need Is Ears*, 186.

4. Du Noyer, *Liverpool, Wondrous Place*, 193–94.

5. Turner, *Beatles '66*, 173.

6. Turner, *Beatles '66*, 174.

7. Turner, *Beatles '66*, 175; Martin, *All You Need Is Ears*, 160.

8. Martin, *All You Need Is Ears*, 160; Turner, *Beatles '66*, 181.

9. Martin, *With a Little Help*, 55.

10. Beatles, *Beatles Anthology*, 207.

11. The Beatles, press conference, Los Angeles, CA, August 29, 1966, The Beatles Interview Database, www.beatlesinterviews.org.

12. Rodriguez, *Revolver*, chap. 1; Badman, *Beatles Off the Record*, 201.

13. Winn, *That Magic Feeling*, 2:19.

14. Lewisohn, *Recording Sessions*, 79.

15. Emerick and Massey, *Here, There, and Everywhere*, 128.

16. Emerick and Massey, *Here, There, and Everywhere*, 128.

17. Emerick and Massey, *Here, There, and Everywhere*, 128; Lewisohn, *Recording Sessions*, 79.

18. Beatles, *Beatles Anthology*, 207.

19. John Wade, "Alan Civil," obituary, *Daily Telegraph*, March 21, 1989, www.hornsociety .org/information-archive/151-hornplayer/hpn-info-archive/636-alan-civil-obituary.

20. Lewisohn, *Recording Sessions*, 79.

21. Wade, "Alan Civil"; Lewisohn, *Recording Sessions*, 79; Beatles, *Beatles Anthology*, 207.

22. Emerick and Massey, *Here, There, and Everywhere*, 129.

23. Turner, *Beatles '66*, 178; Lewisohn, *Recording Sessions*, 79.

24. Beatles, *Beatles Anthology*, 207; Miles, *Paul McCartney*, 289.

25. Emerick and Massey, *Here, There, and Everywhere*, 128; Beatles, *Beatles Anthology*, 207.

26. Emerick and Massey, *Here, There, and Everywhere*, 129; Lewisohn, *Recording Sessions*, 79; Mark Lewisohn, *The Complete Beatles Chronicle: The Only Definitive Guide to the Beatles' Entire Career* (London: Pyramid, 1992), 222.

27. Lewisohn, *Beatles Chronicle*, 222.

28. Maureen Cleave, "How Does a Beatle Live? John Lennon Lives Like This," *London Evening Standard*, March 4, 1966, 10.

6: Abracadabra

1. Lewisohn, *Tune In*, 1:638.

2. Martin, *Playback*, 176.

3. Gregory Paul Martin, interview with author, August 27, 2017.

4. Martin, *Playback*, 176.

5. Martin, *All You Need Is Ears*, 183; Louise Harrison, *My Kid Brother's Band: A.K.A the Beatles* (Morley, MO: Acclaim Press, 2014), 40.

6. Emerick and Massey, *Here, There, and Everywhere*, 118; Everett, *Beatles as Musicians*, 56.

7. Emerick and Massey, *Here, There, and Everywhere*, 118.

8. Emerick and Massey, *Here, There, and Everywhere*, 119.

9. Lewisohn, *Recording Sessions*, 101; Emerick and Massey, *Here, There, and Everywhere*, 123.

10. Lewisohn, *Recording Sessions*, 81; Emerick and Massey, *Here, There, and Everywhere*, 119.

11. Lewisohn, *Recording Sessions*, 81; Emerick and Massey, *Here, There, and Everywhere*, 120.

12. Lewisohn, *Recording Sessions*, 81; Dowlding, *Beatlesongs*, 139.

13. Lewisohn, *Recording Sessions*, 81.

14. Martin, "The *Mojo* Interview: Sir George Martin," interview with Jim Irvin, *Mojo*, March 2007, 39.

15. Lewisohn, *Recording Sessions*, 83.

16. Turner, *Beatles '66*, 213.

17. Rodriguez, *Revolver*, chap. 6.

18. Rodriguez, *Revolver*, chap. 6.

19. Emerick and Massey, *Here, There, and Everywhere*, 130.

20. Emerick and Massey, *Here, There, and Everywhere*, 130; Miles, *Paul McCartney*, 288.

21. Emerick and Massey, *Here, There, and Everywhere*, 130.

22. Rodriguez, *Revolver*, chap. 6.

23. Rodriguez, *Revolver*, chap. 6; Martin, *Playback*, 164.

7: The Jesus Christ Tour

1. Rodriguez, *Revolver*, chap. 6.

2. Rodriguez, *Revolver,* chap. 6.

3. Turner, *Beatles '66,* 239.

4. Rodriguez, *Revolver,* chap. 6; Turner, *Beatles '66,* 260.

5. Turner, *Beatles '66,* 262.

6. Turner, *Beatles '66,* 263; Tony Barrow, "*Revolver* Is Title for New Beatle LP," *KRLA Beat,* August 13, 1966, 1; Leigh, *Love Me Do,* chap. 6.

7. "UA Signs George Martin to Exclusive Long-Termer," *Cash Box,* July 9, 1966, 7, 53.

8. Martin, *Playback,* 176.

9. Martin, *All You Need Is Ears,* 189–90.

10. Martin, *All You Need Is Ears,* 189–90.

11. "Obituaries: Brian O'Hara," *Independent,* July 1, 1999, www.independent.co.uk/arts -entertainment/obituaries-brian-ohara-1103691.html.

12. Mark Lewisohn, *The Beatles Live!* (London: Pavilion, 1986), 192; Martin, *With a Little Help,* 8.

13. Spitz, *The Beatles,* 620; Martin, *With a Little Help,* 8; Ray Coleman, *The Man Who Made the Beatles: An Intimate Biography of Brian Epstein* (New York: McGraw-Hill, 1989), 316–17.

14. Martin, *With a Little Help,* 10, 163.

15. Martin, *Playback,* 164–65.

16. Martin, *Playback,* 164–65.

17. Turner, *Beatles '66,* 264.

18. Turner, *Beatles '66,* 268.

19. Turner, *Beatles '66,* 268.

20. Martin, *All You Need Is Ears,* 164.

21. Turner, *Beatles '66,* 274.

22. Lewisohn, *The Beatles Live!,* 195; Turner, *Beatles '66,* 274; Cleave, "How Does a Beatle Live?," 10.

23. Emerick and Massey, *Here, There, and Everywhere,* 134.

24. Turner, *Beatles '66,* 275.

25. Robert Rodriguez, interview with author, August 2, 2017.

26. Turner, *Beatles '66,* 283.

27. Martin, *With a Little Help,* 9; Beatles, *Beatles Anthology,* 227.

28. Turner, *Beatles '66,* 306.

29. George Martin, introduction to "An All-Star Tribute to Brian Wilson," Radio City Music Hall, New York City, 2002.

30. Turner, *Beatles '66,* 311.

8: Floating on AIR

1. Leigh, *Love Me Do,* chap. 5.

2. Martin, *With a Little Help,* 7; Spitz, *The Beatles,* 641.

3. Spitz, *The Beatles,* 645.

4. Spitz, *The Beatles,* 645.

5. Turner, *Beatles '66,* 314.

6. Coleman, *Man Who Made the Beatles,* 334; Leigh, *Love Me Do,* chap. 7.

7. Martin, *With a Little Help,* 6.

8. Spitz, *The Beatles*, 652–53.

9. Turner, *Beatles '66*, 374.

10. "Beatles Getting Bored: Drift Toward Breakup," *Bakersfield Californian*, November 10, 1966, 19.

11. Turner, *Beatles '66*, 360.

12. Martin, *Playback*, 166.

13. Turner, *Beatles '66*, 360; Martin, *Playback*, 166.

14. Ken Scott, interview with author, June 2, 2017; Turner, *Beatles '66*, 361.

15. Martin, introduction to "Tribute to Brian Wilson"; Turner, *Beatles '66*, 379.

16. Martin, introduction to "Tribute to Brian Wilson."

17. Domenic Priore, *Smile: The Story of Brian Wilson's Lost Masterpiece* (London: Sanctuary, 2005), chap. 10; "It's Beach Boys Over Beatles: Reader Poll," *Billboard*, December 10, 1966, 10.

18. "Beatles Split? . . . Epstein Mum," *KRLA Beat*, December 3, 1966, 1.

9: A Wistful Little Tune

1. Martin, *All You Need Is Ears*, 199.

2. Emerick and Massey, *Here, There, and Everywhere*, 132.

3. Emerick and Massey, *Here, There, and Everywhere*, 132.

4. Turner, *Beatles '66*, 400; George Martin, "The Making of *Sgt. Pepper*" (lecture, Count Basie Theatre, Red Bank, NJ, 1999).

5. Emerick and Massey, *Here, There, and Everywhere*, 135; Martin, *With a Little Help*, 13; Martin, "Making of *Sgt. Pepper*."

6. Martin, *With a Little Help*, 13.

7. Martin, *With a Little Help*, 17.

8. Leigh, *Love Me Do*, chap. 7.

9. Leigh, *Love Me Do*, chap. 7.

10. Rodriguez, *Revolver*, chap. 6; Martin, *With a Little Help*, 17.

11. Emerick and Massey, *Here, There, and Everywhere*, 136; Martin, *With a Little Help*, 17.

12. Lewisohn, *Recording Sessions*, 89.

13. Martin, *With a Little Help*, 38.

14. Lewisohn, *Recording Sessions*, 89.

15. Emerick and Massey, *Here, There, and Everywhere*, 138; Martin, *With a Little Help*, 19.

16. Martin, *With a Little Help*, 19.

17. Martin, *With a Little Help*, 19; Emerick and Massey, *Here, There, and Everywhere*, 138.

18. Martin, *With a Little Help*, 20.

19. Martin, *With a Little Help*, 21.

20. Martin, *With a Little Help*, 34.

21. Martin, *With a Little Help*, 35, 38; Martin, *All You Need Is Ears*, 201.

22. Martin, *With a Little Help*, 21; Emerick and Massey, *Here, There, and Everywhere*, 139.

23. Martin, *With a Little Help*, 21.

24. Martin, *With a Little Help*, 24.

25. Martin, *With a Little Help*, 22; Lewisohn, *Recording Sessions*, 91.

26. Martin, *With a Little Help*, 23.

27. Martin, *All You Need Is Ears*, 44.

28. Turner, *Beatles '66*, 397; Martin, *With a Little Help*, 70.

29. Beatles, *Beatles Anthology*, 253; Emerick and Massey, *Here, There, and Everywhere*, 142.

30. Martin, With a Little Help, 38.

10: Carnivals of Light

1. Brian Southall, *Northern Songs: The True Story of the Beatles Song Publishing Empire*, with Rupert Perry (London: Omnibus, 2009), chap. 2.

2. Martin, *With a Little Help*, 25.

3. Martin, *All You Need Is Ears*, 201.

4. Lewisohn, *Recording Sessions*, 92; Miles, *Paul McCartney*, 309.

5. Lewisohn, *Recording Sessions*, 92; Emerick and Massey, *Here, There, and Everywhere*, 143.

6. Winn, *That Magic Feeling*, 2:81.

7. Emerick and Massey, *Here, There, and Everywhere*, 144.

8. Emerick and Massey, *Here, There, and Everywhere*, 144.

9. Martin, *All You Need Is Ears*, 202.

10. Lewisohn, *Recording Sessions*, 93; Emerick and Massey, *Here, There, and Everywhere*, 145.

11. Lewisohn, *Recording Sessions*, 93; Martin, *All You Need Is Ears*, 202.

12. Derek Johnson, "Most Way-Out Beatles Ever," *NME*, February 11, 1967, 6; "Show Business: Other Noises, Other Notes," *Time*, March 3, 1967, 63.

13. Martin, *With a Little Help*, 26.

14. Beatles, *Beatles Anthology*, 239; Martin, *With a Little Help*, 26; Leigh, *Love Me Do*, chap. 7.

15. Coleman, *Man Who Made the Beatles*, 302.

16. Martin, introduction to "Tribute to Brian Wilson."

17. Mike Love, *Good Vibrations: My Life as a Beach Boy*, with James S. Hirsch (New York: Blue Rider, 2016), 157.

18. *The Making of Sgt. Pepper* (ITV, 1992), television documentary; Emerick and Massey, *Here, There, and Everywhere*, 148.

19. Martin, *With a Little Help*, 53.

20. Martin, *With a Little Help*, 53–54; Emerick and Massey, *Here, There, and Everywhere*, 148; Lewisohn, *Recording Sessions*, 94.

21. Emerick and Massey, *Here, There, and Everywhere*, 148.

22. John Lennon and Yoko Ono, *All We Are Saying: The Last Major Interview with John Lennon and Yoko Ono*, interview with David Sheff, ed. G. Barry Golson (New York: Griffin, 2000), 184.

23. Martin, *With a Little Help*, 55.

24. Miles, *Paul McCartney*, 303.

25. Martin, *With a Little Help*, 63.

26. Martin, *With a Little Help*, 67.

27. Emerick and Massey, *Here, There, and Everywhere*, 151; Ryan and Kehew, *Recording the Beatles*, 156.

28. Martin, *With a Little Help*, 69.

29. Martin, *With a Little Help*, 84; Robert Freeman, *The Beatles: A Private View* (New York: Barnes and Noble, 1990), n.p.

30. Martin, *With a Little Help*, 88.

11: Home and Dry

1. Martin, *With a Little Help*, 68.

2. Emerick and Massey, *Here, There, and Everywhere*, 152.

3. Emerick and Massey, *Here, There, and Everywhere*, 152.

4. Emerick and Massey, *Here, There, and Everywhere*, 149.

5. Martin, *All You Need Is Ears*, 209; Miles, *Paul McCartney*, 327.

6. Martin, *With a Little Help*, 55.

7. Martin, *With a Little Help*, 55–56; Emerick and Massey, *Here, There, and Everywhere*, 153.

8. Martin, *With a Little Help*, 56.

9. Martin, *With a Little Help*, 56.

10. Martin, *With a Little Help*, 56.

11. Martin, *With a Little Help*, 73–74.

12. Martin, *With a Little Help*, 86.

13. Martin, *With a Little Help*, 85; Miles, *Paul McCartney*, 315.

14. Martin, *With a Little Help*, 55–56; Emerick and Massey, *Here, There, and Everywhere*, 165.

15. Lewisohn, *Recording Sessions*, 96.

16. Emerick and Massey, *Here, There, and Everywhere*, 158.

17. Lewisohn, *Recording Sessions*, 96.

18. Martin, *With a Little Help*, 57–58.

19. Alistair Lawrence, *Abbey Road: The Best Studio in the World* (London: Bloomsbury, 2012), 20.

20. Massey, *Great British Recording Studios*, chap. 1.

21. Martin, *With a Little Help*, 57; Lewisohn, *Recording Sessions*, 57.

22. Emerick and Massey, *Here, There, and Everywhere*, 158; Lewisohn, *Recording Sessions*, 96.

23. Emerick and Massey, *Here, There, and Everywhere*, 159; Lewisohn, *Recording Sessions*, 97; Richard Lush, "What Was It Like to Record with Lennon and McCartney? A Conversation with *Sgt. Pepper* Sound Engineer Richard Lush," interview with Riley Fitzgerald, *Hhhhappy*, January 17, 2017, http://hhhhappy.com/what-was-it-like-to-record-with-lennon-and-mccartney-a-conversation-with-sgt-pepper-sound-engineer-richard-lush/.

24. Martin, *With a Little Help*, 56; Emerick and Massey, *Here, There, and Everywhere*, 159.

25. Beatles, *Beatles Anthology*, television documentary.

26. Emerick and Massey, *Here, There, and Everywhere*, 160; Lewisohn, *Recording Sessions*, 98.

27. Beatles, *Beatles Anthology*, 242.

28. Emerick and Massey, *Here, There, and Everywhere*, 166.

29. Martin, *With a Little Help*, 123–24.

30. Martin, *With a Little Help*, 124.

31. Emerick and Massey, *Here, There, and Everywhere*, 167; Lennon and Ono, *All We Are Saying*, 183; Martin, *With a Little Help*, 89.

32. Martin, *With a Little Help*, 91.

33. Emerick and Massey, *Here, There, and Everywhere*, 167; Martin, *With a Little Help*, 91, 92–93; Lush, "What Was It Like?"

34. Martin, *With a Little Help*, 90.

35. Martin, *With a Little Help*, 90–91.

36. Martin, *With a Little Help*, 91–92.

37. Martin, *With a Little Help*, 92.

38. Emerick and Massey, *Here, There, and Everywhere*, 161; Lewisohn, *Recording Sessions*, 99.

39. Emerick and Massey, *Here, There, and Everywhere*, 162.

40. Emerick and Massey, *Here, There, and Everywhere*, 163; Lewisohn, *Recording Sessions*, 99; Martin, *With a Little Help*, 150.

41. Martin, *With a Little Help*, 150.

12: The Song That Got Away

1. Emerick and Massey, *Here, There, and Everywhere*, 169.

2. Badman, *Beatles Off the Record*, 267–68.

3. Lewisohn, *Complete Beatles Recording Sessions*, 100.

4. Martin, *With a Little Help*, 102.

5. Martin, *With a Little Help*, 105.

6. Lewisohn, *Recording Sessions*, 100.

7. Lewisohn, *Recording Sessions*, 101.

8. Martin, *With a Little Help*, 96; Kenneth Womack, *The Beatles Encyclopedia: Everything Fab Four* (Santa Barbara, CA: Greenwood, 2014), 2:1, 292.

9. Lewisohn, *Recording Sessions*, 102; Emerick and Massey, *Here, There, and Everywhere*, 175; Gordon Thompson, *Please Please Me: Sixties Pop, Inside Out* (Oxford: Oxford University Press, 2008), chap. 3; Malcolm Addey, interview with author, December 12, 2017.

10. Martin, *With a Little Help*, 107.

11. Lewisohn, *Recording Sessions*, 102; Emerick and Massey, *Here, There, and Everywhere*, 177.

12. Southall, *Northern Songs*, chap. 2; Giles Martin, interview with Goldman, May 2, 2017; Martin, *With a Little Help*, 126.

13. Lewisohn, *Recording Sessions*, 103; Martin, *With a Little Help*, 127; Emerick and Massey, *Here, There, and Everywhere*, 179.

14. Miles, *Paul McCartney*, 317.

15. Martin, *With a Little Help*, 134.

16. Badman, *Beatles Off the Record*, 283.

17. Southall, *Northern Songs*, chap. 2.

18. Hunter Davies, *The Beatles*, updated ed. (New York: Norton, 2010), 307; Nick Mason, *Inside Out: A Personal History of Pink Floyd* (San Francisco: Chronicle, 2005), 83.

19. Lewisohn, *Recording Sessions*, 104; Martin, *With a Little Help*, 110.

20. Dowlding, *Beatlesongs*, 178.

21. Martin, *With a Little Help*, 141.

22. Martin, *With a Little Help*, 142.

23. Martin, *With a Little Help*, 143.

24. Martin, *With a Little Help*, 147.

13: The Chicken Became the Guitar

1. Martin, *With a Little Help*, 147.
2. Martin, *With a Little Help*, 126.
3. Emerick and Massey, *Here, There, and Everywhere*, 186.
4. Emerick and Massey, *Here, There, and Everywhere*, 179.
5. Martin, *With a Little Help*, 148.
6. Martin, *With a Little Help*, 75.
7. Lewisohn, *Recording Sessions*, 109.
8. Martin, *With a Little Help*, 150.
9. Martin, *With a Little Help*, 149.
10. Lewisohn, *Recording Sessions*, 109.
11. John Lahr, *Prick Up Your Ears: The Biography of Joe Orton* (London: Open Road, 2013), 246.
12. Roy Carr and Tony Tyler, *The Beatles: An Illustrated Record* (New York: Harmony, 1976), 133.
13. Winn, *That Magic Feeling*, 2:102.
14. Martin, *With a Little Help*, 158.
15. Lewisohn, *Recording Sessions*, 109; Barry Miles, *In the Sixties* (London: Jonathan Cape, 2002), 179.
16. Lewisohn, *Recording Sessions*, 109; Gregory Paul Martin, interview with author, September 8, 2017.

14: Good Night, Sweet Prince

1. Martin, *With a Little Help*, 24; Badman, *Beatles Off the Record*, 276–77; Coleman, *Man Who Made the Beatles*, 318.
2. Harriet Vyner, *Groovy Bob: The Life and Times of Robert Fraser* (London: Faber and Faber, 1999), n.p.
3. Norrie Drummond, "Dinner with the Beatles," *NME*, May 27, 1967, in Jay Spangler, "Beatles Interview: *Sgt Pepper* Launch Party 5/19/1967," The Beatles Interview Database, www.beatlesinterviews.org/db1967.0519.beatles.html.
4. Joe Goodden, *Riding So High: The Beatles and Drugs* (London: Pepper and Pearl, 2017), 136; Womack, *Beatles Encyclopedia*, 2:818.
5. Spitz, *The Beatles*, 693.
6. Spitz, *The Beatles*, 667–68.
7. Emerick and Massey, *Here, There, and Everywhere*, 200.
8. Emerick and Massey, *Here, There, and Everywhere*, 201.
9. Paul Gambaccini, *Paul McCartney: In His Own Words* (New York: Flash, 1976), 47–48.
10. Lewisohn, *Recording Sessions*, 110.
11. Lewisohn, *Recording Sessions*, 110.
12. Lewisohn, *Recording Sessions*, 111.
13. Coleman, *Man Who Made the Beatles*, 321.
14. Martin, *With a Little Help*, 162.
15. Tim Riley, *Tell Me Why: A Beatles Commentary* (New York: Knopf, 1988), 205.

16. Christopher Porterfield, "Pop Music: The Messengers," *Time*, September 22, 1967, 60; Leigh, *Love Me Do*, chap. 7.

17. Priore, *Smile*, chap. 13.

18. Priore, *Smile*, chap. 13.

19. Lewisohn, *Recording Sessions*, 114.

20. Beatles, *Beatles Anthology*, 257.

21. Martin, *All You Need Is Ears*, 162; Spitz, *The Beatles*, 700.

22. Andy Babiuk, *Beatles Gear: All the Fab Four's Instruments, from Stage to Studio* (San Francisco: Backbeat, 2001), 206.

23. Badman, *Beatles Off the Record*, 292.

24. Emerick and Massey, *Here, There, and Everywhere*, 206.

25. Martin, *Playback*, 176–77.

26. Martin, *All You Need Is Ears*, 192.

27. Turner interview, July 4, 2017.

28. Emerick and Massey, *Here, There, and Everywhere*, 206.

29. Lewisohn, *Recording Sessions*, 120; Martin, *All You Need Is Ears*, 193; Winn, *That Magic Feeling*, 2:111.

30. Lewisohn, *Recording Sessions*, 122; Coleman, *Man Who Made the Beatles*, 335.

31. Coleman, *Man Who Made the Beatles*, 340; Martin, *All You Need Is Ears*, 194.

32. Martin, *All You Need Is Ears*, 178.

33. Lewisohn, *Recording Sessions*, 122.

34. Martin, *All You Need Is Ears*, 162–63.

15: "We've Fuckin' Had It"

1. Martin, *All You Need Is Ears*, 164.

2. Martin, *All You Need Is Ears*, 164.

3. Martin, *All You Need Is Ears*, 163.

4. Martin, *All You Need Is Ears*, 165.

5. Martin, *All You Need Is Ears*, 165; Coleman, *Man Who Made the Beatles*, 379–80.

6. Lennon, *Lennon Remembers* (New York: Verso, 2000), 25; Spitz, *The Beatles*, 720–21; Tony Barrow, *The Making of the Beatles' Magical Mystery Tour* (London: Omnibus, 1999), 6.

7. Lewisohn, *Recording Sessions*, 122.

8. Emerick and Massey, *Here, There, and Everywhere*, 214.

9. Emerick and Massey, *Here, There, and Everywhere*, 214.

10. Winn, *That Magic Feeling*, 2:121.

11. Lewisohn, *Recording Sessions*, 122.

12. Black, *What's It All About?*, 158.

13. Martin, *All You Need Is Ears*, 191.

14. Emerick and Massey, *Here, There, and Everywhere*, 214; Lewisohn, *Recording Sessions*, 126.

15. Emerick and Massey, *Here, There, and Everywhere*, 216.

16. Lewisohn, *Recording Sessions*, 126; Martin, "'They Were My Boys, the Greatest in the World': An Interview with George Martin (1993)," interview with Bill DeYoung, Bill DeYoung website, January 3, 2016, www.billdeyoung.com/tag/george-martin-beatles/; Ken

Scott, *Abbey Road to Ziggy Stardust: Off the Record with the Beatles, Bowie, Elton, and So Much More* (Los Angeles: Alfred Music, 2012), chap. 3.

17. Lewisohn, *Recording Sessions*, 127.

18. Emerick and Massey, *Here, There, and Everywhere*, 215.

19. Emerick and Massey, *Here, There, and Everywhere*, 215.

20. Lewisohn, *Recording Sessions*, 129.

21. Nick Jones, "New Singles Including the Beatles, Pink Floyd, and Buffalo Springfield," *Melody Maker*, November 18, 1967, n.p.; Richard Goldstein, "Are They Waning?," *New York Times*, December 31, 1967, 62.

22. Steve Turner, *The Complete Beatles Songs: The Stories Behind Every Track Written by the Fab Four* (London: Carlton, 2015), 337; Black, *What's It All About?*, 159.

23. Nick Logan, "Sky-High with the Beatles," *NME*, November 26, 1967, n.p.

24. "Platter Chatter: Albums by the Beatles, Rolling Stones, Jefferson Airplane, Cream, and Kaleidoscope," *Hit Parader*, April 1968, n.p.

25. Martin, *All You Need Is Ears*, 177.

26. Badman, *Beatles Off the Record*, 332.

27. Spitz, *The Beatles*, 734.

28. Badman, *Beatles Off the Record*, 332–33.

29. *Take a Ride Through the Beatles' Magical Mystery Tour* (WCBS-FM, 2011), radio playlist; Martin, *Playback*, 178; Martin, "Making of *Sgt. Pepper*."

16: All That and a Bar of Chocolate

1. Black, *What's It All About?*, 158.

2. Black, *What's It All About?*, 159.

3. "How We Met: Cilla Black and Sir George Martin," interviews with Anthi Charalambous, *Independent*, March 29, 1998, www.independent.co.uk/arts-entertainment/how-we-met-cilla-black-and-sir-george-martin-1153302.html.

4. Du Noyer, *Liverpool, Wondrous Place*, 193–94.

5. Du Noyer, *Liverpool, Wondrous Place*, 193–94.

6. Everett, *Beatles as Musicians*, 153.

7. Lennon and Ono, *All We Are Saying*, 267.

8. Lewisohn, *Recording Sessions*, 133.

9. Lewisohn, *Recording Sessions*, 133.

10. Lewisohn, *Recording Sessions*, 133.

11. Emerick and Massey, *Here, There, and Everywhere*, 221.

12. Lewisohn, *Recording Sessions*, 134.

13. Chris Welch, "Beatles Recall All Our Yesterdays," *Melody Maker*, March 9, 1968, 17; "Spotlight Singles," *Billboard*, March 16, 1968, 78.

14. Al Brodax, *Up Periscope: The Making of the Beatles' Yellow Submarine* (New York: Limelight, 2004), chap. 7.

15. Martin, *Playback*, 186.

16. Martin, *Playback*, 186.

17. Martin, *All You Need Is Ears*, 228.

18. Martin, *All You Need Is Ears*, 35.

19. Martin, *All You Need Is Ears*, 228–29.

20. Nancy Cooke de Herrera, *All You Need Is Love: An Eyewitness Account of When Spirituality Spread from the East to the West* (San Diego, CA: Jodere, 2003), 237, 244.

21. Robert Rodriguez, interview with author, December 21, 2017.

22. Spitz, *The Beatles*, 727–28, 731; Jay Spangler, "John Lennon & Paul McCartney: Apple Press Conference 5/14/1968," The Beatles Interview Database, www.beatlesinterviews .org/db1968.0514pc.beatles.html.

23. Martin, *All You Need Is Ears*, 171.

24. Martin, *All You Need Is Ears*, 172.

25. Martin, *All You Need Is Ears*, 173.

26. Emerick and Massey, *Here, There, and Everywhere*, 234.

27. Emerick and Massey, *Here, There, and Everywhere*, 233.

28. Emerick and Massey, *Here, There, and Everywhere*, 233; John Kurlander, interview with author, November 8, 2017.

29. Lewisohn, *Recording Sessions*, 136.

30. Lewisohn, *Recording Sessions*, 137; Winn, *That Magic Feeling*, 2:175.

31. Emerick and Massey, *Here, There, and Everywhere*, 239.

32. Lewisohn, *Recording Sessions*, 138.

33. Emerick and Massey, *Here, There, and Everywhere*, 242.

34. Lewisohn, *Recording Sessions*, 139; Dowlding, *Beatlesongs*, 250.

17: The Great Tape Recorder Robbery

1. Renata Adler, "*Yellow Submarine*," *New York Times*, November 14, 1968, www.nytimes .com/movie/review?res=EE05E7DF173DAF2CA7494CC1B779948D6896.

2. Beatles, *Beatles Anthology*, 292.

3. Martin, *All You Need Is Ears*, 219.

4. Lewisohn, *Recording Sessions*, 141.

5. Lennon and Ono, *All We Are Saying*, 187; Emerick and Massey, *Here, There, and Everywhere*, 252.

6. Beatles, *Beatles Anthology*, 298.

7. Lewisohn, *Recording Sessions*, 142.

8. Emerick and Massey, *Here, There, and Everywhere*, 255.

9. Emerick and Massey, *Here, There, and Everywhere*, 256.

10. Ken Scott, "Beatles' Recording Engineer Ken Scott Reveals Behind the Scenes Details on Working with the Fab Four," interview with Marshall Terrill, *Daytrippin'*, July 25, 2012, http://daytrippin.com/2012/07/25/beatles-recording-engineer-ken-scott-reveals -behind-the-scenes-details-on-working-with-the-fab-four/.

11. Winn, *That Magic Feeling*, 2:192; Lewisohn, *Recording Sessions*, 144.

12. Badman, *Beatles Off the Record*, 397.

13. Elliot J. Huntley, *Mystical One: George Harrison After the Breakup of the Beatles* (Toronto: Guernica Editions, 2004), 26; Lewisohn, *Recording Sessions*, 145.

14. Lewisohn, *Recording Sessions*, 145; George Martin, "The Producer Series, Part 1," interview with Ralph Denver, *Studio Sound*, January 1985, 58.

15. Massey, *Great British Recording Studios*, chap. 6.

16. Lewisohn, *Recording Sessions*, 146.

17. Martin, "Producer Series, Part 1," 58.

18. Lewisohn, *Recording Sessions*, 146.

19. Beatles, *Beatles Anthology*, 297.

20. Emerick and Massey, *Here, There, and Everywhere*, 261.

21. Beatles, *Beatles Anthology*, 298.

22. Craig Cross, *The Beatles: Day-by-Day, Song-by-Song, Record-by-Record* (New York: iUniverse, 2005), 368.

23. Lewisohn, *Recording Sessions*, 147.

24. Lewisohn, *Recording Sessions*, 148; Scott, *Abbey Road to Ziggy Stardust*, chap. 4.

25. Lewisohn, *Recording Sessions*, 149.

26. Beatles, *Beatles Anthology*, 305.

27. The Beatles, *Beatles Anthology*, 305.

28. Lewisohn, *Recording Sessions*, 151.

29. Beatles, *Beatles Anthology*, 312.

30. Steve Matteo, *Let It Be* (New York: Continuum, 2004), 18.

31. Lewisohn, *Recording Sessions*, 153.

18: Up on the Roof

1. Scott, *Abbey Road to Ziggy Stardust*, chap. 4; Emerick and Massey, *Here, There, and Everywhere*, 261.

2. Scott, *Abbey Road to Ziggy Stardust*, chap. 4; Scott, "Behind the Scenes Details."

3. Leigh, *Love Me Do*, chap. 8; John Van der Kiste, *Jeff Lynne: Electric Light Orchestra—Before and After* (Stroud, UK: Fonthill Media, 2015), chap. 1.

4. Lewisohn, *Recording Sessions*, 161.

5. Lewisohn, *Recording Sessions*, 162; Scott interview, June 2, 2017.

6. Lewisohn, *Recording Sessions*, 162; Scott, *Abbey Road to Ziggy Stardust*, chap. 4.

7. Jann S. Wenner, "Review: The Beatles' *White Album*," *Rolling Stone*, December 12, 1967, www.rollingstone.com/music/features/beatles-19681221.

8. Leigh, *Love Me Do*, chap. 8.

9. Ryan and Kehew, *Recording the Beatles*, 476.

10. Martin, *Playback*, 186–87.

11. Leigh, *Love Me Do*, chap. 8; Spitz, *The Beatles*, 811; Martin, *Playback*, 186–87.

12. Glyn Johns, *Sound Man: A Life Recording Hits with the Rolling Stones, the Who, Led Zeppelin, the Eagles, Eric Clapton, the Faces* (New York: Blue Rider, 2014), 123.

13. Peter Doggett, *Abbey Road/Let It Be: The Beatles* (New York: Schirmer, 1998), 10.

14. Doggett, *Abbey Road/Let It Be*, 78.

15. Turner interview, July 4, 2017; Doug Sulpy and Ray Schweighardt, *Get Back: The Unauthorized Chronicle of the Beatles' Let It Be Disaster* (New York: Griffin, 1997), 74; Doggett, *Abbey Road/Let It Be*, 20; Matteo, *Let It Be*, 48.

16. Martin, *Playback*, 187.

17. Doggett, *Abbey Road/Let It Be*, 24–27, 29, 34.

18. Doggett, *Abbey Road/Let It Be*, 11, 12.

19. Sulpy and Schweighardt, *Get Back*, 124, 170.

20. Tony Barrell, *The Beatles on the Roof* (London: Omnibus, 2017), chap. 2; Martin, *Playback*, 187.

21. Doggett, *Abbey Road/Let It Be*, 33; Sulpy and Schweighardt, *Get Back*, 176.

22. Sulpy and Schweighardt, *Get Back*, 169.

23. Martin, *Playback*, 187; Babiuk, *Beatles Gear*, 263; Barrell, *Beatles on the Roof*, chap. 3.

24. Martin, *Playback*, 187; Lewisohn, *Recording Sessions*, 166; Johns, *Sound Man*, 128; Miles, *Paul McCartney*, 532–33; Barrell, *Beatles on the Roof*, chap. 3.

25. Johns, *Sound Man*, 140; Sulpy and Schweighardt, *Get Back*, 232; Doggett, *Abbey Road/ Let It Be*, 38; Ryan and Kehew, *Recording the Beatles*, 506; Beatles, *Beatles Anthology*, television documentary.

26. Sulpy and Schweighardt, *Get Back*, 227; Lewisohn, *Recording Sessions*, 166.

27. Doggett, *Abbey Road/Let It Be*, 40.

28. Martin, *Playback*, 187.

29. Matteo, *Let It Be*, 83.

30. Martin, *Playback*, 188.

31. Martin, *Playback*, 188; Matteo, *Let It Be*, 86; Ryan and Kehew, *Recording the Beatles*, 506.

32. Martin, *Playback*, 188; Barrell, *Beatles on the Roof*, chap. 4.

19: Come Together

1. Winn, *That Magic Feeling*, 2:263.

2. Martin, *All You Need Is Ears*, 262.

3. Martin, *All You Need Is Ears*, 262.

4. Martin, *All You Need Is Ears*, 263.

5. Martin, *All You Need Is Ears*, 264.

6. Martin, *All You Need Is Ears*, 179.

7. Johns, *Sound Man*, 140.

8. Martin, *Playback*, 188.

9. Leigh, *Love Me Do*, chap. 9.

10. Leigh, *Love Me Do*, chap. 9.

11. Beatles, *Beatles Anthology*, 337.

12. Emerick and Massey, *Here, There, and Everywhere*, 269.

13. Emerick and Massey, *Here, There, and Everywhere*, 271.

14. "Remembering the Forgotten Beatle," *Rolling Stone*, December 5, 2001, 9.

15. Lewisohn, *Recording Sessions*, 173.

16. Lewisohn, *Recording Sessions*, 174.

17. Doggett, *Abbey Road/Let It Be*, 49; Martin, "Producer Series, Part 1," 58.

18. "Stereo Rattles Stations; Mfrs. Strangle Monaural," *Billboard*, January 6, 1968, 1; Martin, "Producer Series, Part 1," 58.

19. Martin, "Producer Series, Part 1," 58; Lewisohn, *Complete Beatles Recording Sessions*, 14; Doggett, *Abbey Road/Let It Be*, 48.

20. Everett, *Beatles as Musicians*, 245; Emerick and Massey, *Here, There, and Everywhere*, 277.

21. Martin, "Producer Series, Part 1," 58–59.

22. Doggett, *Abbey Road/Let It Be*, 59–60.

23. Lennon and Ono, *All We Are Saying*, 202.

24. Lewisohn, *Recording Sessions*, 14.

25. Lewisohn, *Recording Sessions*, 180.

26. Lewisohn, *Recording Sessions*, 181.

27. Lewisohn, *Recording Sessions*, 183.

28. Kurlander interview, November 8, 2017; Lewisohn, *Complete Beatles Recording Sessions*, 183.

29. Martin, "Producer Series, Part 1," 59.

30. George Martin, "The Producer Series, Part 2," interview with Ralph Denver, *Studio Sound*, February 1985, 54; Lewisohn, *Recording Sessions*, 185; George Martin, "To Sir with Love," interview with Larry the O, *Electronic Musician*, January 7, 2009, www.emusician.com /gear/1332/to-sir-with-love/40689.

31. Kurlander interview, November 8, 2017; Emerick and Massey, *Here, There, and Everywhere*, 287.

32. Kurlander interview, November 8, 2017; Emerick and Massey, *Here, There, and Everywhere*, 295; "100 Greatest Beatles Songs," *Rolling Stone*, September 29, 2011, www.rollingstone .com/music/lists/100-greatest-beatles-songs-20110919.

33. Lewisohn, *Recording Sessions*, 13; Emerick and Massey, *Here, There, and Everywhere*, 297.

34. Martin, "Producer Series, Part 1," 62.

35. Lewisohn, *Recording Sessions*, 190.

36. Emerick and Massey, *Here, There, and Everywhere*, 300.

37. Dowlding, *Beatlesongs*, 292; Emerick and Massey, *Here, There, and Everywhere*, 301.

20: Sentimental Journeys

1. Womack, *Beatles Encyclopedia*, 1:4–5.

2. Beatles, *Beatles Anthology*, 347.

3. Leigh, *Love Me Do*, chap. 9.

4. Leigh, *Love Me Do*, chap. 9.

5. Martin, *Playback*, 185.

6. Giles Martin, interview with author, May 2, 2017.

7. Martin, *Playback*, 190; Michael Seth Starr, *With a Little Help* (Milwaukee, WI: Hal Leonard, 2015), chap. 12.

8. Martin, *Playback*, 190; Starr, *With a Little Help*, chap. 12.

9. Martin, *Playback*, 189.

10. Lewisohn, *Recording Sessions*, 195.

11. Derek Johnson, "Next Beatle Album in Depth: NMExclusive," *NME*, November 1, 1969, 11.

12. Leigh, *Love Me Do*, chap. 10.

13. Martin, *Playback*, 189; Gambaccini, *Paul McCartney*, 20; Johns, *Sound Man*, 140; Lennon, *Lennon Remembers*, 101–2.

14. Paul McCartney, press release, London, April 9, 1970, The Beatles Interview Database, www.beatlesinterviews.org; Martin, *Playback*, 189.

15. Leigh, *Love Me Do*, chap. 10; Williams, *Phil Spector*, 148.

16. John Harris, "*Let It Be*: Can You Dig It?," Special limited edition, *Mojo: 1,000 Days of Revolution: The Beatles' Final Years—Jan 1, 1968 to Sept 27, 1970*, March 2003, 132.

17. Martin, *Playback*, 195.

21: The Emerald Isle of the Caribbean

1. Martin, *All You Need Is Ears*, 265.
2. Matthew Fellows, "Studio Profiles: AIR Studios," *Audio Media International*, July 22, 2015, www.audiomediainternational.com/recording/studio-profile-air-studios/04644; Simaen Skolfield, interview with author, August 17, 2017.
3. Black, *What's It All About?*, 222.
4. Martin, *All You Need Is Ears*, 266.
5. Martin, "Listen to My Story," n.p.
6. John Lennon and Yoko Ono, letter, *Melody Maker*, September 4, 1971, n.p.; Martin, *Playback*, 179.
7. Martin, *All You Need Is Ears*, 256; Martin, "To Sir with Love."
8. Martin, "To Sir with Love."
9. Martin, "To Sir with Love"; Martin, *Playback*, 200.
10. Alan Barnes and Marcus Hearn, *Kiss Kiss Bang! Bang! The Unofficial James Bond Film Companion* (London: Batsford, 2003), 110–11; Skolfield interview, August 17, 2017; Martin, *Playback*, 204.
11. Martin, *Playback*, 204–5.
12. Martin, *All You Need Is Ears*, 188.
13. Martin, *All You Need Is Ears*, 189.
14. John Oates, *Change of Seasons: A Memoir* (New York: St. Martin's, 2017), 160.
15. Martin, *Playback*, 201.
16. Martin, *Playback*, 209; Wesley Hyatt, *The Billboard Book of Number-One Adult Contemporary Hits* (New York: Billboard Publications, 1999), 147.
17. May Pang, interview with author, November 26, 2017; John Lennon, "Old Grey Whistle Test," interview with Bob Harris, BBC, March 17, 1975.
18. Martin, "'They Were My Boys.'"
19. Martin, *All You Need Is Ears*, 162.
20. Skolfield interview, August 17, 2017; Martin, *All You Need Is Ears*, 268.
21. Martin, *All You Need Is Ears*, 268.

22: "A Series of One-Night Stands"

1. Martin, *All You Need Is Ears*, 195.
2. Martin, *All You Need Is Ears*, 196.
3. Martin, *All You Need Is Ears*, 196.
4. Martin, *All You Need Is Ears*, 197.
5. Martin, *All You Need Is Ears*, 198.
6. Martin, *All You Need Is Ears*, 198.
7. Martin, *Playback*, 206; Martin, "Producer Series, Part 1," 64.
8. Martin, "Producer Series, Part 1," 62.
9. Martin, "Producer Series, Part 1," 60–61; Martin, *Playback*, 210.
10. Martin, *Playback*, 210.
11. Robert Christgau, "Consumer Guide Reviews," Robert Christgau website, www.robertchristgau.com; Martin, *Playback*, 210.
12. Martin, *All You Need Is Ears*, 146–47.

13. Martin, *All You Need Is Ears*, 146–47.

14. Womack, *Beatles Encyclopedia*, 1:424.

15. Keith Badman, *The Beatles Off the Record 2: The Dream Is Over* (London: Omnibus, 2009), 211.

16. Badman, *Beatles Off the Record 2*, 211.

17. Badman, *Beatles Off the Record 2*, 211.

18. Christgau, "Consumer Guide Reviews."

19. Leigh, *Love Me Do*, chap. 7.

20. Martin, *Playback*, 214.

21. Addey interview, December 12, 2017.

22. Martin, *All You Need Is Ears*, 185.

23. Martin, *Playback*, 215.

24. Peter Doggett, *You Never Give Me Your Money: The Beatles After the Breakup* (New York: Harper, 2011), 256.

25. Martin, *Playback*, 215.

26. George A. Martin, interview with author, October 3, 2017.

27. Christgau, "Consumer Guide Reviews."; Dave Marsh and John Swenson, eds., *The New Rolling Stone Record Guide* (New York: Random House, 1983), 628; Martin, *Playback*, 215.

28. Martin, *All You Need Is Ears*, 268.

29. Stephen Fottrell, "Sir George Martin's Caribbean Legacy: AIR Studios Montserrat," BBC News, March 9, 2016, www.bbc.com/news/entertainment-arts-35761728.

30. Jeremy Hornsby, "Model Fifth Beatle," letter to the editor, *Times*, March 11, 2016, 20.

31. Gregory Paul Martin, interview with author, March 10, 2016.

32. Martin, *With a Little Help*, 24; Philip Norman, *John Lennon: A Life* (London: Ecco, 2008), 783.

23: Here Today, Gone Tomorrow

1. Martin, *Playback*, 233.

2. David Fricke, "Cheap Trick: *All Shook Up*," *Rolling Stone*, March 19, 1981, www.rollingstone.com/music/albumreviews/all-shook-up-19810319.

3. Tim Riley, *Lennon: The Man, the Myth, the Music* (New York: Hyperion, 2011), 630.

4. Martin, *Playback*, 213.

5. Martin, *Playback*, 241.

6. Martin, "Producer Series, Part 2," 58.

7. Laurence Juber, *Guitar with Wings: A Photographic Memoir*, with Marshall Terrill (Deerfield, IL: Dalton Watson, 2014), 222.

8. Tom Doyle, *Man on the Run: Paul McCartney in the 1970s* (New York: Random House, 2013), 211.

9. Emerick and Massey, *Here, There, and Everywhere*, 359; George Martin, interview with Gavin Hewitt, *BBC Evening News*, BBC, December 1980.

10. Martin, *Playback*, 245.

11. Martin, *Playback*, 244.

12. Kit O'Toole, *Michael Jackson FAQ: All That's Left to Know About the King of Pop* (Milwaukee, WI: Hal Leonard, 2015), 247–48; Martin, "Producer Series, Part 2," 54.

13. McCartney, *Tug of War: Paul McCartney Archive Collection* (Hear Music/Concord Music Group, 2015).

14. Stephen Holden, "Paul McCartney: *Tug of War*," *Rolling Stone*, May 27, 1982, www .rollingstone.com/music/albumreviews/tug-of-war-19820527.

15. Martin, "Producer Series, Part 2," 58.

16. Martin, *Playback*, 236.

17. Martin, *Playback*, 235.

18. Martin, *Playback*, 234.

19. George Martin, ed., *Making Music: The Guide to Writing, Performing, and Recording* (New York: Quill, 1983), 8; Steve Morse, "Paperbacks," *Boston Globe*, December 18, 1983, 1.

20. Martin, "Producer Series, Part 2," 54.

21. Martin, "Producer Series, Part 2," 54.

22. Martin, *Playback*, 253.

23. Martin, "Producer Series, Part 2," 58.

24. Martin, "Producer Series, Part 2," 58.

25. Martin, "Producer Series, Part 2," 55.

24: Grow Old with Me

1. Joseph Hudak, "Kenny Rogers on Working with George Martin: 'The Highlight of My Career,'" *Rolling Stone*, March 9, 2016, www.rollingstone.com/music/news/kenny -rogers-on-working-with-george-martin-the-highlight-of-my-career-20160309.

2. George Martin, interview with Richard Buskin, March 3, 1987, YouTube, www.youtube .com/watch?v=evomc1xfM9s&t=103s.

3. David Fricke, "Capitol to Release Beatles CDs," *Rolling Stone*, February 26, 1987, www. rollingstone.com/music/news/capitol-to-release-beatles-cds-19870226.

4. Martin interview with Buskin, March 3, 1987; Robert Rodriguez, interview with author, December 22, 2017.

5. Allan Kozinn, "The Beatles on Compact Disc: A Conversation with George Martin," *Beatlefan* 9, no. 2 (1987): 8–10.

6. Martin, "Producer Series, Part 2," 60.

7. Martin, "Producer Series, Part 2," 60.

8. Martin, *Playback*, 266–67.

9. Martin, *Playback*, 267.

10. Jay Sweet, interview with author, November 26, 2017; George Martin, "Commencement 1989: George Martin's Commencement Address," Berklee College of Music, April 13, 1989, www.berklee.edu/commencement/past/1989.

11. John Kifner, "Devastated by Hurricane, Montserrat Starts to Rebuild," *New York Times*, September 22, 1989, www.nytimes.com/1989/09/22/us/devastated-by-hurricane -montserrat-starts-to-rebuild.html; Martin, *Playback*, 294.

12. Nicholas Lezard, "*Summer of Love*," *Guardian*, June 9, 1995, 6; Robin Blake, "*Summer of Love*," *Independent*, June 18, 1995, 45.

13. Martin, *Playback*, 270; Skolfield interview, August 17, 2017.

14. Martin, *Playback*, 275.

15. Martin, *Playback*, 273.

16. Martin, *Playback*, 288; Anthony DeCurtis, "The Beatles: *Live at the BBC*," *Rolling Stone*, January 25, 1995, www.rollingstone.com/music/albumreviews/live-at-the-bbc-19910125.

17. Emerick and Massey, *Here, There, and Everywhere*, 364; Martin, *Playback*, 293.

18. Martin, *Playback*, 293; Womack, *Beatles Encyclopedia*, 1:90.

19. Martin, *Playback*, 293.

20. "Linda McCartney Service Reunites Three Beatles," *New York Times,* June 9, 1998, www .nytimes.com/1998/06/09/arts/linda-mccartney-service-reunites-3-beatles.html.

21. Martin, *Playback*, 303.

22. Martin, *Playback*, 301.

23. "George Martin," Rock and Roll Hall of Fame, 1999, www.rockhall.com/inductees /george-martin.

24. George Martin, interview with Sue Lawley, *Desert Island Discs*, BBC Radio 4, November 19, 1995.

Epilogue: Swan Songs

1. Mark Espiner, "Sounds and Vision," *Guardian*, June 30, 2001, www.theguardian .com/books/2001/jun/30/books.guardianreview1; Giles Martin interview, May 2, 2017.

2. Press kit for *In My Life* LP, October 1998, courtesy of Mark Lewisohn.

3. Sarah Zupko, "George Martin: *In My Life*," *PopMatters*, October 1998, www.popmatters .com/recent/tv/film/P98740/music/.

4. Martin, *Playback*, 312.

5. Allan Kozinn, "The Beatles' Producer, Still with Stories to Tell," *New York Times*, June 17, 2003, www.nytimes.com/2003/06/17/books/beatles-producer-still-with-stories-tell-george -martin-has-found-life-after.html; Phil Hogan, "Carry That Weight," *Guardian*, March 9, 2003, www.theguardian.com/books/2003/mar/09/biography.highereducation2.

6. Kurlander interview, November 8, 2017; Katie Nicholl, "George Harrison Close to Death," *Daily Mail*, November 14, 2001, www.dailymail.co.uk/news/article-61825/George -Harrison-close-death.html.

7. Peter Hodgson interview, January 27, 2018; Martin, *Playback*, 182.

8. Womack, *Beatles Encyclopedia*, 1:306; Giles Martin interview, May 2, 2017.

9. Womack, *Beatles Encyclopedia*, 1:306; David Stark, interview with author, November 22, 2017.

10. Tom Jamison, "Lives Remembered: Sir George Martin," *Able*, March 2016, http:// ablemagazine.co.uk/lives-remembered-sir-george-martin/; Giles Martin interview, May 2, 2017; Joe Johnson, "Meeting George Martin: A Personal Journey," *Beatle Brunch* (blog), March 10, 2016, https://beatlebrunch.wordpress.com/2016/03/10 /meeting-george-martin-a-personal-journey/.

11. Mark Richardson, "The Beatles' *Love*," *Pitchfork*, November 30, 2006, http://pitchfork .com/reviews/albums/9669-love/.

12. Geoff Emerick, interview with James Marcus, *Netscape*, February 2007.

13. Black, *What's It All About?*, 353, 391–92.

14. Mark Lewisohn, interview with author, August 16, 2014; Gregory Paul Martin interview, March 10, 2016.

15. Sheena McKenzie, "Who Was the Real Fifth Beatle?," CNN.com, March 9, 2016, www .cnn.com/2016/03/09/entertainment/who-was-real-fifth-beatle/index.html; Peter Hodgson interview, January 27, 2018.

16. Scott interview, June 2, 2017.

17. Martin, *With a Little Help*, 46; Leigh, *Love Me Do*, chap. 5.

18. Martin, *Playback*, 189.

19. Martin, *With a Little Help*, xii.

BIBLIOGRAPHY

"100 Greatest Beatles Songs." *Rolling Stone*, September 29, 2011. www.rollingstone.com /music/lists/100-greatest-beatles-songs-20110919.

Adams, M. Clay. M. Clay Adams to Michael Adams, January 10, 1966. Beatles-History.net. www.beatles-history.net/beatles-shea-stadium.html.

Adler, Renata. "*Yellow Submarine*." *New York Times*, November 14, 1968. www.nytimes .com/movie/review?res=EE05E7DF173DAF2CA7494CC1B779948D6896.

Babiuk, Andy. *Beatles Gear: All the Fab Four's Instruments, from Stage to Studio*. San Francisco: Backbeat, 2001.

Badman, Keith. *The Beach Boys: The Definitive Diary of America's Greatest Band, on Stage and in the Studio*. San Francisco: Backbeat, 2004.

———. *The Beatles Off the Record: Outrageous Opinions and Unrehearsed Interviews*. London: Omnibus, 2001.

———. *The Beatles Off the Record 2: The Dream Is Over*. London: Omnibus, 2009.

Barnes, Alan, and Marcus Hearn. *Kiss Kiss Bang! Bang! The Unofficial James Bond Film Companion*. London: Batsford, 2003.

Barrell, Tony. *The Beatles on the Roof*. London: Omnibus, 2017.

Barrow, Tony. "Beatle Rumor Half True." *KRLA Beat*, May 7, 1966, 1.

———. *The Making of the Beatles' Magical Mystery Tour*. London: Omnibus, 1999.

———. "*Revolver* Is Title for New Beatle LP." *KRLA Beat*, August 13, 1966, 1.

Beatles, The. *The Beatles Anthology*. San Francisco: Chronicle, 2000.

———. *The Beatles Anthology*. ABC, 1995. Television documentary.

"The Beatles at Shea Stadium." *Mix: Professional Audio and Music Production*, January 12, 2017. www.mixonline.com/beatles-shea-stadium/429036.

"Beatles Getting Bored: Drift Toward Breakup." *Bakersfield Californian*, November 10, 1966, 19.

"Beatles Split? . . . Epstein Mum." *KRLA Beat*, December 3, 1966, 1, 5.

Black, Cilla. *What's It All About?* London: Ebury, 2003.

Blake, Robin. "*Summer of Love*." *Independent*, June 18, 1995, 45.

Brodax, Al. *Up Periscope: The Making of the Beatles' Yellow Submarine*. New York: Limelight, 2004.

Carr, Roy, and Tony Tyler. *The Beatles: An Illustrated Record*. New York: Harmony, 1976.

Cavendish, Dominic. "The 10 Worst Musicals of All Time." *Telegraph*, February 13, 2015. www.telegraph.co.uk/culture/theatre/3672844/The-10-worst-musicals-of-all-time .html.

Christgau, Robert. "Consumer Guide Reviews." Robert Christgau website. www.robert christgau.com.

Cleave, Maureen. "Did I Break Up the Beatles?" *Daily Mail*, December 18, 2009. www.daily mail.co.uk/tvshowbiz/article-1237097/Maureen-Cleave-Did-I-break-The-Beatles .html.

———. "George Harrison: Avocado with Everything." *London Evening Standard*, March 18, 1966, 8.

———. "How Does a Beatle Live? John Lennon Lives Like This." *London Evening Standard*, March 4, 1966, 10.

Coleman, Ray. *The Man Who Made the Beatles: An Intimate Biography of Brian Epstein*. New York: McGraw-Hill, 1989.

Cross, Craig. *The Beatles: Day-by-Day, Song-by-Song, Record-by-Record*. New York: iUniverse, 2005.

Davies, Hunter. *The Beatles*. Updated ed. New York: Norton, 2013.

DeCurtis, Anthony. "The Beatles: *Live at the BBC*." *Rolling Stone*, January 25, 1995. www .rollingstone.com/music/albumreviews/live-at-the-bbc-19910125.

Doggett, Peter. *Abbey Road/Let It Be: The Beatles*. New York: Schirmer, 1998.

———. *You Never Give Me Your Money: The Beatles After the Breakup*. New York: Harper, 2011.

Dowlding, William J. *Beatlesongs*. New York: Simon and Schuster, 1989.

Doyle, Tom. *Man on the Run: Paul McCartney in the 1970s*. New York: Random House, 2013.

Drummond, Norrie. "Dinner with the Beatles." *NME*, May 27, 1967. In "Beatles Interview: *Sgt Pepper* Launch Party 5/19/1967," by Jay Spangler, The Beatles Interview Database, www.beatlesinterviews.org/db1967.0519.beatles.html.

Du Noyer, Paul. *The Illustrated Encyclopedia of Music*. Fulham, UK: Flame Tree Publishing, 2003.

———. *Liverpool, Wondrous Place: From the Cavern to the Capital of Culture*. London: Virgin Books, 2007.

Emerick, Geoff, and Howard Massey. *Here, There, and Everywhere: My Life Recording the Music of the Beatles*. New York: Gotham, 2006.

———. Interview with James Marcus. *Netscape*, February 2007.

Espiner, Mark. "Sounds and Vision." *Guardian* (US edition), June 30, 2001. www.theguardian .com/books/2001/jun/30/books.guardianreview1.

Everett, Walter. *The Beatles as Musicians: Revolver Through the Anthology*. Oxford: Oxford University Press, 1999.

Fellows, Matthew. "Studio Profiles: AIR Studios." *Audio Media International*, July 22, 2015. www.audiomediainternational.com/recording/studio-profile-air-studios/04644.

Fottrell, Stephen. "Sir George Martin's Caribbean Legacy: AIR Studios Montserrat." BBC News, March 9, 2016. www.bbc.com/news/entertainment-arts-35761728.

Freeman, Robert. *The Beatles: A Private View*. New York: Barnes and Noble, 1990.

Fricke, David. "Capitol to Release Beatles CDs." *Rolling Stone*, February 26, 1987. www .rollingstone.com/music/news/capitol-to-release-beatles-cds-19870226.

———. "Cheap Trick: *All Shook Up*." *Rolling Stone*, March 19, 1981. www.rollingstone.com /music/albumreviews/all-shook-up-19810319.

"From the Music Capitals of the World." *Billboard*, March 5, 1966, 37.

Gambaccini, Paul. *Paul McCartney: In His Own Words*. New York: Flash, 1976.

"George Martin." Rock and Roll Hall of Fame, 1999. www.rockhall.com/inductees/george -martin.

"George Martin in US for Material Hunt." *Cash Box*, February 19, 1966, 18.

Goldstein, Richard. "Are They Waning?" *New York Times*, December 31, 1967, 62.

Goodden, Joe. *Riding So High: The Beatles and Drugs*. London: Pepper and Pearl, 2017.

Hanly, Francis, dir. *Produced by George Martin*. BBC, 2012.

Harris, John. "*Let It Be*: Can You Dig It?" Special limited edition, *Mojo: 1,000 Days of Revolution: The Beatles' Final Years—Jan 1, 1968 to Sept 27, 1970*, March 2003.

Harrison, Louise. *My Kid Brother's Band: A.K.A the Beatles*. Morley, MO: Acclaim Press, 2014.

Herrera, Nancy Cooke de. *All You Need Is Love: An Eyewitness Account of When Spirituality Spread from the East to the West*. San Diego: Jodere, 2003.

Hogan, Phil. "Carry That Weight." *Guardian*, March 9, 2003. www.theguardian.com/books /2003/mar/09/biography.highereducation2.

Holden, Stephen. "Paul McCartney: *Tug of War*." *Rolling Stone*, May 27, 1982. www.rollingstone .com/music/albumreviews/tug-of-war-19820527.

Hornsby, Jeremy. "Model Fifth Beatle." Letter to the editor. *Times*, March 11, 2016, 20.

"How We Met: Cilla Black and Sir George Martin." Interviews with Anthi Charalambous. *Independent*, March 29, 1998. www.independent.co.uk/arts-entertainment/how-we -met-cilla-black-and-sir-george-martin-1153302.html.

Hudak, Joseph. "Kenny Rogers on Working with George Martin: 'The Highlight of My Career.'" *Rolling Stone*, March 9, 2016. www.rollingstone.com/music/news/kenny-rogers-on -working-with-george-martin-the-highlight-of-my-career-20160309.

Huntley, Elliot J. *Mystical One: George Harrison After the Breakup of the Beatles*. Toronto: Guernica Editions, 2004.

Hyatt, Wesley. *The Billboard Book of Number-One Adult Contemporary Hits*. New York: Billboard Publications, 1999.

"It's Beach Boys Over Beatles: Reader Poll." *Billboard*, December 10, 1966, 10.

Jamison, Tom. "Lives Remembered: Sir George Martin." *Able*, March 2016. http://able magazine.co.uk/lives-remembered-sir-george-martin/.

Johns, Glyn. *Sound Man: A Life Recording Hits with the Rolling Stones, the Who, Led Zeppelin, the Eagles, Eric Clapton, the Faces*. New York: Blue Rider, 2014.

Johnson, Derek. "Most Way-Out Beatles Ever." *NME*, February 11, 1967, 6.

———. "Next Beatle Album in Depth: NMExclusive." *NME*, November 1, 1969, 11.

Johnson, Joe. "Meeting George Martin: A Personal Journey." *Beatle Brunch* (blog), March 10, 2016. https://beatlebrunch.wordpress.com/2016/03/10/meeting-george-martin-a -personal-journey/.

Jones, Nick. "New Singles Including the Beatles, Pink Floyd, and Buffalo Springfield." *Melody Maker*, November 18, 1967, n.p.

Juber, Laurence. *Guitar with Wings: A Photographic Memoir*. With Marshall Terrill. Deerfield, IL: Dalton Watson, 2014.

Kifner, John. "Devastated by Hurricane, Montserrat Starts to Rebuild." *New York Times*, September 22, 1969. www.nytimes.com/1989/09/22/us/devastated-by-hurricane -montserrat-starts-to-rebuild.html.

Kozinn, Allan. "The Beatles on Compact Disc: A Conversation with George Martin." *Beatlefan* 9, no. 2 (1987): 8–10.

———. "The Beatles' Producer, Still with Stories to Tell." *New York Times*, June 17, 2003. www.nytimes.com/2003/06/17/books/beatles-producer-still-with-stories-tell-george -martin-has-found-life-after.html.

Lahr, John. *Prick Up Your Ears: The Biography of Joe Orton*. London: Open Road, 2013.

Lawrence, Alistair. *Abbey Road: The Best Studio in the World*. London: Bloomsbury, 2012.

Leigh, Spencer. *Love Me Do to Love Me Don't: The Beatles on Record*. Sleaford, UK: McNidder and Grace, 2016.

Lennon, John. "Beatles Music Straightforward on Next Album." Interview by Alan Smith. *Hit Parader*, December 1969. www.beatlesinterviews.org/db1969.0503.beatles.html.

———. *Lennon Remembers*. Interview by Jann Wenner. 1970. Reprint, New York: Verso, 2000.

———. "Old Grey Whistle Test." Interview with Bob Harris. BBC. March 17, 1975.

Lennon, John, and Yoko Ono. *All We Are Saying: The Last Major Interview with John Lennon and Yoko Ono*. Interview by David Sheff. Edited by G. Barry Golson. New York: Griffin, 2000.

Lewisohn, Mark. *The Beatles Live!* London: Pavilion, 1986.

———. *The Complete Beatles Chronicle: The Only Definitive Guide to the Beatles' Entire Career*. London: Pyramid, 1992.

———. *The Complete Beatles Recording Sessions: The Official Abbey Road Studio Session Notes, 1962–1970*. New York: Harmony, 1988.

———. *Tune In: The Beatles—All These Years*. Vol. 1. Boston: Little, Brown, 2013.

———. *Tune In: The Beatles—All These Years*. Vol. 1. Extended ed. Boston: Little, Brown, 2013.

Lezard, Nicholas. "*Summer of Love*." *Guardian*, June 9, 1995, 6.

"Linda McCartney Service Reunites Three Beatles." *New York Times*, June 9, 1998, http://www.nytimes.com/1998/06/09/arts/linda-mccartney-service-reunites-3-beatles.html.

Logan, Nick. "Sky-High with the Beatles." *NME*, November 26, 1967, n.p.

Love, Mike. *Good Vibrations: My Life as a Beach Boy*. With James S. Hirsch. New York: Blue Rider, 2016.

Lush, Richard. "What Was It Like to Record with Lennon and McCartney? A Conversation with *Sgt. Pepper* Sound Engineer Richard Lush." Interview by Riley Fitzgerald. *Hhhhappy*, January 17, 2017. http://hhhhappy.com/what-was-it-like-to-record-with-lennon-and-mccartney-a-conversation-with-sgt-pepper-sound-engineer-richard-lush/.

MacDonald, Ian. *Revolution in the Head: The Beatles' Records and the Sixties*. New York: Holt, 1994.

The Making of Sgt. Pepper. ITV, 1992. Television documentary.

Marsh, Dave, and John Swenson, eds. *The New Rolling Stone Record Guide*. New York: Random House, 1983.

Martin, George. *All You Need Is Ears*. With Jeremy Hornsby. New York: St. Martin's, 1979.

———. "Commencement 1989: George Martin's Commencement Address." Berklee College of Music, April 13, 1989. www.berklee.edu/commencement/past/1989.

———. Interview with Gavin Hewitt. *BBC Evening News*, December 1980.

———. Interview with Richard Buskin, March 3, 1987. YouTube. www.youtube.com/watch?v=evomc1xfM9s&t=103s.

———. Interview with Sue Lawley. *Desert Island Discs*, BBC Radio 4, November 19, 1995.

———. "Listen to My Story: George Martin Interview with *Melody Maker*." Interview by Richard Williams. *Melody Maker*, August 21, 1971, http://beatlesnumber9.com/martininterview1971.html.

———, ed. *Making Music: The Guide to Writing, Performing, and Recording*. New York: Quill, 1983.

———. "The Making of *Sgt. Pepper*." Lecture, Count Basie Theatre, Red Bank, NJ, 1999.

————. "The *Mojo* Interview: Sir George Martin." Interview by Jim Irvin. *Mojo*, March 2007, 39.

————. *Playback: An Illustrated Memoir*. Guildford, UK: Genesis Publications, 2002.

————. *Produced by George Martin: Highlights from 50 Years in Recording*. Parlophone, 2001, compact disc.

————. "The Producer Series, Part 1." Interview by Ralph Denver. *Studio Sound*, January 1985, 56–64.

————. "The Producer Series, Part 2." Interview by Ralph Denver. *Studio Sound*, February 1985, 52–58.

————. "'They Were My Boys, the Greatest in the World': An Interview with George Martin (1993)." Interview by Bill DeYoung. Bill DeYoung website, January 3, 2016. www.billde young.com/tag/george-martin-beatles/.

————. "To Sir with Love." Interview by Larry the O. *Electronic Musician*, January 7, 2009. www.emusician.com/gear/1332/to-sir-with-love/40689.

————. *With a Little Help from My Friends: The Making of Sgt. Pepper*. With William Pearson. Boston: Little, Brown, 1994.

Martin, Giles. Interview with Scott Goldman, Grammy Museum, Los Angeles, CA, May 2, 2017.

Mason, Nick. *Inside Out: A Personal History of Pink Floyd*. San Francisco: Chronicle, 2005.

Massey, Howard. *The Great British Recording Studios*. Milwaukee, WI: Hal Leonard, 2015.

Matteo, Steve. *Let It Be*. New York: Continuum, 2004.

McKenzie, Sheena. "Who Was the Real Fifth Beatle?" CNN.com, March 9, 2016. www.cnn .com/2016/03/09/entertainment/who-was-real-fifth-beatle/index.html.

Miles, Barry. *In the Sixties*. London: Jonathan Cape, 2002.

————. *Paul McCartney: Many Years from Now*. New York: Holt, 1997.

Morse, Steve. "Paperbacks." *Boston Globe*, December 18, 1983, 1.

Nicholl, Katie. "George Harrison Close to Death." *Daily Mail*, November 14, 2001. www .dailymail.co.uk/news/article-61825/George-Harrison-close-death.html.

Norman, Philip. *John Lennon: A Life*. London: Ecco, 2008.

Oates, John. *Change of Seasons: A Memoir*. New York: St. Martin's, 2017.

"Obituaries: Brian O'Hara." *Independent*, July 1, 1999. www.independent.co.uk/arts-entertain ment/obituaries-brian-ohara-1103691.html.

O'Toole, Kit. *Michael Jackson FAQ: All That's Left to Know About the King of Pop*. Milwaukee, WI: Hal Leonard, 2015.

"Platter Chatter: Albums by the Beatles, Rolling Stones, Jefferson Airplane, Cream, and Kaleidoscope." *Hit Parader*, April 1968, n.p.

Porterfield, Christopher. "Pop Music: The Messengers." *Time*, September 22, 1967, 60.

Priore, Domenic. *Smile: The Story of Brian Wilson's Lost Masterpiece*. London: Sanctuary, 2005.

"Remembering the Forgotten Beatle." *Rolling Stone*, December 5, 2001, 9.

Repsch, John. *The Legendary Joe Meek: The Telstar Man*. London: Woodford, 1989.

Richardson, Mark. "The Beatles' *Love*." *Pitchfork*, November 30, 2006. http://pitchfork.com /reviews/albums/9669-love/.

Riley, Tim. *Lennon: The Man, the Myth, the Music*. New York: Hyperion, 2011.

————. *Tell Me Why: A Beatles Commentary*. New York: Knopf, 1988.

Rodriguez, Robert. *Revolver: How the Beatles Re-imagined Rock 'n' Roll*. Milwaukee, WI: Hal Leonard, 2012.

Ryan, Kevin, and Brian Kehew. *Recording the Beatles: The Studio Equipment and Techniques Used to Create Their Classic Albums*. Houston, TX: Curvebender, 2006.

Scott, Ken. *Abbey Road to Ziggy Stardust: Off the Record with the Beatles, Bowie, Elton, and So Much More*. Los Angeles: Alfred Music, 2012.

———. "Beatles' Recording Engineer Ken Scott Reveals Behind the Scenes Details on Working with the Fab Four." Interview by Marshall Terrill. *Day Trippin'*, July 25, 2012. http://daytrippin.com/2012/07/25/beatles-recording-engineer-ken-scott-reveals-behind-the-scenes-details-on-working-with-the-fab-four/.

"Show Business: Other Noises, Other Notes." *Time*, March 3, 1967, 63.

Snow, Mat. *The Who: Fifty Years of My Generation*. New York: Race Point, 2015.

"Spotlight Singles." *Billboard*, March 16, 1968, 78.

Southall, Brian. *Abbey Road: The Story of the World's Most Famous Studios*. Wellingborough, UK: Patrick Stephens, 1982.

———. *Northern Songs: The True Story of the Beatles Song Publishing Empire*. With Rupert Perry. London: Omnibus, 2009.

Spangler, Jay. "John Lennon & Paul McCartney: Apple Press Conference 5/14/1968." The Beatles Interview Database. www.beatlesinterviews.org/db1968.0514pc.beatles.html.

Spitz, Bob. *The Beatles: The Biography*. Boston: Little, Brown, 2005.

Starr, Michael Seth. *With a Little Help*. Milwaukee, WI: Hal Leonard, 2015.

"Stereo Rattles Stations; Mfrs. Strangle Monaural." *Billboard*, January 6, 1968, 1.

Sulpy, Doug, and Ray Schweighardt. *Get Back: The Unauthorized Chronicle of the Beatles' Let It Be Disaster*. New York: Griffin, 1997.

Take a Ride Through the Beatles' Magical Mystery Tour. WCBS-FM, 2011. Radio playlist.

Thompson, Gordon. *Please Please Me: Sixties Pop, Inside Out*. Oxford: Oxford University Press, 2008.

Turner, Steve. *Beatles '66: The Revolutionary Year*. New York: HarperCollins, 2016.

———. *The Complete Beatles Songs: The Stories Behind Every Track Written by the Fab Four*. London: Carlton, 2015.

Van der Kiste, John. *Jeff Lynne: Electric Light Orchestra—Before and After*. Stroud, UK: Fonthill Media, 2015.

Vyner, Harriet. *Groovy Bob: The Life and Times of Robert Fraser*. London: Faber and Faber, 1999.

Wade, John. "Alan Civil." Obituary. *Daily Telegraph*, March 21, 1989. www.hornsociety.org/information-archive/151-hornplayer/hpn-info-archive/636-alan-civil-obituary.

Welch, Chris. "Beatles Recall All Our Yesterdays." *Melody Maker*, March 9, 1968, 17.

Wenner, Jann S. "Review: The Beatles' *White Album*." *Rolling Stone*, December 12, 1967. www.rollingstone.com/music/features/beatles-19681221.

Williams, Richard. *Phil Spector: Out of His Head*. London: Omnibus, 2009.

Winn, John C. *That Magic Feeling: The Beatles' Recorded Legacy*. Vol. 2, *1966–1970*. Sharon, VT: Multiplus, 2003.

Womack, Kenneth. *The Beatles Encyclopedia: Everything Fab Four*. 2 vols. Santa Barbara, CA: Greenwood Press, 2014.

Zupko, Sarah. "George Martin: *In My Life*." *PopMatters*, October 1998. www.popmatters.com/recent/tv/film/P98740/music/.

INDEX